# RUINS of MODERNITY

**POLITICS, HISTORY, AND CULTURE**

*A series from the International Institute at the University of Michigan*



Sponsored by the International Institute at the University of Michigan and published by Duke University Press, this series is centered around cultural and historical studies of power, politics, and the state—a field that cuts across the disciplines of history, sociology, anthropology, political science, and cultural studies. The focus on the relationship between state and culture refers both to a methodological approach—the study of politics and the state using culturalist methods—and a substantive one that treats signifying practices as an essential dimension of politics. The dialectic of politics, culture, and history figures prominently in all the books selected for the series.

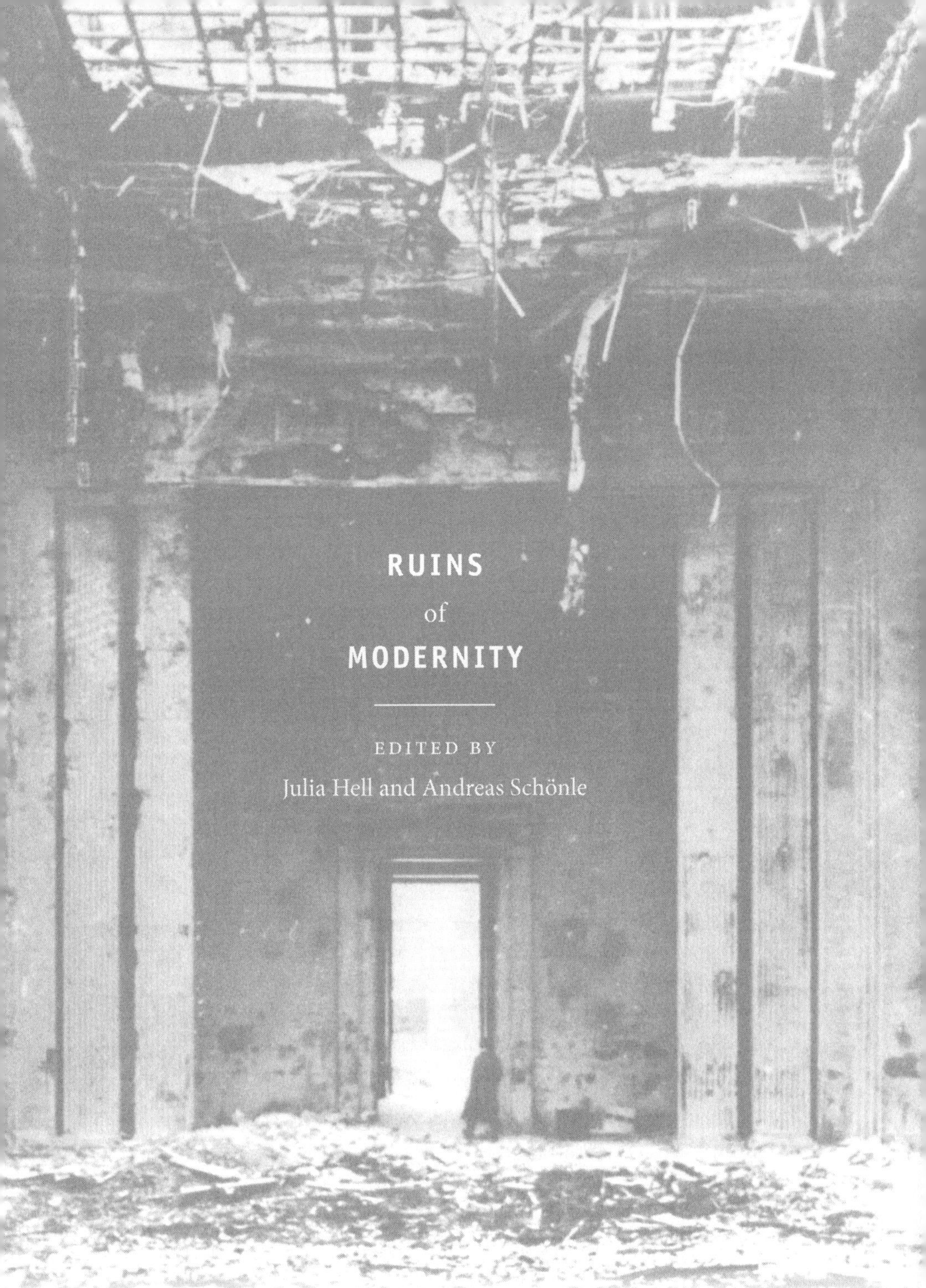

# RUINS of MODERNITY

EDITED BY

Julia Hell and Andreas Schönle

Duke University Press Durham and London 2010

Printed in the United States of America on acid-free paper ∞
Typeset in Minion Pro by Keystone Typesetting, Inc.
Library of Congress Cataloging-in-Publication data appear on the last printed page of this book.
Duke University Press gratefully acknowledges support for the publication of this book from the Regents of the University of Michigan.

## CONTENTS

## LIST OF ILLUSTRATIONS

BOYM



ESHEL

# ACKNOWLEDGMENTS

Ruins may signify the end of the old, or the beginning of something new. In our case, a conversation about ruins in the imperial gardens of Catherine the Great and the remnants of the gigantic steel mills of the Saar and Alsace-Lorraine regions led to a series of seminars, workshops, and finally an interdisciplinary conference exploring the concept of the ruins of modernity. This volume brings to an end our collaborative project, but not the obsession with ruins–signifiers of civilization and barbarism, creativity and destruction. Our initial ideas took shape before 9/11, and we had no inkling, then, that during this project we would witness so much ruination, from contemporary New York, New Orleans, and Baghdad to ancient Balbek.

The project went through several phases, and many people enthusiastically contributed ideas and time. We started with a symposium at which Andreas Huyssen spoke about the British-German author W. G. Sebald, and Thomas Lahusen presented his film about the post-Soviet ruins of Komsomolsk-on-Amur, *Komsomolsk Mon Amour: A City after Socialism.*

We then taught an interdisciplinary graduate seminar, funded by the Horace H. Rackham School of Graduate Studies at the University of Michigan, which enabled us to invite speakers—including Kerstin Barndt, Russell A. Berman, Meilee Bridges, Geoff Eley, Bruce Frier, Peter Fritzsche, Kader Konuk, Artemis Leontis, Kirsten Olds, Helmut Puff, Gustavo Verdesio, and Rebecca Zurier—who all delivered stimulating talks that helped us advance our thoughts.

Our next step was a major interdisciplinary conference held at the University of Michigan in March 2005. The graduate students from the seminar—Michael André, Kathryn Bauss, Victoria Dearman, Paul Dobryden, Philip Duker, Sebastian Ferrari, Courtney Glore, Lauren Graber, Jeffrey Lloyd, John Rowland, and Daniel Stevens—presented papers on the first day, and many of them generously helped us with the organization of the conference. Special thanks go to Kevin Korsyn, who introduced the graduate workshop with a lecture on "Music, Ghosts, and the Ruins of Modernity."

Daniel Herwitz, director of the Institute for the Humanities at the University of Michigan, threw his full support behind our ideas and gave our ambitions a wholly different order of magnitude. The conference was preceded by a series of brown-bag lunches at the institute, at which Erika Naginski talked about the modernity of Piranesi, Bruce Frier exhibited and commented on his collection of Piranesi engravings, and Lars Graebner discussed his ideas for the redevelopment of Detroit. In addition, Sarah Beckwith, another committed ruinologist, was awarded a fellowship at the Institute for the Humanities, and Fredric Jameson was invited to deliver its Marc and Constance Jacobson Lecture. The institute also organized a tour of the ruins of Detroit guided by Lowell Boileau and an exhibition, curated by Elizabeth Paymal, of photographs of Soviet and post-Soviet ruins by Boris Mikhailov, who delivered several presentations as the institute's artist-in-residence.

Our conference took place under the auspices of the Institute for the Humanities and with the generous support of Tom Buresh and the Taubman College of Architecture and Urban Planning, Kenneth Kollman and the Center for European Studies, and Michael Kennedy and the Center for Russian and East European Studies. We also received funding from the Department of Germanic Languages and Literatures; the Department of Slavic Languages and Literatures; the Department of Sociology; the Office of the Vice President for Research; the College of Literature, Science, and the Arts; the Program in Screen Arts and Cultures; the Latin American and Caribbean Studies Program; the Department of English; and the Department of Romance Languages and Literatures, all at the University of Michigan. Last but not least, we would like to thank Barbara Motyka and the German Academic Exchange Service for their interest in and generous support of our project.

Eliza Woodford assumed overall coordination for the conference and all surrounding events. Many other people contributed to its organization, notably Daniela Gobetti, Natasa Gruden-Alajbegovic, Nicola Kiver, Roberta Nerison-Low, Marysia Ostafin, and Elizabeth Paymal, the institute's ruin artist, who created our posters.

The conference could not have happened without the assistance of many colleagues from the University of Michigan who served as chairs or commentators and threw themselves into the discussions: Sara Blair, Tom Buresh, Kathleen Canning, Geoff Eley, Laurence Goldstein, Vassilis Lambropoulos, Artemis Leontis, Marjorie Levinson, Olga Maiorova, Brian Porter, Alex Potts, Scott Spector, Ann Stoler, and Jason Young.

Highlights of the conference included two films: Johannes von Moltke's montage of cinematic ruins and Michael Chanan and George Steinmetz's documentary, *Detroit: Ruin of a City* (2005). We owe special thanks to the Institute for the Humanities, as well as our graduate students and colleagues, who helped us deal with the unanticipated success of the film about Detroit. Expecting an audience of no more than eighty film buffs at most, we were taken by surprise as a line of over a thousand people from campus and the larger Detroit area formed outside the conference building. With Daniel Herwitz deploying strategic talents no one had suspected, we underwent an intense experience of crowd management that left us exhausted and exhilarated. The film, with a soundtrack composed by Michael Nyman, ignited a heated debate and proved once again the controversial politics of ruins. We would like to thank Michael and George for a cultural event that resonated far beyond our campus.

Publication of this volume was enabled by subventions from the Department of Germanic Languages and Literatures; the College of Literature, Science, and the Arts; and the Office of the Vice President for Research, all at the University of Michigan, along with a subvention from the School of Languages, Linguistics, and Film at Queen Mary, University of London. We owe much to Michael Schoenfeld for his support.

Finally, and most importantly, we would like to express our gratitude to Reynolds Smith, executive editor at Duke University Press, who didn't flinch when he saw the size of our project and took it on enthusiastically. Sharon Torian, senior editorial assistant, graciously helped us deal with the odds and ends of manuscript preparation. The design department kindly put up with our technical failings. Finally, we would like to thank Seth Howes for his expert negotiations with several Russian museums.

The facts that so many people contributed to this project and that we made so many friends over its duration testify to the enduring power of ruins and to the debt we owe them. They are remnants of a past that not only made our lives possible, but that also continues to expand the horizon of our modernity.

# INTRODUCTION

On July 7, 2002, the *New York Times* ran an article entitled "Sept. 11 Photo Exhibition Touches a Nerve in Berlin."[1] Apparently this show immediately evoked Berliners' memories of the bombing of German cities at the end of the Second World War. As troubling as these associations are in the specific context of National Socialism and its war of aggression, they are not surprising. The images of New York in ruins resonate with other images of destruction. When history piles wreckage upon wreckage, ruins evoke not only the buildings from which they hail but also a transhistorical iconography of decay and catastrophe, a vast visual archive of ruination. In the era of global media coverage and round-the-clock exposure to visual data, ruins have become ubiquitous. They are images that denote raw reality, yet the way we see them is not raw but framed by a long tradition of ruin gazing. What we see is new, and we might see it in a new way—but not for long. Soon our gaze at the rubble piling up before our eyes is clouded by the iconic wreckage of ages.

### Ruin Gazing I: The (Imperial) Archive

The allusion to Benjamin's angel of history is deliberate. Ruin gazing always mirrors the terror in the angel's wide-open eyes. It always involves reflections about history: about the nature of the event, the meaning of the past for the present, the nature of history itself as eternal cycle, progress, apocalypse, or murderous dialectic process. And as Benjamin—who transformed what Arendt called the "shock of experience" into an enduring and enduringly beautiful image—knew, the aestheticization of ruins is unavoidable.[2] But let us not forget Adorno's caveat about the angel's gaze: his eyes are filled with terror, but they are above all "enigmatic."[3] Benjamin's angel, Adorno reminds us, forces the beholder to choose between submitting to catastrophe and resisting it.

To be seduced by the beauty of ruins is an experience as inescapable as it is old: toward the end of the eighteenth century, the excavation of Pompeii uncovered murals, ruin paintings which made Poussin's landscapes seem like faint echoes. Pompeii, the city of Roman "decadence," quickly became one of romanticism's favorite sites for ruin gazing. The wealth—a veritable explosion—of texts around the city of the dead expresses some of romanticism's core concerns: the political ramifications of the French revolution, an event in Roman (dis)guise that opened a gap between the modern and the premodern worlds; the nature of the modern, its aesthetics, and its philosophies of history; and Rome, both republican and imperial, which constitutes one of the most enduring topoi of the ruin archive, the theme of the rise and decline of empires.

Piranesi comes to mind, of course, but other famous ruin gazers have been obsessed with the fate of past empires: de Volney, the French philosopher, who dreamed up a whole new way of organizing society as he gazed at the ruins of Palmyra; Gibbon, who invested his hopes in the power of enlightened thought to break the cycle of rise and decline; Hegel, the inventor of world history as the dialectics between ruination and refounding; Napoleon, obsessed with the description of Egypt and its majestic ruins; Caspar David Friedrich and his anti-Napoleonic discovery of German ruins; Mary Shelley in her encounter with Valerius, the reanimated Roman, and her celebration of Rome's republican virtues; and Heinrich von Kleist, who created a fierce fantasy about Rome or Paris in ruins; Freud, who had a passion for Hannibal, the Carthaginian general who threatened Rome; Flaubert, with his euphoric, perhaps sadistic, gaze at the bloody obliteration of Carthage; Spengler, who saw twentieth-century Europe as decadent, a culture as petrified as that of the Roman empire; Albert Speer, with his utopia of Berlin in monumental ruins; and Hitler, who visited Italy in the wake of Mussolini's reconstruction of Rome as the city of Augustan imperial power.

Gibbon, convinced that the cycle of rise and decline would be broken, claimed that "humanity" would never again see the devastation of the past.[4] National Socialism proved him wrong. Confronted with the ruined landscapes of postwar Europe, Arendt set out to reinvent politics in her *Origins of Totalitarianism*, and Macaulay wrote her "perverse book" on the history of ruin gazing and *Ruinenlust* in *Pleasure of Ruins*.[5] Twenty years later, Anselm Kiefer reenacted the march of Hitler's army across Europe.[6] Taking photographs of himself in front of the Coliseum, his right arm raised in the Hitler salute, the German painter invoked once more the imperial fantasies of Italian and German Fascism. At his exhibit entitled Chute d'Etoiles/Sternenfall at the Monumenta 2007 in Paris, Kiefer enacted a similar provocative gesture. The exhibit oscillates between unforgettable images and rather heavy-handed ruin kitsch. At the center stand two concrete towers, one falling, the other collapsed, with its rubble strewn across the floor of the Grand Palais. The towers' gray material evokes the bunkers that the Nazis built along the Atlantic Ocean; a miniature submarine stranded among the rubble reinforces the association. But in 2007 two collapsing towers have contemporary associations. Kiefer makes sure that we get his allusion when he comments in the audioguide to the exhibit that "we all know that one day everything will collapse." What distinguishes Kiefer, the neoromantic artist, from us is that he already can see the future in ruins: "I already see the grass growing over New York."

The imperial impulse has even extended into the future, attempting to colonize time for the benefit of mankind and in the process producing more eloquent ruins, of the past as much as of utopian aspirations. Strolling through a forbiddingly cold postrevolutionary Petrograd as small wooden houses were taken apart to serve as heating material, the Russian formalist Viktor Shklovsky noted, tongue in cheek, that the city was beginning to resemble a Piranesi engraving. He relished observing how the city had become more artful than art and thereby defamiliarized official ideology.[7] Mostly left to decay slowly while it conserved a modicum of humanist culture, Leningrad in the Soviet years became a single extended ruin, which underpinned the identity, poetic voice, and historiographic musings of Joseph Brodsky. In contrast, Stalin's Muscovite architectural extravaganzas, his wedding-cake high rises, were intended to subsume the greatness of world civilization in an eternal, glorious present and to thwart the corroding effect of time. Yet after Stalin's death, as their decorative friezes and sculptures quickly began to deteriorate, the high rises acquired a patina and an appearance of decay that belied the future's timelessness. For Muscovites of the 1970s and 1980s, these ruinous buildings signaled the collapse of utopian hubris and fostered a gaze more ironic than melancholic.[8] Yet the most iconic ruin of late-twentieth-century history is surely the remains of the Berlin wall, whose destruction—it is worth recalling—was hailed as the end of history, though for many East Germans it seemed instead to herald an unfriendly imperial takeover that resulted in the devaluation of their lives. Ruins produce more ruins.

This story of imperial legacies, (colonial) empires, and their ruins is familiar, and it seemed to be a story of European ruins. But after 9/11 and the invasion of Iraq, it has become an American story, too. The endless images of Saddam Hussein's palace in Baghdad and the Al-Askariya shrine in Samarra, for example, take us back to the Middle Eastern landscape that de Volney contemplated. The Course of Empire, an exhibit at the Whitney Museum of American Art that combined paintings by Ed Ruscha representing the dereliction of American Fordism with reproductions of paintings by Thomas Cole about the rise and decline of Carthage, revived the discourse about past empires and their ruins. While the exhibit repeated the imperial ruin gazers' melancholy thoughts, it introduced a new topic: industrial decline. More precisely, Ruscha directed our gaze to the end of industrial modernity, particularly the end of America's golden postwar age of Fordist prosperity. Artists across the globe had made de-industrialization "visible," but Ruscha radically transformed this post-industrial gaze into a post-imperial one. America used to set little store by ruins, venerating its prehistoric natural heritage at the expense of historical artifacts. "Many nineteenth-century Americans considered the primeval wilderness morally superior to historical scenes. They preferred a 'hoary oak' to a 'mouldering column.' . . ."[9] Yet in a post-Fordist, post 9/11 reality, the imaginary of imperial ruin and ruination has become pervasive, prompting even the representation of urban decay in coffee-table books such as Camilo Vergara's *American Ruins*.

**Ruin Gazing II: Awakenings?**

While our ruin gaze is informed by centuries of images and their interpretations, each new incidence of massive devastation forces a rereading of previous ones. The sense of exceptionality one naturally ascribes to a catastrophic event is undermined by subsequent wreckage, puncturing our comforting ideological constructions. As the *New York Times* noted in an editorial on September 11, 2005, "We felt that 9/11 had changed our lives in an instant, that we had been jerked out of a pleasant dream. The difference in the blow that Katrina struck was not merely that we could see it coming. It was that, as a nation, we thought we were already fully awake."[10] Just as 9/11 had seemed to be a hard landing in the reality of terrorism without borders, Katrina suddenly revealed social realities that American political discourse had studiously obscured. Nora Gallagher expressed what many felt in an op-ed entitled "Waking from a Sound Sleep": "We got the story of what is really happening in the United States right between the eyes. We got the story of how poor people live and are treated in this country by watching them suffer and die."[11] Or, in Timothy Garton Ash's Hobbesian interpretation of Katrina, "what's under threat here is simply civilization, the thin crust we lay across the seething magma of nature, including human nature. New Orleans opened a small hole through which we glimpsed what always lies below."[12] Each new ruination claims to offer a privileged conduit into reality. Does this betray a sense that in our digitized world, reality can be apprehended only as destruction? Perhaps, but through serialization, such eye-opening catastrophes —the feeling of abrupt awakening that ruination produces—become themselves an effect of rhetoric. Can we make sense of ruins only by granting them an exclusive ontological status?

The reality of ruins at least calls forth a constructive, "manly" rhetoric of looking into the abyss, learning from our mistakes, confronting our enemies, and thus retroactively conferring some modicum of meaning to the senseless destruction. This rhetoric, too, is punctured by the serial recurrence of devastation. As a ruin jolts us into wakefulness, the previous ones seem to recede into the oneiric world. Did 9/11 really wake us up? Will Katrina keep us alert? Or are we addicted to ruins as a stimulant to counteract the numbing effects of the media-induced bubble we live in? Does the thrill of ruins return us to a pre-post-modern feel for reality, despite the fact that so many of us experience the rawness of ruinous reality primarily as a media effect?

### Do We Need an Ontology of Ruins?

This convergence of images and memories—this "touching of nerves" and "waking from a sound sleep"—raises broader questions. The destruction of the world's most famous symbolic icon of capitalist modernity on 9/11 brought to a climax the debate about the ways in which modernity, broadly conceived, seems to have invented, framed, and produced ruins. Is there a possible elective affinity between ruins and modernity? Or is the connection between ruins and modernity even stronger—is there some intrinsic logic of ruin at work in modernity?[13] As Michael Roth argues, only in a secularized world do ruins become objects deemed suitable for study or contemplation.[14] What we now call ruins began to be perceived and preserved as such during the Renaissance, when the awareness of historical discontinuities and the demise of ancient civilizations raised the status of traces from the past. These traces—architectural remnants which had long lost their functionality and meaning—could be invested with various attributes: historical, aesthetic, and political, for example. They reveal an ambivalent sense of time, at once the awareness of an insuperable break from the past that constitutes the modern age and the sense that some valuable trace has endured and needs to be cherished. The dialectic of this temporal self-consciousness is troubling: do we need the trace to highlight the significance of the historical rupture, or do we require the rupture to confer value on the trace? It seems both are necessary.

In recent history, ruins and ruination have become hot political issues. Even when devastation is clearly attributable to so-called acts of God, as with the tsunami in December 2004 and Katrina in August 2005, the aftermath of a catastrophe has wide-ranging political implications, which reveal and disrupt assumptions about the power of individual agency, the role of government and community, and the ideology of social, moral, and economic progress. Here, too, one can historicize the political exploitation of ruins. The desire for preservation in the interest of historical continuity often barely concealed the political exploitation of ruins as signs of past greatness that could be reappropriated. Catherine the Great had fake ruins erected to legitimate her imperial ambitions, allowing her to claim a lineage harking back to Greek antiquity. Ruins, both genuine and fabricated, have served similar purposes in many places and times. Revolutions unavoidably produce a rhetoric of ruin—witness the role of Roman ruins in the iconography of the French revolution—but so do regimes that are bent more on continuity than rupture, from Nazi Germany to contemporary Greece and its political stake in the preservation and refurbishing of its antique ruins.

The ruin is a ruin precisely because it seems to have lost its function or meaning in the present, while retaining a suggestive, unstable semantic potential. The ruin has blurred edges in more ways than one. As an aesthetic and conceptual category, it is uniquely ill-defined. Where does the ruin start, and where does it end? Is a well-preserved but empty building already a ruin because it has lost its practical and social function? And, at the other end of the spectrum, does rubble still qualify as ruin? More broadly, is a ruin an object or a process? Does it signal the loss or the endurance of the past? Does it matter whether ruination is the work of nature or of human action? Is authenticity a necessary condition of a ruin, or are manufactured ruins just as real? And how do we define the authenticity of a ruin in the era of tourist consumption? What is the import of ruins of the future as compared to ruins of the past? Does the ruin evoke nostalgia for the past or shame over it? Faith in future progress? The breakdown of utopia? Does the aestheticization of the ruin belittle the human suffering that it connotes, pushing us into morally dubious territory? Indeed, does the mass reproduction of ruins in various media numb our senses and trivialize horror? Or does it jolt us awake? To make a long story short, ruins "are a paradoxical sign which was attributed to contradictory statements and sensibilities."[15]

### Ruin Gazing III: Reflexivity

The semantic instability of the ruin owes much to the fact that it bespeaks a potential vacuity of meaning. The ruin signals the impending breakdown of meaning and therefore fosters intensive compensatory discursive activity. In its ambivalence and amorphousness, the ruin functions as a uniquely flexible and productive trope for modernity's self-awareness. Indeed, it is one of the master tropes of modern reflexivity, precisely because it encapsulates vacuity and loss as underlying constituents of the modern identity. It is the reflexivity of a culture that interrogates its own becoming.

Theoreticians of various stripes have considered the peculiar status of ruins in modern culture. At the end of the nineteenth century, the political geographer Friedrich Ratzel traced the dissemination of ruins across the entire globe, proposing the concept of *Ruinenländer* (ruin countries)—entire countries ruined by violent conflicts among so-called *Naturvölker* (natural peoples). At the beginning of the twentieth century, Spengler predicted the ruins of modernity: the decline of Western culture into a civilization that leaves an apocalyptic landscape of decaying global cities. Simmel thought that ruins embody the justice of destruction, the reintegration of human design into nature that counteracts human interventions and makes them right. For Adorno and Horkheimer, the process of ruination is an intrinsic component of the dialectic whereby modernity undermines itself and lapses into mythology and self-destruction. Benjamin drew a parallel between the ruin in the realm of things and the allegory in the realm of thought, for both ruin and allegory speak of a disruption in the relationship between form and meaning. In a way, semiotics threatens to become a wasteland. Lotman has considered the ways in which ruins serve the project of cultural self-fashioning. Freud framed the unconscious as a sort of ruined landscape in need of excavation.

More recently, Sebald referred to ruins as master tropes of a traumatic modernity in his scholarly writings, prose poems, and essayistic novels. What texts like *The Rings of Saturn* alert us to is the enormous tension that the representation of ruins seems to provoke, the tension between minute description and grand narrative, between modernist minimalism and metaphysical philosophizing. The ruin's dialectic between absence and presence, fragment and whole, is also one between the visible and the invisible. Close, detailed description seems to suit the representation of this visible remnant just as photography seems to be its main medium. And yet reflections on ruins inevitably seem to lead away from this austere minimalism. At the same time, the reticence of description always seems to undermine the imaginary wholeness of the stories, demanding yet more description and more stories.

This rich body of approaches to ruins teaches us that the ruin is predicated on a particular gaze cast upon it, either modern or postmodern. The beholder defines the ruin, and the ruin could not exist without such creative appropriation. As a result, the ruin is often the playground of speculative strategies that tell us more about the beholder than about the ruin or its original environment. Thus, the questions raised by the responses to 9/11 and Katrina bespeak a culture obsessed with its self-image, struggling to determine what defines its underlying reality once the layers of its self-representation are peeled away. We have not always reacted to ruins in this way. For Diderot, to offer a contrasting example, ruins constitute a subjectivity that society otherwise holds in check. They evoke the great leveling universality of death but allow the self "to make a solitary stand," poised at the edge of "a torrent" that "drags each and every nation into the depths of a common abyss."[16] A ruin "delivers us up to our inclinations," Diderot says. On the site of a ruin, he adds, "I'm freer, more alone, more myself, closer to myself. It's there that I call out to my friend . . . it's there that we'd enjoy ourselves without anxiety, without witnesses, without intruders, without those jealous of us. It's there that I probe my own heart; it's there that I interrogate [hers], that I take alarm and reassure myself."[17] Ruins emancipate our senses and desires and enable introspection. Even more poignantly, they paradoxically invite us to relive in the absence of the lover "the same intoxication that had so completely and deliciously possessed our senses."[18] An emblem of transience, ruins facilitate an imaginary repetition of the past similar in intensity to the original sensations it afforded. The ruin, in short, enables individual freedom, imagination, and subjectivity.

Can Diderot's self-invigorating conclusions be salvaged in a (post)postmodern era? Perhaps not, though translated into a less Cartesian rendition of human subjectivity, they can still alert us to the psycho-political investments that ruin gazers—and ruin scholars, for that matter—make in their object. Drawing our attention to the industrial ruins of post-imperial Britain and protesting against the commodification of history undertaken by the heritage industry, Edensor celebrates the hybridity and transgressive force of ruins in a way vaguely reminiscent of Diderot. Ruins indeed blur boundaries, both spatially, as crumbling structures colonize their immediate surroundings, and temporally, as they articulate the overlayering of temporalities. In Edensor's account, this collapsing of the public order releases energy and creativity: ruins are sites "in which the becomings of new forms, orderings and aesthetics can emerge,"[19] spaces which subvert the overly controlled circuits of human traffic in a contemporary city. Thus the ruin is invoked in a critique of the spatial organization of the modern world and of its single-minded commitment to a progress that throws too many individuals and spaces into the trash. Edensor shares with Diderot the sense in which ruins call into question the legitimacy of the social order, though he is more interested in exploring new forms of collective living and new aesthetic projects than in grounding an individual subjectivity à la Diderot. More importantly—and against all odds—ruins have just as much power to jolt us into wakefulness in the twenty-first century as they did in the eighteenth. This would be wakefulness in Arendt's terms: not a "heroic" confrontation of the abyss, but a willingness to expose ourselves to the "shock of experience"—to face ruins' raw violence and to think of the unprecedented event without taking recourse to old, familiar, worn-out explanations. Benjamin's angel of history does not submit to the course of history, to determinist philosophies of progress or doom.[20] As Arendt argued so passionately in 1944, the angel does not accept the "natural law of ruin."[21]

### Synopses

"Catastrophe, Utopia and the Architecture of Destruction," part 1 of this volume, identifies in the elective affinity between ruins and modernity a difficult relationship with the present, a disenchantment that encourages a leap into heterogeneous temporalities, often embodied in speculation about the future of the past. The self-questioning present represses the awareness of the destructiveness implicit in utopian blueprints. Thus catastrophe, real and imagined, underpins modernity's multilayered sense of history, and ruins can bear witness to, but can also idealize or undermine, modernity's asynchronous temporalities. Reading Piranesi's ruins together with his prisons, and through Adorno and Benjamin's ideas of modernity, Andreas Huyssen argues that Piranesi's works embody the notion of "authentic ruin," understood not as the nostalgic projection of an original past, but as a self-critical awareness of instability that robs the Enlightenment project of any secure historical and axiological footing. Anthony Vidler uncovers the anxiety underpinning modernist architecture since the Second World War, the repressed fear of being bombed out of existence, fed by the extent of technology-aided destruction during the war and reinforced by the fantasies of tabula rasa that inspired the modernism of the 1920s and 1930s. This trauma of anticipatory fear generated an architecture of disillusion, a defensive hunkering down that inspired futurist visions and their articulation of a clean break. Vladimir Paperny discusses architectural modernism's stake in destruction, its relations with autocratic or totalitarian political power, and its intrinsically self-destructive logic. He reviews a number of case studies in America and Soviet Russia leading to the possibility of a nondestructive modernism. Svetlana Boym conceptualizes the current fascination for ruins as a ruin gaze, reflecting back on modernity's utopian aspirations but attentive to the side alleys of twentieth-century history, the alternative heterogeneous perspectives, eccentricities, and asperities that survived despite modernism's single-minded progressivist narrative. To exemplify this off-modern posture, she looks at the afterlife of Tatlin's design for the Monument to the Third International, its recreations and appropriations by late-twentieth-century conceptualist artists, who played with the ruin value of the avant-garde utopia.

"Ruins and the Democratic Polity," part 2, explores the political ramifications of the rhetoric of ruin. Indeed, the ruin can embody both continuity and rupture, thus inspiring contradictory ideologies and programs. Yet as both conservative and revolutionary ruins remind us of our own transience, they throw into relief our need for communal association. Ruins foster imaginary communities, invented traditions, and resonant political rhetoric. Andreas Schönle analyzes Tolstoy's response in *War and Peace* to the destruction of Moscow during the fire of 1812, which in its immediate aftermath energized conservative, isolationist narratives of Russian national identity. Tolstoy uncovers the emancipatory potential of ruins as heterogeneous objects that enable us to overcome historical antinomies and, more to the point, to forswear the totalitarian impulse to direct and control history. Russell A. Berman identifies complicity between democracy and destruction. Narratives of ruination imply human agency, and in modern times the agent of destruction has been the democratic state, acting with missionary zeal to destroy an enemy demonized as the old regime. Berman examines the political ramifications across the ideological spectrum of what he calls democratic destruction and redemption. In his analysis of the Second Republic in Czech history (1938–39), Jonathan Bolton reveals how the defenders of democratic values assimilated a particular rhetoric of ruin in spite of the encroachments of an authoritarian government keen on imposing a total break with the past. For the likes of Karel and Josef Čapek, ruins embody continuity within the modern, democratic state, and partiality to incremental—if messy—change over the deceptive allure of the clean break. In his analysis of contemporary Israeli and German responses to ruins, Amir Eshel traces the ability of ruins to evoke divergent memories and thus to provoke democratic debate, articulate a vision of the future, and prompt meaningful action. Eshel argues for the enduring vitality of ruins and for their paramount importance to a civil society properly cognizant of its own historicity. Finally, Lucia Saks shows how the massive influx of blacks into South African cities brought about the collapse of the apartheid government and how the reconstruction of post-apartheid Johannesburg opened up new life trajectories, identities, and local allegiances, and gave people the sense of being swept into continuous change, which Saks evokes through an analysis of *Joburg Stories*, a documentary by Oliver Schmitz and Brian Tilley.

"Empires, Ruins, and Their Stories," part 3, traces the connection between empires and their ruins from the Third Reich to post-apartheid South Africa and postcolonial India. Julia Hell reads the Nazis' obsession with ruins as symptomatic of the murderous totalitarian logic of this particular form of empire. Hell focuses her analysis on the scopic scenario of the imperial ruin gazer. The first part of her chapter traces the scenario's genealogy backward from Don DeLillo's *Falling Man* through Spengler's *The Decline of the West* to antiquity and Polybius's account of the Punic Wars, arguing that the scenario crystallizes the uncanniness that inevitably accompanies all imperial mimesis. The Nazis' repeated enactment of the scenario responds to this long history, taking on an obsessional, fetishistic quality. Todd Samuel Presner does a "contrapuntal reading" of Hegel's lectures on world history and W. G. Sebald's *The Rings of Saturn*. Presner is less interested in the multilayered representation of empires and their ruins in Sebald's apocalyptic travelogue than in the ways in which the latter turns Hegel's narrative of modernity into a grandiose ruin of its own. Jon Beasley-Murray approaches the narrative ruins of European modernity from a different vantage point, discussing the Inca ruin of Vilcashuamán located in Ayacucho Province, in the highland of Peru. Beasley-Murray examines the ways in which various narratives have accrued around this ruin, from the Incas' imperial expansion through the Spanish conquest, nineteenth-century nationalism, and the civil war of the 1980s. Using the notion of posthegemony, Beasley-Murray argues for the fragility of all narrativizations while considering the relations between ruin and narrative within American modernity. Daniel Herwitz examines the culture of monuments, memorials, and museums arising from the ruins of South African apartheid. According to Herwitz, the African National Congress government was hesitant to begin creating monuments of its own or to tear down the monuments of its predecessors, unlike the case in Eastern Europe after communism. He believes the list of apartheid's victims appearing in the *Report* of the Truth and Reconciliation Commission functions as an alternative, nonmonumental form of commemoration appropriate to the period of transition. The architect Rahul Mehrotra focuses on contemporary Mumbai. Where some might see the ruination of a modernist city, Mehrotra discerns the emergence of a dynamic new kinetic city. If only temporarily, this city reappropriates and gives new functions to the ruins of the modern postcolonial static city. Thus, like Presner and Beasley-Murray, Mehrotra proposes to understand his object as deconstructing the narrative of modernity and modernism.

"(Post-)Ruinscapes," part 4, explores the various ways in which urban landscapes of ruins are created, maintained, used, and represented. The places under discussion range from East Germany's industrial centers to the archaeological sites of the Americas. The different modes of inscription and representation invite or ban specific itineraries and ways of looking while evoking distinctive affective tonalities—the apocalyptic mind-set of the atomic age, for instance, or the melancholic attachment to Fordism in Eastern Europe. Helmut Puff explores a nonverbal medium of representation, the so-called rubble models—scale models of the German cities bombed in the Second World War. He claims they function as means of coming to terms with loss, appearing to offer immediate access to events and experiences that seemed to defy representation. In this medium, destruction is turned into a visual spectacle that offers the beholder scopic control over a cityscape freighted with contradictory emotions. Kerstin Barndt compares the transformation of Fordist regions in East and West Germany into museums and garden landscapes that incorporate industrial ruins. She is interested in whether industrial ruins mount any resistance to their own naturalization or instead succumb to the dehistoricizing impulse of this post-Fordist phenomenon. In a critical reading of Schumpeter's notion of creative destruction, Barndt locates a metaphorical level of the text that naturalizes the economy. The aesthetic transformation of Fordist urban regions into post-Fordist landscapes produces a similar naturalization. Crucial to this argument is Barndt's reading of ruins as postindustrial allegories. However, while she asserts a similarity of transformation in East and West, she traces a dissimilarity of affect: in the West, the pleasures of postmodern spectacle; in the East, a melancholic contemplation of loss prevailing over any sense of new beginnings. George Steinmetz compares the ruinscapes of Detroit and Namibia, focusing on the ways that formerly hegemonic white groups use urban-industrial and colonial ruins. In both places these objects are evocative for these groups, but semiotically underdetermined. White suburbanites use Detroit's industrial ruins to nourish their nostalgic longing for the city's golden era of Fordist prosperity. But nostalgia, Steinmetz argues, does not involve any confusion of past and present: the nostalgic object belongs unambiguously to the past. By contrast, German-speaking Namibians use colonial ruins to cultivate a sense of melancholia that simultaneously denies and acknowledges the end of German colonial power. Jonathan Veitch reports on his journey through atomic ruins at the Nevada test site. He was baffled when he arrived at the site, expecting to find a post-apocalyptic devastation and seeing instead a parklike landscape that naturalizes the memory of the atomic age as a necessary step in the forward march of progress. Veitch asks whether it will ever be possible to use this site to create an understanding of history, or whether the site will inevitably retain its aura of the banality of evil. Finally, Gustavo Verdesio argues that the archaeological sites of the Amerindians have remained invisible due to the ideologically biased regimes of visibility that control researchers' gaze at the remnants of these cultures.

In the last part of the book, "Ruin Gazing," contributors explore the role that the act of gazing at ruins plays in the production of philosophical thought, aesthetics, and aesthetic practice in different media and genres. Alexander Regier probes the way in which philosophical reevaluations of the Lisbon earthquake by Burke and Kant domesticate what eyewitness reports perceived as a formless and unclassifiable excess of devastation. Through the mastery afforded by distance, fragmentation becomes a necessary precondition for the emergence of aesthetic pleasure, for the very act of beholding. The Lisbon earthquake paradoxically acquires foundational value, serving as "stabilizing grounding" for the emergence not only of the Kantian category of the sublime and, through it, the architecture of the three critiques, but also of modern geology as a scientific discipline. Tatiana Smoliarova explores the Russian poet Gavrila Derzhavin's foreboding expressed in his descriptive poem "To Eugene. Life at Zvanka," as he imagines the destruction of his wife's country mansion. Smoliarova connects this vision of ruin to the destruction of Pope's villa at Twickenham and to the emergence of an "anxiety of heritage," the product of modernity's atomistic sensibility, which Derzhavin paradoxically dramatizes through consciously archaic poetic diction and through his infatuation with optical devices and machines. Johannes von Moltke invites us to think about the connection between cinema and ruins. In the first part of his essay, von Moltke pursues the ontological and epistemological affinity between the two. He starts his inquiry with Benjamin's description of cinematic experience as that of the spectator-adventurer traveling among the ruins of tradition, inviting us to reconstruct modern subjectivity out of a ruin aesthetic. Von Moltke turns next to Siegfried Kracauer, continuing the inquiry on an ontological level and proposing that the shared indexical quality of ruins and cinema returns in Kracauer's attempt to theorize the parallels between camera reality and historical reality. In the second part of the essay, von Moltke begins to sketch a ruin aesthetic by tracing the many representations of ruins that have characterized cinema from its beginnings. Cinema's fascination with images of ruins is the most "visible manifestation of cinema's and the ruin's common function to visualize time and history in modernity." Eric Rentschler revisits the genre of the German *Trümmerfilm* (rubble film) in the wake of Sebald's 1997 lectures on "Air War and Literature." Arguing that Sebald's dichotomy of realist description versus aesthetic stylization does not allow us to access the specific cultural work performed by these films, he proposes to explore instead how exactly rubble signifies in these films. "Exercises in the management of shattered identity," the films both look at and look away from the true state of the nation's ruination, as Sebald claims is true of postwar German culture in general. Yet some of these films also stage remarkable moments of confrontation with the catastrophic legacy of National Socialism. More importantly, the films contributed decisively to a form of mythical thinking that is central in the wake of the war that invoked fate and destiny rather than human agency, and whose naturalizing power still informs Sebald's concept of a "natural history of destruction." Helen Petrovsky devotes her chapter to Boris Mikhailov's mutely resistant, amateurish-looking, seemingly meaningless photographs of the late Soviet collective experience of life. Conceived as haphazard series from an open-ended archive, shot from the point of view of a present that looks at itself with retrospective distance and with a sense of both stagnation and completion, Mikhailov's works bring into focus commonplace structures of feeling, a collective private experience of the grayness of time, documenting a habitual, banal existence that normally eludes representation.

## Notes

1. Otto Pohl, "Sept. 11 Photo Exhibition Touches a Nerve in Berlin," *New York Times*, July 7, 2002. The exhibition is "Here Is New York," originally shown in SoHo.
2. Arendt, *The Origins of Totalitarianism*, VIII.
3. Adorno, "Commitment," 194–95.
4. Quoted in Woodward, *In Ruins*, 188–89.
5. Macaulay, *Pleasure of Ruins*, introduction (no page number) and 454.
6. See Huyssen, "Anselm Kiefer: The Terror of History, the Temptation of Myth," in *Twilight Memories*, 215–18.
7. Svetlana Boym, "Peterburg umer. Da zdravstvuet Peterburg!: Ruiny revoliutsii u Shklovskogo i Mandel'shtama," 171–82. See also Kalinin, "Istoriia kak iskusstvo chlenoraz-del'nosti (istoricheskii opyt i meta/literaturnaia praktika russkikh formalistov)."
8. On ruins in the Soviet Union, see the cluster of articles published in *Slavic Review* 65, no. 4 (2006).
9. Lowenthal, *The Past Is a Foreign Country*, 54.
10. "Revising 9/11," *New York Times*, 11 September 2005.
11. Nora Gallagher, "Waking from a Sound Sleep," *Los Angeles Times*, September 9, 2005.
12. Timothy Garton Ash, "The Thin Veneer of Civilization," *Los Angeles Times*, September 8, 2005.
13. To say that the attack on the World Trade Center is a product of modernity is a facile and politically charged statement. Rather than asserting such a connection, we would like to put this very question in the larger context of the role of ruins in modernity.
14. Roth, "Irresistible Decay," 9–11.
15. Assmann, Gomille, and Rippl, *Einleitung*, 11. In his upbeat exploration of the aesthetic experience of ruins, which rests on the thesis that "the ruin can spring forth as an unanticipated aesthetic whole," Robert Ginsberg operates with a particular expansive definition of ruin, which includes nature as well as fragmentary cinematic, literary, or philosophical works. See Ginsberg, *The Aesthetics of Ruins*, xvii.
16. Diderot, *Salon of 1767*, 199.
17. Ibid. As it mistakes the pronouns, the English translation mysteriously conceals the fact that the friend invoked here is a woman.
18. Ibid., 200.
19. Edensor, *Industrial Ruins*, 15.
20. Arendt, *The Origins of Totalitarianism*, VIII.
21. Arendt, "Franz Kafka," 74.

# PART I

# CATASTROPHE, UTOPIA, AND THE ARCHITECTURE OF DESTRUCTION

ANDREAS HUYSSEN

# 1

## AUTHENTIC RUINS

*Products of Modernity*

At a time when the promises of the modern age lie shattered like so many ruins, when we speak with increasing frequency of the ruins of modernity, both literally and metaphorically, a key question arises for cultural historians: what has shaped our imaginary of ruins in the early twenty-first century? For example, do we think primarily of the bombed-out cities of the Second World War and of the decaying residues of the industrial age and its shrinking cities in Europe and the United States? Or does the contemporary love affair with ruins resemble the earlier fascination with the ruins of classical antiquity? Where do 9/11 and the bombing of Baghdad and Falluja figure in this discourse, if at all? And what is the relation of this imaginary of ruins to the obsessions with urban preservation, remakes, and retro fashion, all of which seem to express a fear or denial of the ruination by time? Clearly our imaginary of ruins can be read as a palimpsest of multiple historical events and representations, and the intense concern with ruins is part of the current privileging of memory and trauma both inside and outside the academy.

Given this overdetermination in the way we imagine and conceptualize ruins, I would like to ask whether there can be something like an authentic ruin of modernity. To look for an answer, I will go back to the earlier imaginary of ruins that developed in the eighteenth century's quarrel of the ancients and moderns, was carried forth in romanticism, and privileged in the nineteenth-century's celebratory and deeply ideological search for national origins, only to end up in the ruin tourism of our time. I intend this chronicle to sound like a narrative of ruinous decay, as a move from the authentic to the inauthentic. Key for my argument will be the work of Giovanni Battista Piranesi, which I see as one of the most radical articulations of the ruin question within modernity rather than after it.

My interest in coupling the abstract concept of authenticity with the concreteness of ruins and their imaginary is based on the idea that both the ruin itself and the notion of the authentic are central topoi of modernity rather than results of what Hobsbawm has called the age of extremes. Modernity as ruin was a central topos long before the twentieth century. What I call the authentic ruin is not to be understood as some ontological essence of ruins, but rather as a significant conceptual and architectural constellation that points to moments of decay, falling apart, or ruination as early as the beginnings of modernity in the eighteenth century. Just as the imaginary of ruins was created in early modernity rather than being modernity's end product, the notion of authenticity is a thoroughly historical concept produced by modernity itself rather than referring to an atemporal transcendent essence or to a premodern state of grace. Tied in literature and art to eighteenth-century notions of authorship, genius, orginality, selfhood, uniqueness, and subjectivity, the idea of authenticity became more desirable and intense the more it was threatened by alienation, inauthenticity, and reproducibility in the course of modernization. As a term in that broader semantic field, it had its heyday in the second half of the twentieth century, in the wake of Heidegger's *Eigentlichkeit* and Adorno's claims for the authenticity of modernist art.[1] Its popularity today can be found in retro authenticity, authentic remakes, and authenticity consulting, all phenomena which implicitly though unknowingly deny what they claim to be. At the same time, authenticity has fallen on hard times in intellectual discourse. From Adorno's denial of any authenticity to life in capitalist society to Derrida's critique of any essentialism, authenticity has been disparaged as ideology or metaphysics, tied to a jargon of Eigentlichkeit, pseudo-individualization, and delusions of self-presence.

Nevertheless, I am not ready to abandon the concept altogether, and I take comfort in the fact that even Adorno, one of the most radical critics of the post-1945 form of Eigentlichkeit, still spoke of the authenticity of modernist art as radical negation. His is a notion of the authentic aware of its own historicity. Similarly, I will locate the authentic ruin of modernity in the eighteenth century and suggest that this earlier imaginary of ruins haunts our discourse about the ruins of modernity. At the same time, I acknowledge that the twentieth century has produced a very different imaginary of ruins that has made the earlier authentic ruin obsolete. Even genuine or *echt*—as opposed to authentic—ruins have metamorphosed. The idea of decay, erosion, and a return to nature, so central to the eighteenth-century imaginary of ruins, is eliminated when Roman ruins are sanitized and used as mise-en-scène for open-air opera performances (the Baths of Caracalla in Rome); when ruins of medieval castles or dilapidated estates from later centuries are transformed into conference sites, hotels, or vacation rentals (Paradors in Spain and the Landmark Trust in the United Kingdom); when industrial ruins are made over into cultural centers; or when a museum like the Tate Modern installs itself in a former power plant on the south bank of the Thames. Authenticity itself seems to have become part of preservation and restoration.

Authentic ruins, at least as they existed in the eighteenth and nineteenth centuries, seem to have no place in late capitalism's culture of commodity and memory. Commodities in general do not age well. They become obsolete and are thrown out or recycled. Buildings are torn down or restored. The chance for things to age and to become ruins has diminished, ironically in the same measure that the average age of the populace continues to rise. The ruin of the twenty-first century is either detritus or restored age. In the latter case, real age has been eliminated by a reverse face lifting, whereby the new is made to look old. Repro and retro fashions make it increasingly hard to recognize the genuinely old. Kluge once spoke tellingly of "the attack of the present on the rest of time."[2]

If in the late twentieth century, as Lyotard has claimed, architecture and philosophy lie in ruins, leaving us only with the option of a "writing of the ruins" as a kind of micrology, then the question arises whether the tradition of modernist thought all the way into postmodernism is overshadowed by the catastrophic imagination and imaginary of ruins that has accompanied the trajectory of modernity since the eighteenth century.[3] Architecture in a state of decay or destruction seems to be an indispensable topos for this tradition. Real ruins of different kinds function as screens on which modernity projects its asynchronous temporalities and its fear of and obsession with the passing of time. Benjamin says that allegories are, in the realm of thought, what ruins are in the realm of things; this implies a production principle of modern art, literature, and architecture which is a priori directed toward the ruinous.[4] For Adorno, in analogous fashion, the most authentic works of modernity are those which are objectively and formally determined by the ruinous state of the present. The architectural ruin seems to hover in the background of an aesthetic imagination that privileges fragment and allegory, collage and montage, freedom from ornament and reduction of the material. Perhaps this is the secret classicism of modernism which, however different from eighteenth-century classicism in its coding of temporality and space, is still predicated on an imaginary of ruins.

Classicism in the eighteenth century defined itself through the ruins of antiquity, but aimed at a totality of style and symbolic representation rather than privileging montage, dispersion, and fragmentariness as modernism did. One doesn't have to be a metaphysician of history in order to see, from today's perspective, the field of classical modernism as an oscillating landscape of ruins left from a failed attempt to create an alternative kind of totality that in architecture was called International Style.[5]

As a product of modernity rather than a phenomenon from a deep premodern past, authenticity is analogous to Benjamin's aura. Originality and uniqueness, which characterize the auratic work of art in Benjamin, were made into privileged categories in an earlier age that was already flooded by reproductions, translations and copies of all kinds. Analogously, the ideological value of authenticity rose in proportion to mass culture's inherent tendency toward reproduction and repetition. Even in the transition from a Fordist to a post-Fordist mode of production, we can detect the attempt to return the semblance of authenticity and uniqueness to commodities by means of customization. Aura and authenticity are analogous to each other. Both have to be framed historically rather than ontologically. Modernist decisionism declared both of them dead and gone, but both have proved to be resistant to ideological critique. The desire for the auratic and the authentic always reflected the fear of inauthenticity, the lack of existential meaning, and the absence of individual originality. The more we have learned to understand all images, words, and sounds as always already mediated, the more it seems we desire the authentic and the immediate. A gap opens up between intellectual insight into the obsolescence of authenticity and the life world's desire for the authentic—cuisine, clothing, identity. This longing can be seen as a media culture's romantic longing for its other. Reality TV is its pathetic expression. As we know from the critique of the concept, the positing of stable origins and a historical telos are never far when the authenticity tune is being played. The same is true for the discourse of ruins, which has played such a central role in legitimizing the claims to power of modern nation-states.

Indeed, romantic ruins seem to guarantee origins. They promise authenticity, immediacy, and authority. However, there is a paradox. In the case of ruins, what is allegedly present and transparent whenever authenticity is claimed is present only as an absence. It is the imagined present of a past that can now be grasped only in its decay. Any ruin posits the problem of a double exposure to the past and the present. If the modern ruin is not exhausted by the semantics of pastness, its temporality, which points to past glory and greatness, is clearly different from the claims of plenitude and presentness invariably at stake in the discourse of authenticity. Yet authenticity claims are often contaminated by doubts which then have to be alleviated by further mythmaking. Thus some would claim that authentic authenticity was only possible in the past when the world was allegedly still *übersichtlicher* and not under the shadow of media representation and distortion. We know what kind of ideological phantasms such projections of authenticity have caused in the humanities and social sciences—from the authenticity of the archaic and primitive to the privileging of authentic community as opposed to the anomy and artificiality of modern societies. Especially in the post-Enlightenment discoveries of origins and national identities, the present of modernity appeared—more often than not—as a ruin of authenticity and a better and simpler past. Against this idea of a deep authenticity embodied in the ruins of a glorified past, I posit the idea of the authentic ruin as a product of modernity itself rather than as a royal road toward some uncontaminated origin.

Nostalgia is never very far when we talk about authenticity or romantic ruins. The political critique of ruin nostalgia simply as regression corresponds to the philosophical critique of authenticity as a phantasm grounding stable identities. But such a critique misses the fundamental ambiguity of the ruin and the authentic. However justified it may be to criticize the ideological instrumentalization of authenticity claims, it will not do to simply identify the desire for authenticity with nostalgia and dismiss it as a cultural disease, as Stewart argues in *On Longing*. Neither will it do to understand the modern imagination of ruins and its link with the sublime as expressing nothing but fantasies of power and domination, though that is the case for Speer's theory of ruin value.[6] The dimension present in any imaginary of ruins but missed by such reductive critiques is the hardly nostalgic consciousness of the transitoriness of all greatness and power, the warning of imperial hubris, and the remembrance of nature in all culture.

At stake in the authentic ruin of modernity is not simply the genuineness or *Echtheit* of specific ruins, nor is it some superhistorical memento mori. Genuineness as naturalness in opposition to artificiality and the fake—a topos central to eighteenth-century aesthetics and middle-class culture—is an empirically verifiable criterion of the ruin, and the memento mori dimension is not limited to modernity. We can speak of the modern authenticity of ruins only if we look at the ruin aesthetically and politically as an architectonic cipher for the temporal and spatial doubts that modernity always harbored about itself. In the ruin, history appears spatialized, and built space temporalized. My thesis is that an imaginary of ruins is central for any theory of modernity that wants to be more than the triumphalism of progress and democratization, or the longing for past greatness. In contrast to the optimism of Enlightenment thought, the modern imaginary of ruins remains conscious of the dark side of modernity, what Diderot described as the inevitable "devastations of time" visible in ruins.[7] It articulates the nightmare of the Enlightenment that all history might ultimately be overwhelmed by nature, a fear succinctly represented in Goya's famous etching *El Sueño de la Razón Produce Monstruos*.

Let me use Goya's etching to return to Piranesi, the master of the eighteenth-century ruin. The ambiguity of Goya's title is well known. "El sueño de la razón" means both the dream and the sleep of reason, thus pointing to what came to be known as the dialectic of the Enlightenment. There is, however, a third reading of the title. Let us think of the figure in the etching—who is dreaming or sleeping at his table, upon which we see the instruments of writing—as the artist imagining the other of reason, imagining what will become the etching before us. Let us assume that Goya's figure is Piranesi at the very moment of dreaming the shape of ruins as they will come alive in his etchings. Putting the emphasis on sueño as fantasy and representation rather than simply sleep or utopian anticipation permits me to read Piranesi as the creator of an authentic imaginary of ruins that reveals something central about modernity and its representations.

Piranesi's etchings from the middle of the age of Enlightenment point toward a critical and alternative understanding of modernity that stands against the naive belief in progress and the moral improvement of mankind. Although Piranesi's nightmarish image world had a strong influence on romantic literature, nineteenth-century romantic images of ruins tended to domesticate and beautify ruins by making them picturesque. It is no coincidence that Piranesi's work has been rediscovered in the twentieth century, often in the context of reductively realistic claims that his *Carceri* anticipated the *univers concentrationnaire* of fascism or the Stalinist gulag. Another presentist reading is that these etchings articulate the existential exposure and cast-out state of the modern individual in the face of overwhelming systems. Such interpretations ignore the connection between Piranesi's fantasies of incarceration and the archival documentation of the architectural ruins of the Roman empire which constitutes the major part of his work.

Art historians tended to confirm such views to the extent that they read the *Carceri* as a bizarre creation of the artist as a young man, focusing on Piranesi's role in the eighteenth-century quarrel over whether the architecture of Athens or that of Rome should have pride of place. This question was surely central to Piranesi's archival work in and around Rome, but exclusive focus on this debate ignores the fact that reworkings of the *Carceri* spanned most of Piranesi's career.

It also fails to stress the fact that later versions of the *Carceri* are visually very close to the etchings of Roman ruins.

With the help of an alternative body of Piranesi scholarship, I would like to argue that we can adequately understand the artist's imaginary of ruins only if we read his archive-driven etchings of Roman ruins together with the fantasy-driven spaces of his architecture of incarceration.[8] Only then can we speak of an authentic imaginary of ruins in a precise historical sense. Piranesi's ruins and his jails are artifice through and through. That is what constitutes their authenticity within his dark vision of a modernity still very much in the shadows of a glorious past. It is an authenticity that is captured by Adorno in *Aesthetic Theory*: "The proof of the tour de force, the realization of the unrealizable, could be adduced from the most authentic works."[9] What else are the *Carceri* if not unrealizable as architecture, and tour de force as drawings? For Piranesi and for Adorno, though he never wrote about this Italian artist, the refusal of wholeness and classical closure is a sign of authenticity. Authentic ruins in Piranesi and authentic works of art in Adorno point to an absence, the utopia that cannot be named in Adorno, the nightmarish dystopia that is inscribed in the utopia of neoclassicism. The tour de force in Piranesi's art points to the moment of coercion and violence that is implicit in all authenticity as carrier of authority. Authentic works for Adorno are fragmentary works whose achievement must be located in their lack of completion and whose "failure [is] the measure of their success,"[10] works such as those by Lenz, Hölderlin, Kleist, or Büchner "that succumbed to the terror of idealism's scorn."[11] At first popular in France and England, Piranesi's etchings of the *Carceri* and antique ruins eventually suffered a similar fate because they were irreconcilable with the post-Winckelmann idea of classicism and did not allow for Matthew Arnold's vision of antiquity as sweetness and light.

Piranesi considered the height of authentic architecture to be the monumental Roman temples, palaces, triumphal arches, and tombs of the Appian Way. He captured their overgrown remains with archival precision and in a unique style, from the *Prima Parte di Architetture e Prospettive* and the *Varie Vedute di Roma* (both 1743) to the four volumes of *Le Antichità Romane* (1756) and *Della Magnificenza ed Architettura de' Romani* (1761).

To Piranesi, the monumentality and sublimity of these ruins are more impressive than the miserable present which denies him, a trained architect, any chance to build in a grand style. He mobilizes all available visual tricks to achieve the monumental mise-en-scène of the ruins. In the dedication to *Prima Parte di Architetture e Prospettive* he writes: "I would only say that these speaking ruins have filled my spirit with images of a kind which even the most accurate drawings such as those by the immortal Palladio could never have succeeded in conveying, though I always kept them before my eyes."[12] At stake here is the subjective effect achieved by the representation, the production of phantasms which the ruins bring to life. The ruins flood the senses with images of architectonic space which include views not only of antique Rome but also of the *Carceri*. Especially in their second, significantly darker version, Piranesi's *Carceri* show close affinities with the etchings of antique ruins.

In their spatial configuration, the *Carceri* belong with Piranesi's imagined antiquity rather than with the concentration camps of the twentieth century or the panoptic jails of modern industrial societies. Roman architectural elements such as arcades of columns, broad flights of stairs, large portrait busts, tomb sculptures, and Latin inscriptions fill even the corners of Piranesi's vast jails. In his style of representation, however, the *Carceri* and the overgrown ruins of Rome belong with a present-day modernity, and not just that of the eighteenth century.

In order to understand the formal relevance of the *Carceri* for the modern imaginary of ruins, we must now focus on what, despite their affinities, distinguishes the views of Roman ruins from the prison etchings and stands in productive tension with them. The ruins are located in the urban landscape of Rome and its environs, the Campagna. Their erosion reminds us of that central aspect of the imaginary of ruins which Simmel has emphasized best: the return of architecture to nature.[13] What appears all too romantically as a reconciliation of spirit and nature in Simmel, however, assumes features of the uncanny in Piranesi. He joins masonry and soil to make it look as if the ruins had grown from the innards of the earth.

In their erosion, some of the buildings resemble threatening and inhospitable rock formations. The decaying monuments and remnants of gigantic buildings tower mysteriously and uncannily over a dwarfish present. The voices of the dead seem to speak through Piranesi's images of ruins. Instead of a *nature morte*, Piranesi gives us an *architettura morta*, which not only reminds the present of its own transitoriness but also warns that forgetting the past can be destructive to a culture. While his etchings of antique remnants focus on the intertwining of nature and architecture in decay, his *Carceri* give us pure architectural spaces far from nature, complex interior halls which seem to be partly ruins, partly unfinished buildings.

This impression is exacerbated by the fact that the spatial constriction typical of a prison is shown here not through the absence of space but paradoxically through the opening up of space toward infinity.[14] Passages, staircases, and halls seem to extend in all directions and lack spatial closure. An outside clearly may exist, even though it is not represented. Certainly the natural light streaming into the prisons points indirectly to some outside space. The *Carceri* are so fascinating because both their temporality and their spatiality remain indefinable. Just as the opposition of proximity and distance seems abolished in their confusing spatial arrangements, the borders between past, present, and future no longer seem to obtain. Even though we know that Piranesi was influenced by baroque theater decorations for prison dramas, his mise-en-scène of the prisons has to be read primarily as a formal architectonic proposition rather than as a simple message about the human condition. Reudenbach put it well when he wrote: "We see illogical spatial structures not because the goal is to represent prisons. On the contrary, building on an already developed iconography of prisons, the *Carceri* represent experimental space."[15] Piranesi is interested in prisons as a model for a vast interior space whose representation allows the artist's architectonic fantasy freedom from any realistic limitations. As he has already done in some of the architectonic fantasies in *Prima Parte*, Piranesi ignores the laws of Euclidean space. Units of built space are connected atectonically and illogically. Each etching has several distinct perspectives so the gaze of the spectator never comes to rest. The closer we look, the more disturbed our gaze becomes. In a detailed analysis of the architectural structure of the *Carceri*, Vogt-Göknil has shown how three-dimensional spaces evolve into two-dimensional planes, how depth seems to be pulled apart and breadth shrunk.[16]

Especially uncanny is the relationship between space and a kind of light that seems to produce darkness: "Rays of light leave their natural trajectory. They bend and curve around things, sliding from one object to another, occasionally jumping over interstitial spaces."[17] The walls seem to absorb light instead of reflecting it. The rules of tectonics and central perspective are cancelled. As Walpole puts it, Piranesi "has imagined scenes that would startle geometry."[18] And Goethe emphasizes the difference between his perception of ruins and the effects Piranesi creates.[19]

Contrary to certain claims, Piranesi's strange spaces must not be attributed to some inability of the artist or to simple playfulness. He refuses to represent homogeneous enlightened space in which above and below, inside and outside, can be clearly distinguished. Instead he privileges arches and bridges, ladders and staircases, anterooms and passageways. While massive and static in their encasings, the prisons suggest motion and transition that leave the spectator's gaze unanchored. Instead of viewing limited spaces from a fixed perspective and a safe distance, the spectator is drawn into a proliferating labyrinth of staircases, bridges, and passageways leading into infinity. It is as if the spectator's gaze is imprisoned by the represented space, captured because there is no firm point of view as the eye wanders through the labyrinth. Contrary to what Kupfer claims, this does not suggest that space and time lose all meaning.[20] Instead, Piranesi follows to their logical conclusion the spatialization of history and the temporalization of space which already characterize his etchings of antiquities. In his *Carceri d'invenzione*—the full title is significant here—times and spaces are telescoped and superimposed as if in a palimpsest whereby this complex, temporally fraying imagination of space becomes a prison of invention. It is a tour de force, as Adorno calls the works of art that he finds most authentic.

Tafuri has argued that by breaking with the temporal and spatial perspectivalism of the Renaissance, the *Carceri* point toward basic principles of construction that were developed much later by the cubists, constructivists, and surrealists.[21] It is important, however, to emphasize a fundamental difference between Piranesi and the historical avant-garde. Piranesi's imagination is not energized by some constructive utopian ideal of multiperspectivalism and spatial fluidity (as was Eisenstein), nor does he privilege montage or the fragment. Rather he remains haunted by the threatening aura of ruins, by their oppressive interlocking of past and present, nature and culture, death and life. His work undermines any enlightened and secure standpoint in time or space, and it is quite distant from the avant-garde's ethos of alternative futures. Ultimately, Piranesi's prisons are also ruins, more authentic even than the Roman ruins of the *Vedute di Roma*. The threatening simultaneity of times and spaces, of condensed and displaced perspectives, which are exacerbated in the second version of the prison etchings by the increased presence of instruments of torture, pushes the impression of uncanny space to an extreme only in the *Carceri*.

In their reciprocal tension and their obsessive intermingling of times and spaces, Piranesi's prisons and ruins can be read as allegories of a modernity whose utopia of freedom and progress and of linear time and geometric space they not only question but cancel out. A past embodied in ruined and memory-laden architecture seems to tower over the present of the Enlightenment. In this sense, Piranesi's imaginary of ruins is the product of an age that only slowly escaped from the overwhelming shadow of classical antiquity. In its decay, antique architecture articulates a dialectical constellation of nature and history which posits the changeability and contingency of both nature and history; it does not simply oppose blind mythological nature to history as an ontological space of enlightened human agency. Piranesi's imaginary of ruins thus belongs with a self-critical consciousness that has accompanied enlightened modernity from its beginning. The authenticity I claim for Piranesi's imaginary of ruins lies in this critical aesthetic consciousness and in its articulation in terrifyingly beautiful etchings. If the etchings of decaying classical architecture point to a natural history of destruction in a Sebaldian manner, then the *Carceri* suggest a cultural history of incarceration in an infinite inner space that no longer has any outside.

Reading Piranesi through Adorno's and Benjamin's concept of natural history, which after all is grounded in a philosophy of history, also reveals the historical limits of this authentic imaginary of ruins. As a form of secularized theology with rises and falls, declines and redemptions of cultures, the philosophy of history produced by the Enlightenment stands like a ruin itself in the twenty-first century. Analogously, Piranesi's imaginary of ruins has become a ruin.[22] This argument finds support in modernist architecture, as the building materials of concrete, steel, and glass do not erode or decay in the way that stone does. They refuse the return of culture to nature which was still so central to Simmel.[23] It would have never occurred to Corbusier or Mies van der Rohe to develop a ruin theory of architecture as Speer did, even though by the early twenty-first century much modernist architecture has reached its own ruinous stage.[24] However, the catastrophes of the twentieth century have mainly left rubble behind rather than ruins in Piranesi's sense, even if some of that rubble has lent itself quite well to beautifying representations. The age of the authentic ruin is over. We can write its genealogy, but we can't resurrect it. We live in the age of preservation, restoration, and authentic remakes, all of which cancel out the idea of the authentic ruin.

## Notes

A slightly different version of this chapter was published as "Nostalgia for Ruins," *Grey Room* 23 (spring 2006): 6–21.

1. Knaller and Müller, "Authentisch/Authentizität."
2. Kluge, *Der Angriff der Gegenwart auf die übrige Zeit.*
3. Lyotard, *Heidegger and "the Jews,"* 43.
4. Benjamin, *The Origin of German Tragic Drama*, 178.
5. For a compelling account of modernism as ruin, see Clark, *Farewell to an Idea*, especially the introduction.
6. Speer, *Erinnerungen*, 69.
7. Diderot, *Ästhetische Schriften*, 150.
8. Important for my argument are the following studies: Vogt-Göknil, *Giovanni Battista Piranesi*; Reudenbach, *Giovanni Battista Piranesi*; Kupfer, *Piranesis Carceri*; and Miller, *Archäologie des Traums*.
9. Adorno, *Aesthetic Theory*, 106; "An den authentischsten Werken wäre der Nachweis des tour de force, der Realisierung eines Unrealisierbaren zu erbringen" (ÄT 163).
10. Adorno, *Beethoven*, 220.
11. Adorno, *Aesthetic Theory*, 63; "die unterm Terror des Idealismus der Geringschätzung verfielen" (ÄT 99).

12. Piranesi, *Catalogue*, 115.

"I would only say that these speaking ruins have filled my spirit with images of a kind which even the most accurate drawings such as those by the immortal Palladio could never have succeeded in conveying, though I always kept them before my eyes."

13. Simmel, "Die Ruine," 118–24
14. Tafuri, *The Sphere and the Labyrinth*, 31.
15. Reudenbach, *Giovanni Battista Piranesi*, 44, my translation.
16. Vogt-Göknil, *Giovanni Battista Piranesi*, 40.
17. Ibid., 37–38.
18. Cited in ibid., 28.
19. Goethe, *Italienische Reise*, 452.
20. Kupfer, *Piranesis* Carceri, 46.
21. Tafuri, *The Sphere and the Labyrinth*.
22. Wendorf has made the interesting argument that repetitive mechanical reproduction has produced a material kind of ruination—i.e., that of the copperplate which had to be "reworked in order to offset the graphic loss through printing." Wendorf, "Piranesi's Double Ruin."
23. Simmel, "Die Ruine," 119–20.
24. Jaguaribe, "Modernist Ruins," 327–48.

ANTHONY VIDLER

# 2

## AIR WAR AND ARCHITECTURE

Those who have read W. G. Sebald will understand that my title refers to his *Luftkrieg und Literatur* (Air war and literature), translated into English as *On the Natural History of Destruction.* Sebald investigates the delay in literary response to the impact and effect of the Allies' bombings, notably those of Dresden and Hamburg in 1944, on the German psyche, believing that "those directly affected by the experience neither shared it with each other nor passed it on to the next generation."[1] He looks at images from before and after the reconstruction following the bombings and sees the need for a collective amnesia toward the ruins, a massive—and literal—coverup through the mechanism of architecture. He traces this to a mingling of guilt, embarrassment, and, significantly, the need to demonstrate "rebuilding to be 'greater and stronger than ever before.' "[2] The habit of "looking and looking away at the same time," noted by Sebald, has not been confined to the writers of postwar Germany.[3] It has been extensively noted in Japan, and we can trace it in the United States, the Netherlands, Belgium, and France, despite that country's relative freedom from bombing. While Sebald cites "the culture of the British Isles" as more concerned with history and tradition, we will see that there is no shortage of suppression, repression, and downright delusion in the various British responses to the air war.[4]

What is telling to someone of my generation—I am a little older than Sebald—is that although he was not born until 1944, in a remote Alpine village, and thus was "almost untouched by the catastrophe then unfolding in the German Reich," it "nonetheless left its mark" on his mind.[5] I was born in 1941 and lived on the outskirts of London. The mark left on my mind—by the endless air-raid sirens, bomb blasts, whine of V2 rockets overhead, and taking shelter beneath a steel kitchen table, followed by evacuation (to Coventry no less)—has been formidable. It has been reinforced over the last decades by the nuclear-missile crises of my student years, reports from Korea and Vietnam, sabbaticals in London and Paris during terrorist campaigns, two Iraq wars, and—most agonizingly—by witnessing the fall of the World Trade Center's twin towers from only a few blocks away.

So, taking my cue from Sebald, I want to discuss here the effects of air war—not on literature, but on a more difficult subject, that of architecture and planning. I say more difficult because on the surface there is nothing more simple than seeing architecture as an immediate response to and palliative for the destruction caused by bombing. The reconstruction plans in Europe for London, Coventry, Dresden, Hamburg, and Berlin; in Japan for Nagasaki, Hiroshima, and Tokyo; and for many other urban centers all operated more or less quickly between 1945 and 1950 to erase the traces of attack, clear the rubble, and rebuild according to hopes for a better and more humane world. Certainly if we look at the classic accounts of architectural history after 1945—those of Reyner Banham, Kenneth Frampton, Alan Colquhoun, and Manfredo Tafuri (Leonardo Benevolo's work being a notable exception), all significantly enough written by those who had served in or at least experienced the war—we find little or no mention of the war years. The only mention of the war as an effect on architecture occurs in the always optimistic phrase "postwar reconstruction." Indeed, a Sebald of architectural history would be justified in asking many of the same questions of British writers (and also of French, Italian, German, and American writers) as Sebald himself did of his German literary contemporaries.

If we fast-forward to 9/11, we find no significant change in the rhetoric of reconstruction as a means of demonstrating resilience, resistance, and hope: "to build back higher and stronger than before," to demonstrate a tough and manly response to the "cowardly act" of the terrorists. Indeed, in the responses to the challenge of rebuilding; in the urge to quickly clear the rubble, idealize the process of redesigning the site (in this case, as has become all too clear, as a cover for the underlying economic requirements of the developer and the Port Authority of New York and New Jersey alike), and construe architecture as a form of reply to the attackers; in the very name Freedom Tower, we find ourselves in the world of Ayn Rand's *The Fountainhead*, with the architect as the savior of American individualism. To paraphrase Clausewitz, we might say this represents the consecration of architecture as the continuation of war by other means.

Yet beneath all this architectural bravado, as indeed beneath a great deal of political bravado today, one cannot help sensing anxiety. The fact that the most popular design for the rebuilt World Trade Center, that of Daniel Libeskind, was couched in the architectural language of expressionism—the language of rebuilding after the First World War; of the Glass Chain; of Bruno Taut's insistence on the need for a *Stadtkrone*, or city crown, to symbolize for the modern world what cathedrals and temples had for traditional cities, a crown to be built in the image of Mies van der Rohe's crystalline skyscrapers of 1922—gives us a clue.[6] For was not the language of expressionism also the language of trauma, unmitigated terror, pathological mental states, tormented screams and sexual fears—in popular terms, the language of Caligari? In this sense, as I have noted before, Libeskind's scheme performed a double function: capitalizing on the symbolism of glass, since Paul Scheerbart's encomiums of the 1900s a material representing transparency, democracy, the new society, and above all light; and indicating the trauma of loss and unbearable emotion, suffered by all who survived. The language of the project reveals both an anxiety of achievement—how can we speak as boldly and as confidently as before, thus in a postmodern moment falling back on the ready-made language of before—and an anxiety of loss, crystallized in a language that remembers former losses.

Recent historians of modern architecture have seen similar concerns pervading all architectural production since the Second World War. In a collection of essays by young scholars reformulating the terms for writing modern architectural history, called *Anxious Modernisms*, Goldhagen and Legault, the editors, trace many forms of anxiousness among architects:

> Frank Lloyd Wright is anxious about the "mobocracy"; Le Corbusier is anxious about commercialism and the international dominance of American culture, . . . Bakema is anxious about the palpable challenge to democratic freedom posed by the totalitarian state . . . The architects of the Hansaviertel are anxious about the GDR; the architects and planners of the Stalinallee are anxious about the imperial aspirations of the west. Kisho Kurokawa and his friends are, after the devastation of Tokyo and the annihilation of Hiroshima and Nagasaki, anxious about the very survival of their culture . . . In America, Eero Saarinen and . . . IBM are anxious about the threat computers posed to human dominance over nature . . . Rudofsky is anxious about the globalization of the International Style . . . Rudolph is anxious about how ornament and tradition fit into emerging critiques of the International Style.[7]

"This anxiety," they conclude, "knew no national or local boundaries. It affected the discourse of Modernism as a whole."[8]

Such anxieties, although common in the generation that came to maturity in the decades right after the war, might be termed performance anxieties, stemming from the enormous pressure exerted by the still living modern masters; the architects Alison and Peter Smithson referred to the long shadow of 1918–39, which they called the "Heroic Period."[9] As such professional anxieties occur with every creative act, we might also call them anxieties of influence.

However, the anxieties I wish to discuss here, with their effects on architectural practice after 1945, are none of these types: or rather all of these are part of a much larger anxiety, unmentioned by most architects because it runs directly against the ideology of their profession but nevertheless traceable in much postwar architecture. We all feel it, and it is a simple enough anxiety to describe though its effects are complex. This is the anxiety that emerged in fantasy in the 1880s, in more concrete terms after the First World War, and was reinforced by the technological advances used in the Second World War: quite simply, the anxiety about being bombed into oblivion. The history of this anxiety has been traced by Lindquist in *A History of Bombing*, which constructs what I believe to be the repressed master discourse of the twentieth century: not the trauma of past loss, but the anticipatory fear of future loss; in an age of futurism, the buried response of fear to optimism and hope. Lindquist has provided the backdrop for my inquiry: images of Paris illuminated from the air from "Engineer Robur's flying machine," and another image of his bombing "savages" from the same machine; images of gas attacks on London; and of the staged spectacles by the Royal Air Force, demonstrating on a fine afternoon in 1927 at the Air Show in Hendon how to bomb a native village. Lindquist has carefully built up a massive indictment of those who bombed, or who authorized or planned bombings, in violation of the Hague Convention of 1907, which states unequivocally that "bombardment, by whatever means, of towns, villages, dwellings, or buildings which are undefended, is prohibited," and which is still valid under international law, though always ignored.[10]

The planners speak for themselves. Witness, for instance, F. W. Lanchester (the British mathematician) in 1915: "The critical point and the point to be aimed at as an act of war, is that at which the fire-extinguishing appliances of the community are beaten or overcome. Up to this point the damage done may be taken as roughly proportional to the means and cost of its accomplishment . . . there will always be sentimentalists. To these the destruction of a city of 5,000,000 peaceable inhabitants by fire, with the scenes of horror that would inevitably ensue, will be looked on as the figment of a diseased imagination."[11] Or consider the British Air Ministry in September 1918 on the use of its recently expanded fleet of bombers that in the end had no impact on the outcome of the war: "I would not be too exact as regards accuracy in bombing railway stations in the middle of towns. The German is susceptible to bloodiness and I would not mind a few accidents due to inaccuracy. I would very much like if you could start a very big fire in one of the German towns . . ." The reply from Bomber Command was encouraging: "don't worry, the accuracy is not great at present . . ."[12] Or note the ominous (in retrospect) remarks of Squadron Leader Arthur Harris in 1924: "Where the Arab and Kurd had just begun to realize that if they could stand a little noise they could stand bombing, they now know what real bombing means, in casualties and damage; they now know that within forty-five minutes a full-sized village can be practically wiped out and a third of its inhabitants killed or injured by four or five machines which offer them no real target, no opportunity as warriors, no effective means of escape," which leads Harris to his equally ominous conclusion: "But now that we really were bombing other races, we had nightmares of being bombed ourselves."[13] As Sir John Maffrey, governor of India's Northwest Province, plaintively asked in 1922, "What are the rules for this kind of cricket?"[14]

The physical results, if not the psychological ones, of this *danse macabre* are well known. They are the backdrop, or rather the sites, for architectural developments from 1945 to the present. And I say to the present not simply because we are continuously presented with similar sites, the results of acts of war or terror, but because I am going to argue that no amount of reconstruction, obliteration of the traces, or happy coverups can erase the traces of these sites. They are the evidence we have of both loss in the past and of our anxiety for the future, of our fear of erasure through violence.

These sites, then, were the ground on which a new practice of architecture had to be constructed. While the traditional practice—that represented by Haussmann's reconstruction of Paris, for example—was certainly based on demolition, the scale of the demolition accomplished by the bombs of the Second World War, as well as the terrible human cost of such demolition, had never been experienced before.

The enormity of the destruction, both of human life and urban fabric, was hardly comprehensible and in any case could not be assimilated. Sebald argues that the devastation of Britain, Germany, and Japan, to mention only three of the combatants, was so great as to induce a kind of shell shock that inhibited direct confrontation of social and urban problems and encouraged a strange, almost hallucinatory state of business as usual.

And business as usual meant taking advantage of the large-scale demolition to realize modernists' grand prewar plans. Thus the City of London Plan, prepared during those very raids, mentioned the destruction (in cartoon form, at that) only in order to describe the new spatial order it would permit.

Where did this spatial order come from? It had been developed between 1920 and 1935, largely as a result of the plans for contemporary cities drawn up by Le Corbusier, and adopted as formulas to govern zoning and building by the

Congrès International d'Architecture Moderne after 1928. Le Corbusier proposed to dissolve the urban fabric into a continuous park. He saw the modern city as a system of mechanical infrastructures raised above nature, while the past was either eradicated or transformed, in an eighteenth-century manner, into ruin fragments in the park. Commenting on an aerial photograph of the districts of the Marais and the Champs-Elysées, Le Corbusier asked his reader to "imagine that this swarming mass, till now stuck on the ground like an arid crust, is scraped off, carted away, and replaced by pure crystals of glass." As far as Paris was concerned, such a clearing away necessarily involved the demolition of entire districts; but, Le Corbusier was pleased to note, the happy accident of his chosen grid would spare the churches, which would be surrounded not by houses and shops, but by greenery. With them among the foliage of the new parks, certain historical monuments, arcades, and doorways would be carefully preserved because they are "a page of history" or "a work of art": "And on a lawn stands a Renaissance hotel, trim and gracious. It is a hotel of the Marais conserved or transported; it is today a library, a lecture or conference room, etc." Thus "the vestiges of the past" would be "harmoniously framed by trees and forests." Le Corbusier's tactic is clear, as he fabricates what had been, for much of the nineteenth century, only a critical metaphor: "And yes, things also die one day, and these parks 'à la Monçeau,' are cemeteries, tidily maintained. There one is educated, one dreams and breathes: the past is no longer an evil force that assassinates life; the past has been put in its place."[15] The city has become no more nor less than a cemetery of its own past.

These plans were in a very real sense prepared out of and for the aerial perspective: the view from above—from the Eiffel Tower or from a plane—was crucial to the ability of the planner to understand his field of operation. Le Corbusier even inserts the shadow of the plane on his aerial perspective of towers. He was obsessed by planes: he had witnessed some of the early flights of Louis Blériot; saw planes as the progenitors of a new, streamlined, functional aesthetic; was close friends with Antoine de Saint-Exupéry; and flew across Brazil in 1929 and to Moscow in 1930. He worked closely with the pilot, ethnographer, and sociologist Paul-Henry Chombart de Lauwe, who wrote the first manuals on aerial photography. Chombart had demonstrated to the anthropologist Marcel Griaule how effective aerial surveillance might be in controlling colonial populations. Le Corbusier even wrote a book about planes, published in 1935.[16] But in it we get a slightly more sinister view: he wrote that the plane can become dove or falcon; and as falcon it presents danger—as in the images he published of the aircraft carriers or of the Italian air force on maneuvers. But these images in his book are juxtaposed with even more disturbing images: photographs of the traditional city demolished after bombing. His visions of the effects of bombing are reinforced by his arguments in the 1930s for his own plans as effective defenses against such bombing. He provides the testimony of a German general that his proposed *Ville Radieuse* would withstand any aerial attack and sustain no civilian casualties.[17]

The plans for new modernist cities drawn up after the war were in some sense solutions to the bombing that had occurred. I am certainly not denying their humanitarian purposes as their designs countered disease; allowed for the circulation of air, goods, and people; and exploited new technologies. But I am claiming that there was another, more opportunistic basis for the optimism among planners rampant after 1945. Listen to Hans Scharoun, the German expressionist architect: "What remained after the bombings and final battle executed a mechanical dispersal [that] ruptured the city form . . . [and] gives us the possibility to design an urban landscape . . . Through this it is possible to compose that which is overwhelming and scaleless into manageable parts, and to order these parts into a beautiful landscape—like forests, fields, hills and lakes."[18] Henry Morgenthau, the American Secretary of the Treasury, used a similar tone when he proposed the greening of the bombed German cities in 1944. That was, of course, to be the model of urban reconstruction and later of urban redevelopment from 1945 until at least 1970.

But there was another agenda behind this disurbanization of the urban, beyond the century or more of garden-city ideology and the modernists' visions of radiant cities—an agenda that neatly coincided with these idealized forms of the new city but that was shaped by more urgent pressures. In an incisive article, Galison demonstrates that the decentralization that became planning policy first in the United States and later in Europe was a direct result of the assimilation of the effects of bombing—the assessment of the success or failure of the bombing of German industry, and of the effects of the nuclear explosions over Hiroshima and Nagasaki.[19] Galison demonstrates that these assessments were first explored by the United States Strategic Bombing Survey between 1944 and 1947, under the leadership of the president of the Prudential Insurance Company—an appropriate chairman, given the bombing's destruction of real estate—and with the help of the heads of Standard Oil, General Motors, and similar companies. This team asked why German industry had been so little affected by the British and American campaigns. The answer was decentralization. Decentralization protected industry against bombing; it was also a possible defense against nuclear attack. Galison studies the way in which this report, with other research into network theory and cybernetics, led to a new planning policy for the United States, in which leaflets were prepared for every community urging decentralization of industry and housing, at least for the middle class. The completion of the interstate highway system was urged for the same strategic reasons. Planners were not slow to catch on. Hilberseimer, who had fled Germany for Chicago with Mies van der Rohe in 1939, published *The New Regional Pattern* ten years later; he argued for a mass decentralization of urban areas as a defense against aerial attack. Prefacing his study with images of Nagasaki before and after the nuclear explosion, he developed plans that took wind patterns into account not only to mitigate the effects of industrial smoke pollution but also to avoid radioactive fallout.

The other recommendation of the bombing survey was the construction of fallout shelters. That response of architecture to the consequences not simply of bombing, but of the nuclear threat leads to my second theme: an architecture of disillusion, produced out of the near certainty of total destruction; an architecture that, after the realization of the enormity of what had happened in 1945 in Japan, inspired a sometimes unconsciously—but sometimes very consciously—negative response to the human condition. As Cioran writes in 1960: "Our dreams of the future are henceforth inseparable from our fears . . . Today, reconciled with the terrible, we are seeing a contamination of utopia by apocalypse: the heralded 'new earth' increasingly assumes the aspect of a new Hell. But this Hell is one we are waiting for, we even make it our duty to precipitate its advent. The two genres, utopian and apocalyptic, which once seemed so dissimilar to us, interpenetrate, rub off on each other, to form a third, wonderfully apt to reflect on the kind of reality that threatens us and to which we shall nonetheless assent with a correct and disabused yes. That will be our way of being *irreproachable* in the face of fatality."[20]

This reflection was fully evident in the architecture of the 1960s and 1970s, but it also haunted the work of even those who most wanted to believe in a triumphant, modernist future. As Colomina points out, how else can we look on the *House of the Future* design by Alison and Peter Smithson for the Ideal Home Exhibition of 1955-56 except as a form of safe house?[21] Ostensibly a science-fiction mock-up, its smooth plastic forms evoking images of H. G. Wells, it was also, consciously or not, a shelter. In fact Alison Smithson had written to friends of her experiences in shelters during her evacuation from the bombing.[22] As Colomina notes, "the rooms flow into one another like the compartments of a cave . . . Cave dwelling, like bomb shelters, submarines, and spaceships, corresponds to a time of extreme danger outside. Caves are all interiorized spaces, the first bunkers."[23] As befits a shelter, the interior was to be totally air-conditioned, with temperatures controlled for specific rooms and times. Protected by a hermetically sealed sliding front door, the house was thus furnished with a "private sky" and "unbreathed air." Its totally enclosed courtyard, was, the Smithsons allowed, based on a painting, *The Garden of Paradise*, created around 1400 by the so-called Master of the Middle Rhine. The house is a pod, a shelter, a bunker, with a sealed and private paradise to contemplate while the apocalypse takes place all around.

Yet this vision of a bunker for the future salvation of humanity was almost immediately countered in the Smithsons' work by their *Patio and Pavilion*, erected for the exhibition. This is Tomorrow in 1956. In an exhibit that celebrated the delights of pop culture and consumerism, and whose catalog included an essay by the techno-futurist Reyner Banham, the Smithsons chose to build a shack out of wood and corrugated iron, surrounded by the detritus of civilization, the shards of a post-apocalyptic world. The Smithsons said their construction provided the experience "of walking into a house abandoned by the owners during the course of the evening meal, or into a ruined mine shut down by impending disaster and never reopened";[24] it was a stark contrast to the technological, space-age futurism that surrounded it, which the Smithsons had satirized in their "House of the Future." Tomorrow has become almost unthinkable.

Or at least this is the message my generation received. Who would want a future spent underground, in shelters that were all too like those musty, damp, often flooded holes in the ground, covered with corrugated iron and reinforced with iron bedsteads, that graced the bottom of every suburban garden in Britain —the shelters into which we as protesting children, coughing in the damp and cold, were herded at all hours of the night, shivering under blankets as the air-raid sirens sounded, bombs went off, and we waited for the all-clear? Unless I missed it, the all-clear has not yet sounded.

Our dilemma was summarized for us on the pages of Guy Debord's *Internationale Situationiste* (*IS*). Despite his short-lived romance with Constant, who quickly demonstrates the futility of built, megastructural architecture as another in a long string of impotent utopias, Debord dislikes modern architecture for its pretensions and complicities, implicit spectacles, and explicit functionalism, and its infernal pact with capital. Instead he favors walking through old Paris, exploring inner states of being through the *derivé*, the mapping of the sites of urban tenderness, the psychogeography of the city.

In an unsigned article in April 1962, the *IS* revealed the real irony of the shelter society.[25] In the article, the author shows that the supposed balance of terror maintained by the superpowers equals no more than a "balance of resignation," where a "permanent state of uncertainty" is secured by specialists who ensured the neutralizing of one menace by another.[26] We are preparing not for war but for the indefinite preservation of this balance through upping the stakes: quoting Barry Commoner, head of the U.S. thermonuclear scientific committee, the author warns that after an hour of nuclear war some 80 million American citizens would be killed, and that there was no hope of normal survival afterward.[27] The Joint Chiefs of Staff now count in megabodies, or millions of corpses, admitting that beyond the first half-day after an attack, there is no possibility of calculating any casualties. The Doomsday system has translated the "refusal of history" into precise technical powers that enforce submission and preclude any individual or social emancipation: the author writes that it "prevents people from living while it organizes their survival."[28]

Such a state of half-life is, the author in the *IS* argues, ensured by the development in fallout-shelter technology and the initiative, announced by President Kennedy in his 1961 State of Union address, of a massive civil-defense program to provide some fifty million shelters for American citizens. Seized on by industry—the Peace o' Mind Shelter Co. in Texas, the American Survival Products Corp. in Maryland, the Fox Hole Shelter Inc. in California, and the Bee Safe Manufacturing Corp. in Ohio—the shelter society is promulgated as a consumer necessity and a moral imperative. In this subterranean world, family values are enforced through arguments over whether one should let someone outside the family into one's shelter, with even some priests arguing that family comes first, and people have the right to defend their shelters with firearms. The shelter boom helps sustain the expansion of the domestic economy: "all the appurtenances of life on the surface are to be duplicated for the new duplicate life underground, even to plastic bags for those who die underground with the living."[29] No sooner did you have your American dream house aboveground than you have to buy another one underground. This is, the *IS* argues, "suicide on the installment plan," an air-conditioned vale of tears that had the effect of boosting a neo-Christianity. In the end the new habitat aboveground was no different in quality from that underground which was simply a "lower level of that architecture." Thus, "the concentration camp organization of the surface of the earth is the normal state of the present society in formation; its condensed subterranean version merely represents that society's pathological excess." Such, the author concludes, is the "urbanism of despair."[30]

Other images follow: the *Internationale Situationiste* of August 1964 reports on a June 1963 demonstration in Denmark in protest of a regional government atomic shelter that involved the reconstitution of a former bomb shelter, and in the same issue on the artist J. V. Martin's *cartographies thermonucléaires* made out of burned paper, representing different areas of the globe after an imagined Third World War.

It is with such images in mind that the counter-architectural architectural movements of the 1960s and early 1970s developed. For instance, Hans Hollein and Walter Pichler in Vienna in the early 1960s state nihilistically: "Architecture is the law of those who do not believe in law but make it. It is a weapon. It uses the most powerful means, whatever they might be. The machines are taken over by it, and men are no longer tolerated in its domain . . . The passage from the dream of the megastructure to the nightmare of the radical city closes the ambition of the Modern Movement." Other examples are Hollein's "solid cities" in his Stadt projects of 1960–63, with the carved totems of an uninhabitable city envisaged as megaliths in the landscape; or Pichler's underground city core in a deserted post-holocaust landscape; or Hollein's collage of the American aircraft carrier *Enterprise* stranded on an Austrian wheat field. These are the images that drive the desire of Archigram in the mid-1960s to escape to space, to develop survival pods like the one placed symbolically in a Piranesian ruin by Ron Herron in 1965. Arato Isosaki revisits the site of Hiroshima in 1968, with his "Reruined Hiroshima"; Superstudio in Florence designs underground cities that measure the beat of time in space; Haus-Rucker-Co. designs and tests their Flyhead; while Vittoria Pisani dons a gas mask as an emblem of the radical group Stampo Virile. Finally, OMA, in the form of Elia Zenghelis and Rem Koolhaas at the Architectural Association in London, reimagine London as a prison camp in the style of *1984* in *Exodus, or the Voluntary Prisoners of Architecture*.[31]

In conclusion, I want to go back to my opening remarks that situated the origin of the so-called new architecture in the heart of the war effort. With hindsight—of the kind demonstrated by Sebald—it is possible to recognize what survivors of the war themselves prefer to forget, or at least suppress: that the unbelievable loss of life and cities and the biological damage to the environment accomplished in a few short years by technology was the unspoken, often unthinkable, ground on which a whole generation placed their hopes for the future: the "history of the immediate future,"[32] as Reyner Banham put it, was to be the history of all wrongs put right. Thus we might understand the futuristic programs of Archigram—their little flowering gardens, machines tamed by the forest, metropolises escaping from their static sites, psychological tents and caves, prophylactic suits and tools—as founded on the fears of little boys scared by the blitz and designed to protect them from the greatest fear of all, that of annihilation from the air.

Childish fears, no doubt. But as resistance turns to irony, irony to realism, realism to pragmatism, and pragmatism to solace in spectacular visions, consumerist monsters, development triumphs, and nostalgic dreams, perhaps such anxieties, brought once again to the surface, will stimulate new resistances, desperately needed right now—resistances that will not take the critical understanding of the past as mere pessimism or wrongful authority, but as a salutary instrument against a globalizing development frenzy that insists on burying history.

## Notes

1. Sebald, *On the Natural History of Destruction*, viii.
2. Ibid., 6. Sebald is quoting Robert Thomas Pell.

3. Ibid., ix.
4. Ibid.
5. Ibid., vii–viii.
6. See Taut, *Die Stadtkrone,* and White, Introduction, 1–31.
7. Goldhagen and Legault, eds., *Anxious Modernisms,* 13.
8. Ibid.
9. Smithson and Smithson, "The Heroic Period of Modern Architecture."
10. Lindquist, *A History of Bombing,* 26.
11. Ibid., 39.
12. Ibid., 40.
13. Ibid., 48.
14. Ibid., 112.
15. Le Corbusier, *Urbanisme,* 267–73.
16. Le Corbusier, *Aircraft.* See my "Photourbanism," 35–46.
17. Le Corbusier, *La ville radieuse,* 15.
18. Quoted in Rogier, "The Monumentality of Rhetoric," 167.
19. Galison, "War against the Center."
20. Cioran, *History and Utopia,* 98.
21. Colomina writes that the house of the future "is a kind of bomb shelter" ("Unbreathed Air 1956," 47).
22. Alison Smithson, "Outbreak of War, 1939," 12.
23. Colomina, "Unbreathed Air 1956," 48.
24. Cited in Ibid., 49.
25. [Debord], "Géopolitique de l'hibernation." See also my "*Terres Inconnues,*" which elaborates on the theme of the aerial threat.
26. Ibid., 3.
27. Ibid.
28. Ibid., 4.
29. Ibid., 6.
30. Ibid., 6–7.
31. For a full historical analysis of these projects, see the excellent study by Rouillard, *Superarchitecture,* especially 173–202, and 511–27.
32. See Banham, "The History of the Immediate Future."

VLADIMIR PAPERNY

# 3

## MODERNISM AND DESTRUCTION IN ARCHITECTURE

My point of departure is three pairs of photographs.

The first pair juxtaposes the unfinished frame of Frank Gehry's Walt Disney Concert Hall in Los Angeles with the carcass of Minoru Yamasaki's Twin Towers in New York. We are conditioned to expect a building frame to consist of rectangular elements, or at least to contain some. Gehry's frame has none. Some would see it as a normal rectangular frame twisted and distorted by the creative will of a modernist: the modernist vocabulary, as Anthony Vidler observes, has always included "displacement and fracture, torquing and twisting, pressure and release."[1] Others, however, would see Gehry's frame as a postmodern or antimodern attack on the rigidity of modernist thinking.

The other photo in this first pair shows Yamasaki's rectangular frame deformed by a terrorist act. This violent deformation, as we will see, is also open to different interpretations.

The second pair includes Yamasaki's Twin Towers again, this time with his housing project Pruitt-Igoe as it was blown up by authorities in St. Louis in 1972 after it had been repeatedly vandalized by its residents, and attempts to revitalize it had failed.

The third pair shows the Cathedral of Christ the Savior in the center of Moscow in 1931, in the process of demolition to leave room for the proposed Palace of the Soviets, and the unfinished frame of this palace before it in turn was demolished.

The questions I will try to address are: To what degree, (if at all) is modernism responsible for the violence and destruction of the last two centuries? What is the relationship between modernism and political power? Does modernism have a built-in self-destructing mechanism?

**Howard Roark**

Ayn Rand's *The Fountainhead* is perhaps the most graphic representation of some central modernist categories. Rand was born Alissa Zinovievna Rosenbaum in 1905 in St. Petersburg; she spent the first 21 years of her life in Russia. In the novel, one can see allusions to some themes of the Russian avant-garde.

The hero of *The Fountainhead* is an architect, Howard Roark, who rejects the styles of the past: "I want to be an architect, not an archeologist. I see no purpose in doing Renaissance villas."[2] New technology, he says, should dictate new forms: "Your Greeks took marble and they made copies of their wooden structures out of it, because others had done it that way. Then your masters of the Renaissance came along and made copies in plaster of copies in marbles of copies in wood. Now here we are, making copies in steel and concrete of copies in plaster of copies in marbles of copies in wood. Why?"[3]

The buildings that Roark wants to create have no ornaments and imitate no old styles. They provide "the light, the air, the beautiful logic of the plan in their halls and offices."[4]

There is one important implication of this attitude toward the old: aging is equally bad. To Roark and his friends, it is better for a building to be violently destroyed than to die of natural causes. "I wish that in some future air raids a bomb would blast this house out of existence," says Roark's lover, Dominique, about his creation. "It would be a worthy ending. So much better than to see it growing old and soot-stained, degraded by the family photographs, the dirty socks, the cocktail shakers and the grapefruit rinds of its inhabitants."[5]

Russian futurism provides numerous examples of this anti-aging stance, from David Burliuk's "everyone's young, young, young, a devilish hunger in the stomach,"[6] to Vladimir Mayakovsky's "there's not a single grey hair in my soul,"[7] as well as his often proclaimed desire to die young and never succumb to aging, which may have been one of the reasons he committed suicide in 1930.

In Rand's novel, both the new architecture and Roark's body are made "of straight lines and angles, each curve broken into planes."[8] In contrast, Roark's opposite, Guy Francon, has a face that bears "not a single straight line; it was an artful composition in globes, circles, arcs, and ellipses,"[9] and his building has on its top a replica of the Mausoleum of Hadrian, the cylindrical building in Rome usually known as the Castel Sant'Angelo. The Dana Building, designed by Roark's teacher, Henry Cameron, is made of lines that "were hard and simple, revealing, emphasizing the harmony of the steel skeleton within, as a body reveals the perfection of its bones."[10]

Clearly not every modernist would have subscribed to such dichotomy. Le Corbusier's Villa Savoye, one of the most celebrated examples of early modern architecture, contains round elements despite its overall rectangular structure. Ivan Leonidov's design for the Narkomtiazhprom building in Moscow juxtaposes a rectangular volume and a curvilinear cylinder. Le Corbusier's last masterpiece, the Chapelle de Ronchamp, contains almost no straight lines.

A more precise meaning of the opposition between curved and rectangular would be the distinction between a shape that reveals the harmony of its skeleton and one that does not. Most modernists would agree on that distinction, while most postmodernists would attack it vigorously. The idea of a "decorated shed" put forward by Venturi, Scott Brown, and Izenour is a good example of such an attack, despite the fact that the authors repeatedly deny any affiliation with postmodernism.[11]

Roark's teacher, Henry Cameron, "was among the first and the few who accepted the truth that the tall building must look tall." Cameron "designed skyscrapers in straight vertical lines, flaunting their steel and height."[12] The desire to erect the tallest structure in the world goes back at least to Louis Sullivan, who says: "It must be tall, every inch of it tall. The force and power of altitude must be in it, the glory and pride of exaltation must be in it. It must be every inch a proud and soaring thing, rising in sheer exaltation so that from bottom to top it is a unit without a single dissenting line."[13] With few exceptions, modernists want their buildings to be as tall as possible. Leonidov wants his Narkomtiazhprom building to dwarf the Kremlin and St. Basil's Cathedral.[14] Le Corbusier considers even the buildings of New York of his day "too small."[15]

Closely connected to the idea of reaching for the skies is the desire to fly. Aviation is a major source of inspiration for many avant-garde movements. The futurist Vasilii Kamenskii likes to paint an airplane on his face. Mayakovsky writes a poem called "A Flying Proletarian."[16] When we see Roark for the first time, he is about to jump into a lake. His dive is like flying: "He stepped to the edge, raised his arms, and dived down into the *sky* below."[17]

For Francon, architecture "is a great Art" based on "three eternal entities: Truth, Love and Beauty."[18] Roark, on the other hand, is expelled from a school of architecture for neglecting the artistic side of his craft. "You have been excellent in all the engineering sciences," says his dean at their farewell meeting, "why neglect what may be termed the artistic and inspirational side of our profession and concentrate on all those dry, technical, mathematical subjects?"[19]

The names of many avant-garde movements suggest the same allegiance to technical subjects—for example, constructivism and functionalism. Roark would no doubt agree with Moisei Ginzburg's words: "The best library on contemporary architecture is a collection of the latest catalogs and price lists of technical firms."[20] However, many modernists, especially architects of the Russian avant-garde, have been accused of using references to function and construction to justify their exercises in abstract art. Taut, for example, is shocked to see his Soviet colleagues working like "artists." He writes that they sat "before their drafting tables and, as I observed with astonishment in 1932, very often did not visit the construction site; they did not even know whether the construction had begun and what stage it was in."[21]

Structure, function, construction, technology, machine—all these are, to a large degree, understood symbolically. To many modernists, especially to the members of the Russian avant-garde, these categories represent a new pantheon. Dokuchaev, a member of the rationalist movement, tries to analyze this in 1927: "If in the West, where industry and labor in general are more mechanized and automatized than with us, a romanticism of technology can develop in constructivist artists, then among us, in the years of economic collapse, industrial stagnation, and simple hunger, this romanticism of technology must inevitably acquire a literally mystical strength and significance."[22] Such symbolism and romanticism of technology can be seen in Le Corbusier's work as well. His "machines for living" are, first of all, beautiful sculptures.

"The client," says the dean to Roark, "thinks of that above all. He is the one to live in the house you build. Your only purpose is to serve him. You must aspire to give proper artistic expression to his wishes." Roark disagrees: "I don't intend to build in order to serve or help anyone."[23] He does not notice people and is not interested in their petty lives. "Do you see how many men are walking and living down there?" he asks the dean. "Well, I don't give a damn what any or all of them think about architecture—or about anything else, for that matter."[24] He refuses to let "messy life" interfere with his design process. He also refuses to work with others: "I don't work with collectives. I don't consult. I don't cooperate. I don't collaborate."[25] When his design for housing for low-income residents is altered against his will, he blows the building up. The jury (and obviously the author) finds him not guilty.

Of course, this blatant individualism represents only one side, the Nietzschean, of the modernist attitude to collectivism. The Russian avant-garde provides quite a different picture: one can think of numerous communal housing structures (by Ginzburg, Nikolaev, and others), collective bedrooms (by Melnikov and Kuz'min), and dwelling units designed by the collective Stroikom and published without the names of any individual contributors.[26] On the issue of "messy life," however, modernists—especially the Russian avant-garde—would all be in favor of expelling from new buildings everyday routines, household chores like cooking, laundry, not to mention "the family photographs, the dirty socks, the cocktail shakers and the grapefruit rinds"[27]—everything that is signified by the almost untranslatable Russian word *byt*. Mayakovsky's suicide note even mentions byt: "the love boat has crashed against byt."[28] Characteristically, the postmodern attack on modern architecture begins with Venturi's call "for messy vitality over obvious unity."[29] Modern architecture, he writes, "is dissatisfied with *existing* conditions. Modern architecture has been anything but permissive: Architects have preferred to change the existing environment rather than enhance what is there."[30] It's also worth noting that Meier, sometimes called "the last modernist," has fought with workers of the Getty Museum over their desire to "clutter" his clean white space with their family photos.[31]

Roark does not try to make a good impression on people with power. "Those who want me," he says, "will come to me."[32] The dean tries to reason with him: "You would sound much more convincing if you spoke as if you cared whether I agreed with you or not." Roark replies: "I don't care whether you agree with me or not."[33] In the novel, his strategy works. He does not go to the people with power; they come to him. Strangely, his strategy works in his love life as well: he wins Dominique's love by convincing her to marry two other men before marrying her himself. One of Dominique's husbands is Gail Wynand, a powerful publisher; he becomes one of Roark's strongest supporters and loses his fortune as a result.

The Russian avant-garde seems to have many proud, independent figures like Roark, including Mayakovsky. But we should not forget Pasternak's break with Mayakovsky's journal because it "depressed and repulsed by its excessive Sovietness, that is, its disgusting servility, that is a tendency toward unruliness with an official mandate."[34] Roark does not have an official mandate for unruliness when he plants a bomb, but he has a powerful publisher behind him. A few heroic constructivist and rationalist architects such as Tatlin, Leonidov, and Melnikov refuse to accept socialist realism and choose to become marginalized, like Cameron in Rand's novel. But the leading architects of the Russian avant-garde, like Ginzburg and the Vesnin brothers, not only collaborate with the Soviet government, they become members of it.[35]

### Minoru Yamasaki

The number "two" seems to play a significant role in Yamasaki's life. He has created two sets of twin towers, the first being the Century Plaza Hotel in Century City, California, 1966; two of his major structures were violently destroyed; and there were two terrorist attempts to destroy the Twin Towers in New York, with the first failing to do any significant damage to the buildings. He even married his wife twice. Yamasaki can be defined as a soft modernist. "There are a few very influential architects who sincerely believe that all buildings must be 'strong,'" he writes. "The word 'strong' in this context seems to connote 'powerful'—that is, each building should be a monument to the virility of our society. These architects look with derision upon attempts to build a friendly, more gentle kind of building."[36] He admires Mies van der Rohe's rectangular Seagram Building, saying that it is the building in the United States he would most like to have designed.[37] In fact, the Twin Towers can even be seen as two upside-down Seagram Buildings, with the original 38 floors stretched to 110.[38]

Yamasaki's Pruitt-Igoe residential project was blown up after being vandalized. The architectural critic Charles Jencks blames the project's architecture. "Modern architecture died in St. Louis, Missouri on July 15, 1972 at 3.32 p.m. (or thereabouts)," he writes, "when the infamous Pruitt-Igoe scheme, or rather several of its slab blocks, were given the final *coup de grâce* by dynamite." Pruitt-Igoe, which was constructed in 1952–55 "according to the most progressive ideals of CIAM (Congrès International d'Architecture Moderne)," was a failure, says Jencks, because its modernist "simplistic ideas, taken over from philosophic doctrines of Rationalism, Behaviorism and Pragmatism, proved as irrational as the philosophies themselves."[39] Jencks assumes that the "irrationality of Rationalism" has been sufficiently proven by philosophers. He tries to use postmodern philosophy to legitimize his criticism of modern architecture, but this does not work well: there is almost no connection between postmodernism in architecture and in philosophy. Jencks's definition of postmodern architecture is simple: "the end of avant-garde extremism, the partial return to tradition, and the central role of communicating with the public."[40] Postmodern philosophy is the opposite: it displays a great deal of extremism; breaks with traditions, such as those of the Enlightenment; and is rather opaque to the public.

Even though Yamasaki, unlike Roark, has not blown up his own residential project, he is perceived by Jencks and other postmodernists as the one responsible for the demolition. Perhaps unjustly, he is presumed to be indifferent to people and insensitive to their needs.

"There's nothing revolutionary about the World Trade Center," writes Mumford. "Tall buildings are outmoded concepts—this is Victorian thinking. Skyscrapers have always been put up for reasons of advertisement and publicity. They are not economically sound or efficient—in fact they are ridiculously unprofitable."[41]

The World Trade Center was built by the Port Authority of New York and New Jersey, a quasi-governmental organization with practically unlimited resources and autonomy. The Port Authority was established in 1921 to administer the harbor for the two states; it has jurisdiction over about 1,500 square miles centered on the Statue of Liberty. The World Trade Center grew not from any need for office space in lower Manhattan but from the ambitions of the Port Authority's director, Austin Tobin, and of the chairman of the Downtown-Lower Manhattan Association, David Rockefeller.

There was strong opposition to the proposed World Trade Center from two groups. First were real-estate developers, particularly the owners of the Empire State Building, which stood to lose both its status as the tallest building in the world and possibly its tenants. The developers claimed that the Port Authority was competing unfairly because of its access to public money. Second were the owners of small businesses that would be wiped out by the construction. Yamasaki walked the site and concluded that there was not a single building worth saving.[42] Predictably, the owners resented the Port Authority's power. In the words of Oscar Nadel, who owned a radio shop on Greenwich Street, it felt "just as though we were living in Russia or Cuba, where a man doesn't have anything to say about what happened to him."[43]

The community life in a few blocks that became the World Trade Center was destroyed. "The people building it paid no attention to the consequences of what was happening with the wider idea of what the economy in New York should be like," says Pete Hamill, a New York writer. "And I hated it, you know, I hated that, the arrogance of it, as a kid. I was young and I didn't like that stuff."[44]

Yamasaki worked with Leslie Robertson, a structural engineer. The design they came up with and the design process itself were unique. First, Robertson, in his words, was the only structural engineer in the world using computers in the late 1960s.[45] Second, the structure of Twin Towers was the first skyscraper to be modeled after an airplane. "It was built more like the wing of an airplane," says Robertson. "And in the wing of the airplane, the strength is all in the surface of the wing."[46]

Yamasaki, the soft modernist, acted like Roark when he agreed with the Port Authority's plan to turn a few blocks into the clean slate that eventually became Ground Zero. He wanted the Twin Towers to have open, uncluttered interior spaces uninterrupted by support columns. This modernist desire resulted in an innovative design, but it contributed to the building's destruction. Karl Koch III, one of the builders of the Twin Towers, describes a visit his father, also an experienced builder, paid to the unfinished World Trade Center:

> Dad shook his head. "The design is bad," he said. "It isn't strong. There should be steel columns across the whole floor to keep those ceilings up. Where are the beams and columns?"
>
> "They're spanning the open floor area with trusses, Pop. It's a new, *modern* design."[47]

On 9/11, "the exterior walls performed beautifully, as long as the floors were intact," writes Koch. "It was the ensuing fire that weakened the floor system and then caused them to collapse as if they were imploding."[48]

"Would a less radical departure from traditional key structural elements have yielded a less devastating result?" he asks. His answer is a careful and qualified "yes."[49] In other words, if the office floors had been cluttered with support columns, the Twin Towers might still be standing.

It may be that the modernist worship of technology, understood symbolically, played a role in the destruction of the Twin Towers.

### Frank Gehry

Frank Gehry participated in the Deconstructivist Architecture show, curated by Philip Johnson and Mark Wigley at the Museum of Modern Art in 1988. The title of the show is somewhat misleading. Although the participants are not united by a single style or theory, they are not anticonstructivist, postmodern, or particularly attached to Derrida's deconstruction. "Deconstructivists," as Anthony Vidler observes, "emerge as thoroughly modern and entirely constructive, confirming a century of experimentation and reaffirming a continuity with the Modern movement."[50] Gehry is a modernist with strong ties to Russian constructivism. He has Russian ancestors, spoke a little Russian as a child, and loves Tatlin and Malevich.[51] In 1980 he designed the exposition layout for the show The Avant-Garde in Russia at the Los Angeles County Museum of Art.

Gehry's design process is unique. Like the team of Yamasaki and Robertson, Gehry is advanced in his use of computers. He recently formed Gehry Technologies, "a building design and construction technology company that provides integrated, digitally driven construction practice tools and methodologies to companies and their projects."[52] The company uses IBM software previously used mostly in the aerospace, automotive, and manufacturing industries. Gehry creates a model—perhaps using crumpled paper, cardboard, or clay—which is scanned into a computer. A CAD/CAM system controls the manufacturing of building parts.

Classical architecture stresses the relationship of a building's proportions and scale to those of a human body. Modernist architecture breaks with this tradition. "Our great-grandmothers believed that the earth was the center of the universe and that man was the measure of all things," writes El Lissitzky in 1926. "Learn to see what's before your eyes. Here is man—a measure for tailors, but let's measure architecture by architecture."[53] Socialist realism tries to restore architectural anthropomorphism, arguing that a building should base itself on "the architectonics of a life-loving, healthy, well-built person."[54]

Gehry's case is the ultimate step in the modernist direction. His process is "profoundly indifferent to our presence."[55] The objects are created in virtual space, viewed by the lens of a scanner. An important implication of this process is that the interior space becomes incidental. Unity of the exterior-interior space is a constant modernist motif, which can be seen in such celebrated buildings as Mies van der Rohe's Barcelona Pavilion or Wright's Taliesin West. Gehry's Walt

Disney Concert Hall has been criticized for lack of consistency between the billowing swoop of the exterior's stainless steel and the more traditional wood-finished auditoriums. The usually mild and patient Gehry reacts to such criticism with anger.[56]

His relationship with "messy life" has been equally dramatic. His own deconstructivist house in Santa Monica, California, provoked a strong reaction from neighbors who feared that the unusual house would bring down the whole block's property values. Disney Hall's polished surface had to be sandblasted after its neighbors complained about blinding reflections and heat. In this case, Gehry patiently listened to complaints and agreed to sacrifice the integrity of his design.

### Joseph Stalin

In 1817 the Russian government held an architectural competition for a new Cathedral of Christ the Savior in Moscow to commemorate the victory over Napoleon. The winner was Alexander Vitberg, a thirty-year-old artist with little architectural experience. The site he selected was Vorob'evy Gory (Sparrow Hills), now crowned by Moscow University's 36-story main building. The cathedral was to consist of three parts: the bottom a parallelepiped symbolizing the body, the middle a cube representing the soul, and on top a cylinder with a dome signifying the Holy Spirit.

A century later, almost the same symbolism appears in Tatlin's proposal for the Monument to the Third International, in which a cube represents the body, although this time the legislative, rather than the human, body; a pyramid the executive power, in place of the soul; and a cylinder the mass media, instead of the Holy Spirit. The symbolism underwent yet another transformation two decades later, going back to quasi-religious overtones: in the design for the Palace of Soviets by Iofan, Gelfreikh, and Shchuko, the bottom level represented "precursors of communism" and the middle level, the teaching of Marx and Engels, while the viewer's gaze next, according to the authors, "would turn to the statue of Lenin crowning the building."[57]

None of the three projects—Vitberg's cathedral, Tatlin's monument, or the Palace of Soviets—has been realized. Vitberg's proposed cathedral was 755 feet high, while the tallest building of the day, St. Peter's Basilica, in Rome, was only 462 feet (the Twin Towers were 1,353 feet). Czar Nicolas I set up an architectural commission to investigate the feasibility of Vitberg's design, and the commission declared the structure not feasible. Vitberg was later accused of embezzling funds and wrongly convicted; he spent the rest of his life in exile in Siberia.

The Cathedral of Christ the Savior was eventually erected in 1883, using the design of another architect, Konstantin Ton, on another site, the Prechistenskaia

Embankment, and in another style that could be roughly defined as pseudo-Russian revival. It replaced a monastery that was dismantled and moved to another location, which led some believers to declare the site doomed. The reaction of most art critics to Ton's creation was negative: "Architects lacking inspiration and the understanding of the meaning of church building are always substituting spiritual elements for decorative ones . . . A typical example of such costly absurdity is the Cathedral of Christ the Savior that looks like a huge samovar around which the whole of patriarchal Moscow has gathered cheerfully."[58]

The idea of blowing up the "huge samovar" was introduced in 1924 by V. Balikhin, a member of the rationalist movement. In a procedure which could be described as grabbing the flag from a dead enemy and running with it, Stalinism, having demolished both rationalism and constructivism, ran with the idea of demolishing the cathedral. Numerous attempts to blow it up failed, however, as the brickwork was exceptionally strong. Eventually the cathedral was cut into pieces and removed.

In 1931 an architectural competition was announced for a proposed Palace of Soviets, to be built on the site of the demolished cathedral. The following fall, 160 entries, including 24 from abroad, were displayed in the Pushkin Museum of Fine Arts, in Moscow.

One of the foreign entries came from Le Corbusier; predictably, it was rejected. When Le Corbusier finally saw the winning design, he was appalled: "It is hard to accept the fact that they will actually erect that odd thing which recently has flooded all the journals."[59] When Wright addressed the First Congress of Soviet Architects in 1937, he was very blunt about the "falsity" of the winning project of the Palace of Soviets: "This structure—only proposed I hope—is good if we take it for a modern version of Saint George destroying the dragon."[60]

Le Corbusier and other members of the CIAM wrote to Stalin, asking him to "stop this sensational challenge to the public from being executed."[61] As it turned out, Stalin was the last person they should have asked. The architectural historian Dmitrii Khmel'nitskii has discovered that the winning design was actually by Stalin. The official authors—Iofan, Shchuko, and Gel'freikh—were incapable of such "clear spatial ideas, vigor, strength, dynamism, and at the same time such powerful barbarism, such neophyte courage in dealing with form, function and surface."[62]

If we are to believe Khmel'nitskii, who has studied the subject for many years, Stalin appears to have been a greater modernist than Le Corbusier, Wright, Ginzburg, or Vesnin. His creation did not imitate any known style of the past; his palace was to surpass the height of the Empire State Building by a few feet; he did not collaborate; he worked incognito, just like Roark on the housing project; he disregarded community life and was not interested in people. Moreover, his structure was supposed to resist aging: "Centuries will not leave their mark on it," wrote the official historian of the palace. "We will build it so that it will stand without aging, forever."[63]

The design turned out to be an impossible engineering task, and Stalin ordered the unfinished frame of the palace demolished.[64]

### Mikhail Lifshits

In 1966 the Soviet Marxist Mikhail Lifshits published an article called "Why I Am Not a Modernist," paraphrasing the title of Bertrand Russell's famous essay "Why I Am Not a Christian." Modernism is bad, says Lifshits, because it is "connected to the darkest psychological facts of our time, among those: the cult of force, joy in destruction, love of cruelty, lust for thoughtless existence, and blind obedience."[65]

Lifshits studied under David Shterenberg, the modernist painter, and Pavel Florensky, the religious philosopher, at the famous Moscow avant-garde art school Vkhutemas and worked with Georg Lukács in the Marx-Engels Institute, also in Moscow. Some of Lukács's ideas—especially his belief that Nietzsche's philosophy could be held responsible for Hitler's atrocities—had a profound influence on Lifshits. Both Lukács and Lifshits were repeatedly criticized for their excessive interest in Western philosophy. "In the 'Contemporary Philosophy' section of their library they have books by all the idealist-obscurantists (Spengler, Husserl), but not a single book by or about Lenin," writes one of their colleagues in a secret report to the Institute's director. "Apparently they do not consider Lenin a contemporary philosopher."[66] In the 1950s Lifshits was expelled from the Communist Party, becoming a rare orthodox Marxist in a society where Marxism had been reduced to a ritual.

The article "Why I Am Not a Modernist" was not well received by younger Soviet artists, who in the 1960s were struggling with the rapidly shrinking remains of socialist realism. Lifshits was called a dinosaur. His ideas sounded too similar to the antimodernist attacks of the Stalinist era, when unmasking the "antisocialist tendencies of constructivism, functionalism, and formalism" was a signal for a campaign which led sometimes to the imprisonment, and sometimes to the death, of constructivists and functionalists.

From Lifshits's standpoint, however, such a sad outcome is what Marx calls "the irony of history." Lifshits comments on the fate of thinkers such as Henri Bergson, whose death in 1941 possibly saved him from Auschwitz: "You wanted vitality, you were fed up with civilization, you ran away from reason into the dark world of instincts, you despised the masses in their quest for basic culture, you wanted the majority to be blindly obedient to the irrational call of the superhuman? Well, accept what is due to you."[67]

Lifshits is careful not to give examples from Soviet history, although they are plentiful. For instance, the literary historian Mikhail Gershenzon wrote in 1921, "What joy it would be to dive into Lethe so that memory of all religions and philosophical systems, of all sciences, arts, and poetry would be washed away without a trace, and to come up on shore naked, remembering only one thing from the past—how heavy and constricting these garments were and how light it is without them."[68] Five years later, the newsletter of the All-Russian Central Executive Committee announced: "The housing section of the Central Commission on Improving Living Conditions for Scholars is familiar with several grave incidents when the anxiety, suffering, and ordeals brought on by housing problems led to the untimely death of scholars—including the famous professor and writer Gershenzon."[69] Gershenzon had to accept, to use Lifshits's expression, "what was due to him."

Lifshits is aware of another problem: his position's dangerous proximity to the Nazi aesthetic. Even though one stressed class while the other stressed race, both views had similar reactions to avant-garde art and architecture. For the German architect and Nazi activist Paul Schultze-Naumburg, the new architecture was "immediately recognizable as the child of other skies and other blood."[70] For Soviet critics, Le Corbusier's Tsentrosoiuz in Moscow was an "alien building"[71] and "a cultural anachronism."[72] It looks "gloomy and alienated from its surroundings."[73]

Lifshits tries to deal with this difficulty. First, he says, "the official art of the Third Reich had some elements of a standard Modernist pose." This is an astute observation (preceding Groys's analysis of Stalinism),[74] but to deny its applicability to socialist realism requires some intellectual acrobatics. Second, Lifshits says, "social demagoguery always borrows certain superficial elements from its mortal enemy; according to the old legend, Christ and Antichrist look alike." Third, "the future is always born in agony."[75] Comparing Christ and Antichrist to Stalin and Hitler opens a whole can of potentially explosive questions for a Marxist. No wonder Lifshits was never fully accepted by the Soviet establishment.

He writes with indignation about the reaction of Christian Zervos, a French publisher, to the closing of the Bauhaus in Dessau by the Nazis in 1932. Zervos had written to Hitler: "The National Socialist party, for reasons unclear to us, demonstrates hostility toward genuinely modern art. This position seems paradoxical since this party wants, first of all, to attract the youth. It seems hardly acceptable to take all those young, full of enthusiasm, vital energy, and creativity, and to push them into outdated traditions." "This note reeks of kowtowing," says Lifshits; "it shows the same worship of the alleged barbarian youthfulness which led to the spiritual Munich of the 1930s."[76]

If Lifshits had been aware of Le Corbusier's letter to Stalin, written at about the same time as Zervos's note, he might have felt the same indignation but could not have expressed it publicly. If he had read *The Fountainhead*, he might have taken it as the embodiment of everything he detested: the readiness to discard culture, a reckless fascination with youth, arrogance, the cults of the machine and of the superhero, and the worship of power. If he had been alive when the Twin Towers fell, chances are he would have repeated what he said to the modernists: "accept what is due to you."

### Modernism and Destruction

Peter Osborne, an editor of *The Spectator* and a British television personality, said in 2004:

> If I meet an architect who was active in the 60s I would ask him or her: what were you doing in the 60s? It's a bit like if you meet—you used to meet—a German who had fought in the war you would want to know what they did. Maybe they were honorable people fighting for their country but maybe they were doing something terrible. And the same applies to an architect in the 60s. Were you knocking down town centers for us, thanks very much? Were you knocking down the center of Birmingham for us and putting in a bull-ring? Were you knocking down the center of Cambridge for us and putting in Petty Curie? Were you taking apart eighteenth century town centers and putting in concrete monstrosities? These people did evil things.[77]

Lifshits is more careful in his pronouncements. "I don't have anything against the moral reputation of these people," he says about modernists. "Still, let's judge historical events regardless of our views of individual personalities." His final verdict: "There are good modernists but there is no good modernism."[78] Osborne's stance brings to mind the infamous Soviet interrogations of the 1920s.

There are many interpretations of the events of 9/11. Slavoj Žižek compares the terrorist attack on the Twin Towers to Stalin's show trials.[79] If Stalin turns out to have been a greater modernist than Le Corbusier, then the terrorists who destroyed the Twin Towers might have been greater modernists than Yamasaki. They basically redirected two forces of modernity, aiming them against one another: the most powerful airplane in the world (the result of the modernist fascination with flying) and the tallest buildings in the world (the result of the modernist fascination with verticality and height). If we think of the attack as a show trial, the defendant was modernism. The show unmasked—to use Stalinist terminology—some built-in contradictions of modernism, demonstrating that just as violence leads to more violence, destruction leads to more destruction, possibly including self-destruction. Disregard for existing communities and lifestyles, the desire to start from a clean slate or a ground zero, may lead to Ground Zero.

Coming back to the three questions I posed at the beginning, I must admit that I do not have a definite answer for the first one (To what degree is modernism responsible for the violence and destruction of the last two centuries?). I tend to think that modernists are innocent in this respect. Even the antimodernist Lifshits is careful to stress that he is talking about the logic of history and not about individual guilt. It is true that he was disgusted when Vsevolod Meyerhold asked a security guard to arrest Ilya Ehrenburg with whom he was arguing about aesthetics and who had expressed the wrong views, but it was clear to Lifshits, and it is clear to us, that Meyerhold's silly outburst did not create the Gulag. It is true that Mayakovsky writes in one of his poems "I love to watch children die,"[80] but this "épater le bourgeois" statement has nothing to do with his true beliefs and behavior.

What is the relationship between modernism and political power? In considering my second question, I am afraid that modernists demonstrated, at best, extreme naiveté. Zervos's message to Hitler and Le Corbusier's to Stalin are just two of many examples. In the field of architecture, this issue is more complicated, however. To build, one needs money and power. The so-called Soviet paper architecture of the early 1920s was not an artistic statement but the result of extreme economic chaos. Whenever constructivists and rationalists could find some bricks and mortar, they built modernist buildings, even if reinforced concrete had to be imitated with bricks and plaster. It is hard to accuse Yamasaki (or Libeskind, for that matter) of collaborating with the Port Authority—who else would have the power to convert their architectural ideas into reality? Ernst May, a German, and Hannes Mayer, a Swiss, were perhaps naïve to count on Stalin's support for their modernist ideas, but they had little choice: the Bauhaus in Dessau had been closed, and the whole of Europe was rapidly moving toward what came to be called "activist state" systems.

My third question is: Does modernism have a built-in self-destructing mechanism? Le Corbusier wants to wipe out most of Moscow and to replace it with what Tom Wolfe later called "row after Mies van der row of . . . worker housing pitched up fifty stories high."[81] Mies van der Rohe himself, after moving to Chicago and starting to build there, admits that he "rarely sees the city" because he "takes taxis from his apartment to his office" and doesn't know anything about the "Chicago School."[82] It was the modernists' sweeping architectural gestures and total disregard for what already existed that created a backlash, a good example of which is Osborne's angry diatribe. In this sense, modernism has created its own enemies and detractors.

Modernist excesses created postmodernism in architecture, a distant relative of postmodernism in philosophy, that cousin who was not very bright and died young. Practically no architect whose name has been associated with postmodernism wants to admit the relation. "I am not now and never have been a postmodernist," says the caption for Venturi's portrait on the cover of the May 2001 issue of *Architecture*, paraphrasing language from the McCarthy era.

Did modern architecture die on July 15, 1972, as Jencks proclaims? Far from it. The new generation of modernists—including such architects as Thom Mayne and Steven Holl—having learned from the founding fathers' excesses and failures, have managed to shed arrogance, sweeping generalizations, and a disregard for "messy life." They are coming up with unique creations that combine innovation, vitality, and respect for the *genius loci*.

## Notes

This chapter was published as "Modernism and Destruction" in *ARTMargins: Contemporary East-Central European Visual Culture*, May 5, 2006; used by permission of *ARTMargins*.

1. Vidler, *Warped Space*, 1.
2. Rand, *The Fountainhead*, 22.
3. Ibid., 24.
4. Ibid., 44.
5. Ibid., 287.
6. Burliuk, "Utverzhdenie bodrosti," 21.
7. Mayakovsky, *Polnoe sobranie sochinenii*, vol. 1, 96, my translation.
8. Rand, *The Fountainhead*, 15.
9. Ibid., 28.
10. Ibid., 43.
11. Venturi et al., *Learning from Las Vegas*, 87.
12. Rand, *The Fountainhead*, 44.
13. Quoted in Heyer, *Architects on Architecture*, 20.
14. Leonidov, "Iz poiasnitel'noi zapiski," 539, my translation.
15. Quoted in Vidler, *Warped Space*, 62.
16. Mayakovsky, "Letaiushchii proletarii," 311–61, my translation.
17. Rand, *The Fountainhead*, 16, emphasis added.
18. Ibid., 27.
19. Ibid., 21.
20. Moisei Ginzburg, "Mezhdunarodnyi front sovremennoi arkhitektury," 44, my translation.
21. Bruno Taut, "Kak voznikaet khoroshaia arkhitektura?" (article sent by Taut to the Union of Soviet architects in March 1936), Moscow, RGALI (Russian State archive for literature and art), fond 674, opis' 2, ed. khr. 21, 275, my translation.
22. Dokuchaev, "Sovremennaia russkaia," 199, my translation.
23. Rand, *The Fountainhead*, 26.

24. Ibid., 73.
25. Ibid., 513.
26. See Paperny, *Architecture in the Age of Stalin,* 105–6.
27. Rand, *Fountainhead*, 287.
28. Mayakovsky, "Vsem," 138, my translation.
29. Venturi, *Complexity and Contradiction in Architecture*, 16.
30. Venturi et al., *Learning from Las Vegas*, 3.
31. Richard Meier in an interview with the author, December 12, 2003, http://www.paperny.com/meier.shtml.
32. Rand, *The Fountainhead*, 26.
33. Ibid.
34. Katanian, "O Maiakovskom i Pasternake," 509, my translation.
35. Paperny, *Architecture in the Age of Stalin*, 202.
36. Quoted in Heyer, *Architects on Architecture*, 186.
37. Ibid., 185.
38. The top floors with their wider window openings made the Twin Towers look even more like the Seagram Building, but Guy Tozzoli, the former director of construction at the World Trade Center, indicated that this was done on his insistence and against Yamasaki's will. See *The Center of the World* (New York, episode 8), PBS documentary, September 11, 2003. For transcripts, see http://www.pbs.org/wgbh/amex/newyork/.
39. Jencks, *The Language of Post-Modern Architecture*, 10.
40. Ibid., 6.
41. Quoted in Koch and Firstman, *Men of Steel*, 360.
42. Koch and Firstman, *Men of Steel*, 187.
43. Quoted in ibid., 178.
44. *The Center of the World.*
45. Ibid.
46. Ibid.
47. Koch and Firstman, *Men of Steel*, 339, emphasis added.
48. Ibid., 369.
49. Ibid., 371.
50. Vidler, "Deconstruction Boom," 33.
51. Frank Gehry in a conversation with the author, March 28, 1995, http://www.paperny.com/gehry.shtml.
52. See the company's self-description at http://www.gehrytechnologies.com.
53. Lissitzky, "Iz lozungov ASNOVA. 1926," 146, my translation.
54. Kokorin, "Obsuzhdenie tvorcheskogo otcheta rukovoditelia 10-i proektnoi masterskoi," 79
55. Vidler, *Warped Space*, 253.
56. Frank Gehry in a conversation with the author, December 16, 2004, http://www.paperny.com/gehry2.shtml.
57. Miliutin, "Tematika skul'pturnykh i zhivopisnykh rabot dlia Dvortsa Sovetov," 65.
58. Trubetskoi, "Dva mira v drevnerusskoi ikonopisi," 242, my translation.
59. Le Corbusier to A. Vesnin, August 10, 1934, Vesnin family private archive, Moscow.

60. Wright, "Address at First All-Union Congress of Soviet Architects, 21 June 1937," in RGALI, fond 674, opis' 2, ed. khr. 50, 26–28, Moscow.
61. Le Corbusier, letter to Vesnin, August 10, 1934.
62. Khmel'nitskii, *Zodchii Stalin*, 58.
63. Atarov, *Dvorets sovetov*, 15, my translation.
64. The official explanation for the demolition was that during the Second World War, the steel had to be recycled for military purposes.
65. Lifshits, "Pochemu ia ne modernist?" 2, my translation.
66. Stykalin, *György Lukács*, 79, my translation.
67. Lifshits, "Pochemu ia ne modernist?" 2, my translation.
68. Gershenzon and Ivanov, *Perepiska iz dvukh uglov*, 11, my translation.
69. *Izvestiia VTsIK*, August 31, 1926, my translation.
70. Quoted in Lane, *Architecture and Politics in German*, 134.
71. Kokorin, "Chuzhoi dom," 4, my translation.
72. Arkin, "Dom Corbusier," 3, my translation.
73. Kriger, "Oblik velikogo goroda," 336–37, my translation.
74. Groys, *The Total Art of Stalinism.*
75. Lifshits, "Pochemu ia ne modernist?" 2, my translation.
76. Quoted in ibid.
77. " I Hate the 60s," BBC program, June 12, 2004.
78. Lifshits, "Pochemu ia ne modernist?" 2.
79. Žižek, *Welcome to the Desert of the Real*, 9.
80. Mayakovsky, *Polnoe sobranie sochinenii*, 48, my translation.
81. Wolfe, *From Bauhaus to Our House*, 4.
82. Quoted in Heyer, *Architects on Architecture*, 27.

SVETLANA BOYM

# 4

## RUINS OF THE AVANT-GARDE

*From Tatlin's Tower to Paper Architecture*

The early twenty-first century exhibits a strange ruinophilia, a fascination for ruins that goes beyond postmodern quotation marks. In our increasingly digital age, ruins appear as an endangered species, as physical embodiments of modern paradoxes reminding us of the blunders of modern teleologies and technologies alike, and of the riddles of human freedom.

Ruin literally means to collapse, but ruins are more about remainders and reminders. A tour of ruins leads you into a labyrinth of ambivalent language—no longer, not yet, nevertheless, albeit—that plays tricks with causality. Ruins make us think of the past that could have been and the future that never took place, tantalizing us with utopian dreams of escaping the irreversibility of time. Benjamin saw in ruins "allegories of thinking itself,"[1] a meditation on ambivalence. At the same time, the fascination for ruins is not merely intellectual but also sensual. Ruins give us a shock of vanishing materiality. Suddenly our critical lens changes, and instead of marveling at grand projects and utopian designs, we begin to notice weeds and dandelions in the crevices of stones, cracks on modern transparencies, rust on withered "blackberries" in our ever-shrinking closets.

Since antiquity there has been an isomorphism between nature, architecture, and the human body. In decaying columns one can see tree trunks, while phantom Atlases and caryatids haunt porticos all over the globe. The uncanny anthropomorphism of ruins was discovered as early as the sixteenth century in scenes from the anatomic theater, where the dissection of the human body took place against the backdrop of classical ruins.[2] Vertebrae and carcasses overlap in the double vision of ruins. Ruins embody anxieties about human aging, commemorating our cultural endeavors and their failures.

While half-destroyed buildings and architectural fragments may have existed since the beginning of human culture, ruinophilia has not. There is a historic distinctiveness to the ruin gaze that can be understood as the particular optics framing our relationship to ruins. The ruin gaze is colored by nostalgia, but nostalgia is not what it used to be, either. Its object is forever elusive, and our way of making sense of this longing for home is also in constant flux.[3] In my understanding, nostalgia is not merely antimodern but coeval with the modern project itself. Like modernity, nostalgia has a utopian element, but it is no longer directed toward the future. Sometimes it is not directed toward the past either, but rather sideways. The nostalgic feels stifled within the conventional confines of time and space. The ruins of twentieth-century modernity, as seen through the contemporary prism, both undercut and stimulate the utopian imagination, constantly shifting and deterritorializing our dreamscape.

Ruins have a patina of intense nostalgia, and our historical optics changes together with the symptoms of nostalgia, at one time considered a disease.[4] The contemporary obsession with ruins is neither a baroque meditation on worldly *vanitas* nor a romantic mourning for the lost wholeness of the past. Rather than recycling romantic notions of the picturesque framed in glass and concrete, the ruins of modernity question the making of such a world picture, offering us a new kind of radical perspectivism. From a twenty-first-century perspective, the ruins of modernity point to possible futures that never came to be. But those futures do not necessarily inspire restorative nostalgia. Instead they make us aware of the vagaries of progressive vision as such.

At the beginning of the twentieth century, Simmel formulated a theory of ruins that resonates with contemporary preoccupations. According to Simmel, ruins are the opposite of the perfect moment pregnant with potential; they reveal in "retrospect" what this epiphanic moment had in "prospect."[5] Yet they do not merely signal decay but also a certain imaginative perspectivism in its hopeful and tragic dimension. In the fascination with ruins, Simmel sees a peculiar form of "collaboration" between human and natural creation: "Nature has transformed the work of art into material for her own expression as she had previously served as material for art."[6] Such framing of ruins reveals a multidirectional mimesis: men imitate nature's creativity, but a natural setting endows human creations with a patina of age. The contemporary ruin gaze is the gaze reconciled to perspectivism, to conjectural history and spatial discontinuity. It requires an acceptance of disharmony and of the contrapuntal relationship of human, historical, and natural temporality. Rather than postmodern, we can call it off modern: it involves exploration of the side alleys of twentieth-century history at the margins of error of major theoretical and historical narratives. Most importantly, present-day ruinophilia is not merely a neo-romantic malaise and a reflection of our inner landscapes. Rediscovered off-modern ruins are not only symptoms but also sites for new exploration and production of meanings.

Two centuries ago, Schlegel commented on the pace of transformation of modern ruins: "Many of the works of the Ancients have become fragments. Many of the Moderns are fragments the moment they come into being."[7] The pace of modern time precipitates both construction and destruction, sometimes imploding temporal duration. Modern ruins are particularly poignant because they are belated and contemporary at once. In his reflection on baroque drama, Benjamin commented that in ruins, "human history is physically merged into the natural setting."[8] Looking back at the ruins of the twentieth century, we see other paradoxical mergers: between suprahuman state models and human practices, between individual aspirations and collective pressure, between ascending dreams and down-to-earth survival. The contemporary ruin gaze allows us to frame utopian projects as dialectical ruins—not to discard or demolish them, but to confront them and incorporate them into our fleeting present. The ruin gaze challenges the vision of what Krauss has called "the originality of the avant-garde" in her book of that name, or of the continuity of the utopian vision between the artistic avant-garde and the socialist state described by Groys in *The Total Art of Stalinism.* Instead it reveals the internal diversity of the avant-garde, its singularities and eccentricities that proved to be as historically relevant and persistent as its visionary elements and collective utopianism.

The discourse on Russian identity and the discourse of the avant-garde were strange bedfellows in their antipathy toward ruins. According to the Slavophiles' vision, Russians were a rootless nation, unburdened by the ruins of history, a culture without strong links to classical antiquity—although this view has been contested by many in the twentieth century. Derzhavin's imperative to "venerate the ruin," encoded as an acrostic in his famous poem "The River of Time," was not embraced by later generations of poets. Moscow was burned and then reborn like a phoenix from the ashes. The culture of decadent ruins, although quite prominent in late-nineteenth-century Russia, was explicitly rejected by the avant-gardists who wished to turn the whole country into their "antimuseum."

Nevertheless, twentieth-century Russian revolutions produced many ruins but rarely accounted for them. Their logic was that of destruction and renewal, not of the contemplation of contradictions. Against all odds, the ruins survived the revolutions and formed their own subversive theater that offered a different off-center view of twentieth-century history.

**Ruins of the Revolution: Nature Morte with Tatlin's Tower**

Vladimir Tatlin's *Monument to the Third International* (1919–1925) was meant to be radically antimonumental. As a manifesto of the architectural revolution, the Tatlin Tower challenged both the bourgeois Eiffel Tower and the Statue of Liberty at once. Moreover, it aspired to outdo Peter the Great's urban ambitions with a new attempt to score a victory over unruly nature. The tower of iron and glass consisted of three rotating glass shapes: a cube, a pyramid, and a cylinder. The cube was supposed to house the Soviet of the People's Commissars of the World (Sovnarkom) and to turn at the rate of one revolution a year; the pyramid, intended for the executive and administrative committees of the Third International, would rotate once a month; and the cylinder, a center for information and propaganda, would complete one revolution daily. Radio waves would extend the tower into the sky. Oriented toward the cosmos, the monument would not defy merely the hierarchy of traditional architectural and sculptural styles, but the force of gravity itself. Its dramatically open, spiral shape represented the movement of the liberation of humanity, challenging the old-fashioned figurative allegory of the Statue of Liberty.

In fact, Tatlin's Tower embodied many explicit and implicit meanings of the word "revolution." Originally from scientific discourse, the word first meant repetition and rotation. Only in the seventeenth century did it begin to signify its opposite: a breakthrough, an unrepeatable event. The history of the Tower reflects the ambivalent relationship between art and science, revolution and repetition. Shaped as a spiral, a favorite Marxist-Hegelian form, the Tower culminated with a radical opening on top, suggesting unfinalizability, not synthesis. In fact, the Tower commemorated the short-lived utopia of the permanent artistic revolution, of which Tatlin was one of the leaders. He declares that the revolution did not begin in 1917 but in 1914, with an artistic transformation; political revolutions followed in the steps of the artistic one, mostly unfaithfully.

Punin describes the monument as the antiruin par excellence. In his view, Tatlin's revolutionary architecture reduced to ashes the classical and Renaissance traditions, and the "charred ruins of Europe are now being cleared."[9] Ilya Ehrenburg believes that the Tower was an answer to all those figurative official monuments that he called "plaster idiots," including Marx's "plaster head, which as a tribute to contemporary thought has been trimmed by an Assyrian barber."[10] Tatlin's Tower sabotaged the perfect verticality of the Eiffel Tower, by choosing the form of a spiral and leaning to one side.

Yet uncannily Tatlin's monument was not free from the charm of ruins, despised by revolutionary thinkers and artists from Malevich to Debord. El Lissitsky praises the Tower for the "synthesis between technical and artistic," old

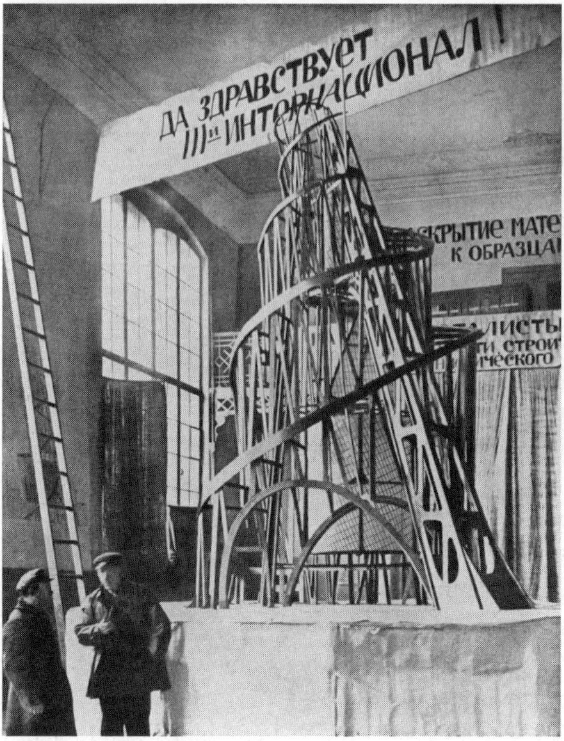


1. Model for *The Monument to the Third International* (November 1920). In the photo are Tatlin and Meerzon.

and new forms: "Here the Sargon Pyramid at Khosabad was actually recreated in a new material with a new content."[11] The project in Khosabad was actually a ziggurat, a pyramidal structure with a flat top that was the probable model for the shape of the Tower of Babel. In its attempt to be the anti-Eiffel Tower, Tatlin's Tower started to resemble the Tower of Babel, which was itself an unfinished utopian monument turned into mythical ruin. Moreover, in the case of the Tower of Babel, the tale of architectural utopia and its ruination is mirrored by the parable about language. The Tower of Babel, we recall, was built to ensure perfect communication with God. Its failure ensured the survival of art. Since then, every builder of a tower has dreamed of touching the sky and, of course, the gesture remained forever asymptotic.

Still, every functional modern tower evokes this mythic malfunctioning of the original communication. Barthes's poetic commemoration of the uselessness of the Eiffel Tower could just as easily apply to Tatlin's Tower. Barthes writes that while Eiffel himself sees his tower "in the form of a serious object, rational, useful, men return it to him in the form of a great baroque dream which quite naturally touches on the borders of the irrational." Much of visionary architecture, in Barthes's view, embodies a profound double movement; it is always "a dream and a function, an exprcssion of a utopia and instrument of a convenience." Barthes's Eiffel Tower was an "empty" memorial that contained nothing, but from the top of it you could see the world. It became an optical device for a vision of modernity. Tatlin's Tower played a similar role as an observatory for the palimpsest of revolutionary panoramas that included ruins and construction sites alike.[12]

Unlike Eiffel's, Tatlin's Tower was never built. Its failure to be realized is due not merely to engineering problems and concerns about feasibility. The Tower was both behind and ahead of its time, clashing with the architectural trends of the Soviet regime. It appeared as an incomplete theatrical set, not gigantic but on a human scale, a testimony to revolutionary transience. Trotsky writes that Tatlin's project gives "an impression of scaffolding which someone has forgotten to take away."[13] In fact, it remained "a scaffolding" for the future architecture. Even the original model of it has not been preserved. All that remain are two photographs from November 1920 and May 1925 that show an unfinished model.[14] In 1920 articles about the Tower appeared in the Munich art magazine *Der Ararat* and caught the attention of the emerging Dadaists. Grosz, Hausmann, and Heartfield proposed the slogans "Art Is Dead!" and "Long Live the Machine Art of Tatlin!" Yet to some extent, the Dadaists' celebration of the death of art via Tatlin's spiral guillotine was an act of cultural mistranslation and a common Western misconception about the Russian avant-garde. By no means is Tatlin a proponent of machine-assisted artistic suicide, especially not at the time of the revolution, when the death of art was more than a metaphor. Instead, he argues against the "tyranny of forms born by technology without the participation of artists." His own slogans—"Art into Life" and "Art into Technology!"—do not suggest merely putting art in the service of life and technology, or putting life in the service of political or social revolution.[15] Rather they propose to revolutionize technology and society by opening horizons of imagination and moving beyond mechanistic clichés and what Tatlin dubs "constructivism in quotation marks."[16]

From the very beginning, the Tatlin Tower engendered its double—a discursive monument almost as prominent as the architectural original. Victor Shklovsky is one of the few contemporaries who appreciates the unconventional architecture of the Tower, which for him is an architecture of estrangement. Its temporal vectors point toward the past and the future, toward "the iron age of Ovid" and the "age of construction cranes, beautiful like wise Martians."[17] To quote Benjamin, in this case "the modern . . . is always citing primal history."[18] The construction cranes, the wise Martians, and Ovid all collaborated in the making of the Tower. Shklovsky ends his essay by laying bare the Tower's unconventional materials: "The monument is made of iron and glass and revolution."[19] The air of the revolution functions as the project's immaterial glue. Thus we find at the origins of modern functionalism in architecture both the poetic function and engineering inventions. Describing the "semantics" of the Tower, Shklovsky speaks of poetry: "The word in poetry is not merely a word, it drags with it dozens of associations. This work is filled with them like the Petersburg air in the winter whirlwind."[20] The Tower is a monument to the poetic function. In its foundation the two meanings of the word "techne"—that of art and of technical craft—continuously duel with one another.

Hence the Tower is not merely an engineering failure but an exemplary case study of constructivist architecture. Architecture is imagined as archi-art, a framework for a worldview and a carcass for futurist dreams. This makes it both more and less than architecture in the sense of a built environment. Revolutionary architecture offers a scenography for future experimentation and embodied allegories of revolution. The most interesting examples of this "archi-architecture" are not built monuments but rather dreamed environments or unintentional memorials. Shklovsky describes his own ludic ruin and construction site that lays a foundation for the subversive practice of estrangement.

It is little known that Shklovsky was the first to describe the Soviet Statue of Liberty, in the same collection of essays in which he reviews the Tatlin Tower. In the essays in *Khod konia* (The Knight's Move), written in Petrograd, Moscow, and Berlin from 1919 to 1921, Shklovsky offers us a parable about the metamorphoses of historical monuments that functions as an alibi for not telling "the whole truth" or even "a quarter of the truth" about the situation in postrevolutionary Russia. In 1918 in Petrograd a monument to Czar Alexander III was covered up by a cardboard stall bearing all kinds of slogans celebrating liberty, art, and revolution.[21] The "Monument to Liberty" was one of those transient, nonobjective monuments that exemplified early postrevolutionary visual propaganda before the granite megalomania of the Stalinist period:

> There is a tombstone by the Nicholas Station. A clay horse stands with its feet planted apart, supporting the clay backside of a clay boss . . . They are covered by the wooden stall of the "Monument to Liberty" with four tall masts jutting from the corners. Street kids peddle cigarettes, and when militia men with guns come to catch them and take them away to the juvenile detention home, where their souls can be saved, the boys shout "scram!" and whistle professionally, scatter, run toward the "Monument to Liberty." Then they take shelter and wait in that strange place—in the emptiness beneath the boards between the tsar and the revolution.[22]

In Shklovsky's description, the monument to the czar is not yet destroyed and the monument to liberty not complete. A dual political symbol turns into a lively and ambivalent urban site inhabited by insubordinate Petrograd street kids behaving unpredictably. (Shklovsky calls them "Petrograd Gavroches," alluding to the French revolution and its representations in fiction, like Hugo's *Les Misérables*.) In this description, the monument acquires an interior; a public site becomes a hiding place. Identifying his viewpoint with the dangerous game of the street kids hiding "between the tsar and the revolution," Shklovsky is looking for the third way, the transitory and playful architecture of freedom. He performs a double estrangement, from both the authority of the czar and the liberation theology of the revolution. The third way here suggests a spatial and a temporal paradox. Caught in the moment of historical transformation, the monument embodies what Benjamin calls the "dialectic at a standstill." The first Soviet statue of liberty is at once a ruin and a construction site; it occupies the gap between past and future in which various versions of Russian history coexist and clash.

In Shklovsky's view, estrangement is an exercise of wonder, of thinking of the world as a question, not as a staging of a grand answer. Thus, estrangement lays bare the boundaries between art and life but never pretends to abolish or blur them. It does not allow for a seamless translation of life into art, nor for the wholesale aestheticization of politics. Art is meaningful only when it is not entirely in the service of real life or realpolitik, and when its strangeness and distinctiveness are preserved. So the device of estrangement can both define and defy the autonomy of art.

Such an understanding of estrangement is different from both Hegelian and Marxist notions of alienation. Artistic estrangement is not to be cured by incorporation, synthesis, or belonging. In contrast to the Marxist notion of freedom that consists in overcoming alienation, Shklovskian estrangement is a form of limited freedom endangered by all kinds of modern teleologies.

By the mid-1920s, the artistic climate in Soviet Russia had changed significantly. Lidiia Ginzburg, the literary critic and disciple of Tynianov and Shklovsky, observes in a diary entry in 1927: "The merry times of laying bare the device have passed (leaving us a real writer—Shklovsky). Now is the time when one has to hide the device as far as one can."[23] The practice of aesthetic estrangement had become politically suspect by the late 1920s; by 1930, it had turned into an intellectual crime. In the late 1920s and early 1930s, Tatlin worked on another monument of avant-garde technology, the artist's namesake—Letatlin (a neologism that combines *letat,'* to fly, and the name of the artist). If the Tower represented a dream of the perfect collective, a new agora for the Third International, Letatlin was an individual flying vehicle. A biomorphic structure, somewhere between a costume and a vehicle, it resembled the firebird from Russian fairy tales stripped to its bare bones. Today its design looks like a vestige of a modern Icarus, a tribute to the dream birds and nonfunctional machines imagined by artists since the Renaissance. Since Tatlin hoped to have his projects sponsored by the aviation industry, he introduced his essay on art and technology with a quote from Stalin: "Technology decides everything." But in Tatlin's case, technology did not function according to the program. Neither a celebration of Soviet engineering nor a solemn statement of Russian cosmism, Letatlin was an intimate artistic vehicle, a graceful monument to a dream, not a journey into another world. There was nothing otherworldly or technological about Letatlin. Most likely it could not fly. Not in a literal sense, at least.

Letatlin and the Tower belong to a very different history of technology, an enchanted technology founded on charisma as much as on calculus, linked to premodern myths as well as to modern science. Yet they are not so alien to the Soviet exploration of space, in which science merged with science fiction, and ideology occasionally sounded like poetry.[24] What remains of Letatlin are the vertebrae of the wings and the drawings that resemble those of da Vinci. What remains of the Monument to the Third International is an architectural skeleton in an old photograph. The monuments appear in retrospect poignantly anthropomorphic and interconnected. The Tower resembles the ruin of a mythical space station from which Letatlins could soar into the sky.

Tatlin's artistic life from the mid-1920s to the mid-1930s is rich in contradictions that reflect the time. He designed the coffin of the revolutionary poet Mayakovsky, who committed suicide in 1930. In 1931 Tatlin received the honor of "distinguished artistic worker," and in 1932 he opened a solo exhibition, the only one in his lifetime, where the critics erroneously observed that he had moved from art to technology. In 1934 the OGPU, a forerunner of the KGB, invited him together with other artists to observe the construction of the Belomor Canal, one of Stalin's early uses of slave labor. After a few other attempts to take part in the design of public architecture, Tatlin gradually retreated from the artistic public sphere; he did illustrations for Kharms and other children's book writers (before some of them disappeared during the purges) and worked on theater design. At the official Artists of Russia exhibit (1933), Tatlin's works were shown in a small hall dedicated to "formalist excesses" (a successful predecessor of the Exhibit of Degenerate Art in Germany). Soviet critics proclaimed that Tatlin's works demonstrated "the natural death of formal experiments in art" and declared him to be "no artist whatsoever."

What do artists do when they outlive their cultural relevance? In the Soviet case, we know very little about the last fifteen years of work of the founders of the visual avant-garde, including Vertov and Tatlin, who died in 1953. What can an avant-garde artist make after his officially declared death?

Tatlin's "postmortem" work consists—literally—of natures mortes, in a brown

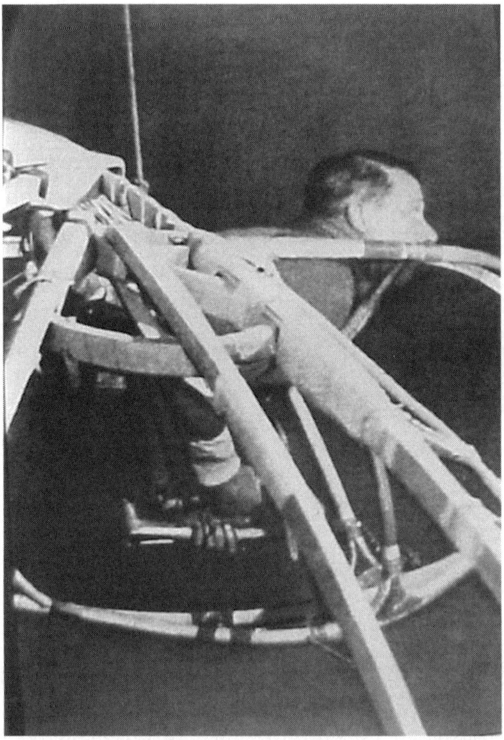

2. Vladimir Tatlin, trying Letatlin (Moscow, 1932)

and gray palette painted on the thinly concealed surfaces of old canvases or icons, and of desolate rural landscapes on the backdrops of socialist realist theater productions, which he painted in the 1940s. At first glance, these works seem untimely and in their technique resemble some of Tatlin's earliest experiments with figurative painting, done before 1914; Tatlin's late figurative works can thus be compared with the late works of his avant-garde rival Malevich. In my view, the belated untimeliness of Tatlin's still lifes and landscapes speaks obliquely of their time—a time of purges and war. While figurative, these works hardly reflect the optimistic tone of socialist realist art, suggesting an existential perspective. Nature morte is one of the ancient genres of world painting that has survived historical cataclysms and artistic and social revolutions. Still lifes are reminders of the nonrevolutionary rhythms of everyday life. They preserve the dream of home, of domesticated nature, and of a long-standing artistic tradition. Tatlin's still lifes are devoid of visual sensuality and represent endless variations on a theme: wild onions and radishes, nondescript garden flowers, knives stuck into the browning flesh of not-so-fresh meat, a skull with an open book. These look like memento mori, foregrounding the fragility of even the most frugal domesticity.[25] There is a subtle tension between the ahistorical still

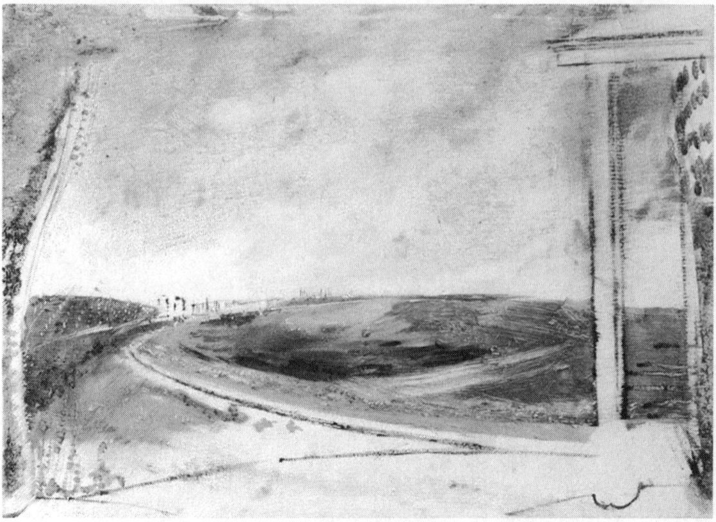

3. Sketch for the set decoration of *Chalice of Joy* (1949–50), a socialist realist theater production.

lifes and the dates on the minimal caption: 1937, 1944. Not politically suspect, still life was one of the few genres on the margins of socialist realism that survived extreme censorship. Strangely, this was one of the favorite genres of prison art, as it promises a temporary escape into a quieter plane of human existence. The maker of still lifes excels in the art of minor variations, performing a manual labor of cultural memory.

Moreover, the closer we look at Tatlin's still lifes, the more they appear to be exercises in double vision, though not in the conventional sense of political doublespeak. There is a tension between the figurative flowers and the abstract background. In the foreground are the sparse still lifes; in the background, the thickly painted planes from which they spring. These unspectacular and belated stage sets were abandoned by the biomorphic revolutionary Icaruses. No Letatlin would land here anymore; no foundation of a revolutionary tower could be laid on this swampy soil of fear. Tatlin's late works resemble a desolate natural setting in which the projects of the avant-garde have turned into the ruins of the revolution.

Artistic works have their own paradoxical lives.[26] Tatlin's Tower was not destined to exist in the open space of the city. Instead it acquired a second life in the form of many models build around the world since the 1960s. One of the most faithful replicas was reconstructed between 1986 and 1991 on the floor of the mosaic factory where Tatlin worked in the last years of his life; the young architects and designers who built it performed a meticulous analysis of Tatlin's

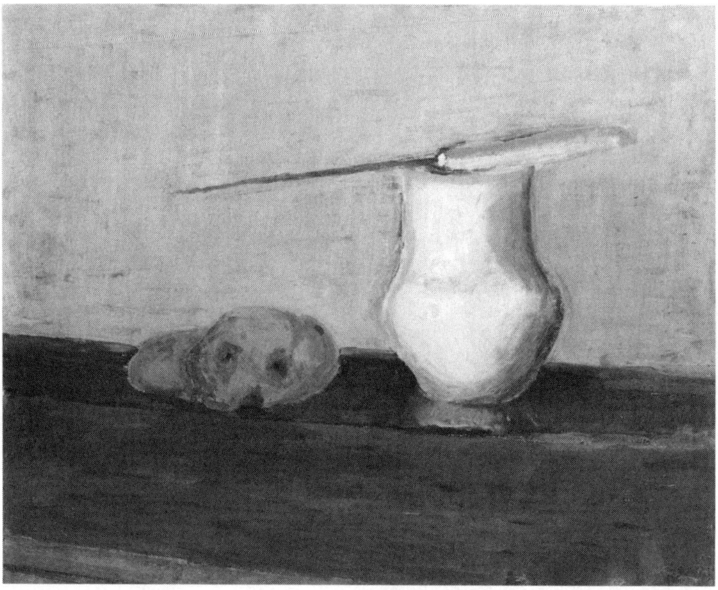

4. Vladimir Tatlin, *White Jar and Potato* (1948–51)

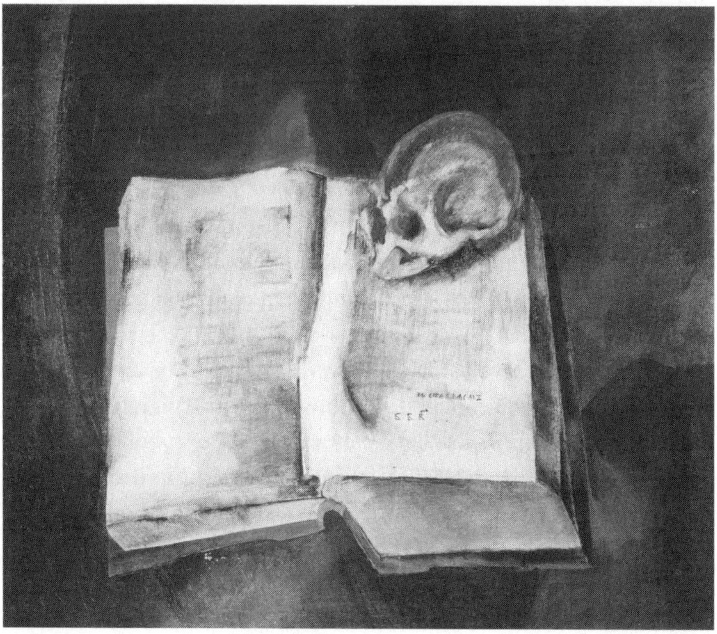

5. Vladimir Tatlin, *A Skull on the Open Book* (1948–53)

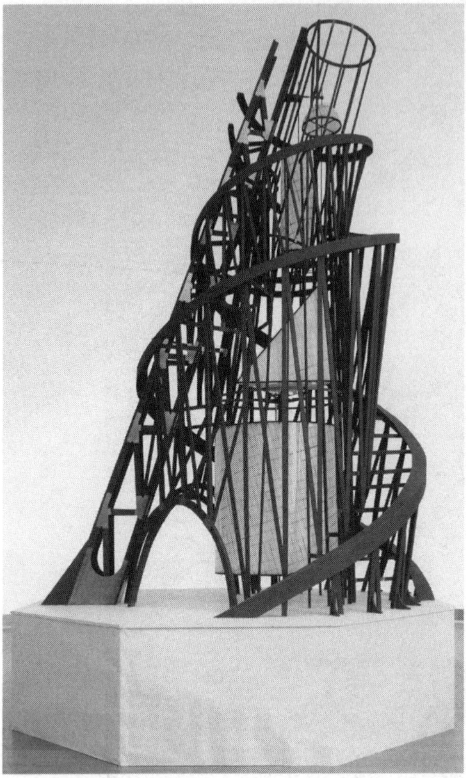

6. Model of Tatlin's Tower in the Moderna Museet, Stockholm

sketches and the 1920s photographs.[27] Faithful to avant-garde technique, Tatlin left no professional architectural drawings of the Tower, leaving space for unpredictability and imagination. The recent Russian tribute to Tatlin coincided with the end of the Soviet Union and the beginning of perestroika and glasnost that hasn't lasted.

Never realized as a radical revolutionary monument, the Tower came into material existence as artistic heritage. Thus uncannily the reconstruction and ruination of revolutionary ideals coincided. The Tower could have embodied the moment when there was still hope that artistic and social revolutions could overlap, but it ended up commemorating its opposite: the collapse of utopian aspiration.

### Phantom Limbs of Nonconformist Art: The Afterlife of the Tower in Conceptual Art and Paper Architecture

In 1996 the Russian-American artist Constantin Boym made a series of souvenirs of missing monuments. There was a little bronze souvenir of the Tatlin Tower, the Palace of Soviets, and King Solomon's Temple. The revolutionary Tower of Babel had a second life as an artistic myth; it became a phantom limb

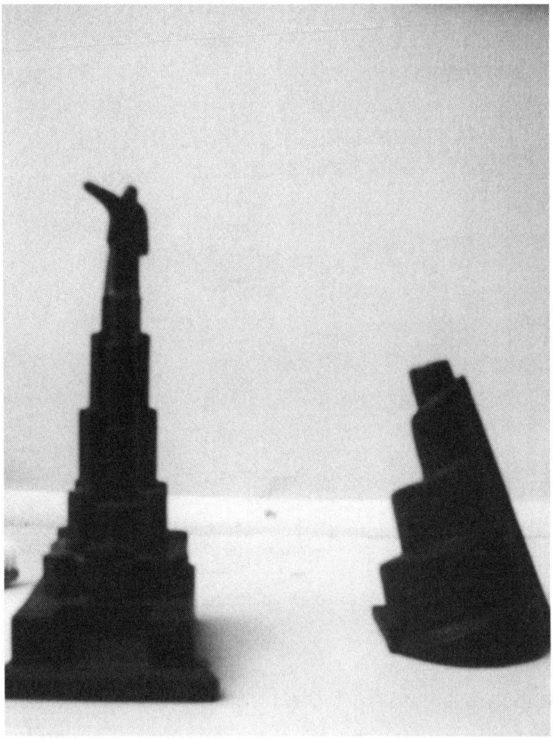

7. Constantin Boym, *Palace of the Soviets* and *Tatlin's Tower* (1996). From the series "Missing Monuments: Souvenirs for the End of the Century."

of the nonconformist tradition of twentieth-century art finding a second life in paper architecture, conceptual installations, and urban folklore.

Many of the artists known as Moscow conceptualists—a loosely organized group that included Kabakov, Sokov, Kosolapov, Elagina, and the team of Komar and Melamid—recycle the symbols of official ideological art, together with everyday Soviet trash and the inspirational icons of the avant-garde. They translate political objects of the Soviet era into artistic signs. If Western artists are often fascinated by the visionary potentials and bold exoticism of the Soviet utopia, Soviet artists confront its metamorphosis in their daily practices of art and life. More deeply connected to their ruins, they are less reverential toward them. They approach avant-garde objects without museum pieties. In fact, in their memory, the international avant-garde was not part of the museum culture or the art market; it had no official museatic sacrality. Instead, it belonged to a reservoir of unofficial utopian dreams.

Sokov keeps mementos of the posthistorical life of the avant-garde. In one of his drawings, he creates an urban still life: a Moscow yard where fragments of Tatlin's sculptures, including the vertebrae of Letatlin, were thrown into the

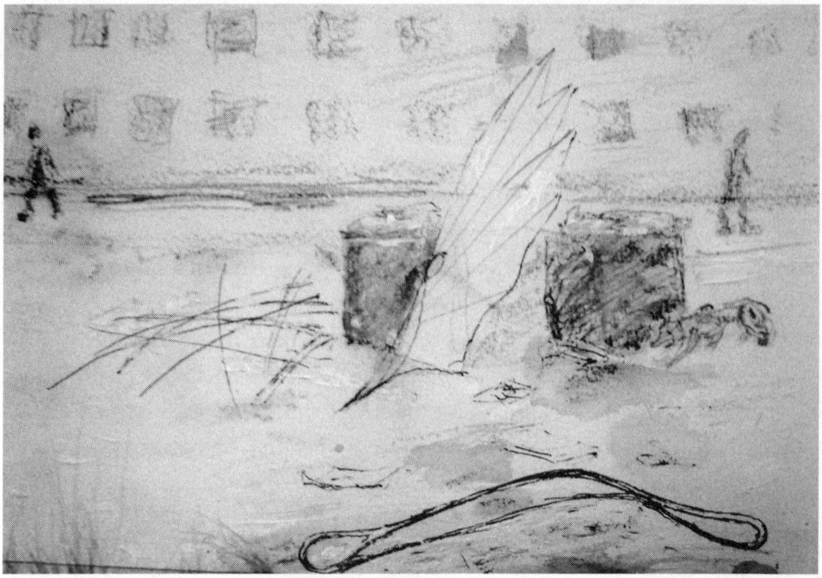

8. Leonid Sokov, *Moscow Yard*, with the fragment from Letatlin drawing. Photo by Svetlana Boym in Sokov's New York studio, 2006.

trash after the artist's death. Some remains of Tatlin's work were actually found among discarded objects by fellow artists. This is a peculiar ruinscape, signifying the irrelevance of the avant-garde during the time of Brezhnev's stagnation in the 1970s. Sokov remakes the vertebrae of Tatlin's project, leaving them as fragments or incorporating them into his own work in a tragicomic manner. Sokov treats the avant-garde as Russia's modern antiquity; he cherishes its ruins but not its dreams.

In Sokov's work the famous ruins of the avant-garde acquires a fragile anthropomorphic physicality. They are no longer made of the thin air of revolution, but of rough wood that leaves splinters under your skin. His is definitely a tactile conceptualism, encouraging the viewer to play with every vertebra of cultural memory and experimental art. Tatlin's Tower appears in Sokov's work as another example of fantastic, dysfunctional technology. His favorite materials, wood and iron, are modern and primitive at once.

In the words of Victor Tupitsyn and Ilya Kabakov, "is Sokov a post-modernist or a folklorist?"[28] His sculptures reveal the corporeality of the utopian ideology, its carnivalesque body.[29] Yet this is neither the traditional folklore (which was highly compromised by the Soviet "lacquering" and restyling since the 1930s) that interests the artist nor the stylized Bakhtinian-Rabelaisian images of carnival; it is impure and hybrid art of everyday Soviet life. It foregrounds layers of nonartistic culture that, according to Shklovsky's and Tynianov's conceptions of filiation and literary evolution, offer new possibilities for artistic innovation that looks not backward or forward but sideways, as a knight moves in chess.

Sokov's rough, unfinished sculptures have another, less mythical source of inspiration. While an art student, Sokov served in the Soviet Army. Looking through the military library, he discovered by chance a book of accounts from the 1930s of artists' and writers' journeys to the Belomor Canal, one of the first "model" industrial construction sites that was a part of Gulag territory. Even though it was official Soviet propaganda, the book produced a lasting impression on Sokov. He was struck by the photographs of the Gulag instruments of slave labor that revealed the brutal, premodern manner in which Soviet industrial might came into being. In his spare time he filled sketchbooks with drawings of these primitive machines and the frightening architecture of the labor camps. In his later work he stages the uncanny metamorphosis of a tower—the Tower of Babel, Tatlin's Tower, an "ur-neo-geo-tower" of the neo-avant-garde—into a hyper-realistic watchtower of the Gulag. Moreover, he makes a life-size sculpture of the contemporary artist as a guard next to the watchtower. This is a revealing cultural self-fashioning: the artist does not present himself as a glamorous nonconformist next to the liberating spiral tower, but as a cog in the system of suppression and surveillance. The relationship between Tatlin's Tower and the Gulag's watchtower is full of paradox and ambivalence. Tatlin's brilliantly drawn but dysfunctional Tower did not evolve into a roughly constructed yet efficient watchtower, nor did it merely exist in the parallel utopian universe. The two towers belonged to the same controversial cultural landscape of Soviet modernity. With the ruins of one pointing to the invisible ruins of the other, they are doomed to historical coexistence.

Sokov's recent *Flying Cage*, made for the exhibit Territories of Terror: Memory and Mythology of Gulag in Contemporary Russian-American Art, at the Boston University Art Gallery, uses the wings of Letatlin to create a juxtaposition of extremes—a liberation of cosmic proportions and an evocation of the claustrophobia of the prison cell.[30] In *The House of the Dead*, Dostoevski's prisoner of the mid-nineteenth century speaks about the "dream of a freer freedom," more liberating than the one dreamed in the "free zone." Yet this particular version of Russian freer freedom is linked to imprisonment. We are reminded of another character of Dostoevski, Shigalev, who begins with a premise of unlimited freedom, and arrives at unlimited despotism. The dream of radical liberation—a cosmic leap into the kingdom of freedom—often goes hand in hand with authoritarianism.[31]

Sokov's version of Letatlin, *Flying Cage*, resembles the flying vehicles of the Russian fairy tales. But Sokov's piece is not merely a didactic vehicle; it's a flying cage" that doesn't fly. Nor does it crash: it is suspended from the ceiling of the

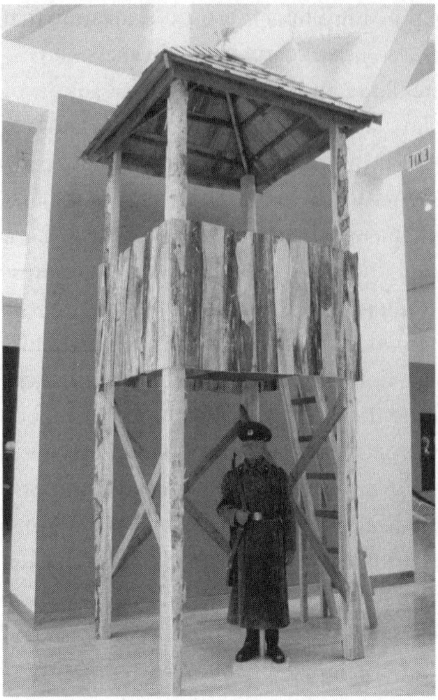

9. Leonid Sokov, *Watchtower: Self-portrait as a Soldier*. Courtesy of the artist.

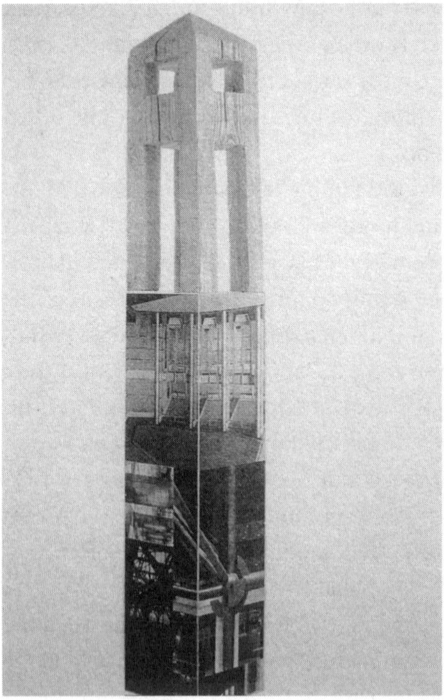

10. Leonid Sokov, *Ur-Neo-Geo Tower*. Courtesy of the artist.

exhibition room. This poetic, dysfunctional machine leaves us in suspense, like the Russian fairy tales Sokov loves that remain elusive and never come true. His UFO from a melancholic, ruinophilic civilization is both a dream and a nightmare.[32]

Sokov is one of the few artists whose works comment on the artistic complicity with the official *ars oblivionalis*, to use Eco's term, and to engage with the surviving ruins of the zone, a seemingly neutral and foreign word that had a special meaning in Soviet Russia. It was a bureaucratic euphemism for prisons and the Gulag. The word became so influential that the world outside the zone was not called the free world but the free zone. Sokov places avant-garde monuments in a new cultural context that is not merely postmodern but border zone—the space of unofficial and informal architecture of fences and locks, of nondescript maintenance buildings, Soviet no man's lands that bear a patina of repressed history. His materials are those of the zone, which he tried to transport into the free zone of his imagination. In Sokov's work, postmodernity quotes prehistory. Or perhaps, as Kabakov suggests, in Sokov's work, postmodernity becomes a living memory, losing its cerebral quotation marks, it turns into an occasion for physical comedy or boundless melancholy. Tatlin's Tower, a virtual ruin, acquires materiality. Its dysfunctionality and virtuality make it not less but more important and credible for the theater of cultural memory. For the artists of the 1970s, Letatlin's bones and the Tower's architectural carcass are no longer mere symbols or models; they acquire a fragmentary body and become part of the ludic cultural archaeology of the twentieth century. To quote Kabakov, "The naive world of Sokov is not so naive."[33]

### Inhabiting Ruins: Paper Architecture and Installation Art

Tatlin's Tower plays a prominent role in the invisible cities of the alternative cultural imagination. It became a central monument in the paper architecture and installation art of the 1970s–1990s. Paper architecture emerged in 1970 as a way of recycling and remembering the utopian dreams of the 1920s. It did not try to make fairy tales come true; quite the contrary. The paper architects were proud to work with paper, not stone or concrete. Many young architects who studied in the Moscow Architectural Institute, the successor of the famous Vkhutemas of the 1920s, led a parallel existence dedicating themselves to international architectural competitions of projects. Many of the winners of the competitions included brilliant young Soviet architects for whom project making, rather than building, was a way of life. Their mythical worlds are extraterritorial and light, and could travel beyond the iron curtain when the architects themselves could not. Immateriality is almost a sign of integrity; the architects do not want to compromise the radicality of imagination and take the life of

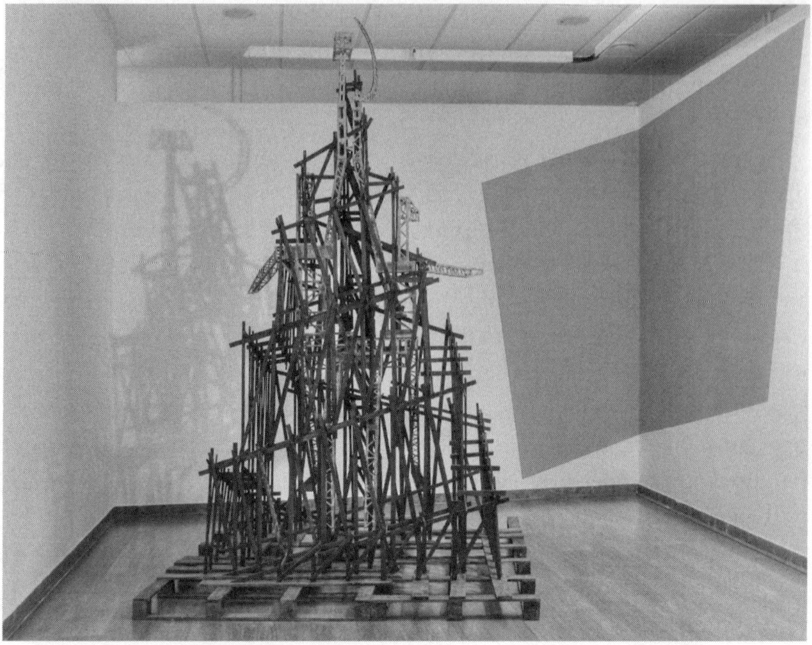

11. Yuri Avvakumov, *Perestroika Tower* (1990), which uses Boris Iofan's and Vera Mukhina's sculpture *Worker and Collective Farmer* (1936–37).

their projects more seriously than any drab jobs in the Soviet architectural industry they might have. While Western followers of the Russian avant-garde embrace the social message and try to see the utopian as possible, the Russian architects embrace the artistic potential, blatantly defying official collective imperatives. They might have shared forms, but not their understanding.

Yuri Avvakumov creates the Perestroika Tower using Boris Iofan's and Vera Mukhina's sculpture *Worker and Collective Farmer* (1936–37), one of socialist realism's masterpieces. As if following Trotsky's description of Tatlin's Tower as a giant scaffolding, Avvakumov makes a monument out of construction cranes that resemble children's toys.[34] His relationship to the tower is affectionate and tender as well as ironic. Tatlin's model turns into a shelter and a habitat which houses unlikely tenants—not only the ideal peasant and worker, but also all the dreamers of the future.

Artistic installations are another form of nonfunctional architecture that provides a refuge for the real and virtual ruins of the avant-garde. Kabakov is one of the pioneers of the total installation that houses ruins, souvenirs, models, and everyday trash.[35]

In one of his recent projects, Tatlin's Tower is not merely a small-scale souvenir of a missing monument. Its shape is evoked in the transitory architecture

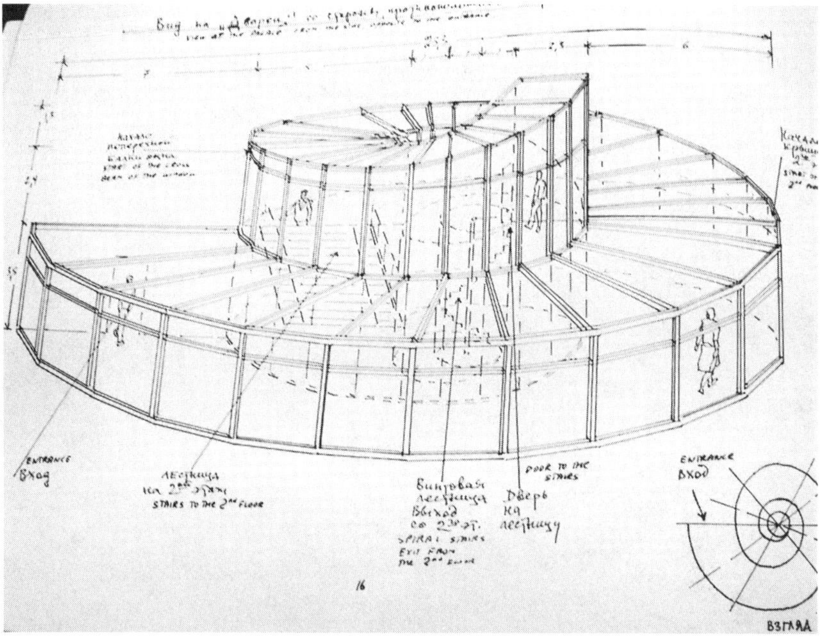


12. Ilya Kabakov, sketch for *The Palace of the Projects* (1999).

of the whole installation. Kabakov's grandiose *The Palace of the Projects*, created in 1998–99, has an ambivalent shape: an ascending vertical spiral which, from above, looks like a snail's shell. On the one hand, the spiral staircase reminds us of institutionalized museum spaces in the Vatican Museums and in the Guggenheim Museum. But there is an additional twist to the architecture of the installation: the spiral does not suggest a Hegelian view of the development of history. For Kabakov, the spiral remains forever open and mysterious, never becoming a pyramid. There is always an empty room and an invisible insect. It is not by chance that the visitor to the exhibit cannot triumph after his ascent; he must go back down the staircase, a journey which inspires private meditations and a bit of humility. Then the visitor may notice that the glowing space of the utopian spiral resembles a snail's shell. It is, after all, our portable home. The architectural shape of the project evokes images of a collective utopian spiral and a protective shell.

The total installation embodies Kabakov's work of memory. It creates a complete environment, including his earlier works and fragments from his albums, paintings, everyday objects, collectibles of obsessive neighbors, sketches by untalented artists, and communal trash. The installation becomes a museum for his earlier work, akin to a set of *matreshka* dolls, with many layers of mem-

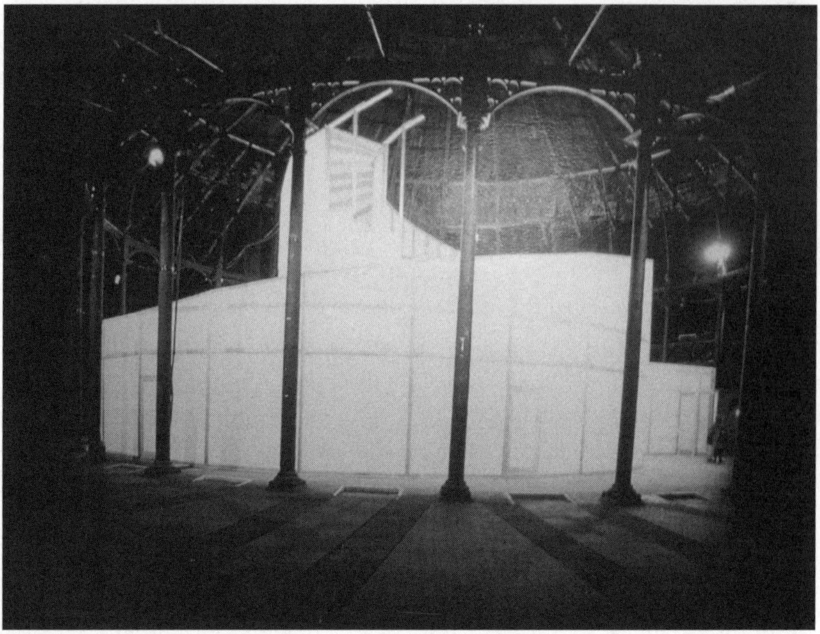

13. Ilya Kabakov, sketch for *The Palace of the Projects* (1999).

ory. Moreover, the artist observes that visitors have begun to leave personal belongings in the exhibit, as if the installation has turned into an international storage space for nostalgic refuse. In another way, it helps people to transform their useless objects into works of art. Kabakov also promotes tactile conceptualism, playing hide-and-seek with aesthetic distance itself.

The installation is a unique museum of dreams, hypotheses, and projects predicated on a shared belief that to "lead a worthy human life is to have one's own project." In Kabakov's view, everyone should be given an equal right to exhibit the models of their desire. Instead of building one group's utopia on a real scale, the artist proposes to give everyone a chance to show their dream worlds—in miniature. If only Hitler could have presented a miniature version of the Third Reich and been applauded by the Viennese artistic establishment, twentieth-century history might have been different.

There are many cosmic dreams here, miniature Letatlins born in the claustrophobic conditions of crowded communal living. Each project has a small room of its own, although there are also empty rooms for the reluctant dreamers of the future and for projects that were submitted belatedly and missed all possible deadlines. There, the visitor can sit in solitude on a chair and inhabit someone else's fantasy, "co-experience it," and become inspired. Almost every project has an author: an ordinary dreamer, a provincial eccentric, an amateur scientist, a self-made philosopher of the universe, an untalented artist, or an unrecognized genius.

*The Palace of the Projects* does not present a museum of Soviet civilization. Here, the utopias are no longer public, but privatized. They are not ruins but models, different in scale from their ideal. In his later works, in exile, the artist's strategy is bicultural. His installations combine the Western language of therapy and home improvement with the Eastern fantasies of flight and escape, practical American dreams with Russian aspirations to change the world. *The Palace of the Projects* is a grandiose hybrid of cross-cultural dreams and obsessions, a combination of utopian projectionism and a ten-step program for self-improvement.

The total installations are Kabakov's homes away from home. They help him to dislocate and estrange the topography of his childhood fears and to domesticate it again abroad. Lyotard suggests an interesting category, "domestication without domus," which I understand to be a way of inhabiting one's displaced habitats and avoiding the extremes of both the domus of traditional family values and the megapolis of cyberspace.[36]

Ultimately, what his projects install is not space, but time. If the past and future are embodied in the installation in the objects' shapes and location, the present is personified by the visitor, pierced by what Kabakov calls the spirals of time, which unwind in different directions.

Kabakov's work is about the selectivity of memory. His fragmented total installations become a cautious reminder of gaps, compromises, embarrassments, and black holes in the foundation of any utopian and nostalgic edifice. Ambiguous nostalgic longing is linked to the individual experience of history. Through the combination of empathy and estrangement, ironic nostalgia invites us to reflect on the ethics of remembering.

While dwelling on his diasporic souvenirs from his Soviet childhood, Kabakov goes to the origins of modern utopia and reveals two contradictory human impulses: to transcend the everyday in some kind of collective fairy tale, and to inhabit the most uninhabitable ruins—to survive and preserve memories. The installation exhibits the failure of the teleology of progress. Instead of a singular, unifying, and dazzling palace of the future, what is on display are the scattered barracks of the past and present. Kabakov's total installations reveal a nostalgia for utopia, but they return utopia to its origins—not in life, but in art.

The fascination for Tatlin's Tower and the ruins of modernity goes beyond the postcommunist condition and the end of the cold war. These post-Soviet ruins are now part of world culture, not only Russia's national heritage. A critical ruin gaze does not aestheticize history. It does not turn it into nostalgic heritage or

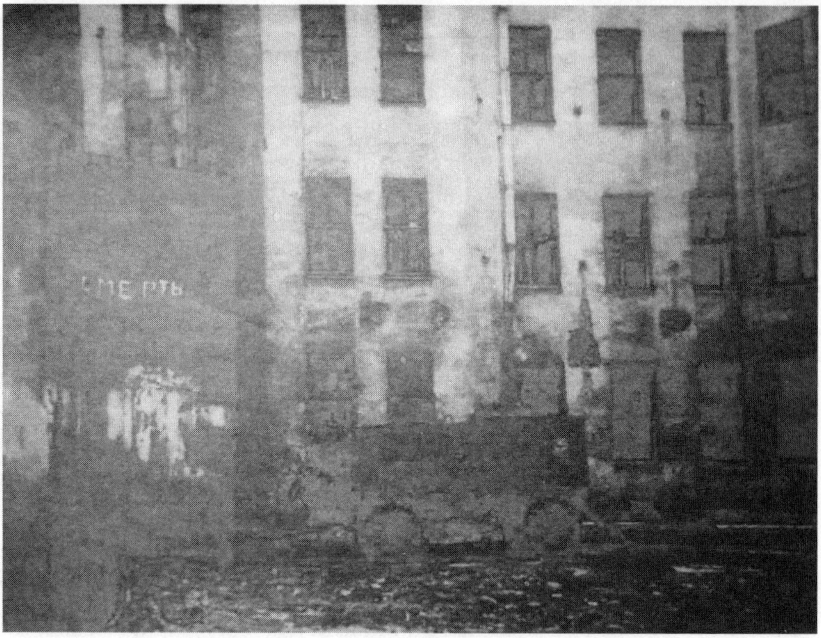

14. Svetlana Boym, "Return Home," from *Nostalgic Technologies*.

yearn for a total restoration. Rather, it remains reflective, pointing at imperfections, gaps, and eccentricities that disturb architectural and teleological designs. This kind of twenty-first-century, off-modern perspective revives the dialectics of thought and perception, of vanishing physicality in the age of digital and virtual reality, of the tension between models and practices. It also signals a return of a certain existential perspective, a human horizon that is superimposed upon intellectual and technological axiologies. In contrast to postmodern fascination for multiplicity and simulation, ruinophilia mourns modern single-mindedness and utopian ambition. It evokes the earlier time when gravity-defying monuments were still dreamed of, but doesn't glorify it. In other words, contemporary ruinophilia harks back not to nature but to the unfinished project of critical modernity, broader than the many isms sharing the common root—be it modernism or postmodernism.

In ruins, monuments become mortal. National and ideological symbols acquire a fragile body and a human scale. Utopian architecture invaded by time and history becomes a habitat for everyday practices. It is recreated, often against the will of the original designer, and becomes a collective artifact over time. It gives a different meaning to the concept of artistic freedom, neither the freedom of an individual artist nor the collective imperative. It brings us back to the idea of co-creation, between human genius and genius loci; between

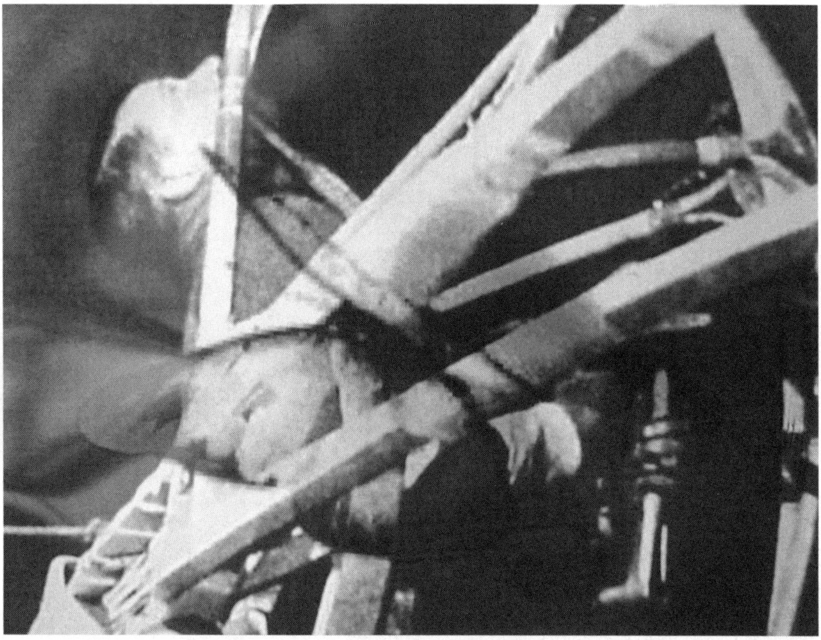

15. Tatlin's Letatlin and Nabokov's Butterfly from *Hybrid Utopias* (2003–6).

history, nature, culture, creative artifacts that defy time, and time that contributes to their metamorphosis. Time transforms them and is contained within them. Social utopias of artistic imagination acquire a second life of recycled dreams and history lessons.

### Personal Epilogue: Immigrant Ruins

When I returned to Leningrad in 1989 after a nine-year absence and immigration, I found my old house in ruins. Everything was in a state of disrepair: not only the façade in the Russian art nouveau style of the early twentieth century, but also the interior yard and the back staircase that led to our communal apartment. I stood numb in front of the familiar ruins. Only when I pulled out my camera to take a picture of my yard did I see the word "death" (smert) on a rusting pipe.

Later I learned that the Leningrad Film Studio was making a film in my half-demolished yard about the absurdist poet Daniil Kharms, whose books were illustrated by Tatlin. I do not know whether the graffiti was a part of the set or the work of an anonymous author. Once when my computer ran out of black ink, I printed the picture of my ruined home, deviating from the printing instructions and using computer errors. I hit the printer several times, letting its unconscious spill out in strange psychedelic colors that made the print un-

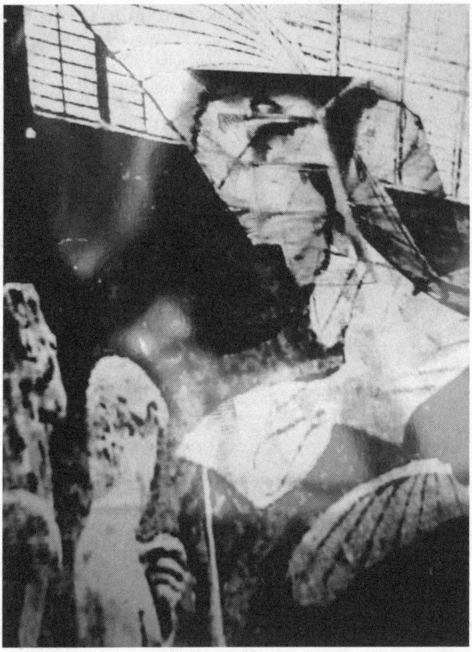

16. Tatlin's Letatlin and Nabokov's Butterfly from *Hybrid Utopias* (2003–6)

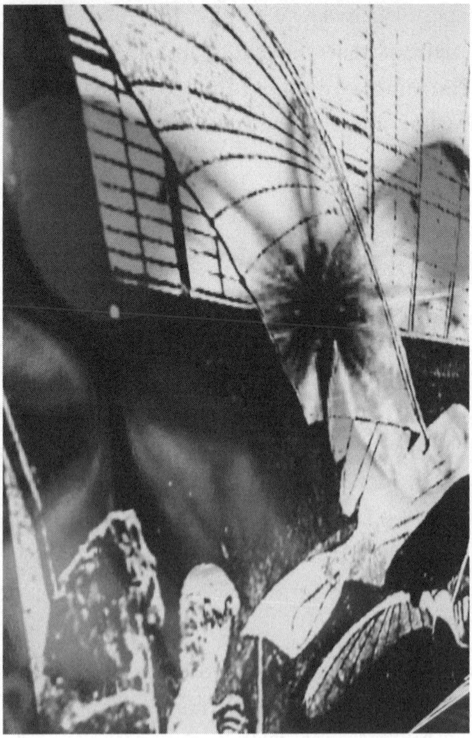

17. Tatlin's Letatlin and Nabokov's Butterfly from *Hybrid Utopias* (2003–6).

repeatable. After all, art's technology is sometimes a broken technology. The error has an aura.

In 2003 I found on the Web a photograph of Tatlin's exhibit of Letatlin in the Pushkin Museum of Fine Arts, in Moscow, and accidentally printed the picture of Nabokov's butterfly on top of it in a different scale. I remembered that in my Soviet school we studied projects of socialist hybridization in biology and beyond, particularly the work of Michurin, who endlessly hybridized pears and apples. I realized that I had accidentally cross-fertilized two different twentieth-century utopian dreams, Nabokov's and Tatlin's, creating a hybrid utopia in which the two can peacefully coexist.

The problem with ruins is that their meaning cannot be controlled. They threaten to imprison us in the unguarded labyrinths of the past, and they also promise to open imaginary escapes. In his prison sketches, Piranesi staged scenarios of exquisite claustrophobia and devised escapes from captivity relying on the power of his designing imagination. Like Houdini, we hope to become escape artists who leave the towers behind at just the right moment.

Ruins are not only anthropomorphic but also anamorphic: in our imagination they morph into different shapes like clouds or stones; they make up the invisible cities of our dreams and nightmares, conjuring them to life; and they reveal the memento mori in every lively tableau, like the skull in Holbein's famous picture. We frame the ruins, and they frame us.

## Notes

Some of the material in this chapter was previously published in Svetlana Boym, *Architecture of the Off-Modern* (Princeton: Princeton Architectural Press, 2008), by permission of Princeton Architectural Press.

1. Benjamin, *The Origin of German Tragic Drama*, 177–78.
2. Roth, Lyons, and Merewether, *Irresistible Decay*.
3. Elsewhere I have defined nostalgia as "a longing for a home that no longer exists or has never existed. The object of nostalgia, home or nostos is forever elusive; we are acutely aware of our loss of home but not sure if the return will cure us or only aggravate the symptoms. Nostalgia is a sentiment of loss and displacement, but it is also a romance with one's own fantasy." Boym, *The Future of Nostalgia*.
4. When nostalgia was first diagnosed as a disease, Europe was struck by an epidemic of feigned nostalgia that was just as difficult to cure as the actual one. In the history of architecture, the fashion for ruins and the discovery of archaeology went hand in hand with the construction of artificial ruins. Moreover, imagined artificial ruins might have anticipated the archeological discoveries. It is not by chance that many seventeenth-century and eighteenth-century paintings of ruins present them as porous architecture;

ruins appear as *vedute*, gateways to the landscape, elaborate man-made frames that mediate between history and nature or between architecture and the elements, the inside and outside of dwellings. The time of the fascination for ruins coincided with the fascination for new optic devices, from lorgnettes to dioramas. Nostalgic vision colored the "ruin-gaze" that required a "progressive lens" for both the myopic and the farsighted.

5. Simmel, "The Ruin," 262. "This is as it were a counterpart of that fruitful moment for which those riches which the ruin has in retrospect are still in prospect."
6. Ibid. Ruinscape reveals the ambivalence of the aesthetic enjoyment that seeks unity and transient perfection but only if it is rooted in something "deeper than mere aesthetic unity—in existential metamorphosis, in the process of becoming."
7. Schlegel quoted in Roth, Lyons, and Merewether, *Irresistible Decay*, 72.
8. Benjamin, *The Origin of German Tragic Drama*, 178.
9. Punin, *Pamiatnik Tret'emu Internatsionalu*, 1, my translation.
10. Ehrenburg, *E pur se muove*, 18.
11. El Lissitsky, "Basic Premises, Interrelationships between the Arts, the New City, and Ideological Superstructure," 188.
12. Barthes, "The Eiffel Tower," 6.
13. Trotsky quoted in Andersen, *Vladimir Tatlin*, 62.
14. The model shown in November 1920 is discussed in the Club Cézanne (that was soon to disappear) where Lunacharsky, Meyerhold and Mayakovsky debated Tatlin's projects.
15. Tatlin, "Iskusstvo v texniku," 5, my translation.
16. Quoted in Strigalev and Harten, *Vladimir Tatlin*, 37.
17. Shklovsky, "Pamiatnik tret'emu internatsionalu," 108–11, my translation.
18. Benjamin, "Paris, the Capital of the Nineteenth Century," 10.
19. Shklovsky, "Pamiatnik tret'emu internatsionalu," 111, my translation.
20. Ibid., 110, my translation.
21. The statue was erected by the sculptor Paolo Trubetskoi in 1909 on Znamensky Square near the Nicholas Station, now Vosstaniia Square near the Moscow Railway Station.
22. This is how Shklovsky introduces the story: "No, not the truth. Not the whole truth. Not even a quarter of the truth. I do not dare to speak and awaken my soul. I put it to sleep and covered it with a book, so that it would not hear anything" (Shklovsky, *Khod konia*, 196–97). For a comparative analysis of Shklovsky's theory of estrangement, see Boym, "Politics of Estrangement: Victor Shklovsky and Hannah Arendt."
23. Lidiia Ginzburg, *Chelovek za pis'mennym stolom*, 59, my translation.
24. Svetlana Boym, "Kosmos: Remembrances of the Future."
25. The contemporary artist Leonid Sokov recalls that during the first Tatlin exhibit since the artist's death, in the 1970s various elderly women who worked in the mosaic factory or in the local theaters brought with them small pictures of Tatlin's forgotten still lifes that the artist apparently gave them in exchange for money and food.
26. Tatlin's legendary Tower found echoes in another unbuilt monument of the twentieth century: The Palace of Soviets (architect Iofan), which was supposed to have been built on the site of the destroyed Cathedral of Christ the Savior. In the Palace of Soviets, the dynamic and open spiral is made static, turned into a terraced colonnade and decorated with a gigantic statue of Lenin. War interrupted Stalin's architectural ambitions, relegat-

ing the Palace of Soviets to the realm of "paper architecture." A replica of the cathedral in concrete was built in 1998.

27. The group included D. Dimakov, N. Debrin, I. Fedotov and E. Lapshina. Previous reconstructions of the tower were made in Sweden (1968), England (1971), France (1979), and the United States (1980, 1983). There was another reconstruction in Russia made in 1975 and 1980 by T. Shapiro, once Tatlin's collaborator.
28. "A Conversation between Victor Tupitsyn and Ilya Kabakov on Leonid Sokov," 15–16.
29. Ibid.
30. Svetlana Boym, *Territories of Terror.* Soviet rocket industry owed as much to science as it did to science fiction. It combined technological achievement with the tradition of enchanted technology and the philosophy of cosmism that survived until the time of Yuri Gagarin; moreover, much of cosmic exploration was done in the "sharazka," the special "elite" Gulag where scientists were kept behind the fence to make the most of their flights of imagination and their scientific research. See Svetlana Boym, "Kosmos: Remembrances of the Future."
31. Sokov offers us his own fantastic version of the story, the rise and fall of the Russian Icarus—Letatlin. He comments that the authorities gave Tatlin money for the Letatlin hoping it would make an ideal Soviet spy vehicle, but Tatlin wanted to make his creature beautiful and gave it wings made of silk. So it became a technological failure.
32. *The Flying Cage* is a post-Soviet, tragi-comic version of Benjamin's and Klee's emblematic "Angel of History," suspended between the future perfect and the past imperfect.
33. "A Conversation between Victor Tupitsyn and Ilya Kabakov on Leonid Sokov," 16.
34. For a more detailed discussion see Constantin Boym, *New Russian Design.*
35. For a detailed discussion of Kabakov's conception of installation and the uses of nostalgia, see Svetlana Boym, *The Future of Nostalgia*; and Groys, *The Total Art of Stalinism.*
36. Lyotard, "Domus and Megapolis." Huyssen, in his book *Twilight Memories*, claims that the current memory boom is not a result of further kitschification of the past, but "a potentially healthy sign of contestation; a contestation of the informational hyperspace and an expression of the basic human need to live in extended structures of temporality, however they may be organized. . . . In that dystopian vision of the high-tech future, amnesia would no longer be part of the dialectics of memory and forgetting. It will be its radical other. It will have sealed the very forgetting of memory itself: nothing to remember, nothing to forget" (35).

# PART II

# RUINS AND THE DEMOCRATIC POLITY

ANDREAS SCHÖNLE

# 5

## MODERNITY AS A "DESTROYED ANTHILL"

*Tolstoy on History and the Aesthetics of Ruins*

> We left the city [Moscow], lit by the most beautiful fire in the world, which formed a gigantic pyramid resembling the prayers of the faithful: its base was on the ground and its tip in the sky. I think the moon was peeking over the top of the fire. It was a grand spectacle, but I ought to have been alone to contemplate it. This is the sad condition that spoils my experience of the Russian campaign: it is that I made it with people who would have belittled the Coliseum and the Sea of Naples.
>
> STENDHAL, *JOURNAL*, SEPTEMBER 14–15, 1812

The burning of Moscow in 1812 created an unprecedented ruin. The magnitude of the destruction called into question an established conceptual order and generated frenzied ideological activity to fill in the void that had opened up. Responses to the burning were many and varied. At stake was not only the adjudication of guilt for the fire, which has preoccupied historians ever since, but also the contentious elaboration of a sociopolitical project in response to the exceptionality of the situation, the need to assign meaning to this senseless event.

This chapter investigates Tolstoy's response to the debate, as with fifty-year hindsight he familiarized himself with the literature on the topic as he wrote the last two volumes of *War and Peace*. Unique among his contemporaries and predecessors in Russia, Tolstoy highlights the aesthetic dimensions of the ruins of Moscow, and the restorative function they can serve. But unlike Stendhal, who romantically desires to differentiate himself from other officers in Napoleon's army through his aptitude for aesthetic appreciation of the devastation, Tolstoy ascribes a transcending force to the aesthetic moment, enabling spectators to overcome their historically determined identities and thus also social and national differences. Through their aesthetic beauty, ruins ground the emergence of a new sense of community while restoring a multilayered sense of time. For Tolstoy, that is, they enable us to escape the mindless and crippling rush onward of modernity. If Tolstoy's plea for the emancipatory potential of ruins escapes the charge of nostalgia, it could well prove as elitist as Stendhal's pursuit of the sublime. In any case, the ramifications of Tolstoy's ideas must be carefully weighed. Nevertheless, as it bears on the difficult and fraught debate about the aesthetic value of ruins, Tolstoy's idiosyncratic voice deserves to be taken into account.

Before we unwrap the layers of Tolstoy's investment in ruins, a survey of the ideological response in Russia to the burning of Moscow is in order. For Admiral A. S. Shishkov, the French occupation, the atrocities committed by French troops in Moscow, and the ensuing fire demonstrate the consequences of the French revolution and drive home the pressing need to reject Enlightenment philosophy so as "to discontinue all moral contacts with the French and return to our pure and immaculate mores."[1] The imputation of the burning of Moscow to the French revolution comes in several variants. Some writers attribute the catastrophe directly to Enlightenment philosophers.[2] Others blame the immorality of the French soldiers, whose eagerness to desecrate Orthodox churches is said to have mirrored the profanation of religious sites during the revolution.[3] For still others, the culprit is the political order that came out of the French revolution and the centralization of power it allegedly enabled. In any case, in this paradigm, the burning of Moscow lays waste to the project of secularization, thus shoring up the religious foundation of Russian society. Orthodoxy serves to unify the Russian people and to underpin the love of the people for the czar. In its inextricable link with autocratic rule, Orthodoxy functions as a principle of legitimacy and stability. This paradigm accommodates a certain degree of diversity. For example, authors differ on the question of whether some notion of enlightenment, if properly framed in a religious sense, is salvageable.[4] Yet they all agree on one central assumption, that the burning of Moscow is a work of human agency.

In tension with this paradigm stands another set of ideas which can be called the providentialist argument, promoted in particular by Fedor Rostopchin, the governor of Moscow, in which the fire represents God's punishment of humanity for its sins. The catastrophe is alternatively presented as punishment for the sins of Russians, who went too far on the path of enlightenment, or as a sign of the chosenness of the Russian nation.[5] The latter reading stresses the facts that the Kremlin, the sacred site of Russian Orthodoxy, remained largely intact and that the fire helped expel the French from Russian territory.[6] The providentialist argument at times goes so far as to compare the burning of Moscow to the crucifixion of Christ, viewing both as necessary sacrifices toward ultimate redemption.[7]

Regardless of the specifics of any reading, the mainstream response to the fire affirmed the exceptionality of the Russian people and sought to gloss over social divisions, promoting a kind of unification of society around a national idea. Stories of self-sacrifice on the side of the nobility and of the unfailing allegiance of serfs toward their masters abound, despite the fact that the reality of social relations during the Napoleonic campaign appears to have been much more complex.[8] We see a heavy-handed ideological appropriation of the catastrophic events, mostly by conservatively minded writers and political actors. Whether they impute historical change to human agency or to divine dispensation, they seek to ward off a fear that looms large in Russian culture, that of an anarchic popular uprising. Indeed, the main concern of many, including the czar, was that the spontaneous patriotic upheaval that consumed the nation, including the emergence of irregular military groups, could lead to attempts by the people—i.e., the serfs—to take matters into their own hands. The mythology of national unification, collective identity, and communal sacrifice was intended to ensure a certain degree of consent to social inequities until the state could reassert its control.

But how did the population of Moscow respond to the city's destruction? In his analysis of eyewitness accounts by Moscow's middle class—minor officials, merchants, and lower-ranking clergy—Martin argues that their response was rooted in premodern attitudes. These groups sought not the emergence of some social value system, but the restoration of their livelihood before the invasion, including the political stability of the old regime. They did not see the French occupation in nationalistic terms or in historical terms, as the result of revolutionary modernity. Instead, victimized both by the invading armies and by mostly lower-class Russian looters, they witnessed the collapse of order and the triumph of the rabble, a calamity of apparently biblical proportion. Their experience of indiscriminate social chaos gave them an acute desire for political restoration. Martin argues that even the looters—many of whom were only trying to survive—did not intend "to challenge the social order as such."[9] At their most ideological, they were motivated by class resentment, but in many cases they were either seeking to settle personal scores or acting indiscriminately. In short, their response to the occupation was mostly devoid of ideology and articulated a pragmatic longing for the stability of the old regime, although without faith in its ideological legitimation—the mutual dependency expressed in upper-class paternalism and lower-class loyalty—which the events of 1812 had largely undermined. The autocracy, at once strengthened and weakened by this outcome, saw the need to preserve the preoccupation social order and to reaffirm its paternalistic ideology but also to implement repressive techniques of social control that seemed to contradict its stated faith in the old regime network of mutual interdependencies and solidarities.

Now let us turn to *War and Peace*. The theoretical part of the epilogue to the novel begins with a refutation of providentialist history, in which Tolstoy goes so far as to assert that teleological metanarratives of human history amount to secularized versions of the same providentialism. By acknowledging "a certain goal toward which peoples and humanity strive," Tolstoy writes, contemporary historians resurrect in veiled form the ancients' notion of *fatum*.[10] Tolstoy stringently rejects such narratives in order to pry history open, but as he does so, he has to account in a new way for the causes of historical events and the degree to which human behavior is historically determined. This problem becomes particularly acute in the narration of extraordinary events such as Napoleon's Russian campaign, with its unprecedented destruction and devastation. Tolstoy writes at the beginning of the third volume of the novel:

> On the 12th of June 1812 the forces of Western Europe crossed the Russian frontier and war began, that is, an event took place opposed to human reason and to human nature. Millions of men perpetrated against one another such innumerable crimes, frauds, treacheries, thefts, forgeries, issues of false money, burglaries, incendiarisms, and murders, as in whole centuries are not recorded in the annals of all the law courts of the world, but which those who committed them did not at the time regard as being crimes.[11]

Explaining the exceptionality of these events without recourse to providentialist or teleological narratives represents a major challenge for historiography. Tolstoy believes such an explanation can succeed only if it postulates the emergence of a totally new type of society and individual. In the epilogue he indicates that Napoleon's campaign presupposed that society be organized into a sizeable military group, that people renounce "all established traditions and customs," and that the leader construct an ideological justification for the violence to be perpetrated.[12] The beginning of this fundamental transformation of French society goes back to the revolution. What Tolstoy has in mind here, of course, is the inception of modernity as an ideology that sweeps aside traditional moral and political representations, institutes a rupture with the past, and defines the present as a transition to the future.[13] For him the rise of Napoleon—"a man without convictions, without habits, without traditions, without a name, and not even a Frenchman"[14]—epitomizes modernity. What worries him in this new epoch is an almost pre-Weberian sense that modernity promotes the centralization of power within the hands of the state, and subjects the social fabric to a system of objectified social relations similar to that of an army, all in the name of progress. Teleological historiography, which folds events into the mold of a march toward an upbeat future, does nothing but propagate the ideology of modernity.[15]

If for its contemporaries, the Russian campaign served as an occasion to revive providentialist paradigms and to strengthen a traditional conception of power, for Tolstoy it calls these models into question. The contemporary response to the burning of Moscow sought to minimize its exceptionality. By drawing parallels with the destruction of Jerusalem recounted in scripture and by embedding the fire into the inscrutable plans of Providence, Russian intellectual elites muffled the conceptual virulence of the events and preempted an inquiry into their moral, political, and philosophical reverberations.[16] Even the apocalyptic interpretation of the events aimed primarily to invigorate the biblical view of history and in no way undermined traditional narratives. The short-lived conviction of Pierre—one of the protagonists in *War and Peace*—that he is called upon to slay Napoleon the Antichrist mocks precisely such conservative interpretive moves. These traditional interpretations of the catastrophe fail to come to terms with the unspeakable novelty of the destruction of 1812. They fail to see the link with modernity. In short, Tolstoy takes issue both with traditionalist interpretations of the events, which turn a blind eye to their uniqueness, and with the teleological reading, which is powerless to ground a critique of modernity's role therein.

Tolstoy sees the French revolution not as a moral aberration resulting from the deleterious impact of Enlightenment philosophy. "How a book like *The Social Contract* can prompt Frenchmen to destroy each other cannot be understood without an account of the causal relation between the new force [of ideas] and events," he writes, positing "mutations of power in time."[17] And his critique of modernity stems from its excessive concentration of power by means of rigid social institutions: "For common action people always unite in certain combinations, in which, regardless of the difference of aims set for the common action, the relation between those taking part in it is always the same . . . Of all the combinations in which men unite for collective action one of the most striking and definite examples is an army."[18] The relationship between the political leader and the mass of people subservient to him or her is mediated by social institutions. Trivial as these findings sound, the literature on Tolstoy rarely acknowledges the sociological dimension of his thinking. Modernity for him is characterized by a sharp increase in the number and effectiveness of institutions of social control. Napoleon's multinational army epitomizes this vision of modernity. Thus, for Tolstoy it is not the French revolution per se, nor the political order that followed, that are to blame for the catastrophe;

rather, it is a broader epochal phenomenon, the emergence of modernity, which acts through constraining social institutions and which affects Russia and France alike.

What does Tolstoy propose in place of discredited modernity? Clearly, blind faith in the chosenness of the czar and the hope for unification of social groups under autocratic rule could hardly satisfy him. In one scene in *War and Peace* during the advance of the French army on Moscow, the czar convenes an assembly of nobles and merchants, ostensibly to consult them on the advisable form of resistance. Thoughtful and earnest as he always is, Pierre—rich, well educated, but perennially off the mark—proposes to demand a full account of the situation of the army so as to make an informed judgment. Reminded of Rousseau's *The Social Contract*, he claims an advisory role for the nobility but is quickly silenced by his peers, who proceed to submit themselves abjectly to the czar. Despite Pierre's remark that such sacrifice amounts to the cruel delivery of others as cannon fodder, they engage in a histrionic competition to pledge as many serfs as possible to the army. Crucially, Pierre ends up blaming himself for the "constitutional drift" inherent in his ideas.[19] Implicit in this parody of the senseless relations between the autocrat and his subjects is a rebuttal of Shishkov's proposal to forswear French ideas and return to Russian traditions.[20]

*War and Peace* features a set of recurrent images that highlight the mechanistic, deterministic functioning of social institutions. Witness, for example, the representation of Mme Scherer's salon as "a conversational machine" in a spinning-mill,[21] or the description of the Russian army as a clock brought into motion by the will of the commander in chief.[22] A similar metaphor applies to the French army. When Pierre is captured, he feels like "an insignificant chip fallen among the wheels of a machine whose action he did not understand but which was working well."[23] It is this mechanical mode of operation that explains how the army can transform good-natured French officers into cold-blooded executioners. Tolstoy calls this machine a "system, an order of circumstances"[24] and a "mysterious, callous force which [compels] people against their will to kill their fellow men."[25] The metaphor of the mechanism pertains both to the French and the Russians, suggesting that Tolstoy conceives of modernity as an epochal phenomenon, and not as a direct consequence of the French revolution or limited to French culture.

Analogous to these metaphors is imagery from the realm of zoology. As Moscow is abandoned by the majority of its population, Tolstoy compares it to a beehive deserted by its queen. In such a beehive, the remaining bees no longer behave according to a regulated pattern: the absence of the queen destroys the social fabric of the hive. In an essay Tolstoy returns to this image, attributing the causes of the incomprehensible destructiveness of the Napoleonic wars to a physiological mechanism: "It was ineluctably necessary, for . . . people fulfilled the same primitive zoological law that bees execute when they exterminate one another."[26] In other words, the causes of the Russian campaign stem from the degree to which social determination succeeded in overriding individual freedom and morality. The zoological metaphor reinforces the mechanistic one.

Of particular interest to me is the metaphor of the destroyed anthill, which occurs twice in Tolstoy's description of Moscow. In the first instance, the trope has roughly the same meaning as that of a beehive deserted by its queen. As the chaos of combat upsets regular military procedures, soldiers threatened by enemy fire "run like ants from a destroyed ant hill, in various uniforms and in various directions at once."[27] It seems as if modernity rests on a sort of existential dichotomy, which allows either for fully determined behavior or for meaningless, random action when the social order collapses.

Yet the ruination of cities and the haphazard behavior that ensues bespeak a more fundamental philosophical breakdown, that of traditional systems of thought. As he witnesses the pointless execution of wrongly accused incendiaries, Pierre reaches the conclusion that "everything had collapsed into a heap of meaningless rubbish. Though he did not acknowledge it to himself, his faith in the right ordering of the universe, in humanity, in his own soul and in God, had been destroyed . . . but now he felt that the universe had crumbled before his eyes and only meaningless ruins remained, and this not by any fault of his own."[28] The ruin of Moscow irreversibly compromised not only the institutions of modernity but also traditional belief. In many ways, Pierre's experience echoes that of the population of Moscow: "the Russian nest was ruined and destroyed,"[29] the world he knew had disappeared. Yet the French occupation forces that he faces are not a lawless rabble but a well-organized military machine. An effect of musical contrast encapsulates the difference between the premodern way of life and the modern order imposed by Napoleon's army: the Russian bells that peal from Novodevichii Monastery, absurdly announcing the nativity of the Virgin to an absent congregation, yield to the "merry sound of regimental music," which to Pierre embodies "a new, completely different, but firm French order."[30] It isn't surprising that, unlike the Muscovite middle class analyzed by Martin, Pierre does not express a longing for the restoration of political stability. The "meaningless ruins" he contemplates seem resistant to nostalgic recuperation.

Yet the ruins of Moscow soon begin to afford the city's inhabitants unique possibilities of moral regeneration. The destroyed anthill acquires a second meaning, in which we see that Tolstoy lays the ground for a theory of the restorative social function of ruins:

> It would have been difficult to explain why, and where to, ants whose heap has been destroyed are hurrying: some from the heap, dragging bits of rubbish, eggs and corpses, others back to the heap; why they jostle, overtake one another, and fight; and it would be equally difficult to explain what causes the Russians, after the departure of the French, to throng to the place that had formerly been Moscow. But when we watch the ants round their ruined heap, the tenacity, energy, and the immense number of the delving insects prove that, despite the destruction of the heap, something indestructible, which though intangible is the real strength of the colony, still exists; and similarly, though in Moscow in the month of October there was no government, and no churches, shrines, riches, or houses—it was still the Moscow it had been in August. All was destroyed, except something intangible yet powerful and indestructible.
>
> The motives of those who thronged from all sides to Moscow after it had been cleared of the enemy were most diverse and personal, and at first, for the most part, savage and brutal. One motive only they all had in common: a desire to get to the place that had been called Moscow, to apply their activities there.[31]

In other words, as an index of the loss of the whole but also of the survival of some priceless remainder, ruins release the energy that contemporaries need to restore the foundation of their lives. Modernity's controlling and leveling mechanisms are swept aside—the state reveals its superfluousness—and individuals reconnect with their "diverse and personal" desires. In this collective fascination with the ruins of the city, Muscovites articulate a spontaneous resistance to the ideology of modernity, and they do it in an anarchically collective manner. Tolstoy glosses over the devastation caused by marauding and looting after the departure of the French army. Rather than depicting a Hobbesian state of nature, he glorifies the social energy unleashed by the spectacle of ruins and the temporary demise of institutions of government.

To summarize, modernity, which Tolstoy represents through highly deterministic metaphors, has through its institutions usurped the ability of common people to affect history. The overdetermined logic of historical change, which we could call the dialectic even if Tolstoy was too strongly anti-Hegelian to use that term, leaves individuals powerless. Institutions of control, such as the modern army, have driven a wedge between history and the everyday, and for Tolstoy, who is committed to affirming the historical responsibilities of individuals, the issue is to reclaim history for common people—i.e., to restore that linkage. The ruins of Moscow serve precisely as an event freeing the people's urge to be themselves, revealing the intangible identity of the city beneath the rubble of its institutions. The ruin is the authentic form of the city, as it were.

The novel depicts two important scenes of aesthetic appreciation of ruins. Characteristically, both scenes occur in a context that briefly suspends socially determined dichotomies. The first is when Pierre is living with his French jailors. The rapport he develops with them, the congenial tenor of their relationship, transcends the antagonism that the logic of history calls forth, and it is at this moment, when history's hold over the mental processing of reality seems suspended, that Pierre opens up to the "soothing beauty" of a "half-burnt mansion occupied by the French," a "befouled house" still surrounded by lilac bushes.[32] Fleetingly, this scene calls forth the possibility of reconciliation, not only between historical antagonists but also in the relationship between nature and humanity. The aestheticization of the ruin here seems to anticipate Simmel's celebration of the "equalizing justice" of the ruin, a leveling of historical hierarchies in the aesthetic sphere, or the aesthetic resolution to a cosmic tragedy.[33] For Tolstoy it is critical that the ruin can emerge as an aesthetic object only as the backdrop of the collapse of existing systems of thoughts, which it denotes figuratively. Beauty arises in the interstices between totalizing systems of thought. This explains the care Tolstoy takes to show how both modernity and patriarchal autocracy compromised themselves in the Moscow fire.

The second scene is later in the novel, after the retreat of the French army. Pierre suddenly discovers in the charred ruins of Moscow an aesthetic quality that he compares to famous West European ruins: "As he drove through the streets past the houses that had been burnt down he was surprised by the beauty of those ruins. The picturesqueness of the chimney-stacks and tumble-down walls of burnt-out quarters of the town, stretching out and concealing one another, reminded him of the Rhine and the Coliseum." Here, too, the setting is one of overcoming historical antinomies, this time between Pierre, as a representative of the aristocracy, and the lower classes. The cabdrivers, carpenters, shopkeepers, and hawkers all acknowledge his presence with "joyful, radiant eyes."[34]

Pierre grew up in Western Europe, and the parallels he imagines here embed his experience of the Moscow fire within a personal biography. The iconography of ruin was then fashionable among the Russian aristocracy. Hubert Robert, who called himself a painter of ruins, received many major commissions by Russian princes, as well as by Catherine the Great. His popularity in St. Petersburg was undoubtedly fed by his proximity to the French court, in particular Marie Antoinette.[35] His proleptic *Imaginary View of the Grande Galerie in the Louvre in Ruins*, painted in 1796, was a self-reflective commentary on the artistic beauty of ruins, but it acquired an altogether different meaning in anti-Napoleonic Russia.

Turning Moscow into a new type of Coliseum brings to mind the complex status of ruins in romantic culture: at once an object of desire, a heroic challenge to unremitting transience, and, more politically, a site invested with the power to call for resistance to a stifling contemporary political order.[36] The ruins of Moscow function as a heterotopia, an embodied otherness that offers an alternative to a constituted social order and throws light on its constructedness.[37] They enable a distancing from modernity that serves not just to afford disinterested aesthetic pleasure, but also to imagine lines of continuity across time and space, to develop a sense of belonging that bridges historical ruptures and cultural divides. For Tolstoy the beauty of the ruins creates a new order of visibility. It reveals the collapse of historical antinomies, whether between the French and the Russian, the West and the East, between the present and the past, or between the individual and the collective.

Thus the ruins help rehabilitate personal identities and restore a multilayered sense of time. This plea for lived heterogeneity implies also a rejection of the ideology of social unification under the aegis of autocratic rule that grew out of the experience of the Napoleonic war. During Moscow's occupation by the French, as he plans to kill Napoleon and imagines proclaiming "it is not I but the hand of Providence that punishes thee,"[38] Pierre feels compelled to "sleep on a hard sofa without undressing and eat the same food as Gerasim," his servant.[39] There are unmistakable parodic tones in Tolstoy's depiction of Pierre's desire to suffer and thus rejoin common mankind. The epilogue demonstrates that despite all the existential wisdom he drew from simple, lower-class Platon Karataev, despite his fascination for Karataev's quietist philosophy, Pierre ultimately rejects this lifestyle, opting instead to assume the moral and political responsibilities of a nobleman and to agitate against the renewed militarization of society he sees at work in the regime of Alexander I.

Pierre's aesthetic appreciation of ruins proceeds from a staunchly elitist position. It is an experience reserved for those whose existential baggage allows for the bifocal vision that sees the present as a palimpsest of the past, burnt Moscow as a likeness of the Coliseum. Yet unlike Stendhal's more radical desire to lift himself out of the collective body to which he belongs, this elitism locates difference within a collective fabric. It fosters an awareness of distinctiveness and privilege, while encouraging bonds of solidarity and responsibility. Framed by an experience of heterogeneity, it rejects the sentimentalism and hypocrisy of the patriarchy for the sake of what we could call compassionate self-reliance, if such words had not been compromised by their use in the Bush administration.

The nobleman affirms and protects his moral and political autonomy from the monarch, while demonstrating solicitude for his servants and peasants.

In her interesting book on the drafts of the novel, Feuer speculates on the possible interest Tolstoy could have taken in Tocqueville's *L'ancien régime et la révolution*.[40] Although Tolstoy could not be more inimical to Tocqueville's overall religious framework, their respective assessments of the French revolution and their emphasis on the commanding role the nobility should play in the social order of their countries overlap in many respects. Tocqueville faults the revolution with creating a strongly centralized government, although he acknowledges that the drive toward enhanced social regulation had begun during the old regime. Underscoring that "where equality and tyranny coexist, a steady deterioration of the mental and moral standards of a nation is inevitable,"[41] he proposes to strengthen the freedom of the aristocracy. The political convictions Pierre reaches toward the end of *War and Peace* concur with this assessment: "Well, everything is going to ruin! Robbery in the law-courts, in the army nothing but flogging, drilling, and Military Settlements; the people are tortured, enlightenment is suppressed. All that is young and honest is crushed! Everyone sees that this cannot go on. Everything is strained to such a degree that it will certainly break," said Pierre . . . "No independent men, such as you or I, are left. What I say is, widen the scope of our Society, let the mots d'ordre be not virtue alone, but independence and action as well!"[42] Although Feuer maintains that as work on the novel proceeded, Tolstoy's political convictions receded to the background, the epilogue affirms the centrality of political activity as the only sphere capable of counterbalancing the government's drive toward centralization and regulation. Evidently, Tolstoy sees some continuity between the French revolution and the regime of Alexander I after 1812. In response,Tolstoy develops what we could call politics from the ruins of the old regime, a celebration of the remnants of noble freedom and the lived experience of self-reliance vis-à-vis the ruler and solidarity toward the serfs. In Pierre's words, Tolstoy cares for the reinvigoration of a "society of true conservatives,"[43] one for which the ruins of Moscow provide both a visual incitement and a moral imperative.

The heterogeneity of the ruin—enough of a form to bring to mind antecedents such as the Coliseum, yet too decrepit to appeal to aesthetic canons—also speaks to Tolstoy's novelistic experiments. The paradox of Tolstoy's endeavor to represent the past despite ceaselessly affirming the impossibility of historical narrative finds some resolution in the ruin as a poetic analogy. On the one hand, in the third and fourth volumes of the novel, Tolstoy tirelessly deconstructs competing historiographic accounts, repudiating them for the naive assumptions about agency that drive their narrative forward. His authorial intrusions continuously pry open the fictional space of the novel. On the other hand, we cannot ignore the fact that he also tells a story, even it is more discontinuous, less teleological, and less controlled than those of his competitors, historians and novelists alike.[44] His way of telling a story stresses the linkages between history and the everyday, restoring to the world of art some of the unpredictability that defines the everyday, highlighting the eventfulness of seemingly unimportant actions and the triviality of grand historical gestures. In his attempt to resist teleology, he repudiates hierarchical models of history, proposing instead a mathematical formula that gives equal weight and validity to all forces at play—the integration of all differentials of history—thereby flattening out our paradigms of history.

My point is obviously not that Tolstoy turns the novel into a ruin for the purposes of representing history. That would overstate my argument. Rather, he identifies a specific ideology in the form of the novel, that of collapsing history into the everyday and establishing linkages within the heterogeneity of life, which also underpins the ruin.[45] The Tolstoyan novel is the perfect medium to represent the processes of unintended, nonteleological, and uncontrollable transformation that characterize both history and the ruin. Yet his sense of history as ruin is sunnier than Benjamin's reverse teleology of history as catastrophic and irresistible decay, for Tolstoy latches potential for emancipation and creativity onto the loss of control that history brings about in moments of devastation.[46] Arguably, Benjamin's notion of the ruin as an allegory of an absent whole and of the work of art as a "common practice . . . to pile up fragments ceaselessly, without any strict idea of a goal, and, in the unremitting expectation of a miracle, to take the repetition of stereotypes for a process of intensification" gestures in similar ways toward a redemptive moment in the very process of decay.[47] Ultimately, allegory, in a reversal of its negative representation, "faithlessly leaps forward to the idea of resurrection."[48] Nevertheless, Benjamin's overall tone is much more melancholic than that of Tolstoy, for whom history amounts to uncontrollable and unfinalizable transformation, but not necessarily to ceaseless decay. Tolstoy's ruins are the ruins of attempts to bring historical change to heel, but not the ruins of history per se. Their emancipatory value resides precisely in the fact that they remind us of the futility of attempting to achieve control—i.e., of the vanity of interventionism and totalitarianism.

## Notes

1. Quoted in Tartakovskii, "Pokazaniia russkikh ochevidtsev o prebyvanii frantsuzov v Moskve v 1812g.," 255, my translation. For a detailed analysis of Shishkov's position, see Zorin, *Kormia dvuglavogo orla . . .* , 241–66.
2. For example, in a version of history concocted by I. S. Bozhanov, the presbyter of a

Moscow church, Napoleon, the "zealous follower of Voltaire," stole the throne of the Bourbons. "Tetrad' sviashchennika moskovskogo Uspenskogo sobora I.S. Bozhanova," 52–53.

3. "Moskovskie novosti," 64.
4. See, for example, the case for enlightenment made in *Syn otechestva*, vol. 1 (1812), no. 6, 229. Or see the rhetoric of human rights expounded by Izmailov, who witnesses in the liberation of Moscow "the triumph of Russian virtues," grown out of "successes in public enlightenment" visible in the freedom Russian society confers on its members. [Izmailov], "Razvaliny Moskvy," 113–24. Influenced by Rousseau, Izmailov developed a particular religiously inflected brand of enlightenment.
5. In accounts that blame the mores of polite society for the destruction of Moscow, Napoleon hardly seems involved. See "Vzgliad na tepereshnuiu bedu," 278–79. Here one is apprised of the fact that "the just hand of God bore down on us and allowed the walls of Moscow to crumble" (278).
6. See "Zamechaniia na nekotoroe zamechanie o Moskve," 13. Here the material ruins of Moscow respond to the prior moral ruin of Russian society (33).
7. A sophisticated version of the providentialist argument belongs to Metropolitan Filaret. He advances the notion of the redemptive value of the devastation and confronts the apparent inequity of the fire, which struck both the righteous and the sinful. See Filaret, "Slovo o glase vopiiushchego v pustyne i na vospominanie proisshestvii 1812 goda," 55–65.
8. See, for example, Nordhof, *Die Geschichte der Zestörung Moskaus im Jahre 1812*.
9. Martin, "The Response of the Population of Moscow to the Napoleonic Occupation of 1812," 485.
10. References to *War and Peace* are from *Sobranie sochinenii v dvadtsati dvukh tomakh*, vols. 4–7. Quotations from the novel are from the English translation by Louise and Aylmer Maude, amended by me where necessary. All other translations from the Russian are mine. Tolstoy, *Sobranie sochinenii v dvadtsati dvukh tomakh*, 7:310; *War and Peace,* 1268.
11. Ibid, 6:7; *War and Peace,* 645.
12. Ibid., 7:251; *War and Peace,* 1213.
13. The first philosophical conceptualization of this new sense of time belongs to Hegel. See Habermas, "Modernity's Consciousness of Time and Its Need for Self-Reassurance," in *The Philosophical Discourse of Modernity*, 1–22.
14. Tolstoy, *Sobranie sochinenii v dvadtsati dvukh tomakh*, 7:251; *War and Peace,* 1213.
15. To my knowledge, Tolstoy's embryonic theory of modernity, which is central to his conceptualization of the Napoleonic wars, has gone unnoticed in the literature on *War and Peace*.
16. On the reception of the Moscow fire in poetry, see Gasparov, "Voina s Napoleonom," 82–117.
17. Tolstoy, *Sobranie sochinenii v dvadtsati dvukh tomakh*, 7:317, 321; *War and Peace,* 1274, 1278.
18. Ibid., 7:331; *War and Peace,* 1286.
19. Ibid., 6:100–104; *War and Peace,* 725–29.
20. As he worked on *War and Peace*, Tolstoy used Shishkov's *Kratkie zapisi admirala A. Shish-*

*kova, vedennye im vo vremia prebyvaniia ego pri blazhennoi pamiati Gosudare Imperatore Aleksandre Pervom v byvshuiu s frantsuzami v 1812g. i posleduiushchikh godakh voinu.* In 1812 Shishkov became state secretary to Alexander I and thus participated in the formulation of the czar's proclamations.

21. Tolstoy, *Sobranie sochinenii v dvadtsati dvukh tomakh*, 4:16; *War and Peace*, 10.
22. Ibid., 4:325; *War and Peace*, 269.
23. Ibid., 7:42; *War and Peace*, 1028.
24. Ibid., 7:45; *War and Peace*, 1030.
25. Ibid., 7:109; *War and Peace*, 1084.
26. Tolstoy, "Neskol'ko slov po povodu 'Voiny i mira,' " in *Polnoe sobranie sochinenii*, vol. 16, 14.
27. Tolstoy, *Sobranie sochinenii v dvadtsati dvukh tomakh*, 6:124; *War and Peace*, 748.
28. Ibid., 7:49; *War and Peace*, 1034.
29. Ibid., 7:42; *War and Peace*, 1027.
30. Ibid.
31. Ibid., 7:223–24; *War and Peace*, 1186.
32. Ibid., 7:102; *War and Peace*, 1079.
33. Simmel, "The Ruin," 266.
34. Tolstoy, *Sobranie sochinenii v dvadtsati dvukh tomakh*, 7:239; *War and Peace*, 1199.
35. As the Revolution broke out, Catherine invited Robert to come to St. Petersburg, and she was obviously disappointed that he declined. In the initial years of the revolution, Robert took a careful, somewhat ambivalent stance. Many of his drawings of the time failed to express a commitment to the old regime, which may be what prompted Catherine to write in June 1791 that "if this Robert was not a commanding general, nor a demagogue and madman, and if he came here, he would find much to paint, as the whole Tsarskoe Selo is a collection of the most agreeable views one can see." And she went on to comment sarcastically that "as this painter loves most to paint ruins, and has so many under his eyes, he does well not to travel from the country of ruins." *Sbornik imperatorskogo rossiiskogo istoricheskogo obshchestva*, vol. 23 (1878), 548.
36. For the political reverberations of the Coliseum, contrasting the greatness of republican Rome to contemporary fatuity, see, e.g., Byron's Canto IV in *Childe Harold's Pilgrimage*, or Percy Shelley's short story "The Coliseum" and Mary Shelley's story "Valerius: The Reanimated Roman." For German romantics, the ruins on the Rhine served to anchor nationalist opposition to Napoleon's imperial ambitions. See Fritzsche, *Stranded in the Present*, 92–130.
37. Foucault, "Of Other Spaces."
38. Tolstoy, *Sobranie sochinenii v dvadtsati dvukh tomakh*, 6:373; *War and Peace*, 964.
39. Ibid., 6:372; *War and Peace*, 963.
40. Feuer, *Tolstoy and the Genesis of "War and Peace,"* 133–206.
41. Quoted in ibid., 188.
42. Tolstoy, *Sobranie sochinenii v dvadtsati dvukh tomakh*, 7:297; *War and Peace*, 1253.
43. Ibid.
44. On Tolstoy's antisystemic views of history and novel writing, see Morson, *Hidden in Plain View*, 83–189.
45. Ricoeur makes a similar point about the novel as a genre, arguing that narrative serves

as a privileged instrument to "synthesize heterogeneity," primarily by exhibiting the intersection between various non-overlapping temporalities, which gives the reader a glimpse of time. Thus narrative enables the elaboration of a "discordant concordance"; See *Time and Narrative*.

46. Benjamin, *The Origin of German Tragic Drama*, 66.
47. Ibid., 178.
48. Ibid., 233. Buck-Morss has argued that Benjamin intended to subject this baroque "hollowing-out" of meaning to a critique. If that reading is correct, it would bring him closer to Tolstoy. See Buck-Morss, *The Dialectics of Seeing*, 174–75.

RUSSELL A. BERMAN

# 6

## DEMOCRATIC DESTRUCTION

*Ruins and Emancipation in the American Tradition*

Johann Tischbein's famous *Goethe in the Roman Campagna*, painted in 1787, places the poet in a landscape strewn with the ruins of classical antiquity: a broken frieze and toppled pillar in the foreground, vestiges of buildings in the distance. The ruins of the romantic age signaled culture, an aesthetic experience, memories of the past, and the representational principle of the fragment. More than two centuries later, the contemporary discourse of ruins draws on some of these images, but our concerns depend on much more emphatically political imagery: a devastated Dresden, the crumbling World Trade Center, damage to the Iraqi infrastructure. The fascination with landscapes of ruins suggests a widespread public mentality drawn more to destruction than to rebuilding. Yet my intention is not to suggest an equivalency among these different cases, but to note the emphatically political (rather than primarily aesthetic) resonance of contemporary ruins as compared to the romantic Italian landscape for Goethe, escaping Weimar. The nightmares of ruins sustain our daily politics. However, this politicization of the question of the ruin is hardly arbitrary, nor is it unrelated to Goethe's seemingly apolitical Campagna di Roma. On the eve of the French revolution, Tischbein's painting declares the past in ruins. The ruin of the past is the declaration of independence of the present. Modern ruins therefore enact a particular political representation, the ruin as the ruins of an ancien régime. Moreover, the destruction of that regime is the precondition for democracy: the path to the future is strewn with rubble. Democracy requires ruins.

In the question of the ruin, differing aspects coincide: on the one hand, the condition of devastation itself, understood as indicating a loss of former coherence, an erstwhile but now lost state of harmony; on the other hand, the agency of that destruction, the culprit. Far from a mere documentation of chaos, the conceptualization of ruin necessarily projects a historical narrative. Once upon a time a fairy tale flourished until it fell victim to the force of negativity, which left only shards in the place of grandeur. The ruin as devastation stands therefore as a sort of diminished afterlife of a previous glory. The relic testifies that a genuine life, the proper state of affairs, has come to an end and that what remains—for something must remain in order for us to speak of a ruin; the devastation has been less than complete obliteration—points backward to the missing, to that past which has departed from us, like gods leaving the desert of secularization. The ruin is therefore both legacy and mnemonic: the dead reaching out to us, pleading for immortality, which is the mythological formulation for our memory. The ruin marks the death of the prior life, but precisely as ruin it involves us in a process of internalization and therefore a surpassing of death, in remembering. Gazing on the ruin, we revive the past as memory: the ruin is the talisman of resurrection.

Witnessing slides quickly into the question of culpability. Who ruined the past? The examination of the body of the ruin does not merely entail registering the degradation but also calls for a determination of the cause. Why has the devastation taken place? The brute force of the elements has left destruction in its path: the fire, the tornado, the tsunami all devastate buildings, cities, and societies, heedlessly strewing fragments over the pockmarked landscape. Cosmic forces crush us with sublime disinterest. Among the weapons of nature, time deserves a special place, since no distinct catastrophe takes place; without outbreak, outburst, eruption, or collision, the silent and slow demolition of age produces destruction as time passes inexorably, draining vitality from the organism. Abandoned, the building collapses, just as the body decays. To be sure, it is the wind or the rain that slowly wears away a weakened edifice, but they can do their work undoing human achievements only because of the irresistible power of time to level anything that stands.

Nature and time generate ruins only where human activity is involved. We are unlikely to speak of a site of physical nature, like an eroded mountain, in terms of a ruin unless we mean to imply a scenario of ecological devastation due to industrial pollution or the loss of a natural terrain that had been shaped by human hand: a ruined beach. Similarly, the term "ruin" could refer to a landscape that had been transformed into an object of aesthetic contemplation: a ruined forest. Do the charred tree stumps after a forest fire in an uninhabited landscape constitute a ruin? That usage would push the metaphorical standing of the term to an extreme. Equally, at the beach we might speak of sand castles—i.e., human constructions—ruined by the waves, but we would not consider the more extensive scattering of random grains of sand in a storm to be a ruin. Ruin is a result of culture, not of nature.

Not only does the term "ruin" indicate the destruction of prior human construction, it also suggests human agency. Even where we think we might attribute the demolition work to the unbridled elements or the ravages of time, we soon have to concede that cosmic powers won dominion over the ruined body only because no protective hand was available to guard it. In recent years, no natural catastrophe—flood, tornado, tsunami—has taken place without being transformed immediately into political accusation. Our public life remains trapped in premodern superstitions, as if natural calamities could act as magical signs of the fate of the ruler. We imagine that all natural destruction is the result of government failure. The builders are gone, and the old mole gets to work: the ruin indicates a human departure. This dialectic between the artifact and the absent agent suggests that any narrowly aesthetic contemplation of the ruined site, any exclusive focus on the decaying building, misses the larger event that the ruin marks: the destruction of the whole civilization that erected the edifice and then failed to protect it, leaving us to contemplate the burned walls, tumbled pillars, or collapsed roof. The contemplative stance therefore avoids the question of agency and guilt, opting instead for the comfortable aesthetic pleasure that the view of destruction affords. Facing one dead body, we might call the police and peek out the window with voyeuristic curiosity. Facing signs of a dead civilization, we fall into a sublime melancholy that precludes our posing the question of justice: who did this deed, who undid this world? This is the inquiry regularly repressed by the aesthetic vision that reifies the ruin into an allegory of decay as such.

Yet the ruin qua ruin poses a historical question. The ruin indicates an ancien régime, in part recalling the ancients—this is the moment of nostalgia shading into historicism and antiquarianism—but above all marking them as ancien, former, belonging to a time that is no longer now. The question of ruination then becomes the character of the relationship between the *ancienété* of the régime and the historical agency that brought the régime to an end, leaving relics as ruins in the process. This is surely the case for ruins of modernity, a subset of ruins understood not as a historical periodization—i.e., an inquiry into the representation of ruins in the centuries characterized as modern—but as a specific exploration of causality: how modernity produces ruins, or modernization as a generator of ruins. The problem of the regime in decline may be posed in the context of natural catastrophes, where there is no obvious agency: we associate ruin with the Lisbon earthquake of 1755 because the Portuguese empire was already in decline, whereas the San Francisco earthquake of 1906 was just a bump in the road of progress and therefore did not produce bona fide ruins. Surely earthquakes, as natural catastrophes, are not functions of modernity, but where modernity already is bringing a regime to a conclusion, as with the extended agony of the Portuguese empire, tectonic violence produces ruins instead of what, in another context, is just an opportunity for real-estate developers.

Rendering a regime former is nothing other than the political process of modernity, and this is the framework in which the ruin emerges. The ruin is the corpse of the old world that has been conquered by the new, the modern, the progressive and democratic. The ruin is the shadow of democratic progress. To be sure, gothic horror (the secret truth in the crypt of the ruin) and historical optimism (making the world a better place) have always gone hand in cold, skeletal hand. Ruination has long been the evil twin of democracy: democratization unfolds not through consensual discussion but through violent destruction. Ruins are left in the wake of the wars through which democracies have destroyed their undemocratic (or "predemocratic," with all the historical teleology implied by the prefix) foes: Napoleon at Moscow, Sherman at Atlanta, Wilson defeating Wilhelm II, Trotsky's revolutionary visions, the bombing of Germany and Japan in the Second World War as a precondition for the postwar regimes, the shock and awe in Iraq. The concatenation of cases is probably unsavory and controversial, but it is surely worth recalling that democracy itself has regularly been regarded as unsavory and controversial. The challenge is not to identify the weakest link in this chain of examples. Rather, it is to face the central claim that ruin, as a consequence of the destructive power of war, is inherent in democratization.

This association runs counter to received opinion across the political spectrum today, characterized by an effectively universal commitment to the notion of violence as senseless, unnecessary, and incompatible with democracy. The neoconservative argument for the Iraq War was based on an agenda of democratization: if a domino effect would only take place, transforming authoritarian regimes into democracies, these new states would pursue peaceful policies, which is putatively the genuine nature of democratic regimes. Only in democracies may citizens pursue the rational choice of their own self-interest, which is always unlikely to include war, or at least war against another democracy. While the opposition to the war has not maintained any similarly uniform position, at least the opposition is not primarily pro-Baathist as some opponents to the Vietnam War supported Ho Chi Minh; rather, it is hostile to the militarization of foreign policy as such, which is—and this is the key point—hardly a historically leftist position. There is no need to rehearse that full debate here. The noteworthy phenomenon is the priority of arguments for peace both on the right and the left: the right has largely refrained from making arguments based on its own former arsenal of traditions regarding the value of heroic military virtue, and the left appears to have suppressed the speculations about violence and liberation so common a few decades ago: the goal of no more war now includes no more wars of liberation. The era in which progressives might cite Fanon to defend revolutionary war seems long gone: for the left there is no value that justifies violence.

Despite this absolute priority of peace and the revulsion at violence, in different ways, on the right and the left, the democracy agenda—to which both sides claim to subscribe as well—has a history inseparable from bellicosity and destruction: the city on the hill of democratic emancipation has always presupposed a valley in the shadow of ruins. This is no secret: it is inscribed in the anthems of emancipation. "*Aux armes, citoyens*!" and "by the rockets' red glare" —the two paradigmatic democratic revolutions emerge through blood and battle, and this is inescapable from the encounter with destruction and death. Even before the demolition of the city, the first ruin is that of the hero's body, and we can trace this genealogy of democratic destruction through emblematic lyrics from the American Civil War which continue to define civic religion in the United States. The series of textual metamorphoses is complexly layered in the textual history of "The Battle Hymn of the Republic," understood as a primary textual representation of the entanglement of democracy, destruction, and death.

The hymn derives from a camp-meeting song composed by William Steffe around 1856, known as "Canaan's Happy Shore" or "Brothers, Will You Meet Me?" Both titles evoke a sacred journey or Christian pilgrimage which grounds the missionary substance of all following versions. Steffe also originated the refrain of "Glory! Hallelujah!" Soon after the outbreak of the Civil War, soldiers from the Second Battalion of the Massachusetts Infantry at Fort Warren in Boston adapted the melody, maintaining the refrain, while introducing a new content, referencing the 1859 attack on the federal arsenal and rifle factory at Harper's Ferry by the radical abolitionist John Brown. The uprising was suppressed by Marines under the command of none other than Robert E. Lee. Brown was convicted of treason and hanged. Hence the imagery of the ruined body and its afterlife: "John Brown's body lies a-mouldering in the grave/His soul is marching on," indeed marching against his nemesis, Lee. Of particular importance are two points: first, the transportation of the camp-meeting song from the context of a religious revival to a political and military setting amplifies the Christian narrative of death and resurrection: the Union army stages itself as John Brown, returned from the grave. Second, while the heterodox sectarian camp meeting probably had a multiracial character and therefore already challenged the regime of slavery, the transformed text becomes the real "Marseillaise" of the Civil War. The emancipation of the lyrics becomes the lyrics of emancipation, at the center of which remains the passage through death to redemption.[1] This transformation is explicit in Edna Dean Proctor's "The President's Proclamation," a version written in 1863, in which the refrain becomes:

John Brown's body lies mouldering in the grave;
John Brown lives in the triumphs of the brave;
John Brown's soul not a higher joy can crave—
Freedom reigns today![2]

Freedom, violence, and religion are then subsequently reconfigured in at least three different variants. Sojourner Truth's version, sometimes referred to as "The Valiant Soldiers," has become popular again after Sweet Honey in the Rock recorded it. It was written for the First Michigan Colored Regiment and performed by Sojourner Truth in Detroit and Washington. The text interweaves the traditional sacred refrain of "Glory! Hallelujah!" with assertions of black identity in the context of a violent pursuit of democratization. "We are fighting for the Union, we are fighting for the Law / We can shoot a rebel farther than a white man ever saw." The third stanza presents the complexity of the dialectic most boldly:

We are done with hoeing cotton, we are done with hoeing corn;
We are colored Yankee soldiers as sure as you are born.
When massa hears us shouting, he will think 'tis Gabriel's horn,
As we go marching on.[3]

The season of labor has given way to the time of war; this alone implies a dynamic of ruin, of abandoned farms and fields. Production yields to destruction. Yet far from a gothic, melancholy wandering through emptiness, the departure becomes the assertion of a collective, the "we" of the collective scandal of "colored Yankee soldiers." The First Michigan Regiment is not Goethe in the Campagna di Roma. Far from it: their rowdy jubilation in the forthcoming victory will be misconstrued by an inadequate religious sensibility as the day of judgment. On one level the comparison is a boast, implying the plausibility of mistaking their own assertive presence for an archangelic volume. On another level it is a description of ideology and faith. Gabriel may ultimately come, but for now the "soldiers in the army of the Lord"—to use the initial John Brown lyrics—bring their own judgment and justice. What the master misconstrues as divine intervention is in fact the very human realization of divine intent.[4] The content of that intent is the destruction of the old regime: heaven on earth.

It is, however, Julia Ward Howe's version which became the familiar "Battle Hymn of the Republic." Although the song is not an official anthem, it is woven deep in the fabric of American public culture. Anyone who thinks that recent efforts to sort out the roles of religion and politics can fall back on the simple metaphor of a wall of separation between church and state need only review the full lyrics to see the complexity of the matter.[5]

In another context, one might dwell on comparisons between Howe's text and the others: to what extent did she intend to ennoble the song, make it more respectable, move it from the plebeian sensibility of the camp meeting, working-class soldiers, or the free black regiment into a realm of bourgeois decorum? A world of social difference stretches between the low rhetoric of the revivalist song and the high style of the hymn. Sojourner Truth's "we" gives way to Howe's first person singular, "mine eyes." Yet even Howe's embellished and ornamental version remains explicitly a battle hymn, driven by a stalwart Christian missionary zeal, with untroubled faith and sureness of purpose in the warrior's pursuit of freedom. Divine judgment prescribes the destruction of the enemy, defined as sinner and condemned unquestionably and irrevocably to ruin: "He hath loosed the fateful lightning of His terrible swift sword"; "Let the Hero, born of woman, crush the serpent with his heel"; and "He has sounded forth the trumpet that shall never call retreat." The logic is compelling: the war is not one of competing interests but between good and evil, a good confident in its obligation to triumph and an evil seething with anger when it recognizes that it is predestined to defeat and ruination. The moral mission requires full victory and the unconditional surrender of the enemy in order to completely eradicate sin. Ending slavery means burning Atlanta. There is no room for compromise or negotiation in the pursuit of freedom, even at the cost of death, which is a specifically Christian death. Hence the penultimate stanza:

> In the beauty of the lilies Christ was born across the sea,
> With a glory in His bosom that transfigures you and me:
> As He died to make men holy, let us die to make men free,
> While God is marching on.

Death for freedom is ruin in the name of liberation and democracy. Death in the pursuit of emancipation is an imitation of Christ, who moved from crucifixion to resurrection. Howe's lyrics document a stance which became proclaimed policy, clear for all to understand, in Lincoln's second inaugural address:

> Yet, if God wills that it [the war] continue, until all the wealth piled by the bondsman's two hundred and fifty years of unrequited toil shall be sunk, and until every drop of blood drawn with the lash shall be paid by another drawn with the sword, as was said three thousand years ago, so still it must be said "the judgments of the Lord are true and righteous altogether."[6]

Lincoln's sureness of purpose combines a rhetoric of theological justification and democracy with a willingness to use effectively unlimited violence to achieve a just conclusion. The same confluence of Christian idealism and abolitionist politics that drives the metamorphoses of "The Battle Hymn of the Republic" circumscribes Lincoln's rhetoric. The path to emancipation leads necessarily through military campaigns and the ruins they leave in their wake.

All of this emancipation pathos moves ultimately from popular song into incantatory lyric at a foundational moment of American poetry, Whitman's poem on Lincoln's death, "When Lilacs Last in the Dooryard Bloom'd." Only barely hidden, the Christian journey structures the passage of the coffin of the assassinated president through the landscape, prefiguring the pilgrimage through death to rebirth. Whitman's verse elaborates on the discourse of death implicit in the John Brown material. It was never simply about an executed prisoner, or even the prescribed struggle unto death against oppression. Although the destruction of the sinful enemy is at stake, more important is the question of self-sacrifice: John Brown's body moulders, just as the "colored Yankee soldiers" risk their lives, and Howe's Union soldiers are prepared to die. It is not ruining the other that matters, although that happens, too; what counts is the ruin of one's own body, self-sacrifice in the embrace of death. Lincoln's body becomes a metaphor for death and freedom. For Whitman the knowledge of death in the midst of the beauty of nature remains a precondition for remembrance and longing. The rebirth of the lilac presumes the necessity of death: "I mourn'd, and yet shall mourn with ever-returning spring."[7]

For the Hegelian Whitman, death is the indispensable source of negativity, the destruction at the heart of creation. The plenitude of presence depends on a recognition of a force of destruction: "the long black trail, / And I knew death, its thought, and the sacred knowledge of death" (236). This insight sheds light on a central passage in which Whitman adopts the tropes of gothic horror for a descent into a world defined by negativity and absence:

> Then with the knowledge of death as walking one side of me,
> And the thought of death close-walking the other side of me,
> And I in the middle as with companions, and as holding the hands of
> companions,
> I fled forth to the hiding receiving night that talks not,
> Down to the shores of the water, the path by the swamp in the dimness,
> To the solemn shadowy cedars and ghostly pines so still. (237)

Lyric subjectivity depends on the negation of the living as if the work of art implies a ruination of the real, rendered hermetic through abstraction and redeemed only by the silent grace of form. Through the darkness of "shadowy cedars" and the minatory quiet of "ghostly pines," the poet hears the song of a bird, a "carol of death," which, in an italicized poem within the poem, announces the project of mortification:

> Come lovely and soothing death,
> Undulate round the world, serenely arriving, arriving,
> In the day, in the night, to all, to each,
> Sooner or later delicate death. (237)

The wholeness of the world, embraced in undulations, is subject to the power of retraction that death carries: to take back life from all, with the patient inexorability of "sooner or later." Yet both poetry and life are defined by this internalized, constitutive negation, an ever-present imminence of retraction. The totality of being is cancelled and preserved in the negation, for "death," wrote Hegel, "is the absolute master."[8] This death does not play out solely in the mode of an aestheticized, romantic desire for death. On the contrary, the poem proceeds to graphic and realistic accounts of the battlefields of the Civil War:

> I saw battle-corpses, myriads of them,
> And the white skeletons of young men, I saw them,
> I saw the debris and debris of all the slain soldiers of the war,
> But I saw they were not as was thought,
> They themselves were fully at rest, they suffer'd not,
> The living remain'd and suffer'd, the mother suffer'd,
> And the wife and the child and the musing comrade suffer'd,
> And the armies that remain'd suffer'd. (238)

Passages like this, replete with war's horror, demonstrate that Whitman is no triumphalist celebrator of the violence of the war, even if he recognizes it to be a war of liberation. Cultural progress proceeds through death—emancipation proceeds through the ruin—but that does not diminish the pain of suffering. Hence there is a dialectic of war, between a *via dolorosa* and a miraculous redemption, between "the white skeletons of young men" and the fragrant sprigs of lilac. Whitman evokes a synthesis in the closing couplet:

> Lilac and star and bird twined with the chant of my soul,
> There in the fragrant pines and the cedars dusk and dim. (239)

Clearly the pines (formerly "ghostly" but now "fragrant") and the cedars (no longer "shadowy") have been revalorized, as the closing verse reestablishes a tentative balance in the context of a never-ending cycle of death and rebirth. That cycle is productive for poetry, but as a strategy to limit the recognition of the scope of suffering, it becomes unproductive in the sphere of politics. What would it take to have the families of fallen soldiers renounce their mourning and forget the "white skeletons"? No promise of redemption is compelling enough to banish former love. On the contrary, any suggestion that ruins are productive (because they clear the way for progress), or that destruction is democratic (because it topples an oppressive regime) is susceptible to denunciation as ideology. Indeed Howe's canonic depiction of the divinely sanctioned war of liberation was subject to bitter caricature by none other than the anti-imperialist Mark Twain in "The Battle Hymn of the Republic (Brought Down to Date)," written in 1901. In place of the damaged body that guarantees redemption, in place of the imitation of Christ through soldierly virtue, Twain's political skepticism takes a cynical turn toward *cui bono*:

> Mine eyes have seen the orgy of the launching of the Sword;
> He is searching out the hoardings where the stranger's wealth is stored . . .[9]

Gone is the idealism of redemption; in its place is the work of infinite greed, devoid of any values other than monetary. Howe's Christian "beauty of the lilies" undergoes a hostile transformation in Twain's alternative account:

> In a sordid slime harmonious Greed was born in yonder ditch,
> With a longing in his bosom—and for others' goods an itch.
> As Christ died to make men holy, let men die to make us rich—
> Our god is marching on.[10]

Today's suspicion of the rhetoric of democratic redemption is hardly new; it is, so to speak, part and parcel of the history of the rhetoric of emancipation. Any discourse of freedom is susceptible to the insinuation of ulterior motives, all the more so if the cost in ruins is high. This characterization makes the accusation itself neither true nor false, but it does indicate that current resistance to a notionally emancipatory war for reasons of an imputed hidden agenda represents a long-standing hesitation, inscribed in the inherited discourses of political debate. The reductionist stance that views all policy in terms of wealth and gain is a necessarily prefigured chess move in the ongoing political game. Democratic wars, like democracy in general, are always open to the criticism of corruption. Whether democracy is more likely than other political forms to be corrupt is dubious; that democracy—and democratic wars—is more likely to appear to be corrupt might be a consequence of the amplified idealism, the expectation that democracy will realize ideals of civic virtue in a way not expected of other political forms.

The destructive violence of democracy and its potential to leave ruins in its wake is hardly new. On the contrary, the proximity of freedom and violence defined the response to the French revolution. Hegel explores this connection in his discussion of the Terror, as does Burke in his treatment of the revolution well before the Terror. Even Kant, at his most optimistic in "What Is Enlightenment," understands that democracy, in the form of a reasoning public, must submit to arbitrary rule in order to prevent a descent into societal chaos, a constant temptation for democracy because the enlightened world might disintegrate into internecine conflict without an authoritative power. Eventually liberal historiography comes to celebrate certain modes of revolutionary violence, at least in democratic revolutions, leading to the *Sonderweg* account, the paradigmatic critique of German illiberalism understood to be a consequence of the missing German revolution—the absence of revolutionary destruction of the predemocratic order. Because there were no German ruins, either from the absent bourgeois revolution or from Western armies in 1918, antimodern and antiliberal political currents could flourish and contribute to the rise of Hitler. Real German democracy, at least in this account, could not begin until the country lay in ruins.

Such is the liberal association of ruin, violence, and democracy. Until a decade ago, the Western left also largely embraced the association of violence and freedom. What the left—with appeals to Sartre, Fanon, and Leninist anti-imperialism—used to envision as democracy would be achieved, primarily, through violence: hence the fascination with guerrilla fighters rather than with pacifist leaders, Che rather than Gandhi. Hence also the preferred military garb of the lionized leaders: the uniforms of Castro and Arafat. The unabashed apologies for revolutionary violence are part of this picture. But today much, if not all, of the discourse of revolution and violence has been replaced by invocations of peace: the end of tyranny will come about only through soft power and negotiation, since no tyranny is deemed so heinous that its end should be hastened by violence. This politics of delay is built into the dynamic of the proscription on genocide: since any declaration of genocide burdens the international community with an obligation to act, there is a predisposition to resist any such determination, as evidenced recently in the world's failure to act in Darfur. The romantic association of ruins and silence takes on an unexpectedly topical significance when it involves the silence of the international community, watching the destruction of a people. Darfur is the ruin for contemporary contemplation and an allegory of the incapacity to act.

The insight into the destructive process of democratization, the need to abolish the ancien régime by ruining it, generates two distinct critical responses. In a general sense, contemporary objections to democratic violence depend on an accusation of inconsistency: the violence directed against an authoritarian regime lacks credibility because any antiauthoritarian claims made to justify the attack on established authority are deemed insincere or hypocritical. The pursuit of democracy, as in Twain's verse, is regarded as lacking in authenticity, and therefore whatever military violence is deployed loses its legitimacy. In turn, however, this perspective implies a severe limitation on the power of the criticism, for it would seem that a bona fide and convincing campaign for democracy might be acceptable, no matter how destructive it was: Bush's fight for democracy was not credible to some because Bush himself was not believed, but what about such a fight by Clinton or Roosevelt or Lincoln? Or Lenin, for that matter? If critics denounce the ruins of Fallujah, arguing that greed for oil drove the American use of force and that invoking democracy was a pretext, do they also denounce the ruined Reichstag, viewed not as a triumph of democracy over dictatorship, but as a victory for plutocrats in the West and Bolsheviks in the East? (The Nazis certainly described the world situation in terms very much like these.) Like the neoconservatives, the left has a world-revolutionary history, which is why genuine conservatives regard neoconservatives with considerable suspicion. This explains the weakness of the left in mounting an effective criticism of war. The left has a worldview that is neither isolationist nor pacifist and would be predisposed to deploy considerable violence, if it could do so in the pursuit of its own revolutionary goals. What remains then are only half-hearted complaints of inconsistency and implementation. Meanwhile the use of destructive power is denounced as inconsistent: if ruins in Fallujah, why not ruins in Riyadh, too? The fact that the rhetoric of democracy is used to explain violence against some authoritarian states but not against all is taken to indicate that democracy is not actually the goal. In addition, the technical implementation of destructive power is criticized in terms of an inadequate management of the planning processes and insufficient sensitivity in tactics. Neither of these complaints goes to the core of violence. In other words, ruination as a means to an end is evidently quite acceptable, although there is an expectation that destructive violence should be used with greater consistency (which would mean, more, not fewer wars) and efficiency (a norm of technical accuracy, not moral validity).

There is an alternative criticism, culturally much more interesting, that would interrogate the deeper connection between democracy and ruins, emancipation and violence. While a progressive camp fundamentally accepts the link between violence and freedom—"Aux armes, citoyens!"—and worries only about marginal terms of consistency and implementation, a long-standing conservative criticism also identifies the connection and on that basis critiques democracy itself. The democratic war becomes so destructive because it is defined by a specifically democratic rhetoric of high morality; that rhetoric necessitates the vilification of the enemy, who must therefore be eradicated. Compromise is not an option, only unconditional victory. This is the core of Schmitt's critique of

Wilsonianism. States regularly engage in war to pursue their interests. In the context of the post-Westphalian European system of international law, these conflicts between opposing powers were vehicles to achieve limited advantages. For Schmitt, however, the displacement of these *Kabinettskriege* by ideological wars with moral purposes like making the world safe for democracy means the transformation of the foe into an enemy who is the incarnation of evil. Instead of fighting to acquire a specific territory, access to a harbor, or limited natural resources, the goals of war become redemptive and moralistic, part of a necessary change of a way of life. Yet this can only mean the intention to terminate a way of life that is deemed unacceptable. Democracy leans toward this form of warfare because of the greater need to mobilize public opinion; American democracy in particular may do so because of the streak of religion in its public culture. The logic of this argument points to the proximity of democratization and war, a connection which in turn leads to an ultimately conservative field of democracy criticism.

Within a week of declaring solidarity with the United States after 9/11, *Le Monde* began to posit a structural equivalency between what it called fundamentalist Islam and fundamentalist Protestantism. By the latter term, it meant not Bible-belt literalists but the ritual of the memorial service for the victims of the attack in the Washington National Cathedral and the singing of "The Battle Hymn of the Republic." Crucially, the European critique of American sectarianism is not about prayer in the schools or monuments in front of courthouses. The point is the missionary zeal of a derivatively Christian rhetoric as a revolutionary force, which is at odds with the established order of the world. This conflict is classic: it poses a militant form of Christianity against the old world order, with all its complacency. Faith confronts law, in a competition staked out by Paul in his letter to the Romans.[11] Law—not only traditional Jewish law but, much more important for our purposes, the legal code of the Roman empire—is replaced by the redemptive mandate of faith. The fire of that faith mobilizes the masses and, as Nietzsche argues, becomes the basis of modern democracy; it is that same fire that burns the edifices of the ancient regime, and leaves it in ruins.

**Notes**

1. Browne, *The Story of Our National Ballads*, 129–57.
2. Boynton, *American Poetry*, 329.
3. Gilbert, *Narrative of Sojourner Truth*, 126.
4. http://afroamhistory.about.com/library/bltruth_valiant_soldiers.htm (accessed May 13, 2007).
5. Hall, *The Story of the Battle Hymn of the Republic*, 1–2.
6. Lincoln, *Collected Works*, 8:333.

7. Whitman, *Complete Poetry and Selected Prose*, 233 (subsequent page references to this work appear parenthetically in the text).
8. Quoted in Rauch and Sherman, *Hegel's Phenomenology of Self-Consciousness*, 26.
9. Quoted in Zwick, *Mark Twain's Weapons of Satire*, 40.
10. Ibid., 41.
11. See Villey, "Torah/Dikaion," 144–55.

JONATHAN BOLTON

# 7

## THE RUINS OF A REPUBLIC

*Czech Modernism after Munich, 1938–1939*

In evoking a vanished order—and thereby, in some sense, sustaining it—ruins help us pose questions of how, and whether, the past should be remembered and preserved. Ruins can become a symbol of both victory and defeat, depending on who is doing the ruining; they simultaneously signify memory and forgetting; they can herald the creation of a new order or confirm the destruction of an old one, as well as recording its stubborn persistence in truncated form. Ruins are thus likely candidates to become a metaphor for modernity's relationship to the pre-modern, to its own past. Unlike the gleaming skyscraper or clean-lined functionalist villa, on the one hand, or the swampy wasteland of a First World War battlefield, on the other, ruins are an effectively double-edged metaphor—an eloquent symbol of *both* the creative and destructive energies unleashed in the modern world. In looking for links between the idea of ruins and the idea of modernity, we should keep this ambiguous symbolism in mind.

As a student of Czech culture, I was first attracted to the metaphor of ruins because it helped elucidate the political discourse of a period of Czech history that has received relatively little attention from historians, and even less from cultural historians: the so-called Second Republic, which began with the Munich agreement on September 30, 1938 and ended with the Nazi occupation of Bohemia and Moravia on March 15, 1939.[1] One reason the Second Republic has received little attention is that it was such an ignominious failure. Its predecessor, the First Republic, had been a relatively well-functioning parliamentary democracy, a self-consciously modern state founded on the ashes of monarchy when the Austro-

Hungarian Empire collapsed in 1918. In its twenty years of existence, the First Republic had developed an open and thriving cultural life with close ties to both Western Europe and Russia. Although it never fully satisfied the concerns of its two major national minorities, Germans and Slovaks, it had made great progress in incorporating them into a multi-national democracy. While the governments of its Central European neighbors became increasingly right-wing and authoritarian between the two world wars, Czechoslovakia remained the only liberal democracy in the region.

The Second Republic, by contrast, had a short and unhappy life. It began inauspiciously, born of the Munich agreement, in which France and England abandoned Czechoslovakia to Nazi Germany. The terms of this abandonment were severe. The border regions of Bohemia and Moravia—whose large German-speaking population, under the influence of Nazi propaganda and false promises, had been agitating for incorporation into the Third Reich—were given to Hitler outright. Immediately after Munich, Poland and Hungary added their own demands, slicing off more territory in Silesia, southern Slovakia, and Subcarpathian Rus. All in all, Czechoslovakia lost a third of its territory and population. As George Kennan, who arrived in Prague as the secretary of the U.S. legation on the day of the Munich Conference, wrote with characteristic economy: "No other servitudes were mentioned";[2] yet the annexations did more than just slice off Czechoslovakia's borderlands. The country was deprived of its natural mountain defenses, which had been reinforced by a "Maginot Line" of bunkers that were now handed over to Germany with hardly a shot being fired. Czechoslovakia lost some 40 percent of its industrial capacity, including 60 percent of its textile production and 55 percent of its coal.[3] Hitler had drawn up his demands carefully, tracing a border that would cripple internal Czech communications by cutting through important transportation routes; major rail lines now ran through German territory, such that a Czech leaving from Prague needed a passport to reach many places inside the country.[4] Roughly a hundred and fifty thousand refugees from the borderlands—Czechs, Jews, and Germans opposed to the Nazis—"emigrated" to the Second Republic, representing an additional burden for the shrunken economy of the new state. Unemployment more than doubled between October and February.[5]

"Within a period of days after the Munich crisis," writes Kennan, "the great corps of Western correspondents that had descended on Czechoslovakia while the crisis was in progress had dispersed. Western opinion rapidly withdrew its attention from what was regarded as a lost country."[6] The same might be said of the history books, where Czechoslovakia also tends to drop out of sight in October 1938, retreating docilely into the background and waiting to be properly invaded on the Ides of March, when the Germans established a Nazi-run

"Protectorate of Bohemia and Moravia." Discussions of Czech literary and artistic modernism often end here as well, as if the culture of the Second Republic were hermetically sealed off from that of the First. And yet a state existed during these six months, run by an uneasy alliance of conservative politicians (led by members of the Agrarian Party, which supplied the new prime minister, Rudolf Beran), Catholic intellectuals, and occasionally Czech fascists. Both Slovakia and Subcarpathian Rus were given more autonomy from the central government in Prague—among numerous less cosmetic changes, the country was renamed Czecho-Slovakia—but within the Czech lands, *Gleichschaltung* continued apace: the Communist Party was banned, and all other Czech parties were merged into two entities, the government National Unity Party and an increasingly ineffective opposition, the National Labor Party.

In the autumn of 1938, National Unity still had the upper hand, but it was forced to make repeated swings to the right in order to satisfy its own radical authoritarian wing, as well as the demands, explicit and implicit, of Nazi Germany. By February of 1939, elements of National Unity, as well as the fascist movement Akce Národní Obnovy (Action of National Renewal), had launched a campaign to shut down the National Labor Party as an obstacle to efficient, strong government and a survival of now-discredited parliamentary pluralism. Censorship was intensified throughout the fall and spring—ultimately, nearly two thousand periodicals were shut down or ceased to publish[7]—and the government's opponents were often subjected to vilification campaigns in the press. Some formal anti-Semitic measures were introduced. The Second Republic, in accelerated form, thus followed a trajectory similar to that of Czechoslovakia's neighbors like Poland, Romania, and Hungary in the twenties and thirties: a conservative authoritarian government tried to hold off its own radical right wing, as well as to resist the threats and blandishments of Germany, only to find itself pushed further and further to the right anyway. Had Hitler not invaded in 1939, Czechoslovakia may well have slid into fascism on its own—or, as the poet Jaroslav Kvapil put it: "March 15 was actually our salvation; in the second republic, after all, we either would have suffocated in shame or eaten each other alive."[8]

### Ruins of a Republic

Not all Czechs, however, had given up on their twenty-year project of building a modern, multi-national democracy. And for the disoriented democratic forces in the Second Republic, the metaphor of ruins became an eloquent way of understanding their new situation. A sense of Czech attitudes in the fall of 1938 is clear from two drawings by František Muzika in a slim volume that assembled some dozen poems written by leading poets in response to the Munich crisis.

The cover shows a cracked stone slab with the title of the collection, *Český podzim 1938* (Czech Autumn 1938). And the volume's frontispiece shows another image of ruins: in the background, a figure wrapped in a blanket (or shroud?) sits in the doorway of a cracked wall. On a table in the foreground, a gas mask evokes the mobilization of the Czechoslovak army during the week leading up to the Munich agreement. The loaf of bread on the table is a traditional symbol of Slavic hospitality; here it is shown cut in half, perhaps to reinforce the idea that the Germans in the borderlands had refused Prague's attempts to satisfy their demands, perversely insisting instead on leaving the country.

The metaphor of ruins appears often in writing from the fall of 1938 on. One of the most well-known poetry collections from this period was František Halas's *Torzo naděje* (Torso of Hope), the word "torso" here evoking an unfinished or broken statue. Just two days after Munich, the journalist and writer Karel Čapek, one of the leading cultural figures of the interwar period, wrote: "We stand with sadness in our souls, like a farmer in front of a farm that has been partially destroyed, like a farmer who is calculating what all he has lost and how much poorer he has become."[9] And two months later, Čapek wrote: "May this trial, then, enrich us with the self-knowledge that we didn't let ourselves be broken or morally violated, and that, even in a half-ruined house, we didn't give way to small-mindedness and decay. And more than that, may it resurrect in us new and active virtues that would give new honor and hope to our impoverished life!"[10] This mixture of distress and defiance can be seen as well in *1938*, a drawing by Čapek's brother, the artist and writer Josef Čapek: while a looter makes off from a burning house carrying one sack on his back and dragging another along the ground, a woman in the foreground raises her arms in an ambiguous gesture of anger and despair.[11]

### Ruin and Its Counter-Metaphors: Construction and Cleansing

Metaphors function in a web of relationships, rather than independently. When we are considering the discourse of ruins among democratically-minded Czechs who rejected the authoritarianism of the Second Republic, it helps to keep in mind the rhetoric of their opponents. We might expect the new authoritarian regime to invoke the ruins metaphor as well: calling the First Republic a ruin was one way of discrediting it. But in fact the opposite is the case. For the government that took charge after Munich, the First Republic was an unwanted heritage that had to be denied. The metaphor of ruins was less appropriate for this denial, because it might suggest that, even if the old republic had disappeared, its legacy was still present. Indeed, we should remember the homology between the metaphor of ruins and that of heritage or legacy; both metaphors emphasize the remains of an older order, raising issues of loyalty and betrayal.

By contrast, many supporters of the authoritarian Second Republic were heavily invested in the image of a *new* beginning and a total break with the past. In their ideology, the Munich agreement had finally allowed the proper forces to take control of the country and cure it of the fractiousness and weakness born of democratic tolerance. They thus tended to portray the post-Munich state as a cleansing of the messy multinational democracy of the interwar years; they had swept away the past, leaving no traces. In a December speech explaining his party's program, Prime Minister Beran said, referring in particular to the loosening of ties with Slovakia and Subcarpathian Rus, that the new situation had "cleared the way for us to make a definitive accounting with a system inherited, effectively, from before the war [i.e., World War I]. The national idea has freed itself from the web of globalism and foreign ideologies, overcome petty class politics, and allowed new, powerful political currents to arise."[12]

For our purposes, some of the most interesting attacks on the First Republic —attacks that can be suggestively juxtaposed with the idea of ruins—framed the devastation of the state as a source of new strength. The motif of *cleansing* or *purification* was thus prominent in Second Republic discourse. The Agrarian Party magazine *Večer* (Evening) announced a competition for readers to help purge their language by thinking up Czech equivalents for foreign words, and one nationalist group even announced an *Očista* (Cleansing) campaign, calling (unsuccessfully) for all foreign words to be removed from public signs, for fewer translations to be published, and for all citizens to "Czechify" their surnames and prove knowledge of Czech under threat of expulsion.[13] Not everyone went that far, but it became a standard move in official discourse to suggest that the lost population and territory had somehow been an impurity, contaminating the "real" Czech nation. In his 1939 book *Economic Geography of the Second Republic*, Karel Matoušek wrote:

> We have gotten rid of our most ominous former weakness, namely, the strong minorities attracted to our neighbors across the border, and we have become almost a single nation in our second, as it were new republic: *Czechs in the Czech lands, Slovaks in Slovakia, and Rusyns in Carpathian Ukraine*. . . . As you can see, the more territory and people who were lost from our lands in 1938, the more we gained from the viewpoint of national cleansing [*očista*].[14]

And in his discussion of the country's new economic situation, he wrote:

> The 1938 limitation of our state, to a region that was almost exclusively Czech-Slovak-Rusyn, brought a *considerable national cleansing* [*značnou národní očistu*] to our industry. . . . In the diminished state, there have remained only a few German enterprises; although many of them are Jewish,

> they will take on a Czech form, or even pass into Czech hands, particularly into the hands of Czech banks. . . . The Czechification of industry will continue. It will, however, be necessary to take care that Jewish firms, which can no longer exist in the occupied territory, don't move into the diminished Second Republic and found enterprises in it.[15]

More generally, the loss of the country's huge German minority was seen as an opportunity to "return" to a purely Czech conception of nationhood, where the country's national identity would not be tainted by the presence of non-Czech minorities (especially Germans and Jews). Where the First Republic had combined a number of territories—the Czech lands, Slovakia, and Subcarpathian Rus—populated by different national and religious groups, the new state was seen as "returning to" the medieval crown lands of Bohemia and Moravia, in order to "revive" a more limited, nationally pure conception of Czech statehood and free the Czechs from their messy involvement with Slovakia and Subcarpathian Rus.[16] As is so often the case, however, the past to which the country was returning had never really existed, since the crown lands of medieval Bohemia and Moravia had included the very borderlands occupied by Nazi Germany under the Munich agreement—a historical inconvenience that Second Republic ideology rarely mentioned.[17]

Along with the idea of cleansing, the motif of new construction was common in government rhetoric. In November 1938, the Agrarian Party published an editorial called "How to Build the Second Republic." It was a major policy statement by the right wing of the party, printed on the front page of its organ *Brázda* (Furrow). Written all in capital letters, the editorial screamed:

> The future does not rest in the calculations of the old generation, but in what the young generation creates and makes real. . . . The only task today is to build anew and from the foundation a state that is national in its thought, its politics, its economics, and its social structure. To build by means of new and young people, to settle accounts with the past and everything old and bad, to create a strong regime with a new program, led by new people. . . . A national society, social justice, organization of estates, and Christian morality—these are the pillars of any working program for the renewal of the republic. Our working plan is built on them as well.[18]

The emphasis on youth, energy, and strength is tied closely here to the idea of a totally new construction, built "from the foundation" up, completely getting rid of old structures—of ruins. The contrast between authoritarian and democratic rhetoric can be seen clearly if we look at "The Other Side of the Loss," an article in the opposition journal *Kritický měsíčník* (Critical Monthly) written by one of the new regime's opponents, Bohumil Mathesius. Mathesius does present a critical view of the culture of the First Republic: "For foreign eyes we stuck on gilded cornices, little decorations and pedestals made of plaster. We built on the outside, rather than building toward the inside." In using the building metaphor, however, Mathesius does not aim at a wholesale rejection of the First Republic:

> What collapsed in the autumn of this twentieth year of the republic? Only the stucco and gloriettes, the protrusions and outcroppings. A few pedestals will remain empty, a few wings unfinished, but *the foundation* is untouched, the center unshaken, the pillars unmoved. . . . We will emerge from the shock more experienced and mature. . . . We will build in smaller dimensions, but with more stubbornness and poise. Even if what had and has to fall fell, if its fall was simply hastened by the shock, we haven't worked for twenty years in vain.[19]

Instead of youth, Mathesius extols experience and maturity; instead of building, *re*building. These were the metaphors that could provide some consolation to opponents of the new regime, and suggest what tasks awaited a ruined polity.[20]

Karel Čapek, with his usual keen ear for journalistic jargon, took aim at the rhetoric of cleansing and new beginnings in the article we cited earlier, called "Obroda, očista, čistka" (Rebirth, Cleansing, Purge):

> You will find these words in the majority of newspapers. The nation must be reborn. Our life needs a moral rebirth. A purification of our public life must take place, a purification of this or that institution, a purification of this or that office. . . . You'd almost get the impression that before this heavy blow fell upon us, there was nothing here but grime and dirt, that the twenty years of our happier past had been nothing but disgraces and bungling.[21]

Čapek's own images of the half-collapsed house and the partially destroyed farm can be seen as countering the government's rhetoric of purification and renewal. More generally, we can see how the ruins metaphor became a way of coping with the catastrophe of Munich—admitting the weaknesses of the First Republic, while still remaining faithful to twenty years of experience with democracy. "No matter how badly we suffer," wrote Čapek, "we don't have to be ashamed of ourselves and our history—*not yet*."[22]

### Ruins and the Mobilization of Pathos

A month after he wrote those words, on Christmas Day 1938, Čapek died of pneumonia at his country home in Strž, just south of Prague. Čapek had been one of the living symbols of the First Republic, and it was rather difficult not to see his death as a symbol of the republic's demise.[23] He had been one of its most successful playwrights and novelists, as well as a close friend to Czechoslovakia's first president, Tomáš Masaryk, and a consistent supporter of Masaryk's brand of liberal humanism. Both the Second Republic and its opponents considered Čapek a symbol of the old liberal order. Thus, after Munich, he received barrages of hate mail and was subjected to widespread attacks in the press. His death was greeted with hate-filled obituaries—Rudolf Medek in *Tak* called him "a left-wing masonic high priest and agitator for the GPU," while, a tad more moderately, the journal *Cesta* associated him with the First Republic's "decadent liberalism, lack of manliness, praise of mediocrity."[24]

To Čapek's supporters, on the other hand, his death seemed one more example of a defeat from which strength could, and had to, be drawn. Although he died of pneumonia, the idea that he had been struck down by the Munich agreement was almost irresistible; he had also been a great advocate of French and English culture, and just as he personified the First Republic, so did he seem to personify and intensify the Czechs' feelings of betrayal toward their supposed Western allies. It seemed all too fitting when Čapek's country home in Strž was flooded after heavy rains in the autumn of 1938—he spent weeks cleaning up the debris, and during this work he seems to have contracted the pneumonia that killed him. The various parallels were deployed by another centrist democrat, the journalist Milena Jesenská, in her impressively effective obituary:

> Like a flood, the year 1938 washed away the rocks that had previously seemed so firm. One blow fell after another. The loss of French friendship; the loss of faith in the Marseillaise, the hymn of democratic freedoms; the loss of mountains and borders; the crippled nation; the poet's anxious helplessness; and, along with the roar of a house demolished and plunging to the edge of an abyss, the new speech of some Czechs who befouled their own nest. Too much devastation for the heart of a person whose lifelong faith was to build, construct, work. . . . He was too modest and shy a person to die of a broken heart. He died of pneumonia.[25]

The implication, of course, is that Čapek *did* die of a broken heart—or at least of complications brought on by one.

Jesenská's obituary flags a number of themes that were widely associated with Čapek's writing: his devotion to everyday life, to the small-scale virtues of hard work, domestic life, and simplicity, to compassion for the weaknesses and fears of the common man and woman. These "domestic" virtues (which *Cesta* railed against as a "lack of manliness" and "mediocrity") were miles away from the kind of pathos that the forces of authority were trying to mobilize—the pathos of strong young men in uniform, simultaneously soldiers and construction workers, building a new state and a pure society from scratch. Nevertheless, Čapek's death itself became a symbol of a different kind of pathos, as is clear from Jesenská's account of his final weeks at his country home:

> Strž is a stone house beneath the dam of a pond in the Dobříš forest. There are twenty hectares of land around the house, and this clay, this stone, and the view from it onto the hills of Brdy had grown close to Čapek's heart, as if they were something that breathed. The more the world around us fell into ruins, the more feverishly and eagerly he built, dragging rocks, preparing the regulation of the stream, pulling out stumps. . . . Čapek spent six weeks here in the fall, quite alone except for the stonemasons, toiling away at his work.[26]

Here, Čapek's daily and incremental hard work at his estate becomes a symbol of the "everyday" virtues he espoused, which themselves are implicitly placed over and against the pompous rhetoric of the authoritarian Second Republic—the type of rhetoric Čapek had, indeed, always despised and expertly deconstructed. In juxtaposing his personal crisis with the larger national and European catastrophe (the "crippled nation," the house sliding toward an abyss), Jesenská highlights the pathos of Čapek's own "everyday" world by putting it into the context of a world in ruins.

This strategy was entirely in line with Jesenská's many other articles written after Munich.[27] Jesenská had been a Communist in her youth and was always something of a firebrand, but by the later 1930s she had moderated her views enough to write for the weekly liberal journal *Přítomnost* (Presence), closely associated with Masaryk, Čapek, and the circles of intellectuals around them. Her articles during the Second Republic are noteworthy for the way they zero in on individual lives and situations while still sustaining a feeling of European-wide crisis and controlled despair. In "How This Time Has Gotten on Our Nerves," she pointed out:

> In September and October, for example, the number of injuries on the job rose quite noticeably in Czechoslovakia. Work hasn't gone well for people. It has stuck to their fingers like bad luck. . . . In these days there have arisen people who, with mockery and mindless optimism, pronounce a scornful judgment on those who have borne these months badly. . . . Well, could you show me the monster who didn't suffer during these days? . . . Something else is important: how to return a shaken and trembling nation to peaceful and positive thought and action.[28]

And in an article from October 16, 1938, she interpreted classified ads in the final pages of newspapers to sketch out people's personal disasters—houses and factories offered for sale in the occupied territories, relocated doctors and lawyers looking for work in new surroundings, requests for assistance in emigrating to other countries.

Jesenská's attention to small virtues in great times evokes a particular kind of pathos, what could be called a pathos among the ruins. In fact, many political movements can be characterized by the type of pathos they seek to evoke and mobilize in their supporters. The official rhetoric of the Second Republic could draw on the standard 1930s pathos of struggle, construction, and self-defensive purification—topoi that both Hitler and Stalin had perfected long before the Munich agreement. This is the pathos of capital letters, exclamation points, and urgent appeals, and it tended to paint the First Republic as *incapable* of real pathos, buried as it was in corrupt political intrigues, self-serving backroom deals, and the messiness of parliamentary compromise.

The Second Republic's opponents were quite sensitive to this criticism. For example, the Communist Stanislav Kostka Neumann, who despised both republics as agents of capitalist domination, could still invoke the simple courage of the Czech people. Munich may have "buried Czech illusions under the ruins" of the First Republic,[29] he wrote in his introduction to the poetry anthology *Československý podzim* (Czechoslovak Autumn), but "the Czech people—as opposed to the greater part of the so-called intelligentsia—displayed in these most difficult moments so much simple [*nepatetické*, "having no pathos"] greatness and natural courage that we can truly be proud of them."[30] As with Jesenská's denial that Čapek died of a broken heart, the denial of pathos here is meant to evoke a grandeur all its own.

Thus, when Mussolini disparaged the Czechs after the German invasion in March 1939—saying that if they couldn't even make a gesture of protest against the invasion, they had merely gotten what they deserved—his judgment cut many Czech democrats to the quick.[31] In *Kritický mìsíèník*, František Kovárna spoke of "a Czech courage that does not rely on . . . gestures, rhetoric, and mythologization."[32] Against the "great-nation pathos" of Hitler's Germany and Mussolini's Italy, some Czechs still tried to cultivate a kind of "small-nation pathos," based on the ideals of sober hard work and realism in the face of disaster.

### "The Difficult Fate of a Small Nation": Josef Čapek's *Written on Clouds*

The suitability of the ruins metaphor for this type of pathos is clear in a book of aphorisms and short meditations by Josef Čapek: *Psáno do mraků 1936–1939* (*Written on Clouds 1936–1939*). In 1939, he wrote: "For many of us, almost the entire world fell apart that autumn of 1938. We live in the ruins; our ideas about the justice of history, the value of morality, and the firmness of truth have been severely shaken—what wretchedness, and yet—what a task for our lives!"[33] Here again we see the idea that life among the ruins entails its own kind of work ethic, imposing tasks that arise from weakness instead of strength. In the hundreds of interlocking aphorisms in *Written on Clouds*, Čapek builds on this idea in various ways:

> Only someone who knows how to bear defeats also knows how to bear successes.[34]
>
> *The difficult fate of a small nation.* To fear for one's freedom and fight for it—that life stance is morally more worthy than to use one's freedom and not know what it is. Humans are the creation of catastrophes as well as of peace.[35]
>
> A nation afflicted by a great blow must be capable of growing to meet the greatness of its misfortune. If not, this great misfortune was merely a great punishment.[36]
>
> Alas, indeed, life is only what remains.[37]
>
> The more the times are tossed about, the less certain the general foundation is, the more it is necessary to ask about the meaning and value of life. The less certain my existence is, the more shaky and unsatisfactory, the less can it be merely a question of a sheer struggle for survival.[38]

These entries, and many others, explore the idea that failures and uncertainty shape our life struggles in a different way, more meaningfully, than do strength and success. Čapek wrote another entry on a scrap of paper that he had not yet incorporated in his book when he was arrested by the Gestapo on September 1, 1939, on the first day of the Second World War. His posthumous editor placed it at the end of the book, and it is worth quoting at length:

> It's true that a painter must feel and think through his painting. In this way the painter, encountering the world of phenomena, fears for his own world. Fears that it is just an illusion, an agonizing illusion, a vision without any substantial content. Together—the beautiful with the evil—an evil theater.
>
> This is because he lives in the ruins of the world. The ruins of an old world, that is, which is disappearing. Even the Francos who want to maintain it, preserve it, are conducting its demolition through fires, bombing, killing, seiges. This gigantic demolition is going on, and we have no shelter, as it were, no internal residence. Like Madrid under seige. A lot of heroism; the cinemas keep showing movies; when a roar is heard (inside us), we escape into holes and squint longingly after the sun.
>
> The fear that things are empty. That the painter's world isn't worth anything. That it is just a great, collapsing ruin. Happiness, love, truth . . . the

words we use so much cannot be empty words. Not just empty words, a glittering glass bead that art plays with, that the whole world plays with for a moment's entertainment, distraction, sterile romance.

But enough. Life is lived, not written.[39]

Because this entry was not part of the original manuscript, it is difficult to date precisely, although the references to Franco and the siege of Madrid in the Spanish Civil War place it after 1936, like the rest of *Written on Clouds*. In any case, while it may not directly reflect the results of the Munich agreement, it fits well with Josef Čapek's entries from after the crisis, delineating a larger framework for understanding the artist's position among the ruins of a polity.

How are we to understand this passage? For Čapek, the artist fears for his or her creation *because* the real world is in ruins. The Francos of the world—blinded, we might extrapolate, by their own ideological constructions—are destroying it in the name of preservation. Their actions seem to leave only one possible role for art: mere escapism, an "entertainment, distraction, sterile romance," like watching a movie in a dark theater during the bombardment of a city. But Čapek defines and defends a different role for art: it is the painter's essential mechanism for feeling and thinking. Yet this art, if it doesn't escape from the ruins outside, threatens to collapse along with them. The artist lives "in the ruins of the world," and so "the painter's world" itself becomes "a great, collapsing ruin."

The terms of this argument are similar to those we saw earlier. On the one hand, Čapek paints fascism as an ideology that destroys in the name of preservation or renewal. Opposing this ideology is a kind of sober realism, the only defense available, which tries to create something real and lasting even as it realizes that there is no "real shelter," no "internal residence." Homelessness here becomes something like a shadow metaphor of ruins, turning them into a symbol of the absence of a home. Josef Čapek's sense of art as a provisional, weak defense thus parallels his brother Karel's sense of having to live in a half-ruined house—and of wanting to continue living in it, rather than tearing it down and building something new.

These considerations help us move beyond the symbolism of ruins to a better understanding of the surrounding discourse, in which ruins are an image of both weakness and resolution. As should be clear by now, I find the metaphor of ruins, though interesting on its own, to be even more important as a marker of this larger set of issues, involving the pathos of defeat and the effort to ground strength in failure. Josef Čapek's pathos is that of "writing on clouds," of sending out messages whose very transience and instability is part of their meaning. It is an attempt to refuse the temptations of escapism, while still acknowledging the relative weakness of art to oppose the destructive power of our political fictions. I find Čapek's voice here to be very much of its time and place, Europe in the late 1930s, and I am tempted to call it a voice of late modernism—aware of an old order in disintegration, and finding in that disintegration a source of inspiration as well as a horrible premonition. The remnants of Czech liberal culture during the Second Republic shared this inspiration and premonition, filtering it through their own lens of a small nation struggling to understand its own humiliation. In a paradox that by now should be familiar, Čapek's final injunction—"Life is lived, not written"—is both an artist's admission of failure and an attempt to draw rhetorical energy, if nothing else, from that defeat.

## Notes

I would like to thank Chad Bryant, Julie Buckler, Peter Bugge, Benjamin Frommer, Marek Nekula, Scott Spector, and Jindřich Toman for valuable comments on earlier drafts of this chapter.

1. The best works on the Second Republic are Gebhart and Kuklík's judicious *Druhá republika, 1938–1939* (The Second Republic, 1938–1939), and Rataj's more polemical *O autoritativní národní stát* (The Authoritarian National State). Rataj is a shrewd analyst of political rhetoric, but Gebhart and Kuklík offer a more differentiated account of the various shades of authoritarian and fascist discourse. The standard work in English is Procházka's *The Second Republic.* Among the many interesting memoirs of the period after Munich are Zeman's *Československá Golgota* (Czechoslovak Golgotha), Černý's *Křik koruny české* (The Cry of the Czech Crown), and Kennan's *From Prague after Munich.* All translations from the Czech are my own.
2. Kennan, *From Prague after Munich*, xiv.
3. Procházka, *The Second Republic*, 53. For a contemporary account of the population and economic losses, see Matoušek, *Hospodářský zemìpis druhé republiky* (Economic Geography of the Second Republic); see also Gebhart and Kuklík, *Druhá republika, 1938–1939*, 26 and 163–71. Among other suggestive measures documented by Gebhart and Kuklík, we might mention the loss of 90 power plants, 30,000 railroad cars, 10 of the country's 34 airports, and 14 tons of its gold (which Germany absurdly demanded, and received, as "compensation" for the Czechoslovak paper currency taken out of circulation from the occupied borderlands).
4. Gebhart and Kuklík, *Druhá republika, 1938–1939*, 166.
5. Procházka, *The Second Republic*, 53.
6. Kennan, *From Prague after Munich*, vi.
7. Gebhart and Kuklík, *Druhá republika, 1938–1939*, 196.
8. Quoted in Rataj, *O autoritativní národní stát*, 222.
9. Karel Čapek, "Drazí lidé!" (Dear People!), in *Spisy*, vol. 16, 515.
10. Karel Čapek, "Obroda, oèista, èistka" (Rebirth, Cleansing, Purge), in *Spisy*, vol. 16, 532.
11. Josef Čapek's drawing is a kind of study for his 1938–39 cycle of twenty-one oil paintings, *Oheò* (Fire), in which the motifs of the woman, the house, and the looters recur in various forms. The woman, although always faceless, is more clearly defiant in some

paintings, more clearly despairing in others; the house is sometimes in flames, sometimes a charred ruin, sometimes absent. The looters have also been interpreted as refugees leaving the occupied territory with their possessions on their backs, perhaps after having destroyed their own homes. See Slavík and Opelík, *Josef Čapek*, especially 463–81. These polyvalent interpretations of the paintings are quite in keeping with the ambiguous nature of the symbolism of ruins, caught between memory and forgetting, resistance and surrender.

12. Quoted in Gebhart and Kuklík, *Druhá republika, 1938–1939*, 102. For a different take on the role of ruins in totalitarian discourse, see Josef Vojvodík's fascinating discussion of ruins in Czech and European cultural consciousness, in his *Imagines Corporis*, especially "Moderna v ruinách" (The Modern in Ruins), 148–208.
13. Rataj, *O autoritativní národní stát*, 95–96. Cf. Gebhart and Kuklík, *Druhá republika, 1938–1939*, 184–85.
14. Matoušek, *Hospodářský zemìpis druhé republiky*, 42, emphasis in the original.
15. Matoušek, *Hospodářský zemìpis druhé republiky*, 125–26, cited in Rataj, *O autoritativní národní stát*, 114; emphasis in original. Rataj cites Matoušek's book as an example of straightforward authoritarianism, although Matoušek—despite his emphatic anti-Semitism—was in fact more sympathetic to the First Republic than many other thinkers on the right.
16. Rataj, *O autoritativní národní stát*, 166–67.
17. A further element of this cleansing return was the distortion of the "Saint Václav" tradition. The tenth-century Czech Prince Václav, according to one popular legend, had sent an annual tribute to the Saxon king Heinrich der Vogler. This practice was now seen as founding a tradition of Czech vassaldom to Germany, most lately embodied in the Second Republic's generally sycophantic foreign policy toward Nazi Germany. On the Second Republic's uses of the Václav tradition, see Rataj, *O autoritativní národní stát*, 166–181.
18. "Jak vybudovat druhou republiku" (How to Build the Second Republic). The editorial appeared in *Brázda* (Furrow), November 9, 1938. I draw on the facsimile of the front page printed in Rataj, *O autoritativní národní stát*, 70. Cf. Gebhart and Kuklík, *Druhá republika, 1938–1939*, 116–18.
19. Mathesius, "Líc prohry" (The Other Side of the Loss), 387, emphasis in the original.
20. In a similar vein, the poet Josef Hora wrote: "We have lost the leaves of illusions, but not the trunk of faith" (*Lidové noviny*, October 1, 1938, cited in Gebhart and Kuklík, *Druhá republika, 1938–1939*, 200).
21. Karel Čapek, "Obroda, oèista, èistka," in *Spisy*, vol. 16, 532.
22. Ibid., emphasis in the original.
23. See Bugge, "Nákaza svìta" (The Infection of the World), 256–57; and Rataj, *O autoritativní národní stát*, 127–28.
24. Both quoted in Rataj, *O autoritativní národní stat*, 128.
25. Jesenská, "Poslední dny Karla Čapka" (The Last Days of Karel Čapek), in *Nad naše síly*, 161; originally published in *Přítomnost* on January 11, 1939. In the West, Jesenská has long been known primarily as one of Franz Kafka's correspondents (*Letters to Milena*), and secondarily for her courage and selflessness in the Ravensbrück camp, where she died in 1944. Only recently has she emerged as a more three-dimensional character, a fine

essayist, and one of the more intriguing figures of interwar Czech culture, thanks largely to Sayer's *The Coasts of Bohemia* and Hayes's excellent edition *The Journalism of Milena Jesenská.*

26. Ibid., 164.
27. In fact, she had perfected this strategy even earlier, in her dispatches from a starving and impoverished Vienna, written in the months after the First World War. See Jesenská, *The Journalism of Milena Jesenská*, 49–100.
28. Jesenská, "Jak tato doba zahrála na nervech" (How This Time Has Gotten on Our Nerves), in *Nad naše síly*, 139; originally published in *Přítomnost* on November 16, 1938.
29. Neumann, "Úvodem" (By Way of Introduction), in *Československý podzim* (Czechoslovak Autumn), 5.
30. Ibid., 6.
31. See Zeman, *Československá Golgota*, 213–27; Černý, *Křik koruny české*, 88; and Kovárna, "Rozdíly duše" (Differences of Soul) and *Česká střízlivost a český pathos* (Czech Sobriety and Czech Pathos). Zeman quotes one version of Mussolini's statement: "It's clear . . . that when a nation with a large number of men and an extensive arsenal is not capable of a gesture, it is ripe, overripe for its own new fate" (*Československá Golgota*, 214).
32. Kovárna, "Rozdíly duše," 192.
33. Josef Čapek, *Psáno do mrakù 1936–1939* (Written on Clouds, 1936–1939), 283.
34. Ibid., 185.
35. Ibid., 190.
36. Ibid., 207.
37. Ibid., 133.
38. Ibid., 220.
39. Ibid., 341.

AMIR ESHEL

# 8

## LAYERED TIME

*Ruins as Shattered Past, Ruins as Hope in Israeli and German Landscapes and Literature*

Any attempt to understand why ruins such as those of the Frauenkirche in Dresden, the Stadtschloss in Berlin, or the Twin Towers in New York matter so much should begin with the obvious: we are fascinated by structures that disintegrated or were shattered as a result of human action—buildings, sites, and neighborhoods that were leveled in a calamitous war, or destroyed by forces we call political in the broadest sense. Ruins that signify decay or natural decline, however, are fascinating only in protoromantic and thus anachronistic contexts.

In *Stranded in the Present*, Fritzsche discusses Western notions of history in the aftermath of the French revolution. In previous centuries, Fritzsche claims, ruins signified the dignified presence of earlier epochs and a cycle of life and death resembling natural history. In the modern era, ruins came to be understood as objects of observation and study—in short, a target of historicizing. Ruins became the sign of a new approach to the past: no longer could history be seen as the source of a heritage that dictates how we think about our lives, how we act, and how we envision our future. The past became a way to think about our ability to act and influence the world in "circumstances of contingency."[1]

No longer signifying simply the cycle of life and death, modern ruins ceased to underscore the power of nature over human creation. Faced with an ever growing rate of change, the ruins of the past—the ruin as an object of aesthetic awe and source of inspiration—became "a foundation for an alternative present."[2] Ruins lost their magical appeal and the dark fascination surrounding the dialectics of culture versus nature. The horrors of human history began to be understood as the result of "a specific historical disaster" and not of an abstract "devastation of time":[3] formal insights into the action and mutability of the historical process and into the production of ruins could then be taken to provide, Fritzsche claims, "evidence of abrupt endings and new beginnings, and thereby encouraged the efforts of contemporaries to 'make' or resist history in the present."[4] Not the ruin, he concludes, but "the ruin of the ruin is the hallmark of modernity."[5]

The ruin, in other words, is deprived of its ability to serve as the source of melancholic retreat and aesthetic experience. Unearthed, hermeneutically explained in service of present-day aspirations, the ruin entered a sphere in which every element of signification is made available for a new and immensely powerful thrust forward. Away from the premodern fixation on history as a shaping, nonhuman substance, the world of humans ceased to be thought of as a hostage to the past but rather as what is given to humans of the present to shape as they wish. With this infusion of energy, the way was paved for the cataclysms of the modern era, a time characterized by unprecedented economical, technological, and social advances and by the previously unknown horrific consequences of attempts to create mankind—or a certain race or class of it—anew. This is also, of course, the era of modernism: the notion that artistic creation should free itself from the bonds of known forms and past modes of expression.

It took the devastations of two world wars and the massive deaths resulting from fantasies of a classless world to shake modernity's confidence in its ability to create a world freed of all relation to the past. While the interwar era left intact much of this dream—that we might reshape individual and social spaces in light of futurist projections—the decades following the Second World War were dominated by questions like how we might deal with completely flattened neighborhoods and hollowed-out cities, and how we can make sense of and signify spaces in light of a past of destruction so recent and so unforgettable that it is always at hand. And these questions were asked amid remnants that kept evoking the outcome of some of modernity's most monstrous notions regarding the creation of a new, liberated mankind. In Germany, ruins such as those of the St. Nikolai's Church in Hamburg and the Kaiser Wilhelm Memorial Church in Berlin were left as *Menetekels*: haunting skeletons which never tire of reminding us of the unprecedented scars inflicted by the world wars. If the historical and temporal consciousness of the modern age can be understood as strandedness in the present, then the postwar era—especially the decades following the Auschwitz trials of 1963–65 and the Eichmann trial of 1961—was littered with ruins and remnants that were seen as almost untouchable artifacts, objects which would not allow us to historicize them, objects which found their significance in their command that we must always remember.

In the last decades of the twentieth century, public interest in such ruins and the weighty discussion surrounding sites of memory became a significant facet of what Huyssen aptly describes as a new kind of concentration on things past: it reflects an obsession with the notion that the forward gallop of modernity has caused not only memory but the past itself to begin to slip away. We postmoderns "counteract" the fear of forgetting with "survival strategies of public and private memorialization."[6] Some thinkers even go so far as to describe this new postmodern or late-modern era as barren of a reflective sense of time and history. Jameson, for example, proclaims that our late-modern epoch stands for "the end of temporality";[7] the capitalist machinery of production, consumption, and profit-driven politics radically reduces our imaginations to the realms of the present and the body.[8] The modernist emphasis on the now as a way to rethink present conditions in light of future—if not futuristic or utopian—fantasies is gone, Jameson claims, and in its place is a complete strandedness in the now that leads to an obliviousness of human historicity, to an inability to regard the given conditions as the products of human action, and thus, crucially, to an inability to see these conditions as subject to change.

While many of Jameson's examples support his observations, I would like to suggest a more complex picture in reference to the prominence of ruins such as Dresden's Frauenkirche. I would like to argue that the presence of ruins in the faces of our cities, in significant contemporary literature, in cultural criticism, and in the popular imagination implies a modification of the modern concentration on the now in light of unprecedented historical events, that those occurrences demand a renegotiation between overcoming the recent past and maintaining its memory as a way to avoid inhuman modernist fantasies. Furthermore I will suggest that our cultivated ruins—which serve as memorial sites and as multifaceted objects of cultural production and political dispute—demonstrate that space has never completely shattered the modern concern with time and temporality. In other words, the ruins of our postwar era—ruins, that is, of post- or late modernity—are not the material manifestation of a fascination with destruction and demise, not only sites in which memory qua memory is ritualistically celebrated. The sites also enable us to think about the historicity of our condition and even experience hope. The significant ruins of our time indicate both the persistence of the catastrophic and the fact that humans—weak and restricted as we might be—are still agents of our histories. Negotiating past and present, these ruins reveal the possibility of thought along lines that move through different temporal realms—between what occurred, what persists, and what can still occur—and thus suggest the potential for change. What such ruins denote, I will conclude, is not melancholic retreat from human action in time, but rather an awareness—not universal, but not deniable—of the inscription of time, the inscription of human agency in space.

Established in their current political form in the late 1940s, both Israel and Germany have cultural and political discourses that are shaped to a large extent by debates surrounding questions of history and memory. At the center of many of these debates, we find the difficulty of deciding between alternative understandings of what the countries' pasts signify. What does a site of memory denote, and what should it denote? What are the meanings and lessons of the narratives surrounding such sites? What might be the implications of those narratives for the future of the state—its social formation, political discourse, and cultural institutions? In both Israel and Germany, the debate regarding the signification of the past is thus unsubtly related to thorny questions about the present and the future. In Germany, debates about the material remnants of sites such as the Frauenkirche often touch on the tensions inherent in the role of today's German national consciousness in light of Germany's nationalistic past: does the reconstruction of a ruin that for decades symbolized Germany's defeat, the devastations of a war brought about by nationalistic and racial zeal, and the horrific air raids on German cities mean that Germany is now moving away from that past and assuming a new, assertive role in Europe?

Grounded in the notion that Zionism reconnects modern Jewry to the bygone age of Jewish political independence in the Holy Land, Israel integrated ruins such as Masada and the Western Wall in Jerusalem into aspects of what is essentially the political culture of a modern state. These ruins are often used as settings for national ceremonies, commemorative events, and the taking of military oaths. The underlying narrative of such ceremonies is that of restitution out of destruction: the Jewish state of antiquity is continued or resurrected through the modern sons and daughters of ancient Israel and Judea. The narratives surrounding such remnants as the Western Wall are at the core of many modern political questions. To what extent does the presence of massive stones from Herod's day, excavated and now on public display, indicate the historical right of Jews to settle what has become the Palestinian quarter in Jerusalem? Since the events surrounding the departure of some 700,000 Palestinians from what is now Israel in the 1948 War of Independence are at the heart of the present political struggle over the future of large parts of the Holy Land, ruins and remnants that evoke the flight or expulsion of Palestinians are at the center of bitter political debates.[9]

In addition, the discussion of significant ruins—and hence of the memory of the past—is related in Germany and Israel to their mutual past, the historical event that most significantly informs their cultural and political discourses regarding the past: the Holocaust. In both countries, evoking, presenting, and commemorating past events means rethinking the present in light of both the recent and distant past; in both countries, the Holocaust is one of the most crucial moments that define the current cultural and political landscape. Both material ruins, such as those mentioned above, and ruins in literary works display the layering of time in space, what Koselleck calls *Zeitschichten.* According to Koselleck, historical time is rendered concrete through spatial metaphors. Zeitschichten can be observed in marked places such as ruins which indicate the presence of several historical times in one material stratification; break lines that become visible in marked spaces, going through and sometimes connecting different moments in time to a new layer, as in a geological structure.[10] Both the invocation of historical time and the consideration of the connection between different temporal realms (lines connecting Nazi Germany with current German circumstances; lines relating Jewish antiquity to present-day claims over disputed territories) originate at the turn toward narrative. Through narratives, material ruins gain their chronotopic quality: they signify the inscription of history in space; through narratives, ruins promote conflicting notions of the past.

A telling example is the role of ruins in Zionist culture and ideology. Narratives preoccupied with ruins serve in contemporary Israel as a central trope in fostering a sense of community through a connection to the ancient Jewish past. The founding of Tel Aviv on the eastern coast of the Mediterranean in 1909 was motivated by the desire to build a clean, European neighborhood on the outskirts of Jaffa, which was seen as grimy and Oriental. In Hebrew, *tel* is a mound of ancient ruins, while *aviv* means the season of spring. The name of the new city represents the claim that it was built on the ruins of ancient Jewish civilization in the promised land.

Growing up in Haifa, in northern Israel, I never heard the story of Haifa's pre-1948 past in a manner that emphasized the lives of the city's Palestinian population. The deserted, cemented-up houses in the Arab quarter were left silent: no sign explained their haunting stillness.

The usual story told about the emergence of present-day Haifa is one of creation out of nothing. Haifa's past, as seen in the silent Arab houses, lay literally in ruins. Much has changed in the city over the last two decades, yet these ominous cenotaphs still stand, calling upon all to tell their story. Hardly any national effort has been made to explain what led to their abandonment. On a municipal level, however, Haifa's Jewish population does address them as

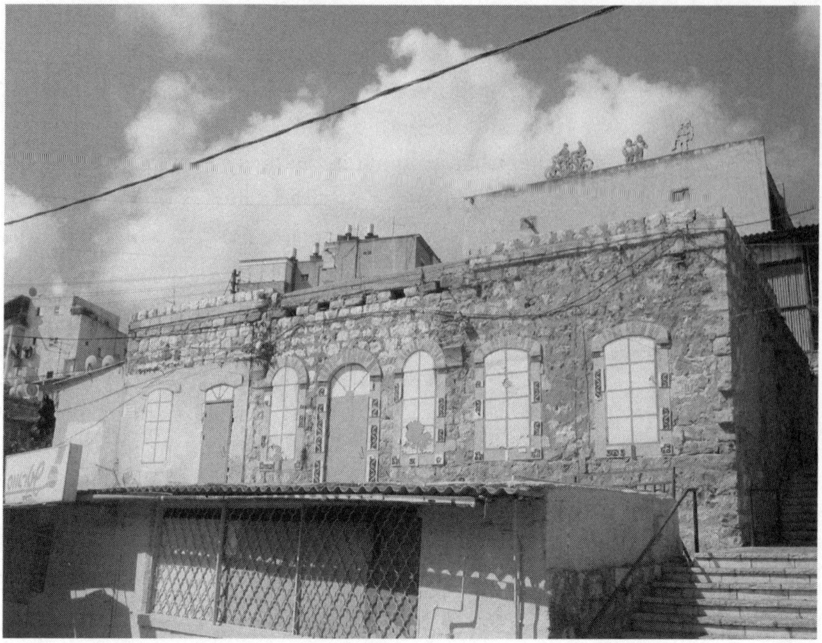

1. Deserted, cemented-up houses in Haifa's Arab quarter, summer 2004. Photo by author.

ruins that memorialize the departure of the city's Muslim population in 1948. In recent years, a variety of street happenings and artistic exhibitions turned some parts of the old Palestinian neighborhoods into an open-air museum of the past and of a future of Arab-Jewish cohabitation. The current artwork near or on the deserted houses indicates not only the traumatic moments of war and exile but also the possibility that new life might emerge in these spaces, and thus the historicity of their present condition. On the walls and windows of one cemented-up Palestinian house, a work by the Israeli artist Igal Shtayim, *Untitled*, brings together images of Haifa's past and of a woman. The images of the woman in the windows project life back into the silent, ruined space, signifying the possibility of a future life in these houses. Where once people used to live, the past and its memory is a haunting presence, yet what is now gone can return through human action. Creating art is one possible action. It does not undo the past but rather suggests adding to it a new layer—a possible new form of life, the return of a vibrant community.

Artwork also covers the walls of other Palestinian houses in Haifa. The windows of some of the houses display poetry—the work of Palestinian or Israeli writers, such as "Le'vad" (Alone), by the poet Nava Semel. Set in Haifa's Arab quarter, the poem disrupts the spatial setting of the decaying wall it is

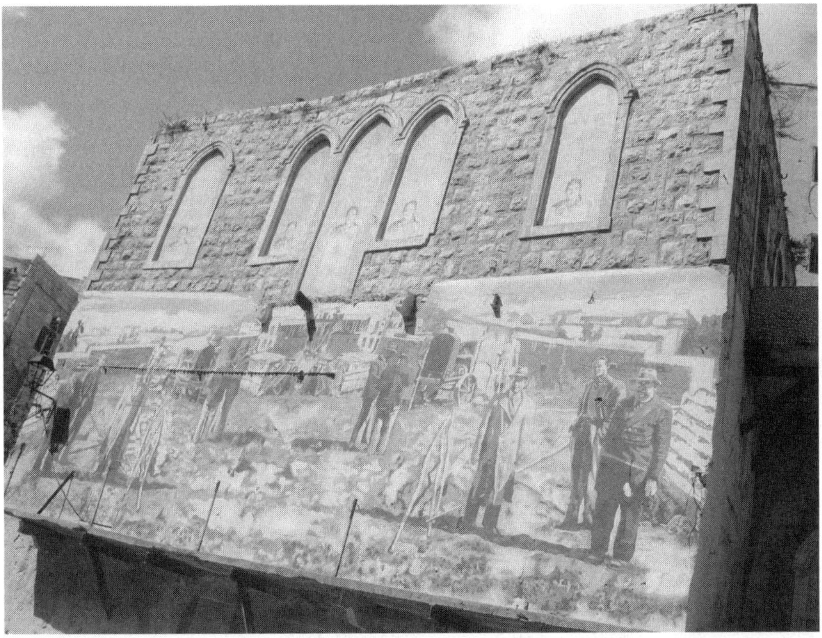

2. Igal Shtayim, *Untitled*, painted on two unoccupied Palestinian houses in Haifa. Photo by author.

attached to. Displayed in Hebrew and in Arabic, the poem also disrupts notions of monolingualism and marks the space as belonging to more than one ethnic group.[11] It proposes that past catastrophes always leave room for hope.

Written by a child of Holocaust survivors who made Israel their home after the Second World War, the poem displays the layering of several times in Israel's metaphorical space: it is written from the perspective of Jewish suffering, but, as it is set in the present and in a new space, it underscores the darkness resulting from the displacement and exile of those who used to live in the cemented-up houses. To be sure, the poem hardly equates the sufferings of those who were exposed to "darkness" in Semel's own biography with the darkness suffered by Haifa's Palestinian population. Instead, it shows that diverging memories can share a single space, and that those who experienced darkness can perceive the sufferings of those around them—in this case, those who lay claim to the same space in what is now Israel.

Another ruin serves as the site around which both remembrance and the possibility of human action in time are considered in a novella by the eminent Israeli writer Yizhar Smilansky, who uses the pen name S. Yizhar. This work gave rise to one of the fiercest public debates in Israeli history, a dispute about the question of Palestinan flight and expulsion during the War of Indepen-

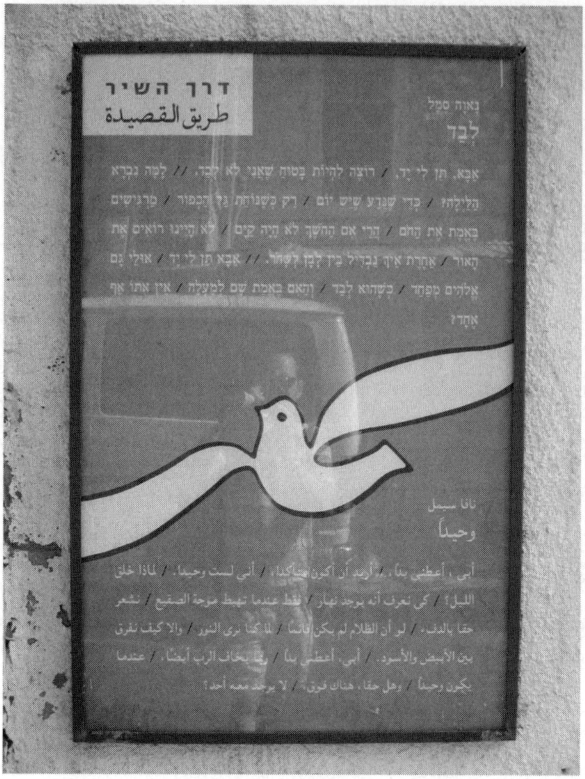


3. Nava Semel, "Le'vad" (Alone), on a wall in Haifa's Arab quarter. Photo by author.

dence.[12] Hirbet Hizah is the name of a fictional Palestinian village.[13] Written in 1949, the story tells of the Jewish occupation of the village as seen from the perspective of a young soldier. The soldiers were ordered to arrest all the men; gather all the women, old people, and children, load them onto trucks, and transfer them behind the demarcation lines; and blow up their stone houses and burn their huts—in short, to turn the village into a ruin.

When the soldiers have carried out those orders, the novella switches from a mode of description and psychological realism to one of metaphor and symbolism, full of allusion and allegory:

> I had to control myself. My guts were screaming. Colonialists. . . . Hirbet Hizah is not ours. Never did the machine gun give [anyone the] right to anything. . . . What didn't they tell us about the [Jewish] refugees. Everything for the refugees, their peace and rescue. . . . Sure, our refugees. Those we expel—that's a different matter altogether. Wait: two thousand years of exile. Whatnot. Jews are killed. Europe. Now we are the masters. Would the remaining walls not scream in the ears of those who would later live in this

village? Would the air not be filled with the shadows, sounds, and gazes, with the sights, the screams that sounded and did not sound, the frightened innocence of shocked cattle, the surrender of the weak, and their heroism, the single heroism of those who don't know what to do and cannot do [anything].[14]

The images of the degradation of Palestinians, which earlier in the novella alluded to images of Jews expelled during antiquity, the Middle Ages, and the recent Holocaust, culminates in this section in the repeated use of *karon*, which in Talmudic Hebrew means a vehicle to transport goods, but in modern Hebrew means rail car.[15] The references collapse together the image of Palestinians awaiting expulsion with that of Jews transported to their death during the Holocaust: "like lambs to slaughter."[16]

Like Semel's poem, the novella does not equate Israelis' actions with atrocities committed against Jews during the Holocaust. Instead it maps the ways in which the observer retrospectively arranges events and invites the reader (through the formal collapsing together of divergent images) to think of the Israeli War of Independence as both clearing the road to Jewish statehood in Palestine and introducing a set of ethical choices never faced before. In focusing on the transformation of a village into a ruin, the story expands the reader's view of the Zionist endeavor and what Gershon Shaked calls the Zionist metanarrative—a narrative assuming the creation of the new Jewish national entity on the ruins of Jewish antiquity in Palestine. The novella does not simply present a critical account of what happened during the 1948 war; it also acknowledges, without moralizing, what the narrator terms "colonialism."[17] In speaking out in the face of destruction, the textual ruin underscores what occurred during the war but also reminds us that the destruction of the village is the result of human action, and that the ruin can thus be seen as challenging us to respond to it.

The novella became a literary site of memory immediately after its publication. The poet Leah Goldberg, for example, expressed an early appreciation for its honesty and "civil courage."[18] The *now* coexists with the memory of what the War of Independence involved—the flight and expulsion of Palestinians—and the significance of this event for any attempt to envision the future course of the Jewish state. In signifying the historical layers of this site, the novella serves as a focus for personal and collective reflection: it is through this and other literary sites that the interdependencies between the occurrences of the past and the constitution of the present are made present, showing us that what occurred is an indication of what can still occur, if we choose to address the circumstances and conditions of our lives.

Collapsing together images of the 1948 War of Independence with those usually associated with Jewish suffering during the Holocaust invited—as a literary provocation—individual and social reflection on the relationship between the recent past in Europe and the options that Israelis and Palestinians are facing in its aftermath amid the difficult circumstances of the Middle East. The novella's implied insistence—that the unprecedented Jewish suffering during the Holocaust marks a turning point in thinking through the moral contingencies of our time—is one of the first literary examples of the process by which the Holocaust has become a crucial element in the discourse of globalization. One of the central scenes of this process of debating the connections between the Holocaust as a global signifier and questions of moral conduct undoubtedly is contemporary German culture—not least through its fascination with ruins. The dramatic paintings of Kiefer and the prose of Kluge and Sebald clearly reflect the significance of ruins in imagining the past and thinking through its relevance to culture and the public sphere.

The German version of the memory boom of the eighties and nineties included a broad public debate surrounding a section of Berlin that came to be known as the Topography of Terror. In the rather small area between Niederkirchnerstrasse (then Prinz-Albrecht-Strasse), Wilhelmstrasse, and Anhalter Strasse, both the SS and the Gestapo had their headquarters between 1933 and 1945. This was the ground on which Himmler, Heydrich, Kaltenbrunner, and their staffs walked. Offices here ordered and controlled the persecution of political opponents, the assimilation of all occupied territories, and the Holocaust itself.

After the badly damaged buildings on this site were torn down in the 1950s, the terrain was cleared of debris, only to eventually become—after the erection of the Berlin Wall—a part of the city's new frontier. When Berlin prepared to celebrate its 750th anniversary in 1987, the site and the rest of the Wilhelmstrasse were redesigned to include information boards that refer to Berlin's manifold historical incarnations. Passersby in the Wilhelmstrasse could now look through transparencies depicting the government buildings that used to be where now generic houses stand. Through the street sign which located the site of the president's palace during the Weimar republic, the present became a layer of the stratification of time and history in space.[19]

The site of the Topography of Terror was made available to the public through an open-air pavilion displaying the documentary exhibition Topography of Terror: Gestapo, SS and Reich Security Main Office on the 'Prinz Albrecht Terrain.' The public interest proved immense, and the exhibition was extended. A commission appointed by the Berlin Senate in 1989 suggested keeping the

Topography of Terror as a site of remembrance and learning, but that triggered an extensive debate over the site's future. Twenty years later, the future of these ruins at the heart of the German capital remains uncertain.

The role of the ruins as initiator of a public debate whose point of departure is the past and whose trajectory is the future becomes evident when one visits the site, analyzes the explanatory texts, and speaks with the staff. The association that manages the ruins has a Web site that provides relevant historical information and displays entries in the guest book by prominent visitors to the site. These entries are reminiscent of the artwork in Haifa's Palestinian quarter: the ruin is recognized as encoding the past, and thus provides a sense of remembrance of the traumatic moment at which a previous form of life came to an end. However, the entries go beyond retrospection to include the decisive element of projection: a consideration of how present-day circumstances might relate to future possibilities. The ruins' potential involves the site's specifics. One view is that the material foundations of the ruins should be solidified as an indication that the past has been integrated into the German consciousness. As the writer Maxim Biller, a German Jew, insists: "In the open-air presentation of the topography of the terror one learns a surprising insight—that during the Nazi period, Germans were tortured by Germans . . . Germans were thus also victims of National Socialism? Why do we know so little about it? And when would this chapter of German history . . . be finally appropriately presented, that is, not only through a few open-air exhibition boards?"[20]

The ruins signify the same future-oriented thought, the possibility of hope, present in the somewhat abstract words of Christina Weiss, culture minister under Chancellor Gerhard Schröder: "Today we draw together again a strength of vision—with firm view of this reality, we hope for a new communicability."[21] For Weiss, the ruins are a powerful source of inspiration, serving to mobilize, energize, and enable a more communicative German discourse. During a visit to the site on November 21, 2002, the current chancellor, Angela Merkel, noted that many people today deplore a sense of widespread amnesia. She then emphasized that the notion of community is lost if modern society remains completely stranded in presentness—that is to say, solely focused on the instantaneous and on consumption. Merkel ties together what is lost (gone because of crimes committed by the site's previous inhabitants), its persistence in the present as remains, and the future-oriented notion that such places also indicate communal values: "Memory creates responsibility. The exhibition . . . clarifies what happened, and makes responsibility tangible. . . . [T]he words of Demosthenes . . . apply: 'for the free, shame over the events is the most enormous source . . . of civil courage. For the liberal community, attention to others and the adherence to human rights remains the highest requirement.' "[22] The ruins serve both as the signifier of an abstract, collective German shame for Nazi crimes that is the encoding of the past, and as a point of departure in a reflection on future human action, the material origin for a foundational agreement reminiscent of the German constitution, which begins with the rather elusive principle "the dignity of humans is unimpeachable."

Encompassing speechlessness in the face of man-made catastrophe and as a point of departure for reflection on the future, the ruins are also at the core of one of the most impressive pieces of postwar German literature on ruins, Alexander Kluge's "Der Luftangriff auf Halberstadt am 8. April 1945" (The Air Raid on Halberstadt on April 8, 1945). Kluge shows both textually and visually how large sections of his hometown, Halberstadt, were turned into a pile of rubble during an Allied attack.

What distinguishes his prose is both its themes and its formal choices: the question of precisely when the historical event we refer to as the Allied air raids began seems to motivate the entire narrative. Kluge answers this question not simply by indicating that the explanation for the air raids takes us back to the Nazis' rise to power but by showing the temporal layering of the moment of attack. He uses a distinctive device to recount the city's demise: a combination of the history of the devastating attack with the plot of a Nazi film being shown in one of Halberstadt's cinemas during the raid. The film, Gustav Ucicky's *Heimkehr* (Homecoming), was commissioned by Goebbels in 1939 and released two years later. It portrayed the Germans living outside the Third Reich as a beleaguered ethnic community "whose survival is threatened by the Poles."[23] Reversing what actually occurred in Poland after war broke out, the film describes the persecution of exiled Germans by Poles, depicting Germans carted away on flatbed trucks, "like animals."[24] At one point, the Nazi film star Paula Wessely says: "Just think, people, what it will be like, just think, when around us there will be lots of Germans—and when you come into a store, people won't talk Yiddish or Polish, but German."[25]

In combining the image of the ruination of his hometown and a movie that reiterates the main elements of the Nazi racial fantasy, Kluge reverses the notion of German victimhood before the outbreak of the Second World War and thus addresses one of the enduring attempts to justify the war. He also makes it difficult to equate the suffering of Halberstadt's citizens with those of the victims of National Socialism.

The weaving together of Halberstadt's demise and the ideologies of racial discourse is made possible by Kluge's chillingly ironic rhetoric throughout the essay: Frau Schrader, the cinema's manager, observes the destruction of her

27

*Heft 2*

**Der Luftangriff auf Halberstadt am 8. April 1945**

I

[Abgebrochene Matinee-Vorstellung im »Capitol«, Sonntag, 8. April, Spielfilm »Heimkehr« mit Paula Wessely und Attila Hörbiger] Das Kino »Capitol« gehört der Familie Lenz. Theater-Leiterin, zugleich Kassiererin, ist die Schwägerin, Frau Schrader. Die Holztäfelung der Logen, des Balkons, das Parkett sind in Elfenbein gehalten, rote Samtsitze. Die Lampenverkleidungen sind aus brauner Schweinsleder-Imitation. Es ist eine Kompanie Soldaten aus der Klus-Kaserne zur Vorstellung heranmarschiert. Sobald der Gong, pünktlich 10 Uhr, ertönt, wird es im

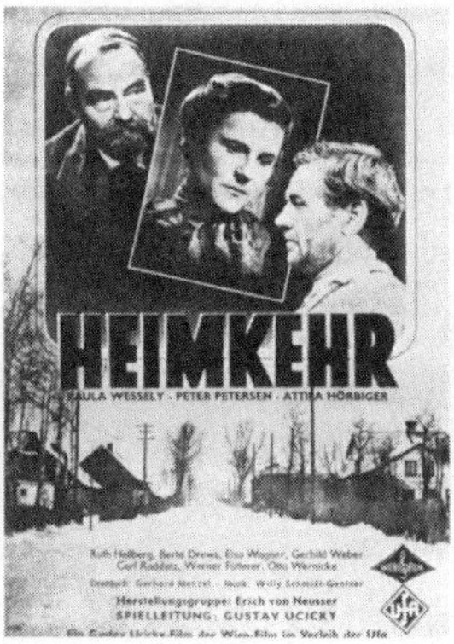


Kino sehr langsam, den dazwischengeschalteten Spezialwiderstand hat Frau Schrader gemeinsam mit dem Vorführer gebaut, dunkel. Dieses Kino hat, was Film betrifft, viel Spannendes gesehen, das durch Gong, Atmosphäre des Hauses, sehr langsames Verlöschen der gelbbraunen Lichter, Einleitungsmusik usf. vorbereitet worden ist.

Jetzt sah Frau Schrader, die in die Ecke geschleudert wird, dort, wo die Balkonreihe rechts an die Decke stößt, ein Stück Rauchhimmel, eine Sprengbombe hat das Haus geöffnet und ist nach unten, zum Keller, durchgeschlagen. Frau Schrader hat nachsehen wollen, ob Saal und Toiletten nach Vollalarm restlos von Be-

4. Facsimile of the first page of Alexander Kluge, "Der Luftangriff auf Halberstadt am 8. April 1945." Reproduced by permission of Suhrkamp Verlag.

town, talking to herself in an idiom that reflects a quasi-scientific distance and an utter numbness to what is going on around her: "the obliteration of the cinema's right elevation cannot be meaningfully related, from a dramaturgical viewpoint, to the film just shown."[26]

Upon arriving in the cinema's cellar, she discovers the bodies of six matinee guests who were trapped there and literally boiled to death by steam coming out of the heating pipes. Kluge shows the absurdity of her reaction: "Frau Schrader wanted to restore order here at least, and placed the loose, cooked body parts, which came apart either through the heating pipes' explosion or through the bombs, in the laundry room's laundry basket."[27] Kluge's irony peaks at the completion of Frau Schrader's meticulous "cleanup." She joins her friends, the Wilde family, in a bunker to eat pepperoni sandwiches and pickled pears while thinking to herself that she was now "simply done."[28]

By opting for irony, Kluge deprives the reader of cathartic empathy or shock and moves significantly beyond the decoding of what was surely a traumatic event in his life. I would like to suggest that the irony turns the reading experience into a process of reflection on the conditions that allowed the world he describes to exist, and that led to the thought processes evident in characters like Frau Schrader. The essay is not merely a reflection of occurrences in time but is an invitation to the reader to reflect on the social, political, and cultural circumstances that led to these occurrences, conditions which—at least as far as Kluge is concerned—persisted through the air raid on Halberstadt. While Kluge might recommend that both the images and their ironic conjuring be described as the workings of instrumental reason, the range of possible readings remains unrestricted. The horror of Halberstadt's fall is one moment in a totality of human cruelty and inhumanity that reaches back in time to the beginnings of human history and stretches through the present and into the future. Kluge warns us that "some stories [in this volume] might appear not to be from our times. They take place, however, in our times."[29] Benjamin emphasizes that "history is the subject of a construction whose site is not homogeneous, empty time, but time filled full by now-time."[30] He follows in this notion the mystical *nunc stans*, which indicates a form of existence not subject to the limitations of time.

Kluge, for his part, refrains from the mystical. He believes that the past never ends; he extends an invitation to regard the now—including the now of the reading experience—as preserving and relating to the presentness of the past. The now metaphorically becomes a geological structure where there and then exist contemporaneously with here and now. That makes Kluge's texts into histories of the present: stories occurring in the now. The radicalism of his figurative choices is that their ironies, allegories, and symbolism unbind events from their restriction to representation, allowing them to emerge during and after the reading process as events of the now, not restricted in time. In the case of the essay on Halberstadt's demise, the end refers to a study that was apparently conducted in the city by the American armed forces in May 1945 and a statement made by one of interviewees: "At a certain point of cruelty it doesn't matter who began it. It should simply stop."[31] Beyond echoing Adorno's and Horkheimer's *Dialectic of Enlightenment* and without falling back on moralism, the essay describes an event that occurs in the present but for the future: "it should simply stop" continues to sound even when the last survivor of the air raid had passed away. The conditions for stopping man-made catastrophes such as that of Halberstadt remain the issue implicitly posed by the essay, and thus an object of possible human action in the future. What is at stake here is not simply a correct or useful working through or representation of a dreadful event, but also a question oriented toward the future: How can we avoid the sort of cruelty displayed in Halberstadt? Even if we don't accept the essay's suggested redescription of the past and present as the manifestation of instrumental reason, its reflexive and self-reflexive mode (irony) allows us to engage in a broad consideration of the cruelty and madness exhibited in Halberstadt—both in itself and in the context of the German past.

I would like to conclude by returning to a material ruin. Majestically dominating the Dresden skyline with its shining colors, the newly reconstructed and reconsecrated seventeenth-century Frauenkirche could easily be misread as a sign of global amnesia. Others might see in the structure a sign of Germany's emergence (especially in the territories of the former East Germany) from its postwar slumber—a potent sign of German suffering during the war and its gradual overcoming of, or rather obliviousness toward, that distress since reunification. Even those who might wish to forget that this structure lay in ruins for some six decades would never be able to ignore all that was lost once they stepped into the building—the new construction is only a shell, waiting to be filled with new life and endowed with new meanings.

Perhaps to indicate that the ruin's recent past cannot be completely obscured, the designers and builders of the reconstructed Frauenkirche chose to use many of the blackened bricks of the destroyed Frauenkirche. The new walls thus appear as a patchwork of the old and new. The interplay between different bricks is the material manifestation of different histories, the layeredness of all temporal moments in this site.

The ruin of the Frauenkirche that symbolized between 1945 and 1989 the recent man-made catastrophe is now gone. The memory of this event is, however, hardly gone. It remains preserved in the new Frauenkirche that emerged at the same site. Visitors will have to take into account the burned bricks and the old cross which is now found inside a new one. In recognizing all the temporal layers of the edifice, visitors will also engage with the story of its birth and with what led to the destruction of the old Frauenkirche.

Here, then, is one way to answer the question of why such ruins of the modern era matter. They matter because they signify the promise of action—our ability to build, destroy, and build again. They matter because they give us the opportunity to endow even those spaces we destroyed with meanings that not only acknowledge their history but gesture beyond retrospection and mourning. Ruins move us because they inspire thought, debate, and engagement with the traumatic moment of their being ruined—and because they allow us to imagine a moment in which the ruin as the material face of human destruction will be replaced by a new human creation. They haunt us not only because of their past but also because they allow us to project onto them our wishes, desires, and hopes for the future: to see them as a space that is still in becoming rather than a site that merely marks what was.

The fact that ruins invite us to reflect on where we come from and where we are headed does not necessarily mean that such reflections will be progressive, as Jameson and others might wish.[32] It does suggest, however, that the visitor to such sites (or the reader of literature dealing with ruins) acknowledges that different times and historical events have flowed through a certain marked space. Such spaces remind us that what is given to us is the result of human action, even if the action seems unintelligible or reprehensible now. Action should be understood here as Arendt conceives it: to act is to begin, to take an initiative, to place oneself as a social actor in the web of human agents that we are born into. The ruin is a material object that displays how people interacted in the past, allows reflection on the preconditions, courses, and disastrous results of human interaction, and offers itself as the substance that invites future action. Ruins indicate the completed actions of the past, and they suggest the possibility of action in the present and the future: turning the rubble of a house in Haifa or of a Berlin synagogue into spaces for human life and comfort. Although, as Arendt never tires of emphasizing, action is neither certain in its outcome nor reversible, it is still the faculty that interferes with the law of mortality, and in our case we can say that it signals the fact of human life after destruction—and the knowledge that what was built anew will also, one day, be gone.[33]

Perhaps more than we care to admit, ruins are thus one of the most distinguished spatial manifestations that humans can use to shape their history; unlike objects subject only to nature, ruins are historical entities. Their signification of the movement through time and space of human action allows us to recognize our historicity—since we are not completely subject to nature, we are agents of our own lives. Through narratives of different sorts, artistic and architectural fantasies, public debates and disputes, ruins lead us to make choices and act in our time, to see even through the abysses of human evil the possibility of hope. To quote Arendt again: "There remains also the truth that every end in history necessarily contains a new beginning; this beginning is the promise, the only 'message' which the end can ever produce. Beginning, before it becomes a historical event, is the supreme capacity of man; politically, it is identical with man's freedom."[34] This is not freedom from the past, but a freedom we should never underestimate: the freedom to shape the present and the future without being stranded in the ruins of the past.

## Notes

This essay draws on a book project I am currently completing on the engagement with the past in contemporary literature and culture. This book examines post–World War II German literature as it invokes Nazism, Hebrew literature as it revisits the 1948 War of Independence and the Nakba, as well as recent Anglo-American literature's dealing with man-made catastrophes of recent modernity.

1. Fritzsche, *Stranded in the Present*, 5.
2. Ibid., 97.
3. Ibid., 96.
4. Ibid.
5. Ibid., 102.
6. Huyssen, *Present Pasts*, 18.
7. Jameson, "The End of Temporality," 718.
8. Ibid., 714, 717.
9. In recent years, this debate expanded beyond the walls of the Israeli academia, where it was a subject of harsh discussions during the late 1980s and the 1990s, and moved on to significant sites of pre-state Palestinian life in the borders of Israel. At this point one should mention the work of the group Zochrot (those who remember), which stages reenactment events such as placing street signs in Arabic where now only Hebrew street signs signify an Israeli space. On the activities of Zochrot and the debates in which they are involved, see http://www.nakbainhebrew.org.
10. Koselleck, *Zeitschichten*, 9.
11. Semel, "Le'vad," in *Yashen Hu Er BeMakom Acher*, 70.
12. Shapira, "Hirbet Hizah."
13. For those familiar with Israeli topography, the inclusion of "ruin" in the village's name comes as no surprise. Many villages and cities in the country are built on ruins and include hirbet in their names.
14. Yizhar, "Hirbet Hizah," 110, my translation. Yizhar completed the novella in November 1948. It was published in 1949 as "Sipur Hirbet Hizah," in a volume that also contained another novella. In this chapter I refer to the version published as "Hirbet Hizah" in *Arbaah Sipurim* (Four Stories).
15. See Shoshan, *Ha'milon he'hadash*, 1222.
16. The idiom "like lambs to the slaughter" was apparently first used in relation to the Holocaust by the Polish-born poet and activist Abba Kovner. See Segev, *The Seventh Million*, 110.
17. Yizhar, "Hirbet Hizah," 109, my translation.
18. Goldberg quoted in Shapira, "Hirbet Hizah," 13.
19. On the Wilhelmstrasse project, see http://www.topographie.de/wilhelmstr.
20. See "Topographie des Terrors" website, http://www.topographie.de.
21. "Topographie des Terrors" website, http://www.topographie.de.
22. "Topographie des Terrors" website, http://www.topographie.de.
23. Von Moltke, *No Place Like Home*, 56.
24. Ibid., 57.
25. Quoted in ibid., 57–58.
26. Kluge, "Der Luftangriff auf Halberstadt am 8. April 1945," 28, my translation. The essay originally appeared in 1977; in this chapter I refer to the reprinted edition in Kluge's *Chronik der Gefühle*.
27. Ibid., 29, my translation.
28. Ibid., my translation.

29. Ibid., 11, my translation.
30. Benjamin, "On the Concept of History," 395.
31. Kluge, "Der Luftangriff auf Halberstadt am 8. April 1945," 82, my translation.
32. Jameson, "The End of Temporality," 710–12.
33. Arendt, *The Human Condition*, 246.
34. Arendt, *The Origins of Totalitarianism*, 478–79.

LUCIA SAKS

# 9

## CITIES, CITIZENSHIP, AND OTHER *JOBURG STORIES*

> Citizens have to define their social and environmental aims and ideals and actively participate in shaping their city so that it relates to their culture, provides for their needs, and is safe and healthy. It is only thus that cities will become culturally relevant, aesthetically satisfying and intellectually rewarding.
>
> AYYUB MALIK, "AFTER MODERNITY"

There is a common accordion effect which cities go through in the twentieth and twenty-first centuries. Power and money tend to be concentrated in expanding cities. If a city fails to expand, capital will not accumulate there; such a city is in decline. The accumulation of capital means that growth is happening, unless the city is becoming totally unbalanced. In a growing city, building is taking place; people are flooding into the city to work; and wealth is accumulating, which leads to consumption, *flânerie*, and the growth of the service sector. This scenario is common, and as it happens, the city moves outward away from the center, with new ground colonized for the purposes of expansion. If life is seen as expansion, cities are essentially chaotic, for there will come a point at which city planning (the effort to manage available resources for circulation, dwelling, commerce, and industry) is overwhelmed by growth. Since the process of growth is ongoing, the accordion is likely to inflate and deflate over and over again, as gentrification takes place, property in the city center comes up for grabs, and property at the periphery of the city becomes costly and overused. Cities are also characterized by the imposition of order through urban planning, which becomes a race to rebuild what is being consistently broken through: city structure, city life, goals for the city that are reasonable given its specific conditions of development and transition. Transition and development create new places and destroy old ones, allow mobility for some people while limiting it for others. As Lefebvre points out, the organization of space is never neutral, but always entangled in complex power arrangements.[1] We have seen this process in cities as different as Caracas, Dakar, Detroit, and New York. Innumerable films like *Escape from New York* (1981), *Blade Runner* (1982), and *Sammy and Rosie Get Laid* (1987) have portrayed the effects of this process on urban life. In African cinema, the move from the country to the city has been a staple theme that addresses a whole set of binaries, such as modernity versus tradition, agrarian society versus industrial society, and belonging versus alienation. A perfect example is Gaston Kaboré's *Zan Boko* (1988), which portrays the expansion of Ouagadougou into the rural areas as a cancer leading to the death of the rural village, along with its concepts of social life and time. Similarly, Donald Swanson's *Jim Comes to Jo'burg* (1949), one of the earliest South African films to have an all-black cast, contrasts the vile, crime-ridden city against the purity of the countryside, as do both versions of *Cry the Beloved Country*, Zoltan Korda's from 1951 and Darrell Roodt's of 1995. Although the two versions were made over forty years apart, in both the city is the object of desire and the instrument of contamination—contradictory functions that embody the characters' ambivalent feelings toward modernity and tradition. Lionel Rogosin's great neorealist exposure of apartheid cruelty, *Come Back, Africa* (1959), uses the buildings and streets of the city as visual evidence of the carceral nature of apartheid for black people. The film opens with modernist images of city skyscrapers, monuments in concrete with blackened, empty windows for eyes as if the architects of the buildings and those of apartheid were one and the same: men dedicated to order, power, and repression of the human soul.

Urban space is differentiated in specific ways, and within it people are exposed, sometimes involuntarily, to different experiences and encounters depending upon the space that they occupy. Aspects of civic society may become more inclusive and embrace the larger picture, reconceptualizing the terms of belonging in broader, less local ways. Thus people are accepted into the society irrespective of their origins, gender, sexual preference, or color. Or membership in the society may become more closed and discriminatory in character as the powers of local governance keep out those who are deemed undesirable. Homeowners' associations, gated communities (in effect, little walled cities), private clubs and schools, laws, and fines can be used as instruments of exclusion and ostracism in the name of order. Both of these trends are present in contemporary Johannesburg, which has become the melting pot for sub-Saharan Africa. A quick tour of the pavement economy in Hillbrow, a hilly section next to the center of Johannesburg that is reportedly the most densely populated square kilometer of urban space in Africa, will bring you into contact with Ethiopians and Congolese street vendors selling watches, bags, food, vegetables, beads, and makeup. A restaurant that used to be Greek has become Angolan. In what was once a hotel in a national chain, a young immigrant runs an Ethiopian restaurant. Apartment buildings that had been filled with young, gay white men determined to turn the area into South Africa's version of Chelsea or Greenwich Village are now occupied by poor black illegal immigrants who see the city as their only chance for survival. They cluster together for safety and comfort, forming enclaves that increase their vulnerability and isolation from the official administrative culture. Many poor residents both celebrate the city's new cosmopolitan status but virulently dislike their foreign counterparts. Rising rates of crime and unemployment, plus the legacy of isolationism due to apartheid, has led to a xenophobic backlash against these *makwerekweres*, the black foreigners who are perceived as stealing jobs from South Africans, using up scarce public resources, and committing crimes. The arrival of democracy in South Africa may have given the country a constitution that sanctifies the notion of human rights, but the expectation that this would be extended to those from outside of the nation's borders has been rudely contradicted, often with dire consequences. Partly in response to the brutal disputes over urban space, post-apartheid filmmakers have begun to make films dealing with xenophobic violence. Thus *The Foreigner* (1997) a short polemical film by Zola Maseko, that centers on the friendship between Koffi, a street vendor in Hillbrow from the Ivory Coast, and Vusi, a young South African street child. Both marginal figures in society, they turn to each other for comfort. The mise-en-scène contrasts the sunny, brightly lit streets of Hillbrow with the threatening attitudes of the South African traders who eventually murder Koffi, leaving Vusi in despair.

### Tales of the City

In this essay I hope to trace the ways in which post-apartheid cinema has expressed Johannesburg's ongoing transformation from apartheid city to African metropolis. My focus is on *Joburg Stories,* a documentary made in 1997 by Oliver Schmitz and Brian Tilley that traces the lives of several people living in downtown Johannesburg and that—in its poetic, moody style—is more like Robert Altman's *Short Cuts* (1993) than the usual documentary. A mining camp in the nineteenth century, Johannesburg grew rapidly and by the mid-1930s was one of the largest cities in Africa. It is now the premier city and financial capital of South Africa, containing 40 percent of the country's population. There is a saying in South Africa that as Johannesburg goes, so goes the country. The product of capitalism, the city has always been entangled with modernity in its economic and social spheres. This is manifested in its spatial configurations, which are based on rationality, fixity, and a homogeneous view of race. The center of Johannesburg is laid out on a grid system like New York, a mimesis that reinforces its connectedness and similarity to the capitals of Europe and America. During apartheid the so-called natives were contained in townships on the periphery of the city, partitioned off from the white center and allowed into the city only to work. The city saw itself as European or Western, for otherwise how could it be a modern metropolis at the bottom of Africa? This is, of course, an idealized and incomplete picture.

There were always leakages in Johannesburg's blueprint, despite the city's attempts at rigidity and containment. Mbembe calls these "disjunctive inclusions" that breached the segregation of apartheid.[2] People of different races met and interacted with each other even at the height of apartheid, but in ways that were marked by power differentials. I am thinking here of the servants of white families that lived in the segregated suburbs, and of the flat boys that lived on the top floors of the apartment houses in the city center. There were also migrant laborers who came to work in the gold mines. They lived in compounds at the mines, and their access to Johannesburg was limited, but they were on the edge of the city and interacted with whites in numerous ways. By the late 1980s, when apartheid lay in ruins and squatters' settlements were spreading from the townships to the city, the patterns of interaction and social relations broke out of the bounds that had been defended for so long. Over the last decade Johannesburg has been undergoing a massive spatial reconstruction as urban planners struggle to realize the dream of a unified city, and beyond that of a unified nation. Johannesburg is plagued by crime, AIDS, inequality, fragmentation, and disjunction, but it is also showing signs of cosmopolitanism, international capital, a resurgence of vibrant city politics, and new imaginaries in the making. As such it is the example par excellence of South Africa's transitional period.

The first image in *Joburg Stories* is a dramatic image of change. A woman framed in medium close-up stands on a tiny balcony of a high-rise building, singing an operatic aria. In the background another high-rise suddenly implodes in a cloud of rubble and dust. The woman cringes in shock. The singing woman and the imploding building are deliberately disparate; their juxtaposition suggests that what follows will be equally characterized by disunity, uneven histories, and fragmentation. No complete story of Johannesburg is promised, and none emerges. Nine years earlier, Schmitz made *Mapantsula* (street slang for "gangster"), a feature film whose main character is a gangster and petty thief called Panic. His *locus operandi* is Johannesburg's city center, which in 1988, during a nationwide state of emergency, is itself a place of panic filled with liminal people remaking the urban geography as they move between township and inner city to avoid detection by the authorities, and live hand-to-mouth in a spiral of change and uncertainty. There is a rent boycott in Soweto, workers' strikes, fights between township residents and security forces, attacks on black police, a school boycott by students, severe restrictions against any form of demonstration, a gag on the media, and jails filled with political agitators being detained without trial. Respectable business enterprises have begun to abandon the city in favor of its northern suburbs, with their fortified enclaves of office parks ringed with leafy trees and protected by electrified walls and armed security guards. At the same time, a wave of black people is moving into the city center. Johannesburg is already spreading outward like a cooking pancake, decentralizing in the manner of Detroit, Los Angeles, Osaka, and Seoul. This race into the city from township ghettos like Soweto is also a race for representation. As new kinds of people move to the center of the city, they almost immediately begin to stake their claim to it, configure it in their images, detach it from the comfort of its past, and turn it into something as yet unknown and unpredictable.[3] Panic, the main character in *Mapantsula*, stakes his claim to the city through violent acts. Like the city he is multilayered and partly unknown, even to himself. Thus, when he is arrested for stealing and thrown into a jail cell filled with black union activists, he is surprised to find himself refusing to "help the police by acting as a stool pigeon" (the price of his release), despite the contempt in which he holds all activists. Earlier Panic has avoided taking any political stance, despite the turmoil of the times. His reaction to the brutality of the system, his way of beating it, has not been through political struggle but through crime, which generates a vicious brutality within him. His radicalization is a gradual process, one that takes place almost by accident as a result of his exposure to his cellmates and to the brutal way the police treat them. Finally realizing that he cannot ignore the struggle, he becomes an unlikely fighter for black freedom.

In *Joburg Stories*, Schmitz returns to the downtown spaces where Panic created panic, to film—with Brian Tilley—the ongoing process of the city's transition. According to the two directors, they were motivated by the idea that the nature of the city lay in its attitude as well as its topography. There is something about Johannesburg, says Schmitz, "that brings everyone down to size." They chose to film people who they felt were naturally dramatic, "people who have a dream, possibly an inflated one, or an illusion, or lead a double life in the city."[4] Vinnie drives a cab and tells stories of being held up by gun-toting passengers. "It's bad. We must shoot the bastards. It's the only way," he says. His girlfriend, Julie, is a nurse who has become a prostitute, although Vinnie does not know what she does for a living. She walks her beat in tight white pants, high-heeled boots, and a halter top, pondering the moral dilemma of being with a white client who is rich but whom she does not love, as opposed to being with her black boyfriend, Vinnie, whom she loves but who does not have money. She is terrified of being poor. "In Joburg," she says, "you have to be first or second class. Otherwise you are dead." Marie, a woman in her seventies, describes herself as a "real city person." She is nostalgic for old Johannesburg, the city of her youth, a city of emporiums with teashops and hotels where she met and danced with young men. She lives in the suburbs now because the city is "too dirty, too noisy, and too frightening," but she still takes cabs into the center dressed in her idea of suitable city attire—a hat, gloves, red lipstick. For Junior, lead singer of a popular rock band in the city, singing has been his ticket out of a life of petty crime. It has allowed him to reinvent himself as a young man about town, driving around in an imported red sports car. He finds the city to be a liberating space, filled with possibilities for reinvention: "Joburg people, they do not give a damn, they don't give a shit who you are, you know. Joburg, you have to be yourself." Thembi, a teenager and part-time singer with Boom Shaka, goes to school in the city and lives in a high-rise in Hillbrow with her mother. She feels ill at ease in the city because of her fame. "Too many people there know who I am," she says. In contrast, Edwin, a middle-aged drag queen, casts the city as his communal family, "an old mistress" giving him "the best years of my life."

In long, fluid shots the camera follows the characters around the city, intercutting their activities with textual shots in blue and red hues of buildings and streets—shots with strong graphic elements pulled out of the cityscape that make it look like an abstract expressionist painting. In the montage the people are as constitutive of the city as are its structures, pavements, cars, windows (often broken), lights, traffic, dirt, skyline at dusk, noise, crime, and empty office space. "This building used to be full four years ago," says the manager of a high-rise with twenty-one stories. He shrugs his shoulders and adds: "now it's empty. That's more or less the same story throughout Joburg." The accordion effect described earlier has been racially marked in Johannesburg with white flight to the suburbs, which are expanding, and an in-filling of the center by blacks arriving from the township ghettos, a migration that is both an escape for them from the township and an extension of the township into the city.

## How the City Got Its Shape

In 1910, just eight years after the Boer War, the British created the Union of South Africa by joining the two Afrikaans republics of the Transvaal and the Orange Free State (the losers of the war) with the two British colonies of the Cape and Natal (the winners). The union greatly increased the state's power to control the urban migration of blacks. The Urban Areas Act of 1923 formalized segregation policies and laid out a plan for the evacuation of blacks from municipal areas to Soweto, an acronym for South West Township. In 1930 the Native Urban Areas Act made it illegal for blacks to rent or purchase property in white areas. By 1933 Johannesburg was proclaimed white. Of the half-million people in the city, over sixty thousand (all black) had been relocated. By the time the apartheid government came to power in 1948 on a platform of separate development of the races, the landscape of segregation was in place. However, apartheid required even more discriminatory laws to achieve its aims, both in the city and in the countryside. It followed a national blueprint that sought to confine African laborers necessary to the economy in satellite townships built outside apartheid cities. Black laborers not needed by the economy were confined to the homelands, conceived of as independent states or protonations with their own legislatures and rules of citizenship. Denied citizenship and political rights in white South Africa, black Africans were expected to realize their political rights within these independent states. Black Africans in the cities were expected to be, as David Smith puts it, "temporary sojourners," tolerated only as long as they were needed by the white economy.[5] Temporary sojourners did not need to have their families with them; hence single-sex hostels were created for black men. Indians and coloureds were also moved to race-specific townships. A graphic of the apartheid Johannesburg would contain the following elements: A focal central business district bisected by an east-west railroad line and encircled by white suburbs to the north and coloured, black, and Indian suburbs in the industrial south. Since only the railroad crossed the city, it became an iconic symbol in many South African films of journeying into or out of the city and of displacement, as people were at home at one end of the journey and foreign or threatening at the other.[6] Rural Africans were forbidden to visit urban areas for more than seventy-two hours without a special permit, and the police were authorized to arrest anybody who did not possess the necessary documentation. In 1975 and 1976, the heyday of apartheid, more than 381,858 Africans were arrested under these laws.[7]

"Black spots," or land owned or occupied by black Africans in white regions, were eliminated and the occupants resettled in either the homelands or the townships. Sophiatown, a multiracial suburb southwest of Johannesburg where black South Africans had owned their own homes since the turn of the century, was bulldozed to the ground and its residents relocated. This tragedy was inadvertently chronicled by Rogosin in *Come Back, Africa*, which he happened to be filming at the time. Often referred to as a docudrama, Rogosin's film shows the dislocation, defiance, and pain experienced by the community. Sophiatown in Johannesburg, Cato Manor in Durban, and District Six in Cape Town were chosen for destruction precisely because they were spatially contiguous with their cities, part of their makeup and thus anathema to apartheid ideology. The occupants of Sophiatown were moved to Meadowlands, which became part of Soweto, a city of more than a million people forty kilometers southwest of the center of Johannesburg.

By the mid-eighties, the system of control was in a state of collapse due to the profound contradictions between the needs of industrialization and those of controlled urbanization. A skilled and sophisticated workforce could not be created from an impermanent and fragmented proletariat. Nor could the needs of the economy for a growing pool of consumers be met. According to Smith, "No matter how carefully the state contrived to control it, [urbanization under apartheid] undermined apartheid itself, bringing South African society and its cities to the brink of significant if still uncertain change."[8] The spontaneous flow of blacks to the cities was already well underway by the time the government finally conceded failure and, in 1986, introduced a new White Paper on Urbanization. Under the slogan of orderly urbanization, which was little more than an attempt to paper over an already uncontrollable situation, the government relaxed constraints on state planning. In effect, the government gave in to pressures from the commercial sector, on the one hand, and pressures of black urbanization, on the other hand. The problem of industrialization was suddenly turned into the solution. The government's new policy was not unique to South Africa: it reflected the Western democracies' turn away from state intervention in welfare matters and toward the privatization of social services, with a new conception of the citizen as a consumer of those services.[9] Under Reagan and Thatcher, for example, homelessness and joblessness were seen as lifestyle choices.

The change from temporary worker to consumer in the conceptualization of the urban African is an important one in the history of constructing black identities in general, but it had specific consequences for the spatial configurations of South Africa's cities. In terms of housing, the government abandoned its role as a provider of planned urban development and put forward the marketplace in its stead. The result was an immense increase in settlements of shacks ringing the major metropolitan areas and an increase in the black population of the inner cities as strict enforcement of the group areas law broke down.

### The Post-apartheid City

Urban planners in post-apartheid South Africa have had to deal with the legacy of apartheid cast in concrete, which—unlike other apartheid aberrations—cannot be legislated away. The planners have also had to deal with a set of new, postmodern conditions that are global in nature, and this has complicated their political policies. As Alan Mabin points out, the fact that emancipatory movements like the African National Congress were formulated in the sixties and seventies under very different local and international circumstances leaves the movements ill prepared to cope with changes that have taken place in industry and urbanization.[10] Old policies promoting unification and integration do not fit well with global shifts in spatiality toward fragmentation and dispersion. New approaches are needed to cope with the ways in which the legacy of apartheid interacts with contemporary patterns of domination and reincorporation in the post-apartheid, postmodern era. Plans for urban renewal change as each vision of the city is superseded by a new one. According to its different constituencies, since the end of apartheid Johannesburg has been imagined as a mecca for international investment and tourism; an African version of Hong Kong, both neoliberal and friendly to business; a declining city with a population that is increasingly black and poor; and a thriving city that would finally, after forty years of exclusion, belong to blacks. Not one of these visions has been wholly realized. White emigration to the suburbs has drained the city of its tax base and altered the racial mix; black immigration from other countries in Africa has turned the city into a cosmopolitan, but not South African, black city.[11] Far from being unified, the city's spaces have become difficult for people to inhabit with a sense of belonging. For the majority of immigrants, Johannesburg's inner city is "neither the preferred nor the final destination."[12]

In *Joburg Stories*, the dialectic of displacement and belonging is played out on the city streets. Despite a pervasive sense of defamiliarization that emerges through the lighting, the night shots, and the beat of rap music with lyrics like "Johannesburg, my city. Dreams come here to die, dreams come here to die," the city is also a locus for the possibilities of new identities, for new images of the self and of how the self is perceived through the perceptions of others. Deep-focus shots offer reflective surfaces for these performative acts, providing a backdrop for the way we represent ourselves as actors on the city's stage. It is the stage for the drama of the self, itself on show, which sets up a consonance between the city and its inhabitants. An extended montage of the characters intercut with reflective images of the city—windscreens of cars, glass cladding on modernist buildings, puddles of water in the streets—reveals people preparing themselves for a night on the town. It is as if the city provides a mirror, a flat surface onto which can be projected an image of the self composed from a set of individual experiences and lived history, but also created through clothing and makeup, so that the body participates as a prop in its own representation.

In another long sequence of shots, the film reveals how deeply our sense of self is formed and manipulated by predigested representations gleaned from advertising, shop windows, looking at others in the crowd—in short, from a cultural cache that is overwhelmingly generated in urban spaces. Junior shows us how he dresses for the city in huge Nikes and baggy pants. Thembi goes through her wardrobe of platform shoes, high boots, and shiny, tight vinyl outfits in a room cluttered with girlish paraphernalia, explaining to the camera how she feels in each outfit. The longest sequence is devoted to Edwin as he gets ready for a drag show. We see him in a mirror, transforming himself with wig, makeup, feather boa, and six-inch heels from a nondescript male of average height into a tall, sexy Marlene Dietrich look-alike. In a voice that parodies drag queens, he talks of himself as a structure, "still in the construction phase." Soon, he promises, "you'll see the most glamorous woman in Johannesburg."

Bauman sketches a dystopic vision of the postmodern city's moral collapse into a space filled with marginal types: the flâneur, vagabond, game player, and tourist. These types, he maintains, hold out little hope for a moral transformation in civic life.[13] The people in *Joburg Stories* are indeed marginal if we are to assume that the center is occupied by those who espouse bourgeois values and live conventional lives. But do such lives form the material for moral transformation in modern life? What Schmitz and Tilley are intent on revealing is precisely the result of a profound moral transformation in South African urban life, the opening up of the city after apartheid to people irrespective of their color, ethnicity, class, gender, or their sexual preference (under apartheid there were repressive laws against homosexuality). Yet despite the city's liberation from the strictures of apartheid, Schmitz's and Tilley's approach is neither celebratory nor condemnatory. Their film is driven by unending change and demonstrates that every transformation has both good and bad in it, exacting a price.[14] While each character has his or her own journey to make, the central character in the film is the city itself, and the central drama is the city's continuing process of self-discovery and reconfiguration.

Junior is an example of a vagabond who has made good in the transformed city. He used to be homeless, living in Joubert Park and supporting himself by breaking into cars and stealing radios. It is hard to imagine him escaping from poverty in the city under apartheid: no doubt he would have remained homeless, gone to jail, or been deported to some homeland to which he did not actually belong. The camera follows him back to his former home, the park, and into a public bathroom filled with homeless men cooking on paraffin stoves, playing chess, gambling, and sleeping on pieces of cardboard. Junior treats them with respect and affection, asking them if he can come inside. "Coming back here, I feel cool," he says, talking directly to the camera. "It's part of me. It's my home. I always tell the guys who are staying here, you can do good. Even my children, I will bring them here so that they can see it's where Daddy came from." With this statement, it is clear that Junior's sense of himself as a member of society is predicated on this place in the city. He has not come to Johannesburg from somewhere else; it is his place of origin in a way that is far more tangible and present to him than is any sense of membership in that more abstract, intangible entity called the nation—a fact that raises the issue, which I will discuss below, of the relationship between cities and the concept of citizenship.

Holstein and Appadurai point out that citizenship as a concept has been historically linked with nationality and the nation-state rather than with "the neighborhood or the city or the region."[15] Yet they note that "although one of the essential projects of nation-building has been to dismantle the historic primacy of urban citizenship and to replace it with the national, cities remain the strategic arena for the development of citizenship."[16] Within these tumultuous arenas, the substance of citizenship as it has been conceived at the national level can undergo such immense changes as to make it unrecognizable in its formal incarnation. These new forms of membership destabilize the social imaginary of the nation in innumerable ways. To show the full force of these changes, it is necessary to discuss here the difference between what Holstein and Appadurai call the formal aspects of citizenship and the substantive ones. Formal citizenship refers to membership in the nation-state, while substantive membership refers to "the array of civil, political, socioeconomic, and cultural rights people possess and exercise, the ability to enjoy the formal rights of citizenship by participating in the organizations and institutions that form the material of national life."[17] Substantive citizenship can take place whether one has formal citizenship or not. We need think only of how easy it is for the rich to establish themselves in a place, or in many places in the world, irrespective of their formal citizenship, to understand the full force of the division between the two types of citizenship. Concomitantly, formal membership does not guarantee one the ability to exercise substantive membership. That is dependent on an array of other factors, such as money, access to the powers of local government, employment, contacts, and support systems, factors clearly absent in the film's characters—the poor and dispossessed, the street kids, the hawkers, the insane, and the old. In a series of static close-ups, which punctuate the camera's movement through the city and create frozen portraits of despair, the film shows these people as witnesses to, but not participants in, the urban drama unfolding before them. It is clear that formal citizenship in the new South Africa has done little to change their lives. As the film shows, they are still harassed by the police and, if they are hawking, fined for breaking the law or forced to give up informal trading and pay rent for space at legally sanctioned street markets.[18]

Holstein and Appadurai's distinction between the two kinds of citizenship points to the emptiness of the concept of the citizen. It is a cold set of institutional arrangements waiting to be filled with passion and loyalties that will make it a factor for self-identification as opposed to identification with the nation.

Citizenship tells me, as McDonald puts it, "what I am, not who I am."[19] That question is expressed in the exercise of substantive citizenship, and the city is the locus for its expression. What are the terms of self-expression in the film? How do the people featured in it stake their claims to freedom and independence in living their rights of citizenship? There are various answers. In one extended sequence, the camera follows the activities of a black man who, in *bricoleur* style, has fashioned a job for himself setting up stalls for the street vendors each morning and dismantling them each night. Since he cannot read or write, he must remember the correct spot for each stall. "Sometimes I dream all the trolleys are being stolen," he says. "Maybe God gave me this job." Over a cup of tea, Marie and her friend John, a gay man wearing a toupee, reminisce about the old days, about how they could walk through clean streets with impunity, window shop, and visit the grand emporiums. The camera closes in on Marie's vintage hat, bright red lipstick, and face, full of wrinkles and age spots. The close-up exploits the human face for all its expressive values, and like a palimpsest gives us glimpses of the young Marie coming through the old. Indeed change becomes the organizing principle of the film in lieu of narrative unity. The montage juxtaposes the present and the past through a series of traveling street shots. The images suggest that the past can best be seen in the architecture of the city, which remains as a testament to the past. We see the remains of what was in Johannesburg's high-rise glass buildings, reflecting the intensity of the sky, and in the carved murals and plinths around the doors and windows of buildings from the art deco period. The past is present in these buildings and, to a lesser extent, in people's conversations, which veer between their present reality and their past memories.

In one scene, the camera tracks along an endless wall of red mailboxes while a postal clerk recalls the days when the Johannesburg post office had over 11,000 boxes and there was a waiting list for more. Now there are "only 2,000 in use," he says. An older white man in a pub dressed in a suit and tie drunkenly recounts the "demise" of the public park near his apartment, a park once specifically set aside for blind white people. Now it is "filled with rubbish," he snarls, "black trash." Edwin, on the other hand, is sanguine about the changes he sees in Hillbrow, accepting them as an intrinsic part of life in the city. "It used to teem with artists, poets, writers like the Village in New York," he tells us, smiling wryly. "Now it teems with new people."

It is in these new people that the present is vested, and we see them at the level of the street. No longer can we see the city as a panorama, a view that we were offered earlier in the film when John (who is white) stepped out on the balcony of his condo in the middle of the city to look around. From his vantage point the city appeared as a planned view, but at street level we are in a more chaotic position. We can see only small bits of the city, which appears unreadable. The space becomes more confused; it is now the space of the pedestrian, produced, as Certeau would put it, through pedestrian enunciations by those who walk the streets.[20] We are shown street vendors and their hastily erected stalls, people putting up and taking down shutters, prostitutes touting for business, street children sniffing glue out of plastic bottles with the tops cut off, uncollected mounds of garbage in the gutters, pools of water, street lights, cars, and the contents of shops for traditional medicine.

Certeau's idea of walking the streets and negotiating one's own urban space (in a sense, being your own cartographer) seems too cheerful to fit the configuration of space in *Joburg Stories*. At the center of this city is violence, a violence accreted from the past but also gestated in the new pan-African metropolis. There is not a single character whose patterns of life do not unfold in a violent setting. Violence penetrates all their stories—from friendship and camaraderie, to styles of independence and autonomy, to aggression. We are shown scenes of violence: a police raid on drug dealers, a section of the city cordoned off with the yellow tape that marks a crime scene, a street child menacing the camera with a knife, and—in what is perhaps the most surreal image of the film—a night shot of an ambulance that has broken down in the center of Hillbrow, being pushed down the road by heavily armed policemen. In another sequence, an off-duty policeman conducts a downtown aerobics class in which at least one of the other characters is present. The camera emphasizes the frantic beat of the exercise, a beat both exciting and terrifying. We see the policeman enter the gym, remove his clothing, put on his gym shorts and top, and place his gun in his gym bag. Next to him is a naked man who is changing his clothes. The policeman is white, the naked man is black, and one cannot help notice the contrast of these two bodies and the strangeness of their being together in this space, which suddenly becomes metonymic of the changing space of the city. Two former adversaries face each other in the banal space of the gym, and there is a moment of possible tension. But it evaporates as the black man takes a shower and the white policeman goes to lead the class, which is mainly composed of black people, all jumping up and down in response to his whistle, which he uses to indicate changes in the routine. There is violence to both the montage and the sound in this sequence, which is echoed in a scene in a jazz club where Boom Shaka performs. This is the beat of a city wrapped in energy and destructiveness, a city whose urban psyche is dominated by violence.

Thembi, the young singer, sits in a clean new vehicle as she waits for her mother to emerge from the aerobics class; she is obviously nervous of hijackers while she is parked and therefore exposed. Women are the chief victims of sexual violence. Junior describes his past of petty thievery and thuggery as something he was racing to get out of "because I saw my friends die." They all speak of muggings, fights, bravery and stupidity in the face of fists and weapons. *Joburg Stories* does not offer an overt explanation for the violence. The reasons lie in the mise-en-scène of the film, the shots of filth on the street, the glue-drugged faces of the homeless children, the marginalization of the poor, the guns, and the poverty. To deny the crime would be to deny the lasting impact of apartheid. I have already noted this legacy in the spatial arrangements of Johannesburg, but it also can be seen institutionally. Post-apartheid South Africa inherited key institutions of the state, and the slow pace of institutional change has led to frustration especially among the poor. In the past, violence that emanated from marginalization due to apartheid was framed as political. Now it is seen as antisocial.

It is a lacuna in otherwise brilliant work by Holstein and Appadurai that while they highlight the role of cities in defining and pushing issues of substantive rights, they put little emphasis on the related, but not identical, issue of the way in which cities are the birthplace of new moral attitudes, new ways of thinking about self, freedom, independence, choice, other people, and the city itself: attitudes which will serve as the new moral capital (or lack thereof) of the new nation, but which are not reducible to issues of rights. Clearly safety is a right, and the film's characters tell stories that touch on questions of safety. Yet the way they are living is not reducible to this right. More important is the kind and the quality of people they are and will become—as Junior puts it, "what they will tell and show their own young." Thus a city becomes the birthplace for the moral capital of the nation. I take this exploration of moral attitude to be far more central and compelling in *Joburg Stories* than any direct claim about rights, substantive or otherwise, that the film makes. Indeed the film completely eschews any such claims, showing us instead a city racing to morally reconstruct itself through new people and new stories. It is the quality and character of the reconstruction that counts.

## Notes

1. Lefebvre, *The Production of Space*, passim.
2. Mbembe, "Aesthetics of Superfluity," 387.
3. The word "ghetto" is a disputed one in South Africa. It has been most frequently used in scientific studies of African American ghettos in the United States. It implies an urban space that is configured in terms of race. Since the apartheid townships were outside of the city and were formally instituted by apartheid, it is unclear how appropriate the term is in the South African context. That is why many scholars use it in conjunction with the word "township." See Jurgens, Gnad, and Bahr, "New Forms of Class and Racial Segregation," 56–70.
4. Andrew Worsdale, "Tales of the City," *Mail and Guardian*, December 11, 1997, 14.

5. David Smith, Introduction, 1.
6. I am thinking of films such as *Fools* (Suleiman Ramadan, 1997), *Cry the Beloved Country* (Darrell Roodt, 2001), *Jump the Gun* (Les Blair, 2002), *Tsotsi* (Gavin Hood, 2005), which use an extended montage of a train entering the city. The train journey fulfills many functions. It indicates that there are two distinctly separate spaces such as the township and the city center, or the country and the city. It works as a symbol of displacement since in each case the characters are at home in one place and "foreign" (*Cry the Beloved Country*) or threatening (*Tsotsi*) in another.
7. Thompson, *A History of South Africa*, 193.
8. Smith, Introduction, 1.
9. Privatization is not without its critics. Anti-privatization protesters recently threw water bombs at government officials in a clash over plans to sell off municipal water delivery services. See Celean Jacobson, "It's the end of the city as we know it," *Sunday Times*, July 23, 2000, 13.
10. Mabin, "On the Problems of Overcoming Segregation."
11. Tomlinson et al., Introduction.
12. Gotz and Simone, "On Belonging and Becoming in African Cities," 130.
13. Bauman, "From Pilgrim to Tourist," 32.
14. By resisting the categorical form of documentation and forgoing the usual didacticism of the earlier South African city films mentioned (*Cry the Beloved Country, Jim Goes to Joburg, Come Back Africa)*, Schmitz's film has been formative in later cinematic depictions of urban life, such as Dumisani Phakathi's *Wa n Wina* (2001), which chronicles Phakathi's return to his old neighborhood in Soweto, and Ntshaven Wa Luruli's *The Wooden Camera* (2003), which charts the story of two fourteen-year-old township kids, Sipho and Madiba, who find a video camera and a gun on the corpse of a dead man. Sipho uses the gun to enforce his leadership in a street gang, while Madiba takes the camera into Cape Town, the big city, to capture it on film. The former comes to a tragic end, but the latter, Madiba, uses the camera to forge a friendship across class and race lines and to overcome his marginality. Khalo Matabane's first feature, *Conversations on a Sunday Afternoon* (2005), uses Joubert Park, the main park in Johannesburg, to emphasize the characters' feelings of displacement, alienation, and homelessness. The main character, a young black writer, searches for a woman he met wearing a blue scarf; this narrative mechanism allows the camera to fluidly follow and record the stories of people in the park and the surrounding streets. The result is a blend of fiction and documentary, depicting an extraordinarily multilayered urban space filled with cosmopolitans, war veterans, transnationals—in short, an African metropolis.
15. Holstein and Appadurai, "Cities and Citizenship," 187.
16. Ibid., 188.
17. Ibid., 190.
18. Hawkers or street traders are part of South Africa's informal trade sector, which employed some 1.8 million people in 1997. Robert Simmonds, "Is Joburg Trading Sense for Apartheid-Era Order?" *Sunday Independent*, April 30, 2000.
19. McDonald, "The Citizen and the Man About Town," 172.
20. de Certeau, "Walking in the City."

# PART III

# EMPIRES, RUINS, AND THEIR STORIES

JULIA HELL

# 10

# IMPERIAL RUIN GAZERS, OR WHY DID SCIPIO WEEP?

> But that's why you built the towers, isn't it? Weren't the towers built as fantasies of wealth and power that would one day become fantasies of destruction? You build a thing like that so you can see it come down. The provocation is obvious. What other reason would there be to go so high and then to double it, do it twice? You are saying, Here it is, bring it down.[1]

In Don DeLillo's novel *Falling Man*, these lines are spoken by Martin, a former sympathizer of the Red Army Faction who is now a successful art dealer. The passage represents the moment when an unbridgeable gap opens in the relationship between Nina, a liberal American art historian, and her European lover. Provoked by Nina's declaration that she does not want to look at "our ruins,"[2] this statement condenses a host of familiar themes: the Tower of Babel motif, the theme of imperial decline, and incendiary comments by Baudrillard and other European intellectuals. Most provocatively, it contains an allusion to the fantasies of imperial ruin of Hitler and his architect, Albert Speer, who set out to build an empire on the model of Rome with a vision of its future ruins in mind.

## A "Dread Foreboding": Scipio the Younger and the Destruction of Carthage

Since the attack on the World Trade Center and the invasion of Iraq, the debate about the nature of an American empire has intensified and comparisons to the British and Roman empires have become ever more frequent. As a consequence, the theme of imperial rise and decline and its apocalyptic ruin imagery seems to have taken hold of the American imagination. Comparisons to imperial Rome tend to conjure up the sight of ruins—the ruins of Rome's enemies and the ruins of Rome. This is what Michael Mann, the eminent British theorist of power and expert on Rome, calls the "potentially disquieting thought" that accompanies all imperial mimesis.[3] This uncanny knowledge, or imperial "melancholy,"[4] has a deep history that we can trace back as far as 146 BC—that is, to the moment when Rome destroyed Phoenician Carthage, its rival city located on the Mediterranean's northern shores. With this victory Rome became heir to the Carthaginians' maritime empire in the Mediterranean, and in the process created its first colony, Africa Proconsularis. As Polybius, the historian who accompanied Scipio Africanus the Younger on his African campaign, reported, the Roman general felt deeply ambivalent about his enemies' surrender. This was a "glorious moment," Scipio told his embedded historian, but one overshadowed by "a dread foreboding that some day the same doom will be pronounced upon my own country." The Roman general's "dread foreboding" signifies more than a mere awareness of the "mutability of Fortune";[5] according to Appian, another Roman historian, Scipio was said to have wept for his enemies as he observed Carthage's destruction. What provoked Scipio's tears? He realized, Appian writes, "that all cities, nations, and authorities must, like men, meet their doom." Like the great Assyrian, Median, and Persian empires, the "prosperous city" of Illium vanished. Appian later reported that when Polybius asked Scipio what he meant: "he named his own country, for which he feared when he reflected on the fate of all things human."[6] As early as 146 BC, thus, we find a transition from what we will later call the vanitas or memento mori trope to a discourse concerned with the inevitable rise and fall of empires. This discourse is already part of all imperial imaginaries and their specific articulations of space and time.

Imperial imaginaries create particular topographies, temporalities, scopic regimes, and modes of representation. Their scopic regimes include what I will call scenarios of imperial ruin gazing—that is, scenes in which the imperial subject contemplates the metropole of a mighty empire in ruins while thinking about the future of his own empire. It should be noted first that what these scenarios crystallize are power relations—between one empire and another, between Romans and barbarians, between conqueror and conquered. Second, these scopic scenarios—for that is what they are: constellations that organize or structure acts of looking, their subjects, and their objects in an imaginary space—articulate these power relations visually. As we will see, they do so in two ways: on the one hand, the object of the gate is the remnants of empires past; on the other hand, the subject viewing these remnants is itself the object of our gaze. Third, these scenarios create their own mode of representation that I will discuss as empiricist realism and derive from the centrality of ruins as objects both visible and invisible.

Scenarios of ruin gazers are thus central to imperial imaginaries and their particular articulations of time and space. In this chapter I will explore the reinvention of the ruin gazer during the Third Reich. This exploration will include an analysis of Hitler's and Speer's so-called theory of ruin value as well as Hitler's rudimentary history of art. I will focus on the ways in which this theory—and the Nazis' architectural practice—reshapes the scenarios of ruin gazing. My thesis is that the Nazis, their theorists, and their artists were preoccupied with strategies to counter the specter of imperial decline raised once again by Spengler's enormously influential *Der Untergang des Abendlandes* (Decline of the West) at the beginning of this century of extremes. Nazi theorists and architects think up strategies of fortification—of architecture and of the imperial subject's gaze itself—however, they also anticipate ruination. Rebuilding Germany as a Reich with the ruins of the future in mind is not only an anticipatory defense against eventual doom, but one of the most glaring symptoms of this new Reich's criminal foundations, its murderous totalitarian logic that sets it apart from all other imperial projects and their imaginaries.

I am thus tracing a particular feature of a particular form of imperial mimesis by foregrounding the ways in which the theorists of the Third Reich attempted to exorcise the specter of decline and fall that clings to their ruinous reinventions. In the next section, I will briefly sketch a genealogy of imperial ruin gazing from the West's most famous epic of empire, Virgil's *The Aeneid* (written around 27 AD during the reign of Augustus), to an exhibit at the Whitney Museum of American Art in 2005–6, entitled The Course of Empire, which juxtaposed a series of canvases depicting industrial dilapidation by Ed Ruscha with reproductions of nineteenth-century landscapes by the Anglo-American Romantic painter Thomas Cole, culminating in the elegiac representation of Carthage in ruins. Ruscha's part of the exhibit consists of five earlier paintings from his 1992 Blue Collar series and five responses to those painted for the 2005 Venice Biennale. The second series shows the same industrial buildings as abandoned, defaced, or even decayed, a haunting commentary on the waning of American Fordism, a mode of production and a way of life associated with the United States in one of its most prosperous periods. Combined with Thomas Cole's smaller paintings, Ruscha's canvases raise the specter of inevitable imperial decline.

### Carthage—Rome—London—New York: The Genealogy of a Scopic Scenario

Appian's remarkable scene is not a scenario of ruin gazing per se but belongs to the archaic genre of the lament for the fallen city.[7] We find such scenes in Virgil's *The Aeneid*, which narrates the story of Aeneas and his men, who left "Asian" Troy to refound the city as Rome, to which Jupiter grants "empire without end."[8] When Aeneas and his men land on Carthaginian shores on their journey to Italy, Aeneas tells his audience about the Trojan empire's demise. At the most dramatic moment of his tale, which recounts the battle that raged in the streets of Troy, Aeneas interrupts his eyewitness account to conjure up the moment when the "ancient city is falling."[9] Virgil thus separates Aeneas's report into a vivid eyewitness account of the battle and a retrospective look at what is left of the capital of an empire that ruled "over the many lands of Asia."[10] The destruction of Carthage itself, which we encounter as a city in the process of being built, only appears in the simile Virgil uses to describe the city's reaction to the death of its queen. Evoking the sacking of the "noble city" that Dido founded, the simile recalls to the reader's mind the event that established Rome's dominion in the Mediterranean.[11]

The eighteenth century, the century that saw the first excavations at Pompeii and rediscovered classical antiquity, also rediscovered ruins—and with them the scenario of the ruin gazer. It is only fitting that Rollin, a historian of the Punic Wars, would claim that the Romans were in the habit of taking visitors through Carthage's urban ruins, Scipio "not being sorry that the miserable ruins of a place should be seen, which had disputed empire with Rome."[12] Gibbon described the genesis of his monumental *The Decline and Fall of the Roman Empire* as he sat musing "amidst the ruins of the Capitol."[13] Gibbon's mind circled around the question of what caused empires to rise and fall. That question also preoccupied the Comte de Volney, a political philosopher, historian, and avid traveler. In 1791, he published a popular text entitled *The Ruins, or Meditation on the Revolutions of Empires and the Law of Nature*. He traveled to Syria and visited the Greco-Roman ruins of Palmyra, about 150 miles northeast of Damascus. In contrast to Gibbon's imperial metropole, Palmyra is a veritable "archive . . . of four empires,"[14] and that ruinous evidence of the rise and fall of empires is what fascinated Volney. Do empires just "vanish," Volney wonders, because of some "blind fatality," or is this destruction the work of men?[15] The lessons that Volney derived from the silent ruins are those of a French revolutionary. Ruins inspire hope because they suggest that new revolutions will topple nations and empires.

Ruins, empires, and the history of the world—this nexus generates in the Enlightenment a whole new gaze at ruins, one tied to the notion of progress and the hope that the cycle of rise and fall may be broken. Or, as Gibbon put it with all the confidence of an Enlightenment historian in humanity's "advances toward perfection," we may safely presume "that no people . . . will relapse into their original barbarism."[16] Why then do we find Volney—a few pages later—again striking the pose of the ruin gazer, but this time much more despondent? It is the vision of his own civilization in ruins that pushes him into this melan-

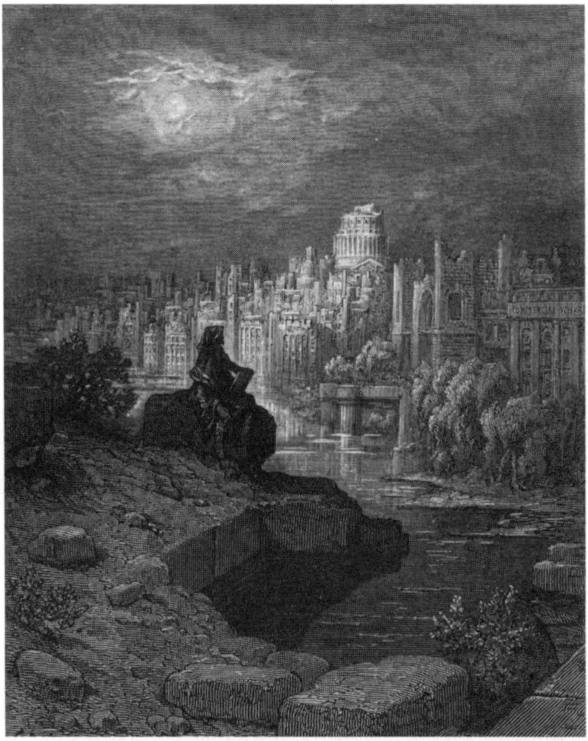

1. Gustave Doré, *The New Zealander* (1872), based on Macaulay's idea of a future visitor to London.

cholic state. "Who knows if on the banks of the Seine, [or] the Thames," Volney wonders, "who knows if some traveller like myself, shall not one day sit on their silent ruins, and weep in solitude over . . . the memory of their former greatness."[17] Volney's meditations at Palmyra about the empires of the past and the republics of the future, about imperial despotism and republican liberty, thus oscillate between hope and despair. Centuries after Scipio learned his lesson at Carthage, Volney learns in the Syrian desert that the sight of empires in ruins transmits an uncanny knowledge—the knowledge that all empires might crumble into ruins, rubble, dust.

This ruin gazer at the very heart of Europe will become a popular icon of the nineteenth century. But the structure of the scenario will change because the European ruin gazer will become the barbarian celebrating the ruin of Europe's empires. In 1840 Thomas Macaulay, the British literary critic, historian, and colonial administrator, re-invented the ruin gazer as a traveler from New Zealand who "shall, in the midst of a vast solitude, take his stand on a broken arch of London Bridge to sketch the ruins of St. Paul's."[18] Looking at Rome, Macaulay thinks of London, a gaze most likely inspired by Volney's *The Ruins*. But there is a crucial difference between the two scenarios: in Volney's version, the future ruin gazer is the self, the European subject. In Macaulay's scenario, the ruin gazer is the other—the barbarian, the colonized subject.

The invention of imperial imaginaries, the haunting knowledge of decline, the strategies to counter this knowledge, and the scopic scenarios of ruin gazing are not historicist or antiquarian topics. As the course taken by the war in Iraq has raised anew the specter of imperial decline, scenarios of ruin gazing are proliferating—the ancient ruins of Carthage have become visible again. Their sudden visibility is an aftereffect—sometimes intended, sometimes not—of a decade-long neoconservative discourse on Washington and Rome that counters the specter of imperial decline with assertions of unprecedented imperial might. In *Incoherent Empire*, Michael Mann analyzes these strategies, observing that while American neoconservatives (and some liberals) abhor the word "imperialism," they seem to have grown quite fond of "empire" with its "noble" connotations.[19] These advocates of a new world order, Mann writes, counter the "disquieting thought" of the demise of the British empire by simply leaving that nineteenth-century predecessor of the American empire out of the story, taking a great leap forward from the Pax Romana to the Pax Americana and considering modern Americans "the noblest imperialists of them all."[20]

While Mann evokes, albeit indirectly, the image of Rome in ruins, Kaplan puts Rome's drawn-out conflict with Carthage on center stage. Kaplan asks us to understand the Second Punic War as the equivalent of the Second World War. Just as the Romans' victory over the Carthaginians established the Roman empire, the Second World War, he argues, made the United States a "universal power."[21] The Hobbesian state of the world requires an imperial power, which in turn requires a dose of heroic patriotism and a sense of imperial destiny—virtues rooted in the kind of "historical imagination" that Churchill possessed, a worldview informed by the ancient Greek and Roman historians.[22]

What happens if the United States does not heed Kaplan's advice? Churchill raises the specter of decadence: if a nation lacks the basic sense of insecurity that motivates its struggle to conquer more worlds and destroy its rivals, it will, like Rome, eventually "sink to actual eroticism and ultimate decay."[23] It is the victorious Rome of the Punic Wars that Churchill and Kaplan admire. Ruinous decay would be the fate of this Rome if it were to give up its quest for imperial power. Carthage signifies not only as Rome's enemy, but as a Cassandrian warning about the fate of London and Washington, cities that might end up like Berlin, their barbarous adversary in the Second World War.

As Churchill's musings about decadent Carthage indicate, the Phoenician city is one of the sites of the most excessive Orientalizing in the nineteenth century. In order to fully comprehend the meaning of Carthage, we need to turn to another critic of empire, the French historian and fierce critic of Napoleon, Jules Michelet. In his view, the Punic Wars were a struggle between two races, the indo-Germanic and the Semitic: the Carthaginians were part of the Semitic world—the world of Jews, Arabs, and Phoenicians—characterized by the spirit of work, commerce, and navigation; Rome represented the spirit of heroism, art, and lawfulness. At stake in this conflict of "enemy races" was the fate of the entire world.[24] What was it about Carthage that merited this annihilating violence? To Michelet, the Phoenicians are an "impure race," their cities modern versions of Sodom and Gomorrah.[25] A "mercantile tyranny," Carthage started exploring the world for profit, not power or knowledge, Michelet writes, like the "English nabobs" of the nineteenth century who plundered their colonies.[26] This perverse imperial world deserved ruination, and our nineteenth-century ruin gazer looks with deep satisfaction at the ruins of Carthage.

Let us skip ahead a century to the Whitney Museum's The Course of Empire, one of the most successful exhibits in post-9/11 New York. This exhibit also conjured up images of barbarous, decadent Carthage, but with a difference: Ruscha took the exhibit's title from Cole, who painted his The Course of Empire series in the 1830s. Ruscha's paintings confront the viewer with a sight often seen yet rarely made the subject of a work of art: industrial modernity in decay; Cole's work thematizes the rise and fall of empires. Cole's first and second paintings show us unspoiled, pastoral landscapes; the third painting, *Consummation of Empire*, celebrates urban civilization at its height with a luminous representation of a rich, busy ancient city. In the next painting, *Destruction*, Cole's prosperous city is the site of a fierce battle. The series ends with *Desolation*, a melancholy scene of former grandeur in which the few remnants of the ancient city have been overgrown by nature.

While Cole painted in the United States, his concerns and style are clearly formed by European romanticism and its obsession with the rise and fall of empires. Yet it is not Rome but Carthage that Cole's paintings refer to: with *Consummation of Empire*, Cole deliberately alludes to two paintings by Turner, *Dido Building Carthage* and *The Rise of the Carthaginian Empire*; Cole's *Destruction* takes its inspiration from Turner's *The Decline of the Carthaginian Empire*, which Turner exhibited just a year after the collapse of the Napoleonic empire and which depicts France's Oriental decadence. But Turner's apocalyptic vision also stands as a dire warning at the beginning of the era of Great Britain's greatest wealth and power in the wake of its victory over Napoleon in 1815. Cole's *Destruction* thus still transports that meaning of imperial decline—in the 1830s and in the early twenty-first century. And the Whitney's The Course of Empire mobilizes this tradition, turning us into present-day ruin gazers—gazing at ruins both present and absent. For between Ruscha's images of rusty, shabby, derelict industrial landscapes and buildings and Cole's elegiac evocation of the sublime ruins of the great city of Carthage hover the images of the World Trade Center.

As we have seen, the exhibit also evoked the Orientalist trope of Carthage. My later discussion of the Nazis will demonstrate how easily Carthage can be mobilized for a populist critique of capitalist decadence with strong anti-Semitic overtones. As part of the so-called *Aktion Ritterbusch*, an interdisplinary initiative among German academics to support the war effort, Joseph Vogt, a classicist, argued in 1943 that the conflict is racially motivated by "blood heritage" leading to a merciless "war of annihilation."[27] Bervé, Vogt's colleague, who argued that Europe's new order required a new image of antiquity,[28] delivered a lecture entitled "Rom und Karthago" more than thirteen times. Bervé's audiences ranged from academics to Wehrmacht officers. Rome, Bervé argued, annihilated "Semitedom" in the Mediterranean, thus saving the *Abendland*.[29] A model for the Nazis, this war remained a testimony to "fanatical enmity among races."[30] Nevertheless, even Bervé began to articulate imperial unease. The end of Rome's struggle for hegemony hints at the danger of an imperialism destroying its own roots.[31]

The obsession with the annihilation of Carthage was not a mere quirk of some isolated academics. Goebbels wrote in his diary on March 1, 1945, that Hitler had asked him to publish statements on the Punic Wars as the greatest example of a "world-historical decision" whose impact lasted for centuries.[32] Immersed in reading Mommsen's *Römische Geschichte* as his war neared its catastrophic end, Goebbels most likely imagined himself as Scipio overlooking Carthage's ruins. Yet we may also safely assume that he was plagued by visions of another ruin gazer, a Carthaginian barbarian triumphantly surveying the smoking remains of Speer's reconstructed Berlin, that Germania which the *Führer* expected to be completed by 1950. The Nazis' reinvention of the imperial ruin gazer derives from the problematic raised by these scenarios of non-German, non-Aryan ruin gazers. The Nazis set out to build an empire knowing that empires crumble and that their enemies might one day gaze triumphantly at the rubble. Their scopic reinventions represent scenarios of identity—that is, scenarios in which the ruin gazer in the present imagines another ruin gazer like himself looking at the ruins in the future. Hitler's and Speer's ultimate goal was to construct an imperial imaginary that keeps the other—the non-German, the non-Aryan—out of sight. As we will see, what accounts for this obsession with ruination is their fear of retaliation.

### Spengler's Ruins of Modernity, or the Return of the Barbarian

Spengler's *Decline of the West* is best known for its conservative and often deeply anti-Semitic critique of European modernity as decaying, or the moment when organic *Kultur* is gradually sliding into inorganic *Zivilisation*.[33] More importantly for our context, Spengler also theorizes empire (as the political form that all late civilizations take) and its ruins for the twentieth century.[34] In the process, he stages the author as modernity's most perspicuous ruin gazer, predicting a world more desolate than any shown in Cole's or Turner's ruin paintings.

By asserting the identity of ancient and modern fates, Spengler contributed decisively to the thinking of Germany's so-called conservative revolutionaries like Carl Schmitt, Ernst Jünger, or Gottfried Benn, who disdained Weimar democracy; celebrated dictatorial states, warriors, and wars; and were enthusiastic about a new Reich and new technologies. Spengler also influenced their thinking in terms of rising and declining empires with the attendant cultural racism and anti-Semitism. Unlike Schmitt, Jünger, and Benn, Spengler maintained his distance from National Socialism. Nevertheless attracted to Spengler's analysis of modern Germany's decay, Adolf Hitler and his theorists of empire critically appropriated his work: like van den Bruck, whose *Das dritte Reich* provided the Nazis with the vocabulary for their political metaphysics, they fiercely debated Spengler's pessimism, arguing that Germany is one of the "young" peoples destined for rebirth and a new Reich.[35] Hitler's and Speer's theory of ruin value with its scenario of imperial ruin gazing responded to Spengler's uncompromising embrace of modernity's ruination.

Spengler writes world history in terms of space, not time, replacing the Hegelian tripartite scheme with a study of eight autonomous world cultures: for example, Faustian (the culture of the Occident), Apollonian or Greco-Roman, and Magic or Arab. The relation between these *Kulturkreise,* or cultures, is defined by a "feeling of profound alterity";[36] each culture consists of different peoples that are often at war but that unify as soon as they encounter members of a different culture. This encounter generates the barbarian—someone only outwardly belonging to one's culture, someone with a different soul.[37] The Jew comes to embody this barbarian, or "parasite," among his occidental "host people."[38] Like Carthaginians, Jews belong to the Magic culture.

According to Spengler, each culture unfolds around an archetype or soul, which finds its clearest expression in a culture's style—particularly its architecture, with its specific spatial imagination and visual regime.[39] Although this spatialization of history is a latently relativist move, Spengler clearly privileges Faustian culture, whose soul is animated by a desire to conquer "empty space":[40]

Faustian culture is above all a culture of explorers and a culture obsessed with the past—territories beyond the borders of the visible. It thus comes as no surprise that Spengler celebrates the Faustian desire for expansion, as long as it serves political, not economic, goals; the collective interests of the nation, and not the private motives fueling imperialism. More specifically, Spengler advocates one core nation's expansion and eventual hegemony within its culture, but not into territory belonging to other, foreign cultures.

The desire to see and conquer far-away countries is thus part of this Faustian soul, as is the desire to see the far-away past. It is in this context of Faustian fascination with infinite space that Spengler theorizes ruins, their particular epistemology and aesthetics. Faustian culture is obsessed with the ruins of the past, its gaze responding to their provocation to recreate what is no longer visible.[41] Spengler describes his Faustian fascination with the fragments of the past as a kind of scopophilia: they invite the eye to fill the empty space.[42] But let us explore Spengler's particular scenario of ruin gazing, whose object is the ruins of the Roman and German *Spätzeit* (late period or end period). The Roman empire constitutes the centerpiece of his theory of late European modernity. In a controversial chapter dealing with the deadly nature of the megalopolis as a symptom of civilization's decay, Spengler presents his explanation of Rome's decline. This backward gaze at ruined Rome is simultaneously a gaze at the ruins of the future, for Spengler predicts Germany's decline into late Roman civilization.

"Imperialism," Spengler argues, "is pure civilization."[43] In Spengler's iron logic of civilizations, empires will end up as "dead bodies," and the end result of this process will be what the political geographer Friedrich Ratzel called "ruin countries":[44] like Rome, London, Paris, and Berlin will become "petrified world cities" that will eventually disintegrate into ruined urban deserts, their inhabitants ruled by emperors interested only in unending wars fought for gain.[45]

In Spengler's view, Rome's golden age was the era of the First Punic War and "great Scipio," when Rome was culture and Carthage civilization.[46] Carthage lost, Spengler writes, because the Carthaginians subordinated politics to their economic interests. With the victory of Scipio, Rome enters its imperialist era, when "money triumphs in the form of democracy," eventually leading to chaos and a new form of political rule, Caesarism, with its endless wars for the "private possession of the world."[47] Spengler thus admires the Rome of Scipio Africanus the Elder, yet advocates Caesarism as a model: like the *Imperium Romanum*, Europe might ward off its ruinous fate—albeit only for a while—with the help of the Prussian state that would hegemonize Middle Europe.[48]

Empires, Spengler coldly affirms, are uncanny, and their inevitable decline needs to be confronted with a cold, sober gaze. At times this gaze, with which the anorganic intellectual scrutinizes the petrified remains of what once was an organic culture full of life, shades into a gaze enthralled by decay, expressing a kind of sublime elation. Yet this heroic, detached stance crumbles when faced with the sight of the urban ruins of the late Roman empire. This particular passage does not resonate with heroic pathos but is filled with a profound sense of grief. Spengler's detached gaze thus disintegrates, resonating with the emotions of centuries of ruin gazing: grief, awe, and terror. The fate of Rome matters—even to Spengler.

Spengler situates himself as Europe's very last ruin gazer, while leaving open the possibility of a different scenario—the barbarian ruin gazer from a foreign culture. Hitler and Speer, however, project themselves into the future, thereby asserting German mastery over ruination—while keeping Spengler's barbarian out of sight. Sharing Spengler's assessment of contemporary Germany as decadent, the Nazis endeavor to build a new Reich against Spengler's tragic vision of Europe as an apocalyptic ruinscape. Hitler and Speer fantasize about building ruins to enthrall the future Aryan ruin gazer with the sublime spectacle of everlasting imperial power.

### Reinventing Empire: Space, Spatial Imaginary, Slavery, and Genocide

Above all, the Nazis fantasized about creating a new Germanic Reich. Carl Schmitt contributed decisively to the debates about this new Reich, as do Vogt and the political geographer Karl Haushofer.[49] These thinkers reinvented empire for the context of twentieth-century Germany: while Britain and France had carried their civilizing mission to the non-European world, Germany would create its own territorial empire centered on Middle Europe. Vogt made the case for imperial expansion in the East by taking his readers into a "foreign historical zone":[50] the Roman concept of empire, he asserts, has never been as valid as now. Reich, or empire, designates a power, which regulates questions of domination and service for many peoples in a wide-ranging space. Beyond taking care of material arrangements, a Reich also provides its members with a sense of protection and of meaning for their sacrifices;[51] a Reich thus requires a unifying spiritual bond.

In Vogt's view, the basis of the Romans' success in creating an empire was their conception of space. History is a struggle among empires, he writes, and their will to dominate space. A strong people, the Romans had a particularly "alert spatial instinct";[52] its leaders always kept in sight a far-away goal that they connected to the imperial core.[53] What sets Vogt apart from Hitler, Alfred Rosenberg, and other hard-core Nazi theorists of Lebensraum were two things:

his idea that the Roman empire rightly refrained from expanding further east, into a "volk-dom of a fundamentally different nature";[54] and that a Reich is primarily defined culturally, not racially.

One of those theorists was Haushofer, who traced a hidden optimism in Spengler's European "ruin landscape."[55] Haushofer wrote a veritable handbook of imperial politics, in which he argues the need for an imperial imaginary. This imaginary, the ability to imagine one's own place "in a large space" which the Romans mastered so exceptionally well,[56] has to be practiced: once a month, every German ought to imagine his or her exact position in the world, starting from their German Lebensraum—while keeping their eye on Germany's long-term geopolitical goals.[57] Haushofer's imperial imaginary predictably included a ruin gazer scenario, one of astonishing melodramatic swagger: Germans, Horace proclaimed, had no choice but to face up to the "deadly depths" of world politics.[58] Quoting the Roman poet—"Even if the entire globe should crumble, the fragments will hit him unafraid"—Haushofer promised that his "world-political self-education" will allow Germans to perish "knowingly."[59]

In 1939, Schmitt enthusiastically welcomed the advent of a strong Reich with its Middle European *Grossraum* that put an end to a system that relied on the continent's "weak core."[60] Schmitt theorized the specificity of the new Reich, frequently referring to Ratzel's, Haushofer's, and Vogt's writings on Rome. While the history of international law is a history of empires and their *Grossräume*,[61] Schmitt argued, the concepts of empire, *Imperium*, or Reich, are not easily translatable. The universalism informing the older international order guaranteed by the British empire was pure formalism. Space, Schmitt claimed, is always historically concrete—that is, connected to a specific *Volk* and the reality of its specific "origin, blood and soil," not "empty space."[62] The German Reich is thus in its very essence *völkisch*, because its core is always constituted by a particular Volk.

With his völkisch conception of a Reich as an entity that transcends the nation-state, Schmitt came close to making National Socialist ideas the core of his theory. His definition of Grossraum uses a slightly different terminology: it is a "cultural and economic-industrial-organizatorial" sphere of influence belonging to a particular Reich.[63] This new Grossraum, he argued, will respect the particularity of other peoples in the East. Moreover, it will obey a political logic of agreement among powers, not economic motives.

In the end, Hitler and Himmler had very different ideas about Germany's *Weltreich* than Vogt, Haushofer, or Schmitt. The latter, when asked why he collaborated with the Nazis until the attack by the SS in 1936, compared himself to an ethnologist discovering "a new tribe of Kaffirs."[64] This "new tribe" that turned out more murderous than any "Kaffir" also looked to Rome for inspiration, but they do not model their empire on Vogt's idealized version; they reinvent slavery and genocide. In October 1943, Himmler addressed an audience of SS officers and police commanders at Posen, defining the Nazis' ultimate goal as a "Germanic Empire" and the Second World War as a "means to open the east for German settlement."[65] Possessing an astute sense of what it means to build and maintain an empire, Himmler planned to teach Germans how to be imperialists—not, as Haushofer suggested, by imagining themselves as the center of the world, but by honing their skills in administering native policies. Germans were still learning how to rule their newly acquired empire, Himmler claimed; they were still committing lots of errors when it comes to "how to act with regards to foreign peoples, the domination of the foreign-blooded masses by a small minority of the upper crust."[66] Unlike the English, Germans lacked the experience of ruling millions, but Himmler's elite will learn how to rule because their racial superiority ultimately protected them from error.[67] Himmler's institutions will teach them the mind-set required to dominate inferior races, who will be "slaves" and to whom it is wrong to attribute "our good nature."[68] The SS knows that its "duty is to our Volk, and to our blood," and they will face the "problem of all foreign, non-Germanic peoples" with utter "indifference."[69] This native policy will be based on "Asiatic laws."[70] Such a detached attitude is all the more necessary for the SS's ultimate mission, the "eradication of the Jewish people."[71]

The section of the speech entitled "The Evacuation of Jews" is at the core of many interpretations of the Nazis' genocidal politics. LaCapra, for instance, interprets this as an example of the negative political sublime—that is, the Nazis' claim to a unique historical mission requiring a form of transgression which has never been practiced before and which evokes a kind of "sublime horror."[72] LaCapra focuses on Himmler's description of the task of the SS and police units, who will confront a sight that others would be unable to bear. Many Germans speak about the "extirpation" of the Jews, says Himmler, but "not one has seen it happen, not one has been through it."[73] What distinguishes the SS elite from other Germans is that they have seen the piles of dead bodies. The SS and the police units in charge of executions were hardened by going through that, but they "have kept [their] integrity."[74]

With his emphasis on the integrity of the SS, Himmler tried to bring together decency and mass murder. The passage also hints at a kind of "elation" that comes with the transgression it describes and, most importantly, betrays the full knowledge of the extent of that transgression.[75] Although I don't agree with LaCapra's understanding of this negative political sublime as the return of repressed religious sacrifice, and of the Holocaust as a form of "deranged sacrificialism," I do find enormously insightful his concept of the negative political sublime, with its emphasis on the perverse pleasure involved in transgression and the knowledge of its criminal nature.[76] At the same time, we need to see the section of the speech in context: Himmler is commenting on the Nazis' imperial project. What this speech tells us is that like many empires, the Third Reich was founded on a crime—but that unlike other empires, its foundation was a crime of monstrous proportions. More importantly, the Nazis were fully aware of this fact. It is this awareness, and the anticipation of retaliation that comes with the awareness, that drove the Nazis' ruinomania, their perverse "Ruinenlust" as Macaulay called it after the war.[77]

### Hitler's Grand Tour, or the Führer as Imperial Ruin Gazer

The Nazis developed their imperial ambitions in contrast to those of England and France; the Third Reich would be continental, its civilizing mission directed at the vast regions east of Germany. Yet while Hitler compared colonial India to the colonized "space of the East,"[78] he also frequently resorted to comparisons with the Roman empire.[79] Views of the Forum by Hubert Robert, who also painted an imaginary view of the Louvre in ruins when it was still under construction, decorated Hitler's cabinet room at the Reichstag.[80] Rome—with its imperial reach, monumental architecture, and equally monumental ruins—was thus the Nazis' model. Given the discourse about the Third Reich as a new Rome, a visit by Hitler to Rome was only logical, and he arrived there on May 3, 1938, with a large entourage. Mussolini's technicians of resurrectional realism staged this visit as a journey through Rome's ruins, displaying the imperial city's past and present.[81] Ending at the spectacularly lit Colosseum, the route that Hitler took that night led past Rome's most significant ruins, all ablaze with lights. Pushing the modern parts of the city into the background, this elaborate mise-en-scène recreated the core of the ancient city, with the ruins that Mussolini's urban restructuring had "liberated" from the clutter of decadent modernity so that they might "loom larger."[82]

Gothic seems the appropriate name for the particular mode in which the ancient ruins were resurrected. The fiery glow of the flickering red flames illuminating the past was at once a tribute to the Nazi flag and part of a ceremonial rite to honor the blood sacrificed by Italian Fascists. Mussolini's technicians used all the means at their disposal to take the spectators back into a city of ruins, while suggesting with their lighting that it be imagined as whole. Moreover, Mussolini's mise-en-scène of imperial power made its participants into imperial ruin gazers who occupied a position both of scopic mastery and of the mastery that comes with giving life to the past. These travelers had access to an unencumbered view of Rome's urban center and also a god's-eye view that allowed them to look both backward and forward—to their imperial past and to the future of their empire.

This Fascist spectacle opened a space, an imperial imaginary in which the boundaries of past, present, and future had collapsed. On that night, imperial Rome became real, its "heroism in ruin" a renewed presence.[83] Most importantly, however, the specter of barbarian ruin gazers had been chased from the urban ruinscape: it was Mussolini who had orchestrated the scenario and Hitler who looked at Rome's ruins, reoccupying Spengler's position.

The Nazis appreciated Mussolini's fantasy and used the visit for their own purposes. Ribbentropp's foreign ministry published *Der Schlüssel zum Frieden* on May 17, 1938, documenting Hitler's state visit from the moment he left Berlin's Anhalter Bahnhof—today one of the city's most spectacular ruins—to his return, triumphantly staged at the Brandenburg Gate.[84] The book is a collage that resembles one of the Nazis' weekly newsreels. Its text tells two stories: the story of the triumph of Hitler, the statesman, and the story of the grand tour of Hitler, the artist. The book's title thematizes the politics of the axis, its subtitle—*Führertage in Italien* (Führer's Days in Italy)—the narrative of Hitler as artist on a grand tour.[85] The lavishly illustrated travelogue stages the Führer as contemporary ruin gazer triumphantly testifying to the possibility of imperial rebirth—in Italy, where, Hitler tells his audience, Mussolini "founded a new Imperium" and in Germany, where a "new Germanic Reich" has arisen.[86]

What the Germans wanted to communicate through their account of the journey was that Mussolini was not the only imperial leader. This explains the overall frame of the political narrative, the Führer's triumph.[87] Like a Roman emperor, when the Führer returned to his capital and stepped through the Brandenburg Gate, he was greeted by the masses. While this story positions Hitler as following the path of Rome's emperors, the narrative of the grand tour takes up the Roman theme from a different angle. Rome visited is always Rome revisited. Thus Thomas Macaulay, the inventor of the Maori on a grand tour, admires the "majesty" of the Colosseum on his own journey in 1838.[88] *Führertage* presents the Führer as an Italian traveler in the tradition of Goethe.[89] Among other things, this section contains an excerpt from Goethe's *Italienische Reise* and concludes with *Coliseum*, a 1760 drawing by Piranesi, the master of ruin art.

A separate section documents Hitler's visit to Rome. As we know, the highpoint of Hitler's visit was his tour of the ancient city at night. The core of this section consists of a photograph of the Führer in a carriage with the Italian king, and three photos of the dramatically illuminated ruin sites displayed for Hitler's gaze. The political story of *Der Schlüssel zum Frieden* thus is one of the triumphant rebirth of empires south and north of the Alps.

The story of Hitler on his Italian tour is inextricably linked to imperial politics. The Nazis' repetition of Mussolini's dramatic mise-en-scène of ruin

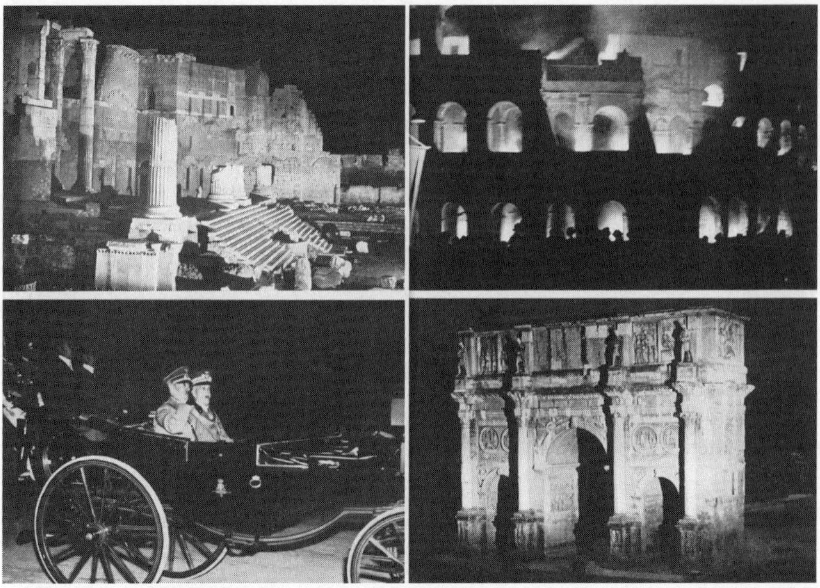

2. Adolf Hitler with the Italian king in Rome, May 3, 1938. Reproduced from *Der Schlüssel zum Frieden: Führertage in Italien*, ed. Heinrich Hansen (Berlin: M. A. Klieber Verlag, 1938), no page number.

gazing—the display of photograph after photograph of the Führer in the ruins of Rome—has an obsessional, fetishistic quality to it, if we understand fetishism as the confrontation with an unbearable knowledge that paradoxically creates a memorial to the sight the fetishist needs to disavow—placing the memorial at the very site that produces this uncanny knowledge.[90] For all imperial projects, that traumatic site is Rome.

Hitler toured Rome in the year when he was preparing for his expansionist war. In this context of empire building, the scenario of ruin gazing takes on the meaning of a fetish: in *Schlüssel zum Frieden*, Ribbentrop's propagandists reinstalled the Occidental ruin gazer in his position of mastery, hoping that Spengler's barbarian would recede from the horizon of the imperial imaginary they were constructing. At a strategic moment, the book thus promised a Reich that will not decline.

### Building a Future in Ruins: Hitler's and Speer's Theory of Ruin Value

At the time of Hitler's visit to Rome, Walter Benjamin created his famous angel of history. Was it Mussolini's grandiose historicist parade through Roman ruins that Benjamin had in mind when he wrote "Theses on the Philosophy of History" in Paris? Did this spectacle prompt him to argue that the resurrection of the past had to be in the service of the defeated, not of the victors? Was it Mussolini's ideological junk heap of dehistoricized rubble that piled up in front of Benjamin's angel, terrifying him to death? Or, more intriguing yet, did the exiled philosopher of history reconceptualize Spengler's barbarian–its eyes ripped wide open?[91]

With their neoclassical architecture, the Nazis wanted to create an imperial gaze, not a panicked stare. The director of the German Archaeological Institute in Rome, Gerhart Rodenwaldt, celebrated the inscription of this new Fascist gaze into urban space as Roman, as a way of seeing "in a Roman way and with Roman eyes."[92] Speer and other Nazi architects will be in charge of this scopic transformation of space, a project that amounts to the creation of an imperial space with a strong metropolitan core. In 1940, Hitler sent a memorandum to his architects, saying that "Berlin must as soon as possible receive its new architectural form as capital of a strong, new Reich." Hitler saw this construction as "the most important contribution to the final securing of our victory" and announced it will be completed in 1950.[93] He outlined his rather derivative theory of art and architecture, promising that the new Reich will replace the degenerate architecture of Weimar's weak state, characterized by the dominance of capitalist over state architecture. In a Spenglerian vein, Hitler argued that large department stores, hotels, and skyscrapers were signs of urban decadence.[94] In contrast to these "fractured" cities, Greek and Roman cities possessed a "spiritual center."[95] Lamenting this lack of "symbols of national community" in Weimar's cities, Hitler outlined his apocalyptic vision of the ruins of the future: "If Berlin were to meet the fate of Rome," he wrote, "then the coming generations could one day admire the department stores of some Jews, and the hotels of some corporations as the most imposing works of our time, the characteristic expression of the culture of our days."[96] According to Hitler, modern cities would thus leave Jewish, modernist ruins behind—ugly remnants of the particularist interests of Jewish capitalists.

Ranting against modernism's "Jewish artistic temperament," Hitler promised that the "young German Reich" will revive a genuine national art representing its "pure German essence."[97] The pretext for Hitler's Munich speech was a planned theatre festival, to be directed by Max Reinhart. The plans, Hitler argued, are motivated by tourism—*Fremdenverkehr*, or "traffic of foreigners," a word that prompted him to free-associate about the dangers of foreignness: Berlin's modern architecture, for instance, expressed "foreign artistic temperament," whose origin he traces to Poland.[98]

Hitler created a second scenario of ruin gazing: what do we learn, he asks, when we look at the "gigantic fields of ruins" that antiquity left us?[99] No pyramid, no temple, no palace was ever built with "foreigners" in mind. In contrast to the ruins that Weimar's modernist cities would leave behind, in Hitler's one-track mind ancient ruins are non-Jewish ruins—as would be the ruins left behind by the new Reich.

Hitler insisted again and again that his architects build for "eternity."[100] We do not know whether Hitler and Speer expected their monuments to slowly disintegrate over time, be overtaken by nature, or be sacked by enemies. But we may safely assume that they did not expect them to be reduced to rubble by Allied air raids within four years. One of Speer's most famous buildings was his monumental Reichskanzlei (chancellery). Completed in 1939, the building was bombed and then razed by the Soviets. The bombs left the chancellery looking very unlike what Hitler and Speer had intended. This was no noble, heroic ruin but a "Jewish," modernist one: the modern building materials were exposed, leaving a skeleton of metal and concrete.

According to Speer, his theory of ruin value arose in response to Hitler's definition of architecture as a "bridge" across time which would "transmit his time and its spirit to posterity."[101] With an eye on Mussolini's resurrection of Rome's "heroic spirit," Hitler argued that "periods of weakness" inevitably follow the "great epochs of history," but a nation at its "lowest ebb" can be inspired by the relics of a great age.[102] To achieve this effect, Speer would use materials that would last and, more importantly, go to ruin as "clearly recognizable ruins," not rubble.[103]

In Speer's account, his theory was born when he observed the demolition of buildings in Nuremberg to make room for the Zeppelin Field. Looking at the remnants, Speer realized that modern buildings would make "dreary ruins."[104] He did not want to be responsible for "rusting heaps of rubble"; he wants to create "structures which even in a state of decay, after hundreds or (such were our reckonings) thousands of years would more or less resemble Roman ruins."[105] To make his point, Speer prepared a "Romantic drawing" in the tradition of Hubert Robert and Joseph Gandy, the architect who in 1798 showed the newly constructed Bank of England in picturesque wreckage;[106] Speer's drawing depicted the Zeppelin Field's reviewing stand (modeled after the Pergamon Altar) after "generations of neglect": "overgrown with ivy, its columns fallen, the walls crumbling here and there, but the outlines still clearly recognizable."[107] While Hitler's entourage was outraged by Speer's ideas, the Führer was fascinated by his architect's invention, "this 'law of ruins.' "[108] Hitler could, like Speer himself, easily "conceived of a period of decline for the newly founded *Reich* destined to last a thousand years."[109]

In Speer's and Hitler's imaginary, the future ruin gazer would be an Aryan

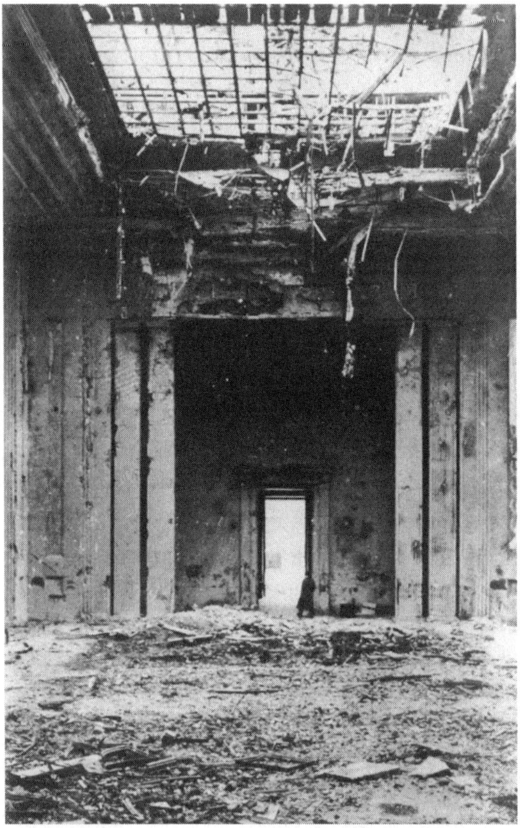

3. The Mosaic Room in Albert Speer's Chancellery, Berlin (ca. 1945).

German; they did not imagine the ruin gazer to be the empire's victorious subject—the one who would be gazing at *Germania* would not be a Pole, or Russian, or Jew. As I mentioned above, Hitler saw one of the functions of the ruins of Speer's Germania as a bridge across generations, reminding Germans in times of weakness of their mighty imperial past. Moreover, in 1941 Hitler fantasized about an annual triumph through Germania: once a year, the German masters would lead natives from the East through Berlin, filling their minds with the power and grandeur of the Reich. It turns out that when Hitler thought about his subjects in the eastern territories, the image of the "Maori" readily came to his mind.[110] One of the monuments the barbarians would encounter would be the gigantic Arch of Triumph that Hitler had been planning since 1936.[111] But behind this awed and cowed ruin gazer lurk the uncanny shadows both of Spengler's barbarian ruin traveler from another culture who scrutinizes the remnants of a dead civilization, and of Macaulay's colonized subject who contemplates the ruins of the empire's metropolitan center. Who was to guarantee that it would be an Aryan whose gaze would rest triumphantly on the remains of the Third Reich? Who was to guarantee that it would not be one of the barbarians forced to participate in Hitler's ritual?

In this new imperial imaginary, the imperial ruin gazer coexisted with the cowed and awed subject, the idea of ruination with the idea of a strong new Reich. Like the project of building a Reich with exceptionally solid foundations, the scopic structure of the Nazis' ruin fantasy and its fetishistic deployment indicate that we are dealing with yet another attempt to deal with the anxieties raised by the uncanny nature of empire. But as I argued with respect to Himmler's speech, there is much more at stake in the Nazis' fetishistic obsession with ruination. Let us once more return to Carthage, this time via Mommsen's *Römische Geschichte*. "The ruins burnt for seventeen days," Mommsen tells us. Then he adds: "but Scipio, whom nature had destined to a nobler role than that of executioner, stared in horror at his own work." Why does Scipio Africanus the Younger recoil from his own victory? Because, Mommsen wrote, the Roman general was seized by the fear that retaliation would inescapably follow such a monstrous deed.[112]

The Nazis' imperial imaginary crystallized around a scenario which simultaneously promised an exceptionally solid imperial foundation and sublime ruins. This articulation of imperial creation and destruction is unique to the Nazis. The symptom of an empire driven by a totalitarian logic of mass murder, it sets the Nazis' imperial project apart from all others. Like Mommsen's Scipio, Hitler, Himmler, Speer, and others were aware of their crimes, and afraid of the brutal retaliation that awaited them. It is this fear of retaliation that their obsession with ruins and ruination betrays. And it is this monstrous peculiarity of the Nazis' Reich and its aesthetics of sublime ruination that Martin, Don DeLillo's postfascist ruin gazer, willfully denies when he looks at their ruins.

## Notes

1. DeLillo, *Falling Man*, 116.
2. Ibid.
3. Michael Mann, *Incoherent Empire*, 10.
4. Mayer, *Among Empires*, 13.
5. Polybius, *The Histories*, 437.
6. Appian, quoted in Polybius, *The Histories*, 439.
7. On the lament, see Reed, *Virgil's Gaze*, 135.
8. Virgil, *The Aeneid*, 56.
9. Ibid., 13.
10. Ibid., 94.
11. Ibid., 150.

12. Rollin, *The Roman History from the Foundation of Rome to the Battle of Actium*, 220. On the representation of the destruction of Carthage, see also Ridley, "To Be Taken with a Pinch of Salt."
13. Gibbon, *The Decline and Fall of the Roman Empire*, vol. 3, 1085.The work was originally published 1776–88.
14. Quote from Traill, a nineteenth-century traveler mentioned in Macaulay, *The Pleasure of Ruins*, originally published in 1953.
15. Volney, *The Ruins*, 6 and 20.
16. Gibbon quoted in Woodward, *In Ruins*, 188–89.
17. Volney, *The Ruins*, 8.
18. Quoted in Edwards, "Translating Empire? Macaulay's Rome," 80.
19. Michael Mann, *Incoherent Empire*, 9.
20. Ibid., 10.
21. Kaplan, *Warrior Politics*, 32.
22. Ibid., 18.
23. Quoted in ibid., 26.
24. Michelet, *Histoire Romaine*, 204. All translations in this chapter are mine.
25. Ibid., 205.
26. Ibid., 208 and 213.
27. Joseph Vogt, *Rom und Karthago*, 7 and 5. On Aktion Ritterbusch, see Rebenich, "Alte Geschichte in Demokratie und Diktatur," 474–75.
28. Bervé, *Das neue Bild der Antike*, 9.
29. Quoted in Rebenich, "Alte Geschichte in Demokratie und Diktatur," 484.
30. Ibid.
31. Ibid. See also Joseph Vogt, *Rom und Karthago*, 5.
32. Goebbels, *Die Tagebücher von Joseph Goebbels*, 394. See also Reuth, *Goebbels*, 342.
33. Spengler, *Der Untergang des Abendlandes* (Decline of the West), 45. English translations from this work are mine.
34. Spengler's title was inspired by Otto Seeck's six-volume *Geschichte des Untergangs der antiken Welt (1897–1921)*, vols. 1–6 (Stuttgart: Metzlersche Verlagsbuchhandlung, 1966). Spengler transformed Seeck's biological racism into cultural racism, often sliding back into biological terminology. See his polemic against race biology, 952.
35. Van den Bruck, *Das dritte Reich*, 15–16. Van den Bruck also uses the three categories of *Kulturkreis*, the "soul of race and *Volk*," and "barbarity." See his *Das Recht der jungen Völker*, 194 and 195.
36. Spengler, *Der Untergang des Abendlandes* (Decline of the West), 953.
37. Ibid., 761.
38. Ibid., 40 and 953.
39. Ibid., 234.
40. Ibid., 329.
41. Ibid.
42. Ibid.
43. Ibid., 51.
44. Ibid.; and Ratzel, *Anthropogeographie*, 510.
45. Spengler, *Der Untergang des Abendlandes* (Decline of the West), 43 and 782.

46. Ibid., 50.
47. Ibid., 1101 and 1106.
48. Spengler, *Das Jahrzehnt der Entscheidung*.
49. Franz Neumann discusses earlier advocates of eastern expansion, such as Friedrich Naumann, the national-liberal author of *Mitteleuropa* (1915), or Ratzel, who argued the "law of the growth of spaces," that is, a "trend toward giant empires" (Franz Neumann, *Behemoth* [1942], 138ff.). See also Geoff Ely, "Empire by Land, or Sea?"
50. Joseph Vogt, *Vom Reichsgedanke der Römer*, 5.
51. Ibid., 5–6.
52. Ibid., 38.
53. Ibid., 49. See also 41: the Romans organized many expeditions acting as "the eyes of the senate."
54. Ibid., 63.
55. Haushofer, "Kulturkreis und Kulturkreisüberschneidungen," 97.
56. Joseph Vogt, *Vom Reichsgedanken der Römer*, 38.
57. Haushofer, *Weltpolitik von heute*, 259 and 11; see also 20–23.
58. Ibid., 260.
59. Ibid., 259. In 1942 Schmitt wrote that, unlike many of his contemporaries, who experienced this moment as the end of their world, he saw the emergence of a new "nomos" (*Land und Meer*, 79). Schmitt thus coldly gazes at Europe's ruinscape from the vantage point of a new order.
60. Schmitt, "Völkerrechtliche Grossraumordnung," 306. On the status of this essay in Schmitt scholarship, see Joseph W. Bendersky, "Carl Schmitt's Path to Nuremberg," 17.
61. Schmitt, "Völkerrechtliche Grossraumordnung," 309.
62. Ibid., 306. Schmitt's discussion of this idea of "empty space" is anti-Semitic; see 318–20. In *Land und Meer*, Schmitt discusses space and "Raumrevolution," or spatial revolution, in Spenglerian terms. See his *Land und Meer*, 37–44.
63. Ibid., 309.
64. "The 'Fourth' (Second) Interrogation of Carl Schmitt at Nuremberg," 41.
65. Himmler, "Posener Rede vom 04.10.1943 (Volltext)," available in German at www.nationalsozialismus.de/dokumente/textdokumente/. English translations are mine.
66. Ibid., 6.
67. Ibid., 7.
68. Ibid.
69. Ibid.
70. Ibid.
71. Ibid., 20
72. LaCapra, "History and Memory," in *Representing the Holocaust*, 36.
73. Himmler, "Posen Speech."
74. Ibid.
75. LaCapra, "History and Memory," 35.
76. Ibid., 38.
77. Macaulay, *The Pleasure of Ruins*, 454. Nazi aesthetics in general is not an expression of some death drive but is related to their imperial project. See, for instance, Featherstone

on the Nazis' "ideological necrophilia" in his "Ruin Value," and Lacoue-Labarthe and Nancy, "The Nazi Myth," 303.

78. Quoted in Hildebrand, *Vom Reich zum Weltreich*, 715.
79. See Hitler, *Mein Kampf*, 470 and 731. See also Scobie, *Hitler's State Architecture*, 20.
80. Woodward, *In Ruins*, 30. On Hubert Robert, see also Andreas Schönle's chapter in the present volume.
81. Scobie, *Hitler's State Architecture*, 24.
82. Ibid., 9. On this "surgical clearance," see also Tung, *Preserving the World's Great Cities*, 61–63.
83. Walter Pater quoted in Kennedy, "A Sense of Place," 23.
84. H. Hansen, *Der Schlüssel zum Frieden*. On the story of the Anhalter Bahnhof, see Presner, *Mobile Modernity*, 31–33.
85. See Spotts, *Hitler and the Power of Aesthetics*, 3.
86. H. Hansen, *Der Schlüssel zum Frieden*, unnumbered page.
87. Ibid.
88. Quoted in Edwards, "Translating Empire?" 79.
89. On the intertextual nature of travel to Rome, see Kennedy, "A Sense of Place," 19ff.
90. Pollock, "The Image in Psychoanalysis," in *Psychoanalysis and the Image*, 10.
91. In *The Origin of German Tragic Drama*, Benjamin critically engages Spengler's view of modernity as ruined culture.
92. Rodenwaldt, *Kunst um Augustus*, 8.
93. Quoted in Spotts, *Hitler and the Power of Aesthetics*, 351.
94. See, for instance, Hitler, *Mein Kampf*, 292, on cities as "desolate" symptoms of "sinking culture" suffocating in the "service of money."
95. Hitler, "Rede auf NSDAP-Versammlung in München, 9. April 1929," 192.
96. Quoted in Ladd, *The Ghosts of Berlin*, 126.
97. Hitler, "Rede auf NSDAP-Versammlung in München, 9. April 1929," 193 and 168.
98. Ibid., 178 and 175.
99. Ibid., 186.
100. Hitler, *Mein Kampf*, 291.
101. Speer, *Inside the Third Reich*, 55.
102. Hitler quoted in ibid., 56.
103. Ibid., 56.
104. Ibid.
105. Ibid.
106. On Robert, see Macaulay, *The Pleasure of Ruins*, 23; on Gandy, see Woodward, *In Ruins*, 162.
107. Speer, *Inside the Third Reich*, 56.
108. Ibid.
109. Ibid.
110. As he told friends in 1942, the Romans' first contact with Germanic tribes resembled the Nazis' encounter with Poles and with other primitive people east of the Altreich. "Die Versetzung nach Germanien war für den Römer etwas ähnliches wie für uns eine Zeitland die Versetzung nach Posen." It seems Hitler had read Tacitus' account of the

Roman conquest of Germania: "Man stelle sich vor: ewige Regenzeiten und das ganze Gebiet in einen Morast verwandelt." He then extended the analogy by equating Germanic tribes to the Maori, whom he mistakenly identifies as "Neuseeländer, Negerstamm." The Germanic tribes were "auf keiner höheren Kulturstufe wie (heute) die 'Maori' "—although superior in one aspect: "das griechische Profil [war] bei ihnen zuhause wie der römische Caesarenkopf." Picker, *Tischgespräche im Fuhrerhauptquartier 1941–1942*, 173.

111. Spotts, *Hitler and the Power of Aesthetics*, 317.

112. Mommsen, *Römische Geschichte*, 443–44.

TODD SAMUEL PRESNER

# 11

## HEGEL'S PHILOSOPHY OF WORLD HISTORY VIA SEBALD'S IMAGINARY OF RUINS

*A Contrapuntal Critique of the "New Space" of Modernity*

Before his death on December 14, 2001, W. G. Sebald—the expatriate German author, who garnered much acclaim in the United States and Great Britain for what has been called his "literature of memory"—published four major novels, which navigate the haunting and labyrinthine topographies of destruction in Europe after the Second World War. Through complex interrelationships between text and image, literature and history, and biography and autobiography, all four novels—*Schwindel, Gefühle* (1990; translated as *Vertigo,* 1999), *Die Ausgewanderten* (1992; translated as *The Emigrants*, 1996), *Die Ringe des Saturn: Eine englische Wallfahrt* (1995; translated as *The Rings of Saturn*, 1998), and *Austerlitz* (2001)—are extended meditations on the uncanny, physical presence of the ruins of modernity. In images of dilapidated train stations, abandoned industrial lands, wrecked ships, discarded colonial objects, bombed-out buildings, and decaying institutions of power, Sebald reveals the violent underbelly of progressive hopes of modernization: the exploitation of nature, the genocidal legacy of European imperialism and overseas empires, and the human and natural catastrophes of warfare. But in reading Sebald, we quickly recognize that the ruins of modernity are not just physical ruins or material remains: they are the ruins of certain kinds of narratives. What Sebald also draws our attention to—and perhaps this is somewhat less obvious—are the ways in which the project of modernity has been variously rendered as a narrative, and the ways in which these narratives demand to be reevaluated.

As Huyssen argues in his chapter in this volume, an imaginary of ruins is necessary for any theory of modernity, if it is to be more than just another progress philosopheme.[1] Destruction and ruins, then, are not simply the endpoint or culmination of the project of modernity, but processes that are present at every stage of modernization.[2] For this reason, it makes more sense to speak of iterations of a dialectic of modernity. On the one hand, modernity builds upon and disseminates certain universalist values stemming from the Enlightenment; it facilitates the attendant ideals of progress through modernization and the production of a strong, autonomous, rational subject; and it engenders new possibilities of emancipation. On the other hand, modernity fosters the growth of disciplinary power and surveillance, the fragmentation of the subject, the capacity for destruction and mass death on a scale never before possible, and the creation of new ways of subjugating people and controlling society.[3] The latter critique, of course, owes much to the work of Foucault, the Frankfurt school theorists, and, most recently, scholars of cultural and postcolonial studies who examine the uneven, discrepant, and countercurrent experiences of modernity.[4] As Geoff Eley points out, historians have only recently become interested in articulating "modernity's dark side,"[5] the nexus of knowledge and power, culture and catastrophe, that comprises the dialectic of modernity.

Taking my cue from Said's notion of "contrapuntal analysis"[6]—a reading of texts which attempts to draw out and give voice to what is passed over, silenced, or excluded in cultural production—I seek here to articulate this dialectic by reading two key narratives of modernity against one another: Hegel's *The Philosophy of History* and Sebald's *The Rings of Saturn*. I propose that Hegel's narrative of modernity must be examined contrapuntally, by elucidating its imperial-colonial imaginary from the perspective of the ruins that modernity wrought. According to Said, once "Western cultural forms [have been] taken out of the autonomous enclosures in which they have been protected, and placed instead in the dynamic global environment created by imperialism," we can reread the cultural archive "not univocally but contrapuntally, with a simultaneous awareness of both the metropolitan history that is narrated and of those other histories against which (and together with which) the dominating discourse acts" (*CI*, 51). Not unlike Benjamin's idea of "[brushing] history against the grain,"[7] Said proposes that the critic must give an account of the pressures and counterpressures of a text, "[opening] it out both to what went into it and to what the author excluded" (*CI*, 67). In his ambitious and compelling study, Said shows how cultural production—particularly the development of the European novel in the late eighteenth and early nineteenth centuries—is fundamentally connected to empire building, industrial capitalism, and imperialism. For

Hegel, as we will see, it is the figure of the ship which gives the philosophy of world history its forward motion as the ruins of one empire are progressively overcome by the end of one civilization and the birth of another, until the last stage of history—the Germanic nineteenth century—is reached. As an overdetermined figure of the dialectic of modernity, the ship guides the direction of world history by facilitating the spread of the universal as well as signifying the violence of imperial exploitation.

The contrapuntal analysis of Hegel and Sebald that I am proposing differs, at least at first glance, from the readings examined by Said in *Culture and Imperialism* because I do not call upon a non-European author to deconstruct Europe. I show how Sebald—a German expatriate living and writing in Great Britain—critiques the "European geographical centrality" (*CI*, 59) of Hegel's philosophy not only by virtue of his status as a writer outside the nation, to use Seyhan's term,[8] but also by virtue of his privileged status as a writer inside the nation, one who is aware of the stakes of turning the European tradition on itself. Sebald goes to the very heart of the West's imperial imaginary—the seacoast of Great Britain—in order to construct a new, geographically inflected philosophy of history, which is radically contiguous with its places of exploitation, ruin, and destruction. Rather than diminishing the role of the non-European, this contrapuntal reading of Sebald and Hegel actually underscores Said's point that Europe is already divided against itself, internally fractured by and comprised of the very forces that it supposedly believes exist only outside.

I begin my analysis with a brief overview of the conceptual semantics of modernity (or *Neuzeit* in German, literally meaning "new time"), bearing in mind that the word is, first and foremost, a temporal designation; thus, we think about the ruins of a particular temporal structure and the meanings associated with this ruin. After that, I turn to what I see, using Hegel and Sebald, to be the specific new space (*Neuraum*) of this new time: the colonial sphere.[9] The argument that follows has two parts. First, I consider Hegel's *The Philosophy of History* as an emblematic narrative of modernity, one in which the spirit of world history manifests itself through a progressive, geographic overcoming of bygone empires. The story Hegel tells is essentially a seafaring narrative in which the movement of the World Spirit from East to West, from ancient times to the Germanic nineteenth century, proceeds as a nautical voyage of discovery. The second part of my argument focuses on Sebald's *The Rings of Saturn*, taking seriously the German subtitle: "an English pilgrimage."[10] Read contrapuntally, I consider Sebald's travel narrative through the countryside of Suffolk as a postcolonial philosophy of history, which takes the ruins of the British empire as the specific site for examining the dialectic of modernity.

**Spatiotemporal Axes of Modernity, or Hegel and the Sea**

In his study of the semantics of historical time, Koselleck argues that a new time, a new understanding and function of time, was condensed in the saddle-time period between 1780 and 1820. Time then was no longer eschatological, with the future already determined, but was newly imagined as a space of possibility, openness, and unfixedness. Koselleck chooses the terms "space of experience" and "horizon of expectation"[11] to demonstrate how the presence of the past became distinguished from the presence of the future. As both a period and a reconfiguration of temporality, modernity signaled a new time. Concepts like progress, acceleration, and revolution (the latter no longer meaning return but now rupture) were possible only with the invention of a future-oriented view of the passage of time, one that facilitated the idea of one temporal period as quantitatively different from and better than another. This reorientation could take place only when Christian eschatological time, predicated on the definitive and determined arrival of the Second Coming and Judgment Day, was superseded by the unbinding of the future from the past. The idea of progress, certainly the hallmark of modernity, took root when "the expectations that reached out for the future became detached from all that previous experience had to offer."[12] In effect, this shift from an eschatological predetermination to an open space of possibility inaugurated a new approach to the temporalization of events and the practice of writing history. History is no longer the collecting of knowledge but becomes the charting of progress, the designation of development, advancement, and evolution over time.

While Koselleck draws our attention to the temporal axes of modernity, he pays scant attention to its geographic or spatial dimensions, despite his use of terms such as "space of experience" and "horizon of expectation" to articulate this reconfiguration of the world. Said justifiably maintains that "most cultural historians, and certainly all literary scholars, have failed to remark the *geographical* notation, the theoretical mapping and charting of territory that underlies Western fiction, historical writing, and philosophical discourses of the time" (*CI*, 58). Hence, cultural criticism of the beginnings of modern imperialism, which Said situates in the saddle time around the end of the eighteenth century, needs to "affirm both the primacy of geography and an ideology about the control of territory" (*CI*, 78). While Koselleck is right to speak of the newness of time during this period, for critics such as Said, Gilroy, and Appadurai, modernity cannot be understood apart from geography since empire building, industrial capitalism, imperialism, and colonialism make up the spatial matrix of modernity. Gilroy's "black Atlantic" and Appadurai's "global ethnoscapes,"[13] for example, are two important geographic studies of the interconnected, transnational new spaces of modernity that have come in Said's wake.

In his reflections on the ruins of modernity, it is no coincidence, then, that Sebald begins his final novel, *Austerlitz*, with a literal invocation of the complex interplay between new time and new space through the image of a "mighty clock . . . with a hand six feet long . . . blackened by railway soot and tobacco smoke" in Antwerp's Central Station.[14] As the condition of possibility for the other "deities of the nineteenth century—mining, industry, transport, trade, and capital," world standard time, he writes, "reigns supreme among these emblems" (A, 12). The great Belgian railway station functions as one of the dialectical sites for this spatiotemporal reconfiguration of the world, and it emerges as the overdetermined locus of the hopes and catastrophes of modernity:[15] World standard time—a coordination of experience and expectation—was first conceived in England in the 1840s and was adopted globally several decades later as the expression of the progress of modernization.[16] As Sebald shows, this new time—represented in the hall of the Antwerp train station—also bears witness to a new space, as the station was a product of Belgium's colonial expansion in the Congo. Sebald explains:

> Belgium, a little patch of yellowish gray barely visible on the map of the world, spread its sphere of influence to the African continent with its colonial enterprises, when deals of huge proportions were done on the capital markets and raw-material exchanges of Brussels, and the citizens of Belgium, full of boundless optimism, believed their country . . . was about to become a great new economic power . . . It was the personal wish of King Leopold, under whose auspices such apparently inexorable progress was being made, that the money should be used to erect public buildings, which would bring international renown to his aspiring state. (A, 9)

Funded by the Belgian colonial enterprise in the Congo and modeled on the great dome of the Pantheon in Rome, the railway station was opened to an awestruck public in 1905—nearly three decades after the scramble for Africa began in earnest, following an international meeting in Brussels in 1876 to explore the continent and introduce European civilization.[17] As a product of the colonial enterprise, the Belgian railway station is a testament to the dialectic of modernity, both its new time (progress and catastrophe) and its new space (civilization and genocide, from Belgium to the Congo).

Conceived a couple of years before the opening of the first railway line in England in 1825 and several decades before the European powers carved up Africa at the end of the nineteenth century, Hegel articulates the tensions of this new spatiotemporal configuration of modernity in a set of lectures delivered at the

University of Berlin in 1822–23.[18] According to Hegel's narrative, world history is divided into four progressively higher stages based on geography: the "Oriental world," the "Greek world," the "Roman world," and the "Germanic world." Africa is actually the first geographical space that Hegel mentions; however, because the land has "remained impenetrable," "enveloped in the dark color of night," and filled with "the most thoughtless inhumanity and disgusting barbarism" (*V*, 120–21/91–92), the African people are "no historical part of the World" (*V*, 129/99). Hence, Hegel quickly dispenses with them, and they are not part of the narrative procession of world history. The final stage, on the other hand, corresponds to the highest development of the family, civil society, freedom, and the state, having emerged from abstract rights and morality based on mere laws. This four-part formulation provides the geographic basis of the direction and movement of the World Spirit, which proceeds in a singular direction and toward a specific, predetermined goal until universal knowledge and the consciousness of freedom are attained: "World history travels from East to West, for Europe is absolutely the end of history, Asia the beginning" (*V*, 134/103).

In Hegel's account of the progress of spirit, each phase of the world—with the notable exception of the Germanic world—emerges at a particular time, reaches maturity, and eventually comes to its demise. Corresponding to a narrative with a beginning, middle, and end, these worlds function as dialectical counterparts to one another, building on the ruins of bygone empires in a steady progression. Hegel remarks that apprehending the ruins of empire may initially elicit a melancholic sorrow: "When we see the evil, the vice, the destruction that has befallen the most flourishing of kingdoms which the mind of man ever created, we can scarcely avoid being filled with sorrow . . . we retreat into the selfishness that stands on the quiet shore, and, from the safety of a distant gaze, enjoy the massive rubble confusedly hurled." (*V*, 34–35/20–21). This sorrow, however, ends with the realization that the progress of the World Spirit has a purpose, direction, and ultimate goal: the ruins will give rise, in dialectical fashion, to a new life and a higher level of historical development. Hegel explains:

> What traveler among the ruins of Carthage, Palmyra, Persepolis, or Rome has not been stimulated to reflections on the transiency of kingdoms and men, and to sadness at the thought of a vigorous and rich life now departed . . . But the next consideration which allies itself with that of change is the fact that change not only brings dissolution but also involves at the same time the rise of new life . . . Spirit—consuming the envelope of its existence—does not merely pass into another envelope, nor rise rejuvenated from the ashes of its previous form; it comes forth exalted, glorified, a purer spirit. (*V*, 97–98/72–73)

Through a process of ever-increasing glorification and purification, the crumbling of the Oriental world gave rise to the possibility of the Greek world; the destruction of the Greek world gave rise to the Roman world; and, finally, the ruination of the Roman world set in motion the spread of Christianity and the advent of the Germanic world. However, the rise of the Germanic world is "entirely different from that sustained by the Greeks and Romans. For the Christian world is the world of completion; the grand principle of being is realized; consequently, the end of days is fully come" (*v*, 414/342). In other words, the Germanic world will not go to ruin because it represents "the world of completion," a world without temporal extension or historicity. Essentially, it cannot be part of a dialectic. Unlike the other worlds, the three periods of the Germanic world do not correspond to the narrative categories of beginning, middle, and end, or birth, rise, and decline; instead, they correspond, in Hegel's terminology, to the "Kingdoms of the Father, the Son, and the Spirit" (*v*, 417/345). In effect, this progressive narrative of world history ends by overcoming narrativity itself through the eschatological logic of Christianity. Here, we notice a decided tension in Hegel's story: On the one hand, the modernity of the narrative underscores the progress of history and the acceleration of time through the dialectical procession of spirit; on the other hand, the narrative is fundamentally eschatological insofar as it announces the arrival of the end time, the Germanic world of the nineteenth century as the *telos* of history. What we are left with at the end of Hegel's narrative of modernity is pure space—a Germanic empire that extends outward in all directions, something that also explains the primacy that Hegel gives to geography in his conceptualization of the advancement of the World Spirit.

To better understand the centrality of geography in Hegel's philosophy of world history, we need to focus on his comments about seafaring and the expansive, outward spread of the spirit. For him, the figure of the ship and seafaring bear out the progressive advances of world history, both its new time of progress and new space of empire. World-historical people, he argues, are intimately connected to the sea because nations become great colonial powers—and, hence, world-historical—only when they undertake voyages of discovery and conquest. World-historical people have a connection to seafaring and ship travel, whereas nonhistorical people are basically landlocked and condemned to wander on the ground. In his discussion of the history of the Greek and Roman worlds of antiquity, Hegel shows how the Mediterranean Sea played a critical role in the development of these civilizations by facilitating the emergence of a national identity and civil society and, more expansively, by spreading the universal outward. In Hegel's words, "the Mediterranean Sea is the heart of the ancient world, for it is what conditioned and vitalized it. Without it, world history is inconceivable, just as Rome or Athens would be unimaginable without the forum" (*v*, 115/87). In the Oriental world, however, "this stretching out of the sea beyond the limitations of the land is missing" (*v*, 119/91). Hegel is even more explicit in another version of the lectures: "The sea has no meaning for Asia; quite the opposite: The Asian peoples have closed themselves off from the sea." By contrast, "the relationship to the sea in Europe is important . . . [because] only through a connection to the sea can a European state become great."[19]

Africa, treated by Hegel in a couple of pages, is not even a part of the history of the world because it does not have a colonial relationship to the sea.[20] Hegel explains that Africa "has no movement and development to exhibit" (*v*, 129/99) due to the fact that it has remained geographically "impenetrable" (*v*, 120/91). Not only do Africans not undertake voyages of discovery, but the Europeans (at least as of 1823) "have scarcely [been able to penetrate] into the interior of Africa and Asia because travel by land is much more difficult than travel by water" (*v*, 118/90). But more importantly, in Hegel's view, Africa is not a part of world history because it can neither colonize nor be fully colonized. As he says bluntly, Africa is "the unhistorical, undeveloped spirit, still involved in the conditions of mere nature, and which had to be presented here only as on the threshold of the world's history," for it "is no historical part of the world" (*v*, 129/99).

World-historical nations, on the other hand, are characterized by their power to master the expansiveness of the sea and their ability to undertake voyages of conquest. Hegel writes:

> The sea gives us the idea of the indefinite, the unlimited, and the infinite, and insofar as man feels this infinite within himself, he is emboldened to go beyond limits. The sea invites man to conquest and plunder but also to trade and commerce . . . Courage must be contained within trade and bravery is at the same time bound with cleverness . . . the ship—that swan of the sea which cuts the watery plain in agile and arching movements or circles upon it—is an instrument whose invention does the greatest honor to the boldness of man and his faculty of reason. (*v*, 119/91)

Western Europe emerges as the telos of world history because it is here that the highest levels of development and the expansive spread of the World Spirit have been realized through voyages of discovery: "the English have undertaken the weighty responsibility of being the missionaries of *civilization* to the entire world; for their commercial spirit urges them to traverse every sea and land, to form bonds with barbaric peoples, to awaken needs and stimulate industry, and above all to establish the conditions necessary for commerce, namely the relinquishment of violence, the respect for property, and hospitality" (*V*, 538/455). In other words, the English have selflessly assumed the burden of spreading civilization to the dark, inhumane reaches of the globe, turning the barbarians into civilians who will respect property, accommodate European colonists, and facilitate the imperial project of spreading industrial capitalism across the world.

The Germanic world—by which Hegel seems to mean "Western Europe," including England[21]—is the culmination of world history, the product of all the dialectical movements of spirit from East to West, and itself the fount of an outwardly realized, civilizing, colonial mission. He considers the Germanic world to exhibit the highest level of development in world history, and it is here that the World Spirit radiates out from Europe in order to bind distant people to the universal. The history of spirit thus proceeds from the African threshold, making its way from the first world-historical peoples in the East toward the West, from which voyages of discovery and colonial expansion facilitate the spread of the European idea of the Christian state back to the rest of the world. With "this urging of Spirit *outward*"—through "the maritime heroes of Portugal and Spain who found a new way to the East Indies and discovered America," through the spread of Christianity to the New World, and through the discovery of a passage to India by the Cape—the Germanic stage emerges as the universal (*V*, 490/410). World history thus has a direction and finality, culminating in the universality and absoluteness of the imperial European state.

For our purposes, what is significant about Hegel's account is that the philosophy of history is a colonial travel narrative, in which the ruins of past empires merely confirm the progress of spirit and propel its march forward in a seascape that moves from overcoming the temporality of destruction and ruin to the permanent spatiality of a global Christian empire. As a part of a grand narrative that unfolds geographically, the non-European is simply accorded a place outside of world history (as in the case of Africa) or treated as a colonial space reachable by ship and thus to be subsumed into the progress of civilization and the expansion of empire. After all, as Hegel indicates in his discussion of the English in India, "it is the necessary fate of Asiatic empires to be subjugated by the Europeans" (*V*, 179/142). In its essential form, then, *The Philosophy of History* is a geographic narrative of the imperial imaginary and the subjugation of the non-European other. As Said writes in *Culture and Imperialism*, "to think about distant places, to colonize them, to populate or depopulate them: all of this occurs on, about, or because of land. The actual geographical possession of land is what empire in the final analysis is all about" (*CI*, 78). Hegel's narrative of world history is, in the final analysis, all about the spread of empire and the geographic possession of new spaces.

**Sebald and the Sea, or Another English Pilgrimage**

Like Hegel's *The Philosophy of History*, Sebald's *The Rings of Saturn* is organized geographically and highlights the relationship between Europe and the colonial sphere in its historical narrative of modernity. However, unlike Hegel and despite the cosmological expansiveness of the title, Sebald's story takes place in an extraordinarily limited, ostensibly inconsequential space: a walk along a thirty-mile stretch of English coast from Somerleyton to Orford Ness in Suffolk. It is a landscape characterized by remarkable emptiness, with pockets of ruins periodically encountered among long stretches of barrenness and decay: the traces of industrial lands, the decline of shipbuilding and seafaring, the ruins of natural decay, and the destruction caused by the exploitation of nature. Upon being "confronted with the traces of destruction," the narrator tells us that he was stricken by a "paralyzing horror" (*RS*, 3), something that results, a year after his travels in Suffolk, in his hospitalization. It is at this time—just as he begins to write the account of his travels—that the traces of destruction confine him to bed. The travel narrative thus begins with the paradoxical theme of the narrator's immobile body and lack of spectatorship, as he can perceive only what looks to be "a sea of stone or a field of rubble" from his hospital window (*RS*, 5). The narrator likens himself to the ill-fated Gregor Samsa, as he crawls to the window and assumes "the tortured posture of a creature" (*RS*, 5) condemned—not unlike the ruined landscapes he surveyed—to incomprehensibility, death, and oblivion.

Far from the determinate progress of the World Spirit moving from East to West and culminating in the necessity of universal history, Sebald's narrative is a disorienting, compressed, and peripatetic journey through Suffolk, which takes decline and destruction as its organizing principles: "On every new thing there lies already the shadow of annihilation. For the history of every individual, of every social order, indeed of the whole world, does not describe an ever-widening, more and more wonderful arc, but rather follows a course which, once the meridian is reached, leads without fail down into the dark" (*RS*, 24). As we move from Somerleyton to Orford Ness via Southwold, Dunwich, Middleton, and Woodbridge, the English coast opens up onto a world-historical geography of decline and catastrophe, something that, at first sight, seems vaguely Hegelian in scope. But upon closer inspection, the novel's explosion of geographic confinement, coupled with the narrator's embodied, unsystematic, and contingent encounters with the ruins of modernity, turns the travel narrative into a philosophy of history with a decidedly anti-Hegelian thrust. As Beck has astutely observed, "this is not a dialectical movement that trundles toward some telos of understanding; it is a particular kind of destabilizing orderly disorder that trawls time and space . . . [it] does not build toward an organized structure of control but to further instability and disappointment."[22] The disembodied progress of Hegel's spirit gives way to a radically embodied, historically contingent walk along the coast of Suffolk. What Sebald's narrator encounters on the ground is a function of chance, the product of what happens to be left of the grandiose—and grandly catastrophic—processes of industrialization, modernization, and colonization.[23]

The story opens with the narrator arriving by train at Somerleyton from Norwich, observing the desolate coastal landscape, punctuated by the remains of wind pumps, windmills, and old manor houses. As he wanders through Somerleyton Hall, describing the history of the manor house and its former owner, Morton Peto, an industrialist, he encounters a store of colonial objects (African masks, spears, safari trophies, engravings of Boer War battles) and reflects that one "is not quite sure whether one is in a country house in Suffolk or some kind of no-man's-land, on the shores of the Arctic Ocean or in the heart of the dark continent. Nor can one readily say which decade or century it is, for many ages are superimposed here and coexist" (*RS*, 36). A couple of pages later, the narrator strikes up a conversation with the estate's gardener, a man who tells him that during the Second World War, "every evening I watched the bomber squadrons heading out over Somerleyton, and night after night, before I went to sleep, I pictured in my mind's eye the German cities going up in flames, the firestorms setting the heavens alight, and the survivors rooting about in the ruins . . . Braunschweig and Würzburg, Wilhelmshaven, Schweinfurt, Stuttgart, Pforzheim, Düren, and dozens more. In that way, I got to know the whole country by heart; you might even say it was burnt into me" (*RS*, 38–39). It is in these two passages, for the first time in the narrative, that another geography opens up, one that stretches far beyond Suffolk County and links present-day England with the dialectic of modernity: Somerleyton is connected to both the colonial enterprise in Africa and the firebombing of German cities during the war.

As the narrator continues his journey, this other geography will impose itself over and over again, connecting the thirty miles of coastline to the catastrophic underside of world history. Not only will Suffolk become connected to Belgium, various German cities, and "the dark continent" via the massacres in the Congo and the scramble for Africa, but it will also become connected to the Dutch East Indies via the sugar dynasties, South America via the Amazon Trading Company, Bengal via the Opium Wars, and many other places in the imperial imaginary. As a kind of spatial counterpoint to Bloch's "simultaneity of the non-simultaneous"(*Gleichzeitigkeit des Ungleichzeitigen*),[24] we might call Sebald's modernist geography the contiguity of the noncontiguous, the *Gleichräumigkeit des Ungleichräumigen*, to emphasize the spatial coexistence and connectedness of these noncontemporaneous and noncontiguous geographies. Sebald is attempting to retrieve the many different geographies coexisting with and historically impacted in the Suffolk coast. In effect, his narrative does two things here. First, he is endowing place with a layered temporality, not unlike what Koselleck calls, in another context, "Zeitschichten" (time layers), a particularly modernist understanding of the simultaneity of multiple, coexisting, asynchronous temporalities and spatialities.[25] And second, Sebald is creating a new cultural geography, one which reconnects the thirty miles of Suffolk coastline with the spatially expansive, colonial-imperial project of modernity.

Unlike the inexorability of the Hegelian dialectic of world history, Sebald's novel represents a kind of "multilayered," "multivoiced," and "multispatial dialectic"[26] that takes noncontemporaneity and noncontiguity as its organizing principles. There is no triumphal finality in Sebald's novel, only an attempt to recognize and comprehend the destruction wrought by the world-historical powers through the European colonial project. In Sebald's multilayered and multispatial dialectic, Somerleyton is connected to the spaces of the Arctic shore, the African continent, and the firebombed cities of Germany, thereby rendering it contiguous with geographies that are ostensibly noncontiguous and synchronic with histories that are ostensibly nonsynchronic. Far from undertaking any kind of voyage of discovery or seafaring adventure leading to foreign lands and the subjugation of native peoples, Sebald's narrator never leaves England; instead, he walks along the shore of the origin, the places of departure for an empire that at one time reached out, embraced, and conquered much of the earth.

The results of this remapping of colonial space are apparent in the two chapters dedicated to Southwold, a coastal town dominated by a giant lighthouse. Upon arriving in this town, the narrator climbs up to "Gunhill" and gazes out to sea. Invoking the aesthetic illusion of an accessible past, Sebald's narrator says: "I felt as if I were in a deserted theater, and I should not have been surprised if a curtain had suddenly risen before me and on the proscenium I had beheld, say, the 28th of May 1672—that memorable day when the Dutch fleet appeared offshore from out of the drifting mists, with the bright morning light behind it, and opened fire on the English ships in Sole Bay." He goes on to describe the way in which the townspeople might have experienced the spectacle at sea from the safety of the shore: "As the battle continued, the powder magazines exploded, and some of the tarred hulls burned down to the waterline; the scene would have been shrouded in an acrid, yellowish-black smoke creeping across the entire bay and masking the combat from view" (RS, 76). Not unlike his account of the firebombing of Hamburg,[27] the narrator suggests that the accounts of eyewitnesses are actually "unreliable" and the pictorial representations mere "figments of the imagination" (*RS*, 76) because they "fail to convey any true impression of how it must have been to be on board one of these ships" (*RS*, 77). A different kind of representation—and, therefore, a different kind of viewing and narration—is required, perhaps an "artificial and synoptic view" of the totality of the destruction or a kind of modernist realism, which highlights the tension between the realist fantasy and the modernist narrative.[28]

To accomplish this, Sebald creates a narrative form in which his character is connected to the catastrophe through its ruins in the present, and inside the processes of describing through the artificiality and contingency of his perspective, limited in geographic and historical terms. This narrative form does not create a spectator who observes a catastrophe from the sidelines and attempts to recount what happened from an outside, objective, or transcendental perspective.[29] Sebald not only refuses to create a surrogate spectator; he also refuses to lift the curtain on the past. As the narrator declares with regard to "the representation of history," "it requires a falsification of perspective. We, the survivors, see everything from above, see everything at once, and still we do not know how it was" (*RS*, 125). Even if we stand atop the greatest monument and look down, the past cannot be encapsulated or recreated as it really was. The narrator continues: "Are we standing on a mountain of death? Is that our ultimate vantage point? Does one really have the much-vaunted historical overview from such a position?" (*RS*, 125). For Sebald, there is no "historical overview" or Hegelian progress or World Spirit. Instead, the narrator wanders on the ground among the ruins at the edge of the sea, trying to connect them—in a most unsystematic way—to the violence of modernity.

In an interview, Sebald refers to Blumenberg's "emphatic configuration in which shipwreck at sea is set beside the uninvolved spectator on dry land"[30] as a fundamentally flawed epistemological and ethical stance. Unlike Hegel, who maintains a disembodied position of detached spectatorship to observe and even enjoy the ruins of empire "on the quiet shore . . . from the safety of a distant gaze" (*V*, 35/21), confident that the end of history will bring the universality of the Germanic world, Sebald creates an embodied narrator who is contingently and yet intimately connected to the ruins he encounters on his journey. With regard to this desire to observe the catastrophic from the safety of distance, solid ground, and enjoyment, Sebald says: "It is certainly a question of one of the fundamental conditions of artistic work itself: that one stands on the edge of the catastrophe, looking and reporting how it is, how it was. It is obvious that this results in a certain moral problematic for the author or spectator. In this constellation, one warms one's hands on the misfortune of others, one somehow feels happy—although this would never be confessed—that one was not there."[31]

In replacing Hegel's disembodied, relentlessly progressing World Spirit with the corporeality and fragility of the narrator's peripatetic journey, Sebald negates the safety of external spectatorship in order to evoke the buried horrors contained in the noncontiguous geographies of the Suffolk landscape.

The narrator remarks that although "it has never been determined which of the two parties in the naval battle fought off Southwold to extort trading advantages emerged victorious," the English were able to commence, on that day, "the sovereignty of the sea" (*RS*, 78). This sovereignty of the seas, which Hegel would make the centerpiece of his geographic explanation of world-historical peoples, was the condition of possibility of the British empire, whose power and dominance are detectable today only by its ruins. Here, Sebald is evoking the other history and geography of the sea journey: not Hegel's ship as a "swan of the sea . . . an instrument whose invention does the greatest honor to the boldness of man and his faculty of reason" (*V*, 119/91), but rather the ship as a trope for empire and its central role in reconfiguring the space of the world.[32] As Gilroy points out, "the ship provides a chance to explore the articulations between the discontinuous histories of England's ports, its interfaces with the wider world. Ships also refer us back to the middle passage, to the half-remembered micropolitics of the slave trade and its relationship to both industrialization and modernization."[33]

For Sebald, the contiguity of the noncontiguous is both a method of preserving historiographic complexity and an expression of the dialectic of modernity. What this means for the temporal field is that multiple, nonsimultaneous histories are considered as if they were simultaneous; for the spatial field, it means that multiple, noncontiguous geographies are linked together as if they were contiguous. This is because the postcolonial philosophy of history must start by reconnecting the noncontiguous geographies and nonsimultaneous histories, however tentatively, in order to expose the underside of modernity and the consequences of colonialism.[34] Sericulture, for example, was not only a vital part of British industrialization and England's ascendancy as a global power; it was also connected to the economies of warfare, race science, and theories of degeneration—all of which were betrayed by the contiguity of the noncontiguous. Sebald's novel takes this logic as its organizing principle: the postcolonial philosophy of history forges connections that have long since been lost or forgotten.

This is perhaps nowhere more evident than in the chapter explicitly devoted to the so-called scramble for Africa. During his second night in Southwold, the narrator falls asleep while watching a BBC documentary on the meeting between Joseph Conrad and Roger Casement, a British consul who brought the crimes committed by the Belgians against the native people in the Congo to public attention in 1903 (*RS*, 127). The narrator tries to piece together Conrad's family story, giving particular attention to his stay in Suffolk and his work for a trading company called the Société Anonyme Belge pour le Commerce du Haut-Congo, and as the commander of "a steamer that plied the upper reaches of the Congo" (*RS*, 116). In accordance with Hegel's depiction of the African continent as "impenetrable," the Congo was then indicated by nothing but "a white patch on the map of Africa" with no railway lines, no roads, and no towns: "cartographers would often embellish such empty spaces with drawings of exotic beasts, a roaring lion or a crocodile with gaping jaws" (*RS*, 117). Under the direction of Leopold II, king of Belgium, the Congo was ruthlessly exploited, with enormous profits for European trading companies built on exterminating or enslaving the indigenous peoples. It is here that Sebald's narrator reflects most pointedly on the dialectic of modernity: the goal was "to open up the last part of earth to have remained hitherto untouched by the blessings of civilization. The aim, said King Leopold, was to break through the darkness in which whole peoples still dwelt, and to mount a crusade in order to bring this glorious century of progress to the point of perfection" (*RS*, 118). Sebald thus unmasks the dark side of progress, civilization, and Enlightenment in the colonial imaginary.

In calling his novel "an English pilgrimage," Sebald consciously places it within the history of the colonial imaginary as well as in dialogue with the ideology of the mission of civilization. But unlike the expansive, world-historical pilgrimages of conquest undertaken in the Congo under the direction of Leopold II or those that departed the Suffolk coast for the East Indies, the Amazon river basin, China, and countless other places, Sebald is creating a pilgrimage of memory, one undertaken by a German expatriate in England who attempts to reconnect the space of the present with the horrors of the past—in effect, to render the ruins of empire contiguous with the noncontiguous spaces of imperial exploitation. In this respect, Sebald's novel is a dialectical counterpart to the outward spread of the Hegelian world spirit; it represents a journey in reverse, one which never departs from the ruins of the English coast, while always being long since departed. In this regard, Sebald consciously fashions himself as a postcolonial critic, following in the footsteps of thinkers such as Arendt[35] or of novelists such as Hans Christoph Buch and Peter Schneider.[36]

For Sebald, the figure of Conrad mediates between Hegel's expansive philosophy of world history and Sebald's own English pilgrimage. Conrad's *Heart of Darkness*, arguably the most enduring and horrific novel of the exterminatory violence of the European colonial mission in the Congo, was published in 1899, shortly after Conrad's own voyage to Léopoldville and Stanley Falls.[37] Narrated by an Englishman named Marlow to a small group of his compatriots aboard a British vessel anchored at the mouth of the Thames, Conrad's novel begins with a reflection on the expansive possibilities of seafaring and the distant geographies that became part of the European imperial project. Marlow tells us that the Thames is "an interminable waterway . . . leading to the uttermost ends of the earth" (HD, 7–8), with ships that explore the world over. Very much in line with Hegel's glorification of the ship as the means of bringing courage and reason to the far reaches of the world, the vocation of seafaring is connected to "the dreams of men, the seed of commonwealths, the germ of empires" (HD, 8). As Marlow relates the story of his trip to the Congo, "the glories of exploration" (HD, 11) means filling in the "blank" spaces on the map of the world, of penetrating the "darkness" and bringing the bounty of "progress" to all (HD, 12–13). Once again, the new time of modernity—its ideology of expansive progress, the forward movement of the civilizing mission—is explicitly connected with the new space of modernity, the colonial sphere.

And it is precisely here that Conrad, like Sebald, will reveal the violent underside of the dialectic of modernity. Marlow links the European "pilgrimage" to the interior of Africa with the nightmares of slavery and genocide: just before telling his compatriots about slaves starved and kept in chain gangs, Marlow says that his journey "was like a weary pilgrimage amongst hints for nightmares" (HD, 17). While the pilgrimage reveals the human, economic, and natural exploitation of the Congo, it simultaneously maintains faith in the civilizing process. After all, the "pilgrims," as Marlow calls them repeatedly, are there to establish order: "each station [along the river] should be a beacon on the road towards better things, a centre for trade of course but also for humanizing, improving, instructing" (HD, 34). The "pilgrims" believe that they are "taking possession of an accursed inheritance," of land that is already theirs and must only be retaken, improved, and saved. Indeed, as Casarino points out, " 'pilgrimage' is associated with some of the most brutal chapters of imperialist exploitation" in *Heart of Darkness*.[38] Even on his deathbed, Marlow comforts Kurtz—the architect of the "great plans" realized through exterminatory violence—by telling him that his "success in Europe is assured in any case" (HD, 65). In effect, the history of the pilgrimage would be written by the victors. Sebald's English pilgrimage is an attempt to turn this victory on its head, to travel among the ruins of empire and salvage the knowledge of destruction before the onset of oblivion.

Let me conclude. Although a travel narrative, Sebald's *The Rings of Saturn* is not about traveling to distant lands or even about leaving England; instead, read as a philosophy of history, it is about linking the ruins of modernity—emblematically encountered along the eroding Suffolk coast—with the historical spaces of imperial exploitation and, thereby, halting the forward-moving oblivion called progress. Sebald's narrator is intimately connected to the objects he is describing, so much so that they run together as a radically unsystematic accumulation of detail, digression, and chance. The narrative does not finally lead anywhere; instead, it opens up onto a new consciousness of the geography of modernity, one in which the faraway colonial spaces become reconnected to the decaying topographies of the English coast.

This novel, like so many of Sebald's other works, is a meditation on the physical, conceptual, and narrative ruins of modernity and its empires. The "trash of history" (*Abfall der Geschichte*), to use Benjamin's phrase,[39] includes exploited lands, nameless victims, sunken ships, sailing logbooks, navigational instruments, model ships, crumbling piers, colonial relics, and remains of the shipbuilding industry. The novel is also a meditation on the ruin of certain world-historical narratives organized according to the progressive advancement of technology, industry, or sea power. *The Rings of Saturn* betrays the ruins that have been erased or forgotten in the Hegelian philosophy of history: in its "contiguity of the non-contiguous," Sebald's narrative exposes the "refuse" of world history, the ruins and trash, the leftover remains of empire and domination. It is not just a Benjaminian project of "brushing history against the grain," for Sebald is also dissecting the systematicity of the Hegelian project, particularly its developmental narrative of unstoppable progress, by showing how the ruins of new time (*Neuzeit*) are fundamentally connected to the colonial-imperial new space (*Neuraum*) of modernity. In reconnecting Suffolk with the expansive, colonial geography of modernity, Sebald writes the other history of European empire, beginning where Hegel left off and with what he left out: the contiguity of England with the noncontiguous, non-European spaces. Hegel's geographic imaginary is the starting point, even if Suffolk is never explicitly invoked in *The Philosophy of History*. Sebald is not simply anti-Hegelian; he tracks the ruins of modernity precisely because of the success of the project. Considered contrapuntally, *The Rings of Saturn* is both the revocation of Hegel's philosophy of world history and its horrible underside.

## Notes

1. See in this volume Huyssen, "Authentic Ruins."
2. Perhaps the most famous image of the dialectic of modernity is Benjamin's angel of history, who perceives catastrophic destruction and the accumulation of wreckage in place of the progress of history. Benjamin, "Theses on the Philosophy of History," 257–58.
3. The seminal proponent of modernity as an unfinished project of the ideals of the Enlightenment is Habermas. See his *The Philosophical Discourse of Modernity: Twelve Lectures*. The seminal proponent of modernity as engendering ever more subtle and dangerous mechanisms for monitoring individuals and regulating society is Foucault. Among other works, see *Discipline and Punish*.

4. See, for example, Appadurai, *Modernity at Large*; Said, *Culture and Imperialism*; and Gilroy, *The Black Atlantic*.
5. Eley, "German History and the Contradictions of Modernity," 96.
6. Said, *Culture and Imperialism*, 66–67. All further references to this work will be cited parenthetically in the text as *CI*, followed by the page number.
7. Benjamin, "Theses on the Philosophy of History," 257.
8. Seyhan, *Writing Outside the Nation*.
9. This corresponds in some ways to the argument Bhabha makes in the concluding chapter of *The Location of Culture*, esp. 236–56.
10. Sebald, *The Rings of Saturn*. Quotations come from the English translation. All further references to this work will be cited parenthetically in the text as *RS*, followed by the page number.
11. Koselleck, *Futures Past*, 268.
12. Ibid., 279.
13. Appadurai, *Modernity at Large*, 48–65.
14. Sebald, *Austerlitz*, 8. Quotations come from the English translation. All further references to this work will be cited parenthetically in the text as *A*, followed by the page number.
15. In my *Mobile Modernity*, I map German-Jewish intellectual history onto the railway system in order to use cultural geography to examine various iterations of the dialectic of modernity.
16. At the end of the nineteenth century, Greenwich was chosen as the zero meridian for the purpose of dividing the earth into twenty-four time zones, establishing the precise length of the day, and standardizing time across the globe. Greenwich effectively represented the spatiotemporal locus of modernity. For a discussion of this, see Kern, *The Culture of Time and Space*, 10–15. With respect to Sebald, see Eshel's discussion in "Against the Power of Time."
17. For a compelling analysis of the geographic and human consequences of this meeting and the subsequent division of the African continent by the European powers, see Mudimbe, *The Idea of Africa*, esp. chapter 4.
18. Hegel, *Vorlesungen über die Philosophie der Weltgeschichte* (1970), which is based on an 1840 reconstruction by Karl Hegel. The English translation is *The Philosophy of History*. I have consulted the English translation but have opted to give my own translations of Hegel throughout. All further references to this work will be cited parenthetically in the text as *V*, followed first by the page number from the German edition and then by the page number from the English translation.
19. Hegel, *Vorlesungen über die Philosophie der Weltgeschichte* (1996), 111, my translation. Although differing from the standard edition published in 1970, this edition is based upon a new reconstruction of the lectures, using three sets of lecture notes from the winter semester 1822–23.
20. For a critical assessment of Hegel's relationship to colonialism and views on Africa, see Bernasconi, "Hegel at the Court of Ashanti."
21. According to Taylor, "the Germanic world" does not refer to Germany per se, but rather to the "barbarians who swarmed over the Roman empire at its end and founded the

new nations of Western Europe. There is no particular chauvinism in this use of the word German." Taylor, *Hegel*, 398.

22. Beck, "Reading Room," 82.
23. Over the past few years, the literature on Sebald's journeys and his reworking of the genre of travel literature has blossomed. Some key studies are Theisen, "Prose of the World," and Zilcosky, "Sebald's Uncanny Travels" and "Lost and Found."
24. Bloch, *Erbschaft dieser Zeit*, 125.
25. Koselleck, *Zeitschichten*. The German word for history, *Geschichte*, contains the word for layer (*Schicht*), which can refer to class strata or spatial layers.
26. Bloch, *Erbschaft dieser Zeit*, 125–26, my translation.
27. Sebald, *On the Natural History of Destruction*. The original is *Luftkrieg und Literatur.*
28. For a discussion of how Sebald portrays the reality of the firebombing through decidedly modernist literary strategies, see my " 'What a Synoptic and Artificial View Reveals.' " For another account of Sebald's spectatorship, see Hell, "The Angel's Enigmatic Eyes."
29. In her discussion of Adorno's injunction that "the permanent threat of catastrophe no longer permits any detached watching," Hell points out that the position of the realist narrator or uninvolved bystander has its roots in the bourgeois theater but is no longer a viable option for representing the catastrophes of modernity. See Hell, "Ruins Travel."
30. Blumenberg, *Shipwreck with Spectator*, 10.
31. Sebald, "Katastrophe mit Zuschauer" (interview with Andrea Köhler), 52.
32. For a fascinating study of the ship as the "heterotopia par excellence" of modernity, see Casarino, *Modernity at Sea*, esp. 11–17.
33. Gilroy, *The Black Atlantic*, 17.
34. Such a strategy can also be found throughout the classic literature of postcolonialism, including, for example, Said, *Culture and Imperialism*; Bhabha, *The Location of Culture*; Spivak, *The Post-Colonial Critic*: and Appadurai, *Modernity at Large*.
35. See Arendt, *The Origins of Totalitarianism*, 186–97. In a subsection of this work called "The Phantom World of the Dark Continent," Arendt describes the colonial enterprises of Europeans and the genealogy of race-based political movements. Referring to Conrad's *Heart of Darkness*, she argues that the origins of "superfluous" men and thereby the roots of totalitarianism were to be found in the catastrophes of the European colonial projects in Africa during the nineteenth century.
36. For a discussion of these novelists and the history of German postcolonial literature, see Lützeler, *Postmoderne und postkoloniale deutschsprachige Literatur*. An extensive body of literature on German colonialism has developed in recent years. Some of the key studies are Berman, *Enlightenment or Empire*; Zantop, *Colonial Fantasies*; and Friedrichsmeyer, Lennox, and Zantop, eds., *The Imperialist Imagination*.
37. Conrad, *Heart of Darkness*. All further references to this work will be cited parenthetically in the text as *HD*, followed by the page number.
38. Casarino, *Modernity at Sea*, 23.
39. Benjamin, "Konvolut N," 577, my translation.

JON BEASLEY-MURRAY

# 12

## VILCASHUAMÁN

*Telling Stories in Ruins*

There is no such thing as an ancient ruin, for the ruin is always a modern concept. Ruination and modernity go hand in hand: the modern displaces the ancient and marks it as irredeemably part of the past precisely by construing it as ruined. Ruins are the site of what we have left behind. But they remain front and center, for modernity occasions a sometimes anxious reflection on the conditions and effects of progress, on this process of temporal displacement for which the ruin serves as memento mori. Modernity creates the ruin as something to be discarded but also to be read, its story obsessively recapitulated. We moderns construct and interpret ruins as judgment on the past and warning for the future. "Men moralize among ruins," observes Benjamin Disraeli, "or, in the throng and tumult of successful cities, recall past visions of urban desolation for prophetic warning. London is a modern Babylon; Paris has aped imperial Rome, and may share its catastrophe."[1] A sign of modernity's success and vitality is that past civilizations are in ruins all around; but these ruins also remind us that there can be no guarantee that today's proud edifices will not, in turn, crumble and decay. Ruins demonstrate that whole cultures, just like the lives of mortals, are transient. Hence they are invented by cultures that feel their own transience. And no culture feels more transient than the American.

Though the Americas have been envisaged as the New World, and despite Goethe's assertion that "America, you have it better / Than our old continent; / You have no ruined castles / And no primordial stones,"[2] in fact the hemisphere has more than its share of ruins. This should be no surprise: modernity was after all abruptly conceived in the encounter between Old and New Worlds and built upon the ruins of the civilizations encountered by Spanish conquistadors. The traces of Spanish (and Portuguese, British, and French) imperial grandeur are now themselves ruined, and where there are no ruins easily to hand, often they have been built from scratch or substitutes have rapidly been found. From Hearst Castle or Collegiate Gothic—with steps made of soft stone so they wear down quickly—to the dinosaur bones collected by tycoons such as Andrew Carnegie, as the United States became the dominant world power at the end of the nineteenth century and in the first decades of the twentieth, it increasingly sought out its own ruins. Frequently, those ruins were south of the border: this was also the heyday of a burgeoning archaeology, and the discovery of "lost" cities in rain forests and remote valleys throughout the hemisphere. Today ruins are big business—think of Tikal or Tenochtitlán—even as big business leaves its own ruins behind, from the Rust Belt to reclaimed factories.

In this essay I focus on what is now the small and apparently insignificant Peruvian village of Vilcashuamán, built in and around the ruins of what was once a major Inca site. But its lasting importance for a range of political projects has been underlined and reinvoked by a series of stories and discourses told by the Incas themselves, Spanish conquistadors, republican nationalists, and even Maoist guerrillas in a somewhat bizarre dialogue with the contemporary state. Residues of these stories linger on, and Vilcashuamán's ruins carry traces of the distinct pasts that they narrate, of their continuities sustained by the material presence of the ruins themselves, and of their discontinuities and dislocations. I trace how the ruins in this quiet corner of Ayacucho Province shed light on the pasts that they have served to memorialize or represent. I am interested in the ways in which these ruins have provided the occasion for memorialization; in how they conjure up multilayered, sometimes contradictory narratives of American modernity; in what they tell us of the sacrifices and silences inherent in the modernization process; in the traces of alternative modernities that they preserve, however faintly; and in the diverse readings of history that they offer. Above all I am interested in what these ruins tell us about power and sovereignty in American modernity, and in the relationship between their brute materiality and the more tenuous stories that aim to secure a power that is no less brutal. For to talk of ruins is always to talk of power: ruins inspire and legitimate narratives of power, and sometimes also of counterpower. But perhaps our task—the task of what I term posthegemony—might be their denarrativization, their further ruination. Perhaps these ruins are not yet ruined enough.

**History, Narrative, Posthegemony**

My three guiding concepts are history, narrative, and posthegemony. First, the ruin emerges from and sustains a particular way of thinking historically, even as it undercuts the very notion of history that it establishes. Ruins are presented as foundation, and ruination as necessary clearing out to enable the birth of the new. Ruins legitimate and ground the structures that are built upon them. Sometimes this foundation is literal, as when the stones of earlier constructions are built over or recycled for new buildings. But this recycling threatens to undercut the linearity of the history that it otherwise anchors: if one civilization can fall to ruin, then so perhaps can—or must—each subsequent one. And the succeeding cycles of construction and ruination may suggest that all progress is in danger of being reclaimed by the desert, the jungle, and the creeping threat of what Walter Benjamin terms "irresistible decay."[3] Ruins incarnate the persistence of the past as much as its obsolescence and the possibility that the past may catch up with the present, returning us to some new stone age or reinvigorated barbarism. They can imply that all talk of progress is but another unfounded story. (We should not forget that in Spanish, the language of most of the discourses I will be discussing, *historia* can mean a fictional story, as well as supposedly factual history.)

There is another tie between ruination and history. If the ruin is a concept invented and reinvented by cultures at particular times and in particular places, we can map that concept's changing fortunes—perhaps even its contemporary ruination—through time. Benjamin famously notes "the baroque cult of the ruin."[4] But it is in Romanticism that ruins come into their own. Think of Shelley's "Ozymandias" or Wordsworth's "Tintern Abbey," to take but two examples of the romantic obsession with these temporal remnants, history become nature. Still, it is not as though the romantics treated the objects of their obsession with great respect: Byron, for instance, notoriously inscribed his name in the stone of the Temple of Poseidon at Sounion. Such cavalier attitudes changed over the nineteenth century, as ruins became the object of scientific study with the invention of archaeology as a discipline. In the early twentieth century, burgeoning popular interest made celebrities out of figures such as Howard Carter, the excavator of Tutankhamen's tomb. Then the First and the Second World Wars produced ruins of their own, some of which, such as Coventry Cathedral or Berlin's Kaiser Wilhelm Memorial Church, were preserved as an exercise in public memorialization. Today ruins are financial investments for collectors and the heritage industry alike, as well as a matter of political controversy. The claims of literature or science upon the ruin are disputed—in very different ways—by commerce and mass tourism, and by the descendants of those whose cultures modernity ruined. In short, the concept of the ruin should itself be historicized, by examining the different stories that it provokes or enables at different times.

Second, ruins inspire narrative. This is the obverse of Benjamin's observation that "allegories are, in the realm of thoughts, what ruins are in the realm of things."[5] As should already be evident in the stress that I am putting on the stories told about them, ruins are incessantly seen as pointing beyond themselves, to some absent totality. That totality has then to be narrated. Stories fill in the gaps left by the ruin's material remains, to tell the tale of the splendor that once was and the catastrophe or slow decline that led to its downfall. Ruins are not themselves immediately legible: they have to be spoken for, interpreted, and supplemented by a guided tour, a cautionary inscription, an informative notice, a historical reenactment. These narratives restore the ruins before our very eyes, allowing us to imagine them, once again, complete, and to understand and learn from the process that led to their current dilapidated state. Hence we have a paradox: though stubbornly material, the mute remainder of a culture whose representatives may now be missing, and though they do not come with a narrative of their own, ruins have consistently to be ventriloquized. Narrative accretes around them, purporting to complete them. It is as though we can never see the trees for the forest.

The stories that ruins are made to tell are almost always stories of power. Precisely in their fragmentariness, ruins evoke the sublime. The narratives that claim to complete the ruin can sketch out a totality all the more awe inspiring in that it is a work of the imagination. To quote Benjamin yet again, "in the ruins of great buildings the idea of the plan speaks more impressively than in lesser buildings, however well preserved they are."[6] The discrepancy between the ruin, with its absences plainly present, and the totality whose presence is felt through those absences, magnifies still further the grandeur of the absent whole. In a ruined abbey whose roof is no more, one can imagine the walls reaching up to the skies. (Think also of the endless columns of light that temporarily replaced New York's World Trade Center towers.) There is no limit to the sublime dimensions of the edifice that ruins imply. In evoking dreams of totality and sublimity, ruins have been read as particularly vivid allegories of power and sovereignty—and their vicissitudes. Shelley's "Ozymandias," for instance, relates the tale of the toppled remains of a vast sculpture of power, on whose pedestal is inscribed: "My name is Ozymandias, king of kings: / Look on my works, ye Mighty, and despair!"[7] The mighty could now be tempted to perceive in the desolation of this broken monument the temporary nature of even the most overweening despotism. But the fact that Ozymandias's declaration, however ruined, endures even though the civilization over which he presided has faded without a trace, could also suggest that the signs of transcendence prevail over the most calamitous of social and natural catastrophes.

Third, is this chain of associations that links ruins to hegemonic projects an inevitable one? Can we forestall the narrative seduction that seems so relentlessly to convert material fragment into ineffable sovereignty? In what follows I offer a posthegemonic analysis of American ruins. By posthegemony I mean two things: first, that discourses that aim to secure hegemony no longer have the purchase that they once had, now that we inhabit a cynical, postideological age. In Žižek's formulation, we "know very well" what we are doing, "but still, [we] are doing it."[8] Ruins can no longer be relied upon to serve as the material supports of an intangible totality that we "know very well" to be impossible. Their legitimating power is weaker than ever before, in part because of the Babel-like confusion of competing discourses that have built up around them. Rather than securing hegemony, ruins are now troubling reminders of an alternative modernity that the dominant would rather ignore. They are mute witnesses rather than vital points of articulation. In these posthegemonic times, ruins function more as a fragment of an inexpressive real: an excrescence that indicates the absences and exclusions of social and political projects that fail to achieve even the illusion of hegemonic fullness. To understand the persistence of social order (the problem to which the concept of hegemony sets out to respond), we should turn to other concepts, such as affect and habit. But why assume that these other forces were not also operative in a preceding era in which hegemony appeared to offer some explanation? Why concede the notion that hegemonic projects were ever viable or effective? Second, then, by posthegemony I also mean a radical skepticism toward all claims for hegemony as an explanatory concept, even before the advent of contemporary cynical consciousness. Drawing on the lessons learned from our current epoch, in which hegemonic projects clearly no longer convince, I question the efficacy of the narratives spun around "primordial stones" in the past. Perhaps the stories that ruins provoked were never really hegemonic, though they may have offered a simulacrum of something like hegemony. Indeed, the ruin offers a case study for the failures of hegemony, for its stubbornly material limits. These stories of power soon became ruined themselves, while there were always other ways of inhabiting or cohabiting with material ruination, and the affects and habits that it induces. This is the underside of modernity's grand claims. And in archaeological spirit, to reach that underside I will scrape off layers of discourse to reveal the ruins in themselves.

### Vilcashuamán

I start with a story of my own. Having some time to spare in Vilcashuamán, Ayacucho, highland Peru, I climbed the pyramid that looms over the village. I was with a group of anthropologists and aid workers, most of whom had business to discuss with the local authorities. During a lull in proceedings, a young NGO employee and I made our way up the pyramid, then sat and looked at the ragged little town below, gently fending off the attentions of the inquisitive children who had followed us up the stone steps. Not much was going on that day in the village—or indeed, it seemed at first sight, on any other day. But Vilcashuamán (also known simply as Vilcas) was once a significant Inca cultural and administrative center, occupying a strategic location at the intersection of the trade routes that crisscrossed the Inca empire: it was where the road from Cuzco to the Pacific met the empire's main north-south highway. Moreover, according to the Spanish chronicler Pedro Cieza de León's report of native accounts, the town was at the geographical midpoint of the Tawantisuyu, the Inca empire, "for they state that it is the same distance from Quito to Vilcas as from Vilcas to Chile, the limits of their empire."[9] Vilcas is now a town full of ruins, though one might also say that the place is a set of ruins that enclose a town, as it can be hard to judge where the ruins end and the town starts. Houses and shops nestle up against or are perched upon Inca walls and stones, and are themselves made of this same recycled material. As a result, the site is, in the words of Gasparini and Margolies, in an "advanced state of destruction and deformation."[10] Vilcas remains, however, undeniably impressive, in part because everywhere you go in the village, you are up against and on top of the ruins. There is no measured distance between contemporary life and sacrosanct historical artifact: no ropes, no fences marking off the museal from the everyday. The ruins of Vilcashuamán are fully if sparsely inhabited; they show no signs of their exceptionality. In John Hemming's words, they conjure up a scene of desolation, "Vilcashuamán is now a small village, remote on its hill-top, perched on the ruins of the great Inca city whose temples have been pillaged for building blocks, and surrounded by rolling, hilly country with few trees and little population."[11] History seems to have passed it by, to have set it free from whatever stories it once inspired. Certainly, when I had learned that I was going to Vilcas for the day, I had had no idea I would end up climbing a pyramid.

Indeed, these are hardly the most famous ruins in Peru and are far from being the most visited, meriting at best a couple of lines in the guidebooks. Rather, that honor goes to Machu Picchu, perhaps the foremost tourist attraction in all South America, which attracts around 450,000 visitors a year and has

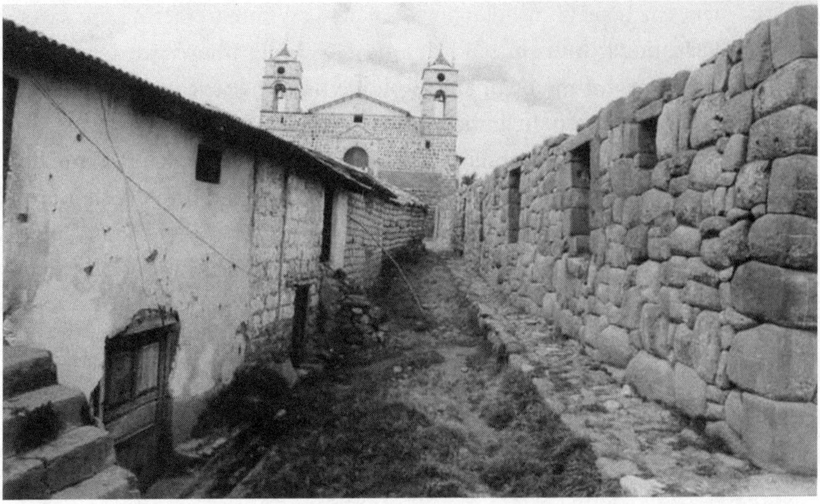

1. Vilcashuamán. An Inca wall is to the right, village houses are to the left, and the colonial church is in the background. Photo by John Servayge. Reproduced by permission.

come to stand synecdochically for Peru, sometimes even for Latin America as a whole. Arguably, Machu Picchu is a more modern set of ruins, having been discovered—or better, invented—only in the early twentieth century by Hiram Bingham's Yale-sponsored expedition of 1911. Bingham was feted for having discovered the so-called lost city of the Incas. That claim, however, rings hollow when it is realized not only that it was a local tavern proprietor and landlord, Melchor Arteaga, who led the archaeologist to the site when promised "a whole silver dollar," but also that Bingham himself noted graffiti on the stones: "the name, 'Lizarraga,' and the year, '1902.' "[12] Bingham gave this Lizarraga credit for the discoveries in his first book about the expedition, *Inca Land*, but by the time of his later account, *Lost City of the Incas*, Lizarraga's name disappears.[13] Meanwhile, Bingham's opinion of indigenous knowledge can be inferred from his own comment that "readers of *Inca Land* will remember that Professor Harry W. Foote and I had often been obliged to add, when discussing reports of 'noteworthy and important ruins'—'but he may have been lying.' "[14] The locals are untrustworthy, telling tall tales to make up for their ignorance. Bingham goes on to observe that the indigenous *campesino* does not mark the ruins in any particular way: "Presumably, to him and his kind, Inca ruins of temples and palaces built by their remote kindred are not in themselves interesting but merely evidence that the latter found the land worth occupying and cultivating."[15] In this sense, Bingham's achievement was less to discover Machu Picchu than to put it into discourse: to articulate its stones, to make them speak in the recognizably modern idiom of ruination.

This, then, is where Vilcashuamán is different. Without entering the narratives of international tourism, and despite remaining unexcavated until the 1980s, Vilcas's ruins have a much longer history of being repeatedly articulated and rearticulated by competing stories about Peruvian modernity, almost from the moment of Spanish conquest and thus their initial fall into ruin. We might therefore say that Vilcas is more eloquent about Peru's modernity than Machu Picchu is, especially now that the latter has assumed the status of a brand, a signifier almost without content—like the Nike swoosh or the McDonald's golden arches. Machu Picchu says "Peru" or "Latin America," but it says almost nothing about these places. By contrast, in the to and fro of the conflicting versions of what Vilcas's ruins might be made to say, a whole series of narratives have been advanced about historicity and hegemony, modernity, and, more to the point, the (still essentially modern) lament that Peru has failed to become modern. Vargas Llosa famously opens his monumental novel *Conversation in the Cathedral* with the question "At what precise moment had Peru fucked itself up?"[16] We might not know when; but it would not be far-fetched to argue that Vilcashuamán may be that precise place *where* Peru fucked itself up. Vilcas is marked by the series of interruptions that indicate the fuckups Vargas Llosa would claim have stalled progress toward modernity. These interruptions—symbolized, or better materialized, in the strewn stones of Inca edifices—have served as fissures within which variously confident, wistful, and messianic narratives have sought firm footing, like weeds in the dirt. Yet the interruptions have also brought these stories to their own ruination, their disarticulation.

### Incas and Chancas

But let us go back. Vilcas first became significant because it was built upon the site of the destroyed capital of the Chanca confederation, the Incas' now somewhat mysterious enemies, during the first period of imperial expansion. Ruins upon ruins: the discourse of ruins knows no other foundation. The Chancas (or Chankas) gave the Inca empire its founding narrative. Means provides the traditional account, that the Chancas were "a strong and warlike folk . . . a numerous and a bellicose people."[17] The story continues that sometime after 1400, while the Incas were still confined to the territory around Cuzco, the Chancas assembled an army and, "with a savage brandishing of weapons and a wild chorus of battle cries," set out to destroy the Inca heartland.[18] Cuzco's inhabitants abandoned their city, leaving behind only eight warriors, among them the future Inca Pachakuti, who would become Inca historiography's and mythology's single most important figure. Aided by the god Viracocha, who sent warriors to their aid as if from nowhere, Pachakuti and his men succeeded in beating back the Chanca challenge. Over the course of the subsequent Chanca wars, the Incas advanced into their enemies' territory, setting into motion a process that led to further conquest and so their rapid rise and territorial expansion, converting a city-state into an empire, and even (as Rostworowski argues) establishing the Inca state per se. But against this traditional story, we should set the fact that, as Terence D'Altroy notes, "despite the many accounts of the Chanka wars, scholars disagree about their authenticity."[19] Some even suggest that "the Chankas may have been built up as the consummate but largely mythical foil, used to glorify Pachakuti and to provide a divinely inspired foundation for the empire." D'Altroy himself tends to agree that "the sagas of the Chanka wars may still be mostly a glorious epic invoked to burnish the image of the empire's father."[20] In Rostworowski's words, "the legend of the Chanca wars met the Incas' need to explain a reality, to account for the events that gave rise to Inca expansion. . . . So the story is somewhere between myth and reality," providing justification for "an elite of capable men who were able to take advantage of circumstances to advance the rise of a powerful state."[21]

Fortified by this narrative of divine blessing and elite heroism, the Incas took over the territory to their north and reterritorialized what had been the Chanca capital, establishing in the place they now called Vilcashuamán (meaning "sacred falcon") a complex of buildings including the pyramid I climbed, also known as an *ushnu* and, according to Hemming, "the only surviving Inca structure of its kind,"[22] one of several aspects of Vilcas's architecture found nowhere else. For Reiner Zuidema, the ushnu at Vilcas was "perhaps the most splendid of the Incas";[23] and "in the conquered and subjugated territories," the ushnu "was supposed to produce a visual impact that would evoke the power of the Incas."[24] In addition there were (and remain, in ruins) temples to the sun and the moon, and between them a large plaza. All this marked Vilcas's special place within the empire: Vilcashuamán became a key link in the "long rosary of the *qhapaq-ñan*," the road between Quito and Cuzco.[25] It therefore became the site of a large military garrison (up to 30,000 soldiers according to some accounts, though D'Altroy questions that figure),[26] with, we are told, 700 storehouses. Accompanying therefore the legitimating myth of heroic conquest, and on the ruins of the Chanca town, the Incas mobilized formidable works of civil and military engineering.

But again, as well as physical power, the place encoded and concentrated symbolic power. It was the site of significant festive and ritual occasions reinforcing the tenets of Tawantisuyu social structure. On feast days and for celebrations, up to 20,000 people would gather in the plaza at Vilcas, to witness animal and human offerings conducted on a sacrificial stone. It is said that the pyramid was the site of an ornate throne, covered in gold, on which the Inca himself and his wife would sit to preside over the ceremonies. The entire space was marked out as a repository and stage for the performance of symbolic, religious, cultural, and juridical power: the lineaments of that power were expressed in its monumental architectural configuration as well as in the ornamentation it boasted and the treasure it held. Cieza de León, who frequently refers to Vilcas and underscores its importance, tells us that:

> The temple to the sun was large and finely built. . . . To one side . . . , toward the rising sun, there was a shrine for the Lord-Inca, of stone, from which small terraces emerged, about six feet wide, where other enclosures came together, and at the center there was a bench where the Lord-Inca sat to pray, all of a single stone so large that it was eleven feet long and seven feet wide. . . . They say this stone used to be covered with jewels of gold and precious stones to adorn this place they so venerated and esteemed. . . . The *Orejones* and other Indians tell that the image of the sun was of enormous value, and that there was great treasure both in the temple and buried, and that these palaces had at their service over forty thousand Indians.[27]

Size, quality of workmanship, the presence of the Inca himself, the use of precious metals, the value of specific objects, and the population dedicated to the complex's upkeep: all confirm the chronicler's interest. They are designed to dazzle and to impress. Moreover, it is clear that the Incas had thoroughly obliterated whatever ruins of the Chanca capital remained. What counts is the presence of these monuments of Inca prestige. Any Chanca "real" had faded into mythic prehistory. For the Incas, it seems, stone could mean only permanence, a bedrock for power, rather than the anxious reminder of their own possible transience.

### Spaniards

The Spaniards encountered Vilcas early—naturally enough, given its strategic position. It was the site of an ambush that caught Hernando de Soto and his men by surprise in their initial 1533 march on Cuzco.[28] But the Incas' "bold attack" was ultimately futile, killing only one Spanish horse, wounding another, and also wounding one of the men.[29] By contrast, and typical of the one-sided combat that characterized the conquest, the Spaniards killed over 600 indigenous soldiers and quickly advanced on the Inca capital, which fell within ten days of the battle of Vilcas. As Hemming notes, "the four battles on the road to Cuzco—Jauja, Vilcashuaman, Vilcacongo, and the pass above Cuzco—. . . demonstrated the immense superiority of mounted, armoured Spaniards over native warriors."[30] Vilcas became a watchword for indigenous defeat and for the futility of armed resistance. When, later, in the "great rebellion" of 1536, the Inca Manco did attempt a counterattack, the Spaniards took advantage of Vilcas's strategic location to station a garrison there while reprisals were under way.[31] A "determined attack" was beaten off nearby, as the rebellion continued through 1537.[32] And though Manco continued to menace the Spaniards from his stronghold in neighboring Vilcabamba until his assassination in the mid-1540s, Vilcas remained securely in the conquistadors' hands the whole time.

The Spaniards took no care to maintain the architectural heritage they had taken over. By the end of Manco's rebellion, Vilcas must already have been in ruins, as Cieza de León, writing as early as around 1550, is fascinated by how rapidly its monuments had degenerated. It is the ruins that fascinate. Or rather, it is not the site's glory that is of most interest, but the contrast between its recent magnificence and its current sorry state. Having described the rituals and splendor he learns had been regularly on display, Cieza de León ends with a salutary commentary on the discrepancy between past splendor and present ruination: "What can be seen are the foundations of the buildings, and the walls and enclosures of the shrines, the stones I have mentioned, and the temple with its stairways, even though it has fallen into ruins and is overgrown with grass and the storehouses have fallen down. In a word, it was once what it no longer is, and by what it is, we can judge what it was."[33]

Already, then, fewer than thirty years after the Spanish conquest, and less than a decade after the pacification of what would become the province of Ayacucho, Vilcashuamán is marked as a site of lament, even for those who brought down the regime that had constructed and populated the buildings now in ruins, "overgrown with grass." "It was once what it no longer is," writes Cieza de León: Vilcas is the site of an interruption, an indication (already) of the pastness of the past. It is a memento mori indicating the traumatizing effects of the clash between what can now be cast as ancient and what is emerging as modern.

From being the site of the Inca's judgments, then, the ruins of Vilcashuamán become a sight to enable judgment on the Inca: "by what it is, we can judge what it was." One story is over, but another has begun, a new story that can claim to correct the earlier narrative's errors precisely because the ruins signal the silencing of that narrative—and in their irreversible ruination, the impossibility of any appeal. In their finality, ruins enable an assessment of the past, but they also imply that history has already been judged, and been found wanting. As nature overtakes the temples and terraces, the Spanish judgment on Inca civilization is itself naturalized. The residues of that civilization offer up what is literally an object lesson on the way in which history has passed by Inca culture. The ruins confirm that the Spanish interruption into Peruvian history is irrevocable: the legacy of this most central of Inca sites is only an overgrown residue that serves as moral pedagogy. As such, however, the ruins can and should be preserved: the Spaniards seldom attempted to eradicate entirely the traces of what they had overturned. In fact, they were usually keen to take advantage of and—literally and figuratively—build upon the ruins of what they had supplanted. Spanish modernity was never presented as a creation ex nihilo; it took the interruption that indigenous ruins represented as foundation, but one that had to be permanently on display: less mythic bedrock, then, than tangible reminder of history's lessons. It is with this historical consciousness, forged for the Spaniards in their encounter with the civilizations of the Americas, that the ruin as ruin comes into its own. So, although Peter Fritzsche argues that in Europe it is only after the French revolution that the ruin comes to be seen as "the debris of quite specific historical disasters, not simply the general devastation of time,"[34] surely in the Americas the new masters of Vilcas recognized the historicity of ruination almost 300 years previously. Nature's encroachment on the ruins confirms Spanish ascendancy, but it also provokes a somewhat melancholy reflection on history.

Of course, the Spanish empire hardly allowed itself to wallow in such melancholia: that would be the contribution of a romantic sensibility still to come. Rather, the Spaniards constructed new rituals, in ways that incorporated and acknowledged the ruins over which they held sway. They seemed to recognize the power of place, and particularly the power of this place. Before long the invaders would return in rather different circumstances, in their own way rejuvenating the overgrown remains of former Inca glory. The indigenous chronicler Felipe Guaman Poma de Ayala tells us that in 1570 Viceroy Francisco de Toledo came to the province, visited Vilcashuamán, ascended the steps of the same pyramid that had been the focus of Inca celebrations, sat on the Inca's throne, and "was received by the principal lords as though he were the Inca himself."[35] In part, Toledo was responding to a visit that the Inca Manco's son had made to the site a mere two years earlier, when "the natives paid homage and tried to relive their glorious past."[36] The viceroy was demonstrating that the privileges of power had passed to the Europeans: he told his own narrative of continuity and rupture in the overgrown stones of Vilcas. Likewise recoding or overcoding the town's architecture, and with it the geography of power in the region, the Spaniards built a church dedicated to Saint John the Baptist directly on top of the Inca temple to the sun. The colonial church lording it over the remains of the Inca temple served as another history lesson, a constant reminder of indigenous defeat and Spanish dominance. As Valerie Fraser puts it, by recycling the stone from indigenous temples and building upon them, the Spaniards "effectively suppressed not only idolatry but native culture and society as well."[37] Yet Fraser also notes that the colonial silence about this practice may betray a certain anxiety, "related to the whole prickly question of the

Spaniards' right to conquer by force of arms."[38] Or the anxiety may relate instead to the limits of their force as a whole, for by building upon the ruins the Spaniards thereby fixed them: keeping them in place, confirming their durability and strength. In the case of Vilcas in particular, the church is rather precariously perched on what is still a very solid and much larger indigenous base. So precarious is the church's perch that, as Gasparini and Margolies report, around the end of the nineteenth century the entire colonial structure could be, and was, reoriented by ninety degrees so that it now faces toward the ancient plaza rather than parallel to it.[39] A twist in the tale, one might say, of the Spanish effort to situate a hegemonic project on Inca ruins.

**Peruvians**

As the Spanish empire drew to a close and especially after Peru's independence, to contemplate Inca ruins, and the ruins at Vilcashuamán in particular, was to indulge in lamentation and nostalgia at best. Over the centuries following Viceroy Toledo's visit, Vilcas was little more than a backwater in one of Peru's poorest and most overlooked provinces. Modernity seemed to be taking place elsewhere, anywhere but in this increasingly remote corner of the increasingly remote province of Ayacucho, whose name fittingly translates as "the corner of the dead." The region's population remained overwhelmingly Quechua-speaking indigenous peasants, barely surviving on subsistence agriculture or small-scale animal husbandry. The town lived in the disparity between the former glories indexed by its ruins and the reality of its impoverished present. Run-down houses still nestle between these ruins and the inevitable comparisons they attract. When I visited, the young NGO worker who climbed the pyramid with me commented on the apparent contradiction, pointing to the indigenous children scrambling on the stones around us, many trying to sell us chewing gum, soda, or ornaments, or simply asking for small change. "Look," he said, "can it be that we are the same people who built these monuments so long ago?" The question expresses a sense of cognitive dissonance: the Inca ruins indicate a history of uneven development, of repression and stagnation, that breaks with conventional understandings of causality and temporal sequence. (In *Chariots of the Gods?* and subsequent books, the Swiss author Erich Von Däniken provides a fantastic, because overly literal, resolution to this dissonance in his suggestion that Peru's monuments were the work not of indigenous peoples, but of ancient astronauts: another interruption, this time on an interplanetary scale.) Somehow Peru must have fucked itself up.

The romantics put these matters more delicately, but their consternation was no less heartfelt. With the end of the Spanish empire, and precisely because of its remoteness, poverty, and isolation, Vilcas becomes central to a discourse of lament that encrusts itself over the ruins and the shabbiness of Inca and Spanish masonry alike. As a matter of fact, the battle that signaled the final victory in South America's struggle for independence took place not far away, but this never turned Ayacucho into a place of celebration. Rather, Vilcas came to symbolize now not Inca power or Spanish modernity, but the failure of the Peruvian nation to assert its own supremacy or arrive at its own modernity. By the early twentieth century, Vilcashuamán had become something like a *locus classicus* of lament for Peruvian cultural nationalists. In discussing contemporary British postcolonial melancholia, Baucom claims that "in some strange way to be English is, often, to be a member of a cult of the dead, or, at the very least, a member of a cult of ruin."[40] Such a melancholic sense of nationhood grips Peruvian cultural identity more strongly still, in part because it was forged in a crushing military defeat at the hands of Chile, in the late-nineteenth-century War of the Pacific. Not thirty years later, the writer and politician José de la Riva Agüero, grandson of one of Peru's first presidents, retreated to the Andean *Perú profundo* or "deepest Peru" and still found no solace.

Riva Agüero toured the southern Peruvian Andes on muleback in 1912, and Vilcas occupies a central role in his resultant book, *Paisajes Peruanos* (Peruvian Landscapes). On the occasion of his visit to the village, it is as though time and space themselves reflect and intensify the misery and disgrace of the ruins, viewed "in the luminous sadness of a June afternoon."[41] He provides the standard narrative—taken mostly from Cieza de León—of Vilcas's former glory, which he proceeds to contrast with its current degradation. All around is filth and dirt. It is as though, he tells us, the contemporary inhabitants had completely forgotten all habits of hygiene and cleanliness. "It is possible," he suggests, that as in the fall from ancient Rome to the European Dark Ages, "degradation should have caused them to lose the habit of cleanliness."[42] So the material ruination of the built environment leads, as though by contagion, to the moral as well as physical decline of a whole people. Riva Agüero's observations of Vilcas's ruins, and the ways in which he claims they have in turn led to a people in ruin, provokes then a sustained meditation on this empty heart or dead center of the Peruvian nation. From the vibrant core of the Inca Empire, Vilcas has come to stand for the desolation of the present republic, itself in ruins as fragments (the provinces of Tacna and Arica) are parceled out to Chile, its history evacuated as the entire contents of the national library are shipped south to Santiago. Peru can be understood, Riva Agüero suggests, in the combination of former wealth and contemporary degradation for which Vilcas's ruins provide a striking synecdoche:

I have never felt such a piercing and heartrending sensation of decadence. The village's silence was deep, because almost all its inhabitants were still in the fields. Only the warble of birds, the humble noise of the animal pens, the cackle of hens, and the footfalls of a mule train disturbed the solitude that had once listened to songs of adoration to the Sun and frenetic praise for the Inca. . . . Remains of a great historic shipwreck under the light of the setting sun, one could say that the ruins of Vilcas sounded out a desperate melody, more destitute and anguished than the music of the native panpipes. Extinct opulence, and a legendary, mournful sorrow, two notes that sum up the soul of the Peruvian Andes.[43]

The whole landscape, the whole region, resonates with the "desperate melody" provoked by Vilcas's ruins. The place's emptiness makes it serve all the better as a sounding board within which laments for a failed modernity reverberate. Riva Agüero conjures up the ghosts of those who had filled the space and suggests that Vilcas was also the site where the Spaniards' downfall was sealed: he recounts the story that it was in Vilcas, in the midst of a thunderstorm, that a condor settled on Pizarro's baggage train, full of title deeds and letters, all the bureaucracy of imperial reterritorialization. The condor represented, we are told, a "funereal omen," and though "Pizarro laughed the augury off, with his taciturn indifference,"[44] he was to die but a year later, in a mutiny of his own men. "Peru," Riva Agüero concludes his chapter on Vilcas, "has always been the country of tragic outcomes."[45] No wonder the book is lacking its final pages, and that it should have gone unpublished in the author's lifetime. How could it end but in the tragedy foretold by the melancholy ruins at Vilcashuamán? Modernity had failed precisely because, as Guha says of India, of the "historic failure of the nation to come to its own":[46] it had failed to secure a hegemonic project that would bind the nation together. And the pain of that failure could be felt most keenly at Vilcas.

### Liberators

Now a final set of stories woven around Vilcashuamán's battered stones, in a strange dialogue or fable that might perhaps have put a halt, however temporary, to all such fables. After its long isolation, Vilcas came back into the news (and then just barely) only in the early 1980s, when it was the site of some of the earliest armed engagements between the Maoist guerrillas of Sendero Luminoso (Shining Path) and the forces of law and order. Vilcas was one of the first places in which Sendero gained support and organization (as is revealed by an intelligence report from 1979, before the war had even broken out).[47] It is therefore unsurprising that Vilcas should become a flash point in the initial period before the state's regular forces essentially deserted the rural highlands, and while the government still claimed to be upholding a national project motivated by Enlightenment modernity. One engagement in particular found a special place in Sendero's own mythology, and Vilcas found itself the site of a remarkable dialogue between state and insurgency, an exchange of symbols in this most symbolic of places, a dialogue and strangely revealing manifestation by this most intransigent, silent, and invisible of guerrilla groups. In late March 1982, a brief skirmish in Vilcas left one policeman slightly wounded. Impulsively and against the advice of his staff, the Peruvian president, Fernando Belaúnde, decided he would visit Ayacucho, and he took an unannounced helicopter flight to land at Vilcashuamán. With his interior minister and other senior officials, he made his way to the central square. As Gorriti reports, "their arrival was so unexpected that no one went to meet them." Quickly, once they realized that the president had paid them an unexpected honor, the local police raised the national flag, and the troops presented themselves for review. Like a modern-day Spanish viceroy, Belaúnde then "met briefly with some local people at the entrance to the ruins of the temple of the Sun."[48] There he delivered the following remarkable assurance that he was personally committed to keeping the town and its ruins within the light:

> They told me that there was alarm the night before in Vilcashuamán. That the town was in darkness—its electrical generator blown up by terrorists a year ago—and that these elements took advantage of the shadows to attack once again with sharpshooters, skilled in marksmanship, quick to escape. I could not resist the impulse to come and see them without delay to tell them that I am with them and those who defend order.[49]

Vilcas becomes once more the symbolic heart of the nation, of all that has to be defended against the new threat of violence, fleeting and shadowy. To defend Vilcas is to side with modernity against barbarism, to uphold the integrity of the nation against its impending fragmentation. The temple of the sun is the site of a renewed proclamation of authority and hegemony: the Peruvian president takes up the place occupied first by the Inca and then by the colonial viceroy, to announce a power that turns out to be little more than symbolic.

By way of reply, on August 22, 1982, Sendero attacked and overran the police station, killing four policemen and wounding three others. Putting the lie to the president's declaration, the guerrilla demonstrated the real physical as well as ideological weakness of the Peruvian state in these remote parts of the central highlands. But a strange discovery in the wake of the attack showed that there was something more to this flexing of muscle. Next to the destroyed police station, a bag was found containing some of the personal effects of Abimael

Guzmán, Sendero's mysterious leader, of whom at that stage very little was known and of whom there were as yet no photographs in public circulation. The bag contained Guzmán's "university identification, issued by the University of Huamanga, two copies of his law degree, and a certificate of conditional freedom, renewed by the police department's judicial Zone II."[50] In response to Belaúnde's personal visit to the ruins of Vilcas and his declaration of order, the bag left behind by Sendero indicated that Guzmán had also visited Vilcas in person, to take up and return the challenge. But that return was also a depersonalization, a shedding of the legal accoutrements of identity and professional qualification. After all, the former university professor now went by the nom de guerre of Comandante Gonzalo, maximum leader of the Revolution. Suffering from altitude-exacerbated psoriasis, Guzmán was in a state of physical semi-ruination himself, applying medicinal creams to ensure that he did not shed his skin. But in this ruinous site of so many narratives of identity, nationhood, and justice, he happily cast off the skin of official identity, to become mythic, to become the avenging angel who would truly, once and for all, bring the country to ruin. Far from the enlightenment that Belaúnde asserted, Gorriti portrays the effect of this clandestine exchange as a visible darkening over the Andes: "What scene better describes that violent encounter after centuries of neglect than to see that square that Riva Agüero had imagined beautiful, shining, and filled with thousands worshipping the Inca . . . submerged in shadow even in the midst of light, alone and arrayed only in private fears and furtive glances. And the scarlet tint was not sacred, but, in that still-smoking building, the blood of two dead guardsmen, humble, hurting, defeated."[51]

Gorriti shares in Riva Agüero's romanticism. The centuries of neglect and the blood that had been shed at Vilcas, before and after the coming of the Inca, could not be so simply excised by Belaúnde's *fiat lux*. As the police pulled out and the guerrilla and then the state's counterinsurgency troops moved in, small towns and villages such as Vilcashuamán became the scene of atrocities committed by both sides in an increasingly dirty war of attrition and intimidation. For most of the 1980s, rural Ayacucho became a no-go area, as any image of postcolonial serenity was shattered and rural economies, livelihoods, and customs were devastated. Ruins upon ruins.

Many years later, in 2003 at the close of the civil war, and in the wake of the 70,000 lives lost in the conflict, Peru's Truth and Reconciliation Commission decided to organize a photography exhibition in conjunction with issuing its final report on the crimes committed during the war. This exhibition featured press and other pictures of the violence that had wracked the country. Its purpose was to tell those who lived in Lima the story of a conflict that long went relatively unremarked and unreported on the coast—a region that has always

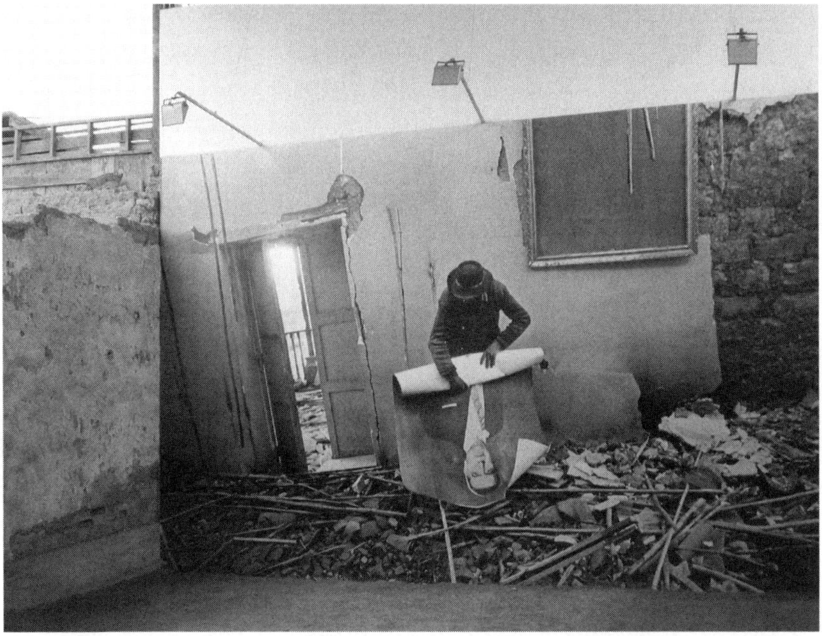

2. A portrait of Peru's President Fernando Belaúnde is recovered after a terrorist attack on municipal offices in Vilcashuamán in August 1982. Photo by Oscar Medrando. Reproduced by permission of the journal *Caretas*. The photo of its installation at the Casa Ríva Agüero, as part of the "Yuyanapaq" exhibition, is by Jill Lane and reproduced by permission.

counted itself more modern than the Andes and its physical and social ruination. The exhibition's title was Yuyanapaq, Quechua for "to remember." It was curated in an old colonial house in Chorrillos, a former fishing village that is today a fairly upscale suburb of Lima. The house, a mansion overlooking the ocean, now owned by the Universidad Católica, was in a state of severe disrepair. As Forero notes in his review of the exhibition, "the plaster is peeling, the floors are made of cement and the walls rot."[52] The place was, in short, a complete ruin. "But Peru's past is alive here," continues Forero, "in riveting, raw photographs intended to recall the horrors of a 20-year terror war."[53] Again, then, ruination and violence, life and death, storytelling and memory, come together in the same place. "The walls are part of the exhibition," the curator is reported to have said. "The house permits you to see and understand the images. There is a marriage between the house and the images." The house is named after its most distinguished former owner and occupant: it is the Casa Riva Agüero. Among the largest photographs, covering "an entire wall" of one of the mansion's rooms, is a picture of ruins, the rubble of a bombed-out municipal headquarters "where a diligent worker rolls up a huge photograph of Fernando Belaunde, then the president, after a Shining Path attack. 'It's symbolic because it's complete destruction and amid the rubble a peasant is trying to care for his president.' "[54] The village where this photograph was taken is, of course, Vilcashuamán.

## Notes

1. Disraeli, *Tancred*, vol. 2, 138.
2. Quoted in Lowenthal, *The Past Is a Foreign Country*, 110.
3. Benjamin, *The Origin of German Tragic Drama*, 178.
4. Ibid.
5. Ibid.
6. Ibid., 235.
7. Percy Bysshe Shelley, *Selected Poems*, 11.
8. Žižek, *The Sublime Object of Ideology*, 29.
9. Cieza de León, *The Incas*, 126.
10. Gasparini and Margolies, *Inca Architecture*, 112.
11. Hemming, *Monuments of the Incas*, 187.
12. Alfred Bingham, *Portrait of an Explorer*, 6, 13.
13. Ibid., 26.
14. Hiram Bingham, *Machu Picchu*, 10.
15. Ibid.
16. Vargas Llosa, *Conversation in the Cathedral*, 3.
17. Means, *Ancient Civilizations of the Andes*, 237.
18. Ibid., 244.
19. D'Altroy, *The Incas*, 65.
20. Ibid.
21. Rostworowski, *Pachacutec y la leyenda de los Chancas*, 12, my translation.
22. Hemming, *The Conquest of the Incas*, 103.
23. Quoted in Gasparini and Margolies, *Inca Architecture*, 269.
24. Quoted in ibid., 280.
25. Ibid., 99.
26. D'Altroy, *The Incas*, 210.
27. Cieza de León, *The Incas*, 126–27.
28. Hemming, *The Conquest of the Incas*, 103–4.
29. Ibid., 103.
30. Ibid., 109.
31. Ibid., 199.
32. Ibid., 215.
33. Cieza de León, *The Incas*, 127.
34. Fritzsche, *Stranded in the Present*, 96.
35. Guaman Poma de Ayala, *El primer nueva corónica y buen gobierno*, 447, my translation.
36. Hemming, *Monuments of the Incas*, 186.
37. Fraser, *The Architecture of Conquest*, 68.
38. Ibid.
39. Gasparini and Margolies, *Inca Architecture*, 115.

40. Baucom, *Out of Place*, 175.
41. Riva Agüero, *Paisajes Peruanos*, 70. All translations from this work are my own.
42. Ibid., 71.
43. Ibid., 71–72.
44. Ibid., 76.
45. Ibid., 77.
46. Guha, "On Some Aspects of the Historiography of Colonial India," 43.
47. Gorriti, *The Shining Path*, 51.
48. Ibid., 221.
49. Quoted in ibid.
50. Ibid., 229.
51. Ibid., 229–30.
52. Juan Forero, "Peru Photo Exhibit Captures Pathos of 20 Years of War," *New York Times*, June 27, 2004.
53. Ibid.
54. Ibid.

DANIEL HERWITZ

# 13

## THE MONUMENT IN RUINS

Nothing is more monumental in the landscape of the twentieth and twenty-first centuries than ruins. Cities reduced to rubble, wrecked bunkers, roadways, skyscrapers. Rivers poisoned by battle or industry. Huge factory complexes abandoned, their cavernous spaces accumulating dust. Waste bespeaks our craving for the monumental.

Where ruin is monumental, there will also probably be monuments: the terms of our gaze demand them. Monuments in modern times are often forged out of experiences of ruination, which stir communities to monumental changes in their terms of empowerment. When monuments address ruins, rubble, loss, or decimation, they tend to convert these experiences into communalizing memory, public resolve, power. The ashes of the past, acknowledged as irreparable, become symbolically reconstructed into something else: the hard currency of stone. Around the physical solidity of the thing, the ensuing process of mourning becomes a process of solidarity, of resolution. The power of the stone becomes the occasion for the genesis of power.

Had there been no Boer War in South Africa, there would have been no apartheid state. That war took place because Cecil Rhodes rode in on his fine horse to claim England's share of booty from the poor Afrikaans farmers who, by chance, had unearthed a boundless treasure of gold and diamonds. The Boer War, fought between 1899 and 1902, was the opening act of the twentieth century. Already going full force when the champagne bottles of the new century were uncorked, it proved a model for the bombs, bunkers, ruins, rubble, and wrecks that were to follow. It featured the first concentration camps: Lord Kitchener, furious that a ragtag group of Afrikaners carrying tattered Bibles could stump his best Commonwealth troops, burned the Afrikaners' farms so that nothing could grow there again, and placed their women and children in concentration camps, where many died of disease. The Afrikaner population never forgot this humiliation, or that the English had started the war for the sake of gold and diamonds. Their radicalization took place around the memory of the war. They grew more racist, more xenophobic, deeply attached to the rising German fascism. The Afrikaners' experience of English concentration camps led to the master plan for apartheid. Like concentration camps, apartheid is a way of concentrating and controlling people, of regulating work, leisure, circulation, and dwelling. So one architecture of humiliation becomes another. The Afrikaner, once the last apostle of colonial rurality, becomes the new master of state power.

When the apartheid state came into being with the National Party's rise to power in 1948, the Voortrekker Monument was built in the town of Valhalla, between Johannesburg and Pretoria, to celebrate it. The monument, unveiled in 1949, was designed by the architect Gerard Moerdyk, himself imprisoned in the Standerton concentration camp during the Boer War. It was commissioned by the state to commemorate the so-called great trek of the early nineteenth century, when a band of Afrikaners drove their ox wagons into the interior of the country and established themselves in the Transvaal, fighting off Zulus cowboy style. These settlers drew their ox carts into a "Laager," a tight circle through which the Zulu enemy could not penetrate, and from which they could fire their rifles from positions of relative security, again reminiscent of the American West. It is because of the great trek, the mythology goes—because of what the brave and simple Afrikaner did, as opposed to the actions of the English dandy and thief—that the great nation of South Africa was founded. We and not you, the monument declares, are the origin of the nation.

The monument's encircling outer wall is covered with ox-wagon reliefs. On the inside a series of paintings depict the trekkers. An inner circle cut out from the first floor allows the visitor to see a cenotaph of fire and funereal stone below, emblazoned with the words "Ons vir ju Sud Afrika" (We are for you, South Africa). There is a marriage of male and female in this monument, with its rings of encircling maternal spaces and its rising phallic forms—the shaft of the building, the upright flame within. Safety and force, nurturance and power converge in a religious gesture.

Moerdyk drew his inspiration for the building from Bruno Schmitz's Völkerschlachtdenkmal (memorial of the battle of the people) in Leipzig, and there is a special dialogue between these two monuments around ruination. The Leipzig monument was built at the beginning of the twentieth century to commemorate Germans fallen during the Napoleonic wars. Its construction began at the time of the Boer War, allowing Afrikaners to identify its memorialization with their own. I would call the German monument the architectural unconscious of the Afrikaner one. Through identification with the passion of the Leipzig memorial, the Voortrekker Monument claims a double origin for the new state, in the great trek and the humiliation of the Boer War—thus converting hardship into resolve, indeed, victory at the moment of the National Party's ascendancy. Something between an art deco radio tower and a Romanesque church, the Voortrekker Monument proclaims this in a pro-German voice right at the end of the Second World War, as if taking over the mantle of the fallen Third Reich.

It would seem that nothing could be farther from this monument than the utopian plans of the modern architect, with his or her clean, rational spaces and desire to enhance living through better cities, houses, roads, and workplaces. When Le Corbusier developed his *Plan Voisin* in 1925 for the reconstruction of Paris, he intended to replace the chaos of modern urban life with more rationalized systems of leisure, dwelling, work, and circulation. In his city human thinking, living, work, and enjoyment would be uplifted, Platonized. These plans are well known, and it is fascinating to revisit them in the light of the brutality of monuments like the Voortrekker Monument. That monument proclaims the conversion of ruins into state power and state plans. Le Corbusier hardly does that. But he does arrogate to modern architecture the right to reduce Paris, the most cosmopolitan city in the world, to ashes so that something more ideal can be built in its place. In South Africa, this was a typical apartheid procedure. On top of the ashes of Sophiatown—that vibrant, mushrooming city for people of color at the edges of Johannesburg, destroyed between 1955 and 1960 to prevent a hybridized black modernity from forming—the apartheid state built a working-class Afrikaner town called Triomf. This arrogation of the right to ruin places and dispose of people in a game of social perfectionism, whether fascist or Platonist, is a hallmark of the thinking of modernity. Not even the Nazis were willing to bomb Paris; only the genius architect was ready to get the job done.

In modernity, monuments and utopian plans are two sides of the same coin: monuments signal the conversion of ruins to power, and utopian plans signal the power to ruin modern life so that it may be converted into something more monumental. Neither side of this coin could have been engraved were it not for the fact that Europe lay devastated by war, haunting everyone, inviting radical change. In a larger sense the coin is made possible through the broad work of that complex system called modernity. "All Europe contributed to the making of Kurtz," Conrad tells us in *Heart of Darkness*.[1] By "Europe" he means philosophy, religion, science, society, racialism, economy, technology, and war. One might say that all Europe contributed to the making of Le Corbusier, even if his goal was to give us more gardens in cities, easier circulation, more efficient and pleasurable work spaces, and more humanized homes.

Le Corbusier's vast plans have been realized only outside of Europe and America, in places like Brasilia, Chandigarh, and Dhaka.[2] It is easier, and more enthralling, to produce the grand sweep of modernity when what existed before it was shack and tenement, village and empty plain. Le Corbusier never rebuilt Paris, but Niemeyer and Costa built Brasilia. Mies van der Rohe was given a chance to build the Illinois Institute of Technology south of the center of Chicago; Wright more or less filled a relatively open suburb of Chicago, known for its many oak trees, with little masterpieces. In general, though, when cities destroyed in the Second World War were being rebuilt, or when American suburbs were being citified with big buildings, the tune was called by the corporate builder, who wanted to build quickly, conservatively, and for maximum profit. Only in the colonies, with their open land and relatively undeveloped cities, could the modern architect realize his dream of a city constructed from scratch. The third world rather than the first became the site of utopian design. Similarly, modernism could infest the second world, with its war-ravaged cities and technocratic five-year plans: from Moscow to Budapest, lives would be lived in freezing conformity in massive, unornamented apartment blocks.

A book could be written about the Wagnerian impulse to fill the so-called empty spaces of the third world with modernist masterpieces and utopian, modernist cities. In this gesture, perhaps the final gasp in colonialism's long history, power seems to find a clean slate, but only because it fails or refuses to notice what it has cleared away in its grand modernist sweep. Few people except architects would have taken the destruction of Paris seriously as an option, and Le Corbusier's plan derives its charm and force from its complete impracticality. But where the world is believed to be empty, as in the third world, power is assumed to move with the implacability of gravity and the speed of light. There we find sites of modernity without resistance, of avant-garde rationality without limitation. Or so it seems, but only because what was there was reduced to the status of primitive or anachronistic.

When Chandigarh was being built by Le Corbusier and his associates, the process was reportedly delayed because some villagers refused to move. When Nehru, then the prime minister of India, heard they would consider leaving their homes only if he talked to them, he quickly went to meet them and hear what they had to say. They asked him: "If we do not move, will you kill us?"

Nehru was deeply liberal, but he thought about the question for a while and answered, "Yes." "We just wanted to hear you say it," they replied. They then moved, and the project was completed. It is worth noting that later, local people used it in their own ways, thus subverting its claim to mold them in accord with the strictness of its modernist ideals. Between population and buildings a dialectic emerged, according to which each exerted its will over the other, and each became essentially different through the force of the other. This dialectic is one of power and its medium of expression. One finds it at work in the history of Brasilia,[3] and earlier in the architecture of the South African missionaries and its use by local Twana populations.[4]

Le Corbusier's cities aim for permanence. It is hardly an easy thing to imagine dismantling Brasilia or Chandigarh now, and the presumption of such radical change would simply be a perpetuation of the thinking of the utopian planner, like Le Corbusier, or the apartheid administrator. We can take no more seriously the idea of razing and remaking whole cities than we can the idea of displacing whole populations. Thou shalt not produce rubble on a monumental scale should be the credo of modern times. However, this does not mean we must accept the human or urban landscape exactly as it is. The very ideas of architecture and of human progress negate this. Monuments may be torn down, streets remade. Authoritarian power may be diffused or dismantled.

Velvet revolutions are often about tearing down the icons of authoritarian monumentality, and most of us have seen images of crowds gleefully ripping down the Berlin Wall or a statue of Lenin. Hungary gathered up its statues and placed them in a theme park at the edge of Budapest, for people to visit as they do zoos, natural history museums, and amusement parks. In contrast, Rossi argues that the landscape of a city ought to retain its fascist past, for example refusing to tear down monuments to Mussolini because such physical traces keep the public's memory alive. Moreover, buildings can change their uses, unlike most monuments: an office built to house a fascist ministry can become home to something else. Following Rossi's thinking, the most critical buildings of apartheid—the huge, brutal, edifices of national power asserting themselves like bunkers the size of the Pentagon—can have new lives in the post-apartheid era and ought be retained.[5]

Until around the year 2000, the post-apartheid era was a time that banned the making of anything monumental in stone, granite, bronze, or marble. This was crucial to the transition from apartheid. The period, which included the work of the Truth and Reconciliation Commission and the drafting of a new constitution, emphasized language and ignored monuments. David Bunn describes it as a moment of "reluctance" regarding monuments:

> We [in South Africa] have arrived at a transitional moment in the language of monuments. There are few grand plans for memorial buildings in post-Apartheid South Africa, and the dust of absurdity has begun to settle over some of the more venerable historical edifices. But for many, including the millions displaced from their homes under apartheid, and the relatives who died at the hands of the security police, there is a complete disjunction between personal suffering and public memory. Apartheid's worst torturers relied absolutely on the fact that it was possible to kill, maim and massacre without any record of their actions passing into the public domain . . . When policemen like Gideon Niewoudt burnt the bodies of Siphiwe Mtimkulu and Topsy Madaka, wrapped the ash and bone fragments in rubbish bags and dumped them into the Fish River, they expected the waters to obliterate all traces of their victims . . . Some months ago, the widows and children of the men murdered by Gideon Niewoudt finally learned, in confessions before the Truth and Reconciliation Commission, what became of those who were thought erased from the historical record. Some time after the hearing, a simple ceremony was held at the approximate site where the bone ash was thrown into the river. Those who had gathered to remember, tossed wreaths into the water and watched them carried away towards the sea.[6]

To appreciate this story of the widows of Mtimkulu and Madaka, one must understand that many South African religions hold that the souls of the dead live in or near the bodies of the dead for a time, after which the souls gradually disperse. Many Africans expressed a desire simply to find the bodies of their loved ones when they gave testimony before the Truth and Reconciliation Commission. They wanted to be with their dead loved ones' souls, which they believed lingered near the bodies. The ritual of casting wreaths into the river is one of making contact with the souls of the dead. It is also one of cleansing sorrow by enacting the gesture of relinquishment, which is what happens to the souls when they float away to oblivion. Monuments in stone are utterly foreign to such gestures.

There remains, however, the matter of the more general reluctance during the heady days of early post-apartheid South Africa to create monuments, and this goes beyond the question of distinctively South African styles of memorializing. The explanation is complex. It would have to refer to a general tendency in the world to demonumentalize, from Europe after communism to America. It would have to refer to the fact that in many ways our postmodern monuments are our skyscrapers, malls, theme parks, and places of business where information circulates on computers in offices touching the sky—hence the monumental terror of attacking the World Trade Center. It would have to refer to a global climate in which the media has demonumentalized materials like granite and stone by virtue of its rapid systems of circulation and mass production: the plasticity of images has taken power from eternal statues and buildings, privileging transient appearance over monumentality. More simply, it has been a special sign of nation building at a moment of transitional justice that South Africa has now reclaimed the desire for the monumental unlike many transitional democracies elsewhere—such as those in Eastern Europe, which have had enough of monuments, it seems. Given this reclaiming of the desire for the state to monumentalize, the question of why it did not happen during the early stages of transition, from about 1994 to 2000, becomes of special interest. This goes beyond the important fact that both the landscape of monuments and styles of monumentalization have little to do with the majority of African citizens in the country, because the state—most of whose citizens are black Africans—now wants to create monuments again.

Why were monuments temporarily out of favor? Social transition required a symbolic break from the monuments of the past, given their complicity in forms of hegemonic power conveyed through symbols like the Voortrekker Monument. These styles of monumentalization were written in the script of the settler. They speak to the excluded majority only as confirmations of its exclusion. It is not surprising, then, that a hybridized style of African monumentalization did not emerge during those years, and that Africans in South Africa (unlike Francophone Africa) developed little interest in the culture of monuments.

Hence the importance of refusing monuments and all they stand for at the moment of transition. However, there is more to the refusal having to do with the moment of transition itself and the trauma unearthed. This moment (1996–2002) in South Africa favored script over monument, recitation over construction. The fifth volume of the Truth and Reconciliation Commission's *Report* (1998) contains a list of all the victims of gross human-rights violations whose names appeared in the Commission's database as of August 30, 1998. Arranged in three columns, the list is nearly a hundred pages long. It is a factual compendium, for one crucial purpose of the Commission was to gather evidence of atrocities in the name of the nation. It is also a memorial, not unlike the Vietnam Veterans Memorial of Maya Lin in Washington, D.C. The Vietnam memorial is about the trauma of that war, not simply for the dead, but for the veterans who came home to a country disgusted with them and who slid into despondency and drug addiction. It is also a memorial for the nation, which has never been able to quite celebrate its narcissistic monumentality in the same way after Vietnam, in spite of the jingoism of the Iraq wars that followed. The reduction of the Vietnam Veterans Memorial to names and dates is right, for a name is nothing but a point of reference apart from a context, and here the context is trauma. By giving only names and dates, suffering remains powerful in its silence, its refusal to monumentalize according to utopian vision or nationalistic achievement. The list of victims in the *Report* is not cast in stone like the names in Maya Lin's memorial, but in the abstraction of the printed page. Nevertheless, when read as a memorial rather than a mere compilation of facts, and when read as a distillation of the powerful history of the Commission, the list in the *Report* takes on an aura akin to that of Lin's memorial. Those names are linked to the trauma of the past, are its living sign, its haunting absence. Again the book refuses monumentality.

The communal spirit that this script of names in the *Report* aims for is Tutu's spirit of reconciliation, eschewing excesses of power and their history of ruination. This is the essential spirit of the break with the past that is the inauguration of social transition in the South African moment of the 1990s.

There is something necessary about the refusal of monuments when the moment is characterized by this kind of acknowledgment. Where the context is one of trauma, the appropriate form of acknowledgment is to say nothing and to resist monumentalization. As Adorno has noted, there can be no poetry after Auschwitz. At least, not immediately after. Equally, when you make a museum to the Holocaust in Berlin, it must resist being a monument, as Daniel Libeskind's Jewish Museum there does; it should be a building uneasy with its status as building, a museum refusing the coherent shape of a museum, attaining a coherence through this deconstructive reluctance or refusal.

This might seem enough to make out the story, but I think there is more. In spite of Coombes's fine work,[7] I am dubious that the government of the African National Congress, dominated by black Africans, is terribly interested in the question of monuments, although—as I shall discuss shortly—it is now, fifteen years after the end of apartheid, interested in the idea of the monumental and its relation to state power. Why do I say that the government lacks interest? Partly because, although there have been vague plans for reworking the extant landscape of monuments and producing new ones, there has been little sustained discussion of those plans. This could change: we contemporary historians all write in fear of being proven wrong at the next historical turn. But, having lived in South Africa from 1996 to 2002, when I was the chair of the philosophy department at the University of Natal (now University of KwaZulu-Natal) and involved in public affairs, and having visited the country often between 1991 and 1996 and again after 2002, I am inclined to doubt it. I sense relative indifference, and that is because monuments are and always have been so foreign to black African cultures. Again, this could change at any moment, but to argue my point, I would ask why the Voortrekker Monument has not been torn down—to keep Afrikaans rightists at bay? Why, ten years after the end of fascism in South Africa, has not a single monument been torn down, defaced, or altered in any way? In Hungary, the Czech Republic, Germany, France, and the United States, that would be virtually unthinkable. I believe that indifference is why the transitional gesture has not taken place in South Africa over the monuments of the past and their ruination, although cities, streets, and buildings are changing their names.

If the monuments of the past such as the Voortrekker Monument remain extant, in isolated irrelevance, that must mean that they never meant very much to black Africans. Yes, the Voortrekker Monument epitomized Afrikaner identity politics for the National Party, but it was a white thing, aimed at settler populations. The monument hardly seems to have affected native populations at all, in spite of its desire to symbolically humiliate them. Perhaps one day, retrospectively, it will, at which point it will be torn down. For the moment the moral seems to be that one group's ruin is hardly another's; one group's symbol converting ruination to power can strike those it tries to strike out with little or no force, even if it plays a role in the articulation of monumental or fascist state power at the time within the ruling elite.

History changes, sometimes rapidly. But the African National Congress remains relatively indifferent to the past landscape of settler monuments. This does not mean that the state is not again thinking in monumental symbols of power, but its current focus is the museum, which it sees as a monument to the struggle against apartheid. That museums honoring the struggle are now being designed and built—that the South African state in conjunction with industry desires them—is a sign that the new ruling party wishes to confirm its state power by monumentalizing its own past struggle.[8] Moreover, the state is weak vis-à-vis the economic sector, lacking internal legitimacy because of its problems in delivering social services. The state is ready to monumentalize itself, and it needs to do so.

This is hardly easy to do, however, since museums are also, inevitably, memorials, and the desire to refrain from monumentalization—because of the memory of ruination which suffused the spirit of the Truth and Reconciliation Commission—also remains active in the state. So the state finds itself caught between the desire to monumentalize its history and thereby concentrate its power, and the desire to memorialize without monuments, as it did in the days immediately after transition. Moreover, there are such intense political debates about the details of these museums—for instance, about how to tell the story, who should be included, and why, debates which are remnants of divisions within the history of the anti-apartheid struggle—that the state can hardly manage to get anything built at all. The state is diverse to a degree hardly imaginable in North America, and it caters to constituencies of even greater diversity. It is well nigh impossible to build museums that do not alienate some of these diverse voices, especially those marginalized by the old regime.

The state is doing best when, ironically, it outsources museum building to industry. A law requires every corporation that builds a new casino to also build a museum honoring the struggle, or a new monument. One wonders if the monuments will be situated in between the crap tables. The Apartheid Museum at Gold Reef City, outside of Johannesburg, is the first pass at such a museum. Although designed and executed by business rather than the state, it presents the state narrative with amazing faithfulness. As one passes from room to room, the story of apartheid and its liberation features the faces of the stars—Mandela, Sisulu, and others—culminating in a final image: Thabo Mbeki, seen as heir to all that came before. Apparently the story of apartheid and its overthrow irrevocably leads to him. The narrative unfolds in a blaze of media images (posters, film clips, multimedia installations), focusing on crowds (showing struggle and resistance) and iconic individuals (the victim, the ordinary person living during this tumultuous time, the hero).

Museums are also being developed by local communities. This is very much in the populist spirit of South African resistance politics. It celebrates a state elected by diverse constituents, with each group meant to have a voice in the new politics of justice. Possibly the most successful apartheid museum to date is the District Six Museum, an intimate memorialization of a community bulldozed into oblivion in the 1960s, which takes the form of an interactive space with photographs, an archive, and a large map on the floor upon which members of the former community can put their names where they used to live. The museum solves the problem of what story to tell by focusing on a particular community, using its single voice to bring mood to memory. Small community projects are easier. However, they are not the elaborating narratives in the name of the nation, not the big picture that seems to be a crucial ingredient in the transition. Ruins are acknowledged, not converted into anything other than remembrance in the spirit of a community mourning.

On August 2, 2002, the day I left South Africa after seven years to return to the United States, an advertisement appeared in a prominent South African newspaper announcing: "The Apartheid Museum Now Does Lunch."[9] This indicates that a process of commodification in line with global information systems is already in place in South Africa. The commodification of the past began as early as 1996 with a television commercial widely broadcast during South Africa's bid to host the 2004 Olympic games. The commercial featured a former political prisoner from Robben Island recalling the importance of intramural games for prisoner morale during the terrible days of his imprisonment, while a camera lovingly lingers on the now empty site of the prison—the point being to sell the idea of having the games in Cape Town under the banner of South African liberation.

There is now a burgeoning tourist industry at the island, which includes a tour of the cells of Mandela, Sisulu, Seybukwe, and Govan Mbeki, father of the current president—complete with politically correct sound bites that, perhaps unavoidably, provide little nuance or complexity. In many ways these tours are a good thing. They bring in money, contribute to moral tourism, and spread the message of what the island was to South African children. However, the Robben Island Museum is not free of commodification. During the millennium celebrations, Mandela returned to his cell, along with a host of CNN set designers and an African chorus, and he passed a torch to Thabo Mbeki in front of the cameras. This is the commodification of the political by way of image as icon and advertisement. The island is gradually turning into a theme park, where nostalgia overwhelms past reality and the past appears as a joyful sham. This demonstrates that South Africa exists in the global postmodern condition, and that memorialization is increasingly guided by the forces of mass commodification. It certainly does not suggest that Robben Island is no longer of value. But one fears that some day that monument to history will replicate its new aura by opening a branch down the street from Euro Disney. At that point in the history of South Africa, the site of memory will have become a theme park converting the experience of ruination into the monumentality of global capitalism. What is at stake is maintaining the acknowledgment of ruins against such gigantic forces.

## Notes

Versions of this chapter have been presented at the University of Michigan, the University of Natal, and the University of Toronto. I wish to thank Andre Dutoit and Deepak Mistrey for their helpful comments.

1. Conrad, *Heart of Darkness*, 86.
2. For a fascinating discussion of the Brasilia project and its subversion by local people, see Holston, *The Modernist City*.
3. Ibid.
4. See Comaroff and Comaroff, *Of Revelation and Revolution*.
5. Rossi, *The Architecture of the City*.
6. Bunn, "Whited Sepulchres."
7. See Coombes, *History after Apartheid*.

8. Physical monuments tend to be created either by fiercely independent, often aggrieved groups, or by the state when it wants to assert its power. The moment before the concentration of state power, which has taken place only during the Mbeki regime, was indeed a moment when attitudes of *healing* were vital to the transitional process—transmuting the deep strife between social agents and groups into what Tutu called "restorative truth," or reconciliation focused on victim acknowledgment. The victims were not stridently trying to assert their group identity in autonomy from the larger nation. Those who took part in the TRC had signed on to a game of national unity eschewing such assertions of separate identity as captured in monuments. And it should be recalled that the TRC took place during a state of on-again off-again political violence (between Inkatha and the ANC, and between other groups), and it was the work of the Truth Commission to salve these eruptions of malcontent through ideals and images of unity and harmony rather than through assertion of monumental power.
9. *Johannesburg Star*, August 2, 2002.

RAHUL MEHROTRA

# 14

## SIMULTANEOUS MODERNITY

*Negotiations and Resistances in Urban India*

Urban India has been one of the most interesting sites for the modern project—a place where the notion of modernity was simultaneously embraced and resisted, creating a highly fractured and fragmented landscape. In fact in India, societal modernity and aesthetic modernity often took different trajectories in how they were introduced and absorbed, sometimes collapsing together, but most often operating independently. Societal modernity, or the process of modernization, was unleashed in colonial India and has developed a well-documented body of scholarship. Aesthetic modernity emerged later through the process of industrialization, with shifts in material production. Its most obvious presence was realized only when architecture and the arts embraced the new sensibility and aesthetics of modernism. It is this aspect of its codification in architecture that is a crucial area for discussion as architects and urban designers grapple with and make sense of the emerging built landscape of India.

Following its introduction to India in Mumbai (then called Bombay) in the 1920s, art deco was the harbinger of aesthetic modernism. Through the medium of film and a wealth of public sites that dazzlingly combined consumerism and entertainment, Western cultural modernity—or aesthetic modernism—influenced all of urban India.[1] Leaders of India like Nehru, who clearly embraced modernism as the appropriate vehicle to represent the country's future agendas, encouraged the spread of modernism. The elite patrons of architecture and town planning found it attractive, as it was devoid of references to the past and brimming with optimism about the future. In fact, Nehru's orientation made India the most vibrant site of the modern project, where the East-West relationship was constantly redefined and where the modernizing experience was a key to forming the identity, or at least the architectural identity, of the nation. The culmination of this process was the invitation extended to Le Corbusier to design Chandigarh, the new capital of the Indian states of Punjab and Harayana. His designs became the symbol of the modern independent India of Nehru's imagination.[2]

But India's independence, while closing the debate on architecture and identity, did not produce the society that the nation had yearned for. Instead all efforts were directed to dealing with the splintered society the nation inherited, a society fractured by caste, class, and economic disparities; rural-urban divides; and a multitude of religious affiliations. "Independence unleashed waves of violence that seemed to be the wrath of supernatural powers. Indeed, in a metaphorical sense, the violence embodied the Indian philosophical tenets of creative and destructive forces—the cycle of chaos leading to order only to return to turmoil. Although modernity claims to decry chaos, its determination to oppose tradition breeds confusion"[3]—a phenomenon that continuously resurfaced and played itself out in far more potent manifestations as the nation evolved.

In the coming decades, the greatest challenge for modernity as the ideological project of independent India, and urban India in particular, will be resistance by subaltern cultures and their negotiations with the state. In the Indian city space many modernist urban systems spread to several other cities and formed startling combinations. We see two major axes of modernity: The first is the axis of the divide between East and West, which has produced distinct variants of modernity; we now recognize that this relationship is much more complex and subtle than the endless repeated world of simple, determinable substitutions. The second axis is that of the asymmetry between hegemonic and subaltern cultures, which continues to produce more ruins and cause an incredible mutation of the original intent of both aesthetic and cultural modernity. This is a fascinating area, and one that is becoming increasingly evident in the emerging urban landscape in India.

Urban India has become the new site for this negotiation between hegemonic and subaltern cultures where a recycled modernity has emerged. This modernity is fluid and mocking. It belongs to those estranged from the elite domains of the formal modernity of the state. It is a pirate modernity, slipping past the legality of the city to create a survival strategy without any particular self-conscious attempt at constructing a counterculture.[4] This is in contrast with the many historical legacies of modernity in India, where instruments such as the state plan (borrowed from Soviet planning paradigms) controlled, determined, and orchestrated the built landscape. With the dramatic retreat of the state in the 1980s and 1990s, the new space of the everyday is where struggles are articulated—a space that has been largely absent from the cultural discourses on globalization in the urban and architectural contexts, which have tended to focus on elite domains of production in the city.

Today, Indian cities clearly contain two components in the same space. The first is a static city, built of more permanent material such as concrete, steel, and brick; comprehensible as a two-dimensional entity on city maps; and monumental in its presence. The second is a kinetic city, which is incomprehensible as a two-dimensional entity, but perceivable as a city in motion—a three-dimensional construct of incremental development on the ground. Built of recycled waste, plastic sheets, scrap metal, canvas, waste wood—juxtaposed with items like dish antennas, webs of electric wire, and cable—this city represents a kaleidoscope of the past, present, and future compressed into an organic fabric of alleys, dead ends, and labyrinths; it is a mysterious streetscape that, like a living organism, constantly modifies and reinvents itself. The kinetic city is not defined by its architecture but by its spaces, which hold social values and support lives—and it is this pattern of occupation that determines the form of the city and how it is perceived.

In Mumbai, for example, it is commonly believed that about 70 percent of the population works in the informal economy. This number has risen as the fragmentation of urban labor curtails workers' bargaining capacity. Approximately 60 percent of the population of Mumbai lives on approximately 10 percent of the land, in the city's interstitial spaces: beside roads, in drainage pipes or ditches, on the edges of railway lines, on sidewalks under plastic sheets, or in houses with walls made of empty storage drums. This is the kinetic city, which like a twitching organism locates itself through the city in perpetual motion—a fluid and dynamic city that leaves no ruins.

The kinetic city, like a bazaar in its form, can be seen as a symbol and metaphor for the physical state of the emerging urban Indian condition. In fact it is from the kinetic city that Indian cities derive their image today. The processions, festivals, hawkers, street vendors, and street dwellers all create an ever-shifting streetscape—a city in constant motion, whose physical fabric is kinetic. In contrast, the static city, which depends on architecture for its representation, is no longer the single image by which the city is read. Thus architecture is perhaps no longer the spectacle of the city or its dominant image.

In fact in the kinetic city, the very expression of the city is temporal in nature: it is in constant flux. Festivals—including Diwali, Dussera, Durga Puja, Ganesh Chaturthi, Muharram, and Navrathri—are emerging as the spectacles of the kinetic city, and their presence on the everyday landscape pervades and dominates the popular visual culture of Indian cities. In Mumbai, for example, the popularity and growth of Ganesh's festival have been phenomenonal. During the festival (which occurs sometime in August or September because it is based on the lunar calendar), numerous neighborhoods transform themselves temporarily with lights and decoration. For ten days, entire spaces are created with an array of paraphernalia to house the idol of Ganesh. During this festival period, family, neighborhood, and city events mark the celebrations, and on the last day the idol is taken to be immersed in the sea, in processions that literally mobilize the entire city. The processions weave through assigned routes in the city, and through their scale, they showcase the intensity of their following in a competitive spirit with other processions emerging in other neighborhoods of the city—a truly spectacular format! The processions wind their way to the nearest waterfront to immerse the idol of the God and bid it farewell amid chants inviting Ganesh to resurrect his presence the following year.

The final act of immersing the idol is a wonderful metaphor, where through immersion the idea encoded in the spectacle disappears with the clay from which the idol is made, dissolving in the water. Thus there are no static or permanent mechanisms to encode this spectacle. Here the memory of the city is an "enacted" process—a kinetic moment, as opposed to buildings that contain the public memory as a static or permanent entity.[5] When this double coding of static and kinetic moments takes place in the same space or building, the city and its architecture can no longer be presumed to contain a single meaning. In the kinetic city, meanings are not stable. Like buildings and space, they are consumed, reinterpreted, and recycled, even if only momentarily. The ruinous quality of the city of modernity is recycled to create a new spectacle.

This idea takes on a critical dimension when we contemplate the preservation of the built environment in these contexts. Debates about the conservation of the ruins of modernity often revolve around the idea of cultural significance. This notion as an all-encompassing idea emerged clearly during the conservation debates of the 1980s. To be more precise, this notion of cultural significance first arose in what is referred to as the Burra Charter, adopted in Burra, South Australia, in 1979—one of the many resolutions made by the International Charter for the Conservation and Restoration of Monuments and Sites (known as ICOMOS) to define and guide conservation practice. The Burra Charter defined cultural significance as a site's aesthetic, historic, scientific, or social value for past, present, and future generations. Implicit in this definition is the belief that significance is static. The definition centers on the object and is devoid of life, with the debate rooted in ideas about antiquities from the Renaissance. What is the validity of such a notion in cases where cultural memory is an enacted process, as in the kinetic city, or where meanings are as fluid as the kinetic city itself? This incongruity is often complicated by the fact that the creators and custodians of historic environments in the static city hail from different cultures than those which created the environments.

What is our cultural reading of the kinetic city, which now forms a greater part of our urban reality? In this dynamic context, if the production or preservation of architecture or urban form has to be informed by our reading of cultural significance, it will necessarily have to include the notion of constructing significance, in debates about architecture as well as conservation. Here the idea of significance will not be a static notion, but rather one that is continuously reinvented to respond to the shifting cultural landscape. In fact, an understanding that significance evolves would clarify the role of the architect as an advocate of change rather than a preservationist who opposes change, defining the architect as someone who can engage with the kinetic and static cities on their terms. An architecture created in that spirit would reduce the symbolic import of the architectural landscape and deepen architecture's ties to contemporary realities and experiences. Conventional architecture and urban typologies would be transformed through intervention and placed in the service of contemporary life, realities, and emerging aspirations. The static city would embrace the kinetic city and be informed and remade by its logic.

Clearly the static and kinetic cities must establish a much richer relationship both spatially and metaphorically, one where affinity and rejection are simultaneously played out in an equilibrium held together by a seemingly irresolvable tension. They must negotiate with the modernity that simultaneously accepts and resists them, so that modernity becomes a basis for identity construction and the kinetic city understands itself only through the degree to which it embraces this modernity.

The ruins of modernity are a fascinating intersection where the static city, encoded in architecture (the symbols of aesthetic and cultural modernity), becomes modernity's ruins and creates a moment for contemplation. The ruins are positioned between their former newness, as symbols of optimism, and their ultimate implosion as they are engulfed by a landscape that they set out to remake. Alternatively, the static city reengages with the chaotic kinetic city, in which it was inserted as a symbol of reason. With these simultaneous pulses of the urban landscape, the modernist ruin dissolves its utopian project and becomes a monument that symbolizes our historical trajectory by fabricating multiple dialogues with its context. To borrow the words of Gaonkar, "one does not retreat, one moves sideways, one moves forward, all this is creative adaptation."[6]

Here, then, modernity reinforces the idea that contradictions and contentions are its fundamental qualities. Modernity is conceived both as something that is encountered and as something that is strived for—sometimes both simultaneously. Then modernity's ruins are not just ruins, they are allegories of the paradoxical crossings in which ruptures and discontinuities are inherent. They are about negotiations that create adaptations and resistances simultaneously. This reading celebrates the dynamic and pluralist processes that shape the urban Indian landscape, creating a kaleidoscopic representation of modernity. It is this celebration that is critical to internalizing the ruins of modernity and rebuilding them, even if only temporarily.

## Notes

Some sections of this essay were previously published in "Negotiating the Static and Kinetic Cities," in *Other Cities, Other Worlds: Urban Imaginaries*, edited by Andreas Huyssen (Durham, N.C.: Duke University Press, 2009).

1. Gaonkar, "On Alternative Modernities."
2. Mehrotra, "The Architecture of Pluralism."
3. Tagore, "The Legacy of Anti-Tradition," 36.
4. Sundaram, "Recycling Modernity."
5. Mehrotra, "Bazaar City."
6. Gaonkar, "On Alternative Modernities," 22.

# PART IV

# (POST)RUINSCAPES

HELMUT PUFF

# 15

## RUINS AS MODELS

*Displaying Destruction in Postwar Germany*

"Amerika kennt keine Ruinen"—America has no ruins—according to an essay written in 1935 by the art historian Horst Janson.[1] No other statement could better capture the power of ruins to occasion definition, reflection, and affective engagement. In the essay, "Amerika," ruins function as an emblematic divider. They are said to divorce the old world, with its penchant for aesthetic appreciation of the past, from the new and ruinless world of modern, industrialized North America. This text powerfully illustrates the central place accorded to ruins in a centuries-old discourse—a discourse that ultimately is not about the material remains themselves but about self-assurance and alienation.

As is well known, ruinous material remains have been made to serve many master discourses. The fact that ruins are versatile matter, discursively speaking, is one of their most enduring features. Between Petrarch and Rose Macaulay, Augustus Hare and W. G. Sebald, writers have mobilized ruins in a variety of contradictory ways. Ruins are said to articulate lessons on ancient morality, ruminations on artistic creativity, and political allegories.[2] Since the Renaissance, ruins have also connected that which is incommensurate: art and nature, past and present, history and sensual experience.[3] In "Amerika," however, ruins provide an analytical prism. The theme brings to the fore a plethora of scattered observations on such diverse topics as the use of particular building materials, patterns of land use, capitalism, historical consciousness, and, of course, culture. To make a case for America as a culture sui generis is one of the text's key points.

The essay was not intended for publication. It is an essay in the original sense of the word: an attempt, an experiment, an exercise in thought. Its authors documented a conversation, one of many during their friendship. Yet the tone of debate has been replaced by beautifully incisive, rigorous, and concise prose. As academic "wanderers between the worlds," the art historians Horst Janson (1913–1982) and William Heckscher (1904–1999) were familiar with both worlds, the old and the new.[4] Somehow this essay, with all its impressive erudition and its assertive style, echoes the authors' own liminality, their tenuous status as messengers between the continents—continents they were mapping with stunning ease. Forced into exile from Nazi Germany, they had just started a new life abroad, making English their primary linguistic vehicle. Yet for the purpose of this conversation on ruins they returned to the common language they had largely abandoned, at least academically: German.

Skillfully, Janson worked to cordon off ruins as a recognizable cultural form. The evocative absence of contemporary ruins in "Amerika" thus reminds us of, among other things, the difference between rubble, the unformed mass of debris, and the ruins that are a well-framed window into the past.[5] Rubble is material without significance; it is matter destined to be removed. By contrast, the term "ruins" evokes traditions, visual codes, and a wealth of significations.

Not surprisingly, discourses on ruins were and are contested terrain. Vergara's *American Ruins* provides an excellent example. The author, a Chile-born photographer and writer, seems to proclaim emphatically that America *has* ruins. Daringly, Vergara weds his exploration of post-industrial urban decay in America's inner cities to a European aesthetic of ruin. When he suggested turning downtown Detroit into a "skyscraper ruins park," his proposal sparked an outcry.[6] For much of its history, the dominant gaze on ruins directed itself primarily to traces of the distant past, a past whose inhabitants had vanished long ago. To bring this overdetermined, complex code to bear on a present moment continues to challenge social, visual, and discursive conventions. The fact that the term "ruins" has kept its power to divide points to the workings of the word. Its various semantic layers vacillate between process and stasis—that is, between ruination and the remains of decay and destruction; between material base and its metaphoric overlay of various moralities. It speaks of materials, people, behavior, institutions. It conjures up abject as well as ennobling states. Such meanings are permeable; their membranes are thin, and at times seem to collapse. Thus viewed, the term "ruins" transports the flotsam of its own history. Layers of usage over time have sedimented into its current configuration.

In this essay, I propose to excavate the semiotics of a particular, nonverbal discourse on ruins. I am investigating scale models representing urban ruins. The dust of oblivion has covered these intriguing objects. Created since the end of the Second World War, three-dimensional renderings of bombed-out cities provide eerie glimpses of the destruction and devastation caused by the war. Yet the existence of such models—I know of twelve—in German city halls and local history museums has gone largely unnoticed. As visual discourse, they promise to provide immediate access to events and experiences that seem to defy representation, translating large-scale destruction into an object.

In light of the recent fascination with the air raids on German cities,[7] the neglect of scale models of urban ruins is surprising. It is my contention that these artifacts offer themselves to viewers as a way of coming to terms with loss (*Verlustbewältigung*):[8] the terrible loss of lives, the human suffering, and the urban devastation wrought by the raids. These so-called rubble models[9] create a visual echo and thus a memory of the bombings. As objects—many of the models have little verbal explanation to accompany them—these maquettes allow for a variety of gazes and forms of engagement. The pleasure of viewing is central to the experience. The models thus function as a complex repository of reflections and emotions, sites where one can invoke memories of a lost past, the experience of destruction, and a future that never came to be.[10] Viewed thus, rubble represented in scale can, by virtue of cultural resonances and the conditions of presentation as well as representation, metamorphose into ruins.

Here I am interested in the models themselves, their properties as a group of objects, their relationship with other forms of representation, and the codes that govern their public presentation. An analysis of how ruined urban spaces have been modeled and displayed will work against the ever alluring repression thesis. Sebald has argued that the bombing of German cities amounted to a taboo subject in postwar German literature: in light of German atrocities, including the Holocaust, the traumatic sufferings of civilians during the air raids could not be expressed publicly.[11] This focus on supposed radical turning points recommends itself as a recovery of what has been lost for too long.[12] Instead, I seek to refocus the debate on the complexities of the intertwined realms of memory, history, and representation as they have unfolded between 1945 and the present.

### From Rubble to Ruins

The fixity of the models stands in marked contrast to the meaning of the Latin word *ruina*: a collapse, or rather a collapsing—that is, a process. Using a three-dimensional model to depict actual destruction with shifting piles of rubble, unstable facades in danger of collapse, and the omnipresence of dust and ash, not to mention stench and vermin, is a material paradox. Years of labor go into making a permanent image of something that was itself impermanent. This paradox is nothing if not arresting.

Models of urban destruction freeze a moment in time into an object ready for visual consumption and investigation. It is hard for the viewer familiar with German history not to fall into meditation, at least for a few moments. With their precise details, the models can lay claim to documentary status. They do not seem to require further elucidation. After all, models are "the least abstract of all representational types." Unlike maps, they can be appreciated "from many different angles." They are even said to be "accessible at first glance to the untrained eye."[13] Thus, three-dimensional renderings in miniature have rarely been subjected to rigorous critical reflection. Yet such models ought to be approached as complex simulations of an abstract, multiperspectival reality.

Models executed to scale make urban space experiential in a particular fashion. Unlike actual cities, models are devoid of human life. Models show the city as *urbs*, or built environment, rather than as *civitas*, or urban community, to quote an ancient distinction that Kagan has taken up.[14] Space as expressed in urban models typically drowns out the multitude of social relations encoded in actual cityscapes: the ownership of buildings or lots, for instance, or the areas defined by specific human activities such as markets or by the professional topography of the urban environment. The particular abstraction at play in city models thus veils the social makeup of urban spaces, turning them into a realm of pure representation. The social meanings of models are therefore articulated through a geometrical conception of space. Devoid of human interaction and social signification, the city model presents itself as an instrument.

Three-dimensional urban portraits are "conceptualized space, the space of scientists, planners, urbanists, technocratic subdividers and social engineeers," to quote Henri Lefebvre.[15] Put differently, scale models invite us to imagine the lived urban environment—an imagining that extends beyond the present into an unseen and unbuilt future. Through the lens of models, future forms of habitation become imaginable. Full-scale models thus interpellate the viewer in a particular way, namely as maker, architect, or ruler.

It is only fitting, then, that city models accord the viewer a position of privilege. Importantly, he—I am intentionally using the male pronoun—is able to position himself as he pleases in relation to the represented space. He may stand high above the model, surveying it as a whole; he may gaze at or zoom in on particular areas or details; he may lower his eyes to the model's horizon in order to view the urban skyline from various directions; he may move about or stand still. As motionless objects, scale models allow a variety of gazes: a quick glance here and there, a systematic scanning, a measured view. The viewer's is a privileged gaze in that it not only entails unrestrained visual control over space but also a dynamic relationship to space—a flexibility possible only under the conditions of an "as if." While architectural spaces often position the subject, especially the preeminent subject, in particular ways (a process splendidly illuminated by Starn),[16] represented space of this kind allows the viewer's gaze and, as a consequence, imagination to roam freely. The model does away with the various impediments, technical or social, that limit access to actual, inhabited spaces.

### 1945 and 1960

Reconstruction had barely begun in Frankfurt when a model of the city's downtown destruction was made, though it is unclear who commissioned the model and whether it was shown to the public at the time.[17] The Römerberg district appears almost completely leveled. Only the walls of large historical buildings—the Kaiserdom, the Paulskirche, and the city hall (the Römer)—stick out of the rubble; Haus Wertheym is a notable exception to the destruction.[18] In the model, the debris is rendered in a kind of high realism. The streets are covered with rubble; passage seems impossible. The model's coloring reflects one of the city's primary building materials, red sandstone, but it also evokes the afterglow of a fire like the one that ravished the city after the attacks.

In all its emotive qualities, this model shows a haunting vision of Frankfurt in ruins rather than the grim reality of destruction—a feature acknowledged in the model's latest presentation in Frankfurt's Historisches Museum (history museum).[19] Its mode is visual hyperbole which, at least in the immediate postwar context, bolstered the argument for radical reconstruction, and seemed to suggest: "Nothing is left of the old city, we need to start from scratch and build anew." This argumentative dimension of models becomes particularly evident if we compare the model of Frankfurt with an exhibit in Vienna.

In 1946, the exhibit "Niemals vergessen!" (Never Forget) opened its doors to the public in Vienna's Künstlerhaus after more than a year of planning. As an antifascist manifesto—one organized primarily by Austria's left—it was an educational event, meant to pave the way for a new society and better future. But as Kos argues, the exhibition was dated by the time its doors opened—a fact evident in the exhibit's heavy reliance upon pre-1934 political propaganda for its pictorial repertoire. Nonetheless, 260,000 visitors saw the exhibit during the fourteen weeks it was on display. Upon entering the exhibit, visitors were confronted with a large-scale panorama of the bombed-out city, with its landmark cathedral in front of a dramatic sky. An image of Hitler in the clouds of smoke indicted National Socialism and the Führer for the disaster. Urban devastation served as a complex symbol of social, political, and moral ruin. In another room in the same exhibit, by contrast, the city in ruins formed the backdrop for a heroic appeal to the future: a stonemason and his female companion work to clear a ruinous cityscape featuring some of Vienna's most famous buildings.[20]

Argumentative uses of models are not peculiar to postwar Germany and Austria. Such propagandistic framings occur throughout the medium's history.

Since the fifteenth century, models have been produced not only to please aesthetically but to survey a realm, particularly a territory's fortifications; to plan military campaigns; and to impress foreign rulers or other viewers in a sort of specular containment policy.[21] Time is one of the argumentative dimensions of rubble models.

In the immediate postwar years, ruins referenced a multilayered temporality. To be sure, they were reminders of a fraught past. Yet this temporal-symbolic nexus relied on absences—that is, it obfuscated the specifics of individual guilt or collective entanglements behind an all-encompassing cipher of disaster. At the same time, however, ruins operated as an appeal for their removal. In other words, they conjured up the construction worker as a figure central to the imaginary of the late 1940s and 1950s, possibly with the vague promise to remove the past with the rubble.[22]

No wonder, then, that during the reconstruction of Germany the rhetorical force of city models acquired a specific edge. Commonly, public presentations coupled a model of the city at its worst, most ruinous state with a model of the rebuilt city; that was the case in Kassel, Heilbronn, and Hannover. While one can also encounter such juxtapositions in museums, this arrangement has been particularly popular in city halls. By inviting comparison, pairs of models with their mutual referentiality highlight a city administration's efforts to restore buildings for its populace. Ironically, the model of Kassel's postwar rebirth was constantly updated and, as a result, reduced to its present ruinous state; thus the model of Kassel in ruins is now on display in the local history museum, while the remnants of the model of "Kassel rebuilt" have been relegated to storage.[23]

In Frankfurt, for instance, the rubble model is displayed with a meticulously crafted model of downtown Frankfurt. Between 1926 and 1955, the brothers Hermann and Robert Trenner used builders' records to create the model of Frankfurt before the raid. Because of the city's demise as a result of the air raids, their model changed from an image of the present city into a monument to a place that no longer was.[24]

Hannover's Rathaus, built in a commanding historicist style and opened to the public in 1913, was one of the few buildings to survive the devastating air raids of the last years of the Second World War; today it provides a grand setting for an impressive group of city models. In its monumental central court, four models of the city—showing it in 1689, 1939, 1945, and today—are on display. No exhibit interrupts or, rather, frames one's encounter with these objects. Visitors are left to make sense for themselves of Hannover's urban history, including its destruction,[25] and to contemplate what has been lost. Without commentary, rubble models are likely to reinforce existing narratives, rather than challenge or transform them.

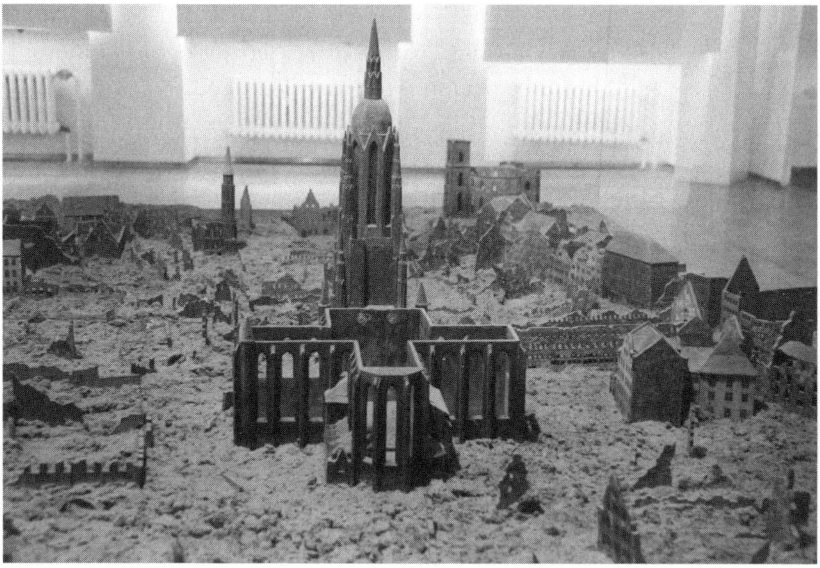

1. Rubble model of Frankfurt (1946?), Historisches Museum, Frankfurt. Photo by author.

In Heilbronn, three city models, one of them showing the city in ruins, are on display in a monument constructed in 1960 to commemorate the lives lost in the war, the devastating air raid of December 4, 1944, and those inhabitants who were persecuted because of their "race, faith, and their beliefs," as an inscription on the monument specifies. The models are installed in a two-storied structure between the old and new city halls. Austerely white, the exhibit space speaks of devastation and loss, accentuated by the unfiltered light breaking in through the windows from the outside. An inscription on the wall opposite the windows puts the manifold losses together in an attempt to articulate meaning and to create a bridge, however tenuous, to the future: "May the will to do good arise from the memory of the dead."[26]

### Absences and Presence

As mentioned before, all the city models are utterly devoid of people. To be sure, this absence is generic: it distinguishes models from dioramas. Yet when it comes to representing ruins in the form of models, this absence accords with iconic representations of fragmented material remains. These pictorial conventions can be traced back to paintings by Claude Lorrain and Caspar David Friedrich, and etchings by Giovanni Battista Piranesi, to name a few of the artists whose work shaped the poignant visual code for representing ruins—and whose images have depicted the tension between absence and presence, past and present, with nostalgia and desire.[27]

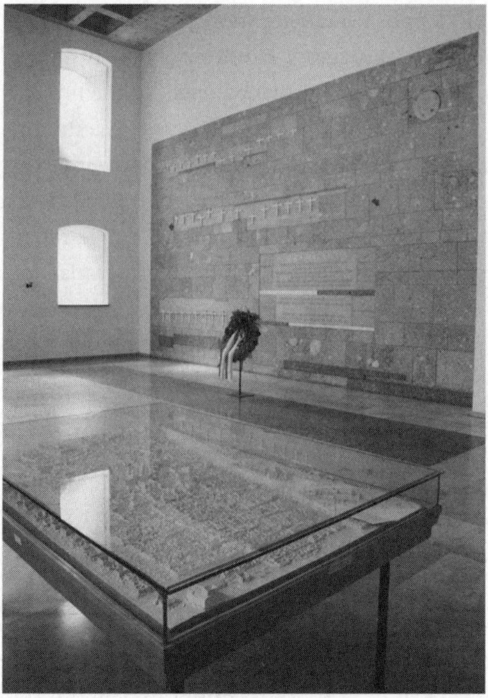

2. City models of Heilbronn (1960), City Hall, Heilbronn. Photo by author.

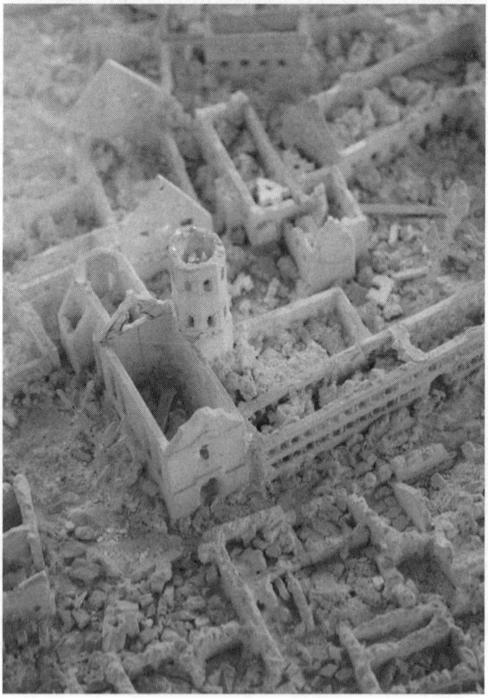

3. Detail of the model of Heilbronn in ruins (1960), City Hall, Heilbronn. Photo by author.

Yet these classic invocations of ruinous beauty are more multivalent than a mere emphasis on their aesthetic qualities suggests. However obliquely, images of ruins gesture toward the disastrous events that turned once-flourishing settlements into deserted heaps of stone. In fact, depictions of more recent disasters often make use of a similar imagistic register.[28] Fritzsche has contended that since the early nineteenth century, ruins have increasingly been imbued with a historicist spirit—namely, a past that promises to be different from the present. "Ruins," he writes, "were increasingly regarded as the sites of particular and knowable historical events."[29] Yet the revolutionary ruptures might not have been as clear-cut as this comment suggests. Ruins did not lack references to concrete events before the Napoleonic Wars, nor did the ruins of modernity exclude the moral reflections typically associated with classic ruins.

In a study on photography in the immediate postwar period, Dagmar Barnouw observes that for the war photographer Margaret Bourke-White, "The fascination of the photograph was the distance that allowed her to see only one-dimensional shapes forming intriguing patterns undisturbed by human fears and hopes."[30] Iconic images of German cities at the end of the war regularly evoke the vast emptiness of uninhabitable, hollow spaces that the viewer knows—the architectural skeleton of a city is recognizable after all—once teemed with life: a past which seems, due to the degree of destruction, irredeemably lost, except for a ruinous reflection. The material ruins thus function like a synecdoche for the people who once lived there, and the urban space that continues to exist only insofar as it is enshrined in personal memory or historic documentation. The horrors of destruction are cloaked in renderings that, as is often remarked, generate a silence of eerie beauty. Hardly anyone appears in such photographs to tell the disaster's story. If there are people to be seen, they gaze over the vast desert of devastation, magnifying the spectacle of destruction by their detached, shadowy presence.[31]

Not accidentally, several exhibits—for instance, in Frankfurt, Heilbronn, Kassel, Münster, and Würzburg—interlace two-dimensional photographic representations with three-dimensional reconstructions, thus inviting visitors to make comparisons between photography, a medium often associated with authenticity, and what is obviously a reconstruction, a city model.

An industry has sprung up based on images of bombed-out cities. In Frankfurt, numerous postcard vendors in the city's rebuilt heart sell aerial views of the Römerberg district, the city's center, at unspecified dates after the war.[32] One postcard, captioned "Frankfurt: yesterday and today," was included in Sebald's *Luftkrieg und Literatur*, juxtaposing a ruinous past with the rebuilt present in the form of photographs.[33] One may wonder what buyers write on the cards when sending them to friends and loved ones. The popular appeal of such

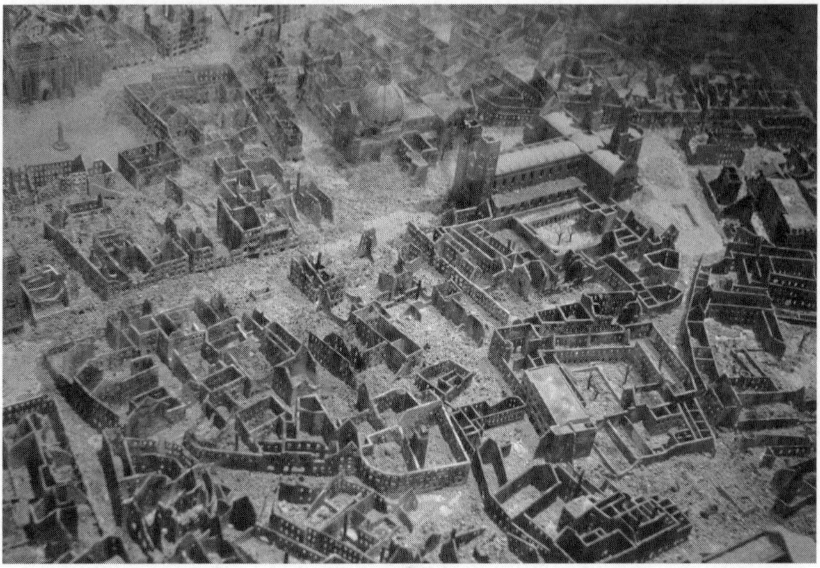

4. Detail of rubble model of Würzburg (1989), memorial to the air raids, City Hall, Würzburg. Photo by author.

postcards for today's visitors to Frankfurt may lie not least in their connotations of an antitourism that, as Buzard remarks, has always been the mark of the true tourist.[34] These postcards may provide an ironic commentary on postwar Frankfurt. But they emerged from the aesthetic and emotional nexus alluded to above and show pride in a quick reconstruction and return to civic urbanity.

Absences invite interpretive pirouettes—acts that give meaning and fill the void. Therein lies one of the appeals of ruins, be they real remains or artifacts like models. The attempt to see the bombed-out German cities as ruins rather than as piles of rubble began almost immediately with their large-scale destruction. When, in 1943, vast parts of Kassel had been reduced to ashes, Joseph Goebbels hastened to give meaning to the smoldering remains of the city. Beyond making the destruction a sign of the enemy's barbarity, Goebbels's speech recast loss and human suffering as a sacrifice for a better future: "[After a German victory] you will march through the fields of rubble in happiness . . . You will view these ruins as pledges and guarantors of victory. You will stand still in front of every house and say: we have sacrificed this house, too, for the victory."[35] Note how buildings as signifiers mask the more lurid aspects of what many people in the audience must have witnessed themselves. Note also how the text proceeds from "rubble" to "ruins." This act of signification elided the present and envisioned the future as a time that would be better than the lost past.

As Benjamin puts it, "In the ruin history has physically merged into the setting."[36] In the case of models, the viewer's response to this dialectic invocation of presence and absence depends, at least in part, on what is physically present—the model's materials. Different material modes generate different viewing experiences. Plaster models, like the ones of Heilbronn, possess few contrasts, which makes it hard to identify specific places and causes the details to recede into an overall impression. As a result, the models' very material evokes absence. The uniform texture and off-white color may in fact remind us how futile it is to attempt to recover what has been lost. The models of old, postwar, and ruinous Heilbronn blend into a melancholic engagement with the past and the present, appropriate for the models' location in a memorial to the city's dead.

Traditionally, however, models are made of painted wood, a material capable of depicting the details that lend these objects an aura of reality.[37] In Bielefeld's Historisches Museum, the representation is ruptured in a way that makes only the ruins seem real: buildings that remained intact are represented as mere wooden blocks, while ruins are painted. This difference helps the viewer assess what and how much was destroyed.

Quite a different effect is achieved in a museum on the history of Münster (Stadtmuseum) that opened to the public in 1979. Among the museum's more than twenty models is one showing the city at the end of the Second World War. While models of earlier versions of the city feature bright, cheerful colors like red and green, this one is in shades of brown, indicating dirt, detachment, and, ultimately, what has to be left behind.[38]

### Absence and Agency

Palpable absences conjure up notions of loss—most prominently, unimaginable human loss. Notably, some of the exhibits—at Frankfurt, for instance—feature no factual account of this loss in the war. Like the victims of the bombings, however, the agents of destruction are also absent in three-dimensional objects. Questions of who bombed the city, why, and how are addressed in the text that frames the objects, or not at all. The exhibits provide a variety of answers to these questions or refuse to answer at all.

Importantly, destruction was not only caused by the Allied attacks. Once German cities had been bombed, Nazi officials seized the opportunity to clean up the urban slate for projected reconstructions in a Nationalist Socialist future that never came. That was the case in Kassel, although there is no mention of this in the extensive exhibit surrounding the model.[39]

But the issue of agency also touches on viewing and the viewer. Because of their nature, most city models assume a rather static relationship to the beholder. Although the models are displayed at varying heights, they tend to invite the visitor to assume the standard position that, in a radically different context, Pratt calls the "monarch of all I survey."[40] Spread out before one's eyes, the city model opens itself to a bird's-eye view, drawing the viewer into its minutiae, inviting inspection, arresting the gaze. Postcards of models give the viewer scopic control over a long vanished urban space, with pictures that underline the models' claim to realism.[41] Although the installations are themselves immovable, viewing models suggests the actions of collapsing as bombs fell. Not surprisingly, architectural models are a favorite backdrop for images of rulers. The static nature of the city models is particularly striking if we compare them with models of urban disasters other than the bombings of German cities. The Museum of London, for instance, offers visitors an interactive exhibit called London's Burning: The Great Fire of London 1666: "a combination of models, lighting effects and sound," accompanied by a recorded narrative that brings to life this long-past catastrophic event.[42] Similarly, the model of the great fire of Hamburg, formerly on display in the Hamburg Historisches Museum, hints at the unfolding of the destruction rather than its aftermath. For reasons of comparison, I also want to bring up a model of a fictional devastated city. In 1960, the Katastrophenschutzschule des Bundes (German School for Disaster Management) in Bad Neuenahr commissioned a model of Bonn that displays various forms and degrees of destruction after a supposed atomic strike on the city's Kennedy Bridge. While Bonn's downtown is presumed to have been erased and is therefore not shown at all, the model depicts the city's northern suburbs, where survival would have been possible.[43] This feature calls attention to a commonality of all the models discussed so far: they focus on urban centers. To be sure, these parts of cities were often hit most dramatically, especially in places like Heilbronn, Pforzheim, and Würzburg, with their premodern timber-frame structures. But the models evoke city centers as symbolic spaces, especially cathedrals as focal points of their communities.

In Bielefeld's Historisches Museum, set up in a former factory in 1994, the curators decided to dramatize the visitor's encounter with a 1985 model of the city during, rather than after, the war.[44] It can be viewed almost cinematically. Installed in an angled, sloping position in front of windows at the end of a room, and bounded by lockers on one side and steel machinery on the other, the model is protected only by a railing and can be approached at close range, as in a low-level flight. Hung from the ceiling, an actual bomb adds to the dynamism and the staged quality of the design. The installation's cinematic effect is further heightened by color photographs which are attached to the railing and arranged to look like film stills. Strangely, this exhibit turns the visitor into a pilot. Whether one imagines flying an Allied or German plane, the installation

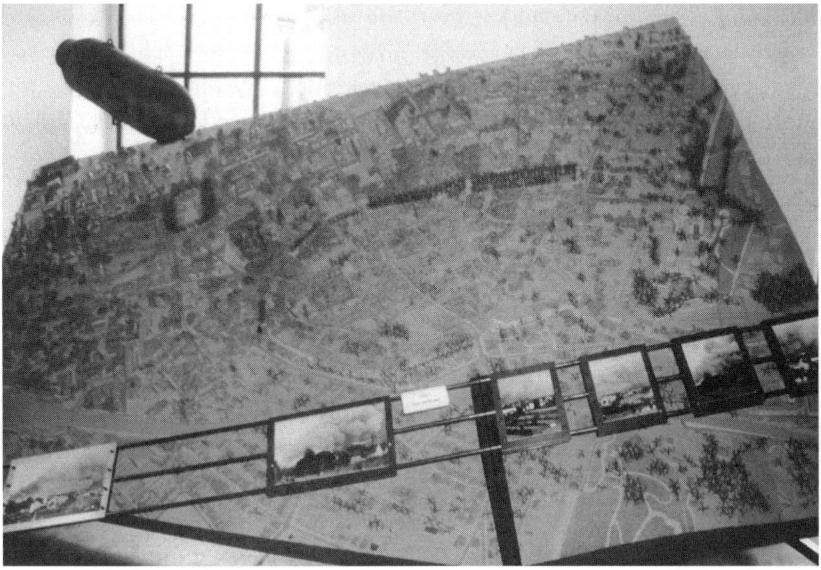
5. Model of Bielefeld (1985), Historisches Museum, Bielefeld. Photo by author.

counters a narrative of mere victimhood while conveying, at the same time, the unsettling sensation of a world turning upside down.

More than sixty years after the end of the war, rubble models have apparently ceased to speak for themselves. Increasingly, younger visitors do not have access to personal narratives of destruction from family members, one of the key modes of disseminating knowledge on the air raids in the immediate postwar period—when public memory was limited in scope and rarely went beyond local commemorations.[45] Notably, the postwar era has become the object of intense historical research. Public debates on the air raids in the wake of Sebald's Zurich lectures have led to further reflections on the topic. A wave of publications has moved the air war to center stage with the German public, a public with a knack for military history.[46]

Germany's network of local history museums has begun to take up the challenge of creating displays on the war and postwar periods. New forms of presentation have come into existence. Older models, including those originally made for city halls, have become part of up-to-date exhibitions with extensive coverage of the air war on German cities, as in the Kassel Stadtmuseum (city museum). Exhibits in Würzburg's Mainfränkisches Museum, the Museum für Hamburgische Geschichte, and elsewhere feature models built especially for displays on the war. New exhibits are currently being planned for museums in Frankfurt and Dresden whose collections include rubble models. The Bielefeld

Historisches Museum provides a novel viewing experience, countering standard ways of displaying such models in memorials and museums.

As a result, verbal information increasingly frames, or rather encroaches on, one's encounter with these artifacts. Originally displayed with little commentary, scale models of bombed-out cities have become embedded in various explicit historical contexts. As didactic tools, the models will continue to play a role in shaping the perception of the air raids, as well as raise questions about the interplay between visual and textual histories.

As I have argued, the history of the meticulously crafted objects discussed here registers a subtle semantic shift, from rubble model to the term used for Würzburg's model in the 1980s, "city of ruins." Regardless of what we call them, the three-dimensional models contribute to a mode of seeing loss which helped to transform rubble into ruins. Scale models of ruined cityscapes turn destruction into a visual spectacle, offering the postwar viewer scopic control over a cityscape pregnant with painful memories and emotions. Viewed thus, rubble models cannot escape their status as a medium of representation, despite their naturalism. They promise immediate access to the past, yet they position the viewer at a comfortable distance from the disastrous events that occasioned their making. Their muteness or abstraction is striking. On the one hand, their visual form shows the anxiety of those who commissioned them that memories of the air raids were virulent. On the other hand, the models' documentary precision serves as an antidote to the lure of forgetting the past altogether.

Devoid of human life, rubble models conjure up a host of visual traditions in representing ruins. They bear visible traces of a particular aesthetics, what Young calls a "rhetoric of ruins,"[47] while summoning a variety of other representational genres, including the architectural model and wartime and postwar photography. In combining various codes, the maquettes have also created a tradition of their own. The latest among them, currently under construction in Pforzheim, has, like the model in Würzburg, been inspired by its ancestor, the Frankfurt rubble model.[48]

Germany, unlike America, has ruins: this is what Janson and Heckscher signal, if only indirectly, in "Amerika." The city models discussed here attest to the presence and importance of German ruins.

## Notes

Profuse thanks to Elizabeth Sears and Charlotte Schoell-Glass for having shared their lucky find with me. Thanks also to the Janson estate for allowing me to publish my thoughts on an unpublished essay by Horst Janson.

1. Horst Janson, "Amerika." See Charlotte Schoell-Glass and Elizabeth Sears, *Verzetteln als*

*Methode*, 71–74; and Charlotte Schoell-Glass and Elizabeth Sears, "'Amerika kennt keine Ruinen': Horst W. Jansons Amerikabild," *Zeitschrift für Ideengeschichte*.

2. Woodward, *In Ruins*, serves as a good introduction to this topic.
3. Bredekamp, *The Lure of Antiquity and the Cult of the Machine*, 44–45.
4. Wendland, *Biographisches Handbuch deutschsprachiger Kunsthistoriker im Exil*, 271–75; Sears, "The Life and Work of William S. Heckscher," 107–33.
5. I am grateful to Julia Hell for having first pointed me in this direction, as she has done for other contributors to this volume.
6. Quoted in David Walsh, "Detroit in Ruins: Downtown Detroit: An American Acropolis," May 5, 1997, World Socialist Web Site, http://www.wsws.org.
7. See, for instance, Friedrich's widely read and much debated *Der Brand* (*The Fire*).
8. This term, with its echo of *Vergangenheitsbewältigung* (coming to terms with the past), is heuristically valuable. I am aware of the problems that continue to trouble the use of Vergangenheitsbewältigung, among other things because of its suggestion that it is possible to bring to a close the memory of Nazi atrocities.
9. This is the name of the model of downtown Frankfurt, on display in the city's Historisches Museum.
10. In a larger project, "City in Ruins: Modeling German History," I will approach the museological form of scale models of ruinous spaces through the lens of the historical traditions on which they rely.
11. Sebald, *Luftkrieg und Literatur* (On the Natural History of Destruction).
12. Huyssen has contextualized Sebald's text in a desire for "Rewritings and New Beginnings," symptomatic of the ongoing traces of historical trauma in German public life and writing. Read thus, *Luftkrieg und Literatur* does not indicate the radical turning point in coming to terms with the suffering of the air raids that Sebald claims. See Huyssen, "Rewritings and New Beginnings: W. G. Sebald and the Literature on the Air Raid," in *Present Pasts*, 138–57.
13. Buisseret, "Modeling Cities in Early Modern Europe," 141.
14. Kagan, "*Urbs* and *Civitas* in Sixteenth- and Seventeenth-Century Spain."
15. Lefebvre, *The Production of Space*, 38.
16. Starn, "Seeing Culture in a Room." From this article, I took the three modalities of seeing mentioned in the text: the glance, measured view, and scan.
17. This model is 2.1 by 1.86 by 0.4 meters.
18. There is a strong resonance with the aesthetic concept of preserving individual historical buildings in a context that often differs radically from the buildings' original neighborhood. This emerged as one of the dominant concepts for monument preservation in the 1950s in response to wartime destruction. See Koshar, *Germany's Transient Pasts*.
19. The caption for the model describes it as "Plastische Skizze der zerstörten Altstadt von Frankfurt—sogenanntes Trümmermodell: . . . Das Modell wurde offensichtlich als 'Argumentationshilfe' in einem städtebaulichen Wettbewerb 1946 eingesetzt: je größer der Grad der Zerstörung, um so leichter die Überzeugung zum absoluten Neubeginn. . . ." The term "plastische Skizze" (three-dimensional model sketch) derives from the original description on the object itself: "Plastische Skizze von der durch Kriegseinwirkung 1939–1945 zerstörten Altstadt von Frankfurt am Main." So far, I have not been able to substantiate the caption's claim about the context for the making of the model.

Apparently, there was no urbanistic exhibit in Frankfurt in 1946. The fact that the model is barely mentioned in the extensive discussions on the city's future between 1945 and the present raises the question whether the model was ever on display before it was discovered in the attic of the state of Hesse's construction department in the mid-1970s and subsequently transferred to the museum. The model was cleaned and restored for the current exhibit, which has been open to the public since 2002. The previous exhibit in the museum's lobby did not mention the distortion.

20. Kos, "Die Schau mit dem Hammer," in *Eigenheim Österreich: Zu Politik, Kultur und Alltag nach 1945*, 22–24. See also Kos, "Zukunftsfroh und muskelstark: Zum öffentlichen Menschenbild der Wiederaufbaujahre," in the same volume, 59–150.
21. Buisseret, "Modeling Cities in Early Modern Europe"; Andrew Martin, "Stadtmodelle."
22. On "Frankfurt oder Bonn?" *Rhein-Neckar-Zeitung*, 30 June 1949, a cartoon by Schaal, see Bauer, "*Seid einig für unsere Stadt*," 70.
23. Karl-Hermann Wegener, Director, Kassel Stadtmuseum, interview by the author, May 22, 2003. The model, first on display in the city hall (1953), was first exhibited in the Kassel Stadtmuseum in 1983. The current exhibit opened its doors in 1993.
24. The model of the city before the raid is 4.5 by 1.7 meters. Its scale is 1:200, while most of the models under consideration here use the scale of 1:500.
25. See Steinweg, *Das Rathaus Hannover*, 6.
26. "Aus der Toten Gedächtnis erwachse der Wille, das Gute zu wirken."
27. For introductions to this topic, see Roth, Lyons, and Merewether, eds., *Irresistible Decay*; and Dekkers, *The Way of All Flesh*.
28. Contemporary images of the destruction wrought by the great fire of Hamburg in 1842 work within the representational frame of romantic ruins. I have chosen this event as an example since it occurred shortly before the medium of photography transformed the representation of disasters. See Horbas and Pelc, eds., *Es brannte an allen Ecken zugleich*.
29. Fritzsche, *Stranded in the Present*, 101.
30. Barnouw, *Germany 1945*, 101.
31. This is evident, for instance, in an oft-cited view of Dresden, with its many religious overtones, shot in 1945 from the city hall: "Dresden nach der Zerstörung am 13.2.1945: Blick von Rathausturm nach Süden," in Sächsische Landesbibliothek, Abteilung Deutsche Fotothek. See also David Crew, "Buildings or Bodies? Using Photographs of the Bombing of Dresden, 1945–1975," talk presented at German Studies Association meeting ("Indelible Images: The German Visual Archive after World War II"), September 18, 2003. There is a different kind of photo that foregrounds survival; yet they often did not achieve iconicity. See Hauschild-Thiessen, ed., *Die Hamburger Katastrophe vom Sommer 1943 in Augenzeugenberichten*.
32. This is also true of Cologne, though not to the same degree.
33. Sebald, *Luftkrieg und Literatur*, 15. The caption for "Frankfurt—Gestern + Heute," designed in a font suggesting a person's handwriting, says: "Frankfurt am Main Blick zum Römer 1947"; "Frankfurt Heute"; "Blick zum Römer 1997." As in his other works, Sebald comments little on the image. Sebald reads this postcard as an example of pride in having rebuilt Germany "bigger and better," comparable to the forms of display of "rubble models" in German city halls in the postwar period.

34. Buzard, *The Beaten Track.*
35. Goebbels's speech, quoted in Dettmar, "Kassel im Luftkrieg," 11, my translation.
36. Benjamin, *The Origin of German Tragic Drama*, 177–78.
37. Frankfurt's rubble model is made of wood, cardboard, and sand. More recent models, like that of Würzburg, seem to use plastic.
38. See *Münster im Modell*, 62–65. A similar effect is achieved in Hannover.
39. Sascha Winter, e-mail message to the author, January 29, 2003. The issue of agency also concerns the makers of the models, who frequently are not acknowledged in the exhibits—an issue I will not address in this chapter.
40. Pratt, *Imperial Eyes*, 204–5.
41. See, for instance, "Braunschweig um 1671 im Stadtmodell: Umgebung des Altstadtmarkts" and "Braunschweig um 1671 im Stadtmodell: Burggelände" (undated postcards) or the large-format postcard of the destroyed city on sale at the Stadtmuseum Münster: "Stadtmodell 1945, Modellbauatelier Steiner, 1966" (undated photo, Stadtmuseum Münster, Tomasz Samek).
42. See www.museum-london.org.uk.
43. Baumunk and Brunn, eds., *Zentren, Residenzen, Metropolen in der deutschen Geschichte*, 431. The model is now held at the Haus der Geschichte in Bonn. It has been shown only as part of special exhibits in 1989 and 1999. Wolfgang Kreutzer was kind enough to send me two digital photographs of it (the Baumunk and Brunn volume does not include an image of the model).
44. The model, Modellbauwerkstatt der Stadt Bielefeld, is from 1985.
45. To date, no systematic study of such activities exists (regular or annual church services, city commemorations, lectures).
46. Sebald, *Luftkrieg und Literatur*. Here is a small selection of recent publications: Ballerstedt and Buchholz, *Es regnet Feuer!*; Deppert and Engels, *Feuersturm und Widerstand;* Kanther and Olejniczak, *Bomben auf Duisburg*; Keller, *Mannheim im Bombenkrieg*; Kempowski, *Der rote Hahn*; Peschke, *Zwickau und Planitz im Bombenhagel*; Serup-Bilfeldt, *Ins Gedächtnis eingebrannt*; and Trost, *Eine gänzlich zerstörte Stadt.*
47. Young, *Texture of Memory*, 119–54.
48. Information from Christian Groh, Associate Director, Stadtarchiv Pforzheim, e-mail message, January 30, 2003.

KERSTIN BARNDT

# 16

## "MEMORY TRACES OF AN ABANDONED SET OF FUTURES"

### *Industrial Ruins in the Postindustrial Landscapes of Germany*

In the once bustling industrial heartland of Germany, the Duisburg North Landscape Park has brought new fame to the economically distressed region. Built around an abandoned steelworks the park has reclaimed vast industrial land for the public. Like ruins in the classical gardens of the eighteenth century, the defunct factory now sits among flowers, trees, fountains, and theater stages as part of a larger aesthetic whole. At night, beams of colored light enliven the works and turn them into a postmodern spectacle. Where workers once produced millions of tons of steel and slag, at an immense cost to the environment, the scenery has become quiet, green, and contemplative. As work has moved out, nature and art have moved in.

A similarly self-conscious play on ruin aesthetics is on display in a park in Saarbrücken, just a few hundred miles southwest of Duisburg. Here the same landscape architects have transformed an abandoned inner-harbor island, formerly used to load the region's rich coal output onto ships, into a park that integrates artificial ruins into the transformed industrial wasteland. The architectural structures, designed to appear frozen in a state of degeneration, merge with a natural environment of regeneration. As signifiers of a specific historical time and economic regime, these residual architectural traces of Germany's Fordist industrial past are embedded in natural cycles of birth and death, growth and decay.[1] Among the ruins of Fordism, romantic concepts of regeneration meet contemporary discourses of economic and national transformation, asking us to decipher the cultural logic of this eclectic mix.

Ruins are palimpsests that invite us to contemplate a layered temporality. Koselleck usefully glosses such layering in his concept of history as "levels of time of differing duration and differentiable origin, which are nonetheless present and effectual at the same time."[2] The parks in Duisburg and Saarbrücken, as well as other important contemporary projects in Germany, make this temporal palimpsest visible by integrating defunct industrial buildings and machinery into elaborately conceived landscapes. Since the revolutionary year of 1989, two large-scale International Building Exhibitions (Internationale Bau-Ausstellung or IBA)[3] in western and eastern Germany, respectively, have undertaken the Herculean task of transforming abandoned landscapes devastated by heavy industry and mining into regenerated postindustrial recreational gardens and lake districts. Combining a historicizing impulse with the intention to renew and naturalize broad swaths of the German countryside, they draw not simply on the semiotics of ruins themselves, but also on their place within landscapes as projective surfaces that have their own aesthetic history, dating back to romantic garden traditions. Situated within these landscapes, the industrial ruins recall specific historical experiences (of Fordism, unemployment, and industrial pollution) but at the same time resignify those experiences by placing them within the contrived natural environments of parks, lakes, and gardens. Aesthetically contained and sublimated by their new environment, these ruins contribute to an elusive sense of historicity in nature, imbuing the landscapes with a grandeur that exceeds any immediate meaning or purpose—whether we think of the latter as ecological reclamation, public recreation, or simply the recycling of industrial wasteland.

Spanning the first two decades after 1989 and aiming at the ecological renewal and structural transformation of former industrial regions, the two IBA projects offer a unique vista onto the process of national unification. Taking a sustained look at specific industrial ruins preserved by the two projects, this essay assesses their historical and aesthetic appeal, as well as the layers of time and history they put into play. I draw on landscape theory, historiography from Benjamin to Koselleck, and literature on the aesthetic of ruins to examine the relationship between social history and natural time, asking in particular whether the industrial ruin mounts any resistance to its own naturalization: how is industrialization naturalized and nature historicized by the presence of the ruin?

In pursuing this question, I ultimately propose an allegorical reading of the industrial ruin, following Benjamin's famous assertion that "allegories are, in the realm of thoughts, what ruins are in the realm of things."[4] Both allegories and ruins are symptoms of epistemological uncertainty and the collapse of time. For Benjamin, allegorical readings emerge with secularization, a historical rupture that shattered the theological paradigm of salvation and its attendant certainties. The loss of these certainties caused the temporal order to collapse into a dark history of nature, dominated by disaster, decay, and death. While Benjamin develops his theory in dialogue with the baroque tragic drama, his ideas are refracted through the lens of modernism and modernity. Extending Benjamin's line of thought into the present provides some perspective on our own time of "fertile decay" and its recourse to natural history. Like the allegories of death and decay in baroque tragic drama, today's industrial ruins are material signifiers of a very specific decline: as postindustrial allegories, they mark the decline of Fordism as an economic and sociopolitical regime that sustained postwar reconstruction and social stability in the Federal Republic of Germany, as well as dreams of socialist and economic progress in the German Democratic Republic. Significantly, the landscape designers responsible for these new parks and ruins frequently resort to organic metaphors that inevitably reflect the growing disparity between a conception of the modern subject as autonomous, free, and self-constituting and the conditions of this subject's existence. Peter Latz, the lead architect for the Duisburg and Saarbrücken parks, uses the biological concept of metamorphosis to reflect on his work: "our working method is one of adaptation and interpretation, a metamorphosis of industrial structures without destroying them."[5] The reference to biological metaphors diffuses the agency of the landscape architect: Latz's conception of adaptive metamorphosis harks back to romantic notions of the artist as genius who mediates between nature and the viewing or reading subject. Concurrently, it stresses the process as creative rather than rational, and it elides the difference between social history and natural time. I will return to this latter point in particular, but we should note here that Latz's conceptualization, as well as his practice of integrating structures of postindustrial decay into a landscape of renewal, is similar to claims about the logic of capital—for example, Schumpeter's economic paradigm of "creative destruction." In terms recalling those used by Latz, Schumpeter uses metaphors such as "perennial gale" and "circular flow" to characterize the capitalist dialectic of destruction and innovation.[6] Both conceptualizations focus on self-generating change from within nature and the economic process, respectively; indeed, both tend to elide the differences between these two realms. In the postindustrial landscapes of contemporary Germany, economy and nature, opposing forces in the process of modernization, seem to be reconciled. The destructive force of political and economic historical processes appears appeased in the pleasing aesthetics of the parks. The entrepreneur for Schumpeter, and the landscape architect for Latz, merely function as mediating agents, unleashing the autochthonous forces of nature or the economy. The vitalist impulses implicit in these naturalizing metaphors not only ideologically suture capitalism to nature; they also hark back to earlier ruin discourses of romanticism and expressionism and constitute the overdetermined historical contexts for the contemporary industrial ruin.

In the eyes of practitioners such as Latz, landscape arc[illegible] justifiably an art form. As such, it relies on the viewer as much a[illegible] the profound natural and cultural transformations ultimately affect [illegible] position of the viewer and landscape dweller much more than that of the [illegible] Landscapes are culturally produced artifacts; as second nature, they invite us t[illegible] appreciate them aesthetically. As Dorrian and Rose suggest, "the operation of landscape can be seen in terms of a screen between a material potentiality and a subject making meaning, feeling and fantasy from it."[7] As a protective screen against natural (and, we might add, historical) processes, landscape mobilizes a viewing subject supposedly freed from the necessities of collective history and nature. The transformation of former landscapes of labor into landscapes of recreation represents a postmodern project in keeping with Dorrian's and Rose's emphasis on feeling and fantasy: combining a contemplative mode with one of playful and phantasmagorical appropriation of Germany's postindustrial landscapes sets the stage for a transformation of the subject and exhibits it as an ongoing process.

These landscapes exhibit the layers that make up Koselleck's understanding of historical time. Informed by geology, the conceptualizing of history as layered time avoids the pitfalls of linear, teleological, or circular historical narratives and accounts for the plurality and nonsimultaneity of historical times.[8] Dorrian and Rose echo Koselleck's concept in their description of the temporal structure of landscapes as "traces upon layers of lines and marks, each left at a particular moment and still resonant, awaiting decoding."[9] The landscape's natural palimpsest foregrounds the *longue durée* of geological time which would exceed any notion of human historical processes and memory formations—be they defined as industrialization, fascism, socialism, or individual and generational history. The slippage between the historical saturation of the postindustrial landscape on the one hand and its embeddedness in geological time is highly suggestive and speaks to our postmodern condition, in which playful, individual appropriation ostensibly trumps the discarded master narratives of history, the nation, the collective. Our task as decoders of time in landscape, then, is to put the nonsynchronous back into play by questioning the ostensible equilibrium of natural time and by working out the contradictions between different temporal layers, material remnants, and human experiences.

### A New Way of Seeing

Let us trace some of these temporal layers by taking a closer look at industrial ruins in the West German Ruhr district, one of the cradles of European and German industrialization, near France and bordered by the Rhine, Lippe, and Ruhr rivers. Since the 1960s, this area has undergone radical structural change

…ng and steel production) to a service economy. …e, citizens, artists, and politicians worked toward …ned industrial sites, turning the former industrial …ndscape of art, education, and consumption. The …t has fueled this endeavor can best be compared with …*eimat* or homeland museums at the end of the nine- …lso provided sites of local identity designed "to reclaim

…dustrial ruins to be saved by a local citizen's initiative from … Zollern II/IV colliery in Dortmund-Bövingshausen. Today, the colli… of the Westphalian Industrial Museum, which has permanent exhibits on mining, preventive medicine, and workers' hygiene. The colliery ceased production and was closed for good in 1966. When wrecking crews began destroying the crumbling buildings three years later, a group of citizens—among them the photographers Bernd and Hilla Becher—made public the architectural and artistic value of the facility. As a result of their efforts, historians of technology and architecture now view the mine as a model colliery. It is the only coal-mining facility from the late nineteenth century to have survived intact, with administrative buildings, workshops, horse stables, machine hall, and worker settlements.

Around the time when the Bechers documented Zollern II/IV, the couple started to organize their collection of hundreds of photographs of European industrial buildings according to taxonomies of form and function. In the process, they coined the term "anonymous sculptures" to signal that "their peculiarities originate not in spite of, but because of lack of design."[11] In contrast to the documentation of the Zollern mine, these photographic series of industrial vernacular forms—water towers, winding towers, gas tanks, and blast furnaces—clearly challenged conventional aesthetic parameters. While the abandoned water tower already has the characteristic of a ruin in succumbing to the natural forces of gravity and decay, the photographic record resurrects and elevates the defunct structure on aesthetic grounds. Documenting these anonymous sculptures in two-dimensional prints, the Bechers invest them with aesthetic value, instilling in the viewer a "new way of seeing" that would extend outside the gallery space and into the open of the changing industrial landscape.[12]

The aesthetic pleasure that derives from the Bechers' typological series on industrial buildings is based on abstraction and distance. While there is an awe-inspiring quality to the sheer numbers and seemingly endless iterability of the Bechers' subjects, their photography does not engage the technological sublime that David Nye describes as a characteristic feature of the North Ameri-

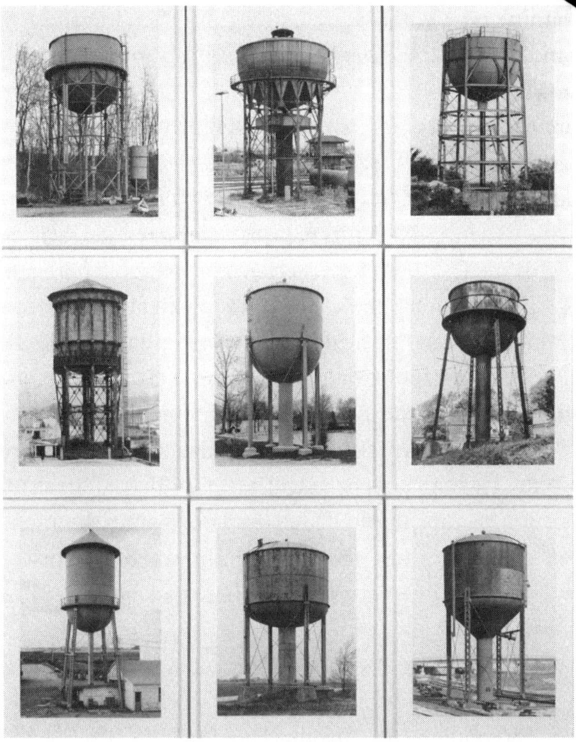

1. Bernd and Hilla Becher, *Water Towers* (1980), Solomon R. Guggenheim Museum.

can Fordist imaginary. Where Nye detects in the work of photographers such as Charles Sheeler an underlying celebration of rationality and progress, we can observe a characteristic emptiness in the post-Fordist compositions of the Bechers.[13] The images are void of signs of life: there are no workers in sight; to the degree that trees and bushes enter the frame at all, they appear barren and dead (see figure 1).[14] Although few photographs depict actual ruins, the overall photographic record bears the signs of abandonment and historicity. The viewer knows that most of these structures have already disappeared and survive only as images. These black-and-white images foreground the function of photography as memento mori: through their formalism and aestheticism, they bear witness to a lost industrial past in an expanded, postindustrial present. The Bechers remove these remnants of industrialization from their historical context into an aesthetic realm of frozen time. Contemplating the photos in a gallery, the viewer is asked to charge these structures with new meaning. In trying to describe the quality and the temporal logic of this encounter, I have found Dürer's figure *Melencolia* very suggestive: are we, the viewers of the Bechers' photographs, not trapped in the same position as *Melencolia* vis-à-vis the "utenhrase, that surround her? Like her, we take up a omed to melancholic contemplation as the only dge."[15]

isplay, however, embeds the individual image in a phs. Inviting an analytical gaze based on comparison function inherent in these vernacular structures, the ges ultimately undercuts the work's melancholic register. gallery refracts our perception and poses a powerful melancholic contemplation of any individual photograph a Suspended between the arresting of time and the energetic moveme alization, the Bechers' photographs prompt us to move our conception and perception of the industrial structures out of the ordinary. As a result, "their sober and seemingly neutral images of industrial architecture devoid of humans have left such traces in our visual memory that, if we drive through the Ruhr district for example and encounter remnants of the monstrous technical twentieth century, we do not think of Thyssen or Krupp, of Hoesch or Mannesmann, but rather of Hilla and Bernd Becher: a late victory of art over the conditions for its existence."[16]

Sachsse goes so far as to credit the Bechers with inaugurating industrial archaeology in Germany.[17] Parallels between the cultural work performed by the Bechers' documentary photography and the function of classical landscape paintings underscore Sachsse's point. In both cases, the artistic framing of a two-dimensional landscape view teaches the public to imbue the same view in nature with heritage value and to see that the space contains projections of sublime power, and of national and regional imaginaries. Landscape, Schama notes, "is the work of the mind. Its scenery is built up as much from strata of memory as from layers of rock"[18] (and of steel and brick, we might add). The Bechers' photographic archive brings a new visual layer to the landscape of memory associated with the Ruhr district, challenging our perception of the region as a landscape of labor, coal, and smog.

## Diving in History

The new cultural and aesthetic perception of the changing industrial landscape prompted by the Bechers' work was taken up by the organizers of the IBA's Emscher Park. Between 1989 and 1999, the IBA produced 120 local projects in seventeen cities at a total cost of two billion dollars; during that decade, it promoted lasting changes in the infrastructure and landscape of the Ruhr district.[19] The projects encompassed not only what I would call the culturalization of industrial ruins, but also the ecological restoration of a polluted river, the founding of an Industrial Culture Route that networks the sites for tourists, and the renovation and construction of apartment blocks. With the help of artists, architects, and landscape designers, Emscher Park created a series of very visible monuments and new public spaces, ranging from artworks on top of slag heaps to postindustrial landscape parks and open-air festival spaces among industrial ruins.

There are many ways of interpreting the IBA's cultural, social, and political effects; its landscape architecture; and its landmark art. Urban planners point to the compensatory role that the IBA played in the process of deindustrialization. Ganser, the project's director, articulates this function succinctly when he proudly notes that:

> the attitude in the Emscher region has changed. After ten years of the IBA Emscher Park, people have the feeling that their region is back on the map. After all, a number of beautiful things have evolved. And people are appreciative of this too, because now they can take their visitors there. Moreover, the media has provided quite positive coverage of what has been done here in the past ten years. People feel better, even though objectively the economic situation remains unchanged.[20]

Without irony, Ganser notes the compensatory function of this particular post-Fordist landscape project. As a "screen in between matter and subjectivity," the deindustrialized landscape in the Ruhr district buffers the material consequences of structural change for residents and visitors alike.[21] It can do so, however, only as long as financial compensation—such as early retirement and continued unemployment benefits—remains in place. The landscape becomes a resource for local citizens, redirecting their former workplace-based class identification to an affective relationship with the region's location and history. Moreover, the new landscape attracts tourists, which might eventually lead to new economic uses and profits. In sum, the far-reaching affective functions of the new landscape contradict Lyotard's assertion that "in order to have a feel for landscape you have to lose your feeling of place."[22] The transformation of the Ruhr landscape does not necessarily entail the loss of homeland or place, but it arguably strengthens local and regional identifications.

However, what is lost in this transformation is the idea of the working class as a source of collective identity. Here, too, the elevated markers of land art that now dot every other slag heap in the region can serve as indicators, for they inscribe the disappearance of labor into their scopic regime. The new vantage points invite adventurous climbers to rise above the reconstructed landscape and contemplate the view. This privileged and individualized vision is significant in the context of post-Fordist modernization. The new landscape of affect encoded into the visual regime of elevated artworks and other spectacular

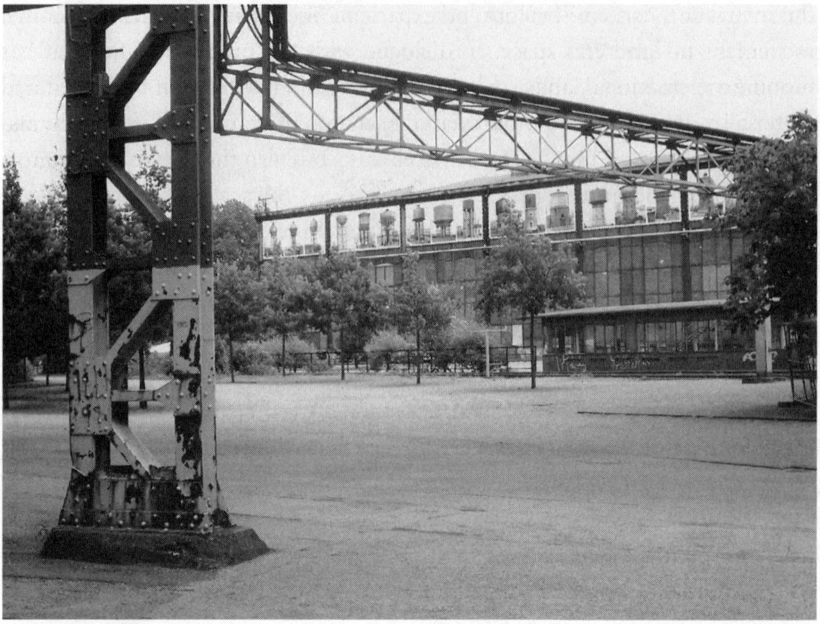

2. Power station, Duisburg North Landscape Park. Series of "Water Towers" by Bernd and Hilla Becher. Photo by author

industrial sites in the region symbolically enables visitors to rise above local history. The elevated artworks create conditions of possibility for "setting the subject free" of systemic structures and long-lived traditions—a development that, according to Beck, Giddens, and Lash, characterizes late-capitalist societies of "reflexive modernization."[23]

To give a more nuanced view of how this production of landscape (and subjectivity) works at a particular site, I would like to turn to one of the more prestigious projects, the Duisburg North Landscape Park. I have also chosen this particular project because of its conscious reference to the tradition and iconography of classical ruins. However, in light of the photographic history sketched above, it may be worth noting that, before visitors reach the heart of the park with its romanticized landscape behind an enormous blast furnace, they pass a frieze of enlarged photographs by Bernd and Hilla Becher on the outer walls of the former power station (see figure 2). Linking the Duisburg site to the Bechers' artistic legacy, the landscape park harks back to the beginnings of preservation efforts of industrial culture in the Ruhr district. Moreover, the frieze establishes the industrial site as an object worthy of aesthetic contemplation. But the perceptual modalities in the park are obviously different from the photographs at its entrance. Whereas the Bechers' photographs arrest time and space in two-dimensional representations of architectural forms, the park's layout invites the visitor to explore and experience industrial architecture through movement in time and space. In dialogue with the production site that has become a recreational landscape, the abstract formal shots gain in context and materiality. It is as if the photos reverted back into three-dimensional space, and in this process, not only the former steelworks but also the photos come into a new aesthetic and historical focus.

The site creates an eclectic play with history. In contrast to the seriousness of the Bechers' work stands the new leisure-time usage of the former gasometer: filled with water, an artificial reef, tunnels, and wrecks of cars and ships, this structure has become the largest artificial diving center in Europe. In a prime example of contemporary experience culture, the athletically inclined are invited to a "diving experience with history at its center."[24] Other visitors may come to the park to attend performances of music, drama, or dance on one of several indoor or outdoor stages. To highlight the focus on the performing arts, the blast furnaces are center stage during a nightly show created by the lighting designer Jonathan Park. In a distant echo of the immense power of the machines, beams of colored light encircle the gigantic furnaces and create an illusion of Promethean vigor. Quite literally, the iron and steel plant now shines in a new light.

With the transformation of a formerly dirty and noisy factory into a postindustrial landmark of leisure-time activities, aesthetic contemplation, and thrills, the process of cultural appropriation and resignification seems complete. The spectacle of recreation in historical industrial settings sidelines the workings of Fordism itself. The relationship between past realities and present myths that this site envisions is loose and imaginative; to the degree that historical consciousness plays into the visitors' outdoor activities, it is characterized by postmodern play and fun. The site tends to pacify history, rather than mining it for criticism and reflection.

However, a look at the rear of the furnace complicates this picture. A smooth transition between the furnace and the surrounding garden architecture dominates the furnace's back. The architects opened, emptied, and environmentally cleaned up the massive ore bunkers to insert a huge slide. Other walls were opened up for rock climbing (see figure 3). As with the diving center in the former gasometer, it first appears that the theme of recreation trumps the history of a former industrial site; but here it does so with a degree of ironic self-reflection. When rock climbers reach the top of the wall, for example, they encounter a cross to mark the summit as Monte Thyssino, in reference to the Thyssen steel firm that previously owned and operated the furnace complex.

Confronting the desire for recreation with a playful historical allusion, the new environment offers the user different viewpoints of the same site. Simi-

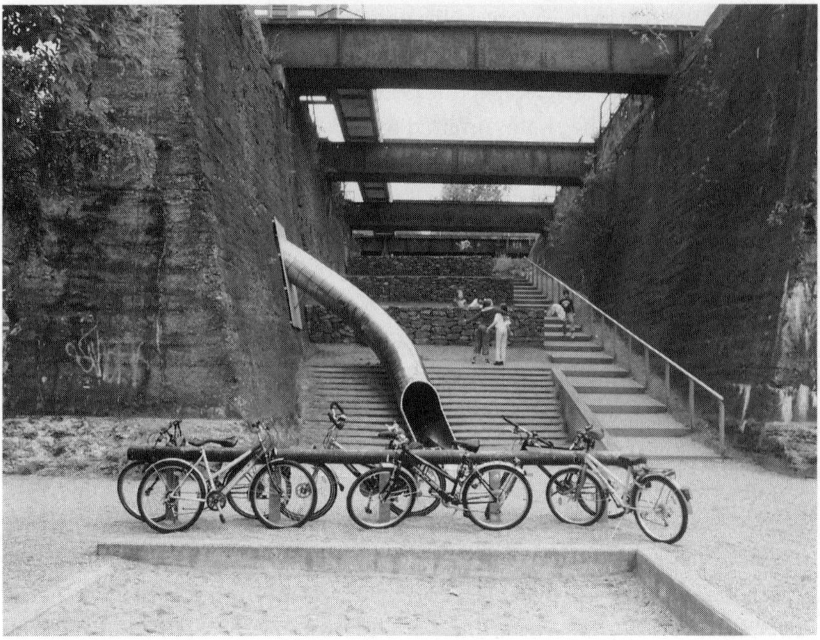

3. Slide through the wall of the ore bunker, Duisburg North Landscape Park. Photo by author.

lar to British gardens from the eighteenth century, with their sweeping vistas and hidden temples, the new landscape in Duisburg features labyrinthian pathways, inviting visitors to discover surprising details and spectacular open views from atop a bunker or footbridge, or to explore the gardens and playgrounds in the bunkers below. One step further down in the terraced landscape of the industrial park, the theme of active recreation turns more contemplative, and the vista opens toward a garden scene among ruins (see figure 4). Seen from the elevated Blue Footbridge that horizontally divides different layers of the terraced landscape, the former sinter bunkers resemble an archaeological excavation site. This impression is offset by the miniature gardens and playgrounds that the firm of Latz & Partner inserted into the structure. The site's postmodern eclecticism challenges the interpreter with elements ranging from clipped hedges to wildflower gardens, from the industrial ruins and public space of an amphitheater to playgrounds and recreational facilities.

According to Latz, this assemblage intentionally transgresses the artificial boundaries between different garden traditions: "I don't happen to be of the opinion that Classicism, Romanticism and other cultural movements are alternative functions, but believe that they can exist synchronously. So it's not always possible to strictly separate the rational and the romantic."[25] Duisburg's new landscape palimpsest stresses the dialectics of the enlightenment by focusing on

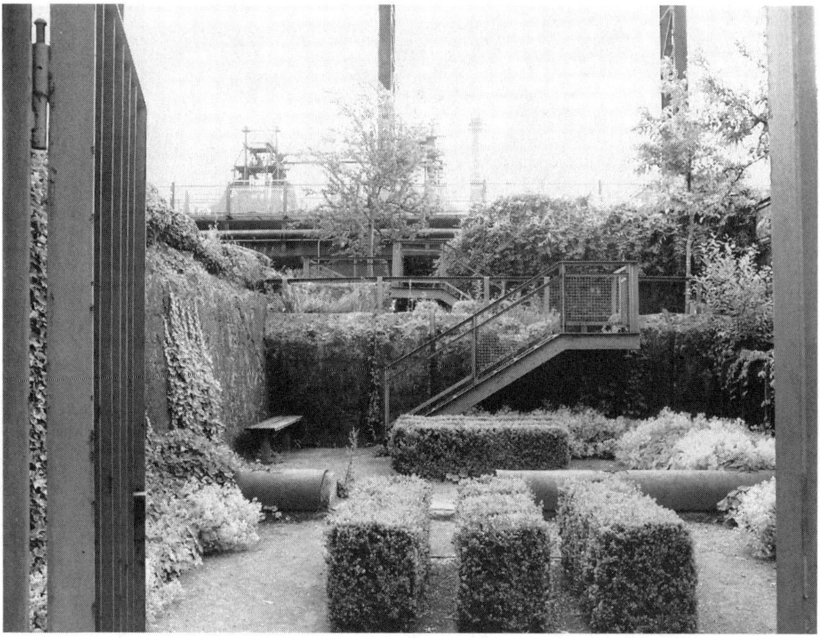

4. Garden in the ruin of the Sintering bunker, Duisburg North Landscape Park. Photo by author.

the layering of nature and culture, geological and industrial time, devastation and ecological reclamation. The organic appeal of this dialectical move, however, smoothes the rough edges of the processes, and the overall sense is one of theatricality in which visitors act out unscripted parts. For gardens, in Dean's words, "are places of heightened energy. They have the character of a stage. Such a work of art can be a place of intensive self-experience for the visitor."[26] The garden reveals itself as a place of memory, evoking the passing of time and history.

If, as Peter Fritzsche argues, the "eighteenth-century landscape configured both the opposition of art and nature and the ultimate reintegration of art into nature,"[27] doesn't the Duisburg park simply prolong this logic by reintegrating not art but industrial remnants into nature? Incorporating wild vegetation in this process of naturalization, Latz & Partner are literally counting on nature to grow over or heal historic destruction. However, the landscape architects used remnants of the industrial processes, such as special steel plates that once lined the casting pits in the foundry, to build the Piazza Metallica, a new public space in the midst of the steelworks (see figure 5). Reminiscent of Carl Andre's avant-garde metal floor pieces from the 1960s, this piazza challenges the sculptural imagination of its visitors.[28] But whereas Andre moves industrial material out of its context and into the art gallery, Latz's place making is specific to the site. It

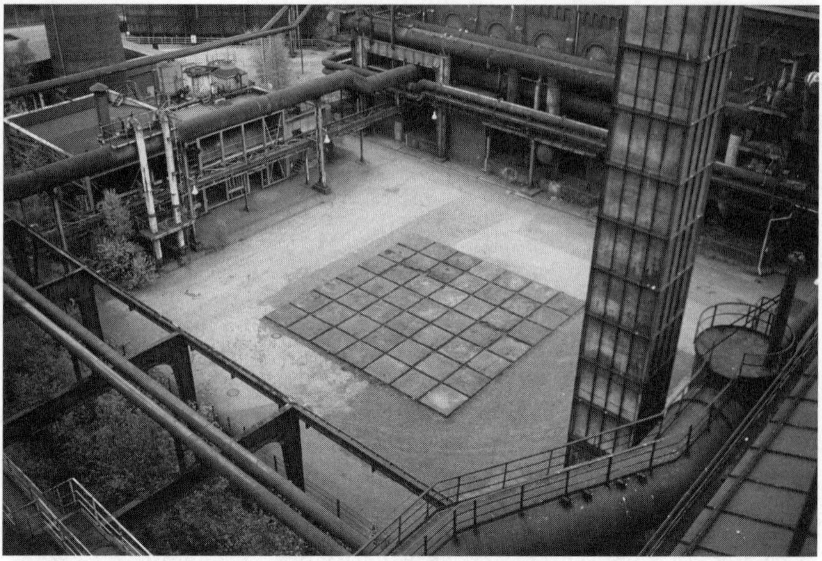

5. Piazza Metallica, Duisburg North Landscape Park. Photo by Michael Latz.

transforms the abandoned material into art to enliven and frame the dead factory. Informed by the Bechers' way of seeing, both the artificially constructed piazza and the enormous furnace around it evolve as anonymous sculptures. In playing with natural and industrial materials, the landscape designers offer surprising new perspectives on a multilayered landscape, which repositions the visitor vis-à-vis Duisburg's monumental piece of industrial heritage.

**Frozen in Time**

With projects like the Duisburg North Landscape Park and its art, the IBA Emscher Park incontrovertibly changed the public's perception of the remnants of industrial culture in the Ruhr district. In this respect, the ten-year project is a success story and serves as a model for a subsequent building exhibit, the IBA Fürst-Pückler-Land in eastern Germany, begun in 2000 and planned for completion in 2010. But while deindustrialization in the Ruhr district has spanned decades, that process started only a few years ago in the industrial regions of the former GDR, leaving ever more factories defunct and landscapes ruined by mining and industrialization. The suddenness of this process has sent shock waves through the region. A closer look at these abandoned industrial landscapes and the plans to transform them culturally shows once more a focus on the figure of ruins and the attendant experience of loss. As in western Germany, though within slightly different social, political, and historical parameters, this loss is at once historically specific and temporally vague, located in a postindustrial present and bound to nature's generative cycles of birth, growth, and decay.

During the period when Germany was divided, millions of cubic meters of earth were moved in the course of lignite mining in the region of Lusatia, an industrial powerhouse of the GDR. Subsequent reclamation works have likewise involved massive landscaping efforts: deindustrialization and the ongoing IBA projects have turned this region into the largest landscape construction site in Europe. In Lusatia, 80 percent of all industrial production sites were declared uneconomical and closed down after 1989. In contrast to the heavily populated Ruhr district, which still boasts the largest concentration of people anywhere in Germany, Lusatia has only half a million inhabitants, and the number is constantly shrinking.[29] With their large-scale landscape projects and local development programs, the organizers of the IBA in the former GDR are working toward what they hope will be a sustainable future for the area.[30] The IBA projects will completely change the landscape of the region once again, notably by flooding nine gigantic holes left by lignite mining. As Rolf Kuhn, the IBA's director, points out, the result "will be a vast, interconnected lake district with a total water surface of about 7,000 hectares, different nature and leisure spaces and a broad range of uses that is very likely to be unique in Central Europe."[31] Kuhn rightly stresses the man-made character of the future chain of lakes, but he also asserts that the visible artificiality of the lakes will bear witness to the region's industrial past.[32]

Given the complex interplay between temporality, history, and landscape already evident in the Ruhr district, Kuhn's claim demands further investigation. We need to look beyond the submersion of vast stretches of land which, contrary to Kuhn's claim, might be seen as the wholesale erasure of any traces of industrial culture, and look instead at some temporary projects of the IBA that emphasized a temporality of loss, shock, and change. The exhibit Landscape and Mining: Lusatian Art of the 20th Century was one such project. In 2004, this extraordinary show was on view in the Plessa power station, which had operated continuously for sixty-six years before being shut down in 1992. The temporality of instant rupture and shock that characterized the demise of the GDR was visible in the installations, photography, and art exhibited in the small town of Plessa.

When I traveled to Plessa to see the exhibit on a sunny day in June, I was the only visitor. The towering halls of the power station met me with silence, exuding an atmosphere of contemplation similar to the sacred space of a church. The interior arrangement of instruments, machinery, and furnishings gave the impression that the power station had just stopped working. It instilled a sense of loss: before my eyes, a forlorn past and its objects were frozen in time.

Although I might have been able to reach out and touch the objects, my own sense of temporality clashed with their reality. As a viewer, I found myself in a different present, and this realization placed the objects at an epistemological distance, turning them into historical signifiers with a surreal quality. The black-and-white photos hanging from the ceiling and on the walls—a displaced evocation of the Bechers' canvases in Duisburg—deepened this sense of dislocation and melancholia (see figure 6). I was locked into this space of the past and confronted by the gaze of "The Last Shift," as the title of a photographic series by Christina Glanz has it. There was a pervasive sense of claustrophobia in dark rooms where Jürgen Matschie's large-scale photographs in upright frames merely mimicked the idea of windows. All I could decipher on (rather than through) these windows were barren landscapes like deserts (see figure 7).

One floor up, I encountered artworks hung in better light. Instead of walls, windows allowed a panoramic view of the outside world and of the main machine room in the building. Several empty administrative rooms functioned as gallery space for a retrospective of Lusatian art devoted to landscape and mining. Although the earliest work was from 1920, the majority of the paintings retrospectively provided an overview of modernism in the GDR, ranging from socialist realist to neo-expressionistic engagements with regional landscapes and people.[33]

But what captured my attention even more than this art-historical cross section of mining views was the fully furnished director's suite. An exhibit modeled on the concept of living-history museums, the room was arranged with attention to detail: the desk was set with pens, papers, and a framed personal photograph. The requisite portrait of Erich Honecker, the former GDR head of state, adorned the wall, alongside a tapestry in ocher and light brown that blended in with the brownish furniture. Closets and shelves were filled with a collection of objects relating to work and recreation: beer mugs and wineglasses, books, a yellow safety helmet and pennant, a set of Russian dolls. Even a blue work jacket was hanging outside a closet, as if ready to be retrieved at any moment. Finally, a wall calendar from 1975 helped authenticate the historicity of the installation.

Contrary to the installations and photos on the first floor that captured the moment of the power station's abandonment, the director's suite nostalgically presented a time of relative economic stability. With Benjamin, we might define the diverging historiographic approaches of the two floors as examples of historicism and historical materialism. The eternal, historicist image of one particular GDR workplace hermetically presented on the second floor stood in stark contrast to the installations on the first floor, which could be described as staging the industrial fall of the region after 1989 as "a memory as it flashes up at

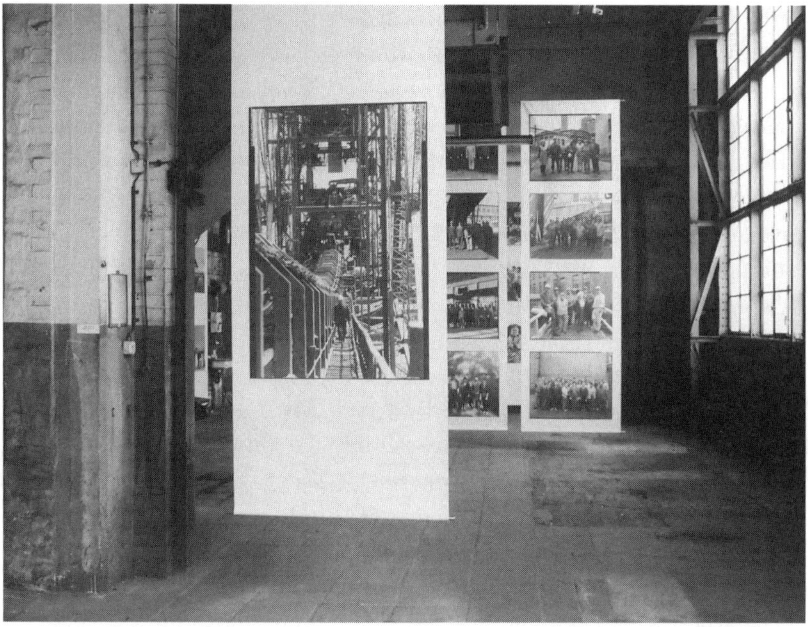

6. In foreground, work by Jürgen Matschie, *Conveyor Bridge: Open Pit Nochten* (1989); in background, work by Christina Glanz, *The Last Shift* (1990–92); both on exhibit in 2004 at the Plessa power station. Photo by author.

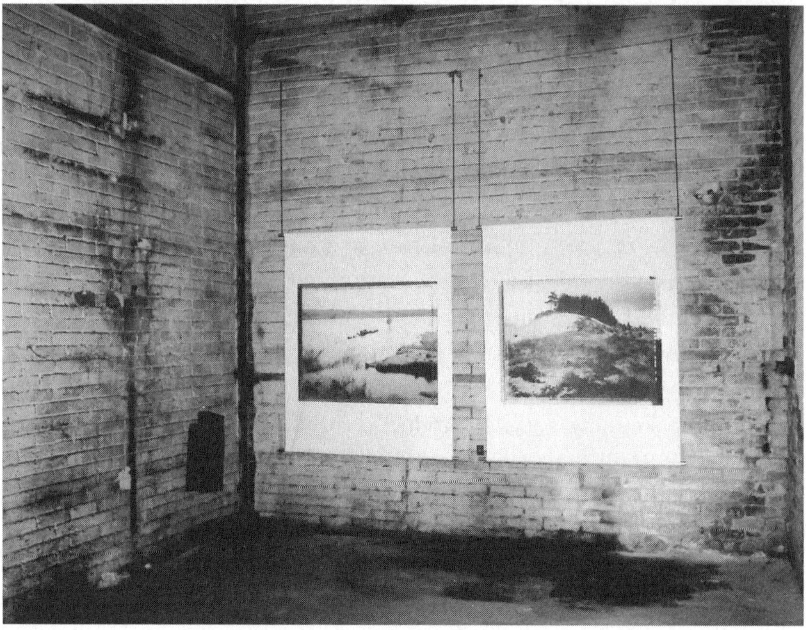

7. Jürgen Matschie, *Flooding: Open Pit Greifenhain* (2001) and *Dune: Open Pit Nochten* (2001), on exhibit in 2004 at the Plessa power station. Photo by author.

a moment of danger."[34] Then again, these installations patently lacked the dialectical rescue of the revolutionary experience that is also the object of Benjamin's *Theses on the Philosophy of History*.[35] Melancholia prevails over any attempt to associate the end of the power station with a new beginning. The exhibit in Plessa make it look as though the end of the GDR did not occur through the revolutionary uprising of its people in 1989, but rather through the closing of its factories and plants a few years later. As long as the citizens of the former GDR still had work, it appears, their lifeworld did not change drastically. Only with the winding down of its industry did the GDR as everyday experience come to an end.

This memorialization significantly elides the GDR's repressive state apparatus and even its demise: secret security forces, closed borders, and censorship are not part of the display and do not enter into the consciousness of the visitor. The effect of this elision is to reinforce the localism of the exhibit as well as its emphasis on the quintessential Lusatian lifeworld—the everyday work of the lignite miner. The elegiac sense of ruination in Plessa attaches not so much to the worker's state, but more specifically to the worker's factory and its culture.

The experience of existential loss precedes mourning and melancholy. According to Benjamin, the baroque's aesthetic fascination with the melancholy of ruins derived from the loss of eschatological coherence and divine order in the aftermath of the Thirty Years' War and from the intense feelings of "grief in the face of rubble."[36] The power plant in Plessa similarly confronts us with a dying world and its forms of labor. Still visible as order, documented in the form of carefully posed workers in uniform in Glanz's photographs or in the staged authenticity of the director's room, this world is relegated to a past era. As such, the order of labor that is on display and becomes framed as an object of mourning retains historically specific contours: visitors are asked to contemplate the demise of a form of labor linked to a full-scale production economy where the worker occupies center stage. Beyond the specific regulation imposed by the socialist state, this form of labor lies at the heart of a Fordist mode of production. As such, it retains its links to the capitalist version of the same model in the West. Both economies were primarily driven by production; factories, plants, coal mining, and steel production provided work for many and thus contributed centrally to patterns of subjectivity and identity formation. Consequently, the end of the GDR and the subsequent processes of political and economic unification have forcefully made visible a host of consequences for communities and individuals associated with the transition from Fordist to post-Fordist economies. In this perspective, unification merely reveals and exacerbates a broader transition that had already begun with deindustrialization in the Federal Republic before 1989.

In Plessa, the unevenness in presentation between the two floors of the power station emphasizes the process of the station's musealization. A fixed form has not yet been achieved; the ruin remains visible as a material sign with historical dimensions. The art installations within the ruin further imbue the space allegorically. The artists' use of the space stresses the experience of loss as ongoing, touching the present. The history of the power station and its labor regime has not yet been fully buried. Will the future use of the building lay this past to rest? Or will it continue to function, in Robert Smithson's words, to preserve the "memory traces of an abandoned set of futures?"[37] The plan for Plessa's future calls for the preservation of the power station as a technical monument. The machine hall will be transformed into an event space, with rooms reserved for permanent and special exhibits; additional attractions will include a microbrewery and a cider mill for various regional fruits. It remains to be seen whether this specific eastern German version of event culture will eventually succeed in filling the "eternity of hopelessness"[38] that the photo exhibit and the director's room instilled in its visitors.

**Interim Landscapes**

The IBA's logo features the word "see," combining the English verb "to see" and the German noun "See" (lake). While the former explicitly stresses the role of aesthetic perception in landscape design, the latter serves as a reminder of the final goal of the reclamation process—that is, the production of a vast lake district. As this goal gradually takes shape through man-made and natural processes, the IBA has chosen to accompany reclamation by exhibiting different stages of the work with a stress on interim landscapes. Given the fact that they will disappear within the coming decades, the financial and cultural investment in these interim landscapes and the attendant projects is striking. However, the decision to provide an aesthetic accompaniment to the lengthy process of reclamation is a rational one: the creation of the lakes will take years, and the IBA hopes to construct a new regional and cultural identity for Lusatia in the meantime. From the perspective of cultural history, these interim landscapes have enormous significance, raising fundamental questions about the temporalities of deindustrialization, the demise of the GDR, and cultural memory: If the interim landscapes of the IBA are designed to disappear, what do they preserve? What will be laid to rest with their flooding? What forms of mourning might they facilitate, or must we read the process rather in terms of repression, naturalized again in the process of flooding?

A particularly visible example that allows us to explore the implications of such interim landscapes within the context of the IBA is on view at Großräschen-Senftenberg. Framed by newly built IBA exhibition cubes called the IBA Terraces,

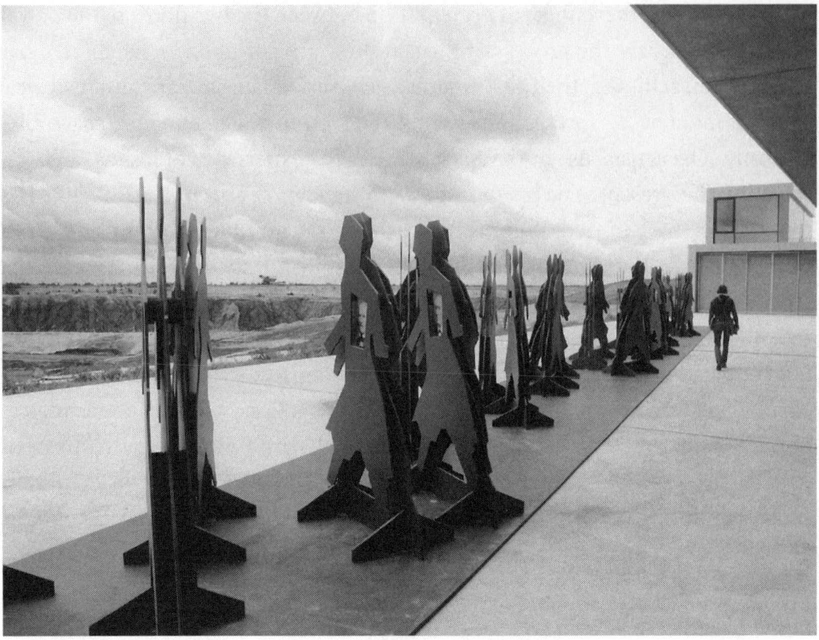

8. Exhibition terraces with a view of a former strip mine. IBA Fürst-Pückler-Land project. Photo by Dieter Barndt.

a former strip mine stretches into the distance (see figure 8). Deck chairs invite the visitor to contemplate the horizon over the enormous pit. In the near future, this gaping hole will be flooded with water and turned into a lake, literally submerging any signs of the industrial past in a massive land-art project.

When I visited the IBA Terraces in the summer of 2004, the three Bauhaus-style white exhibition cubes welcomed visitors to a show entitled Time Machine Lusatia. The exhibit concentrated on the major phases of the region's industrialization process. Significantly, it also explored Lusatia's cultural history, from the minority culture of the Sorbs to Count von Pückler-Muskau's landscape gardens, from model workers' colonies to Bruno Taut's architectural legacy in Senftenberg, from local performances of Goethe's *Faust* to the start of the reclamation of former lignite mines. Most striking was the odd place of the GDR itself in the exhibition narrative. After all, the GDR had turned Lusatia's industry into the country's main powerhouse. Having lost the rich coal resources in the Ruhr district to the Federal Republic, the GDR concentrated on producing its own energy. At the heart of these efforts stood an enormous lignite-processing enterprise, the state-owned Kombinat Schwarze Pumpe (combine black pump), an oft-cited model socialist plant.[39]

Significantly, the exhibit alluded to the substantial increase in the region's mining activity after 1949 only in its use of the official state symbol for the second five-year plan under which Kombinat Schwarze Pumpe was built, two text panels (in a fairly dark corner), and a few seemingly misplaced pieces of lignite coal. Production and its related orders and culture of work were not the focus of Time Machine Lusatia; key aspects of local and industrial history, and the forty-four years of the GDR more generally, were subsumed in the exhibition narrative as only a minor chapter. Moreover, rather than tracing the region's defining patterns of production, the exhibit stressed forms of recreation and consumption: well-lit glass cases displayed goods from other industries (such as glass and textile), presented the region's soccer association and theater, and drew attention to Senftenberg lake, a former mining hole turned into a recreational area, as a model for the future of Lusatia.

These curatorial decisions also had implications for issues of mourning and memory. In clear contrast to the exhibit in Plessa, the IBA Terraces do not mourn a lost mode of production or forms of labor, but look back to a disappearing private sphere. An antique wooden rocking chair, an old trunk, and an old-fashioned child's bed are allowed to stand metonymically for devastated towns and living spaces lost to the ruination of landscape through lignite mining. Although this destruction began in the 1920s, most of the places remembered in the exhibit were destroyed between 1960 and 1989, in the years of the GDR. In the logics and mise-en-scène of the exhibit, however, this specific historical time frame recedes into a broader temporal framework of industrialization from the nineteenth century onward. A second exhibit at the IBA Terraces made this relativizing gesture even more explicit by vastly increasing the temporal horizon. Entitled Land in Motion, the 2005 show situated the regional projects of the IBA within a narrative of the genesis of coal, reaching back to the ice ages. In a self-promoting effort to mark the halfway point of the ten-year-long IBA, the exhibit showcased "the transformation of landscape."[40] Although the curators were at pains to cite notions of industrialization and postindustrialization, these concepts remained empty signifiers within the construction of the exhibit, appearing devoid of historic specificity, and integrated only into the all-encompassing regime of geological time.

If we compare the open horizon of the evolving postindustrial lake district in the former GDR with the density of postindustrial markers and signposts in the Ruhr region, it is striking how much more elusive the eastern landscape and its industrial heritage remain. To a large extent, of course, this is due to the shrinking population in eastern Germany. Moreover, while industrial museums have become an integral part of the Ruhr district's cultural infrastructure, Lusatia has hardly any equivalent institutions to enrich our understanding of the region's industrial history and to balance the postindustrial spaces. But the elusiveness of the eastern landscape must also be traced to a topographical distinction between postindustrial transformation in eastern and western Germany. The open-cast mining in the east produces quite different industrial ruins: the material nature of these ruins, deep cuts into the earth's surface, do not hold much power to resist their further naturalization. The flooding of the pits will erase any referent that might have once pointed toward the industrial past. The reclamation process radically alters the landscape, and the complete submersion of any visible signs of industrial history has few equivalents short of actively tearing down industrial buildings. To be sure, most of the furnaces, gasometers, and winding towers that characterized the Ruhr district's industrial life and landscape survive only in the black-and-white photographs of Hilla and Bernd Becher. These photographs become doubly important as visual signifiers of socioeconomic change. Looking back at the Bechers' oeuvre, we realize how the rupture of 1989 and its material ruins have only deepened a preexisting melancholia. Both IBA projects culturally and economically frame a process of destruction and renewal. What is striking about the IBA Fürst-Pückler-Land project, however, is the amount of celebratory and aesthetic energy that it invests in its interim landscapes, in the ruins of strip mining due to be flooded and fully reclaimed as recreational sites. We are invited to experience this kind of intermediacy, the in-between-ness of the landscape, in aesthetic terms. Contemplating the horizon above the empty pit beyond the IBA Terraces, the former worker or producer, *homo economicus*, is literally confronted with a new perspective on the natural environment that was until recently a site of labor. By adopting this perspective, the inhabitants of Lusatia—and, by extension, interested tourists—are asked to take leave from a past and an identity bound to the labor of mining. That past implied ecological destruction, to be sure, but it was also saturated with the political and economic legacies of the GDR. This particular part of German history, however, remains largely invisible in the context of the IBA. Instead, the IBA's aesthetic education revolves around the inevitability of historical change as a natural process. The flooding will come, and this unique space of contemplative reflection, if not of working through the past, will soon be lost.

Opening up rupture and transition to aesthetic experience, the projects discussed in this chapter offer differing views on how to engage the memory landscape of the abandoned industrial complex or mine. While the postindustrial park in Duisburg calls upon the regenerative forces of nature in a mode that we might label ruin optimism, Plessa's exhibit gives us a melancholic arrest of time. Imbedded in an interim landscape full of industrial deserts that are slowly morphing into a lake district, this power station will soon look even more estranged from its changed habitat, remaining one of only a few material relics of a bygone era. Both case studies, however, reveal the profound historical stakes involved in these projects: as the designers gradually transform the landscape, they mobilize different layers of time and history, intervening aesthetically in the politics of unification and its attendant historical narratives.

The opening of the borders between the GDR and the Federal Republic closed a chapter of Germany's history that had begun in the years immediately after the war—also among ruined landscapes. Just as both postwar German states had worked hard to superimpose new foundational narratives over the ostensible zero hour of 1945, so has the Berlin Republic been generating new images to smooth the rupture of 1989. In different ways, the two projects discussed in this essay have powerfully contributed to this new visual archive.

While the revolution of 1989 revitalized Germans' confidence in historical agency and progress, the neoliberal present of unified Germany has disillusioned many: unemployment soared, poverty prevailed, and cities shrank. For a brief reprieve, the economic upswing around 2007 reversed this state of affairs and leveled economic inequalities between eastern and western Germany. But the most current global recession soon followed and Lusatia as well as the Ruhr region are again struggling with its effects. Against this emerging backdrop of perpetual and ever quicker market swings, the massive investment in producing and staging Fordist ruins in western and eastern Germany attests to the continued decline of an industrial era as it had been known and lived in both German states. Since 1989, the transformation of the Fordist landscape of production into a post-Fordist landscape of recreation has opened up the historical horizon and allowed a glimpse at an archaeology of the present that this chapter has aimed to excavate.

## Notes

1. On modern ruin sensibility, see Simmel, "The Ruin," and Starobinski, "Melancholy among Ruins." For an extension of the discourse on ruins to encompass British industrial ruins, see Edensor, *Industrial Ruins*.
2. Quoted in Zammito, "Koselleck's Philosophy of Historical Time(s) and the Practice of History," 125.
3. These building exhibits continue the tradition of international trade fairs exhibiting progress in the building trades, architecture, art, and design. Since the 1920s, this tradition has taken a unique turn in Germany, with entire city districts reconceived and reconstructed under the auspices of the IBA and the international architectural

avant-garde. (Examples include Stuttgart 1927, Hannover 1951, and Berlin 1957 and 1987; Emscher Park was the first IBA project to foster economic and ecological renewal of an entire region.)

4. Benjamin, *The Origin of German Tragic Drama*, 178.
5. Latz, "Landscape Park Duisburg-Nord," 151.
6. Quoted in Zukin, *Landscapes of Power*, 8.
7. Dorrian and Rose, Introduction, 15. See also Soper, "Privileged Gazes and Ordinary Affections," 338–48.
8. Koselleck, "Zeitschichten," 19–20.
9. Dorrian and Rose, Introduction, 17.
10. Confino, *The Nation as a Local Metaphor*, 169. A crucial distinction between homeland and industrial museums lies in their respective class politics. Whereas the homeland museum promoted a "bourgeois social milieu of memory" (ibid., 211) at the expense of proletarian culture, the industrial museum (of the 1970s, at any rate) is designed to write proletarian culture into local and national memory culture. But of course this emphasis on the working class comes—like the celebration of the homeland—only at the moment of its demise.
11. Bernd and Hilla Becher, *Anonyme Skulpturen* (Anonymous Sculptures) (1969). Quoted in Zweite, "Bernd and Hilla Becher's 'Suggestion for a Way of Seeing,' " 9.
12. Quoted in Zweite, "Bernd and Hilla Becher's 'Suggestion for a Way of Seeing,' " 9.
13. Nye, *American Technological Sublime*, 37–39.
14. Sachsse, *Hilla und Bernhard Becher*.
15. Benjamin quoted in Hanssen, "Portrait of Melancholy," 80.
16. Bussmann, "Hilla und Bernd Becher," 69, my translation.
17. Sachsse, *Bernd und Hilla Becher*, 42.
18. Schama, *Landscape and Memory*, 7.
19. On the ecological and economic program of IBA Emscher Park, see Shaw, "The International Building Exhibition (IBA) Emscher Park, Germany."
20. Quoted in Schröder, "An Outdated View of Modernism," 85.
21. Dorrian and Rose, Introduction, 17.
22. Lyotard, "Scapeland," 215.
23. Beck, Giddens, and Lash, *Reflexive Modernization*.
24. *Diving Center*, brochure advertising the diving center in the gas tower (in author's collection, acquired in 2004).
25. Latz, "The Syntax of Landscape," 129.
26. Dean, "Places against Oblivion of the Self," 9.
27. Fritzsche, *Stranded in the Present*, 99.
28. Potts, *The Sculptural Imagination*, 309–35.
29. Kuhn, "Den Mond bewohnbar machen," 194.
30. See the official Web site for IBA Fürst-Pückler Land, http://www.iba-see.de/web.net/2/Englisch.html (accessed July 17, 2007).
31. Kuhn, "Landscape Change in Lusatia," 8.
32. Ibid.
33. Nelken, *Zeitmaschine Lausitz*.
34. Benjamin, "Theses on the Philosophy of History," 255.

35. On Benjamin's messianism, see Buck-Morss, *The Dialectics of Seeing*, 241–45.
36. Quoted in Emden, "Walter Benjamins Ruinen der Geschichte," 82.
37. Smithson, "A Tour of the Monuments of Passaic," in *Robert Smithson*, 23.
38. Benjamin, *The Origin of German Tragic Drama*, 224.
39. See, for instance, Reimann, *Ich bedauere nichts*, and Heiner Müller, *Die Korrektur*.
40. Kuhn, "Landscape Change in Lusatia," 8.

GEORGE STEINMETZ

17

# COLONIAL MELANCHOLY AND FORDIST NOSTALGIA

*The Ruinscapes of Namibia and Detroit*

If all material objects are semiotically underdetermined, the ruin is particularly open to differing representations. What seems to one observer in Germany after the Second World War to be mere rubble is an evocative ruin for another, a memento mori that conjures associations from the deep archive of ruin imagery.[1] In this article I examine the uses of two different ruinscapes: one in Namibia, a postcolonial African country; the other in Detroit, a city that is no longer Fordist but not yet post-Fordist.[2] More specifically, I examine efforts by politically disempowered white groups to make these two ruinscapes produce particular meanings. In both cases, members of the previously dominant white groups have created detailed itineraries of the ruins. But these ruinscapes are mobilized to nourish two differing psychopolitical postures: melancholia and nostalgia.

## The Ruins of Namibia and Detroit

Most of the Namibian ruins are the remains of the German colonial state, which lasted from 1884 to 1915. For most African Namibians, this German colonial detritus is either noxious or invisible. It is the 20,000 or so German-speaking Namibians who have elevated this rubble to the more exalted status of ruins, through preservation, publications, and guided tours.[3] In recent years, some German Namibians have expanded their focus to encompass the ruins of Namibia's precolonial past. This emerging interest in Africanizing the ruinscape is more than an extension of the European discourse of ruins into new settings. It also marks a division between German Namibian ruin gazers for whom the ruin functions primarily as an object for cultivating a posture of colonial melancholia, and those who have tried to integrate themselves into the postcolonial Namibian polity.

The dominant German Namibian use of colonial ruins, however, is oriented toward a specifically melancholy stance. These ruins allow the ruin gazer to disavow the Germans' permanent loss of the colony. This involves a ghostly projection onto the ruins of the Germans' erstwhile colonial state. The privileged objects used for such projections are the colonial state's defensive structures—its fortresses, police stations, fortified houses and mission settlements, and prisons. The representation of these objects as ruins is one way of admitting that they will not be restored to their earlier functions. The ruinscape thus resonates with an ambivalent psychopolitical stance that simultaneously disavows and acknowledges the Germans' permanent loss of political sovereignty. This is a melancholic stance in the Freudian sense insofar as it cycles continuously between denial and recognition of loss, without ever settling into a mournful bereavement.[4]

Detroit is widely known as the most impoverished and abandoned major city in the United States. The city's ruination is the result of racialized disinvestment and relocation, and the exodus of more than a million people to the suburbs and beyond since the 1950s.[5] Most of the city's residents perceive the abandoned factories, office buildings, theaters, train and bus stations, stadiums, and houses as mere rubble or as breeding grounds for crime. A smaller group in the city, including the artists Tyree Guyton and Lowell Boileau, represents these same structures as ruins. Most of the ruin gazers, however, are outsiders—suburbanites from the metropolitan Detroit area and visitors from farther afield. Architects and urban planners have been fascinated by the possibilities of reusing Detroit's voids and ruins in ways that accept population decline.[6] The photographer Camilo Vergara has documented the decay of Detroit and other cities in the northern United States, and called for the creation of an "American acropolis" of abandoned office buildings in Detroit's downtown.[7]

In Detroit as in Namibia, there is an established itinerary of ruins. Boileau offers guided tours and has created a Web site called "Detroit Ruins Maps."[8] On nice weekend days there is a steady stream of suburban visitors to Guyton's outdoor installation of rubbish art in and around Heidelberg Street. Suburban photographers can be found at the abandoned factories. In 2006 an article in the travel section of the *New York Times* advised visitors to Detroit to view the Michigan Central Railroad Station. The author explicitly invoked an aestheticizing ruins perspective: "Despite some recent progress, decades of economic struggle have left many once-grand Detroit buildings in ruins. But like ruins in Greece or Italy, these once mighty structures can exude a dilapidated wonder."[9] The author then draws attention to the "most dramatic" of Detroit's ruins, "the former Michigan Central Depot, its 18 blown-out floors looming against the sky, its railroad station interior looking like an abandoned Roman settlement."[10] The largest group visiting Detroit's ruins are suburbanites who moved out of the city themselves, or whose parents and grandparents fled a generation or two ago. Their perception of Detroit's abandoned structures seems initially to resemble the German Namibian stance on ruins in Namibia. Many follow a trail through the city's ruins that conjures up the Fordist metropolis in its golden age. Bookstores in Detroit's suburbs carry shelves of paperbacks with sepia-toned covers published by Arcadia, a company that describes its books as being "pretty much all nostalgia."[11] These volumes revisit the lost world of industrial prosperity and trace the arc of the city's rise and fall. The volume *Detroit's Statler and Book-Cadillac Hotels* concludes with a chapter called "The Hotels Today" that describes their decay. The photograph of the Statler Hotel's Grand Ballroom shows it littered with debris. The caption accompanying this image reads: "Once a center of activity, only the sound of passing People Mover trains breaks the silence."[12] The ballroom of the Book Cadillac Hotel appears even more decrepit in a photograph in the book, taken before that hotel's recent renovation (see figure 1). The volume on Detroit's abandoned train station concludes with photographs shot through broken windows and images of "ghosts of former travelers" inside the ruin (see figure 2). Local documentaries about Detroit almost invariably follow a similar rise-and-fall narrative structure, in which a description of the vibrant life of a neighborhood, building, or institution is followed by a mournful disquisition on its decline.[13] For example, a locally made film on Hudson's department store culminates in its dramatic demolition in 1998.[14]

Suburban ex-Detroiters tend to be less ambivalent about their ruins than German Namibians do. Most of the relevant texts, films, and tours that resurrect Fordist Detroit are unambiguous about the fact that it belongs clearly to the past. Admittedly many of these representations imply a continuing sense of ownership over the city. The monthly magazine *Detroit Hour* is aimed at the residents of Detroit's wealthy suburbs and is filled with glossy advertisements for plastic surgeons and expensive restaurants in the suburbs, but it organizes its system of representations around the signifier Detroit. The belief among many African American Detroiters that suburban whites want to retake the city is reflected in a widespread conspiracy theory concerning an alleged fifty-year plan to depopulate and recolonize Detroit.[15] Nevertheless, the Fordist city serves more as an object for historical contemplation than as the projection of wishful fantasies of resettlement. Most suburbanites believe they are better off than their urban ancestors and do not want to return to the past. They have transferred their deeper investments, both psychic and economic, to the suburbs and

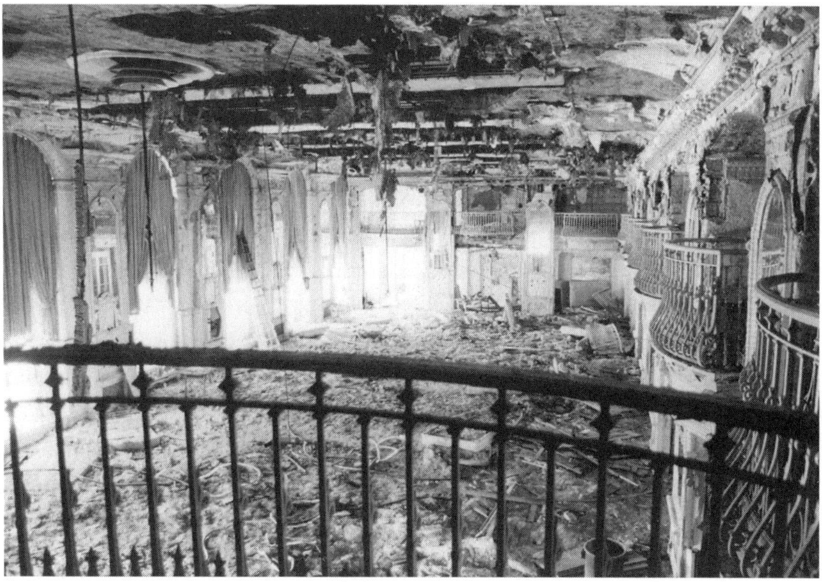

1. Ballroom, Book Cadillac Hotel, Detroit. Reproduced by permission from David Kohrman, *Detroit's Statler and Book-Cadillac Hotels: The Anchors of Washington Boulevard* (Chicago: Arcadia, 2002), 121.

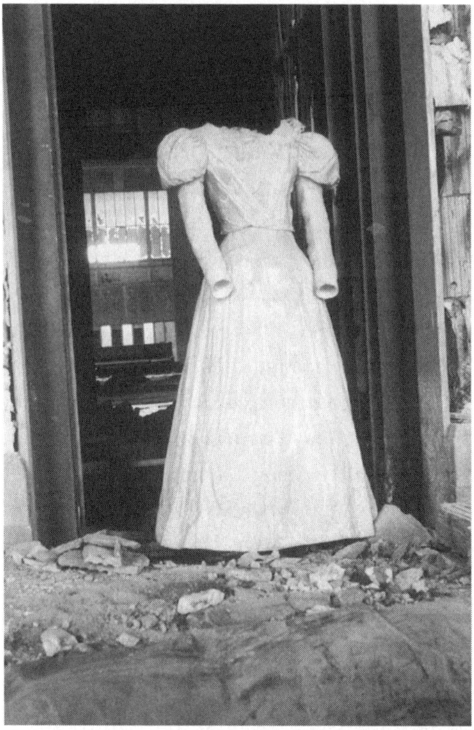

2. Contribution of Deborah Riley to *Cathedral of Time*, multiple-contributor installation by Irina Nakhova, exhibited in 1995 at Old Central Michigan Train Station, Detroit. Reproduced by permission from Kelli B. Kavanaugh, *Detroit's Michigan Central Station* (Chicago: Arcadia, 2001), 118.

beyond.[16] The dominant emotional condition is a simpler nostalgia for Fordism, a desire to relive the past, to reexperience the prosperous metropolis as it is remembered or has been described.

In contrast, most German Namibians have no home other than Namibia, even if they visit Germany frequently. Their unofficial national anthem, "The Southwestern Song," proclaims their love for the African country many still call Southwest, as do most of their literary, historical, and artistic productions.[17] During the past ninety years, they have constructed an ethnic culture that is more than a simple copy of metropolitan German culture.[18] Their identity is rooted in a deep admiration for their own colonial past, which tends to be understood not as genocidal or imperialist but as having laid the foundations for Namibian development. The introduction to a volume published in 1985 by the Interest Group of German-Speaking Southwesterners (*Vom Schutzgebiet bis Namibia, 1884–1984*) (From Protectorate to Namibia) emphasizes the group's "pride" in "the contribution of Germans to the development of German Southwest Africa, Southwest Africa, and Namibia."[19] Most German Namibians see themselves as inherently superior to African Namibians, although postapartheid political culture has made it more difficult to express such feelings openly. According to one German Namibian, many German Namibians continue to "reveal a deeply rooted refusal of 'the Other,' especially the Black."[20] The fantasy of regaining their dominant position as the country's rulers coexists with sober realization that attaining that goal is impossible.

I use the phrases "German Namibians" and "suburban ex-Detroiters" to discuss dominant tendencies in those groups, not to generalize. No matter how much governments and social movements insist that nations or ethnic groups are internally homogeneous, it is a sociological truism that no group is entirely uniform. Indeed, as Bourdieu argues, social practices tend to configure themselves into semiautonomous fields of action that are defined by heterogeneity, conflict, and hierarchies of valued symbolic capital.[21] During the German colonial period, government officials were divided among themselves with respect to their views of African Namibians and to the preferred approach to colonial governance. Officials also differed from missionaries and settlers, who in turn disagreed among themselves.[22] Part of the heterogeneity within any group consists precisely in disagreements about the group's boundaries. The category of white German Namibians is the historically constituted result of strategies of inclusion and exclusion during and after the colonial period.[23]

After the First World War, Southwest Africa came under the control of the Union of South Africa, which governed it as a League of Nations Class C colony. The German Namibian population became more cohesive at this time. It lost its status as the largest white group in the colony and began to press for political representation and cultural autonomy. Yet even during the 1930s, when 80-95 percent of the Germans in Southwest Africa supported Hitler, members of the older generation opposed the Nazis for conservative and monarchical reasons.[24] In the late 1970s, some German Namibians formed the above-mentioned Interest Group, which encompassed less conservative tendencies.[25] A delegation of its members met with Sam Nujoma, leader of the South West Africa People's Organization, and some German Namibians even joined Swapo, including Hanno Rumpf, the former Namibian ambassador to Germany, and the engineer and amateur historian Klaus Dierks.[26] Nonetheless, the main German Namibian newspapers, magazines, and publishing houses continue to articulate the melancholic colonial position discussed here.

Suburban ex-Detroiters are also divided with respect to their views of Detroit, as I discovered while making the film *Detroit: Ruin of a City* and screening it locally.[27] Some white suburbanites acknowledge the racism and class exploitation that permeated everyday life in Detroit during the Fordist era; they are less prone to idealize that period. Many others blame the African American majority for Detroit's deterioration.[28] The dominant attitude, however, is nostalgia for the city's period of growth and prosperity.

Like melancholia, nostalgia reveals hysteresis, a desire to continue inhabiting imaginary identifications that are out of joint with present-day social-symbolic realities.[29] Both psychic processes are rooted in dissatisfaction with the present. Nostalgia was originally considered to be a medical condition among Swiss mercenaries in Europe; the word combines two Greek words, "nosos," meaning "to return to native land," and "algos," meaning "suffering or grief."[30] Current uses retain this original reference to loss. Nostalgia should not be equated with bereavement or the loss of a loved person, however; it is better defined as the sense of having lost an entire sociohistorical context and the identifications that accompany it, and the related desire to reexperience that social past. Nostalgia may be universal, but it is accentuated in rapidly changing, highly mobile social situations. The tourist and culture industries have successfully tapped into wellsprings of nostalgia, as have social movements from the left and the right that reject the present. Contemporary far-right movements try to direct nostalgia for Fordism into assaults on people and groups described as responsible for the socioeconomic plight of the working class.[31]

Melancholy is a more complex and ambivalent subjective posture. The term referred originally to an illness caused by an excess of "black bile," but by the seventeenth century it was understood as a more psychological malady.[32] According to the contemporary Freudian definition, melancholia combines disavowal and recognition of the loss of a loved one. The melancholic may form identifications that are symbolically "illegal," clinging to objects that were "loved not as separate and distinct from [himself] but rather as a mirror of [his] own sense of self and power."[33] The similarity between melancholia and fetishism, as discussed by Freud, is that both involve a simultaneous acknowledgment and negation of loss.[34] This suggests that the melancholic may become oriented toward fetish objects like the German Namibian ruins. Indeed the ruin seems ideally suited for this purpose as it is intermediate between culture and nature, life and death. The ruin partly hides the disappearance of the cathected object and the wider chain of social relations and individuals that the object symbolizes.

My juxtaposition between a postcolonial African country and a postindustrial North American city is intended to compare and contrast the emotional posture of former white ruling groups and the symbolic role that ruins come to play for them. What the two groups have in common is their loss of political sovereignty to representatives of a majority African or African American population (Namibia's population is 95 percent African; Detroit's is 85 percent African American). In neither case has the white group in question disappeared entirely from the scene. In both situations these groups are unusually interested in the material debris left behind by the sociopolitical formation they dominated. For the groups currently in political power, the same ruins bring to mind an objectionable, even disastrous history. There is thus a basic disagreement about the ontological status of these remainders—whether they are ruins, forensic evidence, or simply garbage.

The two politically displaced white groups differ in several fundamental ways. One relates to their assessment of the present. The German Namibians' focus on colonial defensive structures and military history is indicative not just of an obsession with the colonial period but of a more acute sense of immediate danger. These settlers experienced the African independence movements as an escalating series of threats.[35] Today they are concerned with the possibility of occupation of their land, the Africanization of employment, and crime. German Namibians' central shrine to their collective colonial memory, the old fortress in Windhoek, is now occupied by a display on the Namibian struggle against colonialism and apartheid. The German Namibians' emphasis on ruined fortresses expresses a fortress mentality. And while the colonial-era forts gesture toward protection, their ruination alludes to the group's vulnerability.

These two contexts differ with respect to their inherited understanding of ruins. The Germans who initially settled in Namibia during the nineteenth century were heirs to a firmly established European discourse on ruins. In the United States, by contrast, ruins are rarely restored and even less frequently preserved in the half-decayed equilibrium that Simmel characterizes as epitomizing the ruin.[36] The fact that the United States has only ever known a future-oriented capitalism obviously helps explain this relative lack of fascination with ruins. Even the emergence of postmodern tourism to historical heritage sites tends to emphasize fully restored and sanitized preindustrial destinations like Colonial Williamsburg.[37] None of the sites in the continental United States on the UNESCO World Heritage List are ruins of postconquest Euro-American buildings, and only three World Heritage Sites are ruins of Native American civilizations.

Another difference between the two contexts has to do with colonizers' perceptions of the status of ruins among the colonized. In each case, the colonizers and their descendants differentiated themselves from the colonized through ruins. In America and Asia, early colonizers often regarded ruined temples and abandoned cities as signs of a civilization in decay.[38] Sub-Saharan Africa was long described as being almost devoid of the physical remnants of ancient civilizations. The Great Zimbabwe ruins were an exception, but from the moment of their rediscovery in 1871 by a German, Carl Mauch, they were inscribed "with meanings that confirmed old beliefs" in a lost city of Africa, which confirmed their alleged singularity.[39] Pre-Columbian "artifacts and ruins" in America were "reviled" and often "hastily reburied," since they "represented the barbarous and primitive religions of the pre-colonial."[40] Confronted with the abandoned Great Pyramid of Cholula in Mexico, the Spanish colonizers built a church on top of it. All of this began to change during the nineteenth century with the growth of scientific archaeology and the emerging belief in the inevitable extinction of colonized peoples, which transformed the Native American from "a bloodthirsty demon into a noble savage."[41] That led to increased interest in the "stately edifices" of the "American race," which "speak to us so eloquently of a noble culture," as the *North American Review* put it in 1880.[42]

Detroit and Namibia also differ in a number of more obvious ways. Their population was approximately the same in the middle of the twentieth century, but Detroit was at the cutting edge of industrial modernity, while Southwest Africa was organized around agrarian and extractive economies. Policies of genocide and apartheid in Southwest Africa cannot be equated with the racism practiced in mid-twentieth century Detroit. Southwest Africa was a minor colony in the European view of the world, while Detroit occupied a central place in the imaginary of twentieth-century industrial modernity.[43]

Before asking in more detail how ruins are related to melancholy and nostalgia, we need to briefly reconstruct the set of possible strategies for dealing with ruins—or, more precisely, for dealing with rubble.

**Rubble Strategies**

The ruin's transient and processual character—the way it seems to display natural decomposition as gaining the upper hand over human accomplishment—is essential to its aesthetic effectiveness, according to Simmel.[44] Any attempt to reestablish human control over nature by freezing a ruin in a condition between intactness and utter decomposition is potentially self-defeating, since it may eliminate the charm of this ruin effect.[45] Slow decay is "ruin time" proper, since it is most likely to reveal the inexorability of nature's reconquest of human achievements.[46] Gradual dereliction resulting from quasi-anonymous human forces such as disinvestment from an urban center can also produce hybrid mixes of culture and nature that look like ruins which are generated naturally (see figure 3).

Various techniques have been used to prolong, intensify, or call attention to the ruin effect. For several decades, Tyree Guyton has created a metacommentary on Detroit's ruination by transforming and decorating abandoned houses along Heidelberg Street with commentaries on lynching, the O. J. Simpson murder trial, and other traumatic political events, creating what are in effect hyper-ruins. Painting, photography, and film allow images of irresistible decay to be permanently preserved. The physical decay of the canvas, print, or celluloid adds another layer to this experience, a ruined frame for images of ruination (i.e., another sort of hyper-ruin). This is illustrated by the use of digital effects to simulate the decay of the film stock in films about societal degeneration such as *Grindhouse*, written by Quentin Tarantino and Robert Rodriguez.

Merewether describes the architectural work of Daniel Libeskind, especially the Jewish Museum Berlin, as seeking a point that is "neither restoration nor erasure." Libeskind, Merewether writes, believes that "to build over the place of ruins would be suppression and a denial" of history. Instead, Libeskind seeks to "frame what is missing" by building an empty space into the heart of the museum itself.[47] As Libeskind himself says, "The void and the invisible are the structural features which I have gathered in this particular space . . . The experience of the building is organized around a center which is not to be found . . . What is not visible is the richness of the former Jewish contributions to Berlin. It cannot be found in artifacts because it has been turned into ash."[48] Here the ruins of history have been contained, framed, or evoked with no attempt to restore or efface them. The photograph at the end of the published version of Libeskind's lecture (see figure 4) shows the museum under construction from above and missing its roof. In this picture the museum itself appears to be in ruins.

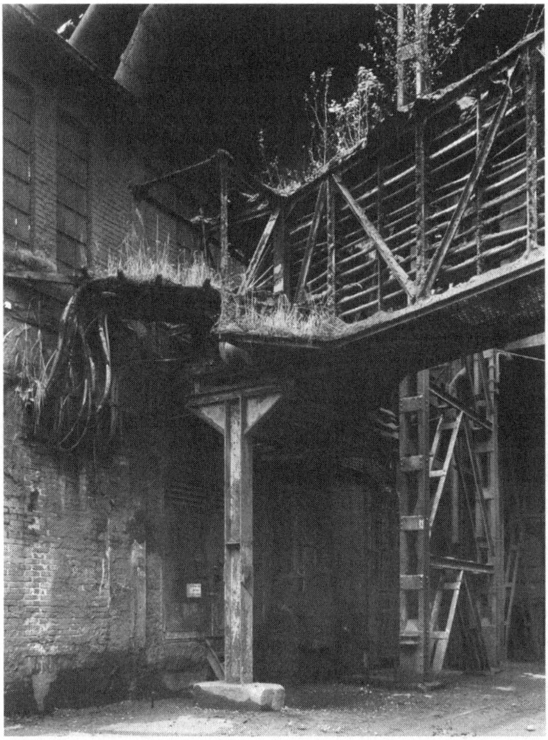

3. Abandoned ironworks, Völkingen, Germany. From Lucius Burckhardt, Georg Skalecki, Hans Meyer-Veden, and Johann Peter Lüth, *Alte Völkinger Hütte* (Stuttgart: Edition Axel Menges, 1997), 27. Reproduced courtesy of Edition Axel Menges.

The more typical practice of patching up ruins in an effort to stop time is revealed a few blocks away from the Jewish Museum, in the shattered facade of the Anhalt Railway Station (see figure 5, showing two large patches in the railway station's interior facade). A similar practice is evident in the keystone placed in the gateway of the Temple of Bacchus at Baalbek by the British in 1870, intended to prevent its collapse.[49] The serpent figures at the Temple of the Feathered Serpent at the Mexican Teotihuacan ruins were propped up by archaeologists during the nineteenth century. More recently, some of these figures have been removed to museums, and the entire ruin has been stabilized with concrete and rocks. At the French "ruins of Oradour," as they are described in the Oradour Memory Centre's official publications, piles of stones have been cleared away so that visitors can move freely, and walls have been partly repaired, leaving the site in a state of suspended but not disorderly decay.

At another extreme, governments often choose to demolish ruins and clear away rubble. With a few exceptions, this approach was taken in German cities after the Second World War and in Detroit since the beginning of the city's decline. When Guyton transformed abandoned houses into artistic political commentary, Detroit officials initially responded by tearing down and clearing

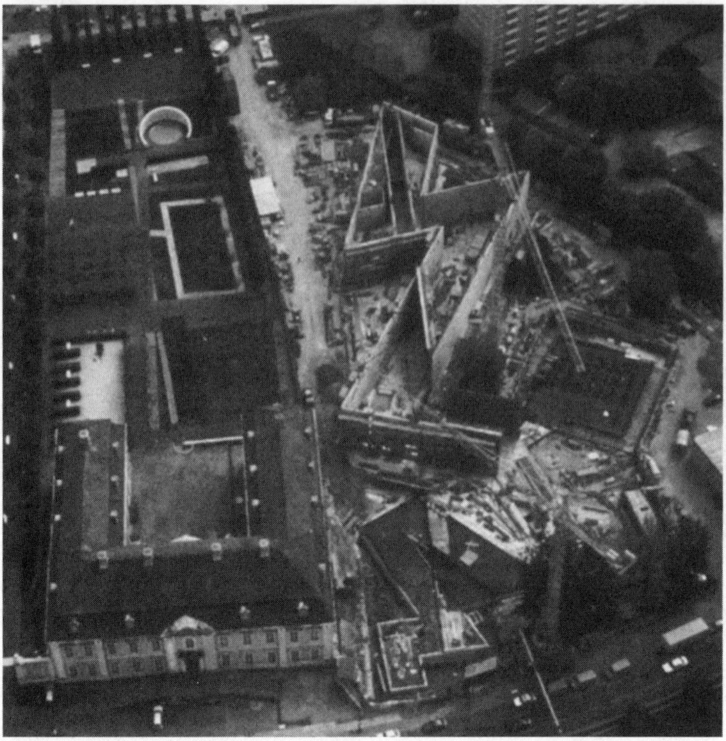

4. Aerial view of the Jewish Museum Berlin, under construction. From Daniel Libeskind, *Traces of the Unborn*, 1995 Raoul Wallenberg Lecture (Ann Arbor: College of Architecture and Urban Planning, University of Michigan, 1995), 41. Reproduced courtesy of Taubman College of Architecture and Urban Planning, University of Michigan.

away these hyper-ruins. (More recently, the city has declared a truce with Guyton, and his installations have expanded into adjacent streets).

We can thus distinguish six different ways of dealing with rubble, not all of which are mutually exclusive: demolishing and removing all traces of the remaining structures; allowing ruins to continue along their natural course of decay; building metacommentaries on ruination into the ruins; trying to sustain ruins in their intermediate, half-decayed condition through the use of patches, supports, or protective coverings; building on top of old structures, with the ruins remaining visible or retaining some sort of presence underneath; and restoring dilapidated structures to their imagined original condition.

### The German Namibian Ruin Cult

The German-speaking Namibian community has been largely responsible for creating Namibia's register of national monuments and ruins. After the National Party won the South African elections in 1948, the German Namibians

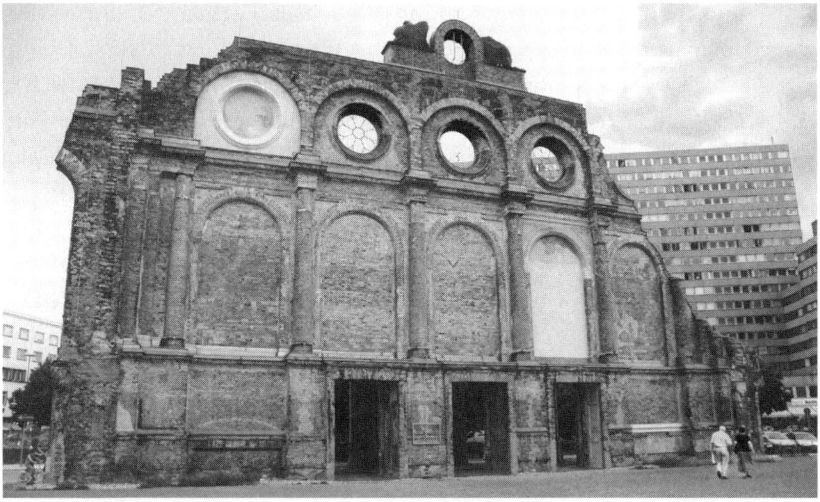


5. Interior facade, Anhalter Bahnhof, Berlin, showing patching, June 2007. Photo by author.

were turned into a "pillar of the new . . . Apartheid society in Southwest Africa," and the Historical Monuments Commission for Southwest Africa, created in October 1948, was dominated by German Namibians.[50] Of the 117 sites declared as national monuments between 1950 and 1990, 77 were German structures from before 1918. After an initial burst of classifying non-German sites as national monuments in the 1950s and 1960s, nearly all of the objects (61 out of 72) so classified after 1968 were from the German colonial era.[51] A project sponsored by the Namibian Architects Institute during the 1980s inventoried every German colonial building in the country's five main cities.

Starting in the 1940s, the Scientific Society's yearbook printed photographs and discussions of colonial ruins.[52] The German Namibian historian N. Mossolow published photos of the German military and missionary ruins. His books usually follow the familiar rise-and-decline narrative structure also found in the Arcadia books on Detroit. Mossolow's books conclude with photos of the German ruins in the 1950s and 1960s; their covers were sometimes printed in the nostalgic sepia color also found on the Arcadia books.[53] Andreas Vogt, one of the most active German Namibian preservationists in recent years, published his dissertation on colonial military structures in 2002. Vogt insists that the list of officially protected monuments in Namibia "should not be understood as an expression of a colonial mentality."[54] His most recent book treats non-German ruins and monuments alongside German ones, but the treatment of the latter is still melancholic.

The Germans' loss of colonial power and their weakened political status after the First World War meant that most of the pre-1918 defensive structures began to fall into rubble immediately. Until 1943, however, German Namibians continued to hope that they would regain control over the colony, and they avoided treating their rubble as ruins. The Nazis promised to "bring Southwest back to the Reich."[55] After the battle of Stalingrad, however, Hitler dissolved the Nazi Colonial Office, and after the war, it became obvious that Germany would not regain control over its former colonies.

The German Namibians thus developed a new approach toward the ruins. They created a ruinscape that functioned as a kind of melancholic apparatus, an ideological machine designed to cultivate a melancholic structure of feeling around their colonial past. On the one hand, the ruins and the rituals performed by German Namibians around these sites conjure up a ghostly reminder of the German colonial state, stimulating a kind of colonial dreamwork.[56] This is linked to a collective disavowal of that state's demise. On the other hand, by preserving many of the ruins in a half-decayed state or by letting them dissolve back into the earth, the German Namibians acknowledge the pastness of the colonial state.

With their ruins and monuments, the German Namibians have contributed to the haunting of the postcolonial Namibian nation.[57] However politically disempowered and few in number, these settlers are engaged in a subtle symbolic interference with the cultural foundations of the Namibian polity. Most African Namibians would love to be rid of the German Namibians and their ruins, rituals, and ghosts. Sam Nujoma, the former Namibian president and Swapo leader, is close to Robert Mugabe, who was invited to Namibia for an official four-day visit in February 2007. Swapo members in the Namibian National Assembly "refused to even listen to an opposition motion on rights violations in Zimbabwe" at the time. The current lands minister has warned that the "willing-buyer, willing-seller concept" has been unable to satisfy Namibians' land hunger, hinting at more aggressive measures to come.[58] But Namibia's leaders know that African states cannot expropriate white-owned farms and businesses without running the risk of international ostracism, disinvestment, and loss of aid.[59] The German Namibians are the country's wealthiest ethnic group, and the German government is Namibia's largest source of international development and technical aid. This is one reason why there has also been little movement to rid the landscape of the physical remains of colonialism, although the government has added new monuments linked to anticolonial struggles.

The German Namibians' fetishization of the Namibian ruinscape perpetuates their sense of loss indefinitely. The persistent denial by some of them of the 1904–8 colonial genocide is related to this melancholic "inability to mourn." The 2002 edition of the volume *From Protectorate to Namibia* attempts to establish a new consensual framework for German Namibians. The volume recycles the colonial trope of Germany "pacifying" Namibia and treats the German-Ovaherero war solely from the standpoint of German sacrifices.[60] The chapter on General von Trotha's massacre of the Ovaherero insists that "modern warfare has become deliberate genocide" and compares von Trotha in 1904 to the "extermination pilots" who bombed Hiroshima and Dresden, and to Russian soldiers who carried out "orders to rape and murder" Germans in 1945, thereby equating German perpetrators with their victims.[61] The volume ostensibly acknowledges the end of colonialism and apartheid but perpetuates colonial ways of thinking about history. Its publisher, Klaus Hess Verlag, has also published colonial-era memoirs by German settlers and soldiers as well as Peter Moors's *Fahrt nach Südwest*, an ultraracist novel about the German-Ovaherero war.[62]

## Defense Mechanisms

Several colonial historians have argued that the original, core structures of a colonial state are the military station, the fortress, the barracks, and the prison.[63] This seems debatable even for Southwest Africa, where the original protocolonial and colonial structures were missionary stations, trading outlets, and copper mines. Nonetheless, it is true that even the locally active Rhenish mission society did not abstain from military violence. One of the oldest mission stations to the Ovaherero was founded at Otjimbingwe in 1849. It became an early site of European settlement in the 1850s, after copper was discovered in the area. The owner of the Matchless Copper Mine, Charles John Andersson, built a series of forts with cannons at Otjimbingwe. Andersson sold his properties to the Rhenish Missionary Society in the 1860s. German missionaries contributed to the escalation of internal violence during the 1860s by selling weapons and arming the Ovaherero for their so-called war of liberation in 1863 against domination by Khoikhoi Orlam groups.[64] A photograph from the period makes it obvious that the first mission church at Okahandja was like a small crenellated fortress.[65] In 1872 the mission created a defensive tower at Otjimbingwe. In 1950, its first year of activity, the National Monuments Council designated this tower a protected monument, and it was restored in 1993.[66] This tower is not in ruins, of course, but the rest of the colonial-era German military structures at Otjimbingwe have disappeared without a trace, and Otjimbingwe is a melancholy shadow of its former self.

The Germans built dozens of forts and police stations in the colony. Many have vanished, but they have been catalogued tirelessly by German Namibian historians. The first fortress was erected at Tsaobis in October 1898 and was already abandoned by 1905. Except for a few traces of the foundation, it has now disappeared altogether.[67] The fortress at Gochas, at the edge of the Kalahari

Desert on the border to Botswana, was evacuated in 1915 and never used again, and the entire complex was in ruins by 1923. Not a trace of it remains today. But it has been catalogued by Andreas Vogt, and there are photos of it in the National Archives of Namibia—an important storehouse for German Namibian collective memory.[68]

Several fortresses have been partly reconstructed without being restored to their original configuration. The colonial army built a fortress in 1890 at Heusis, west of Windhoek, to protect the road from Otjimbingwe to the new colonial capital. This fort was declared a national monument in 1957. Its return to nature has been stopped and all overgrowth removed, but the structure has not been rebuilt and its original roof is missing (see figure 6). The Naiams fortress (see figure 7) was built in 1898 and housed one officer and fifteen soldiers. As can be seen in figure 8, this fort was severely deteriorated by 1967, when it was made into a national monument. Since then it has been partly reconstructed (see figure 9), but the roof and other attached structures that are visible in the early image have not been restored.[69] The Eros Fort has had a similar history. Built near Windhoek during the first German war with the Witbooi in 1893, this was originally a roofless redoubt with a small tower. It was declared a national monument in 1951 and was restored during the 1950s by the Windhoek Municipality.

Other forts are in worse condition. The German army's "Eros lookout post" at Au||gei|gas (see figure 10) is not officially protected and has not been fully restored, though the German Namibian members of the Historical Monuments Commission "already began early on to concern themselves with [its] preservation and maintenance."[70] As the photo shows, this fort is more dilapidated than the two just discussed. But it is better preserved than the German police posts at Hohenfels and at the Waterberg, neither of which has been maintained at all (see figure 11).[71]

Sand is one of the main sources of ruination in Namibia, as can be seen most dramatically in the ghost towns of the old diamond-mining area along the Atlantic coast south of Lüderitz. After diamonds were discovered in 1908, the colonial administration created a restricted area that encompassed the towns of Kolmanskop, Elizabeth Bay, Pomona, and Bogenfels. In 1944 the main diamond company, Consolidated Diamond Mines (CDM), moved its operational headquarters from Kolmanskop to Oranjemund on the South African border, leading to the complete desertion of the colonial-era diamond-mining towns. In 1980, CDM restored some of the old buildings and established a museum, marketing Kolmanskop and Elizabeth Bay as tourist destinations. More interesting in the present context is the way these mining towns were ignored until recently by the guardians of the German Namibian collective memory, with the excep-

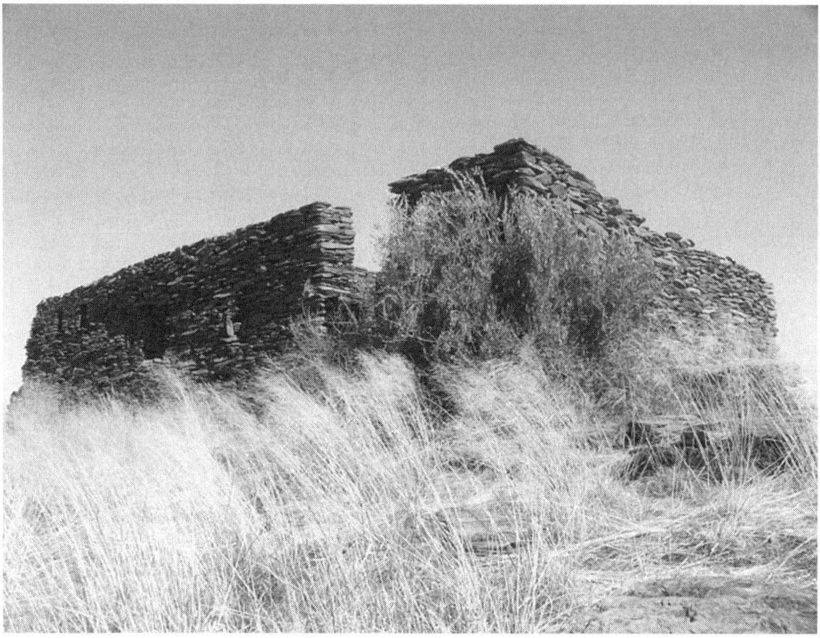

6. Ruins of the German colonial fortress at Heusis, Namibia, present condition. Reproduced courtesy of Klaus Dierks (http://www.klausdierks.com/images/khomas_heusis_francois_fort_1.jpg).

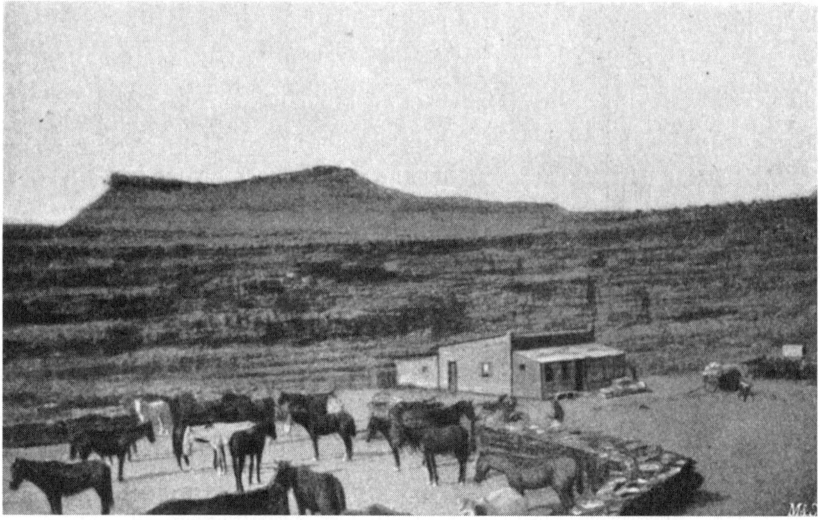

7. Fortress at Naiams, original condition. From Grosser Generalstab, *Die Kämpfe der deutschen Truppen in Südwestafrika. Auf Grund amtlichen Materials bearbeitet von der kriegsgeschichtlichen*, Abteilung 1 des Großen Generalstabs, vol. 2, *Der Hottentottenkrieg* (Berlin: Ernst Siegfried Mittler und Sohn, 1907), 113.

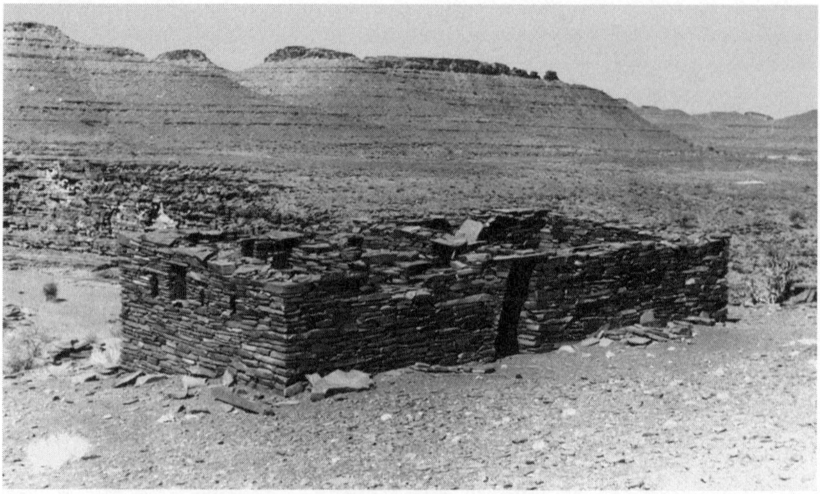

8. Ruins of the fortress at Naiams before 1967. Reproduced courtesy of National Archives of Namibia (photo number 2635).

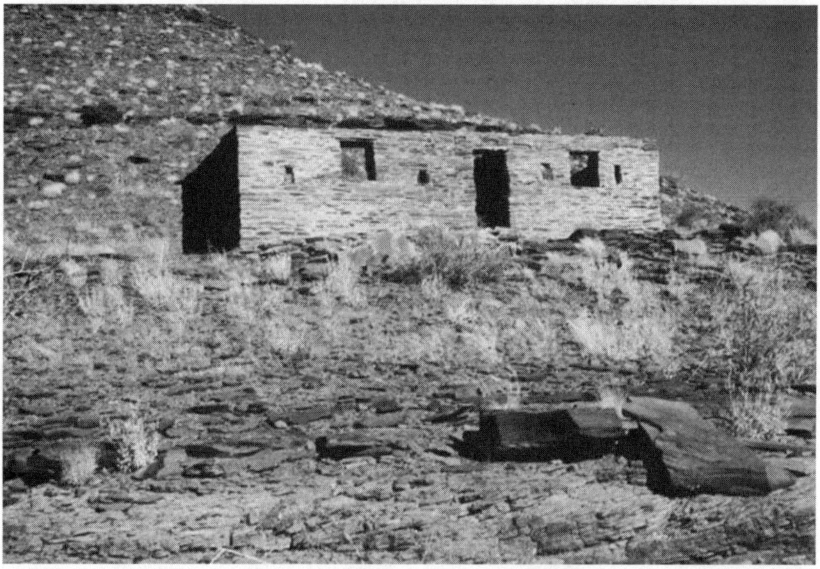

9. Partially restored ruins of the fortress at Naiams, 1992. Reproduced courtesy of Andreas Vogt.

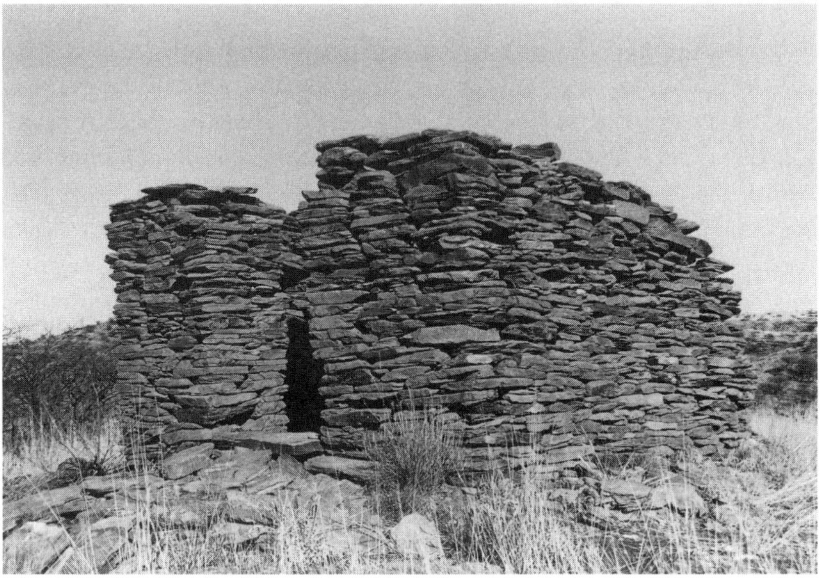

10. Ruins of German colonial army "Eros" lookout post at Au||gei|gas, Namibia, 1997. Reproduced courtesy of Andreas Vogt.

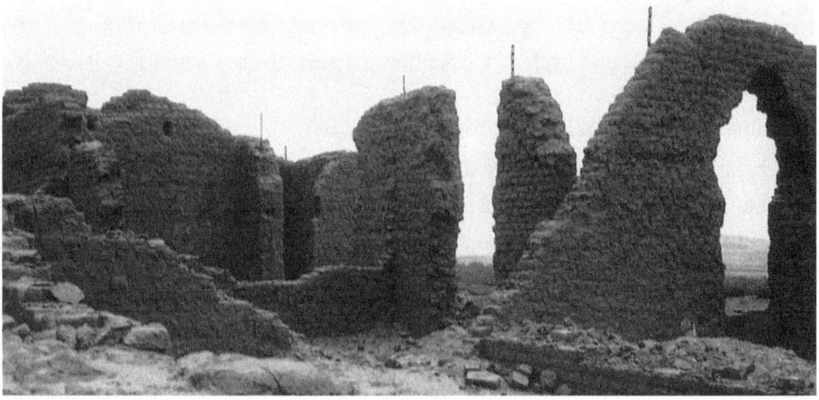

11. Ruins of the former German colonial police post at Hohenfels, Namibia, present condition. From Rothmann, Sakkie, and Theresa, *The Harsh and Forbidden Sperrgebiet Rediscovered* (Swakopmund: ST Promotions, 1999).

tion of Lüderitz, where some of the German diamond prospectors' villas were declared national monuments before 1990.[72] German Namibians do not seem to associate these sites with the heroic militarism that is so central to their colonial imaginary.

One collection of military rubble that is felt to be extremely meaningful is the prisoner of war camp at Aus, where German troops, noncommissioned officers, and members of the colonial police were interned by South African Union forces during the First World War after the Germans' capitulation in 1915. As the literature on this camp emphasizes, the prisoners constructed their own dwellings from mud bricks they made themselves and from salvaged pieces of corrugated iron. Thus "the ruins of the POWs' huts" are said to "bear testimony to how these POWs, under extreme conditions, showed initiative and made their life in the camp more dignified." Though they had surrendered to the South African forces, the Germans "did not surrender to the harsh challenges of Aus."[73] The site was declared a national monument in 1985, and a memorial stone was unveiled with a bronze plaque depicting a German colonial soldier. But the original structures have been allowed to continue eroding. This is noteworthy, since for German Namibians the Aus camp represents both the last chapter of their heroic military phase in the colony and the beginning of their long series of defeats during the twentieth century. A book on the site by a member of the Historical Monuments Commission comments laconically that "little remains to be seen of these huts except some ruins" and continues in a distinctly melancholic vein: "the transitory nature of . . . the inanimate constructions" focuses the visitor's attention on the transitoriness of "their interwoven human stories."[74] Photos in this book show that the camp was already in ruins in 1920 (see figure 12). Those who commemorate the suffering of the German POWs seem to prefer to leave the site in ruins (see figure 13).

## The Ruins of Detroit and Fordist Nostalgia

Whereas German Namibians are drawn most powerfully to the ruins of military structures, suburbanites around Detroit focus on the vestiges of the social system of Fordism. By Fordism I am referring to the regime of capitalist accumulation and social, political, and cultural regulatory practices that was hegemonic roughly between 1945 and 1973 in Western Europe and North America.[75] Fordism does not refer here specifically to the production processes or company policies of the Ford Motor Company, even if the concept did originate with the system pioneered by the company in the first decades of the twentieth century. Although many regulation theorists have focused on countries like West Germany and Sweden, there is no contained region where Fordism was more completely, concretely, and precociously instantiated than in Detroit in the middle third of the twentieth century. The so-called Treaty of Detroit negotiated in 1950 by Walter Reuther of the United Auto Workers with Chrysler, Ford, and General Motors was exemplary of the neocorporatist labor-management agreements that proliferated in Western Europe during the Fordist era. The car manufacturers were protected from strikes while members of the UAW gained health, unemployment, and pension benefits; more vacation time; and "a guar-

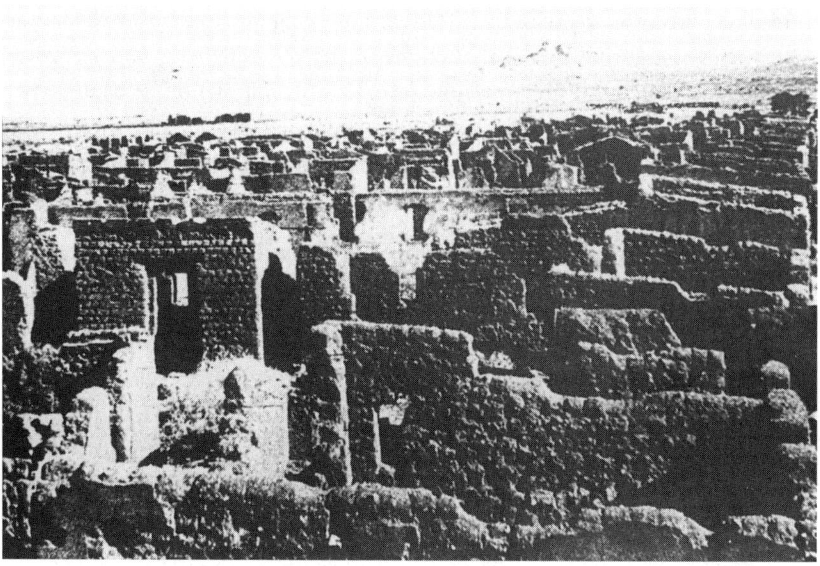

12. Ruins of the German prisoner of war camp at Aus, Namibia, 1920. From J. J. Bruwer, *Prisoner of War Camp Aus, 1915–1919: Establishment, Operation and Closure of the Prisoner of War Camp at Aus* (Windhoek: Namibia Scientific Society, 2003), 29. Reproduced courtesy of National Archives of Namibia.

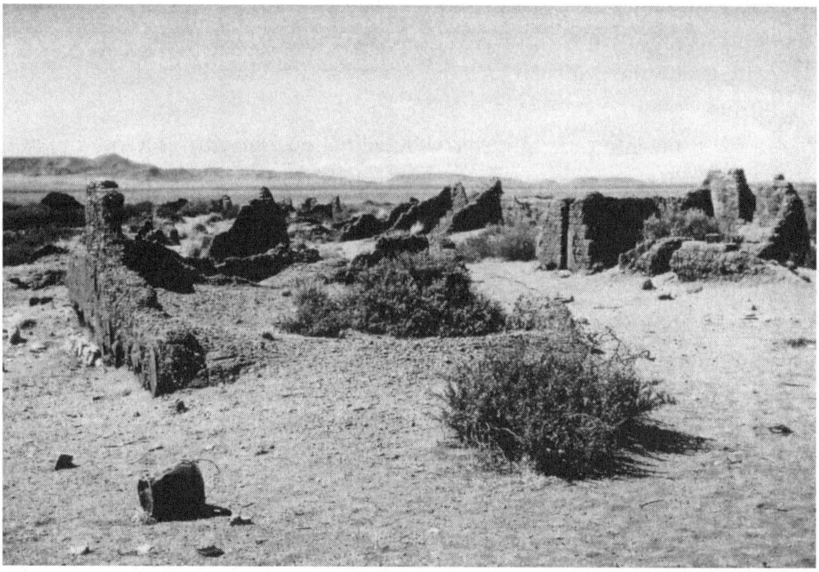

13. Ruins of the prisoner of war camp at Aus, present day. From J. J. Bruwer, *Prisoner of War Camp Aus, 1915–1919: Establishment, Operation and Closure of the Prisoner of War Camp at Aus* (Windhoek: Namibia Scientific Society, 2003), 39. Reproduced courtesy of National Archives of Namibia.

anteed 20 percent increase in their standard of living over the next half-decade, with wages rising due to both increases in the cost of living and improved productivity."[76] Detroit grew rapidly, peaking at a population of around two million in the mid-1950s. And just as the rise of Fordism created twentieth-century Detroit, the demise of Fordism has been responsible for Detroit's extreme impoverishment and for peculiarities of its ruination, such as the large numbers of abandoned high-rise office buildings in the downtown.

Detroit is thus in many ways the ultimate museum and ruin of Fordism. Traffic arteries cut directly through the city, linking Ford's two major assembly-line manufacturing complexes in Highland Park, a municipality surrounded by Detroit, and Dearborn, adjacent to Detroit. But the Highland Park plant has long been shuttered. Scores of automobile and auto-parts manufacturing plants were once scattered throughout Detroit. Today the whole sprawling city is crisscrossed with roads serving the shells of decommissioned factories and leading to empty lots where buildings once stood. Fire hydrants guard the entrances of streets that no longer exist, such as the service drive that parallels Interstate 75, which follows the course of Hastings Street.[77] In addition to Ford's Highland Park plant, major abandoned factories include the Packard plant, the Fischer Body Plant 21, and the Kelsey-Hayes wheel manufacturing plant.[78] Many of Detroit's abandoned factories have burned to the ground, and many others are demolished—including the Uniroyal tire plant, whose destruction in 1985 left only a few skeletal structures on a vast and polluted site along the Detroit River.

Unlike many cities in the eastern United States, Detroit was a low-rise metropolis of working-class houses. Auto workers' comparatively high wages allowed many of them to buy their own homes. White homeowners' associations prevented most large public housing projects from being built in the city. The urban electric railway system was phased out as workers began to purchase their own cars, and the Detroit Master Plan of 1951 projected a network of new urban expressways that would bring suburban workers to and from work in the city.[79] The footprint of this racialized Fordist urbanism is the structural basis of Detroit's utterly forlorn appearance in the present. The movement of jobs and white workers away from the city left behind an ocean of abandoned houses, many of which reveal the charring of recent fires. These ruins have not yet become weathered and do not exhibit the Simmelian equipoise of upward thrusting culture and leveling nature.

As can be seen from aerial photographs, there are almost as many empty lots as built-up ones in many parts of Detroit (see figure 14). These voids are a counterpart to the ruins. Theorists have underscored the danger of using terms like "void," since the people who live near such spaces often insist that they are

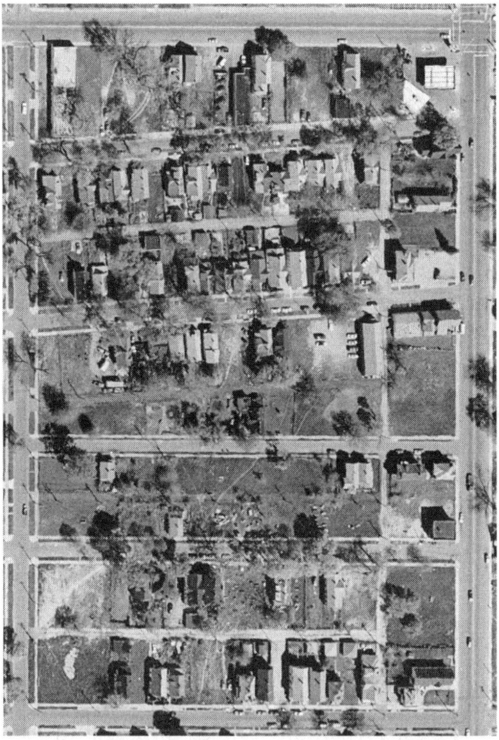

14. Aerial view of Heidelberg Street area, Detroit, 2002. (Image assembled with help from Karl Longstreth from the publicly available DTE Energy maps.)

"actually not a waste at all" but "also an asset."[80] Perhaps a more accurate term for such voids would be "negative ruins." Like "positive ruins," negative ones allow the viewer to imaginatively reconstruct the missing parts, but all that is left is the external frame. These negative forms retain echoes of old cadastral surveys, assumptions about ownership, and the patterns of streets, sidewalks, and railways imposed by city and corporate planners. The effort to ward off the city's ruination through incessant demolition is doomed to produce more ruins, since it leaves behind these negative ones. With their abstract shapes, such decontextualized bits of urban infrastructure are pieces in a jigsaw puzzle that no longer exists. The evolution of Detroit's downtown business district reveals a pattern of voids that reflects the original hub-and-spoke pattern.[81] As Robert Smithson noted with respect to the voids in the suburban landscape of Passaic, New Jersey, "those holes are in a sense monumental vacancies that define, without trying, the memory-traces of an abandoned set of futures."[82]

Detroit has also been largely abandoned by mass culture and mass consumption, both of which were central to Fordism. Tiger Stadium is crumbling and overgrown, having been replaced by a generic new ballpark that cannot become a vessel for collective memories from the Fordist period. In the middle of the twentieth century, Detroit's downtown contained a large number of elegant movie theaters, and there were countless smaller theaters in the residential neighborhoods.[83] Now the city has only one downtown movie house, located inside the fortress-like Renaissance Center, and a single additional first-run multiplex at the city's outer edge. Inside the old Michigan Theater, built on the site of Henry Ford's earliest automobile workshop, cars park near tattered stage curtains and the old projection booth.

Fordism has generated collective nostalgia because it was the launching pad for countless working-class people into middle-class life. Nonetheless, many people currently in the socioeconomic middle experience the neoliberal and hypercompetitive present as a regression compared to the Fordist era of solidarity within the working class and across classes. Yet most of them also recognize that the labor movement will never be as culturally and politically central as it was in Detroit during the Fordist era, and few would like to live in the city even if it were restored to its pre-1960s condition.

## Conclusion

While the ruin seems always to signify transience, mortality, and historicity, its more specific meanings are semiotically underdetermined, varying by context and social group. I have shown how two white populations make very different sense out of the ruins of the historic social formation in which their groups were hegemonic. Whereas the first uses ruins to relive the past, the other uses ruins to deny that the past no longer exists. White suburbanites use Detroit's industrial ruins to nourish their nostalgic longing for the city's golden era of Fordist prosperity. This does not seem to entail any confusion of past and present: the nostalgic object belongs unambiguously to the historical past. By contrast, German Namibians use colonial ruins to satisfy a sense of melancholia that simultaneously denies and acknowledges the end of German colonial power.

Ruins appeal to both groups as particularly evocative objects. Both forms of historical consciousness seem to prefer ruins that are gradually being reassimilated into nature to the fully restored heritage sites and simulacra of the tourist industry. One distinctive feature of the ruin is that it allows the viewer to imaginatively reconstruct its missing and invisible parts.[84] Similar to the Rubin vase/profile illusion, the ruin permits the viewer to see the intact object and its disappearance at the same time. Fully restored buildings tend to present a more predictable, preinterpreted message. The popular Henry Ford Museum and Greenfield Village in Dearborn, for example, a shrine to intense Fordist nostalgia, is "clean beyond reason."[85] The heritage industry feeds on nostalgia, but the result is that nostalgia is diluted, turned into commodity and kitsch. The ruins of Detroit, existing in a seeming no man's land of vague property claims, ambiguous boundary lines, and decommodified labor, refuse any such profit-oriented appropriation.

In Namibia even the fully restored colonial buildings obey a political, not a market, logic. But the most evocative structures for German Namibians are ruins that are left to deteriorate at their own pace, or whose decay is only partly halted. A ruin can point much more powerfully than a restored building to its historical and social genesis. And the ruin's location between culture and nature resonates with melancholia, which is analogously posed between life and death. The constituted landscape of ruins thus functions as a melancholic apparatus.

## Notes

Portions of this chapter were previously published as "Harrowed Landscapes: White Ruingazers in Namibia and Detroit and the Cultivation of Memory," *Visual Studies* 23 (2008): 211–37.

1. Hell, "Ruins Travel."
2. In the regulation-theoretical literature, "post-Fordism" is not just a chronological marker denoting systems that used to be Fordist. It refers to a successor regime to Fordism that is based on flexible production processes, niche-market products, the centrality of credit and financial capital, and privatization of the welfare state. See Jessop and Sum, *Beyond the Regulation Approach*, 76–82.
3. See, e.g., Mossolow, "An Historical and Forgotten Village," "Otjimbingwe," *Otijikango oder Gross Barmen*, *The History of Namutoni*, and *Waterberg*; Walter Peters, *Baukunst in Südwestafrika*; and Andreas Vogt, *Von Tsaobis bis Namutoni*, and *National Monuments in Namibia*. See also Dierks, *//Khauxa!nas*.
4. See Freud, "Mourning and Melancholia," and "The Ego and the Id"; Baucom, "Among the Ruins"; and Gilroy, *Postcolonial Melancholia*.
5. Sugrue, *The Origins of the Urban Crisis*; Chanan and Steinmetz, *Detroit: Ruin of a City*.
6. Daskalakis, Waldheim, and Young, eds., *Stalking Detroit*; Oswalt, *Shrinking Cities*.
7. Vergara, "American Acropolis"; see also Vergara, *The New American Ghetto* and *American Ruins*.
8. See http://detroityes.com/maps/mapfulldetroit.htm.
9. Kyong Park, *Detroit* (2000–2001, self-produced).
10. Ibid.
11. http://www.arcadiapublishing.com (accessed July 24, 2007).
12. Kohrman, *Detroit's Statler and Book-Cadillac Hotels*, 112.
13. A few documentaries about Detroit on public radio and television adopt a boosterish "fall and rebirth" narrative structure.
14. Glaser, "The Hudson's Building"; a similar atmosphere permeates Woods, "Detroit Remember When."
15. The Detroit artist Kyong Park made a video, *Detroit*, in which images of the city's dereliction are accompanied by a narration by someone who sounds like a businessman, saying: "Most of the buildings and houses have been burnt or demolished, and it won't take much more to 'clear cut' the rest of them. A tabula rasa has been created, so

that we can take back the city dirt cheap." At the Ruins of Modernity conference, Park expressed his belief in the existence of the fifty-year plan. While filming *Detroit: Ruin of a City* between 2003 and 2005, Michael Channan and I heard this story repeatedly.

16. For the sake of argument, I am glossing over enormous differences in social class among Detroit's white suburbanites. However, what is distinctive about the cultural system of Fordism and present-day nostalgia for that system is the belief that it attenuated social stratification. Nostalgic activities around Detroit's industrial history, such as Ford's official presentation at the company's River Rouge plant tour, tap into and nourish neocorporatist public memories in which class differences are symbolically overcome.
17. Walther, *Creating Germans Abroad*, 189; Rüdiger, *Die Namibia-Deutschen.*
18. See Schmidt-Lauber, *Die abhängigen Herren* and *Die verkehrte Hautfarbe*; Förster, "Zwischen Waterberg und Okakarara"; and Wentenschuh, *Namibia und seine Deutschen.*
19. Becker and Hecker, *Vom Schutzgebiet bis Namibia*, 9, my translation.
20. Mühr, "Die deutschen Namibier heute," 244–45.
21. Bourdieu, "Some Properties of Fields," in *Sociology in Question*, chapter 9.
22. Steinmetz, *The Devil's Handwriting*, chapter 3.
23. Schulte-Althoff, "Rassenmischung im kolonialen System."
24. Stuebel, "Die Entwicklung des Nationalsozialismus in Südwestafrika," 176.
25. Hess, "Die IG."
26. Rüdiger, *Die Namibia-Deutschen*, 19; Lautenschlager, "Ich träume auf Deutsch."
27. Steinmetz, "Drive-By Shooting."
28. An extreme version of this was long available on the Web site "Stormfront," which is now inaccessible (accessed July 24, 2007).
29. I am using "hysteresis" in the sense developed by Bourdieu in *Distinction*, 80, 142.
30. Lowenthal, *The Past Is a Foreign Country*, 10.
31. Steinmetz, "Social Class and the Reemergence of the Radical Right in Contemporary Germany."
32. Burton, *The Anatomy of Melancholy*.
33. Hell, "The Melodrama of Illegal Identifications"; Santner, *Stranded Objects*, 2.
34. Freud, "Fetishism."
35. Esslinger, "Anpassung und Bewahrung," 498.
36. Simmel, "The Ruin."
37. Barthel, "Nostalgia for America's Village Past."
38. See, e.g. Stenz, *Erlebnisse eines Missionars in China*, 30.
39. See Shepherd, "The Politics of Archaeology in Africa," 196–97; Martin Hall, "The Legend of the Lost City," 179; and Mauch, *The Journals of Carl Mauch*.
40. Thomas, "Stranded Vessels," 96.
41. Berkhofer, *The White Man's Indian*, 88.
42. "Ruined Cities of Central America," 8.
43. See Terry Smith, *Making the Modern*. The anti-apartheid movement and South Africa's defiance of the World Court increased Namibia's global visibility in the 1970s.
44. Simmel, "The Ruin."
45. Roth, "Irresistible Decay," in Roth, Lyons, and Merewether, *Irresistible Decay*, 8, 18.
46. Hetzler, "Causality."

47. Merewether, "Traces of Loss," in Roth, Lyons, and Merewether, *Irresistible Decay*, 33.
48. Libeskind, *Traces of the Unborn*, 35.
49. Roth, Lyons, and Merewether, *Irresistible Decay*, 67.
50. Quotes in text are from Rüdiger, *Die Namibia-Deutschen*, 15; and Andreas Vogt, "Denk mal, ein Denkmal," 251.
51. Vogt, *National Monuments in Namibia*, appendix 1.
52. E.g., "Pioneer Prospectors of the Sperrgebiet," *South West Africa Annual*, 1948, 91; and E. von Koenen, "Zessfontein," *South West Africa Annual*, 1958, 71, 73.
53. Mossolow, *Waterberg*, 58. Mossolow also published images of the Rhenish mission complex and the government post.
54. Vogt, "Denk mal, ein Denkmal," 254.
55. Rüdiger, *Die Namibia-Deutschen*, 76.
56. Mitchell, "Imperial Landscape," 10. On German Namibian memorial performances in the present, see Förster, "Zwischen Waterberg und Okakarara."
57. On the fate of the German monuments in Namibia, see Zeller, *Kolonialdenkmäler und Geschichtsbewusstsein*, and Steinmetz and Hell, "The Visual Archive of Colonialism."
58. Quoted in "Swapo Refuses to Condemn Mugabe Govt's Rights Abuses," *The Namibian*, March 15, 2007; and "Land Reform to Move into Higher Gear," *The Namibian*, April 27, 2006.
59. Kempton and Du Preez, "Namibian-De Beers State-Firm Relations."
60. Alten, " 'Allzu viele haben sie hier begraben . . .' "
61. Rust, "Der 'Schießbefehl,' " 483.
62. Frenssen, *Peter Moors Fahrt nach Südwest*.
63. King, *Urbanism, Colonialism, and the World Economy*, and von Trotha, *Koloniale Herrschaft*.
64. Andersson, *Diaries and Correspondence of Charles John Andersson*, vol. 2, 157, 164, 236–48.
65. All of the forts and police stations built in Germany's African colonies during the 1890s had crenellated towers and walls. See Walter Peters, *Baukunst in Südwestafrika*, 30, and Schnee, *Deutsches Kolonial-Lexikon*, vol. 1, plates 13 and 89.
66. For an image of the tower, see http://www.klausdierks.com/chronology/.
67. See von François, *Deutsch-Südwestafrika*, 50; Schwabe, *Mit Schwert und Pflug in Deutsch-Südwestafrika*, 13; and Andreas Vogt, *Von Tsaobis bis Namutoni*, 165.
68. Andreas Vogt, *Von Tsaobis bis Namutoni*, 107; National Archives of Namibia, photo 3392.
69. Ibid., 108–10.
70. Ibid., 59.
71. For more images, see http://www.sacktrick.com/igu/germancolonialuniforms/militaria/namibia.htm.
72. Kohl and Schoeman, *Kolmanskop*.
73. Andreas Vogt, *National Monuments in Namibia*, 81.
74. Bruwer, *Prisoner of War Camp Aus*, 3 and 12.
75. See Aglietta, *A Theory of Capitalist Regulation*, and Steinmetz, "Fordism."
76. Quoted in Lichtenstein, *The Most Dangerous Man in Detroit*, 280. See also Bell, "The Treaty of Detroit."
77. For photos, see http://www.paradisevalleyblues.com/tour/hastings0370.html.

78. For photos, see http://www.detroityes.com/home.htm.

79. See Andrews, *Detroit Expressway and Transit System*; and Detroit City Plan Commission, *The Detroit Master Plan*.

80. Doron, "The Dead Zone and the Architecture of Transgression," 247. See also Augé, *Non-Places*.

81. Doxiadis, *Emergence and Growth of an Urban Region*, 157.

82. Smithson, "A Tour of the Monuments of Passaic, New Jersey," 55.

83. Morrison, *Opera House, Nickel Show, and Palace*.

84. Hell, "Ruins Travel."

85. Barthel, "Nostalgia for America's Village Past," 87.

JONATHAN VEITCH

# 18

## DR. STRANGELOVE'S CABINET OF WONDER

### *Sifting through the Atomic Ruins at the Nevada Test Site*

Ours is indeed an age of extremity. For we live under continual threat of two equally fearful, but seemingly opposed, destinies: unremitting banality and inconceivable terror.
SUSAN SONTAG, "THE IMAGINATION OF DISASTER"

Please do not climb on Little Boy.
SIGN ON A SCALE MODEL OF THE BOMB DROPPED ON HIROSHIMA, BRADBURY SCIENCE MUSEUM, LOS ALAMOS

The term "atomic age"—once synonymous with modernity—already possesses a vaguely antiquated feel. In a digital era of miniaturization, hypertext, and virtual reality, there is something about the bomb's big bang that seems crude and embarrassingly literal. Not that we have given up the apocalyptic frame of mind: it simply takes other forms now. Bombs, of course, are still very much with us. But except for fugitive memories of duck-and-cover drills; a handful of names like Robert Oppenheimer, Edward Teller, and Karen Silkwood; the epic drama of the Cuban missile crisis; and Peter Sellers's memorable performance in *Dr. Strangelove*, the era seems to have been forgotten along with the ingredients of its favorite drink: the atomic cocktail (equal parts vodka, brandy, and champagne, with a dash of sherry). As a metaphor for the age, the atom is passé. We have ceased to think with it.

Of course that does not mean that we can afford to think without it. But what exactly would it mean to contemplate the complex legacy of America's nuclear entanglements: a surreal amalgam of secrecy, environmental devastation, scientific hubris, ideological

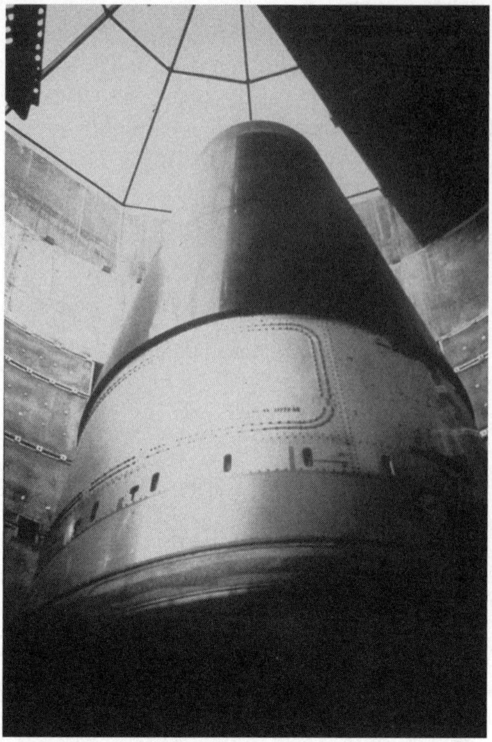

1. Decommissioned Trident missile silo, Tucson. Photo by author.

self-righteousness, breathtaking achievement, utopian aspiration, game theory, and realpolitik? Despite innumerable books on the subject, we have only just begun to put those pieces together. That problem is compounded by the fact that many of the nuclear facilities associated with the cold war (such as Rocky Flats) are now in the process of being decontaminated and decommissioned. Others, like Hanford, Los Alamos, and the Nevada Test Site, are being radically restructured in accordance with the diminished threat from the former Soviet Union and the resulting shift in military priorities. While few people would mourn the adaptation of these facilities to less destructive purposes (if, in fact, that is what is being done), the resulting transformation will mean the loss of an important piece of this country's nuclear history.

Nowhere is this dilemma more amply demonstrated than at the Nevada Test Site, the bull's-eye of America's nuclear weapons program. At 1,370 square miles, the NTS is larger than the state of Rhode Island. It is, in fact, one of the largest secured areas in the United States, giving the military plenty of elbow room. They've needed it. Since 1951 more than 100 atmospheric tests and 828 underground tests have been conducted there, making the site one of the most thoroughly bombed places on earth. At its high point during the cold war, the NTS was credited with pumping a billion dollars a year into the economy of Nevada; moreover, almost 10 percent of the state's workforce depended directly or indirectly on its activities. These were, if you will forgive the pun, literally boom times. But in the last twenty years, the budget for the NTS has declined precipitously: from $1.2 billion dollars in 1990 to roughly $400 million in 2007. Accordingly, the NTS staff is down from a cold war high of 11,000 civilian employees and at least that many military employees to a mere 2,700 people today.

Of course there is still plenty of work being done at the NTS, on projects like the Strategic Defense Initiative, the miniaturization of nuclear weapons, and the development of penetration bombs capable of reaching bunkers buried deep underground. But that, apparently, does not pay the rent. In order to compensate for the loss of income, there have been sporadic efforts to bring in other sources of revenue. Kistler Aerospace has petitioned the government for permission to use the test site to launch satellites for private industry. The NTS has also entered the competition to provide the assembly, launch pad, and landing strip for the next generation of reusable spacecraft, which will succeed the space shuttle *Challenger*. Occasionally NTS facilities are rented out for training exercises conducted by the Bureau of Alcohol, Tobacco, Firearms and Explosives, the Army, and various antiterrorist teams. For these purposes, the buildings are doctored just enough to convey the verisimilitude one would expect to find on a Hollywood back lot: soldiers surround the hospital, bank, or corporate headquarters, and depending on the scenario, negotiate for the release of hostages or storm the interior—just in time, one presumes, to save the day.

As of now, however, the biggest profit center at the NTS is probably what is called the stockpile stewardship program. The argument for the program goes something like this: in the absence of atmospheric or underground nuclear tests, other means must be established to guarantee the safety and reliability of the bombs in America's atomic arsenal. The officials at the NTS liken it to the problem of ensuring that your car will run after sitting on blocks for twenty years. The only difference is that unlike a mechanic working on a car, nuclear scientists cannot start a bomb to verify the results of computer simulations and other experiments. Monitoring America's aging nuclear arsenal is a complicated affair that clearly warrants attention. But it is a far cry from the glory days at the NTS when the media, members of Congress, assorted military brass, and other dignitaries used to gather at News Nob, seven miles from Ground Zero, to watch the tests—along with hundreds of people who simply pulled off the side of the road to watch the sun come up for the second time.

The NTS wasn't at all what I expected, when I visited the site in the summer of 2000. Indeed, to visit it now is to experience a confounding of expectations. There isn't much to mark the entrance except a chain-link fence and a lone security officer, who reluctantly steps out of a weathered guardhouse to check passes. Perhaps another nation "would have made its test site look more like a pillar of empire and less like a maximum security RV park," the critic and activist Rebecca Solnit once observed.[1] The absence of any visible symbols of power is curious. But like Alice in Wonderland, I was about to enter a world that would become "curiouser and curiouser." One of the first curiosities I encountered was a large sign just inside the main gate which warns visitors about the importance of wearing seatbelts. Whether intentionally or not, this sign represents the opening salvo in a series of attempts to diminish public fears of radiation. No doubt there are traffic fatalities at the NTS, but it is hard to believe that the gravest danger one is likely to encounter here comes from other drivers. During my visit to the NTS I saw very few signs warning of radiation, but I saw dozens of signs reminding me to buckle up.

One of the most curious things about the test site is the landscape itself. I don't know what I was expecting—probably something close to the postapocalyptic desert of *Mad Max* and *The Road Warrior*—but the first thing one notices about the NTS is how green it is. "People expect the test site to be a grim, dusty place," Derek Scammell, my escort, observes. "It isn't."[2] Derek works for the Department of Energy's public relations office in Las Vegas, so one would expect him to say something like that. But the fact is that he's right. The NTS looks better than most of the unprotected land one finds along the highway. The test site is proud of that fact and has even proposed turning itself into an ecological preserve. (This is just one of many schemes to secure federal funding I heard about during my visit, and it is by no means the most outlandish one.) The sheer beauty of the place tends to diminish one's fears about the devastation of nuclear weapons. "Here we are at Ground Zero," one thinks, "and it doesn't look half bad!" Of course such sentiments don't take into account the long-term effects of radiation, contamination of groundwater from underground testing, and so on, but that kind of devastation is invisible to the naked eye and, consequently, easy to discount. Hence the conundrum of radioactive contamination: since we cannot see the danger for ourselves, it is sometimes hard to believe it exists. We must depend on experts, often the same experts who gave us the bomb and lied about its effects in the first place. As if to underscore the point, a jack rabbit bolted across the road in front of me. I didn't know what to think. Was this just another example of nature's regenerative capacities? The rabbit seemed healthy enough. Or was it the beginning of a new science-fiction movie, *The Bunny Who Ate Boston?* That was the strange thing about the NTS: both possibilities seemed to be present at once.

**Frenchman's Flat**

Frenchman's Flat is the only part of the NTS that looks even vaguely like the sort of apocalyptic landscape one might expect to find. An uninspiring, dry lake bed of 123 square miles, it is littered with the twisted wreckage of fourteen atmospheric tests from 1951 to 1962, the largest of which was a thirty-seven-kiloton device named Priscilla. Most of the projects conducted here were tests of structural and military effects, which means that they were designed to study the effects of a nuclear blast on a variety of building materials and military equipment. Very little remains from those tests, but what is there testifies to the atom's destructive potential: a railroad trestle has been twisted into the shape of a pretzel; dome-shaped concrete bunkers—more than a foot thick—have had huge holes punched in their sides; buildings of every sort have been reduced to unrecognizable rubble.

The only structure that seems to have survived this unearthly fury is a massive safe, twelve feet high and eight feet wide and deep. Although the safe was assaulted with nearly seventy pounds of pressure per square inch, it remained intact. Designed by the Mosler Safe Company, it was part of a civil-defense project which sought to find ways to protect vital records and valuables. Obtuse to the ironies of their success, the Mosler Safe Company attempted to capitalize on the capacity of its products to survive a nuclear holocaust by displaying this safe (and another one found in the wreckage of Hiroshima) prominently in its advertisements.

J. G. Ballard once observed that "weapons ranges have a special magic, all that destructive technology concentrated on the production of nothing, the closest we can get to certain obsessional states of mind."[3] Nowhere is this obsessional state of mind more visible than in Frenchman's Flat, perhaps best described as a nuclear version of Jurassic Park. Here one finds the same sort of tinkering with nature, with the same outsized and frightening results. It is a landscape of hubris and folly, littered with the detritus of outlandish schemes designed to serve still more outlandish military strategies, concocted to counter unimaginable contingencies: hence its fundamental absurdity, its exaggerated, operatic qualities.

As I was looking over the wreckage, Derek Scammel said to me matter-of-factly, "You're standing on the pad for the MET blast." I looked down at my feet and saw a square of concrete, four feet by four feet, with a metal ring in the center of it. There was nothing to distinguish this spot from any other. Yet on April 15, 1955, a twenty-two-kiloton atomic bomb was set off here, sending up a forty-thousand-foot mushroom cloud that spread radioactive fallout (mixed with silica, iron, and cobalt) from Circleville, Utah, to Boston, Massachusetts.

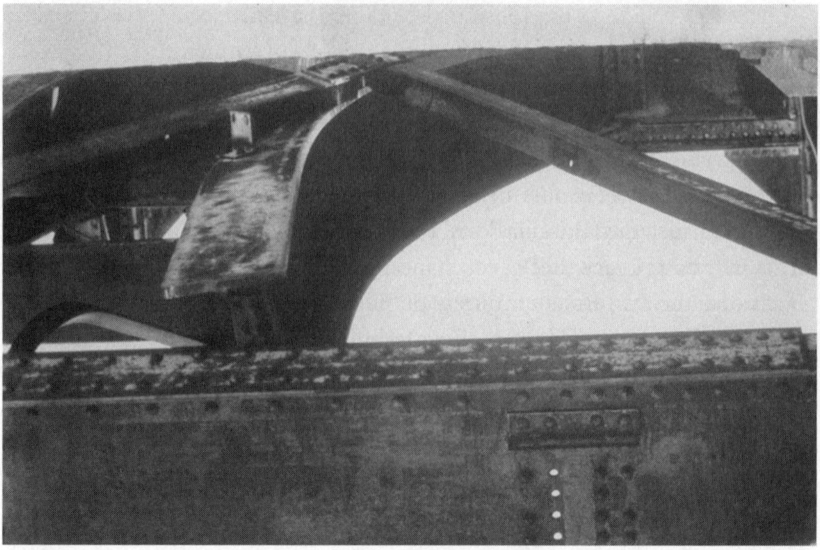

2. Twisted railroad trestle after a structural effects test, Frenchman's Flat, Nevada Test Site. Photo by author.

Thirty-eight scientific projects were associated with the Military Effects Test, many of them involving live experiments. In one experiment, four dozen White Chester swine—dubbed "atomic pigs"—were tethered at various distances from the explosion, dressed in the uniforms of Chinese and Soviet troops. This perverse type of crossdressing sounds as if it were conceived by a Strangelovian 4-H Club. In fact, it was designed by Los Alamos scientists to study how different types of enemy clothing might affect the absorption of radiation by the skin.

Sometimes the military placed soldiers, rather than animal surrogates, in harm's way. The scenario for these war games almost always assumed an enemy was invading the country from the Pacific Northwest. In order to stop their advance, nuclear weapons must be deployed on American soil. In the Military Effects Test, 260 soldiers hunkered down in trenches six miles from Ground Zero. After the blast the troops were commanded to rush in through the hole in enemy lines that it had created and secure the area. Few of the soldiers participating in exercises like these had any idea of the long-term risks involved. In some cases they were told far more about the dangers of rattlesnakes, tarantulas, and scorpions than about those of radiation. Many of the soldiers have suffered from a variety of ailments, including sterility, higher incidences of cancer, and birth defects in their children. But because the government kept such poor records, and because the long-term effects of radiation are difficult to correlate with specific incidents of exposure, the soldiers have had little success in getting either acknowledgment or relief from the federal government.

Once I realized where I was standing, I immediately backed away. Although little remained of the Military Effects Test except for a concrete pad and the steel anchors which held the tower from which the bomb had been detonated, there was something profoundly disquieting about standing in the cross hair of a weapon of such devastation. I didn't like the idea of tempting fate. "Hey, Jonathan, why don't I get a shot of you standing at Ground Zero? It will make a good picture for the dust jacket of your book," Derek suggested helpfully.[4] I felt rather awkward about taking him up on his offer. Throughout my visit to the NTS, I tried to respect the sanctity of these sites by observing an invisible perimeter around them. But there was Derek waiting patiently with the camera, bemused by my reticence. Derek's offer—indeed, the entire tour of the NTS—suggested an entirely different response to places like these. "See," Derek seemed to be saying, "you can walk through the NTS. You can stand on Ground Zero. There is no cause for alarm. It is a place like any other. Some momentous things have happened here. But nothing has transpired that is beyond human comprehension. Nothing you can't take a picture of. Tell your readers that." Maybe he was right. In fact, I never could decide whether opening the site to the public in this way was the beginning of a broader understanding of America's nuclear history or yet another example of what Arendt memorably described as "the banality of evil."

"What's the matter? You chicken?" Derek asked me. No doubt that was part of it. Despite Derek's repeated assurances about the absence of danger from radiation on the test site—"You would have to sit down at Ground Zero for a year or better for it to produce the same amount of radiation you would get from eating off plates of fiestaware"—I *was* chicken, unnerved by an invisible menace. Of course, now that my bravery was called into question—however teasingly—I responded immediately. I heard an imaginary Geiger counter clicking in my ear as I planted both feet squarely on Ground Zero and smiled for the camera. I half expected the ground to open up beneath my feet; needless to say, nothing happened. Instead, I stood there with an absurd, frozen smile on my face for what seemed like an eternity, while Derek positioned himself to get a good shot of the nuclear detritus behind me. A moment later I heard the shutter click, and that was it.

The click of the camera, the click of a Geiger counter: the former replaced the latter in my mind. Somehow, Derek had managed to exorcise the horror of this site with nothing more than a camera in his hands. How could I explain my relief? Surely part of it was due to the mere fact of being released unharmed from the bull's-eye of an apocalypse. But it was more than that. The camera had in a peculiar sense sanctioned my trespass and made the test site available to me in a different way. In "Art in the Age of Mechanical Reproduction," the philosopher Walter Benjamin praises photography for its capacity to do just that. He argues that photography violates the aura of sacred spaces like this one and demystifies the unexamined powers hidden within them. In the process, they become subject to our understanding and, hopefully, to our political will.[5] It is an appealing idea, but of course Benjamin was writing about the revolutionary potential of photography before the world was saturated with its images, and before photography became an indispensable component of tourism.

It occurred to me that perhaps the only way to exorcise the horror of such places is to subject them to incremental attrition through a million photographs like the one Derek took of me. That at least has been the modern solution to the scenes where some of the world's greatest atrocities have occurred, and it has certainly rid them of their horror. But it has rarely led to much understanding. How, I wondered, does one open up a place like this to the public without turning it into a tourist attraction?

### Sedan Crater

We didn't have any trouble finding the Sedan Crater. In fact, you couldn't miss it. The largest man-made crater in the world, it was fashioned by a 104-kiloton thermonuclear blast detonated 635 feet underground, which displaced more than twelve million tons of rock and earth. And it did so in less time than it takes to read this sentence. The force of that detonation released enough seismic energy to create its own small earthquake with a magnitude of 4.75 on the Richter scale. The resulting crater—1,280 feet in diameter and 320 feet deep—is so big that it looks like something one might expect to find on the moon. After witnessing the blast, Edward Teller is reputed to have said, "If you need to move a mountain, drop me a card." Whether or not the line is apocryphal, it goes to the heart of the ethos behind the Plowshare Program, which sought to literally move mountains, dig canals, create harbors, divert rivers, and tap deposits of oil, minerals, and natural gas—all in an effort to develop peaceful applications of nuclear technology. It was an extraordinarily ambitious and strangely naive undertaking which somehow failed to take cognizance of a basic fact: no matter how effective a nuclear explosion might be in moving earth or tapping natural gas, it inevitably left a radioactive residue which was harmful to the environment and the people who came into contact with it. Despite this very obvious fact, the Plowshare Program conducted twenty-seven nuclear explosions and spent billions of dollars before it was discontinued in 1973.

There are many ways to look at this hole in the ground. The skeptic might say

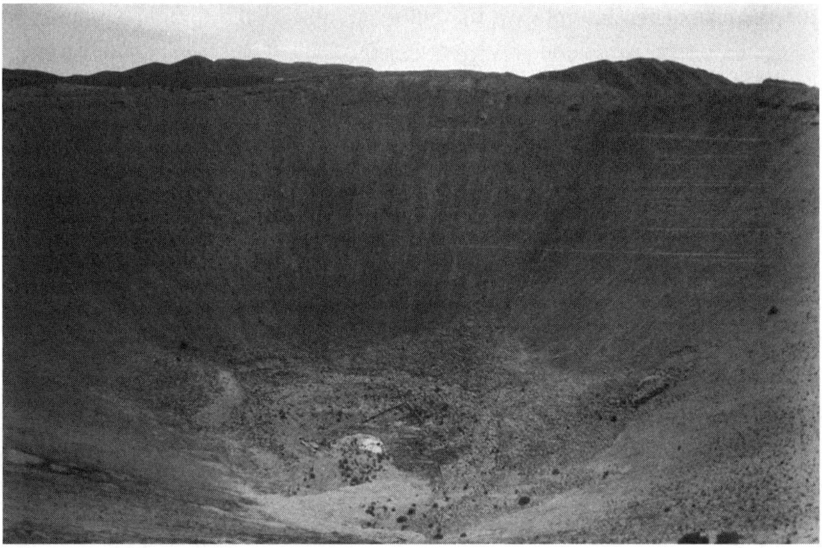

3. Sedan Crater, Nevada Test Site. Photo by author.

that the Plowshare Program was a cynical ploy to counter growing criticism of nuclear weapons. Surely part of what motivated Plowshare experiments like the one that created the Sedan Crater was public relations. The Eisenhower administration had spoken so often about "atoms for peace" that it had to be able to point to some tangible benefits. Even the program's most ardent defenders acknowledged its roots in public relations. Lewis Strauss, head of the Atomic Energy Commission from 1953 to 1958, revealed more than he may have intended when he observed that Plowshare was intended to highlight the peaceful applications of nuclear explosive devices and thereby create a climate of world opinion that was more favorable to the development and testing of nuclear weapons.[6] But to dismiss this program on these grounds alone is to forget the genuine idealism and euphoria that splitting the atom initially inspired. It is easy to laugh at hopes for the atom as a limitless source of virtually free energy, at comic-book fantasies of nuclear-powered trains, planes, and spacecraft. But it is conceivable that if the atom had not been harnessed to destructive impulses from its inception, the history of its use for more progressive purposes might have turned out differently. If this is so, then the Sedan Crater represents more than folly and cynicism; it represents a faith in progress, in the capacity of technology to overcome the recalcitrance of nature. The ebullience of that promise may be hard to recover now, but one cannot understand the genuine idealism behind America's nuclear program without it.

Of course there is a darker side to this ambition, and it possesses a history that both predates and informs the Plowshare Program. More than a hundred years ago, Mark Twain complained about the folly of the Army Corps of Engineers, then attempting to stabilize the route of the Mississippi River:

> One who knows the Mississippi will promptly aver . . . that ten thousand River Commissions, with the mines of the world at their back, cannot tame that lawless stream, cannot curb it or confine it, cannot say to it, Go here, or Go there, and make it obey . . . The Commission might as well bully the comets in their courses and undertake to make them behave, as try to bully the Mississippi into right and reasonable conduct.[7]

It is curious to note that seventy-five years later it is the same Army Corps of Engineers who attempted to harness the power of the atom for essentially the same purposes. Twain reassures us that the engineers have underestimated their adversary. The "Mighty Mississippi" will win out in the end; its beauty and power, he promises us, will endure. But one finds no such assurance in the Sedan Crater. Nature is decidedly routed here. Its face is pockmarked, its secrets plumbed, its basic elements reconstituted and rendered untouchable for eons.

If this is true, then the Sedan Crater may best be understood as emblematic of the hyperbolic ambitions which led to the conquest of the American West. At the Sedan Crater the instrumentalization of nature has been taken to its logical and most reductive conclusion. Indeed, in its most ambitious formulations, the Plowshare Program aspired to move beyond this example of the atom's power, to compel all of creation to submit to this instrumentalizing logic. "We will change the earth's surface to suit us," Teller observes matter-of-factly, and Plowshare was to be the vehicle by which that dream was realized.[8] Nowhere is this more evident than in Teller's "How to Be an Optimist in the Nuclear Age." In that essay, Teller issues an astonishing series of predictions on behalf of the Plowshare Program. He insists that the peaceful applications of nuclear explosions have the potential to reverse the direction of rivers, change the climate and the weather, make deserts bloom, produce "as much oil [in the United States] as can be found in all of Arabia," and induce "genetic mutations . . . in fish, creating new breeds of higher food value." As if that were not enough, he also credits the fission of the atom with the power to make good on the promises set out in the U.S. Constitution and, perhaps most stunning of all, to compress pure carbon into diamonds. "Dreams," Teller reminds the skeptical among us, "do come true."[9]

In the end, it is unlikely that the Sedan Crater will be understood as a sign of either technological progress or ecological devastation. Rather, it is likely to become little more than a tourist attraction. Efforts have been made in that direction already. In the brochures and information distributed by the NTS, the Sedan Crater is touted as "the largest man-made crater in the world." That same

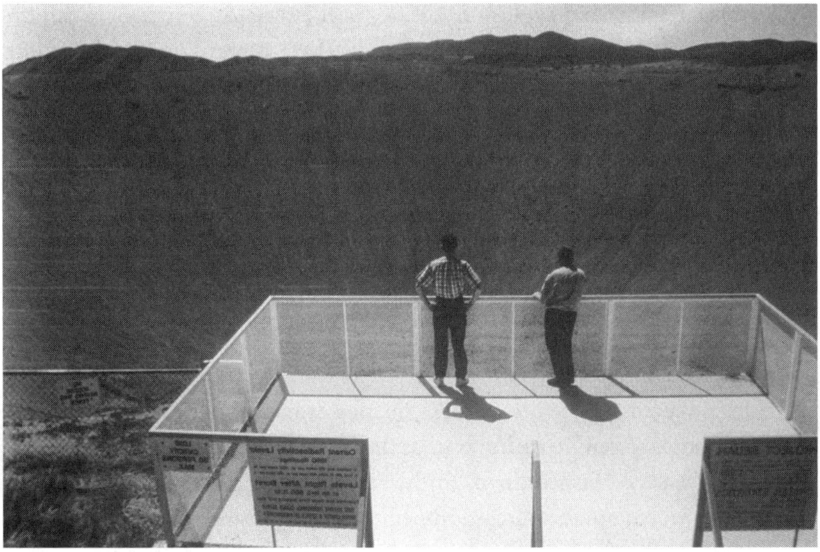

4. Viewing platform overlooking Sedan Crater, Nevada Test Site. Photo by author.

sensibility is carried over into the way the crater itself is framed for visitors. Two viewing platforms have been built on the edge of the site. The second platform is behind the first and raised above it so that visitors can take pictures of their friends and family mugging for the camera in front of the lunar-like landscape. Whatever significance the site might possess is elided by its transformation into this Kodak moment, which will no doubt yield results indistinguishable from comparable photographs of tourists standing before the cataract at Niagara Falls, or attempting to wrap their arms around giant trees in Sequoia National Park. In the process this complex technological artifact becomes another wonder of nature (further blurring an already ambiguous distinction between nature and culture that proliferates throughout the NTS). If the present layout of the site is any indication, these viewing stands anticipate the day when the Sedan Crater will become merely another roadside attraction to be consumed along with any number of nuclear oddities that the NTS chooses to make available to the public. One can already imagine postcards and T-shirts in the inevitable NTS gift shop announcing "Some Pothole!" or "Have a *Blast* at the Nevada Test Site!"[10]

**Doomtown**

Not far from Frenchman's Flat is another set of ruins left from the nuclear experiments conducted at the NTS. Named Operation Cue and conducted in 1955, these tests were primarily civil-defense experiments designed to calibrate the effects of an atomic explosion on a typical American town. The artificial town created for the tests included several different types of houses and motor homes, bomb shelters, "a school, a fire station, a radio station, a library and a utility grid"—virtually everything, in short, but a malt shop and a beauty parlor. Ever mindful of public relations, the Federal Civil Defense Administration (FCDA) dubbed the site "Survival Town," but the macabre nature of the exercise made that kind of official optimism hard to sustain. The participants promptly rechristened it "Doomtown."[11] As at Frenchman's Flat, the ruins from the experiments conducted here are relatively intact. In fact, the whole history of America's civil-defense program can be found telescoped here in all its earnest absurdity.

Perhaps the most absurd feature of the experiments is the passion for verisimilitude they inspired. In order to make the results as accurate as possible, the test houses were furnished down to the last detail, with the aid of corporate sponsors. The bedrooms were equipped with baby cribs (from the Lullabye Furniture Corporation), and mattresses (from Simmons), and the rooms were decorated with colonial reproductions (from the Williamsburg Chair Factory). The living rooms displayed a more up-to-date touch. Shag rugs, and overstuffed sofas and recliners (the latter from the La-Z-Boy Chair Company) set the tone for the décor, which was accented with stylish lamps and Streamline Moderne radios that would now command a hefty price on La Brea Boulevard or in the East Village.[12]

In addition to the furnishings, the houses were stocked to the gills with brand-name favorites of 1950s America: Jell-O; Comet Rice; Del Monte canned peaches and pears; Tree Sweet grape, prune, and apple juices; Pillsbury flour; and several cans of Campbell's mushroom soup. (*Mushroom* soup? Someone in the FCDA clearly had a sense of humor.) The goal of the test was to determine how these products would fare under extreme conditions. The reports found that the radioactive dust which settled directly on the food itself was extremely difficult to brush off. But the FCDA concluded that people might have to eat it anyway because it may be less hazardous to do so than to starve. To no one's surprise, they found that the contaminated food didn't taste very good.[13]

The most bizarre element of the experiment involved the use of mannequins. "Doomtown," as it turns out, was inhabited by a substantial population of mannequins, who could be found conducting a variety of domestic activities on the eve of Armageddon: i.e., listening to a broadcast of *Amos 'n' Andy* on the radio, unloading groceries from the back of a station wagon, or entertaining their neighbors over shrimp cocktails in the dining room. The use of mannequins was a "deliberate attempt to get attention" by the FCDA, according to one of the officials in charge. If so, it worked. "Endless streams of newscasters

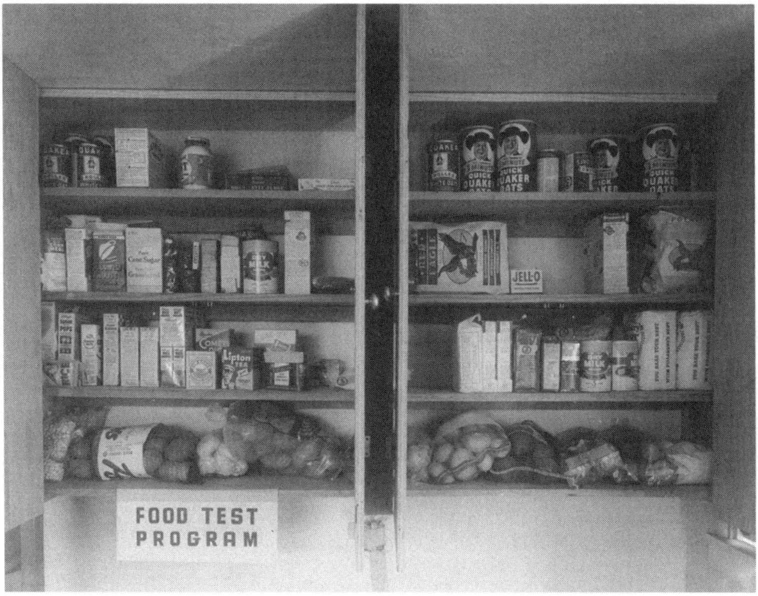


5. Pantry from a test house used in Operation Cue, Nevada Test Site. Photograph #420 in Box 1, 304-oc, Still Photograph Division, U.S. National Archives, College Park, Maryland.

invaded the doomed village, going so far as to conduct one-sided interviews with a mannequin family called the Darlings."[14]

The reporters found the mannequins dressed for the occasion. Dad wore a dress shirt and slacks from J. C. Penney. When he was not in the bomb shelter, he could be found relaxing on the sofa with Sis and Buddy—the latter of whom wore a T-shirt and jeans rolled up at the cuff (presumably so that he could grow into his new pants). Mother was dressed more stylishly: she wore a chic, calf-length evening dress with oversized buttons and checked trim that made her look as if she had been on her way to a cocktail party before she found herself sitting in the basement, waiting for the end.[15] The goal of the test was to enable project personnel to evaluate the degree of absorption or reflectivity of various kinds of fibers, including modern synthetics. But the melodrama of these existential little scenarios tended to obscure the results. Even so, the tests did yield some useful information: in the event of a nuclear attack, the public was instructed to wear layers and eschew tight clothes.[16] The tests revealed that dark fibers burned more easily than light ones. Some of the mannequins were found with the outlines from the printed fabrics they wore tattooed on their bodies, recalling the women in Hiroshima and Nagasaki who found the flower patterns from their kimonos burned into their flesh.

If these scenes induce horror, they also induce an unexpected and disquieting

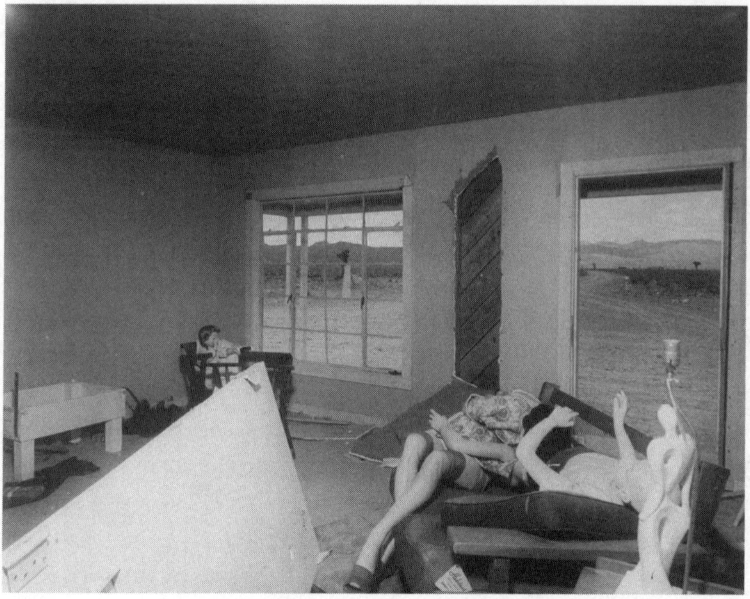

6. "Darling Family" mannequins in the aftermath of Operation Cue, Nevada Test Site. Photograph #BA-3 in Box 1, 304NT, Still Photograph Division, U.S. National Archives, College Park, Maryland.

sort of eroticism. In the film documentary of the event produced by the FCDA, the skirt of one of the mannequins blows suggestively—almost beautifully—out of the doorway of a demolished house: a haunting invitation to love among the ruins. Many of the photographs found in the government archives elicit cruder forms of desire, particularly after the mannequins have been "translated or displaced" by the blast (to use the clinical language of the FCDA). In one photograph a female mannequin lies flat on her bed, her clothes stripped from her by the ravishing force of the explosion. As if in acknowledgment of the titillation this photograph was likely to inspire, her breasts have been blacked out by a priggish censor's ballpoint pen.[17] In several other photographs the force of the blast has twisted the mannequins' limbs into a number of sexually suggestive positions that makes them look like sex dolls after an orgy.

The sexual subtext of the experiment seems to be confirmed by an anecdote told by a technician involved in building Survival Town, who recalls sneaking into one of the test houses at night to rearrange Mother and Dad Darling into positions of conjugal bliss. It was done, he insists, as a practical joke.[18] But the joke begs the question as to whether or not this strange display of eroticism in the midst of a macabre scientific experiment can be seen as an affirmation of life, an embrace of death, or a trivialization of both. Did the atom become the aphrodisiac of the twentieth century? Or have the technologies of destruction become so thoroughly infused with eroticism that the orgiastic frenzy of the atom bomb is no longer an aphrodisiac or even a metaphor for sex, but sex itself?

A Las Vegas news reporter who witnessed the aftermath of the blast vividly describes the scene:

> Along Doomsday Drive, a dirt road 4,700 feet from the blast, everything and everybody suffered heavy damage or death and injury as expected. A handsome two story brick house that could have been a bank president's caved in, bricks sent hurtling in every direction. . . . A mannequin mother died horribly in her one-story house of precast concrete slabs. Portions of her plaster and paint body were found in three different areas. A mannequin tot . . . was blown out of bed and showered with needle-sharp glass fragments. . . . A simulated mother was blown to bits in the act of feeding her infant baby food.[19]

Operation Cue thus turned out to be much more than a civil-defense test: it was a morality tale that told the story of innocence at home and evil abroad. Indeed, the calculated innocence of the mannequins' activities before the blast and the grotesquerie of their deaths afterward heightens the evil of their country's enemies and the righteousness of their country's cause. And it elides their complicity in a nuclear strategy which brought this end upon them. But it told another story as well. So much effort was taken to stock and furnish these houses for no other reason than to destroy them that it is hard not to suspect that at the bottom of it all lay a hidden rage at the aptly named nuclear family. If nothing else, these test houses at the NTS convey, more palpably than any other place I can think of, our longing for apocalypse, the desire to bring everything down around us.

Most of the buildings involved in Operation Cue are gone now. They were either blown to bits, or stripped of valuable building materials and razed to the ground. The only structures that remain are a few of the original houses, which stand in the middle of the desert like lost children. From a distance they look like the kind of modestly prosperous suburban houses you might find in New Rochelle, New York, or Claremont, California—the only difference being that these houses were subjected to the equivalent of 29,000 tons of TNT and enough radiation to kill everything inside them but the cockroaches. They appear to have weathered these catastrophic events surprisingly well. And although they are in a state of disrepair, one could imagine them being described by a real-estate agent as fixer-uppers—nothing a few windows, some fresh drywall, and a new paint job couldn't improve.

I wasn't in the mood to buy. But I did spend a lot of time rummaging through each of the houses: taking note of the closet space, the number of bathrooms, the size of the kitchens and living rooms, the large, unfinished basements that could be adapted to a variety of purposes. When I finished poking around I went outside. It was nearly midday, and the desert sun had grown quite hot, so I found a shady spot against the north side of one test house and sat down. As I ate my sandwich in the shade of the house and pondered the end, I must confess I found it hard to imagine. Despite an intimate acquaintance with a range of spectacular apocalyptic fantasies and prophecies—from Nostradamus and Revelations, to *The Mole People*—all I could think of were the reruns of old sitcoms I had watched on television as a child. The house behind me could easily have been where Beaver and Wally Cleaver grew up, or where Ozzie Nelson hemmed and hawed his way through another episode. I closed my eyes and saw Donna Reed coming down the staircase (forever lovely), and Fred MacMurray looking bemused as he sat in his easy chair—pipe in hand—contemplating the shenanigans of his three lovable sons. These houses provided more than just a set. They provided the architecture of domesticity, an impossible vision of the world that was nevertheless embraced by millions of Americans, who somehow expected it to last forever. How strange to find it in ruins, almost past recall.

As the romantic poets knew, there is nothing sadder than a ruined cottage. Wordsworth wrote one of his greatest poems about one:

> You will forgive me, Sir,
> But often on this cottage do I muse
> As on a picture, till my wiser mind
> Sinks, yielding to the foolishness of grief.[20]

But these American cottages do not elicit grief. How could they? There is no record of lives lived within their precincts. They went from the architect's drafting table to ruin without any human interval. And where there has been no human presence, there is no emotion. These houses were built only to be blown up. Thus they fail to inspire the melancholy one usually associates with ruins. At best they provide a record of hubris and folly, even as they reveal a curious penchant for blowing up the things one professes to love.

Although these ruined cottages fail to inspire grief, they do inspire laughter. Not the laughter that affirms life, but the horrified laughter that recoils from it: closer in fact to Baudelaire's Satanic laughter. Instead of taking my cue from Baudelaire, however, it might be more appropriate to look to the television sets of America in the 1950s for a more homely example of the laughter that ensues from this particular nightmare of reason. I am thinking of Warner Brothers' inimitable *Road Runner* cartoons, a series that was seen in millions of American homes (many just like the test houses) around the same time as Operation Cue. Set in a desert landscape, not unlike that of the NTS, the cartoon may have understood far more about America's nuclear strategy than it knew. If the test houses at the NTS prove anything, they prove how much the Atomic Energy Commission and the Federal Civil Defense Administration—indeed, America's whole nuclear policy—owe to the genius of Wile E. Coyote and his dream of a perfect trap. In all the coyote's attempts to build a device that would stop the roadrunner in his tracks—including slingshots which send him hurtling into space and massive boulders perched precariously on the edge of a precipice—the contraptions always backfired. The greater the coyote's ingenuity, the more exquisite was his pain. The excessive intricacy of the bomb components he received from the Acme Corporation seems to express the futility of it all. Sooner or later the bomb always blows up in his face, leaving the charred coyote gazing mournfully out at us as the roadrunner scoots out of sight. The comic and brutal redundancy of this cartoon allegory was, of course, lost on military planners. But the cartoon's popularity may indicate that the American public was astute enough to recognize itself in the forlorn figure of Wile E. Coyote, standing amidst the ruins of the Nevada Test Site.

## Notes

1. Solnit, *Savage Dreams*, 71.
2. The U.S. Department of Energy, National Nuclear Security Administration, Nevada Site Office, provides free general interest tours on a monthly basis. See www.nv.doe.gov/nts/tour.htm for further information on tours and documents related to the test site. I received a private tour in the summer of 2000 from Derek Scammell, who is the Department of Energy spokesman for the Nevada Test Site.
3. Ballard, *The Atrocity Exhibition*, 10.
4. Scammell is referring to my book-in-progress, tentatively entitled "Colossus in Ruins: Mythic Geographies and Lost Histories in America's 'Defeated' Provinces" (under contract with the New Press).
5. Benjamin, "The Artwork in the Age of Mechanical Reproduction."
6. Quoted in Richard Hewlett and Jack Holl, *Atoms for Peace and War*, 529.
7. Twain, *Life on the Mississippi*, 205.
8. Teller, "How to Be an Optimist in a Nuclear Age," 84.
9. Ibid., 87–82.
10. See Richard Misrach, *Bravo 20: The Bombing of the American West*, 97–118, for a (only half-joking) mock-up of what a museum or "atrocity exhibit" dedicated to sites like these might look like. The book's primary purpose is to present Misrach's hauntingly "beautiful" photographs of a devastated military landscape littered with ordinance.
11. The official account of the test can be found in a 162-page government pamphlet entitled *Cue for Survival (Operation Cue, A.E.C. Nevada Test Site, May 3, 1955), Report by the Federal Civil Defense Administration*. See also the film entitled *Operation Cue* made

by the Federal Civil Defense Administration, which "tells the story" of the test through the eyes of an "average citizen." The film gives a good overview of the test and the narration provides a clue to the way in which the government hoped to position the atomic program and civil defense for the public. It can be viewed at www.archive.org/details/Operatio1955.

12. The list of private corporations that contributed their wares to this exercise includes representatives from the mobile home industry, electronics, frozen foods, furniture makers, can manufacturers, and others, revealing the extent to which military planning and the potential for profit coincided via civil defense. See list of sponsors in Federal Civil Defense Administration, *Cue for Survival*, 160–62.
13. Federal Civil Defense Administration, *Cue for Survival*, 23–29.
14. Uhl and Ensign, *G.I. Guinea Pigs*, 82.
15. There are several good images of the Darlings and the furnishings in the test homes. See photographs #418, #423, #436, #647 in Box 1, 304-OC, Still Photograph Division, National Archives, College Park, Maryland. *Cue for Survival* also reprints a smaller selection of pictures of the test houses and their interiors on 5–6 and 9–10.
16. Federal Civil Defense Administration, *Cue for Survival*, 20, 143.
17. The censored photograph of the mannequin on the mattress can be found in #BA-3 in Box 1, 304 NT, in National Archives. Several more sexually suggestive pictures can be found in photographs #786 and #852 in Box 1, 304-OC. See also #LRA-7 and #LSA-2 in Box 1, 304-NT. The *New York Observer* columnist Ron Rosenbaum has an apt word for this link between eroticism and the bomb. He calls it "nukeporn." *New York Observer*, July 3, 2000, 19.
18. One of the technicians involved in preparing the test site—Alfred O'Donnell—recalls the incident in an interview with a Las Vegas journalist: " 'Because of the type of clearance we had, we could go anywhere on the test site; we could go up in the tower and sit on the bomb and eat our lunch if we wanted to.' As they walked through the houses, it struck them that the mannequins were not as lifelike as they could be. It was, after all, evening, time to retire. 'So we took Pa out of his rocking chair, and took Ma from the kitchen sink and we took them upstairs to the bedrooms.' When the Washington bigwigs arrived to see how tax dollars were being used, they discovered houses full of dummies engaged, as O'Donnell politely puts it, 'in compromising positions.' " K. J. Evans, "Alfred O'Donnell: The Nuclear Measure of a Man," in "The First 100," *Las Vegas Review Journal* (www.1st100.com/part2/odonnell.html). The story is reprinted in *The First 100: Portraits of the Men and Women Who Shaped Las Vegas*. Of course, the links between eroticism and the bomb have a long history, beginning with the picture of Rita Hayworth stenciled on the fuselage of the atomic bomb and the bikini bathing suit named after the tests in the South Pacific.
19. Teague, *Las Vegas Review Journal*, May 6, 1955.
20. William Wordsworth, "The Ruined Cottage" (lines 116–119), 181.

GUSTAVO VERDESIO

# 19

## INVISIBLE AT A GLANCE

*Indigenous Cultures of the Past, Ruins, Archaeological Sites, and Our Regimes of Visibility*

When we think about what constitutes an archaeological site, we ask: how does such a site come into existence, and what is there in a site that makes it a site? But these questions are very difficult to answer, given the wide variety of sites in the history of archaeology as a discipline. Let us try another approach and ask instead about the way in which an archaeological site generates meaning. That is, why not think of a site as a basic unit of archaeological meaning, and ask how that meaning is produced.

Archaeological sites vary dramatically in size and shape, and many different criteria are used to define sites. However, most sites have in common a process that they undergo: excavation. And after decades of academically sponsored archaeological digs, that process has become an extremely codified practice, known as stratigraphic analysis. The practice focuses on a limited space whose dimensions vary from site to site, but which is never very big—at least, not big enough to cover a significant percentage of the surface of the site. The excavated space, with regard to both surface and depth, is but a small percentage of the site, or the unit of meaning to be deciphered.

### A Concept in Ruins? The Archaeological Site and Its Relation to Material Pasts

In my experience teaching archaeological literature, I have frequently encountered an objection from students, both graduate and undergraduate: "how can archaeologists make sweeping statements about entire cultures just from the excavation of such a small surface?" In this chapter I do not feel any need to explain specialists' reasons for making sweeping statements, but I would like to put myself in the shoes of my students.

In fact, it is both impressive and outrageous that archaeologists think they are capable of defining a society's subsistence pattern from the retrieval of, say, a couple of burnt seeds, or a series of tools to which they attribute agricultural uses. Yet further excavations and other technical procedures, such as radiocarbon dating and aerial photography, have often confirmed the assumptions and hypotheses that archaeologists have made based on small pieces of land and scant evidence. Of course, it should be taken into account that confirmations or refutations of hypotheses come from an interpretive system that is shared by the original excavators and those who come after them, regardless of the tools they bring to the research.

But let us forget for a moment the arbitrary nature of knowledge production, not just in archaeology but in all disciplines. Let us instead focus on the definition of a site. What is a site, after all? It could be the Acropolis, Pompeii, the pyramids of Egypt, a settlement pattern in the Amazon basin, or a mound complex in the Mississippi Valley. The first thing that must be defined is, of course, the location of a site. That is, it is necessary to solve the problem of where the site is. Once that question is decided, there is the issue of the site's size. In other words, one should ask how big the site is. I propose to leave the first question for later and tackle the second one now.

According to Ian Hodder and Scott Hutson, "archaeologists are concerned with identifying functional and symbolic meanings and structures from the arrangements of objects (and sites, etc.) over space."[1] They warn, though, that the nature of space is not a neutral variable but something that is qualitatively experienced.[2] If we accept this (as we must, unless we believe space is an objective category—which goes against all we know about it from both science and philosophy), then the issue of space becomes a problematic one. What I mean is that in the archaeological process, at the crucial moment when it is decided what area of space is to be excavated, there are factors that depend on a variable that is not only nonneutral but also extremely subjective. One does not need to be a phenomenologist to accept that our bodies do not always relate to their surroundings in the same way throughout history, across cultural boundaries, and, of course, through space.

This means that different archaeologists in different historical times may not coincide in their evaluation of what area or areas should be excavated. They may not even agree on what the boundaries of the site are. In certain cases, what was originally supposed to be a site has become a tiny part of what is now considered to be the site. That is to say, there are sites whose surfaces have grown dramatically, due to the connections that later archaeologists have made between the area and other territories.

For example, let us consider the territory exploited by an ancient group of hunter-gatherers. Without certain information, archaeologists may not realize that this group included in its subsistence practices the exploitation of aquatic resources—say, the consumption of mollusks and fish. If that is the case, it is reasonable to ask: is the body of water they exploited part of the archaeological site, even if it is forty miles from the rest of the territory? What are the limits of a site? What criteria should prevail in establishing spatial boundaries for the unit of archaeological meaning? What is more important in defining the habitat of a group of humans: the distance they need to travel to get the goods they will consume, or the frequency with which they consume those goods? What conceptualization of territory did the humans have at the time they exploited the area under study? Are their practices something to be considered as archaeologists determine what site should be studied? Is a site better defined by human practices than by geographical traits?

The definition of scale is a crucial one for the kind of analysis to be conducted. This brings us back to the issue of the limits of a site: should the settlement be considered as the privileged unit of analysis? Or should the site be extended to encompass all the places exploited by a culture? For example, it is very difficult to establish the boundaries of sites in the Mississippian culture that flourished in Cahokia during the Lohmann phase. Whether one considers Cahokia a chiefdom or a state, it clearly had relationships with distant lands, as it is shown by the foreign raw materials and manufactured objects found in Cahokia, as well as by the Cahokian objects found in chiefdoms far from the settlement. Then again, what is more important: the place chosen for settlement and exploitation of the land, or the cultural ties and exchanges that a human group maintains with others?

However one answers these questions, it is clear that the delimitation of space entailed by defining an archaeological site is a very subjective endeavor. Consider, for instance, the next choice an investigator needs to make, after defining and delimiting a site: where to start the excavation. One or more very specific spot must be picked for digging, which poses the question why one spot should be preferred over another. Thanks to several factors, one of which is sheer luck, even the best-informed decisions may not lead to choosing the most productive and meaningful spot in the site. Sometimes the evidence archaeologists are looking for may lie a few meters from the main spots that are excavated. An additional problem is that the meanings attributed to the objects contained in the site are equally subject to the gaze of the observer. In other words, the patterns we see in the arrangement and distribution of objects within a site excavated area depend a lot—perhaps too much—on what Hodder and Hutson call "externally derived hypotheses."[3] These are patterns and interpretations imposed by the methods and theories that observers bring to the object of study. In this way, the distribution patterns we see are conditioned more by the domain of the observer than by that of the object observed.

Christopher Tilley and other scholars (I am thinking especially of Felipe Criado Boado) have tried to deal with the issue of archaeological patterns and their relation to the observer.[4] Tilley, known for his phenomenological approach based very freely on Merleau-Ponty's philosophy of perception, has tried to deal with this problem in both theoretical and practical terms. His main object of study is a series of megalithic structures in the British Isles. He tries to understand the space created by humans long ago from the vantage point of a present-day observer who walks through the space and experiences it with his own body. From that very subjective experience, Tilley attempts to restore some meaning to the structures that constitute the site. His approach does not take into account, as Hodder rightly points out, that "how one responds on such a walk would depend on who one is (for example a 'priest' or 'war captive') . . . and on a host of other social factors. These social 'meanings' would have a great effect on the perception of the person walking."[5] Thus, Tilley's proposal to focus on how human beings experience the world through their bodies is problematic not only because of the ahistorical nature of the human experience of space that it implies or presupposes—as Hodder, following Lynn Meskell, has pointed out[6]—but also because it is too strongly based on a subject-object relationship that leaves the burden of establishing patterns in the material record on the side of the subject.

Criado Boado, for his part, has tried to get out of the predicament of phenomenological analysis by putting the emphasis on the material record and on the patterns it imposes on us.[7] In order to do this, the Spanish archaeologist proposes several ways for modern observers to determine the patterns of the material evidence in some Spanish megalithic structures. One way consists of using mathematical and geometric analysis, which Criado Boado believes will help the observer to determine the topographic patterns created by the structures under study. This approach, although promising, calls for the performance of an almost impossible intellectual endeavor: to determine what constitutes a pattern that is independent of our cognitive framework and the theories we bring to the analysis, and to distinguish it from our own projections on what we observe. In spite of its problems, this respect for matter arranged by humans long ago, for a materiality that is not our own, may hold the promise of a more nuanced—at least from a philosophical point of view—approach to the meaning of the objects observed. In other words, this approach takes into account the materiality created by humans in the distant past in a way that gives their work a weight that one cannot find in Tilley's method.

Let us go back to a question I asked earlier: how does one choose an archaeological site? That is, why does one decide that a certain location, a certain point or points in space, is an archaeological site? Archaeologists have always been interested in conspicuous monuments or series of edifices from the past. That is to say, what attracts attention is often a ruin, a material vestige from the past that is visible today. This tells us something about what we see and what we are not so likely to notice. It tells us about what can be called the regimes of visibility—that is, the rules and protocols that determine our gaze and, therefore, what we do and do not see—of our Occidental episteme. It does not tell us much, though, about how local people relate to the ruins they are surrounded by.

### The Colonial Gaze, Local People, and the Creation of Ruins

It is true that some local people have, throughout history, been aware of the existence of ruins in their own quotidian lived space. However, it is no less true that in the majority of cases we know of, the locals rarely view the ruins that surround them as something that is valuable or worth knowing about. In general, locals—at least since the early modern period—have had a more pragmatic take on ruins: what can those material remains be used for? It is the gaze of the foreigner, the outsider, or the professional producer of knowledge that allocates value to that collection of matter that local people see as always having been there, inert, and possibly useless.

Let me offer a couple of examples of the attitudes I am trying to describe here. One of them will require us to go back in time to the Italian Renaissance, when the past was being rediscovered by humanists and biblical scholars alike. Humanism restored value to the achievements of a glorious distant past, some of whose material remains were still present in Rome, Florence, and many other Italian cities. However, as Stiebing has pointed out, this renewed interest in the past did not immediately put an end to centuries of neglect by the locals, who did not see a great use for the ruins with which they had grown up.[8] Nor did the renewed interest have as an immediate result the appreciation or even the protection of the ruins. On the contrary, one of the effects of the ascent of antiquarians and antiquity dealers was that Italian nobles started to search for ancient works of art to decorate their palaces. As Stiebing states, "This passion for classical beauty often resulted in the further destruction of ancient monuments. Many Renaissance buildings were constructed with blocks quarried from the ruins, and used as columns or decoration stripped from ancient structures."[9] This appropriation of the material aspect of ruins has as its correlate the incorporation of remnants of past greatness into projects in the present.

Even when the use of materials from ruins was based on a newly acquired admiration for the Roman past, it is clear that the Italians did not view those ruins solely qua ruins. Most of the buildings that had not been destroyed by nature or humans had survived because they were still in use.[10] Meanwhile, the Spaniards who had invaded Mexico and Peru were involved in similar activities. When confronted with the magnificence and beauty of Incan and Mexican architecture, the invaders allowed themselves a moment of awe and admiration and then set out to dismantle the buildings and put their stones to a more urgent, pragmatic use: the construction of their own palaces and Catholic churches. Those buildings—which were not viewed as ruins by either the local people or the invaders, because they were still in use—quickly became ruins thanks to the destructive actions of the Spaniards.

The ruins left in Europe by the classical Greeks and Romans bear testimony, to Western eyes, of a past grandeur destroyed by the forces of nature—although we know that sometimes humans caused the destruction. The ruins have an additional value, I think: they represent the interruption of that grandeur, the lack of continuity with a glorious past culture, the loss of which—and therefore its unrepeatable nature—makes it even more desirable to the eyes of the observers from the present. In the case of Incan, Mayan, or Mexican ruins, the lack of continuity—whose causes are not understood by most Westerners today—between the culture that produced the ruined edifices and the Amerindians who inhabit the continent in the present makes it even easier for the elites, descended both from local people and invaders, to incorporate such sites as Palenque and Machu Picchu into the cultural heritage they have created for themselves. The lack of continuity and its consequence, the perceived disconnection between Amerindians of the past and those of the present, makes the ruins constructed centuries ago an inoffensive tribute to cultures seen as gone forever.

This is very clear in the case of places like Machu Picchu, whose meanings in the present transcend local, ethnic, and also national boundaries. The site has become a place of pilgrimage for tourists from all over the world, but especially from affluent societies in the northern hemisphere, who appropriate the space as a locus for the sacred or the supernatural. It has also become a place revered by Peruvians in general, regardless of their class or ethnic descent. For the peasants of the region, the ruins are sacred and are used—when possible and allowed by the government—for a variety of everyday activities; for most Peruvians of European descent, the site serves as a focus for myths of national pride in the Amerindians of the past, usually identified only with the Incas.[11] It was this pride, shared by all Peruvians, that led thousands of them to protect the integrity of the site when President Alberto Fujimori attempted to build a cable car that would connect Machu Picchu with the lands below.[12]

Yet it was another politician, a more recent president, who showed how important this archaeological site is for Peruvians today. As a candidate for president, Alejandro Toledo not only promised to protect Machu Picchu from the proposed cable car, but also announced his intention to be inaugurated as president at the ancient Incan site, to show his gratitude to mother earth, known among Andean Amerindians as Pachamama. On July 29, 2001, he fulfilled his promise by participating with his wife in a ceremony dominated by Andean ritual.[13] This is just another example of how the Criollo and Mestizo populations of Latin America now view the indigenous ruins located in the territories of modern-day nation-states as the patrimony of all their citizens. As the case of these Inca ruins suggests, appropriation by the state happens at the expense of—and thus ignoring—the indigenous meanings that present-day Amerindians give them through their continued practices on those sacred lands. We saw above two different responses to monuments produced by other cultures or by ancestors of the present inhabitants. In both cases, the gaze of more recent Westerners led to further destruction of the structures. Yet in other cases, material remains are not destroyed by the foreign or nonindigenous observer. For example, the anthropologist Gastón Gordillo gave a paper at a Latin American Studies Association conference in October 2004, in which he explored the different issues raised by the discovery of the ruins of a Jesuit mission in the Chaco region of Argentina. In that paper, he tells of how he heard about the existence of a building complex that belonged to the Jesuits, and how he sought the help of local people to find and visit the site. He also explores the different attitudes of archaeologists and anthropologists, on the one hand, and the local people, on the other, toward the material remains known as ruins. He alluded repeatedly in the discussion of the panel's papers, as well as in his paper, to the indifference shown by the locals with regard to the ruins, and to their surprise at his interest in the old buildings.

Once Gordillo had been led by locals to the ruins, he witnessed the lack of interest of Juan, one of his guides. Juan not only asked Gordillo what possible interest the ruinous buildings could have for anybody, but he hit the walls to see how sturdy they were. Much to his surprise, Juan saw big chunks of stucco fall from the walls onto the floor, which only encouraged him to continue his destructive endeavor.[14] Gordillo was horrified. However, he realized that he needed to be more understanding of the gap between his view of the ruins and that of the locals.[15] He realized that they thought he was searching for a hidden treasure.[16] We see once again the locals' pragmatic view of ruins: they cannot be worth any attention unless they promise some material profit.

The different attitudes of the guide and the anthropologist should help us think about the wide variety of possible reactions by locals and others: indifference, newly acquired appreciation, destruction, devastation, recovery, or preservation of the material remains. But Gordillo's example does not shed light on another important issue: the creation of the ruin, or how something becomes a ruin rather than a deteriorated building or monument. In other words, how does a ruin become meaningful for local people? Let me give an example of how ruins are perceived by Western observers. As Jeffrey Himpele states in the 1997 movie he directed with Quetzil Castañeda (entitled, in parodic fashion, *Incidents of Travel in Chichén Itzá*), the Maya ruins he visited during the making of the documentary were created by the archaeologists and explorers who cleared the forest and, by doing so, allowed the Occidental imagination to conceive of that area as a city built by Amerindians from the past. That is, what those Western investigators made possible was the emergence of a new object of study and of a series of archaeological sites. The gaze that cleared the landscape to make a city and an object of study emerge is, no doubt, a colonial or neocolonial one.

That is so because of the way in which the gaze resignifies and therefore appropriates the space where an Other or Others once lived. Moreover, it appropriates the space in the name of scientific knowledge, a Western concept, and with total disregard for the views of the descendants of the people who built the ruins. The domestication of a space, used in the past by members of a different culture and ignored or revered by their descendants or other indigenous groups, is achieved through the apparatuses and institutions with which Western knowledge operates and prospers. And those apparatuses and institutions, as well as the desire to produce knowledge about that Other space, are made possible for a simple reason: there is a differential of power, of the same kind that made Orientalism possible, that situates the Western observer in a privileged position vis-à-vis the Other. In other words, there is a geopolitical situation in which a certain culture or society can impose itself on others so that it can produce knowledge on the latter. This production of knowledge is one-sided, generally disrespectful of the Other's opinions (which are often dismissed as mere folklore or superstition), and ultimately destined to educate Western subjects about the Others.

A ruin, then, is not only an object but also a process. It should be understood as both verb and noun.[17] Several agents can participate in this process, but the result is always the same: matter succumbs to the effects of time, whose agents are usually human or nature. One of the consequences of this process is, in Benjamin's words, that a ruin becomes an equivalent of death in the realm of the inorganic.[18] Yet there is, in ruins, a predominance of the inorganic: what is left is the architecture, the product of human action, which remains after its creator. Human beings, then, remain only through the persistence of the material objects they constructed. What is left for us to see and experience is the *ergon*, the product of their actions; the *energeia*, the actions that made that ergon possible and that represent the actions of those human beings at the time when the ruin was not a ruin but a lively social place, is gone forever. The phenomenological experiences of those humans from the past who walked, exploited, and gave meaning to that space—that is, who did all those things that made that space a place for them—are gone. The architectural remains, then, have lost their previous functions and meanings, their human aspects, but new ones await them thanks to the work of professional academics. Now, in this historical moment, in this context, from this domain of observation, they become ruins.[19] This domain of observation is that one that, thanks to its regimes of visibility (themselves a product of the power differential that allows the Western gaze to create a space as a ruin), allows us to see certain things but prevents us from perceiving others.

### Invisible at a Glance: Western Regimes of Visibility and Indigenous Material Pasts

The determination of regimes of visibility is especially relevant when one is dealing with material pasts produced by indigenous peoples. In these cases, the Western gaze is less likely to recognize the hand of human beings in the production of the material landscape. This is why I have proposed, elsewhere, to try to account for indigenous agency in what previously looked like the work of nature. Consequently, I proposed to look at some landscapes—which we, Western subjects, usually view as natural ones—with a different gaze, informed by disciplines such as paleoethnobotany and archaeology. In this way, I intended to unearth (both literally and figuratively) the traces of indigenous agency that contributed to shape the landscapes. In order to do so, I suggested having recourse to some of the sciences that study the past—the very same sciences that have been used, traditionally, to produce or perpetuate the subalternity of indigenous peoples—in order to view the territory in a way that allows us to detect traces of indigenous activities that transformed it into what we see today.

Certain prehistorically cultivated areas in the Americas have not been recognized, until recently, as the product of human activity. A good example of these man-made landscapes are the *camellones* (raised fields) studied by Erickson in Bolivia, which are remains of an ancient form of indigenous agriculture.[20] Another case of territories not even perceived as such until recently is the "fisheries" that Erickson has discovered in the Amazon basin. These fisheries are the result of human modifications of the courses of streams in order to give the Amerindians of the area more control of the reproduction of fish in the streams.[21]

In both cases, the observers who live and produce knowledge in the framework of Western culture had not been able to see a human-made landscape. It was necessary to look at the landscape in a different way in order to see it as such and to acknowledge the work of human labor in its construction. As I said earlier, the complex human labor involved was invisible not because of an impairment of our vision but because of the limits that our ideology imposes upon us. These ideological biases are at the basis of the oppression that present-day Amerindians suffer throughout the Americas. It is that prejudice that places them in a time anterior to ours and a stage of development inferior to ours—described by Fabian as the "denial of coevalness."[22] It is this worldview that makes it very difficult for us to see—sometimes literally—the modifications of nature performed by our indigenous predecessors in the territory we inhabit.

Let us now move to the discussion of two other examples that will, I hope, shed light on what I am arguing in this chapter. The first one has to do with the research conducted in the last fifteen years or so by Tom Dillehay, the archaeologist who studied and dated Monte Verde in Chile, considered to be 12,500 years old and the oldest site with evidence of human occupation in the Americas. One of the most important lines of research for the understanding of the peopling of the Americas is the study of the diet of prehistoric populations. This work suggests that the diet of some ancient peoples of North America differ considerably from the one described for the Clovis culture. This culture, bands of hunters of Pleistocene megafauna, was considered to be the oldest on the continent—which is tantamount to saying it was thought to be the culture that first crossed the Bering Strait—until the archaeological community accepted the date assigned by Dillehay to Monte Verde. The paleodiet studies conducted by Dillehay and his associates reveal that even before the Clovis hunters invented their famous fluted point—a very significant technological innovation—the Amerindians of southern Chile had developed a subsistence pattern based on foraging. The presence of plants at Monte Verde points toward a relationship between nature and humans that differs dramatically from the one proposed by the supporters of the Clovis doctrine.[23] Today, the first peoples of the Americas are represented more like astute exploiters of the environment and less like hunters whose only objective was to hunt huge herbivores for protein. The diversity of their diet reveals a higher degree of complexity in their societies.

These studies have led to the belief that without the adaptations of the late Pleistocene foragers, who settled in forested and wetland environments, the societies they formed would have been less complex, and the evidence found at Monte Verde would not have existed.[24] The picture some archaeologists present today is that of a number of societies all over the Americas that show a great diversity in their technologies, economies, and subsistence patterns.[25] Most of the evidence that supports this picture comes from the study of plant remains, a type of evidence that archaeologists had overlooked and underestimated for years. Again, we now see material remains that went unnoticed and were not expected by our regimes of visibility until very recently.

The last case I am going to comment on may help us see a more complex image of indigenous agency in the Americas of prehistory. I am referring to silviculture in the Amazon basin. For a very long time, silviculture was thought to have been invented in the nineteenth century. However, recent studies of tropical landscapes indicate that many of the places considered to be natural tropical rain forests are, in reality, the product of human activity. Charles Peters has studied several regions and found evidence of human manipulation of tropical rain forests. In order to be able to see that evidence, Peters needed to retrain his way of viewing so that he could see what was not visible at a glance, thanks to our Occidental cultural and ideological blindness. He also needed to retrain his cognitive apparatus to overcome a strictly perceptual difficulty: the exuberance of tropical vegetation makes it very difficult to see any human activity in that environment. The traces or marks of human manipulation look subtle, and their life can be ephemeral. However, Peters has found clear evidence of land manipulation in the form of gardens maintained as annexes to the household; managed regrowth of fallow areas after shifting cultivation; tracts of forest left to recover after being cultivated for years; and managed forests, the most difficult to see of man-made landscapes because the only evidence they leave is the distribution of useful trees in a forest.[26]

According to Peters, present-day Western subjects must overcome another difficulty to see the traces of human agency on the prehistoric landscape: the fact that indigenous peoples of the present, who live in small communities and practice a subsistence level of agriculture and forest resource exploitation, have a very minor impact on the forest.[27] However, Peters avers:

> Given their population density, sociopolitical organization, and intensity of resource use, Precolumbian indigenous communities would have had a significantly larger impact on the forest than their present-day descendants. They probably applied many of the same silvicultural systems, . . . but they would have done so over larger areas of forest, for longer periods of time, at much higher intensity.[28]

It is no wonder, then, that a series of intensive agricultural practices that developed over hundreds or thousands of years has been able to leave some traces that are visible today even in the densest tropical forests, if one looks carefully.[29] To look for them is, I believe, a way of attempting to restore some human agency to the predecessors of today's indigenous peoples. It is also a conscious endeavor whose goal is solidarity with contemporary subaltern subjects.

There exists, according to David Lentz, a common (and, I would add, subconscious) idea among modern scholars: the Americas were, until the arrival of the Europeans, a landscape undisturbed by the manipulation of human agency.[30] This is in consonance with the image of the Amazon basin as pristine rain forest and the associated view of local populations as ineffectual, which results in a representation of Amazonians as profoundly passive subjects.[31] It is also an image related to de Certeau's notion of America as a blank page on which the European subject will eventually make his or her inscription.[32] The studies I have commented on above propose a different relationship between Amerindians and nature—a more hybrid conception of a "natural-cultural" regional landscape, as Raffles and Winkler Prins would have it.[33] They are part of the same trend that can be seen in the studies of present-day indigenous peoples' manipulations of the Amazonian landscape, which has focused mostly on the terrestrial landscape, but which is now paying more attention to human transformations of rivers and streams.[34] It is from studies like these that I think we scholars who deal with the colonial encounter should get our inspiration.

### Making the Invisible Visible

In sum, it is only through a change in the predominant regimes of visibility that scholars have been able to see the fisheries and the Amazonian gardens. This should not make us forget that in the origins of archaeology, and in the most common archaeological practices of today, the regimes of visibility were different. And they were different because of geopolitical reasons. Moreover, I would go so far as to say that those regimes of visibility had their origin in a form of colonialism: it was colonialism, the expansionist drive of European nation-states, that allowed the invaders of distant lands to see old monuments and entire cities in ruins. This same colonialism, which presupposes a power differential between the observer and the observed, is what allowed foreign, imperial eyes, to see and produce knowledge about those decaying material remains of societies from the past.

The archaeological site is becoming a ruin itself, not only because of its limitations from an epistemological point of view, as we saw in the first section of this chapter, but also because it owes its existence to—that is, because it is made possible, as a medium for the production of knowledge, by—a gaze, a way of seeing that can come into existence only thanks to a differential of power created by Occidental colonialism. It is a by-product or consequence of European domination. This is the same colonialism that Kraniauskas sees in Benjamin's acritical relationship to Mexican antiquities.[35] According to Kraniauskas, colonialism becomes a blind spot in Benjamin's critique of modernity and progress, and I would say it is also what makes possible the knowledge produced by Western experts, knowledge developed by what we have come to know as the Enlightenment. If this is the case, then the categories that shape its mode of knowledge production are also affected by the workings of colonialism. The archaeological site, as a meaningful unit of archaeological analysis, should not be immune to this critique.

I am persuaded that it is our duty, as scholars who do not want to become colonizers of the past or the present, to pay more attention to what happened in the Americas before the time of contact with Europeans. In other words, I believe it is necessary to make an effort to perceive the modifications of the territory made by the indigenous peoples of the remote past, so that we can detect indigenous agency in what has seemed to be the work of nature. We also need to revise the ideological prejudices that make it so difficult for us to see some of those traces of human agency. The ruin, in the form of a material presence, has traditionally been the marker of what seems interesting to our Western eyes. The privilege the West has conferred to this kind of visible presence is what is behind our tendency to see other material presences as absences. That is, the limitations of our regimes of visibility are responsible for the way in which we sometimes fail to see the work of human beings who did not leave material traces that qualify as ruins.

By joining forces with practitioners of other disciplines, it will be possible to get a little closer to those local knowledges of the past understood as part of a way of life—understood as living. Past experience is perceived by scholars in the twenty-first century as materiality, vestiges of human activities that could serve as a guide to the practices that produced them. However, one should not lose sight of the fact that past experience is also interpreted by the descendants of the indigenous peoples. I am referring to the oral traditions of the Amerindians of the present, which should be considered legitimate tools to use in the recovery of indigenous pasts. This traditional lore has been acknowledged legally in the United States since the Native American Graves Protection and Repatriation Act became law in 1990. Although the discussions about the law's scope have been vicious and will continue to be so, at least until cases such as that of Kennewick Man are solved in a way that pleases all parties involved, it is undeniable that this legislation has done a lot to establish a balance between Western and Amerindian knowledge. If we do all these things, maybe we will finally become more critical of terms such as "ruin" and "archaeological site" and at the same time keep our thinking from leading to an ethnocentric dead end or, if I may say so, to its own ruin.

## Notes

An earlier version of this chapter was published as "Invisible at a Glance: Indigenous Cultures of the Past, Ruins, Archaeological Sites, and Our Regimes of Visibility," in *Remembering the Past, Retrieving the Future. New Interdisciplinary Contributions to the Study of Colonial Latin America*, edited by Verónica Salles-Reese (Bogotá: Editorial Pontificia Universidad Javeriana, 2005), 70–90.

1. Hodder and Hutson, *Reading the Past*, 178.
2. Ibid.
3. Ibid.
4. Tilley, *A Phenomenology of Landscape*.
5. Hodder, *The Archaeological Process*, 136.
6. Ibid.
7. Criado Boado, "Visibilidad e interpretación del registro arqueológico"; see also Criado Boado and Victoria Villoch Vázquez, "Monumentalizing Landscape: From Present Perception to the Past Meaning of Galician Megalithism (North-West Iberian Peninsula)."
8. Stiebing, *Uncovering the Past*, 119.
9. Ibid., 145.
10. Ibid., 119.
11. Flores Ochoa, "Contemporary Significance of Machu Picchu," 110.
12. Ibid., 117.
13. Ibid., 122.
14. Gordillo, "El sedimento de la historia," 5–6.
15. Ibid., 6.
16. Ibid., 7–8.
17. Stead, "The Ruins of History," 12.
18. Benjamin, *The Origin of German Tragic Drama*, 178–82.
19. See Jaguaribe, "Modernist Ruins: National Narratives and Architectural Forms."
20. For a brief description of these cultivated lands, see my "Forgotten Territorialities." For more information about the raised fields, see Erickson, "Prehistoric Landscape Management in the Andean Highlands" and "The Social Organization of Prehispanic Raised Field Agriculture in the Lake Titicaca Basin."
21. Erickson, "An Artificial Landscape-scale Fishery in the Bolivian Amazon."
22. Fabian, *Time and the Other*.
23. I call it a "doctrine" because its supporters have shown an attitude that is best described as dogmatic or doctrinaire. It is shocking to see the time and energy they have devoted to the desperate defense of the theory that proposes the precedence of Clovis culture—from both a chronological and a developmental perspective—over the other cultures that flourished across the Americas.
24. Dillehay and Rossen, "Plant Food and Its Implications for the Peopling of the New World," 237.
25. Ibid., 238.
26. Charles Peters, "Precolumbian Silviculture and Indigenous Management of Neotropical Forests."

27. Ibid., 214.

28. Ibid., 214–15.

29. Today some scholars believe that as much as 12 percent of the Amazonian forest is currently of biocultural origin. See Raffles and Winkler Prins, "Further Reflections on Amazonian Environmental History, 167.

30. Lentz, Introduction, 1.

31. Raffles and Winkler Prins, "Further Reflections on Amazonian Environmental History," 166 and 168.

32. De Certeau, *The Writing of History*, xxv.

33. Ibid., 166.

34. Ibid., 167.

35. Kraniauskas, "Beware Mexican Ruins!," 141.

# PART V

# RUIN GAZING

ALEXANDER REGIER

# 20

## FOUNDATIONAL RUINS

*The Lisbon Earthquake and the Sublime*

"Have you heard of the earthquake in Lisbon?"

THOMAS MANN, *DER ZAUBERBERG*

In the opening book of his autobiography *Dichtung und Wahrheit* (From My Life; 1811–14, 1833), Goethe records one of his most important childhood experiences by taking a distancing look at himself in the third person: "However, the boy's tranquillity of mind was deeply shaken for the first time by an extraordinary event. On the first of November, 1755, occurred the great earthquake of Lisbon, spreading enormous terror over a world grown accustomed to peace and quiet."[1] Just as this date shakes and severs Goethe's biography, the tremendous impact of the earthquake of Lisbon is a defining moment for the entire eighteenth century. In what follows, I want to take seriously Goethe's image of the disruptive power of this well-known disaster. My argument presents the Lisbon earthquake as an event whose metaphorical force provides a conceptual springboard for a reading of some central texts on the sublime. Although my point of departure is the material circumstance of 1755, its role in these readings is primarily that of conceptual and rhetorical catalyst.

The earthquake of Lisbon is generally understood as an event which marks a crucial and initiating moment in a history linking modernity and increasing secularization, both in the sciences and the humanities (as far as these divisions apply here).[2] Correspondingly, the meaning of the event was, and indeed is, most often theorized in relation to the multidisciplinary complex of issues surrounding the ancient discussion of theodicy. Crudely put, there are two main ways in which Lisbon is presented as a marker of modern European history: First, as swinging general trust from best-of-all-possible Leibnizian worlds to a less optimistic view of life defined by inexplicable suffering. Or, second, as an incentive to show that we should abandon the idea of a wrathful deity who makes the earth tremble in order to adopt a more convincing account that is based on the analysis of natural causes.

In either case, the link between the Lisbon earthquake and the development of our contemporary literary or scientific outlook has proved to be hermeneutically powerful and lasting. Apart from the contemporary journalistic strategy of linking events such as 9/11 or the Asian tsunami in 2004 with the eighteenth-century disaster, the earthquake has had a constant presence in scholarly literature in a variety of fields. A recent example is Neiman's widely discussed study *Evil in Modern Thought*, which links modernity and Lisbon: in fact, Neiman locates "the modern as beginning at Lisbon"[3] and calls the earthquake the "birthplace of modernity."[4] A number of important thinkers and authors are often enlisted as the most distinguished and illustrious proponents of conceptualizing Lisbon in these terms: Goethe and Wollstonecraft write about the earthquake; Kleist and Mann use it in their masterpieces; Adorno, Benjamin, and Russell continue the attempts to understand the catastrophe philosophically. Most of these accounts see the importance of the rupturing moment which the earthquake comes to represent as occupying an exemplary position within a narrative that describes the eighteenth and nineteenth centuries as developing a more secular outlook, particularly in response to natural phenomena. For the purposes of this essay, I will term this the "progressivist narrative." Even the many theologically inflected responses to the calamity, which directly link the disaster to a divine act or word, retrospectively also form part of the framework for this narrative. Whether as independent contributions, or as part of the discussions on theodicy, they are dismantled and superseded by more enlightened arguments—or so the story goes.

### The Progressivist Narrative

The specific literary context of the catastrophe is constructed, at least in part, as a chapter of this progressivist story. Pope's *An Essay on Man* (1733) and its mocking reception by Lessing and Mendelssohn prepare the literary field before the catastrophe hits European intellectual life. In assessing the immediate aftermath, Voltaire's reaction generally serves as the paradigmatic example. His influential "Poème sur le désastre de Lisbonne" (1756)—a classic case of a poem defending a particular position in the debate on the problem of evil—becomes the point of reference for Rousseau's reply on the subject, as well as innumerable other voices.[5] The earthquake retains its power throughout the period as a general foil for imagery, such as in Kleist's *Erdbeben in Chili* (1807). Despite their differences, the representative nature of these "enlightened" texts is firmly established in and through secondary sources.

This general background serves as the context against which my specific argument is situated. My essay will focus on the role played by the aesthetic, specifically the sublime, in the outlined field of responses. The argument will fall into two parts, moving from the particular to the general. In the first section, I will look at reports from the immediate scene of the disaster. The second step links these readings to a much larger complex of aesthetics, via the category of the sublime. By looking closely at some passages from Kant's *Critique of Judgment*, I will attempt to unravel the double nature of the sublime as a taming and domesticating force that ultimately relies on the destructive power of what is best termed fragmentation. Ultimately, fragmentation emerges as the shattering yet foundational force connected to the sublime. Lisbon and its destructive power haunt Kant's theoretical account in unexpected ways. Simultaneously, they complicate the supposedly secular and progressivist character of his argument that has often been taken for granted in secondary literature. In a broad sense, this analysis follows Simpson's remark that "if the earthquake [of Lisbon] can be said to have exposed the dubious status of the doctrines of rational self-sufficiency which the public voice of Enlightenment thought put forward, then it could also be said that it re-emphasized the priority of the gaps upon which that voice was founded."[6] More specifically, the importance of the Lisbon earthquake provides a crucial insight into the structural position of the sublime within a larger Kantian framework. The fragmentation of ideas, to return to Goethe's remark, can be read as the necessary condition for the subsequently rationalizing categories of the sublime. Correspondingly, the common critical narrative allows for its reversal: the "progressive" power of Lisbon relies on something altogether negating and exceeding rationality or secular description; the earthquake's ripples remain more destructive than has been assumed.

## Classification and Excess

Eyewitness accounts of the Lisbon earthquake rank among the more impressive documents of the period. In letters written by inhabitants, traveling merchants, and other survivors of the catastrophe all struggle for words to represent the absolute terror and destruction of the disaster. While the event exceeds classification, the reports attempt to find a language in which to present the destruction that surrounds them. The lack of available vocabulary is evident in a variety of failed attempts to classify the event geographically, historically, and psychologically. An example from each of these areas follows.

The difficulty contemporary observers have in attempting to classify the disaster is striking. It should really have been different. At least England's distant observers seem superficially prepared. In 1750 a mild trembling of the earth in London leads to a publication of an extensive special appendix to the papers of the Royal Philosophical Society dedicated to reports about the event.[7] Hence it is not surprising that the Society is open to reports on the new topic and that earthquakes become a dominant subject of the proceedings for over a year. However, the natural catastrophe in Portugal proves to be of such proportions that it cannot be limited to an appendix. Rather than a catastrophe limited to one place, the Lisbon earthquake immediately becomes an event felt throughout the Western world. The Society stresses that reports about the trembling of the earth arrive from Madrid, Cadiz, and other locations on the Iberian peninsula, as well as Tangier, Arzila, Salle, Fez, Mcquinez, Madeira, and Tasso—the impact of the earthquake is truly intercontinental. And the disaster is not only exoticized: Lisbon is also felt in Derbyshire and Scotland. Once the earth moves from Africa to northern Europe, its aftershock cannot be contained in a single volume. The following years see a continuing interest in geological catastrophes. Reports on movements of the earth reach the Society from Boston, Brigue, Brussels, Dover, Dumbarton, Geneva, Glasgow, Leiden, Maastricht, Neuchâtel, New York, and Philadelphia. It is evident that Lisbon is not simply a localized catastrophe. The event has its epicenter in a particular place, but its impact is far wider. A geographical localization of the event becomes impossible; its power is beyond containment. Lisbon cannot be confined to one geographical space; it is all over Europe.

This difficulty in fixing Lisbon within conventional parameters becomes even clearer when reports attempt to articulate its exceptional status by means of temporal images. The catastrophe is catapulted out of normal history—it does not belong to the generally accepted narrative within which we live, as a letter back home from an English merchant residing in Lisbon illustrates: the earthquake "reduced that whole Metropolis to Ashes; rendering it such a Spectacle of Terror and Amazement, as well as the Desolation to Beholders, as perhaps has not been equalled from the Foundation of the World!"[8] The singularly disastrous character of the catastrophe cannot be "equalled" by anything in the annals of the world. It cannot be domesticated within a common taxonomy of known and memorizable historical events. It becomes an event of biblical proportions, a "disaster" in the most radical sense of the Old Testament. As the eyewitness insists: "I have past through the Ruins of the principal Parts of the City, and they are dreadful indeed to behold. I believe so compleat a Destruction has hardly befallen any Place on Earth, since the Overthrow of *Sodom* and *Gomorrah*."[9]

Normal classification will not do here. Although the beholder does not turn into a pillar of salt, the dimensions of the destruction are suggestive enough. The event is of proportions that go beyond modern records. Through the mythical reference, it escapes the status of a historically locatable event. The reference to Sodom and Gomorrah suggests how far the "compleat Destruction" breaks the usual frame of history. The anonymous *Poem on the Earthquake at Lisbon* (1755) puts it in a similar way when describing the Portuguese King's misery:

> Lo! The good King from out the ruin'd Heaps,
> by Providence Divine, Like *Lot* escapes;
> But *Lot's* Command, while yet the City burn'd,
> The weeping King had disobeyed and turn'd:
> There in Salt Tears congeal'd, he fix'd had staid,
> And, like the Woman, a new Pillar made:
> Forbid his dear *Eurydice* to view,
> Like *Orpheus* he had look'd and perish'd too.[10]

The wild and jumbled mixture of biblical and Classical imagery unwittingly reflects the chaos represented in the scene. In the remainder of the poem the King is likened to Moses on Ararat, Job, and Aeneas beholding "his burning Troy." These comparisons are not only disordered, but they also defy a coherent classification of the collapse and destruction under traditional historical rubrics. People involved in the earthquake, such as the actual King, are taken out of history and transformed into mythical figures. Note that these examples fall outside discourses with open theologico-didactic goals where one might expect, and indeed finds, an abundance of biblical vocabulary, most notably in the innumerable sermons that use the disaster in Lisbon as an argument for the wickedness of its Catholic inhabitants. I want to suggest, therefore, that the earthquake pervades and exceeds the language of its textual reception, catapulting the event out of time and place. Even geological science is not immune from this move. In a letter passed on to the Royal Society a Mr. Perry confirms that "the earthquake at Lisbon, which you gave me an account of, was certainly the most awful tremendous calamity, that has ever happened in the world. Its effects are extremely wonderful and amazing; and it seems, as you observe, to have been felt in all parts of the globe."[11]

More localized reports from the scenes of Lisbon's destruction illustrate the extent to which fragmentation ends in ruin and formless graves. The merchant's report already quoted attempts to capture the process of devastation from the midst of its chaos:

> Not long after my Arrival at the Place I have mentioned, a general Pannic [*sic*] was raised from a Crowd of People's [*sic*] running from the Waterside, all crying out the Sea was pouring in and would certainly overwhelm the City. [V]ast Numbers of them [the inhabitants] ran screaming into the ruinated City again, where, a fresh Shock of the Earthquake immediately following, many of them were buried in the Ruins of falling Houses.[12]

The already "ruinated City" becomes, through a second quake, just as deadly as the nearby sea, locking the inhabitants of Lisbon into a prison of shock, horror, and death. The material fragmentation of the city is repeated twice over. "Ruinated" already, it buries "many" of the "vast Numbers" under its fragments ("the Ruins of falling Houses"). These letters insist on the earthquake's power to form a deadly tomb in which the inhabitants are "buried"[13] or by which they are "dashed to pieces."[14] In the same vein, another eyewitness, Anthony Pereira, reports that "the houses, the streets and alleys were strewed with dead bodies: some had their brains dashed out with the falling of the arches, others were crushed by the tumbling of the walls, most of them were overpowered and suffocated with the weight of the rubbish, in such a heap of rafters and stones."[15] In its collapse, Lisbon becomes a mass grave—in fact, a "third part of its inhabitants was buried in the ruins."[16]

The subject's mind and body cannot cope with these dimensions. In the most extreme instance, the city's total destruction and collapse is mirrored in the bodily annihilation of its inhabitants, as this anonymous letter gruesomely describes:

> Mr. Vincent . . . never left the house he slept in, being suddenly crushed to death before he was dressed, and buried in ruins, which is the only tomb he is ever like to meet with; for his friends, after many fruitless searches, having discovered as they supposed the remains of his body, they found them so putrified, broken and scattered that 'twas impossible to remove them.[17]

The human form is reduced to shapelessness, its body mutilated beyond representation. The very shape of the human subject is "broken and scattered" beyond recognition. "Mr. Vincent," just like Lisbon, is no more. His corpse has been so crushed that it becomes futile to attempt its reconstruction. The only thing left to contemplate and behold are the ruins that function as his memorial. Importantly, the reports correspondingly insist how this material collapse goes hand in hand with a mental breakdown. The reports from Lisbon repeatedly make the "Horrors in the agitated Minds of the Populace" responsible for their running into "ruinated" graves.[18] The mental collapse lies at the epicenter of the disaster: "It would be a vain Attempt to endeavour describing the numberless Miseries, and terrible Distresses of all kinds, occasioned by this dreadful Calamity, as well as the shocking Effects that it had on the Minds of all people."[19] The subject's mind is taken over in the apocalyptic scene, sometimes dangerously close to melodrama. The correlation between mental and material fragmentation is emphasized through these scenes. The material collapse of the city's buildings, churches, and symbols is paralleled by a collapse of inner structures. While the city is "scattered," its inhabitants suffer from mental breakdown and "various Distempers."[20] Mirroring the ruined buildings, people are said to be "sinking under the Anguish of Despair."[21] Descriptions like these—and there are many more—insist that there is a close and complex relationship between the victims' actions, faces, shouts, general confusion, and the already encountered "Horrors in the[ir] agitated Minds."[22] The reason why the mental aspect of these jumbled descriptions is particularly important is that it provides the first, most obvious, but also (as we shall see) problematic link to the aesthetic category of the sublime. The insistence on the mental quality of the experience immediately tempts us to figure the catastrophe and its representations in terms of the sublime, thereby also following a traditional topos, which repeatedly uses the earthquake as a figure in discussing this aesthetic category.

The rhetoric of excess and ineffability also becomes a self-conscious subject in the eyewitness reports. We already know that it is a "vain Attempt to endeavour describing the numberless Miseries, and terrible Distresses of all kinds, occasioned by this dreadful Calamity."[23] Another witness argues similarly that "it would be impossible to pretend justly to describe the universal horror and distress which every where took place."[24] There is no space that could be reserved for controlled representation. An anonymous letter confirms that the earthquake "has made such a scene of desolation and misery, as words cannot describe,"[25] and yet another source succinctly states that " 'tis not to be expressed"[26] what degree the suffering takes. The Nuncio in Lisbon assures that "our Grief and Consternation are unutterable,"[27] just as another anonymous victim reports that, when arriving at the sight of a ruined house, "The new scenes of terror I met with here, exceed all description."[28] Unsurprisingly, the confusion and breakdown are reflected in the texts themselves. The total breakdown of the city makes the activity of orderly writing impossible. Mind and body no longer provide a stable background for the writing of letters: "the scene of misery and destruction is so horrible, that one's blood grows cold at giving you a description of it."[29] One writer, typical of others, "must humbly beg your pardon, Sir, for the disorder of this letter, surrounded as I am by the many in distress, who, from one instant to another, are applying to me either for advice or shelter."[30] Their writing must be "imperfect"[31] because they are in "Hurry and Confusion"[32] while mirroring the fragmentation of the city in their writing.

Only distance permits the development of a vocabulary that can adequately describe the dimensions of the catastrophe. This distancing may be temporal, spatial, or mental. In the realm of aesthetics, the sublime is the category that theorizes the creation of this type of distance and develops a vocabulary of representation. The two most important accounts of the sublime in the period, Burke's *A Philosophical Enquiry into the Origin of our Ideas of the Sublime and Beautiful* (1757) and Kant's *Critique of Judgement* (1790, rev. 1793 and 1799), both insist on the role of distance as vital. In what follows, I want to show how the creation of distance leaves behind the insistence on excess and breakdown in the eyewitness accounts from the scene. Simultaneously, however, the initial importance of ineffability becomes a difficulty that haunts these more theoretical accounts. The main emphasis will be on the aesthetic-philosophic dimensions of the Kantian text. This focus permits me to acknowledge, but ultimately sidestep, approaches that also thematize the interaction of psychic and material event in the realm of language, such as the work by Caruth, Hartman, and LaCapra in the area of trauma studies.[33] In contrast, I want to move the discussion in a direction that is more concerned with the philosophical underpinnings and articulations of the sublime as part of, and articulated within, a larger frame of the aesthetic.

### Beholding the Ruins

It is a given in the secondary literature that almost all theorizations of the sublime insist on distance as necessary to allow for the development of a vocabulary that adequately describes the aesthetic experience. Whether this distancing may be temporal, spatial, or mental, we have to be in a position to "behold" the sublime, or rather its aftermath—the ruins it leaves behind. Once the Lisbon earthquake is categorized as "the sublime" (or rather, its representation), it is conceptualized, rationalized, and framed in a systematic account. An example of how this systematization takes place is the terminology of "beholding the ruins," which occurs with such frequency in the eighteenth century that it becomes a standard phrase in aesthetic discourse.

Both Burke and Kant stress the importance of distance in their texts on the sublime. In the creation of this distance, we leave behind the insistence on excess and breakdown encountered in the eyewitness accounts from Lisbon. Burke and Kant allow us to replace the breakdown with a ruin. Burke's *Enquiry* offers a particularly salient example of the strange and disturbing delight we take in beholding such ruins. In a well-known passage he conjectures that "this noble capital, the pride of England and Europe, I believe no man is so strangely wicked as to desire to see destroyed by a conflagration or an earthquake, though he should be removed himself to the greatest distance from the danger. But suppose such a fatal accident to have happened, what numbers from all parts would croud to behold the ruins?"[34] Burke chooses London as the foil of his example, but the image behind it is clearly the Lisbon earthquake, which had occurred only a year before this passage was written.[35] Thus on first inspection, the reports on Lisbon's "Spectacle of Terror" seem a straightforward (if anachronistic) illustration of the stereotypical Burkean sublime.[36]

Crucially, the ruin is already viewed from a distance, we "behold" it as already aesthetic. Hence the subsequent classification of the event as sublime domesticates it, while enabling an orderly and framing discussion of it in aesthetic terms. The ruins become foundational and serve as a stabilizing grounding in creating a discourse on the sublime. The sublime, understood in this sense, is a taming category. A letter by James O'Hara, a captain visiting Lisbon in 1755, written to his sister in the aftermath of the disaster looks at Lisbon from a distance, providing an example of how the sublime can be understood as taming or domesticating:

> P.s. Since writing the above, I have accompanied Admiral Broderick over most part of the ruins of this city, lately famous for its wealth and commerce. Never did any eye behold so awful, so tremendous a scene. The moon, which was then at the full, shining resplendently on the Tagus, gave us a night view of this wreck of nature. The howling of the dogs, the stench of the dead bodies, together with the gloom which now and then diffused itself around, from the moon's being sometimes obscured, gave me some idea of that general crash, when sun and moon shall be no more; and filled my mind with meditations, that only such a scene could inspire.[37]

The text is a postscript to the inexpressible. The transformation from indescribable scenes to panoramic view is remarkable. The scene on Lisbon's stage has changed utterly. Not that it is a purely pleasant one: in the nearly gothic description, it is still "awful"—but also "tremendous." A city that—like Burke's London—is famous for its splendor and richness has been shattered and suddenly looks like a heap of ancient ruins, waiting for the visitor to enjoy the sublime moonlit scene. Even natural might, which just a few days ago had struck so mercilessly, helps to elevate the scene of ruin. The full moon shines, reflected in the river, lighting up a "wreck of nature," and "being sometimes obscured," gives the perfect lighting to this premature illustration of Burkean sublimity. O'Hara is Burke's imaginary disaster tourist *avant la lettre*.

Reading O'Hara's letter in conjunction with the earlier eyewitness reports and theorizations of the sublime, it becomes evident that there is a tension between the domesticating quality of representations of sublimity, and the fact that they ultimately rely on a moment which escapes any categorization at all.

This simultaneity and interdependence is significant. At one level, Lisbon escapes the modes and possibilities of classification per se, be they temporal, geographic, or aesthetic. At another, this stands in immediate tension with the subsequent mechanisms of control, such as packaging the ruins as a sublime scene. At the very core of the domesticating effect of the sublime that creates the scene of Lisbon lies a shattering moment of fragmentation that exceeds all order and qualification. This interdependence, I want to argue, is sufficiently strong for the fragmentation to be considered structurally and logically necessary for the sublime. Lisbon not only finds its way into the *Enquiry*, but Burke's text can be read as a rationalization of the disaster within a psychology of the aesthetic. The moment of fragmentation becomes the sine qua non for the aesthetic pleasure achieved through the domesticating effect of the sublime.

The tension that we notice in an account of Burkean psychology intensifies when it is transposed to a more formal argument such as Kant's *Critique of Judgement*. Given the nature and position of the dynamic sublime in Kant's thinking, the resulting difficulties in fact extend beyond his account in the *Critique*. In the remainder of this essay, I shall attempt to unravel two aspects of Kant's account and show why it is productive to consider them in connection with the events in Lisbon. First, the analysis will focus on the formal dimension of fragmentation in relation to the dynamic sublime as posited in the *Critique*. Secondly, some of Kant's precritical writings and their reception invite us to reconsider the central position of this aesthetic category.

Like Burke, Kant emphasizes that it is only in safety and with enough distance that we begin to enjoy a scene which would otherwise be simply terrifying. For Kant this distance is not simply spatial; it is also mental, achieved through rationalization of the terror in front of us. If we can conceptually grasp what is terrifying us, we may be able to generate the distance necessary for pleasure to take place. However, once the process of rationalization is begun, there still remains the force that generated the necessity for an ordering movement in the first place. This force, which denies all conceptualization, forms the basis for distance. This makes the process of rationalization especially significant. Kant spends some time explaining how far this process is ultimately necessary and responsible for the pleasure connected to the sublime. In the "Analytic of the Sublime," he argues that both the moment of being utterly overcome, as well as the subsequent rationalization of that moment, are constitutive of the human subject. They provide a valuable way of affirming the special status of this subject within the wider context of the natural world. This affirmation consists of and is performed by the category of rational thought.[38] For Kant, then, the sublime is an instance through which we can define ourselves as rational beings, albeit relying on the "supersensible substrate" that Kant speaks of in 26 of the "Analytic of the Sublime" and "which underlies both nature and our ability to think."[39] The stakes are high: Kant's account places the sublime in a larger framework that concerns itself with the human ability to make judgments and attempts to explain how we place ourselves as rational agents within the natural world.

Although it is not possible to do the matter full justice here, it is important to insist on the Kantian sublime as part of a complex philosophical map. Suffice it to say that the sublime has a deep connection with the epistemological and ethical aspects of the critical framework in terms of which experience is possible in the first place. Leaving aside the extent to which the third *Critique* "crowns" the *Critique of Pure Reason* (1781, rev. 1787) and the *Critique of Practical Reason* (1788), Kant himself insists on how the complex knot of nature and the subject ties them together. This is particularly visible in the roles that reason and subject formation play in Kant's understanding of the sublime. The sublime, then, is where crucial aspects of Kant's thought stand in dialogue with each other. Correspondingly, an unsettling fragmentation will reverberate within both subject formation and the construction of epistemological principles. Just as the sublime begins to connect up with other branches of Kant's thought, the fragmenting quality that underlies the sublime also invades them.

A lot of this has been a cornerstone of discussion in aesthetic criticism since the publication of the *Critique of Judgement*. Here, however, I will veer away from this general discussion to concentrate on a specific aspect that follows from Kant's general idea about the source of the sublime and how it is constructed in ourselves so as to become a defining feature of the subject. Kant insists that sublimity is to be found not in objects but only in our mind:

> Hence sublimity is contained not in any thing of nature, but only in our mind, insofar as we can become conscious of our superiority to nature within us, and thereby also to nature outside us (as far as it influences us). Whatever arouses this feeling in us, and this includes the *might* of nature that challenges our forces, is then (although improperly) called sublime. (28)

The centrality of this claim within the larger framework of aesthetic criticism is widely acknowledged. And once we finish the sentence (Pluhar's version unfortunately breaks it in two, Guyer's retains the semicolon), we see that its final motive lies deeply within the subject's self-construction:

> And it is only by presupposing this idea within us, and by referring to it, that we can arrive at the idea of the sublimity of that being who arouses deep respect in us, not just by his might demonstrated in nature, but even more by the ability, with which we have been endowed, to judge nature without fear and to think of our vocation as being sublime above nature. (28)

This rich passage reflects back on Kant's concern to locate the sublime in a space that understands empirically experienced natural might as explicable within the framework of natural causes. This is an unspoken concern of the *Critique*, which, despite the innumerable commentaries on the role of nature in the text, has received little detailed attention.[40] A little earlier, Kant sketches the background for this argument by positioning the sublime in relation to the subject's relation to nature and creator. He explains that some people mistakenly interpret the idea or manifestation of natural might as a direct and anthropomorphized expression of divine powers:

> This [Kant's] analysis of the concept of the sublime, insofar as [sublimity is] attributed to might, may seem in conflict with the fact that in certain situations—in tempests, storms, earthquakes and so on—we usually present God as showing himself in his wrath but also in his sublimity, while yet it would be both foolish and sacrilegious to imagine that our mind is superior to the effects produced by such a might, and is superior, apparently even to its intentions. (28)

In order to give the sublime the position that Kant wants it to play, catastrophes or other manifestations of natural might have to be understood as being divorced from higher intervention. An earthquake, albeit frightful, is devastating and disastrous, but not an expression of God's anger; to interpret it as such is to misunderstand the workings of both nature and the divine.

Kant's general argument about the interpretation of natural catastrophes is not a new one. He openly and repeatedly rejects vulgar anthropomorphic thinking throughout his works. Even his reference to the earthquake sounds familiar. As early as his precritical writings, Kant elaborates on the mistaken ethics resulting from anthropomorphizing the cause of such events:

> But one contravenes very much against it [our compassion with the victims] if one regards such fates [natural disasters] always as imposed divine judgments, which strike the devastated cities because of their misdeeds, and if we regard these lamentable people as the target of God's revenge over whom all His righteousness pours out its bowl of wrath. This kind of judgment is criminal pertness.[41]

This statement, so very similar to the passage from the *Critique of Judgement*, is taken from the final pages of Kant's treatise on the earthquake of Lisbon, a relatively unknown precritical essay whose title may be translated into English as "History and Natural Description of the Remarkable Occurrences of the Earthquake, which at the End of the 1755th Year shook a Large Part of the Earth." He writes and publishes this essay, and its second part, a year after the disaster, together with a further (more general) treatise on earthquakes.[42]

The objection against interpreting a natural catastrophe, like the Lisbon disaster, as an expression of divine punishment links the third critique and Kant's geological treatise. In both cases he implies that an outraged reaction to an earthquake neglects to see it as part of a complex picture of natural phenomena. The Lisbon earthquake on All Saints Day is the paradigm for a natural disaster that was widely understood in terms of divine punishment or, alternatively, as evidence against traditional theology. Kant's move at least partly sidesteps this discussion, as he follows neither Voltaire nor the majority of contemporary clerical responses. In fact, he goes a step further than either of the parties who defend the "obvious" meaning of the event (divine punishment or the evident impossibility of a benevolent God). Giving his apparently neutral account of natural causes a qualitative spin after all, Kant, outrageously for both the clerics and Voltaire, argues that, first, the horrors in Lisbon could have been limited by careful anticipatory reasoning, and, secondly, that when contextualized in an adequate way, Lisbon's disaster even has a useful side to it. One section of his treatise is explicitly titled "Of the usefulness of earthquakes." Acknowledging that this position will be intuitively unacceptable to most readers, Kant begins: "One will be shocked to see such a terrible punishing rod for humans being praised as having a useful side."[43] He then explains his argument, step by step. First, he makes the point that the extent of the catastrophe is partly due to the way the city was built. In other words, the Portuguese lack of foresight in matters of urban planning partly invalidates their claim to pity. His argument here is a variant of Rousseau's "Lettre à Monsieur de Voltaire" (1756) on the same subject. For Rousseau, too, modern urban planning, as the direct result and marker of questionable developments in civilization, is responsible for the extent of the catastrophe.[44] Kant points out that the Peruvians, doubtlessly less civilized in the Rousseauian sense, build their cities with low houses, thereby reducing the risk of casualties. And in his "Concluding remark," Kant echoes Rousseau, again in moralistic terms: "Man is not born to build eternal huts on this stage of vanity."[45]

This is an exemplary instance of Kant's argument from complexity and recontextualization. It situates the specific earthquake of Lisbon in a scheme of natural phenomena, which, in their totality, ensure the world's continuous fertile existence. A first, "outraged" reaction to a disaster like Lisbon neglects to see it as part of a bigger picture within a complex world. Hence, "however much damage the cause of the earthquakes has ever provoked for humans on the one hand, it [the cause] can easily repair them with gains on the other."[46] It does not matter that the particular basis for this move seems unconvincing to the contemporary reader. (It consists of conjectures about the revitalizing nature of particles in the air and the continuous warmth in the inner regions of the earth, which guarantee fertility of soils.) What is important is the type of argument that Kant is eager to construct and defend. For all his championing of contextualization, Kant clearly limits his explanatory framework to an analysis of natural causes and what they can yield for him. The event, its context, and our possible interpretation of it (as useful, for example), are all to be understood in terms of natural causes. This move helps to blur an underlying problem which comes back to haunt both Kant's aesthetic and its critical reception: the ambiguous position that the Kantian sublime occupies in relation to the progressivist narrative sketched in the introduction.

Benjamin's mythologizing of Kant's treatise on Lisbon illustrates how the connection between Kant's aesthetics and the progressivist narrative becomes significant. In his essay "Earthquake of Lisbon" (1931), Benjamin reconfirms the exceptional nature of the 1755 earthquake. Not only does he point out the special status of Lisbon as a flourishing town, but he also classifies the earthquake as "the most extensive one has ever heard of."[47] Despite dating the event historically, its status is still not totally clear: "however, the earthquake that destroyed Lisbon on the 1st of November 1755 was not just a calamity like a thousand others, but in a lot of ways unique and remarkable."[48] Benjamin also insists that "at that time, nobody concerned himself more with these remarkable events than the great German philosopher, Kant."[49] The special status of the material event combines with the eminence of the philosopher.[50] According to Benjamin it is none other than Kant who, with his treatise on Lisbon, inaugurates modern geology as we understand it: "and a short paper that he [Kant] composed about it was really the beginning of scientific geology in Germany."[51] Kant becomes the founding father of the discipline that helps us categorize the events in Lisbon in such a way that we understand them "correctly." Benjamin posits Kant as the founding father of scientific geology, not only geology as such. The secular character of Kant's text, its insistence on explaining the event in terms of natural causes, creates in its wake a modern discipline as we understand it. Already at its origin, this new system and area of inquiry offer a taxonomy with which it can classify its own founding moment. According to this logic, scientific geology is born through the Lisbon earthquake, but immediately and retrospectively makes that event subject to its rules. In Benjamin's account, Lisbon provokes a Kantian reaction, eventually ending in the secular and scientific "disciplining" of the catastrophe. This will result in a rationalized and domesticated discourse that is intelligible to us. Benjamin's essay is, in other words, a typical instance of the "progressivist" position sketched at the beginning of this exposition.

These secular steps of thought find a parallel in the realm of the aesthetic. The rationalization of the sublime follows a similar movement, insofar as it conceptualizes an unrepresentable instance into a category that we can intelligibly manipulate. For this context, it is insignificant that the final object of a "scientific" enquiry will be, according to Kant, conceptual knowledge, whereas the sublime cannot be based on straightforwardly epistemological categories. The above account stresses the importance of the posited moment that logically precedes the sublime as one of total shattering. This is analogous to saying that the catastrophe of extraordinary proportions is necessary for the birth of the discipline that it will be understood by. Kant's own vocabulary hints at the destabilizing dimension that underlies the domesticating tendency of the sublime. In 27 of the *Critique of Judgement* he writes: "In presenting the sublime in nature the mind feels *agitated* [*moved*, in Guyer's translation], while in an aesthetic judgment about the beautiful in nature it is in *restful* [*calm*, in Guyer's translation] contemplation. This agitation (above all its inception) can be compared with a vibration" (27).

The agitation of the mind can be likened to a trembling, or a vibration. The *Erschütterung* ("trembling," a sense that is lost in both translations) breaks and shakes the innermost moment of the *Gemüt*.[52] This is similar to the trembling with which we began. Goethe's fracturing moment uses the same vocabulary (the *Gemütsruhe*, or "peace of mind," of the little boy is *erschüttert*, "deeply shaken"), thereby mirroring the movement of the earthquake. Kant's argument for the rationalizing "logic" of the sublime has an underlying trembling. The rationalized sublime depends on a shattering that does not allow representation. The foundational ruins in turn must rest on an abyss that cannot possibly form part of any architectural stability. In the same way as at the heart of the "scientific reception" lies the disruptive moment of a nearly mythologized secularization, the sublime relies on the moment of total breakdown—a breakdown that, as Kant's own vocabulary betrays, resembles an earthquake. Here some of Kant's precritical writings, and Benjamin's mythologizing of them via Lisbon, join hands with the explications of the dynamic sublime that we have already encountered in the *Critique of Judgement*. Considering the foundational character of this work for our understanding of the sublime (and modern aesthetics), it is important to see how it is underwritten by a darker dynamic. The secular sublime, together with its ruins, discloses a disruptive and breaking quality at its core.

## Notes

1. Goethe, *From My Life*, 34. For Lisbon's significance for German literature as a whole, see Bohrer, *Nach der Natur*. For standard accounts of the events during the earthquake, see Kendrick, *The Lisbon Earthquake*, and Löffler, *Lissabons Fall*. All translations in this chapter are my own, unless otherwise indicated.
2. The description of this particular link has to remain quite general here. The discussion between Hans Blumenberg and Karl Löwith, for instance, illustrates how difficult it is to describe the connection between secularization and modernity. In this context it is worth remarking that Blumenberg, while insisting on the "legitimacy" of modernity, describes the Lisbon earthquake as "putting an end to the optimism of the first half of the [eighteenth] century" and therefore helping Kant formulate the basis for a subsequent secular outlook. See Blumenberg, *Die Legitimität der Neuzeit*, 244.
3. Neiman, *Evil in Modern Thought*, 4.
4. Ibid., 267. For another relevant and thought-provoking study in this context, see Ray, "Reading the Lisbon Earthquake." Ray links, in quite different terms from Nieman's, contemporary philosophy with the Lisbon catastrophe and Kant's writings on it.
5. See Voltaire, "Poem on the Destruction of Lisbon." The Lisbon episode in chapter 5 of *Candide* (1759) is the poem's variant in prose; see Voltaire, *Candide and Other Stories*.
6. Simpson, *Irony and Authority in Romantic Poetry*, 118.
7. Royal Society, *Philosophical Transactions Being an Appendix to Those for the Year 1750*.
8. Quoted in Nozes, *The Lisbon Earthquake of 1755*, 36.
9. Quoted in ibid., 54.
10. *A Poem on the Earthquake of Lisbon*, 7.
11. Perry, "An Account of the Earthquake Felt in the Island of Sumatra," 491.
12. Quoted in Nozes, *The Lisbon Earthquake of 1755*, 42–43.
13. Quoted in ibid., 42 and 44.
14. Latham, "Extract of Letter V from Mr. J. *Latham*," 412.
15. Pereira, *A Narrative of the Earthquake and Fire of Lisbon of the Congregation of the Oratory*, 5-6.
16. Sacheti, "A Copy of Part of two Letters," 409.
17. Quoted in Nozes, *The Lisbon Earthquake of 1755*, 184.
18. Quoted in ibid., 42 and 44.
19. Quoted in ibid., 52.
20. Quoted in ibid.
21. Quoted in ibid.
22. Quoted in ibid., 42.
23. Quoted in ibid., 52.
24. Quoted in ibid., 116.
25. Quoted in ibid., 150.
26. Quoted in ibid., 140.
27. Quoted in ibid., 238.
28. Quoted in ibid., 178.
29. Quoted in ibid., 196.

30. Quoted in ibid., 76.
31. Quoted in ibid., 188.
32. Quoted in ibid., 132.
33. Caruth, ed. *Trauma and Memory*; LaCapra, *Representing the Holocaust*; Hartman, *Scars of the Spirit*; and Elmer et al., eds., "Trauma and Psychoanalysis."
34. Burke, *A Philosophical Enquiry into the Origin of Our Ideas of the Sublime and Beautiful*, 47-48.
35. In his editorial notes, Boulton links this passage to the 1750 earthquake in London; see Burke, *A Philosophical Enquiry into the Origin of Our Ideas of the Sublime and Beautiful*, 47. Womersley also mentions the link to Lisbon in his introduction to Burke's *A Philosophical Enquiry into the Sublime and Beautiful and Other Pre-Revolutionary Writings*, 448 (note 24). The imagined transposition of Lisbon into London is, in fact, a common rhetorical strategy at the time.
36. The question whether the Burkean sublime could be understood as a "reaction" to the Lisbon earthquake, and how far its historical influences are reflected in Burke's specific account is part of the much larger question of anachronism that this essay cannot cover in detail. In relation to the two philosophical accounts of the sublime I discuss here, the question of anachronism is alluded to in terms of the interdependent presuppositions that describe the tension between empirical (Burkean) and formalist (Kantian) argument. I can only gesture toward this dynamic, reminding the reader of the strong interdependence of Burke's and Kant's accounts, whose ideas are often presented as opposed. It seems to me that not only does Kant openly adopt crucial categorizations from Burke (the division between the beautiful and the sublime, for instance), but also that the empirical experience of the sublime *as a certain type of experience* (which *has* to be empirical) is a necessary stepping stone for Kant's formal argument to take off the ground. Inversely, the characterization of Burke's account as one of purely empirical or descriptive psychology falls short of the analytical (and ultimately formal) claims he makes about the universality and structure of the human experience and mental makeup.
37. Quoted in Nozes, *The Lisbon Earthquake of 1755*, 224.
38. To prevent any misunderstanding, let me note that this "rationalization" is not equivalent to "rationality"; I am not (wrongly) claiming that Kant conceives of reason or even rationality as a domesticating and distancing category; after all, he thinks reason itself needs to be controlled through one's critical faculty.
39. Kant, *Critique of Judgement*, trans. Werner S. Pluhar (Indianapolis: Hackett, 1987). Further references are to this translation, and given in the main text. When alluding to the original German, I refer to the 1793 text of the *Critique* in Immanuel Kant, "Kritik der Urteilskraft," in *Immanuel Kants Werke*, ed. Otto Buek, 11 vols. (Hildesheim: Gerstenberg, 1973), vol. 5, 177–568. Sometimes I also make reference to Guyer's and Matthews's translation; for these see Immanuel Kant, *Critique of the Power of Judgment*, trans. Paul Guyer and Eric Matthews (Cambridge: Cambridge University Press, 2000). All translations of Kant's pre-critical writings are my own.
40. A recent exception is Grant, "Kant after Geophilosophy."
41. Kant, "Geschichte und Naturbeschreibung der merkwürdigsten Vorfälle des Erdbebens, welches an dem Ende 1755sten Jahres einen großen Teil der Erde erschüttert hat" (1756),

in *Immanuel Kants Werke*, ed. Artur Buchenau, 11 vols. (Hildesheim: Gerstenberg, 1973), vol. 1, 439-473 (on p. 471).

42. Kant, "Immanuel Kants fortgesetzte Betrachtung der seit einger Zeit wahrgenommenen Erderschütterungen," in *Immanuel Kants Werke*, ed. Artur Buchenau, vol. 1, 475–84. Also see Kant, "Von den Ursachen der Erderschütterungen bei Gelegenheit des Unglücks, welches die westlichen Länder von Europa gegen Ende des vorigen Jahres betroffen hat," in *Immanuel Kants Werke*, ed. Artur Buchenau, vol. 1, 427–37.
43. Kant, "Geschichte und Naturbeschreibung der merkwürdigsten Vorfälle des Erdbebens," 467.
44. Rousseau, "Letter from Rousseau to Voltaire," 110. On the "theology of earthquakes" in relation to these two thinkers, see Russell, *A History of Western Philosophy*, 689-90. For a link between Kant and Rousseau, see Günther, *Das Erdbeben von Lissabon und die Erschütterung des aufgeklärten Europa*, 42.
45. Kant, "Geschichte und Naturbeschreibung der merkwürdigsten Vorfälle des Erdbebens," 472.
46. Ibid., 468.
47. Benjamin, "Erdbeben von Lissabon," 221. For a more recent exponent of a similar position to Benjamin's, see Oeser, "Das Erdbeben von Lissabon im Spiegel der zeitgenössischen Philosophie."
48. Ibid.
49. Ibid., 222.
50. For Kant's influence on the early Benjamin, see Caygill, *Walter Benjamin*, 27–29.
51. Benjamin, "Das Erdbeben von Lissabon," 223.
52. Just before finishing this essay, I came across Ray, "Reading the Lisbon Earthquake," cited in note 4. To my knowledge, this is the only other place that links this passage of the *Critique of Judgement* to the Lisbon earthquake. See also Ray, *Terror and the Sublime in Art and Critical Theory*.

TATIANA SMOLIAROVA

# 21

## THE PROMISE OF A RUIN

*Gavrila Derzhavin's Archaic Modernity*

"Oh gifted architect!" murmured Arthur, inaudibly to all but Lady Muriel and myself. "Foreseeing the exact effect his work would have, when in ruins, centuries after his death!"

LEWIS CARROLL, *SYLVIE AND BRUNO*

The Venice Architecture Biennale of 2000, the seventh to date and the last in the millennium, was directed by a flamboyant Italian modernist, Massimiliano Fuksas, and bore the catchy title "The City: Less Aesthetics. More Ethics." An article quoted Fuksas as saying "it is not enough to be just an architect" and went on to paraphrase him: "architects must build for the future; they must create more than just buildings."[1] Russian participants in this most prestigious forum of building ideas dedicated their exhibition almost exclusively to various forms of devastation. As if anticipating the terrorist attacks of the following year, the Russian pavilion hosted *Ruins of Paradise*, parallel works by Ilya Utkin and Mikhail Filippov, the leaders of the 1980s paper architecture movement. One Italian newspaper asked, "And what about the Russians? It seems that *their* time is moving backwards. Piranesi's spirit hovers over the room."[2] At the center of Filippov's installation, composed of classical pillars, there was a strange construction inspired by Palladio's Teatro Olimpico, built in 1584 in nearby Vicenza. Utkin wrapped his photo project around an enormous rough stone, with a map of Moscow carved into it. Over the stone, a huge throne composed of pieces of antique furniture was suspended from ropes. Not completely neglecting the future, the artists included a twofold vision of the present called *Future of the Past* and *Past of the Future*, respectively. Although some critics accused the artists of showing off, overall the *Ruins of Paradise* was a success.

**Ruina.ru**

Grigorii Revzin, a leading Russian art critic and the commissioner of *Ruins of Paradise*, explained the philosophical message underlying the project: "Any 'classical ruin' bears in it two major themes: the *ideal image* that existed erstwhile, and the *time* that destroyed it. Observing Piranesian ruins of Rome or a demolished temple pavilion in a park, the beholder immediately visualizes what the debris used to be, and mentally reconstructs the original totality . . . But if the first, 'platonic' constituent of a ruin has been missing from the very beginning, then the ruin's only theme is the destructive force of time. Time as such, its Flow . . ."[3] Revzin's dynamic approach to the ruin and his use of the image of the flow of time help us understand a small yet curious detail: critics reporting on the Biennale events for various Russian art publications all referred, when writing about Utkin's and Filippov's *Ruins of Modernity*, to the same verses about ruins. Everyone quoted a brief poem by Gavrila Romanovich Derzhavin, the foremost Russian poet around the turn of the nineteenth century. Entitled "On Perishability" but better known as "The River of Time in its Stream . . . ," the poem was written down on a slate by the poet three days before he died in 1816.[4] Long thought to be an unfinished fragment, Derzhavin's octet reads:

> The river of time in its stream
> Washes away all deeds of humans
> And drowns in the abyss of oblivion
> Peoples, kingdoms, and kings.
> And if even something remains
> Through the sounds of lyre and trumpet,
> It will be devoured by the muzzle of eternity
> And will not escape the common destiny.[5]

It was not until 1951 that Morris Halle—then a student of Roman Jakobson's at Harvard and later a renowned linguist—observed that the initial letters of the eight lines of the poem formed an acrostic underscoring the theme of the poem, as expressed by its title. The acrostic, consisting of two Russian words (*ruina chti*), hides a message that has been interpreted in at least three different ways, depending on various possible readings of the second word: "the ruin of glory," "read: a ruin," or "a ruin: hold in esteem." Whichever variant we choose, the essence of the acrostic is somewhat oxymoronic as it brings in some additional solidity to the text as a whole; as Eisenstein notes, "in the acrostic the name of

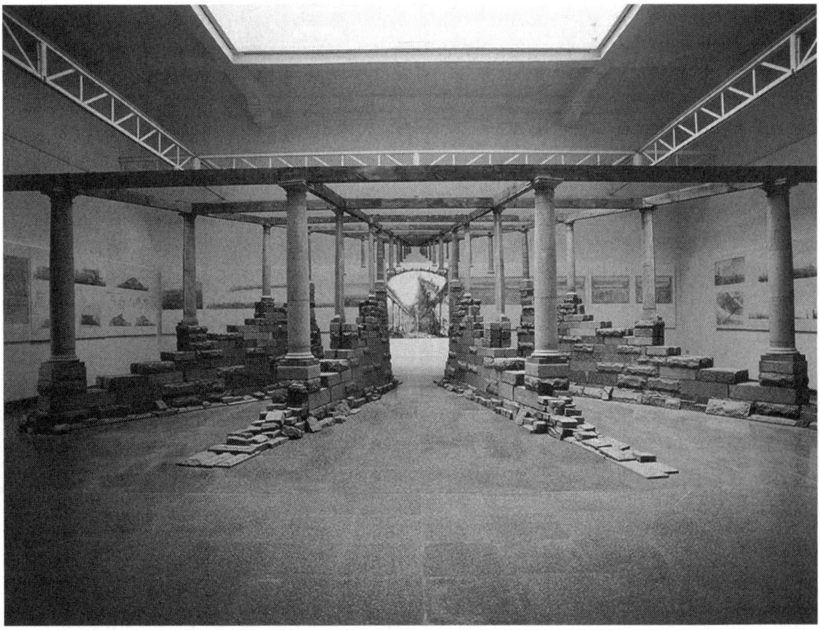

1. Mikhail Filippov, *Ruins of Paradise* (2000), Venice. Reproduced from *Arkhitekturnyi vestnik* 57, no. 6 (2000): 3.

the body holds the body together."[6] The word "ruin" cements the body of the poem—dedicated to the destructive power of time—and foreshadows some paradoxical readings of this text.

Since 1958, when Halle published his discovery,[7] scholars have continued to discuss the semantic value of different constituents of this singularly brief poem, its possible verbal and visual sources, and the obscure message contained in it. Jakobson summarizes its structure and plot in this way: "the dynamic image of the first stanza of time rapidly carrying away things and beings and dooming them to oblivion yields in the second stanza to the static image of everything sharing its common and inevitable destiny of disappearance, or in other, again metaphoric terms, of being swallowed by the muzzle of eternity."[8] Yet one more level might be added to multiple metaphorical interpretations of this text. The so-called solemn ode, the foremost genre of Russian classicism, is always thought of in architectural terms. Unlike the romantics, who look for metaphors and similes in the organic world, classical poets, following Pindar, describe the process of poetic creation as either weaving or building—i.e., putting threads or blocks together.[9]

The metaphorical three-dimensionality of the textual space, conceiving of a poem as a box that can accommodate only a certain amount, is an important feature of the generic consciousness of the eighteenth-century Russian ode.[10] Derzhavin started his poetic career by writing traditional celebratory odes; but by the 1780s he had considerably altered the scope of this rigorous genre, and he almost totally destroyed its rigid canon in the later years of his life (adding yet one more element to the ruined landscape of the classicist genre). A "Poem of a Ruin" being at the same time a "Ruin of a Poem," or, at least, the mode of destruction of a certain literary genre, may be considered a logical development of the eighteenth century's interest in both poetry and architecture.[11] In this sense, embedding the ruin in the very tissue of Derzhavin's last poem seems all the more eloquent.

At the same time, the acrostic ruin was just the last one in a row of ruins that emerged in Derzhavin's poetry, beginning in the late 1790s. One of the first poems dedicated to the destructive power of time and using the ruin as its main symbol was "The Ruins."[12] Without describing any particular ruin, the poem contains an allegorical representation of Tsarskoe Selo, Catherine the Great's favorite residence, in twilight a year after the death of the empress.[13] The poetic ruin that I would like to contemplate now was erected by Derzhavin in 1807, almost half-way between the two framing ruins of 1797 and 1816, in the concluding stanzas of a long descriptive poem "Evegeniyu. Zhizn' Zvanskaya" (To Eugene. Life at Zvanka), his most bluntly autobiographical work in verse.[14] This poem ranks among Derzhavin's best-known works. It is addressed to Bishop Evgenii Bolkhovitinov, a humanist priest and intellectual, who corresponded frequently with Derzhavin in the last decade of his life. Derzhavin's beloved estate of Zvanka in the Pskov region of central Russia was in Bolkhovitinov's diocese, and the bishop occasionally visited the poet there.

It was to commemorate one of these visits that Derzhavin wrote "EZZ" in the late spring and early summer of 1807. Once he had finished the poem, Derzhavin sent it to the bishop with a delicate watercolor by the poet's secretary of the poet's house on the bank of the majestic Volkhov River. The poem begins:

> Blest is that man who least depends on other men,
> Whose life is free from debt and from capricious striving,
> Who goeth not to court for praise, or gold to lend;
> And shuns all vanities conniving![15]

One of the numerous imitations of Horace's second epode, somewhat altered by the influence of biblical poetry, "EZZ" provides us with the first example of a full-fledged Russian country-house poem.[16] "EZZ" stretches the limits of country-house poetry and successfully adapts the genre's norms to Russian soil.

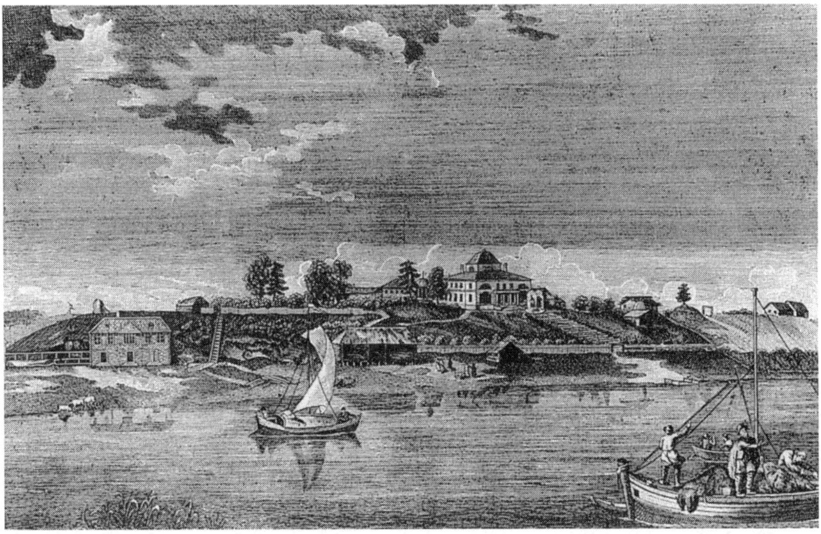

2. *Derzhavin's House at Zvanka* (1810), engraving after a watercolor by Derzhavin's secretary. Reprinted from Priscilla Roosevelt, *Life on the Russian Country Estate: A Social and Cultural History* (New Haven: Yale University Press, 1995).

Besides the long pedigree of Horace's second epode, the Roman poet's name is relevant to the present discussion because of a famous tag, *Ut pictura poesis* (As in painting, so in poetry), taken from Horace's *Ars Poetica* and transformed into an important aesthetic formula by later generations. This concept was still prevalent at the beginning of the nineteenth century in the genre of descriptive poetry. The initial title of Derzhavin's poem, "My Life at Zvanka, or Yet Another Picture of Zvankian Life," was a subtle twist on this representational paradigm.[17]

In the 252 lines of "EZZ," as if practicing the "art of memory" and inviting the bishop to join him in this engrossing activity, Derzhavin gives a detailed account of every corner of his estate and every moment of his day.[18] The archetypal model of a minute description of one's residence may be found in Pliny's description of his favorite Tuscan villa. Establishing a certain isomorphism between the space of the villa described and that of the text describing, Pliny aims at bringing the absent image before his friend's eyes:

> I should have ended before now, for fear of being too chatty, had I not proposed in this letter to lead you into every corner of my house and gardens . . . Besides, I gave my little passion indulgence, for I have a passion for what I have built, or finished, myself . . . Homer, you know, has employed many verses in the description of the arms of Achilles, as Virgil has also in

those of Aeneas, yet neither of them is prolix, because they each keep within the limits of their original design. Aratus, you observe, is not considered too circumstantial, though he traces and enumerates the minute stars, for he does not go out of his way for that purpose, but only follows where the subject leads him. In the same way (to compare small things with great), so long as, in endeavoring to give you an idea of my house, I have not introduced anything irrelevant or superfluous, *it is not my letter which describes, but my villa which is described, that is to be considered large*. But to return to where I began, lest I should justly be condemned by my own law, if I continue longer in this digression, you see now the reasons why I prefer my Tuscan villa to those which I possess at Tusculum, Tiber, and Præneste . . .[19]

Derzhavin could not compare Zvanka to his domains in other parts of Russia, for it was his only estate. And even Zvanka was not strictly his: acquired in 1796 by his second wife, Daria Diakova, a strict and thrifty woman, the estate always expressly belonged to her. What made Derzhavin's heart ache was his childlessness: neither of his two marriages gave him an heir. The image of the "abyss of oblivion," emerging in the third line of "On Perishability," haunted the poet.[20] The poem's picturesque stroll about Zvanka, with its idyllic scenes of hunting and fishing, reading and writing, observing birds and serving dinner, ends abruptly. The pastoral chronotope of the first forty-nine quatrains of the poem is followed by thirteen elegiac stanzas, opening with an almost formulaic lament about the irrevocable passage of time ("Ah! Seeking round, where may I find this fair day fled?") and culminating in a dreary prophesy in stanzas 56–57:

And thus from night to night the brightest stars now blur;
What is this paltry life? My lyre is clay and mortal!
Alas! The dust of my remains shall be dispersed
From off this world by wings of Saturn.

This house shall fall to ruin, its orchard blighted, bare,
And no one shall recall the very name of Zvanka;
From hollow yet shall flash the barn owl's flame-green stare,
And smoke will smolder from the hovel.[21]

Unlike many preromantic landscape gardens, Zvanka contained no ruins, either native or imported, natural or artificial. Where does the grim vision of future devastation come from? Was it inspired by any stone original, or has it emerged from the world of ideas, as a purely "mental construct," to follow the title of Baridon's seminal study?[22] And if the ruin is absent from the physical landscape of Zvanka, how does it come to be in Derzhavin's poetic landscape?

The main literary source of the ruination scene in stanza 57 seems obvious:

the image of the owl's "flame-green stare" piercing the smoke smoldering "from the hovel" echoes the lines of Psalm 102: "I am like a pelican of the wilderness: I am like an owl of the desert. I watch, and am as a sparrow alone upon the house top. Mine enemies reproach me all the day; and they that are mad against me are sworn against me."[23] Derzhavin was simultaneously working on "EZZ" and an imitation of the psalm ("Jeremiad," a free imitation of Psalm 102, appeared in September 1807).[24] The poet's imitation demonstrates his interest in this particular psalm and its specific imagery, and amplifies our understanding of the nexus of ideas in "EZZ." But in stanzas 58-63 the emotional tone of the poem shifts once more, becoming more optimistic:

Or mayhap not, Evgenii! You, who here have caught
The echo of my songs, shall mount to that dread summit,
Concealing deep within its bowels, its narrow vaults,
The tomb of warlord's bard or shaman,

From which you'll hear, as peals of distant thunder roll,
The muffled rumbling of the damask gateposts' shiver,
And copper armor clashing 'neath the forest floor,
The clang of arrows in their quivers.

Dear Pastor! You, perhaps, may seize your Staff again,
And strike the iron tomb, now overgrown with lichen,
Thus banish pallid Envy's coiling serpent den
From off my grove—into the chasm.

You, marking not the turn of woeful days and blithe,
Nor yet the rise and fall of Fortune, gained or squandered,
You shall my name within the hearts of men revive
With Truth alone—through Clio's concord.

Beyond the gloom of endless time, her Trumpet's call
Will hail again this place, where echoes of my lyre
Resounded like a rushing river over holms,
Ravines, and furrowed plains entire.

You heard my songs—you with your pen shall rouse and warn
Our heirs from sleep, in that metropolis due Northward;
And whisper to the trav'ler, like a distant storm:
"Here dwelt God's bard—Felitsa's prophet."[25]

The motif underlying the entire *Exegi Monumentum* tradition—i.e., the belief in defeating the destructive power of time with the creative power of everlasting words—which has just been bitterly rejected ("Alas! The dust of my remains shall be dispersed / From off this world by wings of Saturn") seems to be back.[26] The hope for the forthcoming repair of the ruin expressed in the six concluding stanzas of "EZZ" brings into play a curious coincidence.

## Ruins, 1807: The History of a Coincidence

Derzhavin ranks among the most versatile figures in the history of Russian literature and culture: the variety of genres, styles, modes, meters, and topics in his poetic oeuvre can be compared only to that of Pushkin. Nor can we ignore Derzhavin's impressive political biography: successively a soldier, an administrator, and a governor, he ended up heading the ministry of justice under Alexander I. This uniquely rich experience formed his poetic persona, "the Singer of Felitsa," who did not simply sound the sovereign's praise but told "czars the truth with a kind smile." But Derzhavin's wide-ranging social activities, which he described as of paramount importance to him, vanished in October 1803.

It was in that month that Derzhavin resigned as minister of justice. He did so in great bitterness, feeling betrayed and offended by Alexander I, whose birth he had celebrated some twenty-six years earlier with one of his best odes, in which he wished Alexander to "be humane on the throne." Two months later, Derzhavin lost his long-time friend and close relative, his best company and his "personal enlightener," Nikolai Lvov.[27] During the same pivotal year of 1803, Admiral Alexander Shishkov, the eminent Slavophile and reactionary, published his *Treatise on the Old and New Style of the Russian Language*, a linguistic manifesto of the right wingers. Shishkov's ideas made an impact on Derzhavin's political views and thoughts: the deliberately obscure language, Latinate syntax, archaic vocabulary, and thick layer of Russian folk imagery that Shishkov endorsed were dominant in Derzhavin's poetry after 1804.[28] For Derzhavin, the frontier between the two centuries ran through the sad winter of 1803–4, when the crucial change in his social status became fixed. Henceforth, he was a retired poet, deprived of all his former functions and missions. This gave him freedom and the "pleasures of imagination," but also an intolerable feeling of total uselessness.

How to transform domestic life into creativity? Of all the literary myths and legends of the previous century, Derzhavin in his search for a new identity was particularly attracted to one still relevant in the early 1800s: Alexander Pope, a "retired Poet," "a Poet in his Landscape," the foremost modern heir of Horace.[29]

Pope's writings, especially *The Rape of the Lock* and *An Essay on Man*, enjoyed a great vogue in eighteenth-century Russia.[30] By 1807 *An Essay on Man* had been translated into Russian no fewer than five times (the last translation, published in 1806, was done by Bishop Evgenii Bolkhovitinov). *An Essay on Man* begins with a landscape, serving as a metaphor for the human mind:

> Let us (since Life can little more supply
> Than just to look about us and to die)
> Expatiate free o'er all this scene of Man;
> A mighty maze! But not without a plan;
> A Wild, where weeds and flow'rs promiscuous shoot,
> Or Garden, tempting with forbidden fruit.
> Together let us beat this ample field,
> Try what the open, what the covert yield;
> The latent tracts, the giddy heights explore
> Of all who blindly creep, or sightless soar.[31]

"Gardening is near-akin to Philosophy," Pope wrote in one of his letters to Joseph Addison, and he was almost as famous for his garden as for his poetry. "You may trace [a Man] . . . in the Place where he has lived," Addison responded.[32] Indeed, Pope's villa at Twickenham remained, till the first years of the nineteenth century, one of the most visited poets' homes in Europe. Both before and after his death, dozens of views of the villa were painted, perhaps more than of any other house of the period; numberless engravings, made after the paintings, made Twickenham the most recognized of all the "picturesque sites" of Britain, even as far away as Russia.[33]

Together with the visual records of Twickenham, there existed numerous accounts of the pilgrimages to Pope's house and garden.[34] Derzhavin was undoubtedly aware of at least one of these narratives, by his younger friend Nikolai Karamzin, a poet, writer, and publisher, but first and foremost a historian and the future author of the *History of the Russian State*, a twelve-volume national history, the first of its kind in Russia. In his early *Letters of a Russian Traveller* (1791–1801), written in the wake of his grand tour of Europe and influenced by Sterne's *A Sentimental Journey,* Karamzin describes his visit to Twickenham:

> From Richmond I walked to Twickenham, a sweet little village, where the philosopher and the poet Pope lived. There are many lovely rustic cottages there, but I was interested in the house of the poet (which now belongs to Lord Stanhope). I saw his study, his chair—the place, planted round with trees, where he translated Homer on summer days—the grotto where his marble bust stands, and from where the Thames is visible—finally the century-old willow, which has split in two in an amazing manner, and under the shade of which the philosopher loved to think and the poet to dream; I broke off a twig as a keepsake . . . [35]

The weeping willow, supposedly the first in Britain, was brought to Twickenham by Pope and planted by his own hand. An image of nostalgia per se, the weeping willow died in 1801—ten years after Karamzin "broke off a twig"—in a thunderstorm, as if foreshadowing the future devastation of the entire property. Breaking off a twig "as a keepsake," the sentimental gesture mentioned here, not only exemplifies the style of Karamzin's early prose,[36] but also may have been a response to a poetic prophecy by Robert Dodsley, Pope's longtime friend and devoted publisher. "Pope's dream-vision of Twickenham," writes Morris Brownell, "was composed in large part of the memoirs of the friends who had visited it. To judge from his correspondence the garden was practically identified in his mind with his friends."[37] Dodsley visited Pope at Twickenham in 1743, less than a year before his death, and dedicated the following lines to his famous and cherished grotto:

When dark oblivion in her sable cloak
Shall wrap the names of heroes and of kings;
And their high deeds submitting to the stroke
Of time shall fall amongst forgotten things:

Then (for the Muse that distant day can see)
On Thames' bank the stranger shall arrive
With curious wish thy sacred Grot to see.
Thy sacred Grot shall with thy name survive.—
Grateful posterity, from age to age
With pious hand thy ruin shall repair:
Some good old man to each enquiring sage,
Pointing the place shall cry, "the Bard lived there!"
. . .
Then some small gem, or moss or shining ore,
Departing, each shall pilfer, in fond hope
To please their friends on every distant shore:
Boasting a relic from the Cave of Pope.[38]

Dodsley, whose intuition rarely deceived him, turned to be right not only in the detailed account of the future behavior of strangers from "every distant shore," but also in predicting the future ruin of Pope's villa. As an emblematic background for an anonymous portrait of the poet, an impressive antique ruin first appeared there in the 1730s, based on Pope's design for *An Essay on Man*.[39]

Horace's Sabine retreat—the prototype of poets' dwellings—was a present from his patron, Maecenas. Pope only rented his villa,[40] paying for its improvements with his income as translator and writer:

All this is mine but till I die;
I can't but think 'twould sound more clever
To me and to my heirs for ever . . . [41]

Dwelling in their very similar, temple-like Palladian villas; overlooking, respectively, the Thames and the Volkhov Rivers (a "River at my garden's end" is a requisite for a true Palladian villa); imitating Horace and trying to make him speak "good English" or "good Russian," Derzhavin and Pope also shared the "anxiety of heritage." In both cases, the sense of foreboding was well justified.

After Pope's death in 1744, his villa passed through three hands and was much altered; in 1807 it was bought by its fourth and final owner, Sophia Charlotte Howe, Baroness Howe of Langar.[42] Within a year, inconvenienced by the continuous flow of visitors anxious to see the garden and grotto, the baroness demolished the house and razed the garden. She built herself a new house, about a hundred yards from the site of the original villa. These acts of vandalism caused wide resentment and fury; the baroness was nicknamed "the Queen of the Goths."[43] In the words of R. S. Cobbett, she "blotted out utterly every memorial of the poet."[44] All that survived of Pope's villa was the grotto: Dodsley's words proved to be only too true. His poem became so widely quoted that the references were no longer made to the name of the author.[45]

We possess no direct evidence that Derzhavin was aware of Baroness Howe's deeds. Even if he heard the astonishing news soon after the demolition, it is unlikely that he knew about it at the same time he was predicting the future ruination of Zvanka.[46]

The fact that the real and imagined demolitions were simultaneous seems especially curious given that the final stanza of "EZZ" contains so much of the spirit of one quatrain of Dodsley's poem:[47]

| *Dodsley* | *Derzhavin* |
| --- | --- |
| Grateful posterity, from age to age | You heard my songs—you with your pen shall rouse and warn |
| With pious hand thy ruin shall repair: | Our heirs from sleep, in that metropolis due Northward |
| Some good old man to each enquiring sage | And whisper to the trav'ler, like a distant storm: |
| Pointing the place shall cry, "the Bard lived there!" | "Here dwelt God's Bard—Felitsa's prophet." |

Derzhavin's house and garden were destroyed within several decades of his death. In the early 1860s, Iakov Grot, the best Derzhavin scholar yet, wrote of a visit to Zvanka:

> The center of the oval hill was dominated by the house . . . only the remains of the porch survived, and where the house itself stood, we can see but scattered bricks and stones around. Who thought that Derzhavin's prophecy would prove true so early! . . . Everything here is grim, silent, deserted and obscure: and how lively and noisy was once this very place![48]

Several years ago, Anthony Cross, the founder and longtime devoted leader of the Study Group on Eighteenth-Century Russia, traveled from Petersburg to Moscow, following in the footsteps of Grot, among others. He notes that "Father Time" has ruined the ruins even more:

> We were to sail up river for some six hours as far as Novgorod. We put in at Zvanka, which is now only a memorial plinth on the high promontory, a few walls from the estate church, and the home of snakes and huge mosquitoes and probably still a few unexploded bombs, for it was here during World War Two that the Germans lost 2,000 men and the Russians 4,000 in a bloody battle. We sailed serenely past many other villages of 'eternal Russia' . . .[49]

#### Ruins and Metonymies

Let me now ask what place the image of the ruin occupies in the poetic landscape of Zvanka? In order to find the answer, we must turn one more time to the sad winter of 1803. As already mentioned, at that time Derzhavin turned from an active participant in history into an onlooker, not only incapable of exerting any influence on or predicting events, but gradually even losing a sense of what was going on. This is what his "Magic Lantern" is about. In this poem the lantern is a metaphor for the instability, fragmentation, and unpredictability of real life. "I wrote this poem for my own consolation," Derzhavin confessed in his *Explanations on the Works*, dictated several years later to the daughter of his late friend, Elisabeth Lvov, who became his literary secretary in the 1810s:

> Is not this world a magic play,
> Wherein the lantern shadows change,
> Enchanting and deceiving men?
> Does not some lord or sorcerer
> Or mighty mage divert himself
> Thereby, his prowess vaunting,

As he with idle fingers sets
The planets' course? Does he not call
All earthly creatures to behold
His dreams—and they but dreams themselves?[50]

Twenty years earlier, in 1784, addressing the deity in his most famous ode, "God," Derzhavin had described the "universe so boundless" in totally different, almost Neoplatonic terms:

The Chain of Being Thou comprisest,
And dost sustain it, give it breath;
End and Beginning Thou combinest,
Dost Life bestow in Thee through death.
As sparks disperse, surge upward, flying,
So suns are born from Thee, undying;
As on those cold, clean winter's days
When specks of hoarfrost glisten, shimmer
Gyrate and whirl—from chasms' glimmer
So Stars cast at Thy feet bright rays.[51]

In 1804 "The Great Chain of Being" broke into pieces: too many links were missing, and Derzhavin's optimistic worldview seemed lost forever. The illustration designed for the "Magic Lantern" in the 1808 edition of *Poetic Works*, represented a lantern projecting an image onto a piece of cloth, tossed over the edge of a ruined wall. It is noteworthy that around 1800 in the European, particularly German, iconography, a magic lantern was added to the attributes of Chronos, along with his scythe, hourglass, wings, and nakedness.

In my view, the "optic glass" and magic lantern mentioned in stanzas 31–32 of "EZZ" do not possess the same ontological status as the magic lantern in the poem of that same name. Still, the fact that the two stanzas are in the structural center of the elaborate composition of the poem speaks for the special role they play in its symbolic design:[52]

Through optic glass, most picturesque of views I scry
Of my estates—on scrolls, the cities and the kingdoms
With forests and the seas—Earth's splendors all reside
In eye, displayed through cunning windows.

By lantern's magic then I marvel at the stars.
They trace the billows' dark-blue wake in silent coursing:
In just this way, think I, ablaze do flow the suns,
Thus Wisdom's radiance endorsing.[53]

In his *Explanations* Derzhavin gives a detailed commentary on these stanzas, dwelling at particular length on the spectacle produced by the camera obscura.[54] After he marvels at the optical illusions, in stanzas 33–35 he gives a careful account of Zvanka's domestic manufactures, featuring the latest achievements of engineering thought of the time—a sophisticated sawmill, based on a steam engine; a spinning machine, most likely, the improved version of the spinning jenny combined with a carding engine, which Maria Feodorovna, widow of Paul I, ordered from England in the early 1800s; and a mechanized dye house:

We watch as water thunders from the dam, cascades.
And fuels the mill that splits huge tree-trunks into lumber,
How seething flame two cast-iron poles escapes,
As grinder, fed by steam then rumbles.

Or eagerly we gaze on waves of pure-white fleece,
Which pour like snow through rows of pulleys, wheels and needles:
The weaving-looms knit yards of cloth and fluffy lace,
Thanks to the help of our Maria.

We view the luster, hues diverse of silk and flax,
From our Czarina's precincts comes afresh their splendor;
Or see the rugged steel that melts as crimson wax,
When forged into bright shiny halberds.[55]

The innovative machinery is described in great technical detail, and in equally great syntactic density. Readers are enchanted and at the same time perplexed by the apparent disjointedness of the scene and the complexity of its verbal rendering. Even the most accurate and expressive translation can hardly convey the tumult of the inversions and chiasmi, the overflow of tropes and figures, and the next-to-impossible articulation of these lines in the Russian original. The obscurity of the poetic speech, the need to scramble through the thickets of dense syntax and archaic vocabulary—all criticized by Derzhavin's contemporaries and later scholars—here seem to work on the principle of mimicry, serving as a quasi-iconic representation of the intricacy of working machines.

Surprisingly enough, cunning optical devices and clever machines—the ultimate manifestations of modernity within the pastoral world of "EZZ"—may well belong to the same layer of Derzhavin's poetic imagery as the virtual ruin in the final part of the poem. All these images and motifs stand metaphorically for the poet's overwhelming feeling that the world has become irreparably fragmented. It might, as the six concluding stanzas suggest, eventually regain its coherence, but in a totally different, still unknown way. Perceiving this potential harmony enhances the deciphering skills of the beholder, similar to those used in the close study of the machines, or in reconstituting actual surroundings from the scattered fragments that "reside in one's eye" through "the cunning windows" of the camera obscura. In both these cases, as well as in imagining the potential ruins and their potential repair, bits and pieces should be brought together. Way too much has been said and written on the poetics of the fragment in romantic and preromantic literature and culture.[56] However, what should be emphasized here is that this very "instinct for the fragmentary, the indistinct or the suggestively *incomplete*," as Hunt nicely phrases it, underlies the use of both optical devices and artificial ruins in picturesque gardens all over Europe.[57] As has been already mentioned, no ruins were built in Zvanka's gardens; however, in Derzhavin's poem, optical devices and future ruins coexist.

Numerous studies by both Russian and foreign scholars have been dedicated to Derzhavin's use of metaphors. Metaphors not only outrank other tropes, but they seem to be the only device that can be grasped by rhetorical analysis of poetry. However, Derzhavin's rhetoric is quite diverse and elaborate: alongside metaphors, his verse also contains frequent metonymies, synecdoches, similies, and so forth. The scholarly neglect of rhetorical devices other than metaphors in Derzhavin's poetic diction can probably be explained by the general "rule" set forth by Jonathan Culler in the chapter dedicated to the figure of metonymy in his *Pursuits of Signs*: "Today metaphor is no longer one figure among others but the figure of figures, a figure for figurality; and I mean this not figuratively but quite literally: the reason we can devote journals and conferences to metaphor is that metaphor is not just the literal or proper name for a trope based on resemblance but also and especially a figure for figurality in general."[58] The common view is that metonymies are interesting only when they resemble metaphors: otherwise, they neither forge new links nor uncover new resemblances, and thus they lack expressive power.

The expressive power of metonymies and synechdoches, the tropes responsible for contiguity (as opposed to similarity, in Jakobson's basic contrast of metaphor and metonymy), can hardly be overestimated in Derzhavin's poetry. Although the thorough discussion of the oscillation between "metonymic" and "metaphoric" poles in Derzhavin's poetic work is well beyond the scope of this essay, let us make a quick observation: in creating his verbal pictures, Derzhavin proceeds by selecting one or two representative details. One of the major elements of a country-house poem—a detailed description of the building—is represented in "EZZ" only by its Venetian or Palladian window (unnamed, but suggested by the image of numerous sparkling glasses that reflect the beams of the setting sun) and a balcony (also unnamed, but implied by the self-portrait of the poet, having his evening rest "on the elevation of four pillars"). People in the text are represented by their hands or eyes—on the *pars pro toto* basis. In a similar way, the space of Zvanka metonymically stands for the entire universe, although in this case metaphor and metonymy are barely distinguishable.

As mentioned above, "EZZ" may be read as a lesson in the art of memory. Memory operates metonymically. As James McAllister says in his discussion of the use of metaphors and metonymies in Yves Bonnefoy's poetry:

> The object of memory is necessarily image, a glimpse of a former, now vanished presence. If metaphors describe such an image, building up equivalences between face and earth, metonymy dismisses such comparisons, delivers them to the wind, then retrieves them as mere instances of what is lost. So the metonymic presence of the titular "souvenir" joins the wind of destruction and the "adieu" to unravel the textiles of metaphor.[59]

Representing metonymy (metaphorically!) as a textual counterpart of a material ruin does not seem haphazard at all, for the forms are brought together by the idea of "suggestive incompleteness." Paradoxically, the most striking features of Derzhavin's archaic style—his inversions and chiastic structures, his continuous experiments with "difficult" meters, and the abundance of archaic words and word forms—are instances of discontinuity which serve as signifiers for the nebulous yet enticing signified of modernity.[60]

## Notes

1. Marc Neelen and Marina van den Bergen, "Venice Biennale—Preview," translated by Billy Nolan, *ArchiNed News*, April 2000, http://www.classic.archined.nl/news/endex.html.
2. *La Gazettina*, June 16, 2000; my translation. See also the review by Marcus Binney in the *Times*, June 27, 2000. Binney reported: "Often the conservation messages are the most powerful. The Russians speak from the heart. 'You appeal to a new utopia; but we lived with utopia for 70 years. No architect in the West could ever dream of such opportunities for transforming the city . . . waves of ethics and aesthetics washed across the country without meeting the slightest resistance.' The pavilion contains evocative photographs of Russia's decaying heritage and a stunning series of watercolors and drawings—in the visionary manner of Sir John Soane—by a free-spirited architect in his forties, Mikhail Filippov, who is now building romantic classical architecture of superb quality on the grand scale."
3. Grigorii Revzin, "It's Time to Destroy Stones," *Kommersant*, July 27, 2000, my translation.
4. The slate, still preserving traces of Derzhavin's last poem, is on display in the St. Petersburg Public Library.
5. Derzhavin, "Na tlennost" (On Perishability), in *Sochinenia*, ed. Iakov K. Grot, vol. 3,

178–79. In this chapter all the quotes from Derzhavin are from this edition and are my translations, unless otherwise noted

6. Eisenstein, "Akrostikh i tsenton," 55.
7. Halle, "O nezamechennom akrostikhe Derzhavina" ("On an Unnoticed Acrostic of Derzhavin").
8. Jakobson, "Derzhavin's Last Poem and M. Halle's First Literary Essay," 6.
9. For example, see the famous exordium of Pindar's Sixth Olympian Ode: "Raising the fine-walled porch / of our dwelling with golden pillars, / we will build, as it were, a marvelous hall; / at the beginning of our work / we must place a far-shining front" (*The Odes of Pindar*, 54).
10. The recurrent motif of the "limited holding capacity" of the text stands here for what future romantics would call unspeakable or beyond words: the vast majority of odes claim that the eulogies addressed to the sovereign are too numerous to fit into one text.
11. In the 1740s alone two important architectural treatises based on Horace's *Ars Poetica* were produced: an anonymous poem, later attributed to John Gwynn, *The Art of Architecture*; and Germain de Boffrand's *Book of Architecture* (*Livre d'Architecture*), which is considered one of the major texts of the French architectural theory. Boffrand drew a parallel between the five architectural orders and the five literary genres: "As the genres of poetry are to its chosen subjects, so the orders of architecture used by the Greeks and Romans are to the various genres of building" (11).
12. For an illuminating analysis of this poem, see Golburt, "Derzhavin's Ruins and the Birth of Historical Elegy."
13. Alongside verbal ruins, all kinds of debris dominate the allegorical plates designed for the 1808–16 edition of Derzhavin's poems. Derzhavin paid particular attention to the structure of his books and their artistic decoration. For several years the poet and his friends elaborated sophisticated programs for the vignettes to precede and follow each poem. Emblematic ruins were often mentioned in these programs, to visually amplify poems that might well contain no ruins. It was not until several decades after his death that his plan of a richly illustrated edition was realized by Iakov Grot, in a famous nine-volume edition of 1864–83.
14. In this essay I will refer to the poem as "EZZ."
15. Derzhavin, "To Eugene. Life at Zvanka," in *Poetic Works*, 124. Levitsky and Kitchen have produced extraordinary translations of Derzhavin's poetry, which is extremely difficult to put in English.
16. The genre of country-house poem usually refers to poems in praise of the English country house, and of the way of life of which the country house was the center. This tradition begins with Ben Jonson's *To Penshurst,* is continued by several poems by Thomas Carew and Herrick, by Marvell's *Appleton House,* and finally comes to an end with Alexander Pope. See Hibbard, "The Country House Poem of the Seventeenth Century," and Dubrow, "Guess Who's Coming to Dinner?"
17. Derzhavin, *Zhizn' moia na Zvanke, ili esho inache Kartina Zhizni Zvanskoi*, vol. 2, 412 (commentary in Russian edition).
18. See Yates, *The Art of Memory*. Almost two hundred years later, the French poet and philosopher Yves Bonnefoy wrote about his house at Valsaintes: "I had made the place

the material of a great dream, the dream of being able to live there, simply, in its atemporality and quiet transparency" (Bonnefoy, *In the Shadow's Light*, 163).

19. Pliny, *Letters, and Panegyricus*, 74, emphasis added.
20. His obsession with surviving his own death seems to be one reason for Derzhavin's interest in Pindar's odes, which he translated. See Pindar, Olympia 2, II.15–18, in *The Odes of Pindar*, 5: "Of things that have been done / In justice or unjust, not Time the Father / Of all can make the end unaccomplished. / But forgetfulness may come still with happiness."
21. Derzhavin, "To Eugene. Life at Zvanka," in *Poetic Works*, 133. Golburt describes the similar shift in poetic mood and mode that takes place in "The Ruins" as "a transformation of the odic discourse of presence into the elegiac discourse of absence" ("Derzhavin's Ruins and the Birth of Historical Elegy," 684).
22. Baridon, "Ruins as a Mental Construct."
23. Ps. 102:6–8, Authorized (King James) Version.
24. This psalm is 101 in the Bible he used.
25. Derzhavin, "To Eugene. Life at Zvanka," in *Poetic Works*, 134.
26. Derzhavin's own "Monument" (Pamiatnik) dates to 1795, one year after the death of his beloved first wife and one year before the death of "Felitsa" (Catherine the Great).
27. Lvov was a Russian Renaissance man in the Russian context: poet, artist, and inventor, he was one of the most creative architects of his time and a fervent promoter of *Palladianism* not only as an architectural and gardening style but as an all-encompassing liberal aesthetic paradigm. He did the first Russian translation of the Palladio's *Four Books of Architecture*, of which only the preface and the *First Book* actually appeared.
28. In the years 1811–16 Derzhavin hosted the "Society of Lovers of Russian Word," founded by the same Shishkov.
29. For the most important studies on Pope's horticultural myth, see Mack, "A Poet in his Landscape," 3–29; Hunt, *The Figure in the Landscape*, 58–104; and Batey, *Alexander Pope*.
30. See Levin, *The Perception of English Literature in Russia*, and Cross, *Anglo-Russica*.
31. Pope, *An Essay on Man*, 25.
32. Quoted in Hunt, *The Figure in the Landscape*, 65–67.
33. See Brownell, ed., *Alexander Pope's Villa*.
34. On Russian visitors to Twickenham, see Cross, *By the Banks of the Thames*, 218–26.
35. Karamzin, *Letters of a Russian Traveller*, 444.
36. Karamzin mentions the twig once more, at the very end of his book: "I am going through my treasures with such pleasure: notes, accounts, books, stones, dried plants and twigs, reminding me of the Rhône, 'la perte du Rhône,' the grave of Father Lorenzo, the thick willow under which the Englishman Pope composed his best poems! Agree that all the Croesuses of the world are poor in comparison with me!" (*Letters of a Russian Traveller*, 456).
37. Brownell, *Alexander Pope and the Arts of Georgian England*, 140.
38. Dodsley, "The Cave of Pope," 103.
39. This portrait is reproduced in Hunt, *The Figure in the Landscape*, 61.
40. As a Roman Catholic, Pope was not allowed to own property. See Hunt, *The Figure in the Landscape*, 75–76.
41. Quoted in Hunt, *The Figure in the Landscape*, 33.

42. Sophia Charlotte Howe, baroness of Langar (1762–1835).
43. In one of the *Fraser's* papers, dedicated to the demolition of Pope's villa, Baroness Howe was compared to other inheritors of the "poets' houses," who never dared to alter them, and even to Alexander the Great, who spared Pindar's house in Thebes, for the only reason that it was "the Poet's House."
44. Cobbett, *Memorials of Twickenham*, 287. However, Cobbett also wrote: "poor Lady Howe did not want to be the proprietor of a public exhibition, her tastes were not poetic, nor was her disposition conservative; what she did desire was 'a commodius family residence,' and she certainly provided it for herself" (288).
45. See, e.g., ibid., 292.
46. Certainly Derzhavin could not know how much the demolition of Pope's villa impressed another artist, J. M. W. Turner, who bought land for a house in Twickenham a year later. Turner, a great admirer of Pope, painted two pictures which reflected the intensity of his feelings. The elegiac view of *Pope's Villa at Twickenham during its Dilapidation* (1808) shows workmen with relics from the poet's house in the midst of the pastoral scene. Hamilton, *Turner*, 137–38.
47. Dodsley was not unknown to Russian readers; he was the foremost editor of all the major English writers of the eighteenth century. His own textbook, *The Preceptor: Containing a General Course of Education* (1748), was translated in Russian and published by Karamzin (Levin, *The Perception of English Literature in Russia*, 166).
48. Quote from http://ideashistory.org.ru.
49. For a detailed account of the project *Following Radishchev: A Journey from Petersburg to Moscow*, see http://ideashistory.org.ru.
50. Derzhavin, "Magic Lantern," in *Poetic Works*, 118.
51. Derzhavin, "God," in *Poetic Works*, 18.
52. Crone claims that in "EZZ," too, "the optical arts are a metaphor for poetry. The refracting instrument in poetry is the mind/imagination of the poet." See Crone, *The Daring of Derzhavin*, 104–6.
53. Derzhavin, "To Eugene. Life at Zvanka," in *Poetic Works*, 129.
54. The described optical spectacle looks surprisingly similar to Joseph Addison's account: "The prettiest Lanskip I ever saw, was one drawn on the Walls of a dark Room, which stood opposite on one side to a navigable River, and on the other to a Park. The Experiment is very common in Opticks. Here you might discover the Waves and Fluctuations of the Water in strong and proper Colours, with the picture of a Ship entering at one end, and sailing by Degreed through the whole Piece. On another there appeared the Green Shadows of Trees, waving to and fro with the Wind, and Herds of Deer among them in Miniature, leaping upon the Wall. I must confess, the Novelty of such a Sight may be one occasion of its Pleasantness to the Imagination, but certainly the chief Reason is its near Resemblance to Nature, as it does not only, like other Pictures, give the Color and Figure, but the Motion of the Things it represents." See Addison, *The Spectator*, no. 414, June 25, 1712.
55. Derzhavin, "To Eugene. Life at Zvanka," in *Poetic Works*, 129–30.
56. For a thorough and subtle study of the fragmentary and the incomplete in Russian literature and culture, see Greenleaf, *Pushkin and Romantic Fashion*.
57. Hunt, "Picturesque Mirrors and the Ruins of the Past," 191, emphasis added.

58. Culler, *Pursuit of Signs*, 210.

59. McAllister, "Metonymy and Metaphor in Yves Bonnefoy's Poetry," 154.

60. For a discussion of the same decentralizing tendencies in the theory and practice of the English Romantic poets, who often employed archaisms to resist the hegemony of a denotative, abstract poetic diction (on archaism as an "avant-garde tendency in literary language"), see Richardson, "Archaism and Modernity."

JOHANNES VON MOLTKE

# 22

## RUIN CINEMA

Griffith began it with the Babylon sequence in *Intolerance*, and to this day there is nothing like the thrill of watching all those expensive sets come tumbling down.
SUSAN SONTAG, "THE IMAGINATION OF DISASTER"

Ruins are a way of seeing.
ROBERT HARBISON, "THE RUIN"

At the origins of cinema, we find a play on ruination. In 1895, with their newly invented and patented *cinématographe*, the Lumière brothers staged and recorded *The Demolition of a Wall*. With Auguste Lumière directing from behind the camera and Louis visible onscreen, the single-shot film shows workers using ratchets and sledgehammers to topple a brick wall (see figure 1). The dramaturgy of the filmed attraction is spectacular enough in itself, designed to elicit the astonishment so typical of early reactions to the new medium of cinema:[1] after a prolonged buildup showing mainly the repetitive motions of the workers, the wall suddenly buckles and falls sideways, creating a plume of dust across the entire image. But in a twist testifying to the importance of exhibition during the early years of cinema, it appears that the real appeal of *Demolition* lay in its reversal: after showing the ruination of the wall, exhibitors liked to amaze audiences by running the projector backward. The plume of dust gets sucked into the wall as it assembles itself from a pile of debris and ends up intact.

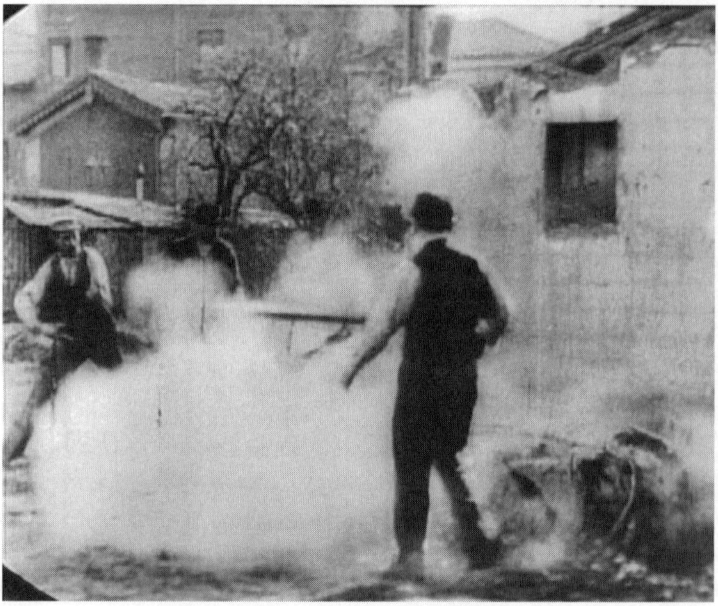

1. Still from *The Demolition of a Wall* (1895).

## Ruins in Reverse

A man-made wall reduced to rubble and then resurrected by the power of the medium: more than just the first of many filmic representations of ruins and rubble, this little episode from 1895 might serve as a cinematic epigraph for the broader aesthetic, ontological, and epistemological imbrication of cinema and ruin in modernity.[2] The following remarks aim to trace these links along a broadly realist representational mode that unites ruins and cinema by virtue of their shared indexical link to the past. In the theorization of cinema as a photographic medium by André Bazin and Siegfried Kracauer, claims about ontology and physical reality resonate directly with readings of ruins from Georg Simmel onward. If we follow this line of inquiry through Kracauer's final book, the posthumously published *History: The Last Things Before the Last*, as I propose to do below, we will find, moreover, that this particular form of realist representation has far-reaching epistemological implications that take us from a theory of film (or of the ruin, for that matter) into the realm of historiography. The cinema and the ruin plough common epistemological ground: as peculiarly modern forms of grasping contingency and temporality, they activate ways of knowing the past and its relation to the present. In this view, the century-long obsession of cinema with the image of ruins, in turn, is but the visible manifestation of cinema's and the ruin's common function to visualize time and history in modernity.

## Gazing and Traveling: Cinema, Ruin, History

In 1895, the cinématographe inscribes the historically new temporality of the modern "event"[3] with a force that Benjamin famously describes as a productive form of destruction. "The social significance of film, even—and especially—in its most positive form," Benjamin argues, "is inconceivable without its destructive, cathartic side: the liquidation of the value of tradition and cultural heritage."[4] Viewed against the backdrop of Benjamin's theses on the destruction of aura and the liquidation of tradition, the intervention of early cinema exhibitors who reversed destruction on film would appear to add another twist to the argument: their action also exposes the inherent historicity of the medium, its power to shape concepts of time and history.[5] This is the same power Benjamin famously attributes to the cinema as a medium that also transforms the logics of perception and lays bare what he calls the "optical unconscious." In a passage that explicitly likens the cinematic spectator to a traveler among ruins, Benjamin writes: "Our bars and our city streets, our offices and furnished rooms, our railroad stations and our factories seemed to close relentlessly around us. Then came film and exploded this prison-world with the dynamite of the split second, so that now we can set off calmly on journeys of adventure among its far-flung debris (*Trümmer*)."[6] In this view (hotly debated in cinema studies as the "modernity thesis"), the cinema both creates and feeds on the ruins of earlier notions of space, perception, and movement.[7] Itself a cinematic event, *The Demolition of a Wall* captures a transient temporal moment—a moment of destruction—and negates the irreversibility of temporality; spectators who have come to marvel at the powers of the new apparatus are struck by the possibility of reversing time, of witnessing the inversion of an event and tracing it back to its origins.

What kind of subject "set[s] off calmly on journeys of adventure"? Benjamin appears to be speaking here of the cinematic spectator who remains stationary in her seat even as she engages in the adventures onscreen.[8] But just as the cinematic spectator is for Benjamin merely emblematic of a far more pervasive mode of modern subjectivity, so does the seemingly paradoxical relationship between passivity and activity, between physiological slackening and imaginary enervation, transcend the confines of the movie theater. Without leaving the cinema behind entirely, the relaxed and adventurous subject is, as Benjamin points out, a ruin traveler. The provocative image of the modern subject that Benjamin conjures here is that of a viewer who is disposed to different forms of perception simultaneously: to the astonishment or shock of (early) cinema on the one hand, and to the calm contemplation or immersion of the ruin traveler on the other.

Following from this implicit link between film spectatorship and ruin travel, further connections become apparent. If the cinema offers new modes of temporality, including the reversibility of time, ruins invite their visitors to travel along related temporal vectors into the past. They offer representations of a bygone time and distant space in the medium of decaying or destroyed architecture. Not only do the remnants index the transient temporal moment from which they survive, but they also serve as the material connection that links the traveler, tourist, or resident of a bombed-out city contemplating (if not living in) ruins to the past as well as to "possible futures that [have] been foreclosed on in past defeats."[9] In the nineteenth century, the ruin emerges as a historiographic marker that ushers in a new historical frame "in which time becomes contingent, not eternally regulated by natural or divine law; ruins themselves are rendered newly visible by these structures of temporality based on disorder and rupture, concealment and half-life."[10] In other words, ruins represent and activate temporalities every bit as complex as those of the cinema as an indexical medium with the ability to (re)structure and reverse linear time.

The related temporal play of ruin and cinema owes as much to their respective production as it does to paradoxically related modes of perception. A mechanical process captures different light values on a chemical emulsion in the case of film; the production of ruins requires the work of nature and the force of gravity—with the latter of particular relevance in cases where nature has been replaced by engineering, as in the aerial bombing of modern warfare. Writing about "our general fascination with decay and decadence" sixteen years after *The Demolition of a Wall*, Simmel observes in ruins a dialectical play of construction and destruction, or between an upward-driving "will of the spirit" and the pull of gravity, the "brute, downward-dragging, corroding, crumbling power of nature."[11] To be sure, Simmel does not envision ruination as demolition; for him, the ruin gains its cultural significance only as a natural process that negates the willful, formative creations of architecture or "the spirit." But upon closer inspection, Simmel's nature becomes a medium with demiurgical powers much like those given to the Lumières' invention. Where contemporary physics would find in the "corroding, crumbling power of nature" a sign of entropy and hence proof for the newly formulated second law of thermodynamics and the irreversibility of time,[12] Simmel insists on the ruin's dialectical *Aufhebung* of decay, and by extension of temporal irreversibility. Through the medium of nature, ruination becomes a process of signification, lending meaning to decay. In this dialectical reading, the reversion of man-made structures to nature becomes legible as a purposive aesthetic movement forward in time. "So long as we can speak of a ruin at all and not a mere heap of stones, [nature's] power does not sink the work of man into the formlessness of mere matter.

*There rises a new form* which, from the standpoint of nature, is entirely meaningful, comprehensible, differentiated. Nature has transformed the work of art into material for her own expression."[13] Through their common ability to "transform rubble into evocative ruins,"[14] both nature and cinema express a fundamental temporal reorientation that couples concerns and anxieties about modern contingency with newfound lessons about history.

As Benjamin and others have suggested, the emergence of cinema participates in, and helps to visualize, a vast restructuring of temporalities. Driven by the ongoing process of modernization, this restructuring can be traced across a wealth of discursive practices to have emerged during the nineteenth century—including statistics and physics, rail travel and telegraphy, psychoanalysis and a new epistemology of contingency.[15] In addition, however, the "emergence of cinematic time" must be considered in relation to those discourses produced by the discipline most directly implicated in the construction of temporalities: history.[16] As Philip Rosen demonstrates in a study of the relationship between cinema, historicity, and film theory, this relationship turns, like the derivative one between cinema and ruins, on the importance of the indexical trace and the mastery of time.[17] At least since Leopold von Ranke, the historian's constructions of the past *wie es eigentlich gewesen* (how it actually was) stake a claim to realism grounded in the indexical quality of the historical source, or trace. On the same ground, early exhibitors advertised the cinematograph as a *historiographe*,[18] and it would not take long for theorists of the new medium to find the same claim inscribed in the very apparatus of the cinema.

Nobody has followed this link between history and cinema more explicitly and in a more sustained way than Kracauer. His *Theory of Film* and *History: The Last Things Before the Last* represent different sides of the same inquiry into "the redemption of physical reality," as he puts it in the subtitle to *Theory of Film*.[19] Fueled by a deep conviction of cinema's powers as a realist medium, Kracauer wants to show how both film and historiography share certain affinities with particular subject matter. Adjusted for their different frames of reference, the two books define these affinities in strikingly similar ways, as if to illustrate the author's sudden realization of "the many existing parallels between history and the photographic media, historical reality and camera-reality."[20] On the one hand, Kracauer sees the cinema ("camera-reality") gravitating toward unstaged, fortuitous aspects of reality that gesture beyond themselves toward an endless, if indeterminate, "flow of life." On the other hand, he sees historical reality as "full of intrinsic contingencies, . . . virtually endless . . . [and] indeterminate as to meaning," which leads him to the conclusion that "camera-reality parallels historical reality in terms of its structure, its general constitution."[21] If some of these general affinities are broad enough to appear somewhat indeterminate themselves, we should remember that Kracauer feels compelled to investigate these parallels by an underlying affinity of his own: "All my main efforts," he says with hindsight, "fall into line—they all have served, and continue to serve a single purpose: the rehabilitation of objectives and modes of being which still lack a name and hence are overlooked or misjudged."[22] In a notebook entry from Marseille, where he met regularly with Benjamin as both were trying to secure safe passage to the United States, Kracauer formulates this affinity for film in ways that resonate directly with Benjamin's notion of the calm spectator-adventurer traveling among the ruins of tradition. Now, however, it is the medium itself that surveys the debris in an effort to reassemble it in a new light, a new medium, a new mode of subjectivity: "Film . . . sets the whole material world into play: . . . it pushes toward the bottom, to gather and carry along even the dregs. It is interested in refuse, in what is just there."[23]

In keeping with this task of rehabilitation—or what *Theory of Film*, closer in some ways to the Frankfurt School, calls "redemption"—the historian must work much like the camera operator, if not like the camera itself: using either short lenses for macrohistorical overviews or long lenses for microhistorical close-ups, and endowed with a "nostalgia for lost causes" that he shares with figures from Buckhardt to Proust, Kracauer's ideal historian seeks to record the unseen, the endless, the fortuitous without preconceptions.[24] But just as the director and cinematographer must seek out (or "scout," in the language of the trade) locations and stage profilmic space, so the historian must travel into the past to retrieve objects she can then discuss. For Kracauer, this journey is not only a complex form of time travel that recalls the overlapping temporalities of the cinema and the ruin sketched above,[25] but also a mythologically overdetermined instantiation of the historian's "mobile self." In a gesture richly evocative of ruin travel (whether literary, cinematic, or real), Kracauer locates the historian's journey in the tradition of Orpheus, describing it as a descent "into the nether world to bring the dead back to life."[26] Julia Hell has linked the walk among the dead, which she defines as a "rudimentary plot structure [of the] (post)war period," to the Orphic logic of ruin gazing as a fascination with death. As she points out, this fascination is fundamentally a visual one, even in the medium of literature.[27] Film theorists from Kracauer to Bazin would bear out this insight at the even more basic level of the medium's ontology.

Cinema, according to the still influential realist theory of the medium, has the power to embalm time. As Bazin famously puts it, "The cinema is objectivity in time. . . . Now, for the first time, the image of things is likewise the image of their duration, change mummified, as it were."[28] Like history as an academic discipline, Bazin's entire film theory "is built on the problem of objectifications of pastness against the flow of time."[29] Bazin consequently derives the ontology of the photographic image from the human desire to mount "a defense against the passage of time" and "to have the last word in the argument with death by means of a form that endures."[30] In an essay on photography that predates *Theory of Film* and that he refers to in *History*, Kracauer links the recording capacity of the camera to the task of the historian, which he defines here as "temporal photography" made possible by the emergent medium of cinema. Accordingly, "historicism is concerned with the photography of time. The equivalent of its temporal photography would be a giant film depicting the temporally interconnected events from every vantage point."[31]

In their overlapping, now canonical answers to the question "What is cinema?" both Bazin and Kracauer base their claims on the photographic properties of the medium; inspired by divergent theoretical and national backgrounds, their conceptualizations of the medium converged on the indexical relationship of the image to profilmic reality. Not only did the image preserve an imprint of that reality in the manner of a fingerprint, thereby testifying to the "that has been" of the referent;[32] more importantly, the cinema could "record and reveal" (in Kracauer's phrase) all manner of temporality—the spontaneity of the unstaged, the fortuitous moment, indeterminacy, and endlessness for Kracauer, and time itself for Bazin.[33] As Mary Ann Doane puts it, "the promise of indexicality is, in effect, the promise of the rematerialization of time—the restoration of a continuum of space in photography, of time in the cinema . . . The indexical sign is the imprint of a once-present and unique moment, the signature of temporality."[34]

As Simmel's insistence on the dialectics of the ruin suggest, ruins rank high among the multiplying indexical traces of the past that achieved "a kind of epistemological prestige in an era of intensifying time consciousness."[35] Like the cinema for the twentieth century, ruins are aesthetic schools of historical thinking in a realist mould for the nineteenth century. Attracting renewed—and new kinds of—attention in the wake of industrialization, ruins and their attendant modes of perception are symptoms of breaks in tradition and historical consciousness.[36] As Simmel's "present form of the past," ruins also "collapse temporalities:"[37] they ask us to contemplate the past within the present, as well as the having-been-present of the past (Kracauer, Simmel's student, speaks of the ability of the photograph to literally re-present the past, even as it hides its full historical dimensions).[38] At their most static, ruins suggest historical closure; thus, for a romantic like Schlegel, the ruin is an index of past wholeness as opposed to the open-endedness of the fragment.[39] At their most challenging, ruins confront us with the foreclosed futures of an earlier era, reintroduce contingency into history, and offer "memory traces of an abandoned set of futures."[40]

## Viewing Ruins

In the temporally charged encounter with the ruin, argues Simmel, "such profound and comprehensive energies of our soul are brought into play that there is no longer any sharp division between perception and thought."[41] How often has the same observation been brought to bear on the cinema and its powers to move the "soul"—whether in order to celebrate its inherent realism, or to critique that same realism as an illusion built on the suspension of our capacity for reality testing? In 1911 Jules Romains had described the cinema experience as a "group dream" in which the spectators lose consciousness of their bodies and take "the haze of visions which resemble life" as reality;[42] for the Kracauer of *Theory of Film*, the spectator "wavers between self-absorption and self-abandonment" in a dreamlike engagement with the images that she or he mistakes for physical reality;[43] and in Jean Baudry's description of the cinema as a "simulation machine capable of offering the subject perceptions which are really representations mistaken for perceptions," one senses a spectatorial experience as overwhelming as the one described by Simmel for the visitor of ruins.[44] Though it would be misleading to collapse the ambulatory experience of ruins in broad daylight into the fixed, almost dreamlike subjectivity of the cinematic spectator in the darkened theater,[45] the areas of overlap would be worth exploring: in terms of the viewing subject, when are ruins cinematic, and when does the cinema evoke the contemplation of ruins?

Given their concern with representational strategies that would allow us to map the corresponding subject positions, these questions can be broached only on the basis of a ruin aesthetic. To be sure, both Kracauer and Benjamin provide leads in this direction: taken together, their investigations of cinema, history, and modernity suggest ample overlap between the imaginary activity of the film spectator and that of the ruin gazer. Indeed, as I argued above, we might locate their theorization of modern subjectivity at precisely this paradoxical intersection between the passive but active viewer whose perceptual apparatus is revolutionized through the shocks of cinema, and the adventurous but calm Orphic traveler who carries along the dregs and contemplates the ruins of tradition. However, barring reductive and unproductive generalizations, the reconstruction of modern subjectivity out of a ruin aesthetic also confronts formidable obstacles: if we attend to the historical variability in the representation, perception, and functionalization of ruins from the Middle Ages to the baroque period, from the nostalgic recuperation of the ruin in romanticism to the apocalyptic ruins of the twentieth century, then the project of a unified ruin aesthetic hardly makes any sense.[46] But what if we narrow our gaze and limit ourselves to one specific form in which ruins have been aesthetically mediated? What if, in this particular instance, we inquire only into the specifically cinematic aesthetics of the ruin? Refocusing the topic of a ruin aesthetic in this manner may allow us to make some broad claims by way of inference, as I will suggest below. But these claims, too, involve a degree of speculative abstraction, as the history of cinema is long enough to raise its own obstacles to generalization. In surveying the representation of ruins in the cinema, as opposed to the historical and epistemological imbrication of ruin and cinema with which I began, at a minimum we must first account for film-historical and generic variations before attempting any sort of synthesis. What are the different historical forms that the cinema's fascination with the ruin takes at the level of subject matter, mise-en-scène, and cinematography? What are the textual functions, the ideological ramifications of ruins in the cinema? Which cinematic genres have taken a particular interest in the ruin, and why? Where do the cinematic aesthetics of ruins intersect with different extracinematic histories of ruination?

### THE NERO COMPLEX

While Simmel's ruin philosophy and its attendant philosophy of history offer intriguing conceptual parallels to the emergent medium of cinema, the natural ruination that he describes does not form a privileged subject of cinematic representation. Of course a famous ruin location like Pompeii features heavily in spectacles about *The Last Days of Pompeii* from the earliest days of cinema, but even among the many films to have used this title, adaptations of Edward Bulwer-Lytton's novel of the same name predominate, suggesting a preponderance of plot over location, and of melodramatic motifs over ruin aesthetics.[47] And rather than ancient ruins or even the nostalgic ruin of romanticism, it is the quintessentially modern ruin produced by aerial bombing that holds pride of place in the ruin iconography of the cinema.[48]

Of this modern ruin, the neorealist moment in Italy and the German Trümmerfilm are the essential repository, though here, too, the melodramatic often dominates. In retrospect the much-touted neorealist return to the streets after years spent in the studios did yield a coherent cinemascape centered on the image of ruination. Wolfgang Staudte's *Die Mörder sind unter uns* (Germany, 1946; see figure 2), Harald Braun's *Zwischen gestern und morgen* (Germany, 1947), Josef von Baky's *Und über uns der Himmel* (Germany, 1947), and Roberto Rossellini's *Germania Anno Zero* (Italy, 1948; see figure 3) are just some of the canonic titles, to which we should add kindred but nationally or generically distinct productions amid ruins such as Billy Wilder's *A Foreign Affair* (United States, 1948) or Carol Reed's *The Third Man* (United Kingdom, 1949) (see figure 4).[49]

In keeping with Hell's claims about the fatal attractiveness of this Orphic

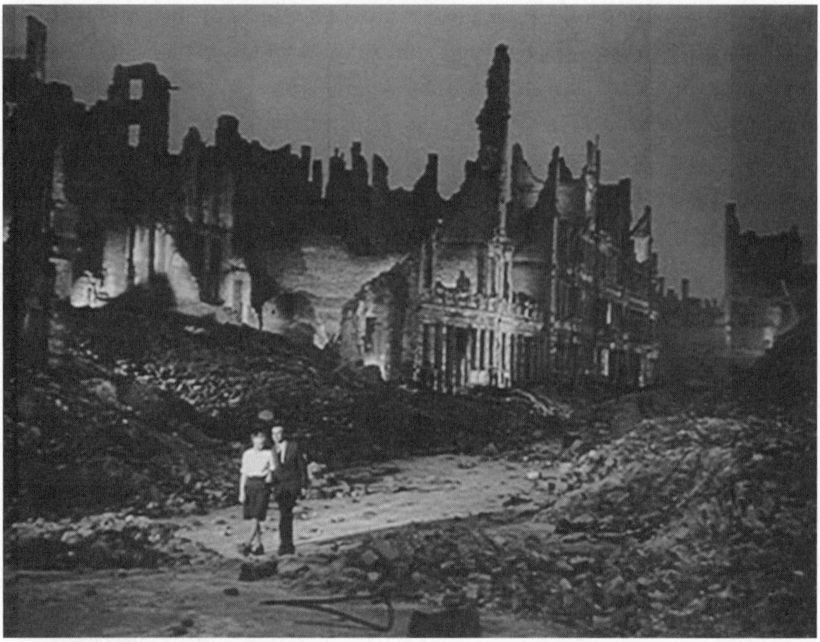

2. Still from *Die Mörder sind unter uns* (1946).

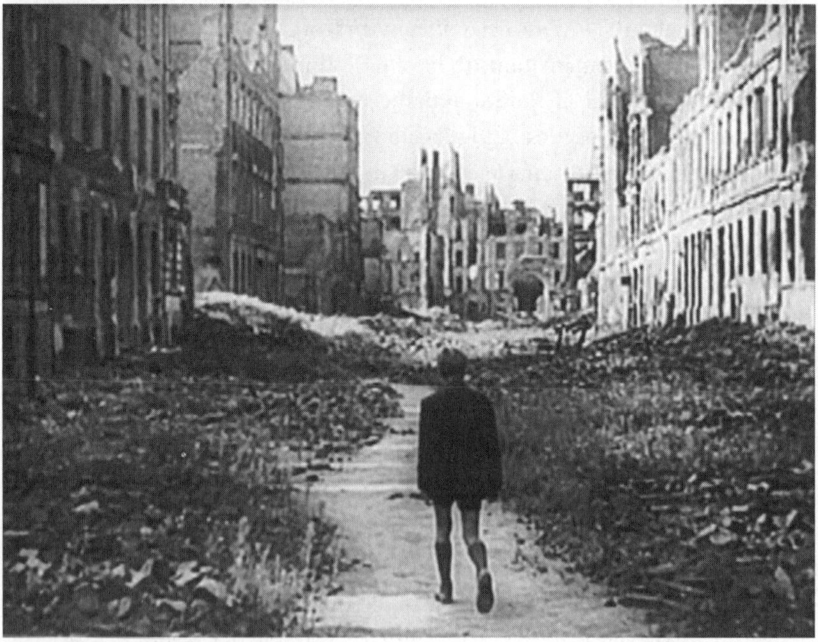

3. Still from *Germania Anno Zero* (1948).

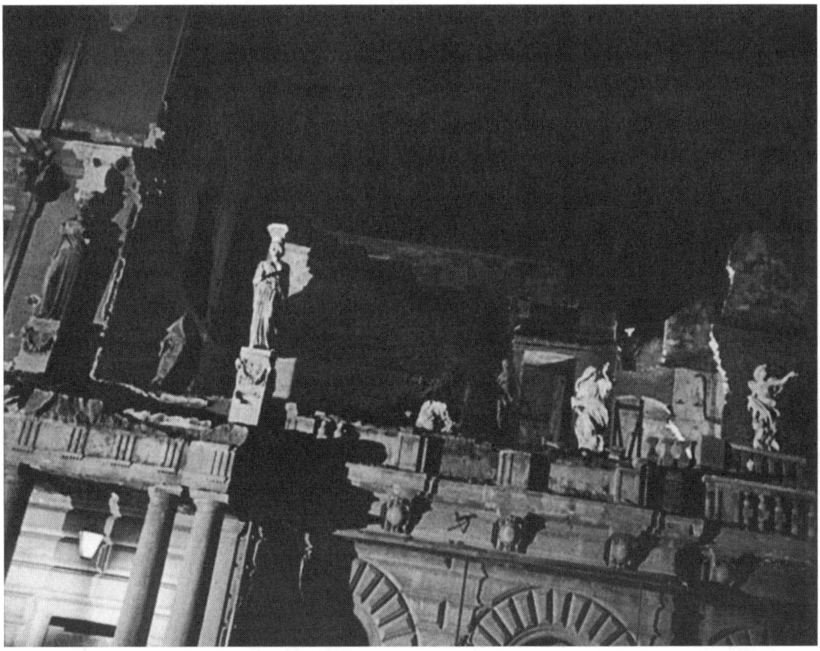

4. Still from *The Third Man* (1949).

space, many of these films stage ruins not only as overbearing but also as aesthetically stunning configurations.[50] It is no coincidence that most of the underworld scenes of Jean Cocteau's *Orphée* (France, 1949) were shot in the bombed ruins of the St. Cyr military academy (see figure 5). But alongside the patent mythologization of ruins, the cinema's specific contribution to a postwar ruin aesthetic must also be sought in a more general effect of the transformation of rubble into representation. Reviewing Frank Capra's roughly contemporaneous educational series *Why We Fight* (United States, 1943-45), Bazin quips that these films have something to do with a "slightly Freudian factor that I would call the 'Nero complex' and define as the pleasure experienced at the sight of urban destruction."[51] What Bazin defines psychoanalytically as pleasure, I would suggest, is the effect of a prior aesthetization of the ruin in the rubble film. As Eric Rentschler outlines in his contribution to this volume, such aestheticization was quickly recognized as problematic by critics from Benjamin onward. Bazin's psychoanalytic emphasis on pleasure points to this problem rather precisely. Far from simply documenting the cityscape in a slice-of-life approach, these films build the ruin into an aesthetic universe and language that invites specific spectatorial attitudes, among which pleasure is certainly a complicated, but plausible, one. Members of the Congressional delegation approaching Berlin from above at the beginning of *A Foreign Affair* may be overcome with the urge to vomit when they see a city reduced to what looks like "a hunk of moldy roquefort cheese" or "chicken innards at frying time." But the spectator is invited to laugh at the comic alignment of the somatic and the historic, the political and the metaphorical within the diegesis (see figure 6). Though Wilder apparently shot much of the material as part of a documentary impulse during his stint as a film officer for the U.S. Armed Forces some years before completion of *A Foreign Affair*, the integration of that material into the fictional film narrativizes the representation of ruins and integrates them into an aesthetic concept aimed simultaneously at comedy and de-Nazifying enlightenment.[52] This is nowhere more apparent than in the tour of the ruins given by Colonel Plummer to the Congressional delegation: an elaborately choreographed rear projection combines Wilder's historical footage of Berlin landmarks (including the Reichstag, the Reichskanzlei, and the Tiergarten) in ruins with the colonel's laconic commentary that Hitler's proclamation of a thousand-year Reich "broke the bookies' hearts," or that the Germans used to treat the Brandenburg Gate as an "arch of triumph—until they got out of the habit." And yet, as Frost, the slightly ridiculous congresswoman, spots one instance of fraternization after another, and the accompanying music makes light of the delegation's tour of the ruins, the traveling shots of ruins in rear projection lend aesthetic weight to the comedic acting and plot.

## GOOD-BYE LENIN: THE POSTSOCIALIST RUIN

Compared to the physical ruins left by the Second World War, the materialization of state socialism's demise in the postsocialist ruin still remains cinematically underexplored. But there are some leads. For all its trivia, the credit sequence of Martin Campbell's *GoldenEye* (United Kingdom and United States, 1995) is among the most memorable of the Bond series to date: the translucent female silhouettes wielding hammers, climbing over oversized sickles, and knocking heads off statues of Lenin, accompanied by Tina Turner's title song, indicate the historical permeability of popular culture even as they ambivalently aestheticize and—rather less ambivalently—sexualize the transformations after 1989 (see figure 7). It is only fitting that the showdown with the villain should take place in a graveyard of socialist statuary: with lighting borrowed directly from *The Third Man*, *GoldenEye* deftly negotiates the end of the cold war and what this entails for the survival of the quintessential cold warrior as a popular hero; it does so by resorting to material and metaphorical images of ruin as a way of prolonging the conflict that drives the series. Having been labeled a "misogynist dinosaur and a relic of the cold war" by his superior, M (played here for the first time by Judi Dench), Bond must shake off the cold war itself as a relic by surviving a climactic confrontation among the ruins of socialism (see figure 8).

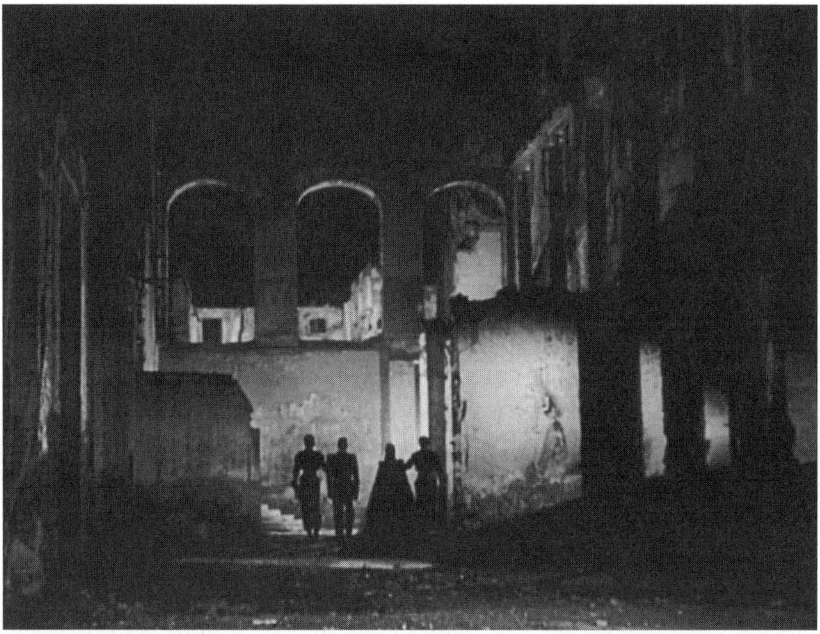

5. Still from *Orphée* (1949).

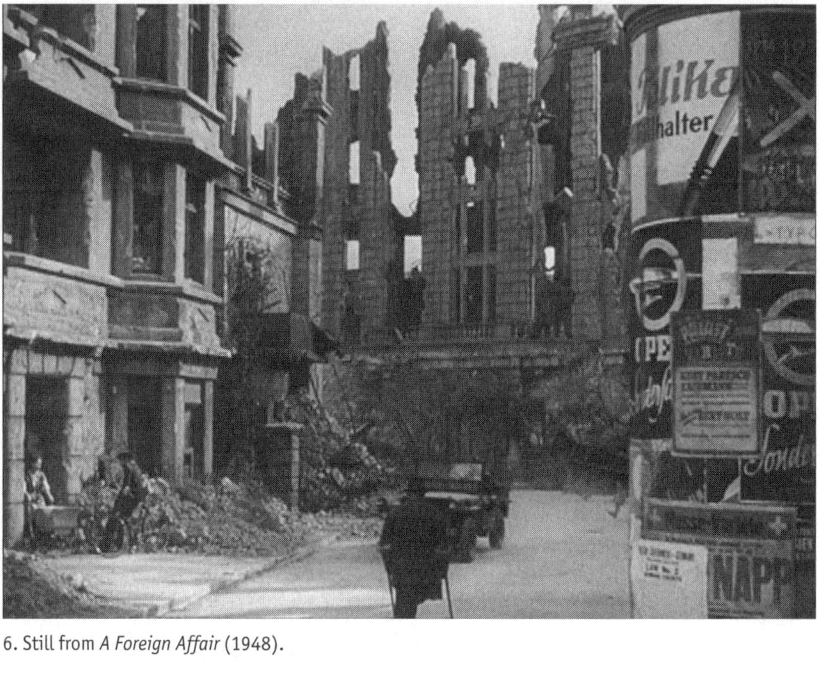


6. Still from *A Foreign Affair* (1948).

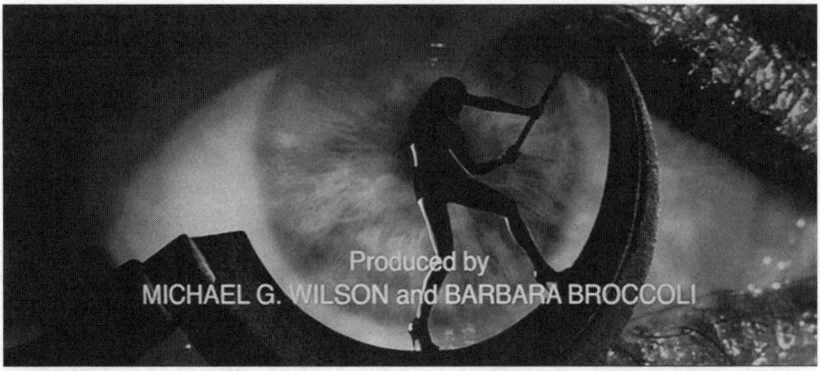


7. Still from credits for *GoldenEye* (1995).

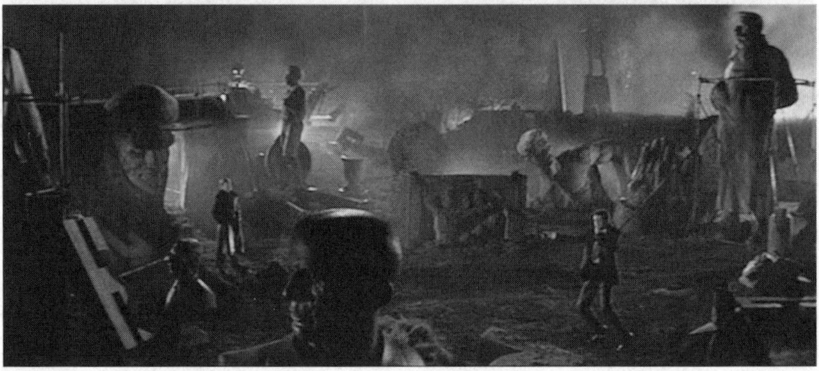

8. Still from *GoldenEye* (1995).

But the quintessential example here must be Wolfgang Becker's *Good-Bye Lenin!* (Germany, 2003). The film belongs in a survey of cinematic ruins not so much by virtue of its vaguely nostalgic plot or its comedic play with *Ungleichzeitigkeit* as because of a single emblematic sequence, in which a helicopter transports a physical remnant of socialism down Berlin's thoroughfares. A distant echo of the ship that carries a statue of Lenin in Theodoros Angelopoulos's *Ulysses' Gaze* (Greece, 1995), the sequence brings the frantic comedy to a halt, marking the dismantling of East German culture as spectacle. But the event is focalized through the oneiric gaze of the mother. The shot's interiority is underlined by the soundtrack, which reduces the ambient noise of the city as the helicopter flies by in slow motion, and for a moment it appears as though the outstretched arm of the statue is in fact waving to the mother: the socialist ruin hails the postsocialist subject (see figure 9).

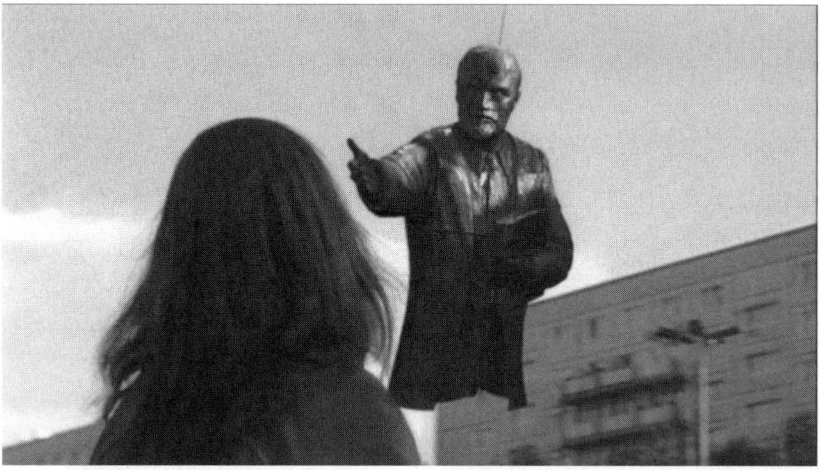

9. Still from *Good-Bye Lenin!* (2003).

## PROLEPTIC RUINS

Operating in the future anterior, the genre of science fiction projects the temporality of the ruin into the future. Where historical ruins memorialize abandoned utopias, science fiction sketches out a future in which the present will have been abandoned as so much historical debris. Mapping the reason for that process—and anchoring that reason in the viewer's present—is part of the genre's raison d'être: whether the nefarious development of present information technologies for autonomous artificial intelligence (*2001*, *Blade Runner*, *The Matrix*, *AI*), the consequences of nuclear proliferation (*La Jetée*, *Dr. Strangelove*, *Planet of the Apes*) or environmental damage (*The Day after Tomorrow*), or a combination of these (*Terminator II*), countless science-fiction plots are built around a cataclysm with roots in the viewer's present and consequences in her or his future, the diegetic present. What remains are ruins, framed within the genre's own "aesthetics of destruction."[53] In the mise-en-scène of *Blade Runner*, we recognize the urban wastelands of today (not to mention the cinematic sets of yesterday) as tomorrow's ruins; the film's now historic cyberpunk aesthetics return in the sets of *The Matrix*, which contrast the rubble of urban existence with the illusory reality of the matrix itself; *Terminator II* unfolds its dizzying time-travel loop from a stunning precredit sequence that pulverizes playing children and reduces a swing set (and greater Los Angeles) to ruin (see figure 10).

A film like Steven Spielberg's *AI* characteristically transmutes trauma into childlike fantasy, though not without a self-reflexive edge: when David, in his

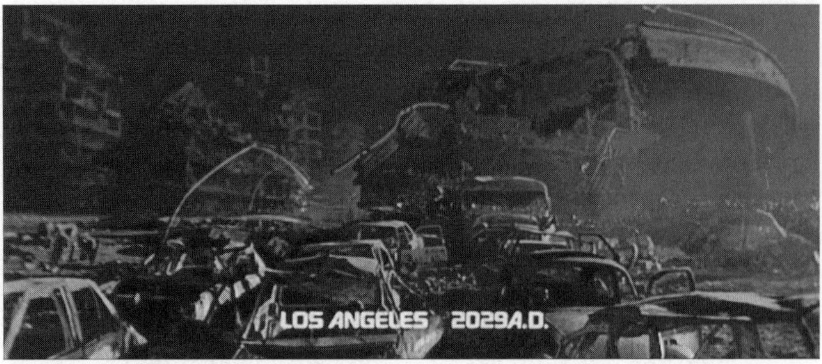

10. Still from *Terminator II* (1990).

quest for authenticity, finally finds the Blue Fairy who will make his dreams come true, it is in a ruin of Coney Island. Paradoxically, the film aims to authenticate its own agenda by projecting the ruination of the entertainment industry within which it operates.

### Toward a Cinematic Ruin Aesthetic

Beyond their conceptual links between cinema and ruin, but also beyond the obstinacy of ruins as a specifically cinematic (cine-genic?) subject, ruins attract our interest for the specific ways in which the cinema directs our gaze toward them, for the how as much as the what of ruin representation. Reviewing the cinema's fascination with ruination over the better part of a century, a few observations begin to suggest the outlines of a ruin aesthetic, formulated in the language of cinema. As Rentschler has noted, in the early postwar works of the neorealists and the Trümmerfilm, this is an aesthetic that draws on other traditions, ranging from romantic iconography to earlier cinematic movements and cycles such as expressionism and the mountain film. Favoring low-angle compositions that privilege the vertical skeletons of Berlin's buildings, a film like *Die Mörder sind unter uns* lets us see how ruins, far from being mere backdrops to a melodramatic plot, become "the function of a studied composition and a director's mise-en-scène."[54]

Rentschler carefully historicizes the emphasis on verticality in a film like *Die Mörder sind unter uns*, pointing to the specificity of Berlin's iron and steel architecture, which made the city's ruins look distinct from those of Cologne or Dresden, for example. But I would propose that the history of ruin representation in the cinema also exhibits a second vector, so to speak. For every vertical arrangement we might identify, we also find countless examples of images whose compositional principles strongly favor horizontality. Among these, the lateral tracking shot constitutes something of an aesthetic dominant: often extended into long takes, these shots suggest a cinematographic affinity for tracking the ruin in order to suggest its extensiveness and invite a specific mode of contemplation on the part of the viewer.[55] In the postwar rubble film, the long traveling shots clearly suggest that the extent of ruination is bounded only by the outer limits of the city itself, where the rubble of the built environment gives way to nature; in this sense, one must think of the German *Heimatfilm* as the ultimate example of the postwar *Trümmerfilm*—a conclusion exemplified by Rudolf Jugert's liminal *Film ohne Titel* (Germany, 1948) that travels from bombed-out Berlin to the countryside.[56]

This horizontal movement may tend toward abstraction, as in the aerial shots from planes gliding over bombed-out cities; it may also emphasize the concrete materiality of rubble and destruction by mimicking passages through the urban wasteland on foot (*Germania Anno Zero, Die Mörder sind unter uns*) or by car (*A Foreign Affair, Der Himmel über Berlin* [Wings of Desire]). The lateral movements of the camera may suggest linear trajectories or describe circles, or they may be aligned with a character's point of view (think of Homer scanning the urban void of Potsdamer Platz in *Der Himmel über Berlin*; see figure 11) or legible as authorial intervention (see the discussion of Andrei Tarkovsky's films below). Whatever the precise aesthetic manifestation of the traveling ruin shot, however, a common spectatorial address begins to emerge. The pleasure that Bazin detected in cinema's "Nero complex" is a profoundly melancholic one: the lingering, tracking cinematography of ruins tends to contemplate these not with the pleasurable nostalgia that Simmel attributed to all ruins[57] or with the projective vigor of the romantics,[58] but with a mortifying gaze that brings the temporal movements of cinema and ruins to a halt. This ruin aesthetic engages the viewer in the space and time of a melancholic mise-en-scène that suspends historicity. This is the spectatorial appeal of a cinematic ruin aesthetic, an aesthetic that takes the viewer on what Kracauer calls the "historian's journey"[59] through the cinematic device of the traveling shot. We can find this appeal literalized in the angelic point of view in Wim Wenders's *Der Himmel über Berlin*, where the contemplative stance outside of history is ultimately equated with melancholic paralysis in the face of historical ruination. The breathtaking opening of Godfrey Reggio's *Naqoyqatsi* (United States, 2002) likewise exudes this melancholic appeal. After a brief shot of Pieter Brueghel the Elder's *Tower of Babel* in ruins, Reggio cuts to a sequence depicting Detroit's abandoned Michigan Central Station in stunning wide-angle shots from a helicopter, which appear to animate the forlorn building even as they maintain a measured melancholic distance. The dominant movement is again horizontal, punctuated by a few tilts that convey the towering height of the building (see figure 12). The flyover of the ruins left by the First Gulf War in Werner Herzog's *Lektionen*

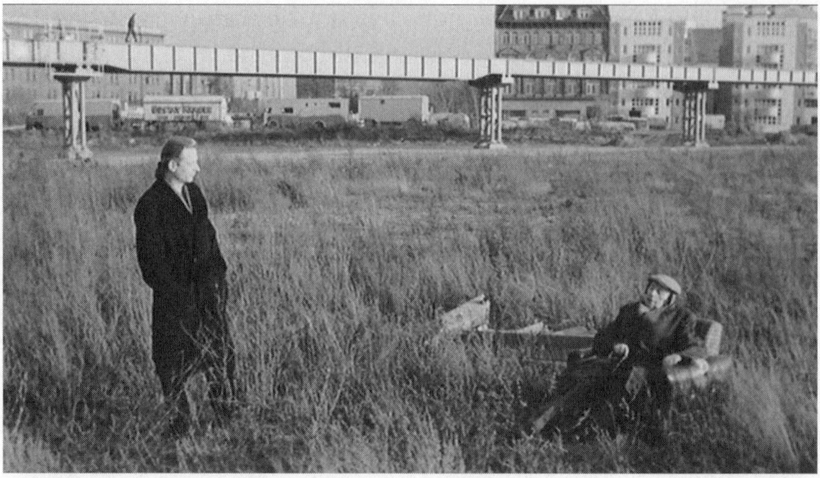

11. Still from *Der Himmel über Berlin* (1987).

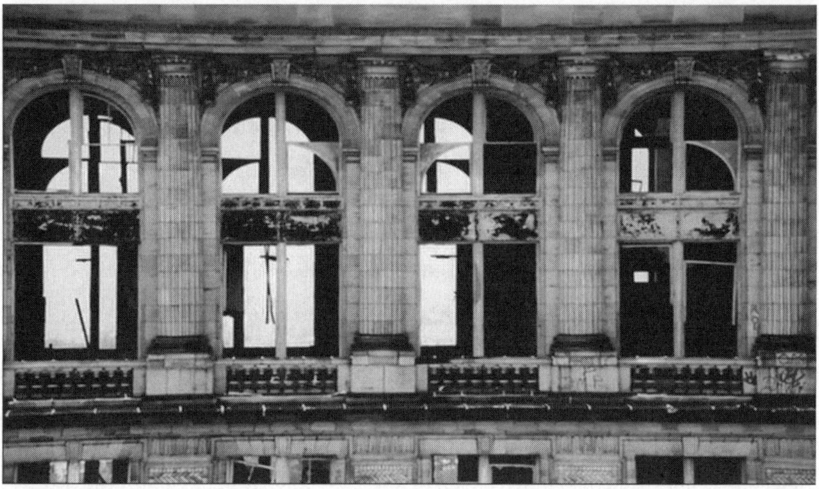

12. Still from *Naqoyqatsi* (2002).

*in Finsternis* (Lessons in Darkness; Germany, 1992) provides a further instance of this melancholic gaze. One of the film's thirteen "chapters" is entitled "Nach der Schlacht" (After the Battle) and offers viewers an extended helicopter flight over the abandoned ruins of the war, from burned-out cars to blasted bunkers and crumpled oil rigs (see figure 13).

Finally, as different commentators have argued, we might consider the work of Andrei Tarkovsky as the locus classicus of the cinema's mortifying gaze at ruins. In the painstakingly long takes of civilization's ruins, Böhme, for one, has discovered Tarkovsky's signature: ruins are "the aesthetic center of his films"[60]

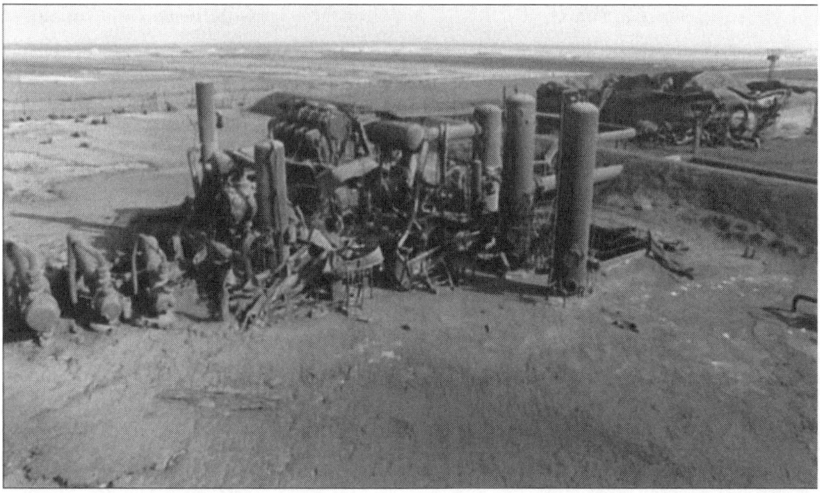

13. Still from *Lektionen in Finsternis* (1992).

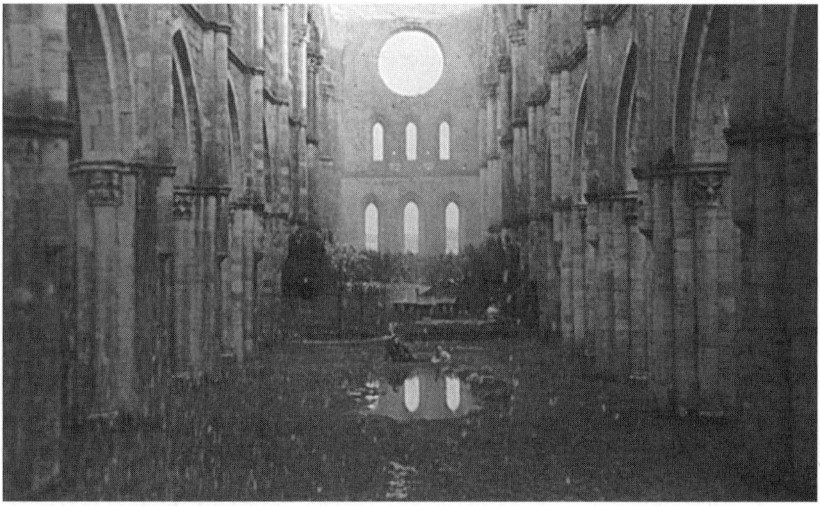

14. Still from *Nostalghia* (1983).

(see figure 14). For Böhme, who argues from the position of critical theory, Tarkovsky's ruins become a sign of melancholia in a productive sense: the melancholic camera's mortifying gaze elaborates a ruin aesthetic that allows the decaying structures to reveal themselves as objects beyond modernity's circuits of exchange, and thus to reveal the underlying laws of history (i.e., the dialectic of enlightenment) that would annihilate any such object. For Böhme, Tarkovsky's use of the long take thus harbors a philosophy of history under the sign of ruin; closely allied with Benjamin's concept of allegory and melancholia,

Tarkovsky's ruin aesthetic turns on a deliberate, melancholic slowing down of progress.

Slow, ostentatious camera movements, long takes, contemplative viewing—the key devices of the cinematic ruin aesthetic that we have been tracing inevitably take us back to Bazin, for whom the long take (along with deep focus) constitutes a dialectical leap forward in the evolution of the language of cinema.[61] But the conceptualization of cinema under the label of ontological realism in the wake of Bazin's influential essays now appears implicated in the philosophies of history generated among the ruins of modernity. If, as Bazin argues, the strategies most suited for the ever more realistic mummification of change resurface in the proliferating attempts to capture ruination on film, we must posit a link between cinema and ruin that extends beyond the conceptual and epistemological and into the realm of the aesthetic itself.

## Notes

1. Gunning, "An Aesthetic of Astonishment."
2. This link between the ruin and cinema finds its way into literature as well, as in a passage in *Slaughterhouse-Five* where Kurt Vonnegut imagines the ruination of (German) cities during the Second World War in reverse. It is difficult to miss the cinematic device of reversing a film, in Vonnegut's ekphrastic description: "American planes, full of holes and wounded men and corpses took off backwards from an airfield in England. Over France, a few German fighter planes flew at them backwards, sucked bullets and shell fragments from some of the planes and crewmen. . . . the formation flew backwards over a German city that was in flames. The bombers opened their bomb bay doors, exerted a miraculous magnetism which shrunk the fires, gathered them into cylindrical steel containers, and lifted the containers into the bellies of the planes" (quoted in Yaeger, Introduction, 9).
3. Doane, *The Emergence of Cinematic Time.*
4. Benjamin, "The Work of Art in the Age of Its Technological Reproducibility," in *Selected Writings*, vol. 3, ed. Howard Eiland and Michael W. Jennings (Cambridge: Belknap, 2002), 104.
5. Other films incorporate the idea of temporal reversibility into their diegesis. See Doane, *The Emergence of Cinematic Time*, 109–39.
6. Benjamin, "The Work of Art in the Age of Its Technological Reproducibility," in *Selected Writings*, vol. 3, ed. Eiland and Jennings, 117.
7. For a useful overview of the debate, see Singer, *Melodrama and Modernity*, 101-30.
8. This is the same viewer whom Jules Romains had discerned in 1911: "The crowd is a being that remembers and imagines," Romains writes, "and while their bodies slumber and their muscles relax and slacken in the depths of their seats, they pursue burglars across the rooftops, cheer the passing of a king from the East, or march into a wide plain with bayonets or bugles." I will return to Romains's prescient analysis of the group dream in the cinema. See Romains, "The Crowd at the Cinematograph," 53.
9. Fritzsche, *Stranded in the Present*, 104.

10. Ibid., 106.
11. Simmel, "The Ruin," 261.
12. Doane, *The Emergence of Cinematic Time*, 108–39.
13. Simmel, "The Ruin," 261–62, emphasis added.
14. Fritzsche, *Stranded in the Present*, 1.
15. Doane, *The Emergence of Cinematic Time*.
16. Philip Rosen, *Change Mummified*, 43–88.
17. Ibid., 143: "Automatically produced indexical images and historiography: these were two regimes of the indexical trace, two masteries of time and pastness, two experiences of knowledge, two kinds of spectacle, both of which achieved contemporaneous and long-lasting cultural success, as well as controversy."
18. This is not simply a question of the oft-noted preponderance of nonfiction subjects in early cinema. See Gaudreault, "The Cinematograph," 95: Even a fiction film is "necessarily compelled to give an account of some sort of reality—that is, the one that appeared in front of the camera—even though it has been disguised in a fiction in order to be recorded. It is indeed by using portions of historical time that cinema builds up fictional time, hence the always-already-given historiographical character of cinematographic time."
19. Kracauer, *History*, 3: "My interest in history . . . actually grew out of the ideas I tried to implement in my *Theory of Film*. In turning to history, I just continued to think along the lines manifest in that book."
20. Ibid., 3–4.
21. Ibid., 45 and 58.
22. Ibid., 4.
23. Quoted in Miriam Hansen, "With Skin and Hair," 438–69.
24. Kracauer, *History*, 79.
25. For Kracauer's discussion of historiographical temporality, see ibid., 139–63.
26. Ibid., 79.
27. Hell, "The Angel's Enigmatic Eyes."
28. Bazin, "The Ontology of the Photographic Image," in *What Is Cinema?*, 15.
29. Philip Rosen, *Change Mummified*, 136.
30. Bazin, "Ontology of the Photographic Image," in *What Is Cinema?*, 15.
31. Kracauer, "Photography," 50. It is important to note that despite the obvious continuities of topics and motifs in Kracauer's writings, his positions on these issues—including the valence of historicism, photography, and realism—undergo significant reversals. On those reversals, see Hansen, Introduction, in Kracauer, *Theory of Film*, and Mülder-Bach, "History as Autobiography."
32. Barthes, *Camera Lucida*, 77: Barthes considers this the *noeme* of photography, whose "founding order" is reference. The fact that "every photograph is somehow co-natural with its referent" constitutes for Barthes "something like an essence of the Photograph."
33. Kracauer, *Theory of Film*, 60–73; Bazin, "Ontology of the Photographic Image," in *What Is Cinema?*, 15.
34. Doane, *The Emergence of Cinematic Time*, 16.
35. Philip Rosen, *Change Mummified*, 115.
36. Assmann, Gomille, Rippl, Einleitung, *Geschichtsvergessenheit*, 7–14.

37. Merewether, "Traces of Loss," 25.
38. Kracauer, "Photography."
39. Assmann, Gomille, Rippl, Einleitung, *Geschichtsvergessenheit*, 10.
40. See Kerstin Barndt's explorations of industrial ruins in this volume.
41. Simmel, "The Ruin," 266.
42. Romains, "The Crowd at the Cinematograph," 53.
43. Kracauer, *Theory of Film*, 158: "Film records physical reality for its own sake. Struck by the reality character of the resultant images, the spectator cannot help reacting to them as he would to the material aspects of nature in the raw which these photographic images reproduce."
44. Baudry, "The Apparatus," 315.
45. Most thoroughly theorized by psychoanalytic critics such as Christian Metz, the topos of film spectator as dreamer is, of course, a larger one in the history of film theory than my examples in the text can suggest. Whether or not we subscribe to the psychoanalytic theorizations of the spectatorial subject, there is compelling self-evidence to this observation, evinced by Barthes's disarming question: "How many spectators slip into their seats as they slip into bed, coat and feet on the seat in front of them?" (Barthes, "Upon Leaving the Movie Theatre," 2).
46. In their introduction to a volume of essays on "ruin images," Assmann, Gomille, and Rippl usefully emphasize this incommensurability of competing historical takes on the ruin. Given that ruins have historically been read as "signs of time *and* of timelessness, of breaks *and* of continuities, of progress *and* of nostalgia," they cannot be integrated into a single system of thought or even grasped through categorization with any degree of conclusiveness. On the other hand, it is precisely this "semantic restlessness" of the ruin that makes it such a productive figure on the cusp between aesthetics and history. See Assmann, Gomille, Rippl, Einleitung, *Geschichtsvergessenheit*, 11.
47. The title *The Last Days of Pompeii* was first used for a film in 1897; that was followed by Arturo Ambrosio's 1908 film, Mario Caserini's 1913 adaptation of the novel, the first Hollywood adaptation by Ernest Schoedsack and Merian Cooper (the makers of *King Kong* in 1935), and further adaptations of the novel in France and the United States.
48. That is not to say that the cinematic representation of modern ruins is devoid of romantic or nostalgic overtones; see Eric Rentschler's chapter in this volume.
49. For a comprehensive account of the rubble film, see Shandley, *Rubble Films*.
50. Hell, "The Angel's Enigmatic Eyes." For a related discussion of Orphic space and vision in a different context, see also Hell and von Moltke, "Unification Effects."
51. Bazin, "On *Why We Fight*," 189.
52. For some of the historical circumstances of the film, see Willett, *The Americanization of Germany, 1945–1949*.
53. Sontag, "The Imagination of Disaster," 213.
54. Quotation, as well as the gloss of ruin aesthetics in the *Trümmerfilm*, comes from Eric Rentschler's sustained analysis in his chapter in this volume.
55. This aesthetic trope is reversed where the camera captures the production of ruins or rubble, as in demolition footage: "an active site of demolition is usually captured by a stationary camera. By contrast, the ruins of a leveled structure are often depicted through the use of a tracking shot. . . . From an aesthetic standpoint, the basic rule of

thumb seems to read: if a compositional subject that rarely shifts is moving, the filmmaker should capture this movement in an unprocessed manner (static camera, tight focus, even exposure). If a compositional subject that rarely shifts is static, . . . it must be accompanied by some sort of aesthetic comment such as a tracking shot or rack focus." Doug Nicholas, "The Aesthetics of Ruin: A Visual Study on the Treatment of Leveling in Film" (senior honors thesis, Department of Screen Arts and Cultures, University of Michigan, 2007), 4.

56. See von Moltke, *No Place Like Home*, 73–78.
57. Simmel, "The Ruin," 259: "Every ruin [is] an object infused with our nostalgia."
58. See Fritzsche, *Stranded in the Present.*
59. Kracauer, *History*, 80–103.
60. Böhme, "Ruinen–Landschaften," 343.
61. Bazin, "The Evolution of the Language of Cinema," in *What Is Cinema?*, 23–40.

ERIC RENTSCHLER

# 23

## THE PLACE OF RUBBLE IN THE *TRÜMMERFILM*

Shots of devastated German cities provide stirring vistas in postwar rubble films (*Trümmerfilme*). As low-angle compositions frame monuments of destruction against the vastness of cloudy skies, the shattered expanses of a depopulated metropolis assume the countenance of natural landscapes. At times the jagged shards of broken buildings bear an uncanny resemblance to the craggy contours of Alpine peaks. It is therefore surprising that discussion of these often studied works has rarely granted their most conspicuous shapes and spaces sustained or close attention.[1] In fact, rubble plays a prominent role in the rubble film. The *Trümmerfilm*—particularly the seminal exercise in this vein, Wolfgang Staudte's *Die Mörder sind unter uns* (The Murderers Are Among Us, 1946)—also figures in a much larger history of rubble representation.

The postwar rubble in Berlin had a different appearance than that in Frankfurt, Hamburg, or Dresden. Modern Berlin, notes Wolfgang Schivelbusch, was less a conventional city than a city machine in which advanced technology did not simply work over old structures, but rather constituted the urban space's prime substance. Unlike other German cities, Berlin was in large part a product of the nineteenth and twentieth centuries, and for that reason steel skeletons undergirded much of its architecture. The capital's buildings (even its conventional edifices from the baroque to the Wilhelminian eras) were so massive that they withstood bombing during the Second World War more readily than those in other cities. The metropolis had been pulverized but not flattened.[2] Decimated Berlin maintained two visages: a vertical one in which towering ruins stretched into the sky, and a horizontal one of vast open fields, the so-called steppes.[3] In *Die Mörder sind unter uns*, it is the former that dominates.

Strictly speaking not a genre, the rubble film is rather a series of feature films produced in Germany between 1946 and 1949 which confront postwar realities. Spanning a number of narrative formulas and employing a variety of styles, Trümmerfilme share a historical situation, a production context, and a political mission. With Germany's film industry out of commission—its studios demolished or seized, and many of its key figures compromised by their Nazi-era activities—the first movies after a year's hiatus (the so-called *Filmpause*) bore the mark of material shortages and artistic uncertainty. Shot largely on location with only restricted amounts of film stock, these films arose under the close control of the Allied occupiers, with different approaches at work in each of the four military zones.[4] Rubble films took stock of a shattered nation and registered a state of physical and psychological ruin.[5]

Exercises in the management of shattered identity, the first German features after the Second World War have an uneven blend of constructive initiatives and critical agendas. They try to envision a better future and work beyond (if not through) the experiences of the Third Reich, a past that, in crucial regards, refused to go away. Their new designs for living responded to the otherwise grim outlooks of demoralized and sometimes homeless people. Regardless of the genre format, Germans usually appear as victims or rescuers, rarely as perpetrators.[6] Guilt belongs to the parties reponsible for the misery of average German citizens and the desperate postwar situation. Although Hitler is referred to on occasion, his name is never expressly mentioned in any of the rubble films. Despite his striking absence, the former leader's legacy is ever present. Exercises in moral rearmament for a population jaded by years of Nazi rule, these tales offer refresher courses in abiding verities and virtues.[7] Above all, Koch argues, the rubble film seeks to foster reconstruction by reinstilling a work ethic and reaffirming the importance of diligence, honesty, punctuality, moderation, and the belief that human beings should recognize and serve a higher power.[8]

Previous commentators as a rule link the Trümmerfilm to various period styles such as expressionism, neorealism, and on occasion film noir, suggesting formal affinities and historical relationships. The influence of expressionism marks a departure from the polish of UFA productions under Nazi rule and a recourse to the venerable legacy of Weimar's "haunted screen"[9] with its lighting effects, animated objects, and eccentric angles, as well as its fixation on the mute world of objects and fascination with city streets. To be sure, one does find stylistic correspondences in selected features from the late Hitler era, exemplars of aesthetic resistance such as Helmut Käutner's *Romanze im Moll* (Romance in a Minor Key, 1943), *Große Freiheit Nr. 7* (Great Freedom No. 7, 1944), and *Unter den Brücken* (Under the Bridges, 1945), and Peter Pewas's *Der verzauberte Tag* (*The Enchanted Day*, 1944), somber mood pieces atypical of the period in which disaffected individuals seek a better life outside of the community.[10] Neorealism would seem to add an international dimension to what we might otherwise think of as the cycle's German *Sonderweg*. There is a common penchant for location shooting (this is also the case for many early films noirs that probe the subterranean reaches and nocturnal haunts of urban spaces) as well as a shared emphasis on the facts of empirical existence and the importance of human solidarity. Both rubble films and neorealist productions reflect the persuasion that a changed world demands new ways of seeing and different means of representation.

Contemporary debates repeatedly contrasted the *Trümmerfilm* with the *Traumfabrik*, pitting a cinema grounded in reality against a cinema of illusion. The designation "rubble film," laments Helmut Käutner, all too quickly became an epithet. This, he elaborated, was the sorry result of unwillingness among German audiences to accept films that probed the aporias of their history.[11] On January 4, 1947, an article appeared in *Der Spiegel* arguing that, with such grim prospects in daily life, depressing images should not also occupy the precious few spaces reserved for German art.[12] Postwar filmgoers eschewed rubble films and instead favored Hollywood features (both reprises and new releases), as well as evergreens from the Nazi era. By 1949 commentators declared that the age of the Trümmerfilm had passed. During the subsequent decade, rubble would all but vanish from the screens of German cinemas.

Even though a host of documentaries made in East Germany right after 1945 had chronicled life amid the rubble,[13] Staudte's film was the first postwar German feature to do so. "Berlin, 1945," reads the opening image. "The city has capitulated." The narrative relates the homecoming of a broken man to a broken city. Hans Mertens, a shell-shocked former soldier, lacks the desire to resume work as a physician and get on with his life. How can a landscape of rubble become a site of Heimat for this depleted *Heimkehrer*? Mertens shares an apartment with Susanne Wallner, who has spent time in a concentration camp but has emerged with a fresh outlook. Unlike Mertens, she seems all but unburdened by her past experiences. In a series of flashbacks, the source of his malaise becomes initially audible and in the end fully visible. He cannot forget the brutal murder of innocent men, women, and children in Poland on Christmas Eve of 1942, an act of violence against which he protested but ultimately witnessed in silence. When he learns that the superior responsible for the massacre, Captain Brückner, is thriving as the prosperous owner of a factory, he reacts with rage and despair. The specter of the past, in the form of traumatic memories and the presence of a murderer, debilitates Mertens and prevents him from finding happiness with Susanne. Only her last-minute intervention will prevent him from taking revenge on his former tormentor.[14]

Staudte's scenario stemmed from a wartime experience. An SS officer had called him a "communist pig" and threatened to kill him. What would happen, Staudte wondered after the war, if he were to meet the man now? Staudte circulated his script[15] among the cultural attachés of the four occupying powers. After rejections from officials in the British and American zones, Staudte finally found support from the Soviets. Even though he was not a communist, his unabashed hatred for the Nazis echoed the Russian antifascist resolve.[16] As a result, the first postwar German film would be made in the Soviet sector and bear the imprimatur of the DEFA studio. It premiered in Berlin on October 15, 1946, fourteen days after the convictions of twenty-two major war criminals in Nuremberg and a week before the resulting twelve executions were to be carried out.[17] Over six million people saw the film; it would go on to be screened in twenty-three countries,[18] which was unusual as most rubble films did not travel abroad and, when they did, they did not travel well.

Many German critics lauded the film as a pathbreaking endeavor; one described it as a work that brought the viewer face to face with "German reality, our reality" and offered a tour "through our clouded psychic landscape."[19] Commentators also praised the film for its return to the legacy of Weimar cinema.[20] Friedel Behn-Grund, the cinematographer, received commendations for his stunning compositions and chiaroscuro lighting touches. Most reviewers granted that the film was a noteworthy effort even if they found reasons to fault it. According to Schnurre, the work was a failure: instead of directly confronting reality, Staudte diverted attention from the true state of things with heavy-handed symbols. Nonetheless, the critic concluded, the film represented a bold start.[21] Subsequent commentators, especially since the 1960s, have faulted the Trümmerfilm for its fuzzy universalism and maudlin self-pity, its response to the question of German guilt with a feeble goodwill and humanistic slogans. The majority of East and West German features from 1946 to 1951, submits Brandlmeier, are more successful in disclosing mental and spiritual residue than they are in probing German history.[22] This is not to say that these films fail to confront the past. A large number of them in fact flash back to the years between 1939 and 1945. (With the exception of Staudte's *Rotation*, however, there is next to no reference to the prewar phase of the Third Reich.)[23] These acts of retrospection are very selective in their terms of remembrance; more often than not, they beg questions of responsibility and pay little attention to the true victims of

German violence.[24] By and large, the rubble film is more concerned with moving forward than with looking back, with reconstructing the nation rather than reconsidering its past.

In crucial regards, the rhetoric of Trümmerfilm criticism anticipates W. G. Sebald's "Air War and Literature," particularly his objection that German authors aestheticized the aftermath of aerial atttacks instead of carefully registering "the true state of material and moral ruin in which the country found itself."[25] The remnants of destruction from the closing years of the war, rather than being fathomed directly and palpably, are filtered through the "half-consciousness or false consciousness" of writers primarily concerned with resuming their careers. Sebald celebrates exceptions to the rule like Hans Erich Nossack and Alexander Kluge, whose work focuses on the cataclysmic results of what he terms "the natural history of destruction." The latter notion is, without question, strangely at odds with Sebald's own call for a dispassionate chronicle of "real conditions."[26] For all his insistence on soberly attending to signs of violence, Sebald's "natural history of destruction" turns away from a national history of violence and fixes on a state of annihilation that appears to be the work of natural forces instead of human agents. This diversion of the gaze resembles what Sebald in another context castigates as "looking and looking away at the same time."[27] Such a shift of focus is, as we shall see, quite common in the rubble film.

One film produced right after the war scrutinized the rubble of Berlin at length and spared the viewer metaphorical contrivances. *Ein Tag im Juli* (A Day in July), a silent, 50-minute documentary made in Kodak color during the summer of 1945, offers a symphony of a bleak city.[28] It was, however, the work of U.S. Signal Corps personnel rather than a German crew. Extended tracking shots capture ground-level panoramas of wasted residential buildings in front of which women clear away debris. A long take traverses the Kurfürstendamm, passing by the shells of former businesses and checking out pedestrians dressed up for an afternoon walk. An American plane soars overhead just as Hitler's aircraft had a decade earlier, in its approach to Nuremberg at the start of *Triumph des Willens* (Triumph of the Will, 1935). The Allied camera claims this landscape for the victors, reworking prominent German documentaries from the Weimar and Nazi eras and in the process updating German history.

The opening minutes of Billy Wilder's *A Foreign Affair* (1948) also mimic Hitler's descent from the clouds to the Nazi Party Congress. We even see a plane, like the Nazi leader's, cast a shadow over the city. The sequence takes stock of German destruction, reviewing a barren landscape while American politicians discuss the alternative futures of the Morgenthau and Marshall Plans. "They

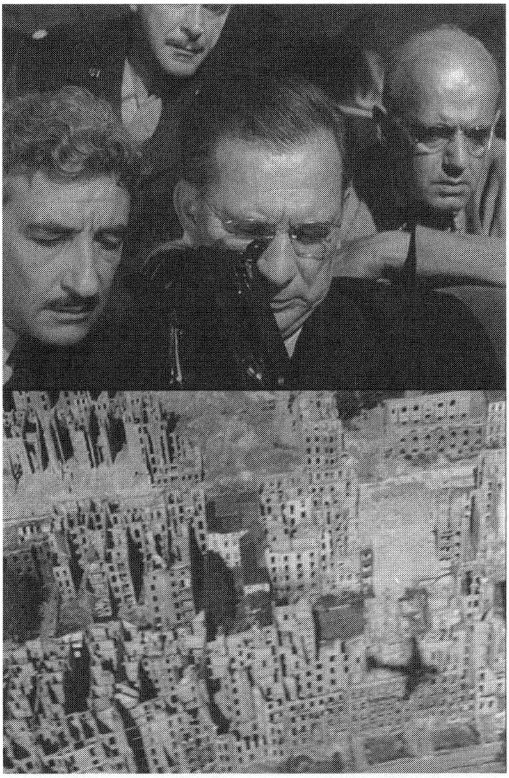

1. Composite image from *A Foreign Affair* (1948). Riefenstahl's film *Triumph of the Will* and Hitler's gaze are replaced by an Allied camera.

ought to scrape it plumb clean, put in some grass, and move in a herd of longhorns," says one congressman. "I say build up their industries and get those smokestacks belching again," responds a colleague. At once looking back and looking ahead, Wilder, an emigrant from Germany and an American occupation officer, self-consciously mimics the celestial prologue of *Triumph des Willens*, replacing Riefenstahl's camera and Hitler's gaze with a regard that is in equal measure awestruck and constructive.[29]

Nazi *Kulturfilme* celebrate architectural grandeur and hail Germany's cities of the future; the era's features very rarely include footage of war ruins. Trümmerfilme frankly exhibit what wartime movies by and large seek to conceal: the amount of destruction caused by Allied aerial attacks. *Die grosse Liebe* (The Great Love) is unusual for a film of 1942 in that it acknowledges nocturnal air raids and shows life in bomb shelters.The protagonists of Käutner's musical, *Wir machen Musik* (We're Making Music, 1942), turn to viewers at the film's end and remind people to darken their windows. In *Die Deggenhardts* (1944), a family from northern Germany closes ranks and stands steady as the war takes its toll on the home front. The final sequence contains elaborate images of destroyed buildings and churches in Lübeck after a particularly severe air raid in March 1942. More typical of the time, however, is Veit Harlan's *Opfergang* (Ride of Sacrifice, 1944), which begins with picturesque views of an intact and picturesque Hamburg, which stood in dramatic contrast to the shattered city in which the film would be screened.

In the final phase of the war, Goebbels commissioned an UFA production on an immense scale, modeled after *Gone With the Wind* (1939) and *Mrs. Miniver* (1942). The only way to mobilize a shell-shocked populace, believed Goebbels at that desperate moment, was to bring people face to face with the harsh facts of reality. *Das Leben geht weiter* (Life Goes On) celebrates the unbroken will of German families despite the horror and devastation of daily air attacks. From the fall of 1944 to the spring of 1945, the director Wolfgang Liebeneiner worked on what was to be a paean for total war. Although no footage remains, the existing storyboards offer vivid tableaux of vast destruction. The closing sequence of the script relates how "from these ruins, life will begin anew." We see burned tram cars, torn electricity cables, collapsed bridges, and a bombed-out train station. People clad in torn and shredded clothing walk down the street wearing goggles and gas masks. In this endeavor the UFA studio technician Gerhard Hottula was sent out to capture location footage of the immense damage. According to the cameraman Günther Anders, Liebeneiner sought to hide the footage of Goebbels's grand rubble film so that after the war it might be transformed into an anti-Nazi production.

Many years later, Alexander Kluge and Peter Schamoni would make *Brutalität in Stein* (Brutality in Stone, 1961), a 12-minute short that contrasts the decayed remnants of Nazi structures in the Nuremberg Zeppelinfeld with the pomposity of Speer's edifices and the giganticism of Hitler's architectural fantasies.[30] The Nazi garbage pile of history provides a testimony in stone: the heroic style, monumental appeal, and large scale of depleted and unfinished structures bear witness to misguided grand illusions. This short documentary recollects shards and reflections of a collective dream, juxtaposing the fragments of today with the immodest designs of Nazi city planners, refashioning historical debris into a deconstructed museum of memories, and concluding with images of building material, rocks, and ruin. These views reveal what is left of the fascist legacy and, in so doing, poignantly enact Adorno's project of dealing with memories of offense and catastrophe by working through them.

Adorno's famous radio lecture of 1959 ("Was bedeutet Aufarbeitung der Vergangenheit?") reflected on Germany's still unresolved relation to the legacy of National Socialism. Have German attempts at public enlightenment, he asked, truly succeeded in addressing a legacy of shame? Or has the insistence on revisiting history been met only with stubborn resistance?[31] The German survivors of the Second World War faced the formidable task of refurbishing themselves and their nation. As agents and symptoms of this reinvention of Germany, the rubble films remain historical artifacts, cinematic counterparts to the postwar era's philosophical "panoramas of cataclysm," particularly the influential interventions of Meinecke and Jaspers.[32] These cinematic scenarios, in keeping with popular sentiment, reaffirm Meinecke's belief that fate had brought upon Germany a great catastrophe. They surely do not support Jaspers's conviction that Germans needed, with all due rigor and integrity, to acknowledge and atone for Nazi misdeeds.

German culture, maintains Meinecke, emerged from the war fundamentally intact, despite "the monstrous experiences which fell to our lot in the twelve years of the Third Reich."[33] The central project of postwar reconstruction would be to revitalize the venerable heritage of *Geist*, to restore culture and religion, to create societies of Goethe venerators that might convey "the most vital evidences of the German spirit" (GC, 120). Meinecke tells how a "frightful catastrophe" (GC, 1) burst upon a noble nation. In Hitler, an "unholy man," "there lay something foreign to us Germans and very difficult to understand" (GC, 58). Precisely because Hitler and the Nazis represented an "extraneous factor in the course of history" (GC, 57), Germany still retained, in spite of what had happened, a sound culture that could not be held responsible for the misdeeds of a small circle of criminals. As in the rubble films, Meinecke's emphasis rests on the German vicissitudes that came in the wake of apocalyptic events. Here, too, we find a contrast between the many who have suffered and the guilty few who have caused the suffering. Indeed, Meinecke distinguishes between the healthy "we" and the murderous "they"—in other words, the murderers are among us.

Speaking from a very different perspective, Jaspers declares that Germans cannot simply banish the shadow of the past.[34] How, though, might a "pariah people" revive itself, particularly if all that Germans now have in common are negative features? How is a gathering of helpless and atomized individuals ever to become a community (QGG, 18)? People in distress, he notes, want to find hope and comfort, not to hear about the past and be burdened with guilt (QGG, 27). In his insistence that all Germans pose the question of their guilt and answer it forthrightly, Jaspers represents a rare voice. During the war virtually everyone suffered losses of family and friends, Jaspers acknowledges, but how one lost them resulted in greatly different inner attitudes. Contrary to the Manichaeism of Meinecke, Jaspers sees substantial distinctions among those who had suffered, depending on the conditions of their suffering. Nonetheless, he posits a community of victims who shared a common situation and faced similar challenges. How is one to remake the world, and on what basis, when everything seems tainted and poisoned (QGG, 114)? There has been a catastrophe (here, too, Jaspers's perspective is fundamentally at odds with that of Meinecke), and for it Germans bear the greatest responsibility. As individuals, he maintains, "we should not be so quick to feel innocent, should not pity ourselves as victims of an evil fate, should not expect to be praised for suffering. We should question ourselves, should pitilessly analyze ourselves: where did I feel wrongly, think wrongly, act wrongly—we should, as far as possible, look for guilt within ourselves, not in things, nor in the others; we should not dodge into distress" (QGG, 114–15).

The Trümmerfilme issue from the same state of emergency that produced Jaspers's call for ethical, moral, and political renewal. Nonetheless, the vast body of rubble films, like their German audiences, ignore Jaspers's proposals. The protagonists of these features do not assume responsibility for the past; instead, they view themselves as objects subject to higher powers. "We can't do anything," says a figure in Rolf Meyer's *Zugvögel* (Migrating Birds, 1947), "things simply happen to us." These films employ a jargon of authenticity that enlists an impersonal destiny as time's driving force and in so doing disavows the subjective factor in history. "I saw a few people," says the voice-over narrator of Käutner's *In jenen Tagen* (In Those Days, 1947). "The times were stronger than they were, but their humanity was stronger than the times." The temporal and geographical indeterminacy of titles—e.g., *Irgendwo in Berlin* (Somewhere in Berlin) and *Zwischen Gestern und Morgen* (Between Yesterday and Tomorrow) —likewise corresponds to the cycle's larger retreat from the disturbing topographies of recent experience.[35] Meinecke's blend of fatalism and existentialism was the preferred response to the catastrophic state of things; Jaspers's call for critical self-reflection and exhaustive soul searching remained most decidedly a minority opinion.

As reflections and symptoms of a spiritual wasteland, rubble films are anything but singular. The tangible presence of ruins dominated postwar urban life in Germany and served as a frequent object of photographers and painters. There was, not surprisingly, a profusion of rubble photography by artists like August Sander, Henry Ries, Max Baur, Richard Peter, and Ewald Gnilka. And these images gave rise to heated debate. Lüdecke's Marxist intervention of 1948, for instance, considers how photography might represent ruins in an appropriate and responsible way. Baur's "Schlossruine in Potsdam" (Palace Ruins in Potsdam), Lüdecke complains, turns heaps of ruins into a romantic vista. Leaves flutter in the wind and clouds billow in Baur's atmospheric panorama of a shattered palace: *memento mori sub specie aeternitatis*. The tableau, anachronistic in its painterly grandeur, transmutes history into a fetish object by concentrating on fragments and not providing a sense of the larger whole—i.e., the Prussian militarism and German war which literally spawned this image. Like the film theorist Béla Balázs, Lüdecke stresses the importance of the *Einstellung*, a word that at once connotes a frame, a mental attitude, and a worldview. The correct Einstellung is the appropriate fix on things; it is in equal measure a formal and a moral disposition. When images of what is yield to metaphorical semblances, we gain art but lose reality. A photographer needs to remain sober and find the proper relationship, both spatially and intellectually, to what is before the camera.[36]

How might one best describe Staudte's Einstellung vis-à-vis the rubble of Berlin? A well-known image from the opening sequence of *Die Mörder sind unter uns* comes to mind, a glimpse at a phantomlike facade framed by a cloudy sky (3:40).[37] This spellbinding take seems to represent what Sebald castigates as "the temptation to make the real horrors of the time disappear through the artifice of abstraction and metaphysical fraudulence."[38] Anyone who transforms the remnants of destruction into an aesthetic reverie lies, argues Lüdecke, because this rubble is a sign of violence that was caused by German aggression: "the consequences of the Second World War are neither idyllic nor romantic."[39] Similarly, Sebald rails against "the construction of aesthetic or pseudo-aesthetic effects from the ruins of an annihilated world." Like Lüdecke, he lauds approaches that are concrete and documentary rather than abstract and imaginary, that provide a sense of "the facts that stare straight at us in the language of those professionally involved in the horror."[40]

A subsequent image of a falling building maintains a compositional symmetry (25:02). The back of the edifice gives way, but the facade remains standing. Swirling dust imparts a *frisson* to the fractured structure, shrouding it in a haze that renders the background barely visible. "No stage decorator," to recall a reproach from Lüdecke's essay, "could have done it more effectively."[41] Staudte's camera, remarks the film critic Werner Fiedler, "creates stirringly beautiful landscapes of ruins." In the process, "incredible painterly effects come into view . . . A wall collapses—hopes fall to pieces. Clouds tower over the ruins—difficult memories darken a countenance. One stumbles, fumbles, and staggers between images and symbols."[42] A contemporary report described how Staudte had combed Berlin trying to discover a location with the most visually arresting ruins. Happening upon a devastated block that made an especially striking impression, he instructed laborers working on a burst water pipe there "not to wreck anything."[43]

Contemporary critics like Friedrich Luft attack Staudte's images for their conspicuous symbolism. The director, maintains Luft, should have spared viewers the metaphors cloaked in shadows and been more concerned with capturing scenes of clarity and verisimilitude.[44] In this regard, it is striking that later commentators have not followed Luft and regarded the film's oft-noted meeting of expressionism and neorealism as a potential conflict of interests, as a formal tension between the desire to probe the secrets of the soul and the wish to picture everyday life amid the ruins. Bazin praises neorealism because it strips away expressionism and eschews montage, granting viewers "a sense of the ambiguity of reality." Although all cinema involves some level of artifice, neorealism, rather than imposing meaning, exercises a formal restraint that allows the world to retain its integrity and richness.[45] All things considered, Staudte's formal approach has little in common with neorealism. What the filmmaker reveals would seem to be more staged than found. Rather than redeeming reality, the rubble film stylizes and transfigures it.

Architectural discourses right after the war, according to Schivelbusch, elaborate how, in a reverse dialectic, the destruction of Berlin might give rise to new configurations that would bring the city and country together: Martin Wagner, for instance, imagines that the former metropolis could become a homeland, a synthesis of city, land, and culture, of modernity and nature.[46] The rubble of Berlin might be understood as a signifier of a vanquished modernity, except we would have to add that the modernity of the former asphalt city was brought down by the modernity of war technology. At first glance, it would appear that Staudte's film, in keeping with the backward movement of the natural history of destruction, retreats from modernity and recasts the ruins of the city machine as an atmospheric spectacle with the sublime grandeur of towering, ice-capped peaks.

Staudte's *Trümmerbilder* contain more than a trace of baroque vanitas in their implied contrast between former greatness and present devastation; there is also something altogether romantic in their evocation of *Stimmung* and the uncanny. They are unquestionably aestheticized, at times downright symbolic or allegorical. This does not mean, as Lüdecke might charge, that they remain incapable of making German history visible. Annie Bourneuf has shown compelling links between Caspar David Friedrich's romantic landscapes and August Sander's postwar photographs of a vanquished Cologne. Consciously echoing Friedrich's *Rückfigur*, Sander often aligns the gaze of the spectator, either overtly or by suggestion, with a vantage point that peers at the city from the top of a fractured edifice. The spatial position of an ethical watcher who looks out over the ruins of war corresponds to the temporal position of a witness or a judge. In their focus on the details of destruction, Sander's cityscapes (like Friedrich's

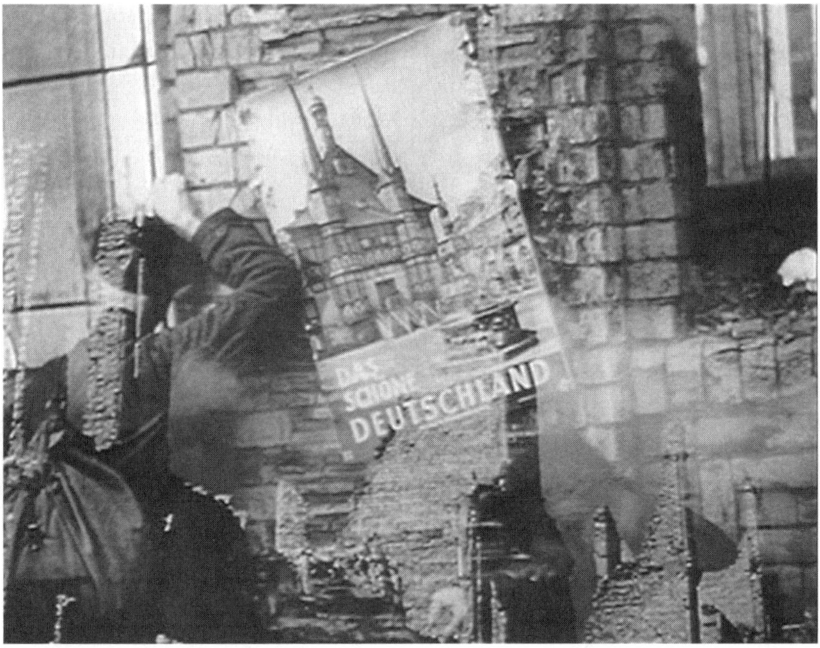


2. Still from *Die Mörder sind unter uns* (1946), a dissolve from a vision of former glory to an image of an altogether different Germany.

landscapes) present themselves as the function of a singular vision. In Bourneuf's estimation, they "draw attention to the seer and lead the viewer to align himself with this seer."[47]

The symmetries in Staudte's view of the shards of buildings described above are anything but arbitrary. They are a function of an aesthetic choice that also determines the placement of the viewer: the director employs composition as well as editing to readjust and complicate how we see what we see. The image in question is preceded by a glimpse of a poster, an element that initially does not stand out in the busy long shot of a crowded waiting room. The camera will, with great emphasis, narrow in on the image and render it the key focus of compositional attention, framing it doubly, between the blasted out windows and human presences that appear on both sides. The two figures, an old refugee and a crippled returned soldier, will recede and allow for an unobstructed view. The poster's vertical composition will finally assume center stage before seguing into a matched dissolve of the rubble ridges. This transition, although visually seamless, is aurally disjunctive. The clang of cymbals provides the sonic equivalent of an exclamation point. The rubble appears like a barren ridge of mountains: unpeopled and atmospheric; both foreground and background, not separated by a middle space; the jagged shards of edifices neatly framed in a medium long shot from a low angle. One shard occupies the center of the composition, and on each side we see three smaller shards, in a symmetry reminiscent of Friedrich's work with its blend of the made and the found.

In gravitating toward the tourist poster of Nuremberg that bears the caption "Das schöne Deutschland," the camera turns the viewer's focus to an artifact of Heimat discourse. As a reminder of the site of the Nazi party rallies and a recollection of shots from *Triumph des Willens*, it becomes an overdetermined ideological signifier. The camera dissolves from a tight view of this idealized vision of former glory to an image of an altogether different Germany, presenting a harsh history lesson and a causal relationship which are underscored by a percussive touch—as if to say that these lies caused these results. That the view of rubble has a distinct beauty of its own does not subtract from its disturbing quality; if anything, the majesty of the image heightens the stark irony of the contrast.

The opening shot of *Die Mörder sind unter uns* presents an askew glimpse at an apparently inebriated Mertens walking down a path between mounds of refuse and mountains of ruins (1:20). In the foreground stands a grave, behind which we see playing children—reminders of the wages of war coexisting with energetic signs of life. The compositional tension anticipates the film's dilemma: how is one to shape a future amid this present and in the face of such a disastrous past? Mertens pauses for a second and turns around before entering *Das moderne Cabaret*, a sanctuary that promises *Tanz Stimmung Humor*, a deferral of present challenges and an escape from past horrors (2:10). The film's point of departure portrays a detour into a locus of alcoholic abandon, sexual indulgence, and honky-tonk music.

Already in the film's initial image, rubble assumes the double guise of a commanding physical presence and an objective correlative for a man who is a virtual wreck. In this regard, rubble functions like the imposing mountains of the *Bergfilm* that, as Balázs points out, possess the distinct physiognomies of "living companions."[48] Rubble, likewise, becomes a character in its own right that is linked to a human drama and the narrative trajectory. A close-up of Mertens accompanies subjective sounds that replay his experiences of war and destruction. As the camera dissolves to an image of rats and ruins (45:34), Mertens's face and eyes spill over into the rubblescape. The camera tilts up from the rodents to an image of the walking ruin, who turns around and staggers drunkenly down the street. In this Trümmerfilm, rubble is more than just metaphoric or symbolic; it is often anthropomorphic.

Painfully dejected, utterly uninvested, unable to love or work, plagued by disgust and nausea, Mertens enters the film as a textbook example of Freudian melancholy. The camera frequently shows him walking through the rubble, a realm of the abject in which he, viewing himself as a pariah, seems far more at ease than in Susanne's flat. At one point the camera tilts up to reveal Mertens's disheveled silhouette and a ravaged building above him, as if the two shapes were parts of a whole (18:56). Mertens is a prodigal son who has come back to Germany, but he has not found a place to call home. "Did I say I felt comfortable here?" he snaps at Susanne. "House, house!" he screams at Mondschein. "Cracks in the walls! Holes in the floor, the windows all boarded up, and the water dripping all the way down to the cellar." He is ruined because his mind is shattered; his traumatic experience in Poland has fundamentally altered his personality. His harrowing past will reappear in a series of flashbacks, memory fragments that the audience, drawing on its own collective experience, is called on to piece together.

The film's initial sequence also shows a second return. Susanne (the role made Hildegard Knef famous) emerges from a train station, a ray of light amid a dark mass of distraught refugees and displaced persons (3:00). Released from a concentration camp, where she has spent the last three years of the war, she makes a beeline for her former residence, her makeup intact and her spirits undaunted. No sooner has she reoccupied her apartment than she goes to work clearing away the debris (22:13). For her the past is not an issue; she is willing and able to leave it behind.[49] From the beginning, her movements and gaze are directed to what is before her. For Mertens, her flatmate, the past is a disease; it afflicts him like a merciless virus. Susanne seeks to comprehend his disaffection by piecing together the fragments of his disturbing memories.[50] She discovers and delivers the letter that reestablishes Mertens's link to Brückner and the wartime act of violence. When she chances on Mertens's journal, she realizes why he seeks revenge against his former superior officer. The facilitator of the memory work that will enable Mertens to confront and overcome the cause of his melancholy, she also intervenes, appealing to his moral conscience. Mertens's shadow briefly merges with that of his former officer, and Mertens too almost becomes a murderer. Interrupting the attempt on Brückner's life, Susanne calls Mertens to order: "We have no right to pass sentence." His shadow recedes (78:55), and, now restored, he agrees with her, adding that "we have the obligation to call the guilty to justice, to demand atonement on behalf of millions of innocent people who were murdered."

The mission of the Trümmerfilme lay in clearing away the rubble, restoring human agency, and creating the conditions for a future community. Toward that end and in a striking recast of the classical myth, Susanne plays a Eurydice who leads her Orpheus away from the realm of the dead and guides him back to the world of the living.[51] In the film's opening sequence, she walks past a shattered statue of a mother and child, untainted and mute witnesses of war's violence (3:53). She will make posters that proclaim "Save the children!" and, like the pietà, is an innocent victim of unseen forces. Unlike Mertens, she will not stand under the sway of rubble again during the course of the film. An angel of history in reverse, she has none of the awe and horror of her counterpart in Benjamin's work because her gaze points in the opposite direction: her aim is to escape a bad history, and in Staudte's narrative, no blast from the past will impede her progress. The eyes of this woman in white focus on the road ahead.[52]

A decidedly uneven and gendered division of labor governs the film's vision of German reconstruction: for the couple (and, by extension, a new civil society) to form itself, the broken man must look back to exorcise the images of horror that haunt and possess him. History becomes a male problem, and woman serves as the midwife who delivers man from its burden. Literally and figuratively a *Trümmerfrau*, Susanne clears away the rubble, both the bombing debris in the flat she shares with Mertens and the residue of the war in her lover's psyche. Mertens's working through the past certainly has little to do with what Jaspers or Adorno had in mind. The film makes visible what he cannot bear to see but needs to see, if he is to restore himself, resume work as a physician, and become a husband. At issue is a German war crime (the thirty-six men, fifty-four women, and thirty-one children shot in Poland on Christmas Eve of 1942), but also Mertens's self-understanding as a noble soldier and a moral being. The deaths that he beholds are not his doing, but the act of violence torments him—particularly the feeling of shame that he was present while crimes were committed in the name of Germany. He is decidedly *not* one of the murderers; the distinction is anticipated in the title and essential to the film's project. Mertens looks back at the past and reckons with the guilty party in order that he might salvage his better self.

The telos of the narrative is for Susanne and Mertens to take leave of the past so that they might occupy a rubble-free future. This hopeful prospect is rehearsed in a night scene where the couple walks through a passage of ruins, the ridges of structures in the background carefully lit in order to provide the most striking impression (35:30). First viewed in long shot, the figures stroll toward the camera. Mertens and Susanne, having progressed to the foreground, look offscreen and up in the direction of the spectator. They step ever closer to the camera, until their bodies finally blot out the rubble and take over the frame (36:30).[53] As the characters extricate themselves from the ruins, Mertens articulates the hope of once again becoming a whole person, capable of love. This

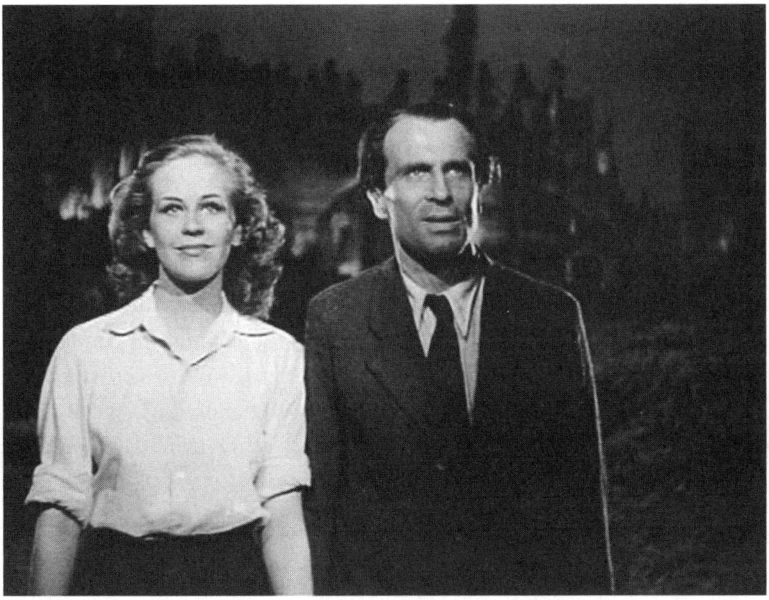

3. Still from *Die Mörder sind unter uns* (1946), leaving the rubble behind and looking toward a more commodious homeland: the manifest destiny of the Trümmerfilm.

dream of restoration, both of living spaces as well as human minds and bodies, is the rubble film's manifest destiny, a fantasy of an intact national corpus that will, of course, find its definitive incarnation in the Heimatfilm.

The vast majority of postwar German feature films, as commentators have often noted, rarely acknowledge the Holocaust. Only a small number of rubble films, in keeping with overarching Allied directives meant to foster cooperation and minimize resentment among an occupied populace, would speak of the Shoah or portray victims of the camps.[54] Staudte's film contains a sequence that, in the context of German productions during the next three decades (particularly in West Germany), stands out as singular and bold. A stark image of silhouetted ruins against a cloudy sky fades to a newspaper headline seen in close-up at the frame's center: "2 Million People Gassed," and below, "Report from a Concentration Camp in Auschwitz" (49:58). The two shots confront the viewer with the inescapable facts of German history (both the site and the report of a crime) and at the same time inscribe the onscreen perspective of a perpetrator who is indifferent to the awful truth. The camera tilts up to a medium frontal close-up of Brückner, who, in a take that lasts a full twenty seconds, eats his lunch with gusto, blissfully oblivious to the newspaper in front of him—which to him, as the composition reveals, is only a wrapper for his sandwich. Brückner does not see the headline, nor does he want to take notice of the rubble. He will later complain about its irritating ugliness, insisting that "the best way to get to know it is to ignore it." Like Mertens, Brückner is a Heimkehrer. But unlike Mertens, he feels at home precisely because neither physical nor psychic ruins have a place in his prosperous new existence.

Brückner embodies the unwillingness to mourn, which is not to say that he has no memories; he fondly recalls "the golden days of freedom in a grey uniform." Owner of a flourishing factory that recycles steel helmets into pots and pans, he anticipates the psychopathology of the economic wonder that never looks back, but instead occupies itself, in the words of the Mitscherlichs, with the "expansion and modernization of our industrial potential, right down to the kitchen utensils."[55] He is, in the double sense of the word, shameless: he feels no shame, and he has no shame. Confronted with his murders, he insists that he is innocent while the camera places him behind bars, and the music indicts him. He is condemned both visually and aurally while Mertens is exonerated. By working through his trauma and relinquishing his desire for revenge, Mertens comes to recognize himself as a victim and to disassociate himself from the perpetrator. For that reason, his final words can assume the moral high ground of a responsible citizen speaking in the name of those who have suffered unjustly. The final procession of victims of the past consists of an old woman and two children, and two wounded German soldiers. There is no indication of Jews or any non-German victims, neither here nor in the closing vista of graves and crosses.

Staudte's film is far less unsettling than *Die Todesmühlen* (Death Mills, 1945), an Allied documentary that put German atrocities on view and that circulated widely during the course of 1946, seeking to impress on people their nation's collective culpability.[56] The work had such a devastating and disturbing effect on German audiences that American officials withdrew it and refrained from further exercises in shock pedagogy. According to Aleida Assmann, these stark images made it impossible for Germans (even if they dismissed the film as Allied propaganda) to disavow or ignore the reality of the camps.[57] *Die Todesmühlen* compiled and publicized incontrovertible evidence of violence and genocide committed under German auspices. Mandatory screenings of the film, Assmann argues, catalyzed a trauma among the nation's citizens—but it was a function of their shame and not their guilt.[58] This trauma was less a response to murders committed by Germans than it was a reaction to the fact that the film had made unspeakable war crimes a matter of public record, and in so doing had exposed and shamed the German nation.[59] *Die Mörder sind unter uns* acknowledges German war crimes, but unlike *Die Todesmühlen*, it denies any collective German culpability for these crimes. Even the Trümmerfilm's most acerbic revisitation of the Nazi experience, which Staudte's film arguably is, seems most noteworthy for the still-resonant way in which it both delimits and reframes the question of German guilt by focusing on the effects of German suffering.

*Die Mörder sind unter uns* resonates differently and strongly in light of Sebald's essay and the recent revival of interest in German wartime and postwar hardship. Seen in this light, the film is hardly dated; it remains, in fact, quite topical. It does not so much describe as reshape and stylize Germany's "state of material and moral ruin" (in Sebald's words) in the hope that it might be overcome. (For that reason, the customary comparison with the verism of neorealism is in a crucial regard misleading.) The first feature film made in postwar Germany beholds the physical destruction of German cities and repeatedly equates it with psychic devastation, suggesting how heavily the past weighed on some, though not all, citizens. Two sorts of ruin become intertwined, the rubble on the streets and the ruin in a returned soldier's mind, material damage and psychic torment, both of which have been caused by outside forces. Rubble, a signifier of destruction, assumes a mythic status within a vanquished nation's fantasy of reconstruction. Myths, as Barthes tells us, may well naturalize. Sebald's "natural history of destruction" is a problematic notion precisely because it revives a long-standing German form of mythical thinking that defers to fate and destiny rather than the power of human agency. It remains, in Huyssen's acute formulation, "closely tied to metaphysics and to the apocalyptic philosophy of history so prominent in the German tradition and recoded in a variety of ways in the postwar period."[60] My endeavor has been to historicize the myths at work in rubble films, especially in their status as cultural productions and compensatory scenarios whose rhetoric continues to exercise an influence on present discussions.

## Notes

1. Exemplifying the tendency of previous discussions, Burghardt argues that most of these films employ images of ruined houses and rubble mountains as a period background that creates the impression of a documentary realism. See Burghardt, "Moralische Wiederaufrüstung im frühen deutschen Nachkriegsfilm," 243. Unless otherwise noted, all translations in this chapter are my own.
2. Schivelbusch, *Vor dem Vorhang*, 15.
3. Ibid., 28–29.
4. Greffrath, *Gesellschaftsbilder der Nachkriegszeit*, 51–137.
5. Of the 47 German features that premiered between 1946 and 1948, 50 percent are set in the shattered streets of a contemporary big city—more often than not, Berlin.
6. Greffrath, *Gesellschaftsbilder der Nachkriegszeit*, 161. Contemporary reviewers generally praised these films for their refusal to point fingers.

7. See Burghardt, "Moralische Wiederaufrüstung im frühen deutschen Nachkriegsfilm."
8. Koch, "Nachkriegsfilme als Werke der Restauration," 6–9.
9. Eisner, *The Haunted Screen*.
10. This is also the case with the French poetic realist classics of the late 1930s and early 1940s, such as Henri-Georges Clouzot's *Le Corbeau* as well as Marcel Carné's *Le Jour se leve*, *Hôtel du Nord*, and *Les Visiteurs du Soir*. See Brandlmeier, "Von Hitler zu Adenauer," 55.
11. Käutner, "Demontage der Traumfabrik," 113–14.
12. "Stimmen aus Parkett und Rang: Man mag keine Ruinen," *Der Spiegel*, January 4, 1947.
13. Prominent DEFA documentaries from 1946 include Kurt Maetzig's *Berlin im Aufbau*, Joop Huisken's *Potsdam baut auf*, Richard Groschopp's *Dresden*, and Kurt Maetzig's and Max Jaap's *Leipziger Messe 1946*.
14. In a crucial regard, Staudte's original scenario was toned down by the cultural attaché of the Soviet sector. The script had ended with Mertens hunting down and killing a war criminal; the revised ending demanded that the guilty be called to justice, but did not allow the hero to fulfill his homicidal desire.
15. An alternative title used in the early screenings of the film is *Der Mann, den ich töten werde* (The Man I'm Going to Kill).
16. Egon Netenjakob, "Ein Leben gegen die Zeit. Versuch über WS," in *Staudte*, ed. Netenjakov, Eva Orbanz, and Hans Helmut Pringler, 24.
17. The October 16, 1946, issue of *Sonntag*, in which a review of the film appeared, featured a lead story about the execution of Nuremberg war criminals. See Mückenberger and Jordan, "*Sie sehen selbst*," 42.
18. Guntram Vogt, *Die Stadt im Kino*, 420.
19. Walter Lennig, "Ein Film der deutschen Wirklichkeit," *Berliner Zeitung*, October 17, 1946.
20. Mückenberger and Jordan, "*Sie sehen selbst*," 44.
21. Wolfdietrich Schnurre, untitled article in *Deutsche Film-Rundschau*, 5 November 1946; reprinted in *Wolfgang Staudte*, ed. Eva Orbanz (West Berlin: Spiess, 1977), 104–5.
22. Brandlmeier, "Von Hitler zu Adenauer," 34. The author, it should be noted, is more favorably disposed toward the cycle than most of his peers, maintaining that several rubble films are small masterpieces.
23. Greffrath, *Gesellschaftsbilder der Nachkriegszeit*, 142.
24. The only films in which victims of the Third Reich assume a central role are *Ehe im Schatten* (Marriage in the Shadows), *Morituri*, *Lang ist der Weg* (Long is the Road), and *Der Ruf* (The Last Illusion).
25. Sebald, "Air War and Literature," in *On the Natural History of Destruction*, 10.
26. Ibid., ix.
27. Ibid., ix.
28. The film is available as an additional feature on the DVD version of Irmgard von zur Mühlen's *Berlin—Ruine 1945—Metropole 2000*.
29. Another notable non-German rubble film by an exiled filmmaker is Fred Zinnemann's *The Search* (1948).
30. Rubble figures strongly in a host of postwar features by noteworthy international di-

rectors such as Akira Kurosawa, Leo Lindtberg, Carol Reed, Alain Resnais, and Andrzej Wajda.

31. Adorno, "What Does Coming to Terms with the Past Mean?"
32. See Rabinbach's *In the Shadow of Catastrophe*, 9. Additional important postwar prospects include Martin Heidegger's "Letter on Humanism" (1947), Erich Fromm's *Man for Himself* (1947), and Max Picard's *Hitler in Our Selves* (1947). There were also numerous literary texts that addressed the burden of German guilt as well as a host of cultural digests such as *Der Aufbau*, *Der Ruf*, and *Die Wandlung*.
33. Meinecke, *The German Catastrophe*, xi. All further references to this work will be cited parenthetically in the text as GC, followed by the page number.
34. Jaspers, *The Question of German Guilt*, 14. All further references to this work will be cited parenthetically in the text as QGG, followed by the page number.
35. Brandlmeier, "Von Hitler zu Adenauer," 33. "The creation of a culture of redemption," Robert Shandley submits, "was the central and perhaps primary work" of the rubble films. See Shandley, *Rubble Films*, 182. See also Elliot Stein's assessment of *Die Mörder sind unter uns* in "Rubble Indemnities," *The Village Voice*, April 10, 2002: "An uneasy mix of shadowy expressionism and doc verisimilitude, this stark film offers little in the way of political analysis, although its moral indignation is somewhat convincing."
36. Lüdecke, "Es kommt auf die Einstellung an," 14. See Balázs, *Schriften zum Film*, 71.
37. The time markings refer to the American DVD of the film, *The Murderers Are among Us*, released in 1999 by Icestorm International and First Run Features.
38. Sebald, "Air War and Literature," in *On the Natural History of Destruction*, 50.
39. Lüdecke, "Es kommt auf die Einstellung an," 12.
40. Sebald, "Air War and Literature," in *On the Natural History of Destruction*, 53 and 60.
41. Lüdecke, "Es kommt auf die Einstellung an," 12.
42. Werner Fiedler, "Der Weg durch die Trümmer," reprinted in Orbanz, ed., *Wolfgang Staudte*, 97.
43. Quoted in Guntram Vogt, *Die Stadt im Kino*, 419.
44. F. L. [Friedrich Luft], "*Die Mörder sind unter uns*," *Die Neue Zeitung*, October 18, 1946.
45. Bazin, "The Evolution of the Language of Cinema," in *What Is Cinema?*, 37.
46. Schivelbusch, *Vor dem Vorhang*, 30.
47. Annie Bourneuf, "The Angel of Photography" (senior honors thesis, Harvard College, 2001), 40.
48. Balázs, "Der Fall Dr. Fanck," *Schriften zum Film*. Eugen Klagemann, Staudte's cinematographer, had in fact produced photographic stills for mountain films of the Weimar and Nazi eras.
49. She says once, "it's so hard to forget," but she never again refers to wartime hardship.
50. Carter, "Sweeping Up the Past," 102.
51. For valuable insights on the pertinence of the Eurydice myth for postwar discourse, see Hell, "The Angel's Enigmatic Eyes."
52. Carter, "Sweeping up the Past," 91.
53. See film script of *Die Mörder sind unter uns* by Fritz and Wolfgang Staudte in the appendix of Peter Pleyer's monograph, *Deutscher Nachkriegsfilm 1946–1948*, 181.
54. Greffrath, *Gesellschaftsbilder der Nachkriegszeit*, 173.

55. Mitscherlich and Mitscherlich, *Die Unfähigkeit zu trauern*, 19.

56. Goergen, "Aufnahmen beglaubigter Kameraleute," 28. See also Chamberlin, "*Todesmühlen*."

57. Assmann and Frevert, *Geschichtsvergessenheit*, 117.

58. Ibid., 122.

59. Ibid., 139.

60. Huyssen, "Rewritings and New Beginnings: W. G. Sebald and the Literature on the Air Raid," in *Present Pasts*, 156.

HELEN PETROVSKY

24

# LOST IN TIME

*Boris Mikhailov and His Study of the Soviet*

In 1928 the pages of *Novyi* LEF (New LEF [Levyi Front Iskusstv or Left Front of the Arts]) included a lively discussion on the theory of photography. At least that is how we would probably describe the matter today. Then, however, the participants found it necessary to establish and affirm a fundamental difference between the painterly isolation or idealization of people and events and the restoration of fact thanks to the camera. The debate featured Alexander Rodchenko, who was rebuffing accusations of plagiarism brought against him by the journal *Sovetskoe foto* (Soviet Photo) and, in response to an open letter by his friend Boris Kushner, explaining the principles of his own photographic aesthetic. This explanation brought a quick response from the editorial board of *Novyi* LEF, which considered the functional approach to be the only one that turned photography into "a means of purposeful action."[1] In the course of this discussion, many insightful thoughts on photography were voiced.

For instance, in Rodchenko's article "How to Photograph," he is not simply against the "summarized portrait," that bad legacy of idealizing and hence subjective painting. He is specifically against the portrait of Lenin produced in this manner (the object of his criticism, though, is mainly hypothetical):

> I assert that Lenin cannot be summed up, and that there is no summary of Lenin that would be the same for everyone . . . But there is a summary of Lenin. That is representation on the basis of photographic documents, books, notes. It should be firmly stated that with the appearance of photographic documents a

single fixed portrait is ruled out. Moreover, a man is never one sum, he is a plurality of sums, sometimes fully at odds with each other . . . So let us not permit art to belie Lenin.[2]

Thus, it is a "big folder" of photographs of Lenin "taken during [his] work and leisure" that necessarily renders futile all attempts to make a painterly representation of him—i.e., to create a subjective and generalized image. Moreover, every single person is not so much a portrait as a multiportrait, first of all a photographic one.

It should be stressed that the folder of photos—together with books, notebooks, shorthand records, and the like—serves as an open archive, delineating in its own right a "truly nonhierarchical collective subjectivity."[3] And seriality, almost by definition, stands for the principle of organization. Indeed, what are these sometimes mutually exclusive "sums" that are the makeup of every human being, and what is the "big folder" consisting of innumerable snapshots—a dossier which challenges the synthetic portrait as both independent and expressly individualistic—if not a representation of the principle of incompleteness and, along with it, interest in the accidental? Such an archive contains gaps. It is extended by elements of series and cannot be invalidated by any ultimate evidence. Its nonhierarchical aspect goes hand in hand with antimonumentality.[4] This, in its turn, has to do with a new mode of storing and transmitting collective memory: its material substrate can no longer be traced to the traditional portrait or monument whose authority depends on removing or suppressing all individual aspects. Instead, the substrate is to be found in the short-lived, albeit totally accessible documentary archive, which the collective memory incessantly augments. Taking Rodchenko's thought to its logical conclusion, such antimonumental propaganda not only corresponds to the image of the new archive keeper, a necessarily collective one, but also allows the keeper to imbue what is kept with emotion: "Lenin cannot be summed up, and . . . there is no summary of Lenin that would be *the same for everyone*" (emphasis added).

Let us recall that Rodchenko fearlessly writes these words while Lenin is being transformed into a new cult object, this time of proletarian origin; while a hardening, crystallizing, or reification of the Russian revolution is taking place, something that Benjamin, who had arrived in Russia a year and a half earlier, clearly saw with his incomprehensive eyes.[5] Rodchenko is writing at a moment of transition which will give rise, aesthetically, to socialist realism, a time that chooses to dispose of photography by rejecting its uncomfortable services. And this can be easily accounted for: the artistic image, a latter-day visual and aesthetic category, contains as much idealization as fact. Moreover, the new fact is conceived to be indissolubly tied to the future, since perception simultaneously embraces both the real (empirical) and the ideal. Photography does not allow for an indispensable projection: it imposes details which in fact (and this is a new understanding of "fact") are no longer viewed separately. In opposition to the LEF theories which championed a restoration of the background—i.e., social movements and relations in the works of art, and the LEF theorists saw photography as a method for representing such formerly disrupted relations[6]—Stalinist culture strictly controlled and signified this background. No surprises were welcome. Stalinist culture is a culture of a totally expanded *studium*, as Barthes would say.[7] It is not a mere return to traditional idealizing painting or the mere fulfillment of a task (LEF theorists enjoyed expatiating upon tasks)—it is a grandiose (anti)utopian project whose implementation goes hand in hand with the emergence of peculiar forms of Soviet mass culture.[8] All painterly masterpieces created at this time—mostly subject to photographic reproduction—are more or less successful replicas of an original which, on account of its being inaccessible (an ideologically pure product could not but be outside the realm of the sensible), is a priori repressed and deferred. Its place will be occupied eventually by new originals, replacing copies in traditional usage—namely, all that anonymous, mediocre art, so tellingly exemplified in the garden sculpture *Maiden Holding an Oar*, depicting a robust female athlete. Let us underline that nothing other than the cliché becomes the true original of socialist realism.

What is at stake, however, is neither influences nor a line of evolution of the kind that an art historian, for example, would like to restore or reestablish. If anything at all is at work here, it is only the principle—a principle which was discussed in theoretical debates as a guideline for the future, and which expressed what had been actually achieved in certain works. What is implied is first of all the multiportrait, seriality, and the open archive, all of which derive from the polyphony of LEF ideologues. Also implied is reportage, which, influenced by leftist art, lasted into the beginning of the 1930s and peculiarly embodied some of Rodchenko's inspired speculations. What we have in mind is one specific series, which immediately gained acclaim. It is A Day in the Life of a Moscow Family, a series of seventy-eight snapshots made by a team of photographers, including Arkady Shaikhet, Max Alpert, Solomon Tules, and their leader and editor, Leonid Mezhericher. But we will return to this later.

The period we are about to turn to is marked by neither tragedy nor heroism. It is the late period of Soviet history, a time of stagnation, reflected and refracted in another series. This time is followed by the time after the end of the Soviet and also, perhaps, of history itself. The photographer who is exploring time is the Ukrainian Boris Mikhailov. Here two things should be kept in mind. First, he is not exploring time as if it were an object: it is not imprinted on things, nor does it form a sequence of chronologically ordered moments. Contemporaneity as retrospection is Mikhailov's vision. He photographs events as if from a time after; contemporaneity is nostalgic of itself. Second, the photographer's identity does not depend on belonging to a certain ethnic group. Indeed, to take pictures so that the present would appear as the past—i.e., in a manner of deferred coparticipation—is something only a Soviet can do. It requires a person whose time is not split into geographical units, a non-national person to be sure. Let us add that today this involves a cosmopolitan dimension: a person who is not only able, but forced, to become ubiquitous.

However, what is the relation of early Soviet experimental, and even filtered Stalinist, photography to all of this? Let us repeat: it is a matter of principles. Or, to be more exact, of that ironic and estranging mode that alone allows us to accept and preserve those principles half a century later. (Strikingly, exactly fifty years separate Mikhailov's series Dance, for which he received the Hasselblad Award in 2000, from the debate in the pages of *Novyi* LEF.) It is in Mikhailov that we will find everything that once had been dreamed of. First of all, in his series openness is underscored not merely by a random number of snapshots—there can be more or less of them, depending on the circumstances—but also by the practice of appropriation, when my archive is supplemented by a stranger's, and the distinction between them is blurred. Of course, appropriation is known as a technique of postmodern art, and for an art historian there is nothing new about it. However, it is worth treating it as something other than a battered device—namely, uncovering that anonymity which provides for actual dynamic equality between artist and viewer: both seem to be incessantly shifting positions and changing viewpoints in the process. Rodchenko's famous vertical—there are two "points of contemporaneity," "from above" and "from below"—gives way to the oscillating horizontal of shooting–perceiving.[9] Let us further note that, again in Mikhailov, the multiportrait is achieved, and quite literally so—only the people posing for the photos, who often adopt postures from the repertoire of painting, are the doomed Kharkov homeless. Finally, Mikhailov is a kind of chronicler of the everyday as well, only his family chronicle—such, in part, is the series *The Unfinished Dissertation* (1984)—is an ironic reversal of the famous photographic narrative of a working family's busy life.

An interesting detail: the Soviet series *A Day in the Life of a Moscow Family* contained a shot depicting a tram ride—everyone is sitting with faces turned to the viewer. Mikhailov, too, shows a tram, and again none of the passengers is standing. But his passengers are showing their backs, and two almost identical photos are accompanied with an inscription: "In the tram. When nothing hurts." Shaikhet was forced to react to an attack on his tram snapshot by ingenuously admitting that the "tram had turned out atypical."[10] No less atypical

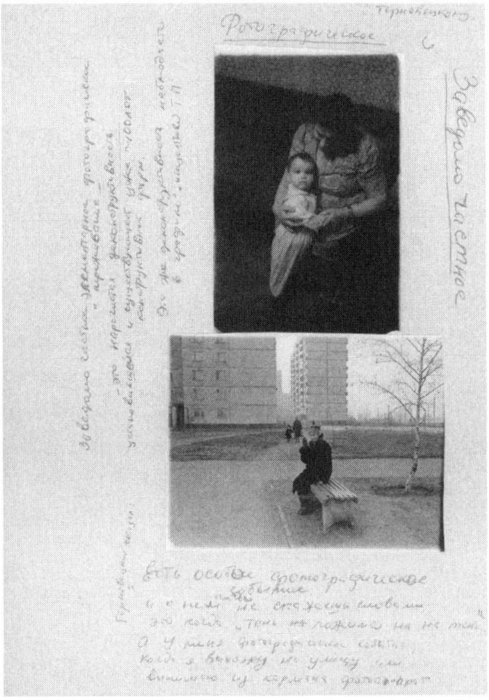


1. Boris Mikhailov, *The Unfinished Dissertation* (1984). All figures reproduced courtesy of the author.

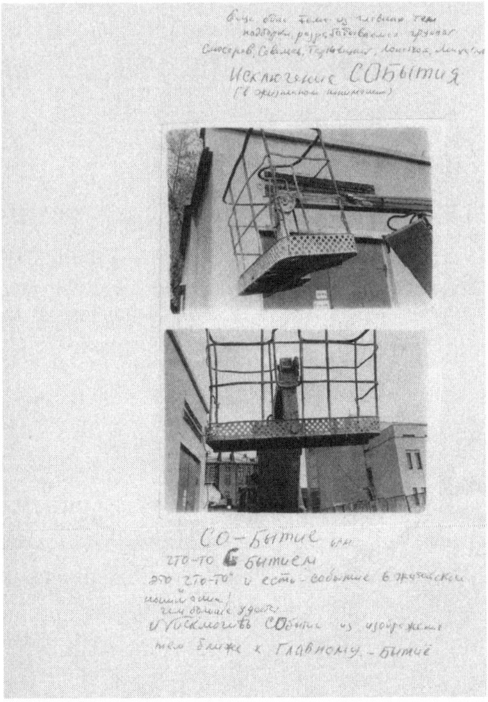

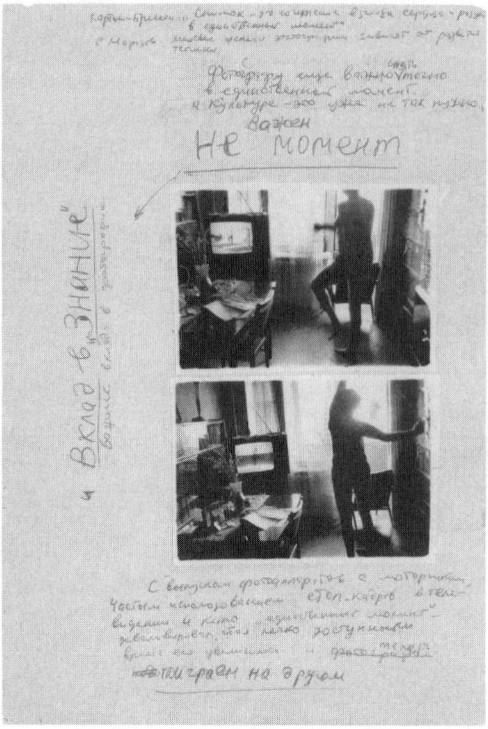

Фотографу еще важно успеть в единственный момент.
в культуре — это уже не так нужно,
важен
Не момент
Вклад в „знание"


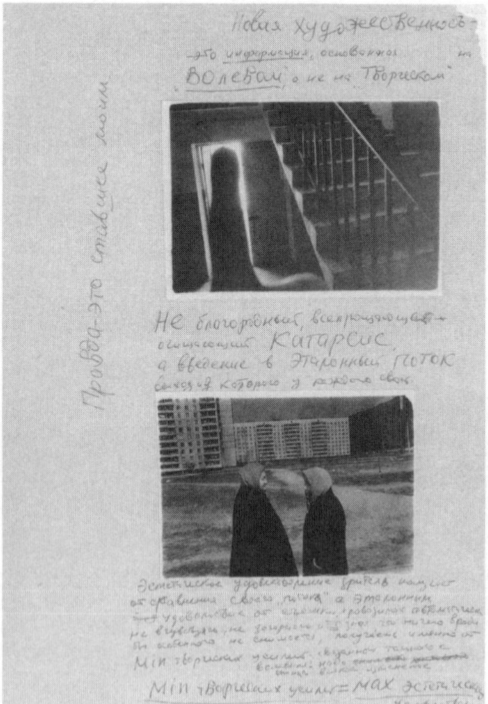

Новая художественность — это информация, основанная на
„волевом", а не на „творческом"
Правда — это ставшее моим
Не благородный, всепрощающий — очищающий катарсис,
а введение в эталонный поток
Min творческих усилий = MAX эстетического удовлетворения

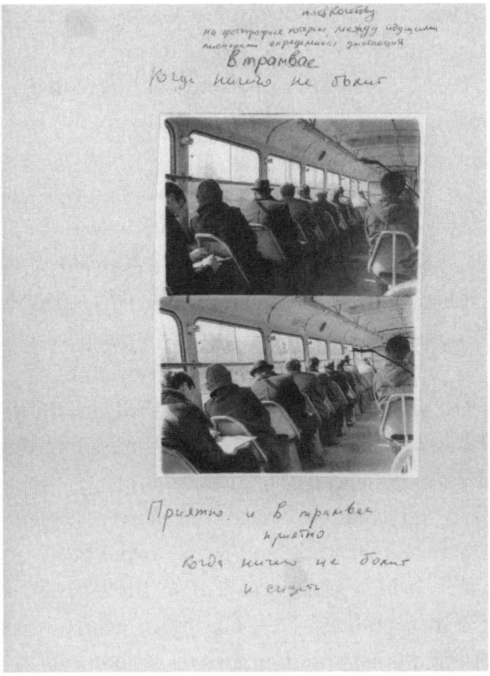


is Mikhailov's late Soviet tram: "It is pleasant. Even in the tram. When nothing hurts. To sit."[11] Let us repeat: the pictures have much in common. But the contrast between them is striking and telling. Intelligent faces are replaced with the anonymity of tired backs, inspired expectations with the complete uneventfulness of the present. Mikhailov's irony has one important feature: it permits estrangement, which makes his position as well as the snapshots—often bleak, faded out, or, in a word, nonartistic—overtly reflexive. This irony comments on and redeems the avant-garde by retracing it in the only possible manner. Moreover, it is intertwined with the artist's self-irony which helps him to identify with his models. Far from being mockery, this is the irony of life itself—a life possibly failed, if placed in a distant historical perspective. It is reality that assumes the role of ultimate commentator here, and it is reality in its maturity and immanent plenitude that Mikhailov presents to the viewer.

To describe the series in words is almost impossible. Such a description would essentially amount to a reconstruction of the scenes, real or enacted, or an enumeration of the elements of fairly unimpressive landscapes. Mikhailov's theatricality, which is often linked to his own appearance in the shots, can be read as both distance and a removal of distance: the photographer belongs to the very world he photographs. Yet, his comprehension of what is taking place has no privilege over the incomprehension of others. And the latter can be easily transformed into its opposite: a war veteran allows someone to inspect his awards with a meaningless meter, and ordinary people pose and perform.[12] This means that the "documentary and conceptual uses of photography are merely different methods or strategies of image making, not necessarily methods in conflict with each other."[13] What Mikhailov seems to do is to raise to the nth power photographic dumbness,[14] the inseparability of picture and visible world—Barthes calls this the stubbornness of the Referent,[15] and we will try to explain why. (Among other things, this leads to the failure of verbalization or, to be more exact, to the limitations inherent in all discursive means. To describe is to assign meaning to what is being described—even the simple contour of meaning, as in the case of the impassive phenomenological first description of phenomena. Mikhailov's snaps, however, are purposely and provocatively meaningless, and the event, whether public or private, is either completely missing from them or is replaced and lowered by accidental comic gesticulation.)

What kind of certitude, stubborn and irreducible, is concealed in these plain, amateurish photos? What makes one return time and again to the beach in Berdyansk, deserted Kharkov courtyards, a seaside swarm in the Crimea, a provincial dance floor, swimmers in a polluted lake, and even the repulsive homeless? What kind of blind spot in all these photographs resists both understanding and a translation into concepts, while powerfully imposing trust in the very image? I would suggest calling this blind spot implied reference. Let me elaborate on the point. First, the term "implied reference" seems to carry an inherent contradiction, for the referent is what is glued to the surface of a photograph, something without which the latter is merely inconceivable.[16] The referent embodies the pointing nature of the photograph; it is the referent's "intractable" presence in the image that immediately triggers a reaction, one expressed in words of recognition: here it is, look, see![17] Thus, to think of the referent, which forms part and parcel of the image, as absent or implied is a problem. There is no way of mending the situation, it seems, even if we give the referent a special reading: one may assume that the photograph shows not so much the referent itself as the rupture which inevitably separates representation from the represented. (Even in Barthes, everything boils down to this: what is the picture it takes him so long to discover, if not a testimony to the fact that photos do not speak the truth or speak only part of it, although their referent seems to be safely in place?) In other words, one can think of the photograph as a structure of deferral—the viewer is given certitude at a spatial and temporal remove. However, in speaking of implied reference, we have something else in mind. On the one hand, we would like to retain Barthes's interest in affect, which is so valuable for our own speculations. It is affect, we recall, that permits him to approach the truth of the photograph, as well as that of the only true image there is for him, the one he purposefully leaves out of his book.[18] On the other hand, Barthes to the contrary, we hope to deindividualize and deprivatize this affect by positing its historical nature. Historical affectivity will necessarily be collective.

Let us take a step further. The implied referent is neither the studium nor punctum. It differs from the former in that there is no strict coding about it—it is impossible to say exactly, to use Barthes's language again, what "rhetoric" the image shall have. There is something in the image that prevents it from being read according to the rules of a dominant culture, or according to the rules of minor or marginal ones. In other words, there is something in the image that remains irresistibly formless, if by form we understand its property of being interpreted. The image seems somehow to oppose "the rational intermediary" of a culture,[19] which also means that it cannot be analyzed exhaustively: it offers mute resistance through what we have earlier named its blind spot—namely, the discursive muteness of representation. However, this is no simple resistance on the part of the visual, no simple trace of a reality organized according to its laws but defying those of language. At the same time, what is in question is clearly not the punctum, no matter how one would choose to read it: a detail that sensitively "pricks me," the photo's power of metonymic expansion, or that intensity which is none other than Time itself.[20] The implied referent differs from the punctum in that it surpasses individual experience, including that of contemplating photographs. It is undoubtedly closer herein to that "reception in a state of distraction" which Benjamin reflects on in terms of a radical, or politicized, aesthetic.[21] We would like to retain two things from Benjamin's notion. First, this mode of perception is posited as collective from the outset (the experience of watching movies is a favorite example). Second, it does not require any effort, because it is born out of peripheral attention, an attention which is, so to say, tangential to its object. These two characteristics should be supplemented by a third: both collectivity and the peripheral nature of perception are brought together (assembled) through affect.

But the following question arises: why are we still speaking of reference? Would it not be easier and more justified to quit this territory altogether, for the referent tends to break the continuity of pictorial representation? And if both the studium and punctum are ways of reading photographs,[22] the referent is a relation between representation and the represented. But it is precisely this point that we would like to preserve in our notion of implied reference. The implied referent is, no doubt, a presence, but a presence of a very special order: it is what the representation contains that makes it visible. It is no secret that many photographs are inert under our gaze—Barthes would place them on the side of the studium.[23] But one can put it more bluntly: the images in question are below the threshold of the studium, for they instantly disappear without having stirred the slightest reaction or interest. In order for something to be seen, it has to be recognized. Recognition is the point where gaze and feeling meet, and where representation develops. The implied referent is the presence of what in a representation *makes* it a representation: it is still unclear what the latter is and how it will be read, but the image has already come into existence. Moreover, it has come into existence as a priori collective. In the act of rising to the surface, breaking into the realm of visibility, it unites the many. Leaving nonbeing behind, stepping out of blackness, the image appears as engendered by collective structures of feeling.

In introducing the notion of structures of feeling, as opposed to the fixed categories of a Marxian analysis of consciousness, the British cultural theorist Raymond Williams wrote: "we are also defining a social experience which is still *in process*, often indeed not yet recognized as social but taken to be private, idiosyncratic, and even isolating, but which in analysis . . . has its emergent, connecting, and dominant characteristics, indeed its specific hierarchies." Structures of feeling reflect social experience as it is lived, ideology as it is in the making—in short, a kind of feeling and thinking which is "social and material" but still in an embryonic condition. It is out of this "practical consciousness," out of this "solution" of affectively colored social experiences that worldview and ideology are later precipitated as social semantic formations. The most significant thing is that during a short span of historical time, usually a "period" or "generation," "values" and "meanings" are spontaneously lived and felt without acquiring any fixed or stable forms.[24] Going back to the implied referent, let us underscore that the photograph is brought to life by these very structures of feeling. Semantically incomplete, what it receives is visual certitude: the photograph enters the field of vision by grasping the sensibility of a collective, and in its turn, it is grasped by this sensibility. In other words, for a representation to exist—for it to reach the threshold of perception—there have to be conditions of perception, and these are the collective structures of feeling; but it is equally important that the collective should recognize itself in the photograph. This recognition will be thoroughly unsystematic, since the collective has no semantic means of expressing what it has seen. On the contrary, one might assume that it is the photograph that provides the means for a preliminary articulation of the essence of a generation.

The implied referent, thus, is at the same time inside and outside. It belongs to representation to the extent that one can acknowledge its existence. However, it also springs from an environment or reality which is basically social, yet is unaware of itself. Its distinguishing feature is the affective openness of experience. This is why the viewer's recognition is as immediate and full as it is wordless—no words can express the truth of this period. But this period is already photographed, for instance by Mikhailov. Again, a clarification is called for. Sociality is neither narrative nor theme, not the main topic of a body of work or the subject matter of an individual representation. Sociality is always already present in the image, which allows it to take on shape and be visually irreducible. In this sense Cindy Sherman's *Fairy Tales and Disasters* series, which communicate the affect of a contemporary body but are also made possible thanks to this affect, are no less social than Mikhailov's Soviet photographic epic. But who says his pictures are Soviet? And what does Soviet stand for in this context? The Soviet, one might conclude, is none other than the specific turn of the implied reference in Mikhailov. The artist gives it his own definition, which is not entirely neutral, however. In *Unfinished Dissertation*, he likes to expand on the "gray."[25]

By now it should have become clear what sort of substance is in question, and why we are both capable and incapable of describing what we see in separate photos. Such, in fact, is the major characteristic of photography in the modern world: it keeps taking us outside the limits of representation proper by forcing us to engage in theorizing, even if influential critics tend to think that the time of photography as theoretical object is long over.[26] It is due to the implied referent that we find ourselves at the intersection of two worlds, the visible and the invisible, and are forced to examine them both. And it is the implied referent that performs the translation of the invisible into the visible when the visible still oscillates with currents born of the raw energies of collectivity.

However, this should not be understood as saying that after a time things settle down, and the implied referent expresses a lack (of meaning, substance, semantics, etc.) which is eventually met. In other words, one should not think that only certain photographs can be treated in this fashion: the implied referent is present even in the most clearly propagandistic pictures. That is what constitutes the time of photography, as I see it, a time which simultaneously develops a visual image and is itself embedded in history. To find this referent is not an easy task, but to articulate it is even more of a challenge. And if, for instance, we choose to assert that the implied referent of Soviet photography was the image of the State or simply its monumental dimensions, we will only be indicating the conditions of visibility, conditions that help us to understand what exactly in those pictures strikes us today as documentary.[27] In fact, the documentary nature of this photography is purely fictional. Indeed, we cannot directly see the idea of statehood imposed from above, or the inhuman scale that is its companion. Yet these ideas are present as affective traces, traces of a certain community, which they help to reveal—either the community of photographers, or the real, and incomparably greater, community behind that.

When Benjamin speaks of a moment of "legibility," he means that with the suspension of linear history one gains access to the past, as well as to its unspoken meaning. At the same time, the past and present combine into a so-called constellation, in which the present completes the past by divining itself in it. This is accompanied by a dropping out of historical linearity.[28] The implied referent is precisely a suspension of the continuity of both thought and history, and it is only in this suspension that the forgotten or unclaimed experience of seemingly lost communities may be retrieved.

Mikhailov provides us not only with a bulk of material but with a language of description. I am not speaking of a visual language, but of a purely linguistic prompt. "Everything is gray now"—these words, borrowed from Benjamin, open Mikhailov's *The Unfinished Dissertation*, a project carried out on the reverse side of someone's real uncompleted paper. The series is made up of a group of yellowed sheets, each of which displays two or three snapshots and accompanying marginalia: observations, anecdotes, citations. These texts have no explanatory power—like the pictures themselves, they seem random. Of course, one can single out a recurring motif or a favorite writer. One example is "gray": from a synonym for "banality" ("The dream no longer reveals the blue horizon. Everything is gray now."), it evolves into the definition of artistic method. " 'Gray' as a fundamental concept of an author," notes Mikhailov, who thus equates gray with that "new artistic sensibility" which prescribes "taking pictures in such a way that the photograph, even before it is made, immediately appears somehow—old, somehow—already known, somehow—seen before." Another entry suggests that "the new artistic sensibility" essentially presupposes a "quiet adjustment" to the world. All these are the overtones of the notion "gray."[29] By referring to "gray" and, most importantly, by taking pictures in full accordance with the method described—none of these snapshots is striking; they could all easily pass for amateur productions destined to fade away, or for waste doomed to irrevocable disappearance—Mikhailov turns photography into a means of reflection. Let us linger on this point.

When philosophy begins to paint "its gray in gray"—an outstanding suprematist metaphor of Hegel's philosophy—this means only that one form of reality "has become old" ("it cannot be rejuvenated") and that philosophy, having arrived belatedly ("the Owl of Minerva takes its flight only when the shades of night are gathering"), completes this reality in its own conceptions.[30] One might say that through its work of conception, philosophy reveals the structure of a completed time. This is what photography accomplishes in its own way. Mikhailov's gray, viewed in this perspective, is a crystallizing of time, a time which for him is nonetheless alive, immediate, and actual. "This time will never ever happen for a second time," he remarks with unconcealed bitterness about the passing moment which he intends to capture.[31] The gray in Hegel is an end and also the beginning of the dusky work of philosophic conception. The gray in Mikhailov is a time which passes as if it were completed. Here we may speak of the specificity of gray in its function of implied reference. This unusual time has to do with the experience of the Soviet community. A gaze which sees its own time as mature, completed, and fulfilled belongs to the viewer, not the photographer. It is because this gaze is recognized that Mikhailov's photographs affect the viewer. In order to see time this way, one has to belong to a community; but seen this way, time is the very affect which constitutes it.

However, "gray" has another meaning even more relevant for Mikhailov. In his analysis of the social functions of photography, Bourdieu characterizes photography, not without disdain, as "middle-brow art."[32] Photography, according to Bourdieu, merely reproduces the image that a group has already formed of itself. Its most important role has to do with the social cohesion of the family, a unit of the middle class. Generally speaking, what is at stake here is social identity, the mechanisms of making stereotypical judgments, rather than artistic value, since photography has no aesthetic criteria proper to itself.[33] Thus, photography is a function of the middle class, whose expectations it popularizes and transmits. Its own aesthetic value, if it has any at all, is "midway" between good and bad, sublime and base. If we free Bourdieu's argument from its recurring social snobbery, we can see a more positive interpretation. Indeed, Mikhailov is a champion of the average or mediocre. According to him, the aesthetic principle of old photography is irretrievably lost. And the "unique moment," the quintessence of this principle, gives way to something else, namely the "obviously private . . . photographic experience."[34] But this experience happens to be embodied in the most habitual and banal—it has no aesthetic of its own, unless it is identified, in an oxymoron of sorts, with the aesthetic of the stereotype. (Hence the interpretation of Mikhailov's snapshots as amateurish or trashy.) All previous photography is replaced with the new, which paradoxically appears to be used. Everything has already happened, been encountered or experienced by someone, perhaps even us. Thus the photograph begins by reflecting on recognition: it recognizes us quicker than we manage to recognize ourselves in it.

The gist of gray in its function of implied reference is the *singularity of the commonplace*. The word "commonplace" means truism or cliché, but we can also think of it as a place open to chance encounters and designed for common, or general, use. Mikhailov's common places include courtyards, lakes, beaches, dance floors, and gyms—even demonstrations, as a ritualized form of state power. All these public spaces include the private, combining with it into a palimpsest. We cannot confuse the private with the public, but they are almost inseparable. Public spaces are sanctioned and strictly defined: leisure is just another affair of the state. But within these spaces—standard, recognizable, and melancholy—private life is lived, a life that, like the dreams it has given up, has turned into kitsch (as Mikhailov says, "a dream transforms into kitsch").[35] This private life has a particular late Soviet dimension—something that Mikhailov grasps and depicts in his art. In order to account for the singular nature of the commonplace, let us turn to the remarks made by Sartre in his preface to a novel by Nathalie Sarraute. For Sartre this word is remarkable in that, expressing our most "hackneyed" thoughts, it simultaneously points to "the meeting place of the community." It is the "place" where I find myself together with the others. "The commonplace" belongs equally to everybody and to me alone; "in me, it belongs to everybody, it is the presence of everybody in me." Since in its essence it is "generality," to appropriate it, I have to carry out a certain act, namely "an act through which I shed my particularity in order to adhere to the general," to become "generality." Sartre makes an important clarification: not to be like everybody, but to be the "incarnation" of everybody. "Through this eminently social type of adherence, I identify myself with all the others in the indistinguishableness of the universal."[36]

The same holds true for the commonplaces in Mikhailov, although they are no longer figures of speech but points of spatial intersection. Their "bleakness" forms a kind of external frame: those are signs of the Soviet. With the help of signs, one can more or less accurately identify a time and place. This is how our gaze is attracted to the public Soviet spaces, for publicity is the sphere of organized and permissible collectives. A public place exists to serve a group. However, in these places no one expects to be like everybody, while everybody is the incarnation of each other—and therefore already non-Soviet. The non-Soviet in the Soviet is a necessary distinction which allows us to discontinue the self-identity of the Soviet and open up the space of affect. This affect is on the side of another banality, invisible and inexpressible—the banality of life itself. The private cannot but point to such an opacity, such a positive absence of form. It is in public spaces that social folds pertaining to another collectivity accumulate. They are the spontaneous entities that defy the collective as an ideological stereotype. They are always half-communes and the only real communities. The dance floor fills up with dancers, the beach with people on vacation, the courtyard with tenants from the neighboring apartment buildings, the gym with gymnasts, the street with demonstrators, and so on. Something changes imperceptibly, which is not accounted for by the mere appearance of people in the snapshots. If viewed separately, the people seem to be an extension of the same ideological signs. One can concentrate on how they dress, what actions they are performing, and so forth. But Mikhailov is a serial photographer, which explains the fact that in him the truth gets stuck somewhere in between—at the interstices of pictures and inscriptions, as well as of the snaps themselves. The truth exists only as a trace, or in the form of an act that Sartre refers to: "I shed my particularity in order to adhere to the general."

Photography, as Rodchenko hoped it would, has transformed itself into a real archive, but it is the archive of a failure. Mikhailov's photographs document the unfulfilled dream of collective happiness as well as of a time devoid of events. However, in this very stasis one may discern the contours of another world or meaning. According to Mikhailov, "I see nothing . . . But sometimes it seems to me that I do not see anything but the point [meaning]."[37] This is what is recognized today by the viewers of other generations. Their own time forms a lacuna which the past seeks to fill in, and the past, by uniting itself with the present, reveals the meaning of both. The implied referent is the incessant work of releasing the time of former presences, and there is nothing in it except for this work.

Let us return to Mikhailov's series. I have already stated that the referent in Mikhailov is connected with time, and that the artist grasped late Soviet private life in its specificity. How can we know this? Just like topoi, the different times constitute a palimpsest. They are similarly immobile. The utopian dream is fulfilled in a present that promises no changes whatsoever. The present, in turn, is free of any kind of projection—it is banal and therefore exhausted. The only thing it can still dream of is private life. But these two times correspond to the two types of social cohesion which I have tried to distinguish above. Utopian time is the time of public spaces which ironically show its dilapidation and decline, whereas the present is the time of private living confined to its short span. However, in the limited perspective of the present, things do happen, no matter how insignificant and dull they may appear. This is time raised to the surface: it expands by filling space with itself. Indeed, there is no other time; we are faced with the expanse of the present. This time is not translated into memory; it seems to be attached to the surface of things, and to the visible world as a whole. While Groys, in uncovering the main tendency of Mikhailov's works, speaks of the "eroticism of imperfection,"[38] I suggest a broader take on the problem, for imperfection has nothing to do with a person's inability to live up to an image from a Soviet poster.[39] Imperfection is an immanent feature of the private, if by the private we mean that which avoids all fixed forms, including those that are social. In late Soviet experience this idea acquires a visual dimension: the Soviet rises to the surface as gray; it objectifies that which seems to resist all objectification. Mikhailov's "gray" simultaneously points to the two conditions. It catches the invisible—the energies of the private, always anti-ideological even if they do not break any norm—and yet it witnesses the transition of these energies into the visible or real. Whatever leaves an imprint—in defiance of ideology and of common sense—carries an inevitable element of the grotesque. Photographs uncover those structures of feeling which, from this moment on, unite us and them, by way of the commonplace.

"The contemporary artistic tradition speaks poetically about mediocre and even poor things," Mikhailov observes with relief.[40] To extend his thought, this leads to the revision of heroic concepts: the unique moment is gone, and so is the archive which preserves, legitimizes, and in the end engenders such uniqueness. If anything is preserved at all, it is useless things, things that clumsily hover between being and nonbeing.[41] In this sense the openness of the archive exceeds all expectations: its totally democratic nature leads it to abandon the idea of value. From now on the archive is quite simply trash, a container of what is denied existence in culture. Trash is the scraps of the private, which has itself been redefined: it is no longer conceived of as the opposite of a genius and his works, which is what the archive preserves and legitimizes. (Strictly speaking, it strategically and consistently endows with the status of a work such formless items as diary entries, marginalia, and notes.) The private, let me repeat, does not stand in opposition to anything at all. It is the triumph of social energies as such. Contemporary art becomes its archive, in a rereading but also a fulfillment of the ideas advanced by Rodchenko.

Just as the notion of the archive is transformed—collective memory closes on itself or, more exactly, on the material forms at its disposal—the conditions of taking pictures undergo a transformation: "the most interesting points of contemporaneity" (to recall Rodchenko) are replaced with Mikhailov's "wandering" look. This look is attracted to the random, partial, and absurd. If it happens to discover beauty in a face, gaze, or figure, it also presents the forces at work in beauty and to what extent its appearance, essentially an optical effect, depends on the raw material of sociality. Let me put it this way: beauty is a culturally designated focus of our gaze, something we are used to seeing as a completed form. What we see is the carcass of beauty, even if the latter is presented to us from new angles—for instance, from above or below. Mikhailov teaches us to see the unseen, what remains outside the limits of culturally framed interests but what is in no way ugly. (This is why one has to be very careful in speaking of imperfection.) Mikhailov's implied referent is located in this interstitial space: it is the private before it falls or splits into the private and its other. The private as element, with no ontology attached; the private as forces constituting sociality in the absence of any opposition, including the purely political one. It is on account of his optics that Mikhailov is unable to take sides: he is neither for nor against but is merged with the everyday, which makes him adopt different angles and looks. He speaks of himself as a spy, but he knows that someone or something is always spying on him.[42] It is here, in fact, that the problematic of the Soviet reemerges. The Soviet, the gray, is grasped by none of the looks alone, but is born at their intersection. As I have written elsewhere, it is the "non-photographic in photography."[43]

This optics also accounts for the transformation of the multiportrait whose concept goes back to Rodchenko. In Mikhailov it is not so much a series of faces or figures, centered as representations of the face, as a set of backs, half-profiles, or averted landscapes. It is the world prior to its (self)presentation. Thus, the face is no longer the center or the bearer of beauty or imperfection. On the contrary, it is a random spot in the social landscape, one of the many figurations of the private. Indeed, the face in Mikhailov's photographs is significant only insofar as it is de-faced, as it is shot through and informed by collective affects. This transformation is made possible by seriality, which shifts the focus away from any single image. It is a portrait in the making, if you will, a dismantled genre which resurfaces each time a figural object appears.

A new photography for a new world—such is its outcome and its evolution. One thing is certain: the loss of the idea or dream of Time does not result in a tragic finale. Time without utopia, as well as time without time (indeed, come to think of it, what else is the infamous stagnation?), is not the disappearance of time altogether. Time is still lived, perhaps in forms that are less alienating. It is lived inconspicuously, and the lack of ostentation, which is not the same as wretchedness, of the Soviet time is what elicits nostalgia. This time is gone. A memory of it is missing (what good things can be remembered of it?) or is being formed. But this is not the memory of knowledge or of an official archive. Rather, it is an attempt to regain oneself by remembering things lost, an attempt to understand how it is possible to remember in principle. Mikhailov redeems not so much what has been lost as what has never happened—to us. Yet this emptiness, this blank in memory, contains the untold history of our parents. Hardly recognizing anything in this other generation, we are unable to tear our glances away: we might know no one in these primitive photos, but they depict our sensibility. The Soviet, as we see it today, does not reduce to a dislike of social institutions or habits that appear unrefined. Rather, it is the constitutive power of the invisible community, that which never stops both separating and combining private and public, general and singular, in the conditions of a closed, crystallized social existence. In contrast, the private is the sphere not only of social nondifferentiation but also of affective ties, of that very community which always seems to be in contradiction to society, although remaining its source.[44] These ties have their own patterns, which sometimes become visible. What we fail to grasp in Mikhailov's photos—and yet what makes us return to them again and again, without hoping to penetrate their meaning or their secret—is precisely the blind field of affect. This blind field, or implied referent, calls for the viewer's participation. Instead of one group aloofly examining another, we participate in the birth of a single community, when the present opens onto the past and allows us to finally discern its contours and meaning. According to Benjamin, this is the emergence of a constellation which unites the past and the present, and is impossible without all those who complete it as interested spectators.

**Notes**

1. *Novyi* LEF 2, no. 12, 40–42. See also nos. 6, 42–44; 8, 38–40; 9, 31–39; and 11, 36–37 (reprint edition of *Novyi* LEF, Munich: Wilhelm Fink Verlag, 1970).
2. Rodchenko. "Protiv summirovannogo portreta za momental'nyi snimok," 15. Unless otherwise noted, all the translations in this chapter are my own.
3. Buchloh, "Residual Resemblance," 60.
4. Ibid., 57.
5. Benjamin, *Moscow Diary*.
6. Brik, "Ot kartiny k foto," 32.
7. According to Barthes, "studium" stands for a continuity of cultural meanings. It is the dominant code of a period rendered visible in the photograph: "It is by *studium* that I am interested in so many photographs, whether I receive them as political testimony or enjoy them as good historical scenes: for it is culturally (this connotation is present in *studium*) that I participate in the figures, the faces, the gestures, the settings, the actions." In contrast, the *punctum* "will break (or punctuate) the *studium*," it is "that accident which pricks me (but also bruises me, is poignant to me)." See Barthes, *Camera Lucida*, 26–27.
8. On the specificity of these forms in the Stalinist era, see my "Sotsrealism," 61–65.
9. [Alexander] Rodchenko, "Puti sovremennoi fotografii," *Novyi* LEF 2, no. 9 (1928): 39.
10. Quoted in Stigneev, "Sud'ba fotografa," 43.
11. Mikhailov, *Unfinished Dissertation*, 132.
12. See primarily the series *The Unfinished Dissertation*, but likewise also *Case History*. also known as "Requiem" (1999).
13. Neumaier, "Re-Representing Russia," 29.
14. Rosler, *3 Works*, 82.
15. Barthes, *Camera Lucida*, 6.
16. Ibid., 5–6, 76–77.
17. Ibid., 5.
18. Ibid., 67–71.
19. Ibid., 26.
20. Let us remember that Time in Barthes is linked to the temporal order of the photograph, which turns it into a distinct type of representation. Also, it is placed not only outside but "against" the flow of history. Ibid., 93–99.

21. Benjamin, "The Work of Art in the Age of Mechanical Reproduction," in *Illuminations*, 240.
22. Barthes, *Camera Lucida*, 41 and 42.
23. Ibid., 26, 27, and 40–42.
24. Williams, *Marxism and Literature*, 132, 130–34. I am indebted to Jonathan Flatley for this important reference.
25. Mikhailov, *Unfinished Dissertation*, 6, 104.
26. Krauss, "Reinventing the Medium," 291–96. However, even for Krauss the "withering" of photography is connected with a liberating effect: precisely because photography disappears—both as object of theory in an earlier version and as image-making technology—it is capable of fulfilling its inherent utopian promise and becoming the ground for the invention of a new, multiple medium. Let us not overlook the fact that the "emergence" of this new "medium" is very much the outcome of reflection, a procedure undertaken by critics and artists alike, and applied to nothing other than photography in an outdated, technologically "obsolete" phase. The "obsoleteness" of photography can be compared to seeing it as losing in importance, which, in turn, I have acknowledged elsewhere through the notion of "whatever photograph" (i.e., any, every photo and even none at all). See my *Antifotografiia*, chapter 1.
27. See Brookman, Afterword, 213: "Today we must *reference* the inauthentic nature of the documentary image in order to seek its authenticity" (emphasis added).
28. Benjamin, "Theses on the Philosophy of History," 253–64.
29. Mikhailov, *Unfinished Dissertation*, 104 (translation modified), 102, and 48.
30. Hegel, *Philosophy of Right*, xvi. See our more extended commentary to this pronouncement in my " 'Seroe po seromu.' "
31. Quoted in Sidlin, "Vremia bomzhei," 11.
32. Bourdieu, *Photography*. The English translation of this work's subtitle, *A Middle-brow Art*, increases the disdainful aspect of the original subtitle, *Un art moyen*.
33. Ibid., chapters 1 and 2.
34. Mikhailov, *Unfinished Dissertation*, 46 (translation modified), 22.
35. Mikhailov, *Unfinished Dissertation*, 6.
36. Sartre, Preface, ix.
37. Mikhailov, *Unfinished Dissertation*, 174.
38. Groys, "The Eroticism of Imperfection," 74–77.
39. Ibid., 76. Incidentally, the conventionality of poster characters from the period hardly need mimicry: the ideal image was so stereotyped that ideological advertising can hardly be compared to commercial advertising, in spite of Groys's optimistically pro-Western assertion.
40. Mikhailov, *Unfinished Dissertation*, 74.
41. Groys and Kabakov. *Dialogi*, Dialogue 8, esp. 109.
42. Mikhailov, *Unfinished Dissertation*, 196, 126, and 150.
43. Petrovsky, *Neproiavlennoe*, 111.
44. For a philosophical reading of community, see Nancy, *The Inoperative Community*.

# BIBLIOGRAPHY


Adorno, Theodor W. *Aesthetic Theory*. Translated by Robert Hullot-Kentor. Minneapolis: University of Minnesota Press, 1997. Originally published as *Ästhetische Theorie*, edited by Gretel Adorno and Rolf Tiedemann. Frankfurt: Suhrkamp, 1970.

——. *Beethoven: The Philosophy of Music*. Translated by Edmund Jephcott. Stanford: Stanford University Press, 1998.

——. "Commitment." In *Aesthetics and Politics*, translated and edited by Ronald Taylor, 177–95. London: Verso, 1977.

——. *Negative Dialectics*. Translated by E. B. Ashton. London: Routledge, 1990.

——. "What Does Coming to Terms with the Past Mean?" In *Bitburg in Moral and Political Perspective*, translated by Timothy Bahti and Geoffrey Hartman, 114–29. Bloomington: Indiana University Press, 1986.

Aglietta, Michel. *A Theory of Capitalist Regulation: The U.S. Experience*. London: Verso, 1979.

Alten, Eberhard von, "'Allzu viele haben sie hier begraben . . . ': Die Schutztruppe in Deutsch-Südwestafrika." In *Vom Schutzgebiet bis Namibia 2000*, edited by Klaus A. Hess and Klaus J. Becker, 234–39. Göttingen: Hess, 2002.

Andersen, Troels. *Vladimir Tatlin*. Stockholm: Moderna Museet, 1968.

Andersson, Charles J. *Diaries and Correspondence of Charles John Andersson*. Edited by Brigitte Lau. Vol. 2. Windhoek, Namibia: National Archives, 1987–89.

Andrews, W. Earle. *Detroit Expressway and Transit System*. New York:n.p., 1945.

Appadurai, Arjun. *Modernity at Large: Cultural Dimensions of Globalization*. Minneapolis: University of Minnesota Press, 1996.

Arendt, Hannah. "Franz Kafka: A Re-Evaluation." In *Essays in Understanding 1930–1954*, edited by Jerome Kohn, 69–80. New York: Schocken, 2005.

——. *The Human Condition*. Chicago: University of Chicago Press, 1958.

——. *The Origins of Totalitarianism*. New York: Harcourt, Brace, 1979.

Arguedas, José María. *Deep Rivers*. Translated by Frances Horning Barraclough. Austin: University of Texas Press, 1978.

Arkin, David. "Dom Corbusier." *Arkhitekturnaia gazeta*, January 8, 1935, 3.

Assmann, Aleida, Monika Gomille, and Gabriele Rippl. Einleitung to *Ruinenbilder*, edited by Aleida Assmann, Monika Gomille, and Gabriele Rippl, 7–14. Munich: Wilhelm Fink, 2002.

Assmann, Aleida, and Ute Frevert. *Geschichtsvergessenheit. Geschichtsversessenheit. Vom Umgang mit deutschen Vergangenheiten nach 1945*. Stuttgart: Deutsche Verlags-Anstalt, 1999.

Atarov, Nikolai. *Dvorets sovetov*. Moscow: Moskovskii rabochii, 1940.

Augé, Marc. *Non-Places: Introduction to an Anthropology of Supermodernity*. Translated by John Howe. London: Verso, 1995.

Balázs, Béla. *Schriften zum Film*. Vol. 2, *Der Geist des Films*. Edited by Helmut H. Dietrich and Wolfgang Gersch. Berlin: Henschel, 1984.

Ballard, J. G. *The Atrocity Exhibition*. San Francisco: Re/Search Publications, 1990.

Ballard, Sebastian, and Nick Santcross. *Namibia Handbook*. 2nd ed. Bath, England: Footprint, 1999.

Ballerstedt, Maren, and Konstanze Buchholz. *Es regnet Feuer! Die Magdeburger Schreckensnacht am 16. Januar 1945*. Gudensberg-Gleichen: Wartberg, 2003.

Banham, Reyner. "The History of the Immediate Future." *Journal of the Royal Institute of British Architects* 68, no. 7 (May 1961): 252–60.

Baridon, Michel. "Ruins as a Mental Construct." *Journal of Garden History* 1 (Jan.–Mar. 1985): 84–96.

Barnouw, Dagmar. *Germany 1945: Views of War and Violence*. Bloomington: Indiana University Press, 1996.

Barrell, John. *The Dark Side of Landscape: The Rural Poor in English Painting, 1730–1840*. New York: Cambridge University Press, 1980.

Barthel, Diane. "Nostalgia for America's Village Past: Staged Symbolic Communities." *International Journal of Politics, Culture, and Society* 4, no. 1 (1990): 79–93.

Barthes, Roland. *Camera Lucida: Reflections on Photography*. Translated by Richard Howard. New York: Hill and Wang, 1981.

——. "The Eiffel Tower." In *The Eiffel Tower and Other Mythologies*, translated by Richard Howard, 3–18. New York: Noonday Press / Farrar, Straus and Giroux, 1979.

——. "Upon Leaving the Movie Theatre." In *Apparatus: The Cinematic Apparatus. Selected Writings*, edited by Theresa Hak Kyung Cha, 1–4. New York: Tanam, 1980.

Batey, Mavis. *Alexander Pope: The Poet and the Landscape*. London: Barn Elms, 1999.

Baucom, Ian. "Among the Ruins: Topographies of Postimperial Melancholy." In *Out of Place*, 164–89. Princeton, N.J.: Princeton University Press, 1999.

Baucom, Ian. *Out of Place: Englishness, Empire, and the Locations of Identity*. Princeton, N.J.: Princeton University Press, 1999.

Baudry, Jean-Louis. "The Apparatus: Metapsychological Approaches to the Impression of Reality in the Cinema." In *Film Theory and Criticism: Introductory Readings*, 5th ed., edited by Leo Braudy and Marshall Cohen, 760–77. Oxford: Oxford University Press, 1998.

Bauer, Thomas. *"Seid einig für unsere Stadt": Walter Kolb—Frankfurter Oberbürgermeister, 1946–1956*. Frankfurt: Waldemar Kramer, 1996.

Bauman, Zygmunt. "From Pilgrim to Tourist—or a Short History of Identity." In *Questions of Cultural Identity*, edited by Stuart Hall and Paul Du Gay, 18–36. London: Sage, 1996.

Baumunk, Bodo-Michael, and Gerhard Brunn, eds. *Zentren, Residenzen, Metropolen in der deutschen Geschichte*. Cologne: DuMont, 1989.

Bazin, André. "On *Why We Fight*: History, Documentation, and the Newsreel." In *Bazin at Work*, edited by Bert Cardullo, 187–92. New York: Routledge, 1997.

——. *What Is Cinema?* Vol. 1. Translated by Hugh Gray. Berkeley: University of California Press, 1967.

Becher, Bernd, and Hilla Becher. *Anonyme Skulpturen: Eine Typologie industrieller Bauten*. Düsseldorf: Art Press, 1970.

Becher, Bernd, Hilla Becher, Hans Günther Conrad, and Eberhard G. Neumann. *Zeche*

*Zollern 2: Aufbruch zur modernen Industriearchitektur und Technik*. Munich: Prestel, 1977.

Beck, John. "Reading Room: Erosion and Sedimentation in Sebald's Suffolk." In *W. G. Sebald: A Critical Companion*, edited by J. J. Long and Anne Whitehead, 75–88. Seattle: University of Washington Press, 2004.

Beck, Ulrich, Anthony Giddens, and Scott Lash. *Reflexive Modernization: Politics, Tradition and Aesthetics in the Modern Social Order.* Stanford: Stanford University Press, 1999.

Becker, Klaus, and Jürgen Hecker, eds. *Vom Schutzgebiet bis Namibia, 1884–1984* (From Protectorate to Namibia, 1884–1984). Windhoek, Namibia: Interessengemeinschaft Deutschsprachiger Südwester, 1985.

Bell, Daniel. "The Treaty of Detroit." *Fortune*,July 1950, 53–55.

Bendersky, Joseph W. "Carl Schmitt's Path to Nuremberg: A Sixty-Year Assessment." *Telos*, no. 139 (summer 2007): 6–34.

Benjamin, Walter. "The Artwork in the Age of Its Technological Reproducibility," translated by Edmund Jephcott. In *Selected Writings*, vol. 3, edited by Howard Eiland and Michael W. Jennings, 101–33. Cambridge: Belknap Press of Harvard University Press, 2002.

——. "Erdbeben von Lissabon." In *Gesammelte Schriften*, edited by Rolf Tiedemann and Hermann Schweppenhäuser, vol. 7, 220–26. Frankfurt: Suhrkamp, 1989.

——. "Konvolut N: Erkenntnistheoretisches, Theorie des Fortschritts." In *Das Passagen-Werk*, edited by Rolf Tiedemann, vol. 1, 570–611. Frankfurt: Suhrkamp, 1983.

——. *Moscow Diary*. Translated by Richard Sieburth and edited by Gary Smith. Cambridge: Harvard University Press, 1986.

——. "On the Concept of History." In *Selected Writings*, vol. 4, translated by Harry Zohn and edited by Howard Eiland and Michael W. Jennings, 389–400. Cambridge: Belknap Press of Harvard University Press, 2003.

——. *The Origin of German Tragic Drama*. Translated by John Osborne. London: Verso, 1998.

——. "Paris, the Capital of the Nineteenth Century." In *The Arcades Project*, translated by Howard Eiland and Kevin McLaughlin, edited by Rolf Tiedemann, 3–13. Cambridge: Belknap Press of Harvard University Press, 1999.

——. "Theses on the Philosophy of History." In *Illuminations*, translated by Harry Zohn, 253–64. New York: Schocken, 1968.

——. "The Work of Art in the Age of Mechanical Reproduction." In *Illuminations*, translated by Harry Zohn, 217–51. New York: Schocken, 1968.

Berkhofer, Robert F. *The White Man's Indian: Images of the American Indian from Columbus to the Present.* New York: Knopf, 1978.

Berman, Russell. *Enlightenment or Empire: Colonial Discourse in German Culture.* Lincoln: University of Nebraska Press, 1998.

Bernasconi, Robert. "Hegel at the Court of Ashanti." In *Hegel after Derrida*, edited by Stuart Barnett, 41–63. London: Routledge, 1998.

Berve, Helmut, ed. *Das neue Bild der Antike*. Vol. 1. Leipzig: Koehler und Amelang, 1942.

Bhabha, Homi. *The Location of Culture*. New York: Routledge, 1994.

Bingham, Alfred. *Portrait of an Explorer: Hiram Bingham, Discoverer of Machu Picchu.* Ames: Iowa State University Press, 1989.

Bingham, Hiram. *Machu Picchu: A Citadel of the Incas*. New York: Hacker, 1979.

Bloch, Ernst. *Gesamtausgabe*. Vol. 4, *Erbschaft dieser Zeit*. Frankfurt: Suhrkamp, 1977.

Blumenberg, Hans. *Die Legitimität der Neuzeit*. Frankfurt: Suhrkamp, 1966.

——. *Shipwreck with Spectator: Paradigm of a Metaphor for Existence*. Translated by Steven Rendall. Cambridge: MIT Press, 1997.

Boffrand, Germain. *Book of Architecture. Containing the General Principles of the Art, and the Plans, elevations and sections of some of the edificies built in France and in foreign countries*. Edited by Caroline Van Eck and translated by David Britt. Aldershot, England: Ashgate, 2002.

Böhme, Hartmut. "Ruinen—Landschaften: Zum Verhältnis von Naturgeschichte und Allegorie in den späten Filmen von Andrej Tarkowskij." In *Natur und Subjekt*, 334–79. Frankfurt: Suhrkamp, 1988.

Bohrer, Karl Heinz. *Nach der Natur: über Politik und Ästhetik*. Munich: Hanser, 1988.

Bonnefoy, Yves. *In the Shadow's Light*. Translated by John Naughton. Chicago: University of Chicago Press, 1991.

Bourdieu, Pierre. *Distinction*. Translated by Richard Nice. Cambridge: Harvard University Press, 1984.

——. *Photography: A Middle-brow Art*. Translated by Shaun Whiteside. Stanford: Stanford University Press, 1990.

——. "Some Properties of Fields." In *Sociology in Question*. Translated by Richard Nice. London: Sage, 1993.

Boym, Constantin. *New Russian Design*. New York: Rizzoli, 1992.

Boym, Svetlana. *The Future of Nostalgia*. New York: Basic, 2001.

——. "Kosmos: Remembrances of the Future." In *Kosmos: A Portrait of the Russian Space Age*, by Adam Bartos, 80–99. New York: Princeton Architectural Press, 2001.

——. "Peterburg umer: Da zdravstvuet Peterburg!: Ruiny revoliutsii u Shklovskogo i Mandel'shtama." In *Sankt-Peterburg: Okno v Rossiiu, 1900–1935*, edited by Ewa Berard, 171–82. St. Petersburg: Feniks, 1997.

——. "Politics of Estrangement: Victor Shklovsky and Hannah Arendt." In *Poetics Today* 26, no. 4 (2005): 581–611.

——. *Territories of Terror: Mythologies and Memories of the Gulag in Contemporary Russian-American Art*. Boston: Boston University Art Gallery, 2006.

Boynton, Percy H. *American Poetry*. New York: Charles Scribner's Sons, 1921.

Bozdogan, Sibel. *Modernism and Nation Building: Turkish Architectural Culture in the Early Republic*. Seattle: University of Washington Press, 2001.

Brandlmeier, Thomas. "Von Hitler zu Adenauer: Deutsche Trümmerfilme." In *Zwischen Gestern und Morgen: Westdeutscher Nachkriegsfilm 1945–1962*, edited by Jürgen Berger, Hans-Peter Reichmann, and Rudolf Worschech, 32–59. Frankfurt: Deutsches Filmmuseum, 1989.

Bredekamp, Horst. *The Lure of Antiquity and the Cult of the Machine: The Kunstkammer and the Evolution of Nature, Art and Technology*. Translated by Allison Brown. Princeton, N.J.: Markus Wiener, 1995.

Brik, O. M. "Ot kartiny k foto." *Novyi* LEF 3 (1928): 29–33.

Brookman, Philip. Afterword to *Propaganda and Dreams: Photographing the 1930s in the USSR and the US*, edited by Leah Bendavid-Val. Zurich: : Stemmle, 1999.

Browne, C. A. *The Story of Our National Ballads*. New York: Thomas Crowell, 1919.

Brownell, Morris. *Alexander Pope and the Arts of Georgian England.* Oxford: Clarendon Press, 1978.

——, ed. *Alexander Pope's Villa: Views of Pope's Villa, Grotto and Garden: A Microcosm of English Landscape.* London: Greater London Council, 1980.

Bruwer, J. J. *Prisoner of War Camp Aus, 1915–1919.* Windhoek, Namibia: Namibia Scientific Society, 2003.

Buchloh, Benjamin H. D. "Residual Resemblance: Three Notes on the Ends of Portraiture." In *Face-Off: The Portrait in Recent Art,* by Melissa E. Feldman, 53–69. Philadelphia: University of Pennsylvania Press, 1994.

Buck-Morss, Susan. *The Dialectics of Seeing: Walter Benjamin and the Arcades Project.* Cambridge: MIT Press, 1989.

Bugge, Peter. "Nákaza svìta: Nemoc a epidemie v dílech Karla Čapka z konce třicátáych let." *Česká literatura* 47, no. 3 (1999): 241–58.

Buisseret, David. "Modeling Cities in Early Modern Europe." In *Envisioning the City: Six Studies in Urban Cartography,* edited by David Buisseret, 125–43. Chicago: University of Chicago Press, 1998.

Bunn, David. "Whited Sepulchres: On the Reluctance of Monuments." In *Blank: Architecture, Apartheid and After,* edited by Hilton Judin and Ivan Vladislavic, unpaginated. Rotterdam: Netherlands Architectural Institute, 1998.

Burger, Richard L., and Lucy C. Salazar, eds. *Machu Picchu: Unveiling the Mystery of the Incas.* New Haven, Conn.: Yale University Press, 2004.

Burghardt, Kirsten. "Moralische Wiederaufrüstung im frühen deutschen Nachkriegsfilm." *diskurs film* 8 (1996): 241–76.

Burke, Edmund. *A Philosophical Enquiry into the Origin of Our Ideas of the Sublime and Beautiful.* Edited by J. T. Boulton. London: Routledge, 1958.

——. *A Philosophical Enquiry into the Sublime and Beautiful and Other Pre-Revolutionary Writings.* Edited by David Womersley. Harmondsworth, England: Penguin, 1998.

Burliuk, David. "Utverdenie bodrosti." In *Rzhanoe slovo: revoliutsionnaia khrestomatiia futuristov,* edited by Anatolii Lunacharskii, 21. Petrograd: IMO, 1918.

Burton, Robert. *The Anatomy of Melancholy.* Oxford: Henry Cripps, 1621.

Bussmann, Klaus. "Hilla und Bernd Becher." In *Bernd und Hilla Becher: Festschrift Erasmuspreis 2002,* edited by Susanne Lange. Munich: Schirmer und Mosel 2002.

——. Introduction to *Bernd und Hilla Becher: Typologien.* Munich: Schirmer und Mosel, 1999.

Buzard, James. *The Beaten Track: European Tourism, Literature, and the Ways to Culture, 1800–1918.* Oxford: Clarendon Press of Oxford University Press, 1993.

Čapek, Josef. *Psáno do mrakù 1936–1939.* Prague: Pražská edice, 1993.

Čapek, Karel. *Spisy.* Vol. 16, *Od èlovìka k èlovìku III* (From Person to Person III), edited by Emanuel Macek and Miloš Pohorský. Prague: Československý spisovatel, 1991.

Carter, Erica. "Sweeping Up the Past: Gender and History in the Post-war German 'Rubble Film.'" In *Heroines without Heroes: Reconstructing Female and National Identities in European Cinema, 1945–1951,* edited by Ulrike Sieglohr. London: Cassell, 2000.

Caruth, Cathy, ed. *Trauma: Explorations in Memory.* Baltimore, Md.: Johns Hopkins University Press, 1995.

Casarino, Cesare. *Modernity at Sea: Melville, Marx, Conrad in Crisis*. Minneapolis: University of Minnesota Press, 2002.

Caygill, Howard. *Walter Benjamin: The Colour of Experience*. London: Routledge, 1998.

Černý, Václav. *Křik koruny èeské: Pamìti 1938–1945*. Brno, Czech Republic: Atlantis, 1992.

*Český podzim 1938* (Czech Autumn 1938). Prague: František Borový, 1939.

Chamberlin, Brewster S. "*Todesmühlen*: Ein früher Versuch zur Massen-'Umerziehung' im besetzen Deutschland 1945–1946." *Vierteljahreshefte für Zeitgeschichte* 29, no. 3 (1981): 420–36.

Chanan, Michael, and George Steinmetz. *Detroit: Ruin of a City*. DVD. Bristol: Bristol Docs, 2005.

Cieza de León, Pedro de. *The Incas*. Translated by Harriet de Onís. Norman: University of Oklahoma Press, 1959.

Cioran, E. M. *History and Utopia*. Translated by Richard Howard. Chicago: University of Chicago Press, 1998.

Clark, T. J. *Farewell to an Idea: Episodes from a History of Modernism*. New Haven, Conn.: Yale University Press, 1999.

Cobbett, Richard Stateley. *Memorials of Twickenham: Parochial and Topographical*. London: 1872.

Colomina, Beatriz. "Unbreathed Air 1956." *Grey Room* 15 (spring 2004): 28–59.

Comaroff, Jean, and John Comaroff. *Of Revelation and Revolution: Christianity, Colonialism and Consciousness in South Africa*. Vol. 1. Chicago: University of Chicago Press, 1991.

*Comprendre Oradour: l'intégrale du parcours de mémoire: documentation, iconographie, témoignages*. Oradour-sur-Glane, France: Etablissement public administratif départemental du centre de la mémoire, 2000.

Confino, Alon. *The Nation as a Local Metaphor: Wurttemberg, Imperial Germany, and National Memory, 1871–1918*. Chapel Hill: University of North Carolina Press, 1997.

Conrad, Joseph. *Heart of Darkness*. Edited by Robert Kimbrough. New York: W. W. Norton, 1988.

"A Conversation between Victor Tupitsyn and Ilya Kabakov on Leonid Sokov." In *Leonid Sokov, Installations, Documents, Articles*, 15–16. St. Petersburg: State Russian Museum, 2000.

Coombes, Annie. *History after Apartheid: Visual Culture and Public Memory in a Democratic South Africa*. Duke University Press: Durham, N.C., 2003.

Cosgrove, Denis. *Social Formation and Symbolic Landscape*. London: Croom Helm, 1984.

Criado Boado, Felipe. "Visibilidad e interpretación del registro arqueológico." *Trabajos de Prehistoria* 60 (1993): 39–56.

Criado Boado, Felipe, and Villoch Vázquez, Victoria. "Monumentalizing Landscape: From Present Perception to the Past Meaning of Galician Megalithism (North-West Iberian Peninsula)." *European Journal of Archaeology* 3, no. 2 (2000): 188–216.

Crone, Anna-Lisa. *The Daring of Derzhavin*. Bloomington: Indiana University Press, 2001.

Cross, Anthony. *Anglo-Russica: Aspects of Cultural Relations between Great Britain and Russia in the Eighteenth and Early Nineteenth Centuries*. Oxford: Berg, 1993.

——. *By the Banks of the Thames: Russians in Eighteenth-Century Britain*. Newtonville, Mass.: Oriental Research Partners, 1980.

Culler, Jonathan. *Pursuit of Signs*. New York: Routledge, 2001.

D'Altroy, Terence. *The Incas*. Oxford: Blackwell, 2002.

Daskalakis, Georgia, Charles Waldheim, and Jason Young, eds. *Stalking Detroit*. Barcelona: Actar, 2001.

Dean, Martin R. "Places against Oblivion of the Self." In *Dieter Kienast*, 6–9. Basel: Birkhäuser, 2004.

[Debord, Guy Ernest]. "Géopolitique de l'hibernation." *Internationale Situationiste* 7 (April 1962): 3–10.

de Certeau, Michel. "Walking in the City." In *The Practice of Everyday Life.*, translated by Steven Randall, 91–110. Berkeley: University of California Press, 1988.

——. *The Writing of History*. Translated by Tom Conley. New York: Columbia University Press, 1988.

Dekkers, Midas. *The Way of All Flesh: A Celebration of Decay*. Translated by Sherry Marx-Macdonald. London: Harvill, 2000.

DeLillo, Don. *Falling Man*. New York: Scribner, 2007.

de Maeseneer, Yves. "Horror Angelorum: Terrorist Structures in the Eyes of Walter Benjamin, Hans Urs Von Balthasar's Rilke, and Slavoj Žižek." *Modern Theology* 19, no. 4 (2003): 511–27.

Deppert, Fritz, and Peter Engels. *Feuersturm und Widerstand—Darmstadt 1944*. Darmstadt: Schlapp, 2004.

Derrida, Jacques. *Specters of Marx: The State of the Debt, the Work of Mourning, and the New International*. Translated by Peggy Kamuf. New York: Routledge, 1994.

Derzhavin, Gavrila Romanovich. *Poetic Works: A Bilingual Album*. Translated by Alexander Levitsky and Martha Kitchen from *Zhizn' moia na Zvanke, ili esho inache Kartina Zhizni Zvanskoi*. Providence, R.I.: Brown University Press, 2001.

——. *Sochinenia*. 2nd ed. Edited by Iakov K. Grot. Vol. 3. St. Petersburg: 1866.

——. "To Eugene. Life at Zvanka." In *Poetic Works: A Bilingual Album*. Translated by Alexander Levitsky and Martha Kitchen. Providence: Brown University, 2001.

Detroit City Plan Commission. *The Detroit Master Plan*. Detroit: n.p., 1951.

Dettmar, Werner. "Kassel im Luftkrieg." In *Leben in Ruinen: Kassel 1943–1948 im Gedenkjahr der Stadt Kassel zur Erinnerung an ihre Zerstörung am 22. Oktober 1943*, edited by Christina Coers-Dittmar and Alexander Link, 11–21. Kassel: Jonas, 1993.

Diderot, Denis. *Ästhetische Schriften*. Edited by V. F. Bassenge. Vol. 2. Frankfurt: Europäische Verlagsanstalt, 1968.

——. *Salon of 1767*. Vol. 2 of *Diderot on Art*, edited and translated by John Goodman. New Haven, Conn.: Yale University Press, 1995.

Dierks, Klaus. *//Khauxa!nas*. Windhoek, Namibia: CASS and Longman, 1992.

Dillehay, Tom D., and Jack Rossen. "Plant Food and Its Implications for the Peopling of the New World: A View from South America." In *The First Americans: The Pleistocene Colonization of the New World*, edited by Nina G. Jablonski, 237–53. San Francisco: California Academy of Sciences, 2002.

Disraeli, Benjamin. *Tancred, or, The New Crusade*. Vol. 2. Leipzig: B. Tauchnitz, 1847.

Doane, Mary Ann. *The Emergence of Cinematic Time: Modernity, Contingency, the Archive*. Cambridge: Harvard University Press, 2002.

Dodsley, Robert. "The Cave of Pope: A Prophesy." In *A Complete Edition of the Poets of Great Britain*, edited by Robert Anderson. Vol. 11. London, 1795.

Dokuchaev, Nikolai. "Sovremennaia russkaia arkhitektura i zapadnue paralleli. 1927." In *Mastera sovetskoi arkhitektury ob arkhitekture*, edited by M. G. Barkhin and Iu. S. Iaralov, vol. 2, 197–205. Moscow: Iskusstvo, 1975.

Doron, Gil M. "The Dead Zone and the Architecture of Transgression." *City* 4, no. 2 (2000): 247–63.

Dorrian, Mark, and Gillian Rose. Introduction to *Deterritorialisations: Revisioning Landscapes and Politics*, edited by Mark Dorrian and Gillian Rose. London: Black Dog Publishing, 2003.

Doxiadis, Constantinos A. *Emergence and Growth of an Urban Region: The Developing Urban Detroit Area.* Vol. 3. Detroit: Detroit Edison Co., 1970.

Dubrow, Heather. "Guess Who's Coming to Dinner? Reinterpreting Formalism and the Country House Poem." *Modern Language Quarterly* 61, no. 1 (2000): 59–77.

Edensor, Tim. *Industrial Ruins: Space, Aesthetics and Materiality*. Oxford: Berg, 2005.

Edwards, Catharine, ed. *Roman Presences: Receptions of Rome in European Culture, 1789–1945*. Cambridge: Cambridge University Press, 1999.

——. "Translating Empire? Macaulay's Rome." In *Roman Presences: Receptions of Rome in European Culture, 1789–1945*, edited by Catharine Edwards, 70–87. Cambridge: Cambridge University Press, 1999.

Ehrenburg, Ilya. *E pur se muove*. Berlin: Gelicon, 1922.

Eisenstein, Sergei. "Akrostikh i tsenton." In *Montazh*, edited by N. Kleiman. Moscow: Muzei Kino, 2000.

Eisner, Lotte H. *The Haunted Screen*. Translated by Roger Greaves. Berkeley: University of California Press, 1969.

Eley, Geoff. "German History and the Contradictions of Modernity." In *Society, Culture, and the State in Germany, 1870–1930*, edited by Geoff Eley, 67–103. Ann Arbor: University of Michigan Press, 1996.

El Lissitsky. "Basic Premises, Interrelationships between the Arts, the New City, and Ideological Superstructure." In *Bolshevik Visions*, edited by William G. Rosenberg, vol. 2, 188. Ann Arbor: University of Michigan, 1990.

Elmer, Jonathan, et al., eds. "Trauma and Psychoanalysis." Special issue, *Diacritics* 28, no. 4 (1998).

Emden, Christian J. "Walter Benjamins Ruinen der Geschichte." In *Ruinenbilder*, edited by Aleida Assmann, Monika Gomille, and Gabriele Rippl. Munich: Wilhelm Fink, 2002.

Erickson, Clark. "An Artificial Landscape-scale Fishery in the Bolivian Amazon." *Nature* November 9, 2000, 190–93.

——. "Prehistoric Landscape Management in the Andean Highlands: Raised Field Agriculture and Its Environmental Impact." *Population and Environment* 13, no. 4 (1992): 285–300.

——. "The Social Organization of Prehispanic Raised Field Agriculture in the Lake Titicaca Basin." In *Research in Economic Anthropology: Supplement 7: Economic Aspects of Water Management in the Prehispanic New World*, edited by Vernon Scarborough and Barry Isaac, 369–426. Greenwich, Conn.: JAI Press, 1994.

Eshel, Amir. "Against the Power of Time: The Poetics of Suspension in W. G. Sebald's *Austerlitz*." *New German Critique* 88 (winter 2003): 71–96.

Esslinger, Dieter. "Anpassung und Bewahrung: Deutsche Regierungsschulen in Namibia." In

*Vom Schutzgebiet bis Namibia 2000*, edited by Klaus A. Hess and Klaus J. Becker, 490–504. Göttingen: Hess, 2002.

Evans, K. J. "Alfred O'Donnell: The Nuclear Measure of a Man." In *The First 100: Portraits of the Men and Women Who Shaped Las Vegas*, edited by A. D. Hopkins and K. J. Evans, 180–82. Las Vegas: Huntington Press, 2000.

Fabian, Johannes. *Time and the Other: How Anthropology Makes Its Object*. New York: Columbia University Press, 1983.

Farmer, Sarah Bennett. *Martyred Village: Commemorating the 1944 Massacre at Oradour-sur-Glane*. Berkeley: University of California Press, 1999.

Featherstone, Mark. "Ruin Value." *Journal for Cultural Research* 9, no. 3 (2005): 301–20.

Federal Civil Defense Administration. *Cue for Survival (Operation Cue, A.E.C. Nevada Test Site, May 3, 1955), Report by the Federal Civil Defense Administration*. Washington: Federal Civil Defense Administration, 1956.

Feuer, Kathryn B. *Tolstoy and the Genesis of "War and Peace."* Ithaca, N.Y.: Cornell University Press, 1996.

Filaret (Metropolitan). "Slovo o glase vopiiushchego v pustyne i na vospominanie prisshestvii 1812 goda." In *Sochineniia Filareta, metropolita moskovskogo i kolomenskogo*, vol. 1, 55–65. Moscow: Tip. a. I. Mamontova, 1873.

Flores Ochoa, Jorge A. "Contemporary Significance of Machu Picchu." In *Machu Picchu: Unveiling the Mystery of the Incas*, edited by Richard L. Burger and Lucy C. Salazar, 109–23. New Haven, Conn.: Yale University Press, 2004.

Förster, Larissa. "Zwischen Waterberg und Okakarara: Namibische Erinnerungslandschaften." In *Namibia-Deutschland, eine Geteilte Geschichte: Widerstand, Gewalt, Erinnerung*, edited by Larissa Förster, Dag Henrichsen, and Michael Bollig, 164–79. Cologne: Minerva, 2004.

Foucault, Michel. *Discipline and Punish: The Birth of the Prison*. Translated by Alan Sheridan. New York: Vintage, 1977.

——. "Of Other Spaces." Translated by Jay Miskiewic. *Diacritics* 16 (spring 1986): 22–27.

——. *The Order of Things: An Archaeology of the Human Sciences*. New York: Vintage, 1975.

Fraser, Valerie. *The Architecture of Conquest: Building in the Viceroyalty of Peru, 1535–1635*. Cambridge: Cambridge University Press, 1990.

Frenssen, Gustav. *Peter Moors* Fahrt nach Südwest. Berlin: Grote, 1907.

Freud, Sigmund. "The Ego and the Id." In *The Standard Edition of the Complete Psychological Works of Sigmund Freud*, edited by James Strachey, vol. 19. Oxford: Hogarth Press, 1923.

——. "Fetishism." In *The Standard Edition of the Complete Psychological Works of Sigmund Freud*, edited by James Strachey, vol. 21, 149–57. Oxford: Hogarth Press, 1963.

——. "Mourning and Melancholia." In *The Standard Edition of the Complete Psychological Works of Sigmund Freud*, edited by James Strachey, vol. 14. Oxford: Hogarth Press, 1917.

Friedrich, Jörg. *Der Brand: Deutschland im Bombenkrieg, 1940–1945*. Munich: Propyläen, 2002.

——. *The Fire: The Bombing of Germany, 1940–1945*. Translated by Allison Brown. New York: Columbia University Press, 2006.

Friedrichsmeyer, Sara, Sara Lennox, and Susanne Zantop, eds. *The Imperialist Imagination: German Colonialism and Its Legacy*. Ann Arbor: University of Michigan Press, 1998.

Fritzsche, Peter. *Stranded in the Present: Modern Time and the Melancholy of History*. Cambridge: Harvard University Press, 2004.

Galison, Peter. "War against the Center." *Grey Room* 4 (summer 2001): 6–33.

Gaonkar, Dilip Parameshwar. "On Alternative Modernities." In *Alternative Modernities*, edited by Dilip Parameshwar Gaonkar, 1–23. Durham, N.C.: Duke University Press, 2001.

Gasparini, Graziano, and Luise Margolies. *Inca Architecture*. Translated by Patricia J. Lyon. Bloomington: Indiana University Press, 1980.

Gasparov, Boris Mikhailovich. "Voina s Napoleonom: nashestvie i nizverzhenie Antikhrista (1812–1815)." In *Poeticheskii iazyk Pushkina kak fakt istorii russkogo literaturnogo iazyka*, 82–117. St. Petersburg: Akademicheskii proekt, 1999.

Gaudreault, André. "The Cinematograph: A Historiographical Machine." In *Meanings in Texts and Actions: Questioning Paul Ricoeur*, edited by David E. Klemm and William Schweiker, 90–97. Charlottesville: University Press of Virginia, 1993.

Gebhart, Jan, and Jan Kuklík. *Druhá republika, 1938–1939: Svár demokracie a totality v politickém, spoleèenském a kulturním životì*. Prague: Paseka, 2004.

Gershenzon, Mikhail, and Viacheslav Ivanov. *Perepiska iz dvukh uglov*. Petrograd: Alkonost, 1921.

Gibbon, Edward. *The Decline and Fall of the Roman Empire*. New York: Modern Library, 2005.

Gilbert, Olive. *Narrative of Sojourner Truth*. New York: Arno Press, 1968.

Gilroy, Paul. *The Black Atlantic: Modernity and Double Consciousness*. Cambridge: Harvard University Press, 1993.

——. *Postcolonial Melancholia*. New York: Columbia University Press, 2005.

Ginsberg, Robert. *The Aesthetics of Ruins*. Amsterdam: Rodopi, 2004.

Ginzburg, Lidiia. *Chelovek za pis'mennym stolom*. Leningrad: Sovetskii pisatel, 1989.

Ginzburg, Moisei. "Mezhdunarodnyi front sovremennoi arkhitektury." *Sovremennaia Arkhitektura* 1, no. 2 (1926): 41–46.

Glaser, Gary. *The Hudson's Building*. Detroit: Urban Garlic, 1997.

Goebbels, Joseph. Speech, November 5, 1943 in the Kassel Stadthalle. Quoted after Werner Dettmar, "Kassel im Luftkrieg." In *Leben in Ruinen: Kassel 1943–1948 im Gedenkjahr der Stadt Kassel zur Erinnerung an ihre Zerstörung am 22. Oktober 1943*. Edited by Christina Coers-Dittmar and Alexander Link. Kassel: Jonas Verlag, 1993.

——. *Die Tagebuecher von Joseph Goebbels*. Vol. 15, part 2. Edited by Elke Froehlich. Munich: K. G. Saur, 1995.

Goergen, Jeanpaul. "Aufnahmen beglaubigter Kameraleute." *Filmblatt* 19–20 (summer/fall 2002): 25–31.

Goethe, Johann Wolfgang. *From My Life: Poetry and Truth*. In *Goethe: The Collected Works*, vol. 4, translated by Eithne Wilkins and Ernst Kaiser. Princeton, N.J.: Princeton University Press, 1994.

——. *Italienische Reise*. In *Goethes Werke*, edited by Erich Trunz, vol. 11. Hamburg: Wegner, 1961.

Golburt, Luba. "Derzhavin's Ruins and the Birth of Historical Elegy." *Slavic Review* 65, no. 4 (2006): 670–93.

Goldhagen, Sarah Williams, and Réjean Legault, eds. *Anxious Modernisms: Experimentation in Postwar Architectural Culture*. Cambridge: MIT Press, 2000.

Gordillo, Gastón. "El sedimento de la historia: ruinas y memorias en la conquista del Chaco en la frontera del Rio Salado (Salta)." Paper delivered at the Latin American Studies Association International Congress, Las Vegas, Nevada, October 8, 2004.

Gorriti, Gustavo. *The Shining Path: A History of the Millenarian War in Peru*. Translated by Robin Kirk. Chapel Hill: University of North Carolina Press, 1999.

Gotz, Graeme, and Abdoumaliq Simone. "On Belonging and Becoming in African Cities." In *Emerging Johannesburg: Perspectives on the Postapartheid City*, edited by Richard Tomlinson, Robert Beauregard, Lindsay Beremer, and Xolela Mangcu, 123–47. New York: Routledge, 2003.

Grant, Iain Hamilton. "Kant after Geophilosophy: The Physics of Analogy and the Metaphysics of Nature." In *The Matter of Critique: Readings in Kant's Philosophy*, edited by Andrea Rehberg and Rachel Jones, 37–60. Manchester, England: Clinammen, 2000.

Greenleaf, Monika. *Pushkin and Romantic Fashion: Fragment, Elegy, Orient, Irony.* Stanford: Stanford University Press, 1994.

Greffrath, Bettina. *Gesellschaftsbilder der Nachkriegszeit: Deutsche Spielfilme 1945–1949*. Pfaffenweiler: Centaurus, 1995.

Groys, Boris. "The Eroticism of Imperfection." Translated by Matthew Partridge, in *The Hasselblad Award 2000: Boris Mikhailov, Dance 1978*, 74–77. Göteborg, Sweden: Hasselblad Center, 2000.

——. *The Total Art of Stalinism: Avant-Garde, Aesthetic Dictatorship, and Beyond*. Translated by Charles Rougle. Princeton, N.J.: Princeton University Press, 1992.

Groys, Boris, and Il'ia Kabakov. *Dialogi (1990–1994)*. Edited by Helen Petrovsky. Moscow: Ad Marginem, 1999.

Guaman Poma de Ayala, Felipe. *El primer "Nueva corónica y buen gobierno"* [1615/1616]. Website of Guaman Poma, 2006. A Digital Research Center of the Royal Library, Copenhagen, Denmark. http://www.kb.dk/elib/mss/poma/.

Guha, Ranajit. "On Some Aspects of the Historiography of Colonial India." In *Selected Subaltern Studies*, edited by Ranajit Guha and Gayatri Spivak, 37–44. Oxford: Oxford University Press, 1988.

Gunning, Tom. "An Aesthetic of Astonishment." In *Film Theory and Criticism: Introductory Readings*, 5th ed., edited by Leo Braudy and Marshall Cohen, 862–76. Oxford: Oxford University Press, 1998.

Günther, Horst. *Das Erdbeben von Lissabon erschüttert die Meinungen und setzt das Denken in Bewegung*. Berlin: Wagenbach, 1994.

——. *Das Erdbeben von Lissabon und die Erschütterung des aufgeklärten Europa*. Frankfurt: Fischer, 2005.

Gwynn, John. *The Art of Architecture: A Poem in Imitation of Horace's Art of Poetry.* 1742. Reprint, Los Angeles: Augustan Reprint Society, 1970.

Habermas, Jürgen. *The Philosophical Discourse of Modernity: Twelve Lectures*. Translated by Frederick G. Lawrence. Cambridge: MIT Press, 1987.

Hall, Florence Howe. *The Story of the Battle Hymn of the Republic*. New York: Harper and Brothers, 1916.

Hall, Martin. "The Legend of the Lost City; or, the Man with Golden Balls." *Journal of Southern African Studies* 21 (1995): 179–99.

Halle, Morris. "O nezamechennom akrostikhe Derzhavina." *International Journal of Slavic Linguistics and Poetics* 1 (1958): 232–36.

Hamilton, James. *Turner: A Life*. London: Hodder and Stoughton, 1997.

Hansen, Heinrich. *Der Schlüssel zum Frieden: Führertage in Italien*. Berlin: M. A. Klieber, 1938.

Hansen, Miriam. "With Skin and Hair: Kracauer's Theory of Film, Marseille 1940." *Critical Inquiry* 19, no. 3 (1993): 438–69.

Hanssen, Beatrice. "Portrait of Melancholy (Benjamin, Warburg, Panofsky)." In *Benjamin's Ghosts: Interventions in Contemporary Literary and Cultural Theory*, edited by Gerhard Richter. Stanford: Stanford University Press, 2002.

Hartman, Geoffrey. *Scars of the Spirit: The Struggle against Inauthenticity*. New York: Palgrave Macmillan, 2002.

Hartmut, John. *Industrie- und Technikmuseen im Wandel: Perspektiven und Standortbestimmungen*. Edited by John Hartmut and Ira D. Mazzoni. Bielefeld: Transcript, 2005.

Hauschild-Thiessen, Renate, ed. *Die Hamburger Katastrophe vom Sommer 1943 in Augenzeugenberichten*. Hamburg: Verein für Hamburgische Geschichte, 1993.

Haushofer, Karl. "Kulturkreis und Kulturkreisueberschneidungen." In *Raumueberwindende Maechte*, edited by Karl Haushofer, 3:91–109. Leipzig: B. G. Teubner, 1934.

——. *Weltpolitik von heute*. Berlin: Zeitgeschichte, 1934.

Hegel, Georg Wilhelm Friedrich. *The Philosophy of History*. Translated by J. Sibree. New York: Dover, 1956.

——. *Philosophy of Right*. Translated by S. W. Dyde. New York: Prometheus, 1996.

——. *Vorlesungen über die Philosophie der Weltgeschichte*. In *Werke*, edited by Karl Heinz Ilting, Karl Brehmer, and Hoo Nam Seelmann, vol. 12. Hamburg: Felix Meiner, 1996.

——. *Vorlesungen über die Philosophie der Weltgeschichte*. In *Werke*, edited by Eva Moldenhauer and Karl Markus Michel, vol. 12. Frankfurt: Suhrkamp, 1970.

Hell, Julia. "The Angel's Enigmatic Eyes, or The Gothic Beauty of Catastrophic History in W. G. Sebald's *Air War and Literature*." In "Extreme and Sentimental History," edited by Vanessa Agnew and Jonathan Lamb, special issue, *Criticism* 46, no. 3 (2004): 361–92.

——. "The Melodrama of Illegal Identifications; or, Post-Holocaust Authorship in Uwe Johnson's *Jahrestage: Aus dem Leben von Gesine Cresspahl*." *Monatshefte* 94 (summer 2002): 209–29.

——. "Ruins Travel: Orphic Journeys through 1940s Germany." In *Writing Travel*, edited by John Zilcosky, 123–60. Toronto: University of Toronto Press, 2008.

——. "The Twin Towers of Anselm Kiefer and the Trope of Imperial Decline." Briefly Noted Column, *The Germanic Review* 84, no. 1 (2009) 84–93.

Hell, Julia, and Johannes von Moltke. "Unification Effects: Imaginary Landscapes of the Berlin Republic." *The Germanic Review* 80, no. 1 (2005): 74–95.

Hemming, John. *The Conquest of the Incas*. London: Macmillan, 1970.

——. *Monuments of the Incas*. Boston: Little, Brown, 1982.

Henriksen, Margot. *Doctor Strangelove's America: Society and Culture in the Atomic Age*. Berkeley: University of California Press, 1997.

Hess, Klaus A. "Die IG: Ein denkwürdiger politischer Beitrag Deutschstämmiger." In *Namibia-Deutschland, eine Geteilte Geschichte: Widerstand, Gewalt, Erinnerung*, edited by Larissa Förster, Dag Henrichsen, and Michael Bollig, 132–23. Cologne: Minerva, 2004.

Hetzler, Florence M. "Causality: Ruin Time and Ruins." *Leonardo* 21, no. 1 (1988): 51–55.

Hewlett, Richard, and Jack Holl. *Atoms for Peace and War*. Berkeley: University of California Press, 1989.

Heyer, Paul. *Architects on Architecture: New Directions in America*. New York: Walker, 1966.

Hibbard, G. R. "The Country House Poem of the Seventeenth Century." *Journal of the Warburg and Courtauld Institutes* 19, no. 1/2 (1956): 159–74.

Hilberseimer, Ludwig. *The New Regional Pattern*. Chicago: P. Theobald, 1949.

Hildebrand, Klaus. *Vom Reich zum Weltreich: Hitler, NSDAP und koloniale Frage*. Munich: Wilhelm Fink, 1969.

Himmler, Heinrich. "Posener Rede vom 04.10.1943 (Volltext)." www.nationalsozialismus.de/dokumente/textdokumente/heinrich-himmler-posener-rede-vom-04-10–1943-volltext.html.

Hitler, Adolf. *Mein Kampf*. Munich: Zentralverlag der NSDAP, 1942.

——. "Rede auf NSDAP-Versammlung in Muenchen, 9. April 1929." In *Reden, Schriften, Anordnungen, Februar 1925 bis Januar 1933*, edited by Klaus A. Lankheit, vol. 3. Munich: K. G. Saur, 166–94.

Hodder, Ian. *The Archaeological Process: An Introduction*. Oxford: Blackwell, 1999.

Hodder, Ian, and Scott Hutson. *Reading the Past: Current Approaches to Interpretation in Archaeology*. 3rd ed. Cambridge: Cambridge University Press, 2003.

Holstein, James, and Arjun Appadurai. "Cities and Citizenship." *Public Culture* 8, no. 3 (1996): 187–203.

Holston, James. *The Modernist City: An Anthropological Critique of Brasilia*. Chicago: University of Chicago Press, 1989.

Horbas, Claudia, and Ortwin Pelc, eds. *Es brannte an allen Ecken zugleich: Hamburg 1842*. Hamburg: Museum für Hamburgische Geschichte, 2002.

Hunt, John Dixon. *The Figure in the Landscape: Poetry, Painting and Gardening during the 18th Century*. Baltimore, Md.: Johns Hopkins University Press, 1976.

——. "Picturesque Mirrors and the Ruins of the Past." In *Gardens and the Picturesque: Studies in the History of Landscape Architecture*, edited by John Dixon Hunt, 171–92. Cambridge: MIT Press, 1992.

Huyssen, Andreas. *Present Pasts: Urban Palimpsests and the Politics of Memory*. Stanford: Stanford University Press, 2003.

——. *Twilight Memories: Marking Time in a Culture of Amnesia*. New York: Routledge, 1995.

[Izmailov, Vladimir]. "Razvaliny Moskvy." *Vestnik Evropy* 69, no. 9 (1813): 113–24.

Jaguaribe, Beatriz. "Modernist Ruins: National Narratives and Modernist Forms." In *Alternative Modernities*, edited by Dilip Parameshwar Gaonkar, 327–48. Durham, N.C.: Duke University Press, 2001.

Jakobson, Roman. "Derzhavin's Last Poem and M. Halle's First Literary Essay." In *Language, Sound, Structure: Studies in Phonology Presented to Morris Halle by His Teacher and Students*, edited by Mark Aronoff, Richard Oehrle, Frances Kelley, and Bonnie Wilker Stevens, 3–6. Cambridge: MIT Press, 1984.

Jameson, Fredric. "The End of Temporality." *Critical Inquiry* 29, no. 4 (2003): 695–718.

Janson, Horst W. "Amerika." October 6, 1953. Unpublished essay, Heckscher Archiv, Warburg Haus, Hamburg.

Jaspers, Karl. *The Question of German Guilt*. Translated by E. B. Ashton. New York: Capricorn, 1961.

Jencks, Charles. *The Language of Post-Modern Architecture*. 4th ed. New York: Rizzoli, 1984.

Jesenská, Milena. *The Journalism of Milena Jesenská: A Critical Voice in Interwar Central Europe*. Edited by Kathleen Hayes. New York: Berghahn, 2003.

——. *Nad naše síly: Češi, židé a nìmci 1937–1939* (Beyond Our Strength: Czechs, Jews, and Germans 1937–1939). Edited by Václav Burian. Olomouc. Czech Republic: Votobia, 1997.

Jessop, Bob, and Ngai-Ling Sum. *Beyond the Regulation Approach: Putting Capitalist Economies in Their Place*. Cheltenham: Edward Elgar, 2006.

Jurgens, Ulrich, Martin Gnad and Jurgen Bahr. "New Forms of Class and Racial Segregation." In *Emerging Johannesburg: Perspectives on the Postapartheid City*, edited by Richard Tomlinson, Robert Beauregard, Lindsay Beremer, and Xolela Mangcu, 56–70. New York: Routledge, 2003.

Kagan, Richard L. "*Urbs* and *Civitas* in Sixteenth- and Seventeenth-Century Spain." In *Envisioning the City*, edited by David Buisseret, 75–107. Chicago: University of Chicago Press, 1998.

Kalinin, I. A. "Istoriia kak iskusstvo chlenorazdel'nosti (istoricheskii opyt i meta/literaturnaia praktika russkikh formalistov)." *Novoe literaturnoe obozrenie* 71 (2005): 103–31.

Kant, Immanuel. *Critique of Judgement*. Translated by Werner S. Pluhar. Indianapolis: Hackett, 1987.

——. *Critique of the Power of Judgment*. Translated by Paul Guyer and Eric Matthews. Cambridge: Cambridge University Press, 2000.

——. "Geschichte und Naturbeschreibung der merkwürdigsten Vorfälle des Erdbebens, welches an dem Ende des 1755sten Jahres einen großen Teil der Erde erschüttert hat." In *Immanuel Kants Werke*, edited by Artur Buchenau, vol. 1, 439–73. Hildesheim: Gerstenberg, 1973.

——. "Immanuel Kants fortgesetzte Betrachtung der seit einiger Zeit wahrgenommenen Erderschütterungen." In *Immanuel Kants Werke*, edited by Artur Buchenau, vol. 1, 475–84. Hildesheim: Gerstenberg, 1973.

——. "Kritik der Urteilskraft." In *Immanuel Kants Werke*, edited by Otto Buek, vol. 5, 177–568. Hildesheim: Gerstenberg, 1973.

——. "Von den Ursachen der Erderschütterungen bei Gelegenheit des Unglücks, welches die westlichen Länder von Europa gegen Ende des vorigen Jahres betroffen hat." In *Immanuel Kants Werke*, edited by Artur Buchenau, vol. 1, 427–37. Hildesheim: Gerstenberg, 1973.

Kanther, Michael A., and Marc Olejniczak. *Bomben auf Duisburg: Der Luftkrieg und die Stadt 1940 bis 1960*. Duisburg: Mercator, 2004.

Kaplan, Robert D. *Warrior Politics: Why Leadership Demands a Pagan Ethos*. New York: Vintage, 2003.

Karamzin, Nikolai. *Letters of a Russian Traveller*. Translated and edited by Andrew Kahn. Oxford: Voltaire Foundation, 2003.

Katanian, Vasilii. "O Maiakovskom i Pasternake." *Russian Literature Triquarterly* 13 (1976): 499–518.

Käutner, Helmut. “Demontage der Traumfabrik.” In *Käutner*, edited by Wolfgang Jacobsen and Hans Helmut Prinzler, 113–14. Berlin: Spiess, 1992.

Keller, Volker. *Mannheim im Bombenkrieg: 1940–1945*. Gudensberg-Gleichen: Wartberg, 2003.

Kempowski, Walter. *Der rote Hahn: Dresden im Februar 1945*. Munich: Goldmann, 2001.

Kempton, Daniel R., and Roni L. Du Preez. “Namibian-De Beers State-Firm Relations: Cooperation and Conflict.” *Journal of Southern African Studies* 23, no. 4 (1997): 585–613.

Kendrick, T. D. *The Lisbon Earthquake*. London: Methuen, 1956.

Kennan, George. *From Prague after Munich: Diplomatic Papers 1938–1940*. Princeton, N.J.: Princeton University Press, 1968.

Kennedy, Duncan F. “A Sense of Place: Rome, History, and Empire Revisited.” In *Roman Presences: Receptions of Rome in European Culture, 1789–1945*, edited by Catharine Edwards, 19–34. Cambridge: Cambridge University Press, 1999.

Kern, Stephen. *The Culture of Time and Space: 1880–1918*. Cambridge: Harvard University Press, 1983.

Khmel’nitskii, Dmitrii. *Zodchii Stalin*. Moscow: NLO, 2007.

King, Anthony. *Urbanism, Colonialism, and the World Economy*. London: Routledge, 1990.

Kluge, Alexander. *Der Angriff der Gegenwart auf die übrige Zeit*. Frankfurt am Main: Syndikat, 1985.

——. “Der Luftangriff auf Halberstadt am 8. April 1945.” In *Chronik der Gefühle*. Vol. 2 of *Lebensläufe*, 27–82. Frankfurt: Suhrkamp, 2000.

Knaller, Susanne, and Harro Müller. “Authentisch/Authentizität.” In *Ästhetische Grundbegriffe*, edited by Karlheinz Barck et al., vol. 7, 40–65. Stuttgart: Metzler, 2005.

Knell, Hermann. *To Destroy a City: Strategic Bombing and Its Human Consequences in World War II*. Cambridge, Mass.: Da Capo, 2003.

Koch, Gertrud. “Nachkriegsfilme als Werke der Restauration: Einige Thesen zur Ideologie des ‘Trümmerfilms’ in Deutschland.” *epd Kirche und Film* 31, no. 2 (February 1978): 6–9.

Koch, Karl, III, with Richard Firstman. *Men of Steel: The Story of the Family that Built the World Trade Center*. New York: Crown, 2002.

Kohl, Helga, and Amy Schoeman. *Kolmanskop*. Göttingen: Klaus Hess, 2004.

Kohrman, David. *Detroit’s Statler and Book-Cadillac Hotels: The Anchors of Washington Boulevard*. Chicago: Arcadia Publishing, 2002.

Kokorin, Viktor. “Chuzhoi dom.” *Arkhitekturnaia gazeta*, 24 January 1935, 4.

——. “Obsuzhdenie tvorcheskogo otcheta rukovoditelia 10-i proektnoi masterskoi.” *Akademiia Arkhitektury* 3, no. 3 (1936).

Kos, Wolfgang. *Eigenheim Österreich: Zu Politik, Kultur und Alltag nach 1945*. Vienna: Sonderzahl, 1994.

Koselleck, Reinhart. *Futures Past: On the Semantics of Historical Time*. Translated by Keith Tribe. Cambridge: MIT Press, 1985.

——. *Zeitschichten: Studies zur Historik. Mit einem Beitrag von Hans-Georg Gadamer*. Frankfurt: Suhrkamp, 2000.

Koshar, Rudy. *Germany’s Transient Pasts: Preservation and National Memory in the Twentieth Century*. Chapel Hill: University of North Carolina Press, 1998.

Kovárna, František. *Česká střízlivost a èeský pathos* (Czech Sobriety and Czech Pathos). Prague: Václav Petr, 1939.

——. "Rozdíly duše" (Differences of Soul). *Kritický měsíčník* 2 (1939): 191–92.

Kracauer, Siegfried. *History: The Last Things Before the Last*. Completed by Paul Oskar Kristeller. New York: Oxford University Press, 1969.

——. "Photography." In *The Mass Ornament: Weimar Essays*, edited and translated by Thomas Y. Levin. Cambridge: Harvard University Press, 1995.

——. *Theory of Film: The Redemption of Physical Reality*. With an introduction by Miriam Hansen. Princeton, N.J.: Princeton University Press, 1997.

Kraniauskas, John. "Beware Mexican Ruins! 'One-Way Street' and the Colonial Unconscious." In *Walter Benjamin's Philosophy: Destruction and Experience*, edited by Andrew Benjamin and Peter Osborne, 139–54. London: Routledge, 1994.

Krauss, Rosalind. *The Originality of the Avant Garde and Other Modernist Myths*. Cambridge: MIT Press, 1985.

——. "Reinventing the Medium." *Critical Inquiry* 25 (winter 1999): 289–305.

Kriger, E. "Oblik velikogo goroda." In *Slovo o Moskve: Literaturno-khudozhestvennyi sbornik*, 317–99. Moscow: GIKhL, 1947.

Kuhn, Rolf. "Landscape Change in Lusatia." In *Bewegtes Land: Internationale Bauaustellung 2000–2010. IBA Werkschau 2005*, ed. IBA Fürst-Pückler-Land, 4–12. Berlin: Aedes, 2005.

——. "Den Mond Bewohnbar machen: Gespräch mit Prof. Rolf Kuhn, Geschäftsführer der Internationalen Bauausstellung Fürst-Pückler-Land." In *Labor Ostdeutschland*, edited by Christina Bauer-Volke and Ina Dietzsche, 193–96. Berlin: Bundeszentrale für politische Bildung, 2004.

Kupfer, Alexander. *Piranesis Carceri: Enge und Unendlichkeit in den Gefängnissen der Phantasie*. Stuttgart: Belser, 1992.

LaCapra, Dominick. *Representing the Holocaust: History, Theory, Trauma*. Ithaca, N.Y.: Cornell University Press, 1994.

Lacoue-Labarthe, Philippe, and Jean-Luc Nancy. "The Nazi Myth." *Critical Inquiry* 16, no. 2 (1990): 291–312.

Ladd, Brian. *The Ghosts of Berlin: Confronting German History in the Urban Landscape*. Chicago: University of Chicago Press, 1997.

Lane, Barbara Miller. *Architecture and Politics in Germany, 1918–1945*. Cambridge: Harvard University Press, 1968.

Latham, J. "Extract of Letter V from Mr. J. *Latham*, dated at Zsusqueira, *Dec. 11, 1755*, to his Uncle in *London*. Communicated by *Peter Daval*, Esq; Secret. R.S." *Philosophical Transactions of the Royal Society of London* 49 (1755–56): 411–13.

Latz, Peter. "Landscape Park Duisburg-Nord: The Metamorphosis of an Industrial Site." In *Manufactured Sites: Rethinking the Post-Industrial Landscape*, edited by Niall Kirkwood. London: Spon, 2001.

——. "The Syntax of Landscape." In Udo Weilacher, *Between Landscape Architecture and Land Art*, translated by Felicity Gloth. Basel: Birkhäuser, 1996.

Lautenschlager, Rolf. "Ich träume auf Deutsch." *Tageszeitung* (Berlin), December 22, 2003.

Le Corbusier. *Aircraft*. London: The Studio, 1935.

——. *Urbanisme*. Paris: G. Grés, 1925.

——. *La ville radieuse*. Paris: Vincent Fréalet, 1933.

Lefebvre, Henri. *The Production of Space*. Translated by Donald Nicholson-Smith. Oxford: Blackwell, 1991.

Lentz, David. "Introduction: Definitions and Conceptual Underpinnings." In *Imperfect Balance: Landscape Transformations in the Precolumbian Americas*, edited by David Lentz. New York: Columbia University Press, 2000.

Leonidov, Ivan. "Iz poiasnitel'noi zapiski k konkursnomu proektu Narkomtiazhproma. 1934." In *Mastera sovetskoi arkhitektury ob arkhitekture*, edited by M. G. Barkhin and Iu. S. Iaralov, vol. 2, 538–40. Moscow: Iskusstvo, 1975.

Levin, Yuri D. *The Perception of English Literature in Russia: Investigations and Materials.* Nottingham, England: Astra, 1994.

Levy, Daniel, and Natan Sznaider. *Erinnerung im globalen Zeitalter: Der Holocaust.* Frankfurt: Suhrkamp, 2001.

Libeskind, Daniel. *Traces of the Unborn: 1995 Raoul Wallenberg Lecture*. Ann Arbor: University of Michigan College of Architecture and Urban Planning, 1995.

Lichtenstein, Nelson. *The Most Dangerous Man in Detroit*. New York: Basic, 1995.

Lifshits, "Pochemu ia ne modernist?" *Literaturnaia gazeta*, no. 110 (October 8, 1966): 2–3.

Lincoln, Abraham. *Collected Works.* Edited by Roy P. Basler. New Brunswick, N.J.: Rutgers University Press, 1955.

Lindquist, Sven. *A History of Bombing*. Translated by Linda Haverty Rugg. New York: New Press, 2001.

Lissitzky, Lazar. "Iz lozungov ASNOVA. 1926." In *Mastera sovetskoi arkhitektury ob arkhitekture*, edited by M. G. Barkhin and Iu. S. Iaralov, vol. 2, 146. Moscow: Iskusstvo, 1975.

Löffler, Ulrich. *Lissabons Fall—Europas Schrecken: die Deutung des Erdbebens von Lissabon im deutschsprachigen Protestantismus des 18. Jahrhunderts*. Berlin: Walter de Gruyter, 1999.

Lowenthal, David. *The Past Is a Foreign Country*. Cambridge: Cambridge University Press, 1985.

Lüdecke, Heinz. "Es kommt auf die Einstellung an." *Bildende Kunst* 2 (July 1948): 12–15.

Lützeler, Paul. *Postmoderne und postkoloniale deutschsprachige Literatur*. Bielefeld: Aisthesis, 2005.

Lyotard, Jean-François. "Domus and Megapolis." In *The Inhuman: Reflections on Time*, translated by Geoffrey Bennington and Rachel Bowlby. Stanford: Stanford University Press, 1991.

——. *Heidegger and "the Jews."* Translated by Andreas Michel and Mark S. Roberts. Minneapolis: University of Minnsesota Press, 1990.

——. "Scapeland." In *The Lyotard Reader*, edited by Andrew Benjamin, 215–19. Oxford: Blackwell, 1989.

Mabin, Alan. "On the Problems of Overcoming Segregation and Fragmentation in Southern Africa's Cities in the Postmodern Era." In *Postmodern Cities and Spaces*, edited by Sophie Watson and Katherine Gibson, 187–98. Oxford: Blackwell Publishers, 1995.

Macaulay, Rose. *The Pleasure of Ruins*. New York: Thames and Hudson, 1953.

Mack, Maynard. "A Poet in his Landscape: Pope at Twickenham." In *From Sensibility to Romanticism: Essays Presented to Frederick A. Pottle*, edited by Maynard Mack, 3–29. New York: Oxford University Press, 1965.

Malik, Ayyub. "After Modernity: Contemporary Non-Western Cities and Architecture." *Futures* 33, no. 10 (2001): 873–82.

Mann, Michael. *Incoherent Empire.* London: Verso, 2003.

Mann, Thomas. *Der Zauberberg*. Vol. 3 of *Gesammelte Werke*. 13 vols. Frankfurt: Fischer, 1960.

Martin, Alexander. "The Response of the Population of Moscow to the Napoleonic Occupation of 1812." In *The Military and Society in Russia: 1450–1917*, edited by Eric Lohr and Marshall Poe, 469–89. Leiden: Brill, 2002.

Martin, Andrew John. "Stadtmodelle." In *Das Bild der Stadt in der Neuzeit: 1400–1800*, edited by Wolfgang Behringer and Bernd Roeck, 66–72. Munich: Beck, 1999.

Mathesius, Bohumil. "Líc prohry" (The Other Side of the Loss). *Kritický mìsíèník* 1 (1938): 386–88.

Matoušek, Karel. *Hospodářský zemìpis druhé republiky* (Economic Geography of the Second Republic). Prague: Česko-Slovenská grafická unie a.s., 1939.

Matthes, Nadja. "Konjunktur: Das kleine Wirtschaftswunder." *Focus*, July 4, 2007, 198–200.

Mauch, Carl. *The Journals of Carl Mauch: His Travels in the Transvaal and Rhodesia, 1869–1872*. Salisbury: National Archives of Rhodesia, 1969.

Mayakovsky, Vladimir. "Letaiushchii proletarii." In *Polnoe sobranie sochinenii*, edited by Institut mirovoi literatury imeni A. M. Gor'kogo, vol. 6, 311–61. Moscow: GIKhL, 1957.

——. *Polnoe sobranie sochinenii*, edited by Institut mirovoi literatury imeni A. M. Gor'kogo, vol. 1. Moscow: GIKhL, 1955.

——. "Vsem." In *Polnoe sobranie sochinenii*, edited by Institut mirovoi literatury imeni A. M. Gor'kogo, vol. 13, 138. Moscow: GIKhL, 1961.

Mayer, Charles. *Among Empires: American Ascendency and Its Predecessors.* Cambridge: Harvard University Press, 2006.

Mbembe, Achille. "Aesthetics of Superfluity." *Public Culture* 16, no. 3 (2004): 373–405.

McAllister, James. "Metonymy and Metaphor in Yves Bonnefoy's Poetry." *French Forum* 19, no. 2 (1994): 149–60.

McDonald, James. "The Citizen and the Man About Town." In *Questions of Cultural Identity*, edited by Stuart Hall and Paul Du Gay, 170–90. London: Sage, 1996.

Means, Philip. *Ancient Civilizations of the Andes*. New York: Gordian, 1964.

Mehrotra, Rahul. "The Architecture of Pluralism—A Century of Building in South Asia." In *World Architecture 1900–2000: A Critical Mosaic*, edited by Kenneth Frampton, vol. 8, 27–30. Vienna: Springer, 1999.

——. "Bazaar City: A Metaphor for South Asian Urbanism." In *Kapital und Karma*, edited by Angelika Fitz, 95–108. Vienna: Kunsthalle, 2002.

Meinecke, Friedrich. *The German Catastrophe*. Translated by Sidney B. Fay. Boston, Mass.: Beacon, 1950.

Merewether, Charles. "Traces of Loss." In *Irresistible Decay: Ruins Reclaimed*, edited by Michael S. Roth, Claire Lyons, and Charles Merewether. Los Angeles: Getty Research Institute for the History of Art and the Humanities, 1997.

Metz, Joseph. "Exhuming Rilke's Orphic Body: Gender and Poetic Voice in 'Orpheus. Eurydike. Hermes' and 'Hetaeren-Graeber.' " *Germanic Review* 79, no. 4 (2004): 247–72.

Michelet, Jules. *Histoire Romaine.* Paris: Belles Lettres, 2003.

Mikhailov, Boris. *Case History*. Zurich: Scalo, 1999.

——. *Unfinished Dissertation*. Zurich: Scalo, 1998.

Miliutin, Nikolai. "Tematika skul'pturnykh i zhivopisnykh rabot dlia Dvortsa Sovetov." *Arkhitektura SSSR* no. 4 (1940): 64–65.

Miller, Norbert. *Archäologie des Traums: Versuch über Giovanni Battista Piranesi*. Munich: Hanser, 1978.

Misrach, Richard. *Bravo 20: The Bombing of the American West*. Baltimore: Johns Hopkins University Press, 1990.
Mitchell, W. J. T. "Imperial Landscape." In *Landscape and Power*, edited by W. J. T. Mitchell, 5–34. Chicago: University of Chicago Press, 1994.
Mitscherlich, Alexander, and Margarete Mitscherlich. *Die Unfähigkeit zu trauern*. Munich: Piper, 1967.
Mommsen, Theodor. *Roemische Geschichte*. Vienna: Phaidon, 1932.
Moreiras, Alberto. *The Exhaustion of Difference: The Politics of Latin American Cultural Studies*. Durham, N.C.: Duke University Press, 2001.
Morrison, Andrew Craig. *Opera House, Nickel Show, and Palace: An Illustrated History of Theater Buildings in the Detroit Area*. Dearborn, Mich.: Greenfield Village Museum, 1974.
Morson, Gary Soul. *Hidden in Plain View: Narrative and Creative Potentials in "War and Peace."* Stanford: Stanford University Press, 1987.
"Moskovskie novosti." *Vestnik Evropy* 65, no. 17 (1812): 63–68.
Mossolow, N. "An Historical and Forgotten Village—Gross Barmen." *South West Africa Annual* 10 (1954): 67–73.
——. *The History of Namutoni*. Windhoek, Namibia: John Meinert, 1971.
——. *Otijikango oder Gross Barmen*. Windhoek, Namibia: John Meinert, 1968.
——. "Otjimbingwe." *South West Africa Annual* (1955), 97–119.
——. *Waterberg: On the History of the Mission Station Otjozondjupa, the Kambazembi Tribe and Hereroland*. Windhoek, Namibia: John Meinert, 1993.
Mückenberger, Christiane, and Günter Jordan. *"Sie sehen selbst, Sie hören selbst . . ." Eine Geschichte der DEFA von ihren Anfängen bis 1949*. Marburg: Hitzeroth, 1994.
Mudimbe, V. Y. *The Idea of Africa*. Bloomington: Indiana University Press, 1994.
Mühr, Stephan. "Die deutschen Namibier heute—Auswanderung, Musealisierung oder Integration?" In *Namibia-Deutschland, eine Geteilte Geschichte: Widerstand, Gewalt, Erinnerung*, edited by Larissa Förster, Dag Henrichsen, and Michael Bollig, 244–55. Cologne: Minerva, 2004.
Mülder-Bach, Inka. "History as Autobiography: The Last Things Before the Last." In *New German Critique* no. 54 (1991): 139–57.
Müller, Heiner (with Inge Müller). *Die Korrektur [von] Inge und Heiner Müller: Hinweise zur Regie von H. Konrad Hoerning*. Leipzig: F. Hofmeister, 1959.
*Münster im Modell: 25 Jahre Verein Münster-Museum e.v.* Münster: Stadtmuseum, 2003.
Nancy, Jean-Luc. *The Inoperative Community*. Edited by Peter Connor and translated by Peter Connor, Lisa Garbus, Michael Holland, and Simona Sawhney. Minneapolis: University of Minnesota Press, 1991.
Neiman, Susan. *Evil in Modern Thought: An Alternative History of Philosophy*. Princeton, N.J.: Princeton University Press, 2002.
Nelken, Nicoletta. *Zeitmaschine Lausitz: Landschaft und Bergbau. Bildende Kunst der Lausitz im 20. Jahrhundert*. Husum: Verlag der Kunst, 2003.
Neruda, Pablo. *The Heights of Macchu Picchu*. Translated by Nathaniel Tarn. New York: Farrar, Straus, and Giroux, 1967.
Netenjakob, Egon. "Ein Leben gegen die Zeit. Versuch über WS." In *Staudte*, edited by Egon Netenjakob, Eva Orbanz, and Hans Helmut Prinzler, 11–129. Berlin: Spiess, 1991.

Neumaier, Diane. "Re-Representing Russia." In *Disrupted Borders: An Intervention in Definition of Boundaries*, edited by Sunil Gupta, 27–41. London: Rivers Oram Press, 1993.
Neumann, Stanislav K. "Úvodem. In *Československý podzim* (Czechoslovak Autumn), edited by Stanislav K. Neumann and Fr. Jungmann, 5–14. Prague: V. Palán, 1939.
Nordhof, Anton Wilhelm. *Die Geschichte der Zestörung Moskaus im Jahre 1812*. Munich: Harald Boldt, 2000.
*Novyi* LEF *II*. Munich: Wilhelm Fink, 1970.
Nozes, Judite, ed. *The Lisbon Earthquake of 1755: British Accounts*. Lisbon: British Historical Society of Portugal and Lisóptima, 1990.
Nye, David. *American Technological Sublime*. Cambridge: MIT Press, 1994.
Oeser, Erhard. "Das Erdbeben von Lissabon im Spiegel der zeitgenössischen Philosophie." In *Elementare Gewalt kulturelle Bewältigung: Aspekte der Naturkatastrophe im 18. Jahrhundert*, edited by F. Eybl, H. Heppner, and A. Kernbauer, 185–95. Vienna: WUV Universitätsverlag, 2000.
Orbanz, Eva, ed. *Wolfgang Staudte*. West Berlin: Spiess, 1977. Oswalt, Peter, ed. *Shrinking Cities*. Ostfildern-Ruit: Hatje Cantz, 2005.
Paperny, Vladimir. *Architecture in the Age of Stalin: Culture Two*. Translated by John Hill and Roann Barris in collaboration with the author. New York: Cambridge University Press, 2002.
Pereira, Anthony. *A Narrative of the Earthquake and Fire of Lisbon of the Congregation of the Oratory, an Eyewitness Thereof. Translated from the Latin*. London: G. Hawkins, 1756.
Perry, Mr. "An Account of the Earthquake Felt in the Island of Sumatra, in the East-Indies, in November and December 1756. In a Letter from Mr. Perry to the Rev. Dr. Stukeley, Dated at Fort Malborough, in the Island of Sumatra, Feb 20. 1757. Communicated by the Rev. Wm. Stukeley, M.D. F.R.S." *Philosophical Transactions of the Royal Society of London* 50 (1757): 491–99.
Peschke, Norbert. *Zwickau und Planitz im Bombenhagel*. Erfurt: Sutton, 2004.
Peters, Charles. "Precolumbian Silviculture and Indigenous Management of Neotropical Forests." In *Imperfect Balance: Landscape Transformations in the Precolumbian Americas*, edited by David Lentz, 205–14. New York: Columbia University Press, 2000.
Peters, Walter. *Baukunst in Südwestafrika, 1884–1914*. Windhoek, Namibia: Vorstand der SWA Wissenschaftlichen, 1981.
Petrovsky, Helen. *Antifotografiia*. Moscow: Tri kvadrata, 2003.
——. *Neproiavlennoe: Ocherki po filosofii fotografii*. Moscow: Ad Marginem, 2002.
——. " 'Seroe po seromu': filosofiia i konets iskusstva." *Iskusstvoznanie*, no. 1 (2001): 106–10.
——. "Sotsrealism: vysokoe nizkoe iskusstvo." *Khudozhestvennyi zhurnal*, nos. 43–44 (2002): 61–65.
Picker, Henry. *Tischgespräche im Führerhauptquartier 1941–1942*. Stuttgart: Seewald Verlag, 1963.
Pindar. *The Odes of Pindar*. Edited and translated by Richmond Lattimore. Chicago: University of Chicago Press, 1976.
Piranesi, Giovanni Battista. *Catalogue*. New York: Smith College Museum of Art, 1971.
Pleyer, Peter. *Deutscher Nachkriegsfilm 1946–1948*. Münster: Fahle, 1965.
Pliny. *Letters, and Panegyricus*. With an English translation by Betty Radice. Cambridge: Harvard University Press, 1969.

*A Poem on the Earthquake of Lisbon*. London, 1755.

Pollock, Griselda. *Psychoanalysis and the Image: Transdisciplinary Perspectives*. Malden, Mass.: Blackwell, 2006.

Polybius. *The Histories*. Translated by W. R. Paton. Vol. 6. Cambridge: Harvard University Press, 1995.

Pope, Alexander. *An Essay on Man*. Edited by Maynard Mack. London: Methuen, 1982.

——. *Imitations of Horace. With an Epistle to Dr. Arbuthnot*. Edited by John Butt. New Haven, Conn.: Yale University Press, 1961.

Potts, Alex. *The Sculptural Imagination: Figurative, Modernist, Minimalist*. New Haven, Conn.: Yale University Press, 2000.

Pratt, Marie Louise. *Imperial Eyes: Travel Writing and Transculturation*. New York: Routledge, 1992.

Presner, Todd Samuel. *Mobile Modernity: Germans, Jews, Trains*. New York: Columbia University Press, 2007.

——. " 'What a Synoptic and Artificial View Reveals': The Modernism of W. G. Sebald's Realism." *Criticism* 46, no. 3 (2004): 341–60.

Procházka, Theodor, Sr. *The Second Republic: The Disintegration of Post-Munich Czechoslovakia, October 1938–March 1939*. Boulder, Colo.: East European Monographs, 1981.

Punin, Nikolai. *Pamiatnik Tret'emu Internatsionalu: Proekt khudozhnika V. E. Tatlina*. Petrograd: Otdel IZO Narkomprossa, 1921.

Rabinbach, Anson. *In the Shadow of Catastrophe*. Berkeley: University of California Press, 1997.

Raffles, Hugh, and Antoinette M. G. A. Winkler Prins. "Further Reflections on Amazonian Environmental History: Transformations of Rivers and Streams." *Latin American Research Review* 38, no. 3 (2003): 165–87.

Rand, Ayn. *The Fountainhead*. New York: Signet, 1952.

Rataj, Jan. *O autoritativní národní stát: Ideologické promìny èeské politiky v Druhé republice 1938–1939* (The Authoritative National State: Ideological Changes in Czech Politics in the Second Republic, 1938–1939). Prague: Karolinum, 1997.

Ratzel, Friedrich. *Anthropogeographie*. Vol. 2. Stuttgart: J. Engelhorn, 1891.

Rauch, Leo, and David Sherman. *Hegel's Phenomenology of Self-Consciousness: Text and Commentary*. Albany: State University of New York Press, 1999.

Ray, Gene. "Reading the Lisbon Earthquake: Adorno, Lyotard, and the Contemporary Sublime." *Yale Journal of Criticism* 17, no. 1 (2004): 1–18.

——. *Terror and the Sublime in Art and Critical Theory: From Auschwitz to Hiroshima to September 11*. New York: Palgrave Macmillan, 2005.

Rebenich, Stefan. "Alte Geschichte in Demokratie und Diktatur: Der Fall Helmut Bervé." *Chiron. Mitteilungen der Kommission für alte Geschichte und Epigraphik des deutschen archäologischen Instituts* 31 (2001): 457–96.

Reed, J. D. *Virgil's Gaze: Nation and Poetry in the Aeneid*. Princeton, N.J.: Princeton University Press, 2007.

Reed, Peter, ed. *Groundswell: Constructing the Contemporary Landscape*. New York: Museum of Modern Art, 2005.

Reimann, Brigitte. *Ich bedauere nichts: Tagebücher*. Berlin: Aufbau, 1997.

Reudenbach, Bruno. *Giovanni Battista Piranesi: Architektur als Bild*. Munich: Prestel, 1979.

Reuth, Ralf Georg. *Goebbels.* New York: Harcourt, Brace, 1990.

Reynolds, Ann. *Robert Smithson: Learning from New Jersey and Elsewhere.* Cambridge: MIT Press, 2003.

Richardson, Alan. "Archaism and Modernity: Poetic Diction, Period Style, and the Romantic Canon." *Southern Humanities Review* 28, no. 3 (1994): 209–28.

Ricoeur, Paul. *Time and Narrative.* Translated by Kathleen McLaughlin and David Pellauer. Chicago: Chicago University Press, 1984–88.

Ridley, R. T. "To Be Taken with a Pinch of Salt: The Destruction of Carthage." *Classical Philology* 81, no. 2 (1986): 140–46.

Riva Agüero, José de la. *Paisajes Peruanos.* Lima: Santa María, 1955.

Rodchenko, Alexander. "Protiv summirovannogo portreta za momental'nyi snimok." *Novyi LEF*, no. 4 (1928): 14–16.

Rodenwaldt, Gerhart. *Kunst um Augustus.* Berlin: Walter de Gruyter, 1943.

Rogier, Francesca. "The Monumentality of Rhetoric: The Will to Build in Postwar Berlin." In *Anxious Modernisms: Experimentation in Postwar Architectural Culture*, edited by Sarah Williams Goldhagen and Réjean Legault, 165–90. Cambridge: MIT Press, 2000.

Rollin, Claude. *The Roman History from the Foundation of Rome to the Battle of Actium.* Vol. 3. London: J. and P. Knapton, 1754.

Romains, Jules. "The Crowd at the Cinematograph." In *French Film Theory and Criticism: A History/Anthology 1907–1939*, edited by Richard Abel, vol. 1. Princeton, N.J.: Princeton University Press, 1988.

Rosen, Philip. *Change Mummified: Cinema, Historicity, Theory.* Minneapolis: University of Minnesota Press, 2001.

Rosler, Martha. *3 Works.* Halifax: Press of the Nova Scotia College of Art and Design, 1981.

Rossi, Aldo. *The Architecture of the City.* Translated by Laurence Venuti. Cambridge: MIT Press, 1999.

Rostworowski, María. *Pachacutec y la leyenda de los Chancas.* Lima: Instituto de Estudios Peruanos, 1997.

Roth, Michael S. "Irresistible Decay: Ruins Reclaimed." In *Irresistible Decay: Ruins Reclaimed*, edited by Michael S. Roth, Claire Lyons and Charles Merewether, 1–12. Los Angeles: Getty Research Institute for the History of Art and the Humanities, 1997.

Roth, Michael S., Claire Lyons, and Charles Merewether, eds. *Irresistible Decay: Ruins Reclaimed.* Los Angeles: Getty Research Institute for the History of Art and the Humanities, 1997.

Rouillard, Dominique. *Superarchitecture: Le futur de l'architecture 1950–1970.* Paris: La Villette, 2004.

Rousseau, Jean-Jacques. "Letter from Rousseau to Voltaire." In *The Collected Writings of Rousseau*, edited by Roger D. Masters and Christopher Kelly, vol. 3, 108–21. Hanover, N.H.: University Press of New England, 1992.

Royal Society. *Philosophical Transactions Being an Appendix to Those for the Year 1750: Consisting of Several Papers Laid before the Royal Society, Concerning Several Earthquakes Felt in England and Some Neighbouring Countries in the Year 1750.* London: 1750.

Rüdiger, Klaus H. *Die Namibia-Deutschen.* Stuttgart: F. Steiner, 1993.

"Ruined Cities of Central America." *North American Review* 131 (1880).

Russell, Bertrand. *A History of Western Philosophy.* New York: Simon and Schuster, 1945.

Rust, Hans-Joachim. "Der 'Schießbefehl.' " In *Vom Schutzgebiet bis Namibia 2000*, edited by Klaus A. Hess and Klaus J. Becker, 480–83. Göttingen: Hess, 2002.

Sacheti, John Mendes. "A Copy of Part of two Letters, written by *John Mendes Saccheti*, M.D.F.R.S. to Dr. *de Castro*, F.R.S. dated from the Fields of Lisbon, on the 7th of *November, and the 1st of* December, 1755." *Philosophical Transactions of the Royal Society of London* 49 (1755–56): 409–11.

Sachsse, Rolf. *Hilla und Bernhard Becher: Silo für Kokskohle, Zeche Hannibal, Bochum-Hofstede, 1967. Das Anonyme und das Plastische der Industriephotographie*. Frankfurt: Fischer, 1999.

Said, Edward. *Culture and Imperialism*. New York: Vintage, 1994.

Santner, Eric L. *Stranded Objects*. Ithaca, N.Y.: Cornell University Press, 1990.

Sartre, Jean-Paul. Preface to *Portrait of a Man Unknown*, by Nathalie Sarraute. Translated by Maria Jolas. New York: George Braziller, 1958.

Sayer, Derek. *The Coasts of Bohemia*. Princeton, N.J.: Princeton University Press, 1998.

Schama, Simon. *Landscape and Memory*. New York: Vintage, 1996.

Schivelbusch, Wolfgang. *Vor dem Vorhang: Das geistige Berlin 1945–1948*. Munich: Hanser, 1995.

Schmidt-Lauber, Brigitta. *Die abhängigen Herren: Deutsche Identität in Namibia*. Münster: Lit, 1993.

——. *Die verkehrte Hautfarbe*. Berlin: Dietrich Reimer, 1998.

Schmitt, Carl. "The 'Fourth' (Second) Interrogation of Carl Schmitt at Nuremberg." *Telos* 139 (summer 2007): 35–43.

——. *Land und Meer: Eine weltgeschichtliche Betrachtung*. Leipzig: Reclam, 1942.

——. "Völkerrechtliche Grossraumordnung mit Interventionsverbot für raumfremde Mächte." In *Staat, Grossraum, Nomos: Arbeiten aus den Jahren 1916–1969*, edited by Günter Maschke, 269–371. Berlin: Duncker und Humblot, 1995.

Schnee, Heinrich. *Deutsches Kolonial-Lexikon*. Vol. 1. Leipzig: Quelle and Meyer, 1920.

Schnurre, Wolfdietrich. Untitled article. In *Deutsche Film Rundschau*, November 5, 1946. Reprinted in *Wolfgang Staudte*, edited by Eva Orbanz, 104–5. Berlin: Spiess, 1977.

Schoell-Glass, Charlotte, and Elizabeth Sears. "Amerika kennt keine Ruinen: Horst W. Janson's Amerikabild." *Zeitschrift für Ideengeschichte* (forthcoming).

——. *Verzetteln als Methode: Der humanistische Ikonologe William S. Heckscher*. Berlin: Akademie, 2008.

Schröder, Thies. "An Outdated View of Modernism: Interview with Karl Ganser, IBA Emscher Park." In *Bauhaus Dessau: Industrielles Gartenreich. Dessau–Bitterfeld–Wittenberg*, edited by Stiftung Bauhaus Dessau, vol. 2, 80–87. Berlin: ex pose, 1999.

Schulte-Althoff, Franz-Joseph. "Rassenmischung im kolonialen System: Zur deutschen Kolonialpolitik im letzten Jahrzehnt vor dem Ersten Weltkrieg." *Historisches Jahrbuch* 105 (1985): 52–94.

Schwabe, Kurd. *Mit Schwert und Pflug in Deutsch-Südwestafrika*. Berlin: Mittler, 1899.

Scobie, Alex. *Hitler's State Architecture: The Impact of Classical Antiquity*. University Park: Pennsylvania State University Press, 1990.

Scribner, Charity. *Requiem for Communism*. Cambridge: MIT Press, 2003.

Sears, Elizabeth. "The Life and Work of William S. Heckscher." In *Zeitschrift für Kunstgeschichte* 53 (1990): 107–33.

Sebald, W. G. *Austerlitz*. Munich: C. Hanser, 2001; English translation: *Austerlitz*. Translated by Anthea Bell. New York: Modern Library, 2001.
——. "Katastrophe mit Zuschauer: Ein Gespräch mit dem Schriftsteller W. G. Sebald." *Neue Züricher Zeitung*, November 22, 1997.
——. *Luftkrieg und Literatur: Mit einem Essay zu Alfred Andersch*. Munich: Carl Hanser, 1999.
——. *On the Natural History of Destruction: With Essays on Alfred Andersch, Jean Améry, and Peter Weiss*. Translated by Anthea Bell. New York: Random House, 2003.
——. *Die Ringe des Saturn: Eine englische Wallfahrt*. Frankfurt: Vito von Eichborn, 1995. English translation: *The Rings of Saturn*. Translated by Michael Hulse. New York: New Directions, 1998.
Seeck, Otto. *Geschichte des Untergangs der antiken Welt*, vols. 1–6. Stuttgart: Metzlersche Verlagsbuchhandlung, 1966.
Segev, Tom. *The Seventh Million: The Israelis and the Holocaust*. Translated by Haim Watzman. New York: Henry Holt, 1991.
Semel, Nava. "Le'vad." In *Yashen Hu Er BeMakom Acher*. Tel Aviv: Sifriyat Poalim, 2000.
Serup-Bilfeldt, Kirsten. *Ins Gedächtnis eingebrannt: Wie Kölner den Zweiten Weltkrieg erlebten*. Cologne: Kiwi, 2005.
Seyhan, Azade. *Writing Outside the Nation*. Princeton, N.J.: Princeton University Press, 2001.
Shandley, Robert. *Rubble Films: German Cinema in the Shadow of the Third Reich*. Philadelphia, Pa.: Temple University Press, 2001.
Shapira, Anita. "Hirbet Hizah: Between Remembrance and Forgetting." *Jewish Social Studies* 7, no. 1 (2000): 1–62.
Shaw, Robert. "The International Building Exhibition (IBA) Emscher Park, Germany: A Model for Sustainable Restructuring?" *European Planning Studies* 10, no. 1 (2002): 77–97.
Shelley, Percy Bysshe. *Selected Poems*. Edited by Timothy Webb. London: Dent, 1983.
Shepherd, Nick. "The Politics of Archaeology in Africa." *Annual Review of Anthropology* 31 (2002): 189–209.
Shishkov, Alexander S. *Kratkie zapisi admirala A. Shishkova, vedennye im vo vremia prebyvaniia ego pri blazhennoi pamiati Gosudare Imperatore Aleksandre Pervom v byvshuiu s frantsuzami v 1812g. i posleduiushchikh godakh voinu*. 2nd ed. St. Petersburg: 1832.
——. *Treatise on the Old and New Style of the Russian Language* (Rassuždenie o starom i novom sloge rossiiskogo iazyka). 1803.
Shklovsky, Victor. "Pamiatnik tret'emu internatsionalu." In *Khod konia: Sbornik statei*, 108–11. Moscow: Gelikon: 1923.
Shoshan, Avraham Even. *Ha'milon he'hadash*. Vol. 3. Jerusalem: Kiryat-sefer, 1991.
Sidlin, Mikhail. "Vremia bomzhei." *NG Antrakt*, December 1, 2001.
Simmel, Georg. "The Ruin." In *Essays on Sociology, Philosophy and Aesthetics*. Edited by Kurt H. Wolff. New York: Harper and Row, 1965.
——. "Die Ruine." In *Philosophische Kultur*, 118–24. Berlin: Klaus Wagenbach, 1983.
Simpson, David. *Irony and Authority in Romantic Poetry*. London: Macmillan, 1979.
Singer, Ben. *Melodrama and Modernity: Early Sensational Cinema and Its Contexts*. New York: Columbia University Press, 2001.
Slavík, Jaroslav, and Jiří Opelík. *Josef Čapek*. Prague: Torst, 1996.
Smith, David. Introduction to *The Apartheid City and Beyond: Urbanization and Social Change in South Africa*, edited by David Smith. London: Routledge, 1992.

Smith, Terry E. *Making the Modern: Industry, Art, and Design in America*. Chicago: University of Chicago Press, 1993.
Smithson, Alison. "Outbreak of War, 1939." Reprinted in Beatriz Colomina, "Friends of the Future: A Conversation with Peter Smithson." *October* 94 (fall 2000): 3–30.
Smithson, Alison, and Peter Smithson. "The Heroic Period of Modern Architecture." Special issue, *Architectural Design* 25, no. 12 (December): 584–90.
Smithson, Robert. *Robert Smithson: The Collected Writings*. Edited by Jack Flam. Berkeley: University of California Press, 1996.
——. "A Tour of the Monuments of Passaic, New Jersey." In *The Writings of Robert Smithson*, edited by Nancy Holt, 52–57. New York: New York University Press, 1979.
Solnit, Rebeca. *Savage Dreams*. Berkeley: University of California Press, 2000.
Sontag, Susan. "The Imagination of Disaster." In *Against Interpretation*, 209–25. New York: Dell, 1966.
Soper, Kate. "Privileged Gazes and Ordinary Affections: Reflections on the Politics and the Scope of the Nature Aesthetic." In *Deterritorialisations: Revisioning Landscapes and Politics*, edited by Mark Dorrian and Gillian Rose, 338–48. London: Black Dog Publishing, 2003.
Speer, Albert. *Erinnerungen*. Frankfurt: Ullstein, 1987.
——. *Inside the Third Reich: Memoirs*. Translated by Richard and Clara Winston. New York: Macmillan, 1970.
Spengler, Oswald. *Jahre der Entscheidung*. Munich: C. H. Beckische Verlagsbuchhandlung, 1933.
——. *Der Untergang des Abendlandes: Umrisse einer Morphologie der Weltgeschichte* (The Decline of the West). Munich: Deutscher Taschenbuch, 2003.
Spivak, Gayatri. *The Post-Colonial Critic: Interviews, Strategies, Dialogues*. London: Routledge, 1990.
Spotts, Frederic. *Hitler and the Power of Aesthetics*. Woodstock, N.Y.: Overlook, 2004.
Starn, Randolph. "Seeing Culture in a Room." In *The New Cultural History*, edited by Lynn Hunt, 208–32. Berkeley: University of California Press, 1989.
Starobinski, Jean. "Melancholy among Ruins." In *The Invention of Liberty 1700–1789*, translated by Bernard C. Swift, 179–81. Geneva: Skira, 1964.
Stead, Naomi. "The Ruins of History: Allegories of Destruction in Daniel Libeskind's Jewish Museum." *Open Museum Journal* 2 (August 2000): 1–17.
Steding, Christoph. *Das Reich und die Krankheit der europäischen Kultur*. Hamburg: Hanseatische Verlagsanstalt, 1942.
Steinmetz, George. *The Devil's Handwriting: Precoloniality and the German Colonial State in Qingdao, Samoa, and Southwest Africa*. Chicago: University of Chicago Press, 2007.
——. "Drive-By Shooting: Making a Documentary about Detroit." *Michigan Quarterly Review* 45, no. 3 (2006): 491–503.
——. "Fordism." In *Encyclopedia of Europe: 1914–2004*, edited by John Merriman and Jay Winter. New York: Charles Scribner's Sons, 2006.
——. "Social Class and the Reemergence of the Radical Right in Contemporary Germany." In *Reworking Class: Cultures and Institutions of Economic Stratification and Agency*, edited by John R. Hall, 335–68. Ithaca, N.Y.: Cornell University Press, 1997.
Steinmetz, George, and Julia Hell, "The Visual Archive of Colonialism: Germany and Namibia." *Public Culture* 18, no. 1 (2006): 141–82.

Steinweg, Wolfgang. *Das Rathaus Hannover*. Edited by Fremdenverkehrsverein. 3rd ed. Hannover: Benatzky, 2003.

Stenz, Georg. *Erlebnisse eines Missionars in China*. Trier: Paulinus, 1899.

Stewart, Susan. *On Longing: Narratives of the Miniature, the Gigantic, the Souvenir, the Collection*. Durham, N.C.: Duke University Press, 1993.

Stiebing, William H., Jr. *Uncovering the Past: A History of Archaeology*. Oxford: Oxford University Press, 1993.

Stigneev, Valerii. "Sud'ba fotografa." In *Arkadii Shaikhet: Fotografii. 1924–1951. Katalog vystavki*. Moscow: Art-Rodnik, 2000.

"Stimmen aus Parkett und Rang: Man mag keine Ruinen," *Der Spiegel*, January 4, 1947.

Strigalev, Anatolij, and Jurgen Harten. *Vladimir Tatlin: Retrospektive*. Cologne: Du Monte, 1993.

Stuebel, Heinrich. "Die Entwicklung des Nationalsozialismus in Südwestafrika." *Vierteljahrshefte für Zeitgeschichte* 1, no. 2 (1953): 170–76.

Stykalen, Aleksandr. *György Lukács–myslitel' I politik*. Moscow: Saganenko, 2001.

Sugrue, Thomas J. *The Origins of the Urban Crisis: Race and Inequality in Postwar Detroit*. Princeton, N.J.: Princeton University Press, 1996.

Sundaram, Ravi. "Recycling Modernity: Pirate Electronic Cultures in India." *Sarai Reader: 2001: The Public Domain*, 93–99. New Delhi: 2001.

Tafuri, Manfredo. *The Sphere and the Labyrinth: Avant-Gardes and Architecture from Piranesi to the 1970s*. Cambridge: MIT Press, 1990.

Tagore, Sundaram. "The Legacy of Anti-Tradition." *Art India* 11, no. 1 (2006): 32–38.

Tartakovskii, A. G. "Pokazaniia russkikh ochevidtsev o prebyvanii frantsuzov v Moskve v 1812g. (K metodike istochnikovedcheskogo analiza)." *Istochnikovedenie otechestvennoi istorii* no. 1 (1973): 232–73.

Tate, Alan. *Great City Parks*. London: Spon, 2001.

Tatlin, Vladimir. "Iskusstvo v tekhniku." In *Vystavka rabot zasluzhennogo deiatelia iskusstv V. E. Tatlina*. Moscow: Ogiz-Izogiz, 1932.

Taut, Bruno. "Kak voznikaet khoroshaia arkitektura?" (Taut article sent to Union of Soviet Architects). March 1936. In RGALI, fond 674, opis' 2, ed. Khr. 21, 275–76. Moscow.

——. *Die Stadtkrone*. Jena: Diederichs, 1919.

Taylor, Charles. *Hegel*. Cambridge: Cambridge University Press, 1975.

Teller, Edward. "How to Be an Optimist in the Nuclear Age." In *The Legacy of Hiroshima*, by Edward Teller with Allen Brown, 79–95. New York: Doubleday, 1962.

"Tetrad' sviashchennika moskovskogo Uspenskogo sobora I.S. Bozhanova." In *Bumagi, otnosiashchiesia do otechestvennoi voiny 1812 goda*, edited by P. I. Shchukin, vol. 4, 49–76. Moscow: Tip. A. I. Mamontova, 1897.

Theisen, Bianca. "Prose of the World: W. G. Sebald's Literary Travels." *Germanic Review* 79, no. 3 (2004): 163–79.

Thomas, Helen. "Stranded Vessels: The Sublime and the Grotesque in American Architecture." *Journal of Architecture* 4 (spring 1999): 95–100.

Thompson, Leonard. *A History of South Africa*. Sandton, South Africa: Radix, 1990.

Tilley, Christopher. *A Phenomenology of Landscape: Places, Paths and Monuments*. Oxford: Berg, 1994.

Tolstoy, Leo Nikolayevich. *Polnoe sobranie sochinenii*, edited by V. G. Chevtkov, vol. 16. Moscow: Gos. Izdatel'stvo khudozhestvennoi literatury, 1955.

——. *Sobranie sochinenii v dvadtsati dvukh tomakh*, edited by M. B. Khrapchenko et al., vols. 4–7. Moscow: Khudozhestvennaia literatura, 1980.

——. *War and Peace*. Translated by Louise and Aylmer Maude. Oxford: Oxford University Press, 1991.

Tomlinson, Richard, Robert Beauregard, Lindsay Beremer, and Xolela Mangcu. Introduction to *Emerging Johannesburg: Perspectives on the Post-Apartheid City*, edited by Richard Tomlinson, Robert Beauregard, Lindsay Beremer, and Xolela Mangcu. New York: Routledge, 2003.

Touraine, Alain. *The Post-Industrial Society: Tomorrow's Social History: Classes, Conflicts, and Culture in the Programmed Society*. London: Wildwood, 1974.

Trost, Ralph. *Eine gänzlich zerstörte Stadt: Nationalsozialismus, Krieg und Kriegsende in Xanten*. Münster: Waxmann, 2004.

Trubetskoi, Evgenii. "Dva mira v drevnerusskoi ikonopisi." In *Filosofiia russkogo religioznogo iskusstva XVII–XX vv*, edited by Nikolai Gavriushin, 220–46. Moscow: Progress-Kultura, 1993.

Tung, Anthony M. *Preserving the World's Great Cities: The Destruction and Renewal of the Historic Metropolis*. New York: Clarkson Potter, 2001.

Twain, Mark. *Life on the Mississippi*. New York: Penguin Books, 1984.

Uhl, Michael, and Tod Ensign. *G.I. Guinea Pigs*. New York: Wideview Books, 1980.

Van den Bruck, Moeller. *Das dritte Reich*. Edited by Hans Schwarz. Hamburg: Hanseatische Verlagsanstalt, 1931.

——. *Das Recht der jungen Völker*. Edited by Hans Schwarz. Berlin: Nahe Osten, 1932.

Vargas Llosa, Mario. *Conversation in the Cathedral*. Translated by Gregory Rabassa. New York: Harper and Row, 1975.

Venturi, Robert. *Complexity and Contradiction in Architecture*. New York: Musem of Modern Art, 1977.

Venturi, Robert, Denise Scott Brown, and Steven Izenour. *Learning from Las Vegas: The Forgotten Symbolism of Architectural Form*. Cambridge: MIT Press, 1994.

Verdesio, Gustavo. "Forgotten Territorialities: The Materiality of Indigenous Pasts." *Nepantla. Views from South* 2, no. 1 (2001): 85–114.

Vergara, Camilo José. "American Acropolis." *New Statesman and Society* 9, no. 385 (January 12, 1996): 16–19.

——. *American Ruins*. New York: Monacelli, 1999.

——. *The New American Ghetto*. New Brunswick, N.J.: Rutgers University Press, 1995.

Vidler, Anthony. "Deconstruction Boom." *Artforum* 42, no. 4 (December 2003): 33.

——. "Photourbanism: Planning the City from Above and from Below." In *A Companion to the City*, edited by Gary Bridges and Sophie Watson, 35–46. Oxford: Blackwell, 2000.

——. "*Terres Inconnues*: Cartographies of a Landscape to be Invented." *October* 115 (winter 2006): 13–30.

——. *Warped Space: Art, Architecture and Anxiety in Modern Culture*. Cambridge: MIT Press, 2002.

Villey, Michel. "Torah/Dikaion." *Krisis* no. 25 (2002): 144–55.

Virgil. *The Aeneid*. Translated by Robert Fagles. New York: Viking, 2006.

Vogt, Andreas. "Denk mal, ein Denkmal: Von der Historischen Denkmalkommission zum National Monuments Council of Namibia." In *Vom Schutzgebiet bis Namibia 2000*, edited by Klaus A. Hess and Klaus J. Becker, 251–56. Windhoek, Namibia: National Monuments Council of Namibia, 2002.

——. *National Monuments in Namibia: An Inventory of Proclaimed National Monuments in the Republic of Namibia.* Windhoek, Namibia: Gamsberg Macmillan, 2004.

——. *Von Tsaobis bis Namutoni: die Wehrbauten der deutschen Schutztruppe in Deutsch-Südwestafrika (Namibia) von 1884–1915.* Göttingen: Klaus Hess, 2002.

Vogt, Joseph, ed. *Rom und Karthago.* Leipzig: Koehler und Amelang, 1943.

——. *Vom Reichsgedanken der Römer.* Leipzig: Koehler und Amelang, 1942.

Vogt-Göknil, Ulya. *Giovanni Battista Piranesi: "Carceri."* Zurich: Origo, 1958.

Vojvodík, Josef. *Imagines Corporis: Tìlo vèeské modernì a avantgardì.* Brno, Czech Republic: Host, 2006.

Volney, C. F. *The Ruins, or Meditation on the Revolutions of Empires and the Law of Nature.* Published from the Peter Eckler edition in 1890. Baltimore, Md.: Black Classic Press, 1991.

Voltaire. *Candide and Other Stories.* Translated by Joan Spencer. Oxford: Oxford University Press, 1966.

——. "Poem on the Destruction of Lisbon." In *The Works of M. de Voltaire*, 4th ed., edited by T. Smollett et al., vol. 20, 219–30. Dublin: Moncrieffe, 1772.

von Däniken, Erich. *Chariots of the Gods? Unsolved Mysteries of the Past.* New York: Putnam, 1968

von François, Curt. *Deutsch-Südwestafrika: Geschichte der Kolonisation bis zum Ausbruch des Krieges mit Witbooi.* Berlin: Dietrich Reimer, 1899.

von Moltke, Johannes. *No Place Like Home: Locations of Heimat in German Cinema.* Berkeley: University of California Press, 2005.

von Trotha, Trutz. *Koloniale Herrschaft.* Tübingen: J. C. B. Mohr, 1994.

"Vzgliad na tepereshnuiu bedu." *Iz bumag Aliab'evskogo arkhiva.* In *Bumagi, otnosiashchiesia do otechestvennoi voiny 1812 goda*, edited by P. I. Shchukin, 5: 278–79. Moscow: Tip. A. I. Mamontova, 1897.

Walther, Daniel Joseph. *Creating Germans Abroad: Cultural Policies and National Identity in Namibia.* Athens: Ohio University Press, 2002.

Weilacher, Udo. *Between Landscape Architecture and Land Art.* Translated by Felicity Gloth. Basel: Birkhäuser, 1996.

Wendland, Ulrike. *Biographisches Handbuch deutschsprachiger Kunsthistoriker im Exil: Leben und Werk der unter dem Nationalsozialismus verfolgten und vertriebenen Wissenschaftler.* Vol. 1. Munich: Saur, 1999.

Wendorf, Richard. "Piranesi's Double Ruin." *Eighteenth-Century Studies* 34, no. 2 (2001): 161–80.

Wentenschuh, Walter G. *Namibia und seine Deutschen.* Göttingen: Klaus Hess, 1995.

White, Ian Boyd. Introduction to *Modernism and the Spirit of the City*, edited by Ian Boyd White. London: Routledge, 2003.

Whitman, Walt. *Complete Poetry and Selected Prose.* Edited by James E. Miller, Jr. Boston, Mass.: Houghton Mifflin, 1959.

Willett, Ralph. *The Americanization of Germany, 1945–1949.* New York: Routledge, 1989.

Williams, Raymond. *Marxism and Literature.* Oxford: Oxford University Press, 1977.

Wolfe, Tom. *From Bauhaus to Our House.* New York: Farrar, Straus, and Giroux, 1981.

Woods, Jim. *Detroit Remember When: Motor City: Memories and Hometown Traditions.* Detroit: WTVS, 1996.

Woodward, Christopher. *In Ruins*. New York: Pantheon, 2001.

Wordsworth, William. "The Ruined Cottage." In *The Norton Anthology of English Literature*, 5th edition, edited by M. H. Abrams, vol. 2, 178–90. New York: W. W. Norton, 1986.

Wright, Frank Lloyd. "Address at First All-Union Congress of Soviet Architects." 21 June 1937. In RGALI, fond 674, opis' 2, ed. khr. 50, 27–33. Moscow.

Yaeger, Patricia. "Introduction: Dreaming of Infrastructure." Special issue, *PMLA* 122, no. 1 (January 2007): 9–26.

Yizhar, S. "Hirbet Hizah." In *Arbaah Sipurim* (Four Stories), 43–112. Tel Aviv: Hakibbutz Hameuchad, 1959.

Young, James E. *The Texture of Meaning: Holocaust Memorials and Meaning*. New Haven: Yale University Press, 1994.

"Zamechaniia na nekotoroe zamechanie o Moskve." *Russkii vestnik*, no. 5 (1814): 11–44.

Zammito, John. "Koselleck's Philosophy of Historical Time(s) and the Practice of History." *History and Theory* 43, no. 1 (2004).

Zantop, Susanne. *Colonial Fantasies: Conquest, Family, and Nation in Precolonial Germany, 1770–1870*. Durham, N.C.: Duke University Press, 1997.

Zeller, Joachim. *Kolonialdenkmäler und Geschichtsbewusstsein*. Frankfurt: IKO, 2000.

Zeman, Adolf. *Československá Golgota: Historicko-politická reportáž* (Czechoslovak Golgotha: A Historical-Political Report). Prague: Jos. R. Vilímek, 1947.

Zilcosky, John. "Lost and Found: Disorientation, Nostalgia, and Holocaust Melodrama in Sebald's *Austerlitz*." *MLN* 121, no. 3 (2006): 679–98.

——. "Sebald's Uncanny Travels: The Impossibility of Getting Lost." In *W. G. Sebald: A Critical Companion*, edited by J. J. Long and Anne Whitehead, 102–20. Seattle: University of Washington Press, 2004.

Žižek, Slavoj. *The Sublime Object of Ideology*. London: Verso, 1989.

——. *Welcome to the Desert of the Real: Five Essays on September 11 and Related Dates.* London: Verso, 2002.

Zorin, Andrei. *Kormia dvuglavogo orla . . . : Literatura i gosudarstvennaia ideologiia v Rossii v poslednei treti XVIII-pervoi treti XIX veka*. Moscow: Novoe literaturnoe obozrenie, 2001.

Zukin, Sharon. *Landscapes of Power: From Detroit to Disney World*. Berkeley: University of California Press, 1991.

Zweite, Armin. "Bernd and Hilla Becher's 'Suggestion for a Way of Seeing.'" In *Bernd and Hilla Becher, Typologies*, edited by Armin Zweite. Cambridge: MIT Press, 2004.

Zwick, James, ed. *Mark Twain's Weapons of Satire: Anti-Imperialist Writings on the Philippine-American War*. Syracuse, N.Y.: Syracuse University Press, 1992.

# CONTRIBUTORS

**Kerstin Barndt** is an associate professor of German studies and an affiliated faculty member of the Museum Studies Program at the University of Michigan. She has published on twentieth-century German literature and cultural history, gender, and museum studies. Her first book, *Sentiment und Sachlichkeit. Der Roman der Neuen Frau in der Weimarer Republik*, was published in 2003, and she is currently completing a book-length study of contemporary museum and exhibition culture, titled "Exhibition Effects: History, Memory, and Aesthetics in Germany."

**Jon Beasley-Murray** is an assistant professor of Latin American studies at the University of British Columbia. He has published extensively in Latin American studies, as well as on questions of social and cultural theory. His book, *Posthegemony*, is forthcoming from the University of Minnesota Press.

**Russell A. Berman** is the Walter A. Haas Professor in the Humanities at Stanford University, where he holds appointments in the Departments of German Studies and Comparative Literature. He is the author of several books, including *The Rise of the Modern German Novel: Crisis and Charisma* (1986), *Enlightenment or Empire: Colonial Discourse in German Culture* (1998), and *Fiction Sets You Free: Literature, Liberty, and Western Culture* (2007). He also edits the journal *Telos*.

**Jonathan Bolton** is an associate professor in the Department of Slavic Languages and Literatures at Harvard University. He edited and translated *In the Puppet Gardens: Selected Poems, 1963–2005* by the Czech poet Ivan Wernisch, and he has published articles on modernist literature and culture, Czech-Jewish literature, contemporary Czech writers, and literary theory. He is currently completing a book on the cultures of dissent in Czechoslovakia after the Soviet invasion of Czechoslovakia in 1968.

**Svetlana Boym** is the Curt Hugo Reisinger Professor of Slavic languages and literatures and a professor of comparative literature at Harvard University. She is the author of *Common Places: Mythologies of Everyday Life in Russia*, *Death in Quotation Marks*, and *The Future of Nostalgia*, as well as short stories, plays, and a novel. The title of her most recent book-length project is "The Other Freedom: Between Aesthetics and Politics."

**Amir Eshel** is a professor of German studies and comparative literature and the director of the Forum on Contemporary Europe at Stanford University. His book, *Zeit der Zaesur: Juedische Lyriker im Angesicht der Shoa*, appeared in 1997, and he has published essays on aesthetics, the discourse of space, German-Jewish literary and philosophical traditions, and major postwar German authors. He is currently completing a book on the literary engagement with the past in contemporary German, Israeli, and Anglo-American literature.

**Julia Hell** is an associate professor of German studies at the University of Michigan. She is the author of *Post-Fascist Fantasies: Psychoanalysis, History, and the Literature of East Germany* (1997). At the moment she is working on a book titled "Imperial Ruin Gazers," which explores European discourses on the rise and fall of empires from the end of the eighteenth century to the aftermath of the Second World War. She and Johannes von Moltke are executive editors of *The Germanic Review*.

**Daniel Herwitz** is the director of the Institute for the Humanities at the University of Michigan. He lived in South Africa during the 1990s, working at the University of Natal, and is the author of *Race and Reconciliation* (2003). He has published widely in aesthetics, with two new books on the topic: *Aesthetics: Key Concepts in Philosophy* and *The Star as Icon*. Two of his short stories about the South Africa of return, exile, and homecoming have recently appeared in the *Michigan Quarterly Review*.

**Andreas Huyssen** is the Villard Professor of German and comparative literature at Columbia University. He is also the founding director of Columbia's Center for Comparative Literature and Society and one of the founding editors of *New German Critique*. His books include *After the Great Divide: Modernism, Mass Culture, Postmodernism* (1986), *Twilight Memories: Marking Time in a Culture of Amnesia* (1995), *Present Pasts: Urban Palimpsests and the Politics of Memory* (2003), and *Other Cities, Other Worlds: Urban Imaginaries in a Globalizing Age* (2008).

**Rahul Mehrotra** is an Indian architect and urban designer trained at the School of Architecture at Ahmedabad and the Graduate School of Design at Harvard University. He divides his time between Mumbai, where he practices architecture, and Boston, where he teaches at the Massachusetts Institute of Technology.

**Vladimir Paperny**, a writer, designer, and cultural historian, graduated from Stroganov Art School in Moscow and received his Ph.D. in cultural studies from the Russian State University for the Humanities. His *Architecture in the Age of Stalin: Culture Two* was published in Russian in 1996 and in English in 2002. He has a design studio in Los Angeles and has been a visiting professor at Bristol University, the University of California, Los Angeles, and the University of Southern California.

**Helen Petrovsky** is a senior research associate at the Institute of Philosophy of the Russian Academy of Sciences. She is the author of *Neproiavlennoe: Ocherki po filosofii fotografii* (The Unapparent: Essays on the Philosophy of Photography, 2002), *Antifotografiia* (Antiphotography, 2003), and *Teoriia Obraza* (Theory of the Image, lecture course, forthcoming). She has translated into Russian Jean-Luc Nancy's *Corpus* and selected writings of Gertrude Stein. Since 2002 she has been the editor in chief of the biannual philosophical and theoretical journal *Sinij Divan*.

**Todd Samuel Presner** is an associate professor of Germanic languages and Jewish studies at the University of California at Los Angeles. His research focuses on European intellectual history, the history of media, and cultural geography. He is the author of *Mobile Modernity:*

*Germans, Jews, Trains* (2007) and *Muscular Judaism: The Jewish Body and the Politics of Regeneration* (2007).

**Helmut Puff** is an associate professor in the Departments of German and History at the University of Michigan. Among his publications are *Deutsch im lateinischen Grammatikunterricht 1480–1560* (1995), *Sodomy in Reformation Germany and Switzerland* (2003), and *Zwischen den Disziplinen? Perspektiven der Fruehneuzeitforschung*, edited with Christopher Wild (2003). His current book project is titled "City in Ruins: Modeling German History."

**Alexander Regier** is an assistant professor of English at Rice University. His study *Fracture and Fragmentation in British Romanticism* (2009) addresses imaginative and philosophical writing. He is the coeditor of *Wordsworth's Poetic Theory* (2009), and has published on Wordsworth, rhetoric, utopianism, and the aesthetics of sport. He is currently preparing a comparative study of theories of language with attention to Hamann, Black, Wordsworth, and Benjamin.

**Eric Rentschler** is the Arthur Kingsley Porter Professor and Chair of Germanic Languages and Literatures at Harvard University, where he also teaches in the Department of Visual and Environmental Studies. His books include *West German Film in the Course of Time* (1984) and *The Ministry of Illusion* (1996).

**Lucia Saks** is an assistant professor in the Department of Screen Arts and Cultures at the University of Michigan. She spent six years in South Africa at the University of Kwa-Zulu, Natal, as the director of media and communications, and has been deeply involved in the transformation of the media in postapartheid South Africa. She has completed a book-length manuscript titled "The Race for Representation: Cinema in a Democratic South Africa."

**Andreas Schönle** is a professor of Russian studies at Queen Mary, University of London. His publications include *Authenticity and Fiction in the Russian Literary Journey, 1790–1840* (2000); *Lotman and Cultural Studies: Encounters and Extensions*, which he edited (2006); and *The Ruler in the Garden: Politics and Landscape Design in Imperial Russia* (2007). He is preparing a book on historical consciousness and the meaning of ruins in Russian culture.

**Tatiana Smoliarova** is an assistant professor of Slavic languages and literatures at Columbia University. She is the author of *Parizh 1928: Oda vozvrashchaetsia v teatr* (Paris 1928: Ode Returns to the Theatre), a study of Diaghilev's 1928 production of *Ode*. Currently, she is at work on two book-length projects: "The Myth of a Poet of Myth: Pindar in France and in Russia" and "The Optical Poetics of Gavrila Derzhavin," a study of visual culture in Russia around 1800.

**George Steinmetz** is a professor of sociology and German studies at the University of Michigan and a foreign corresponding member of the Centre de Sociologie Européenne. His books include *The Devil's Handwriting: Precoloniality and the German Colonial State in Qingdao, Samoa, and Southwest Africa* (2007); *The Politics of Method in the Human Sciences: Positivism and Its Epistemological Others* (2005); *Regulating the Social: The Welfare State and Local Politics in Imperial Germany* (1993); and *State/Culture: State Formation after the Cultural Turn* (1999). With Michael Chanan he directed the documentary film *Detroit: Ruin of a City* (2005).

**Jonathan Veitch** is a professor of English and Comparative Literary Studies and the president of Occidental College. He is the author of *American Superrealism: Nathaniel West and the Politics of Representation in the 1930s* (1997). His current project, entitled "Colossus in Ruins," examines places that were once central to the American imagination—maritime New England, the industrial Northeast, and the Cold War West—but are not so any longer, by examining attempts to frame, preserve, and exhibit their contested pasts.

**Gustavo Verdesio** is an associate professor in the Department of Romance Languages and Literatures and the Program in Latin American Culture at the University of Michigan. A revised English version of his *La Invencion del Uruguay* (1996) has been published as *Forgotten Conquests* (2001). He has edited the collection *Colonialism Past and Present* (2001), with Alvaro F. Bolaños, and an issue of the journal *Dispositio/n* (2005) on the Latin American subaltern studies group.

**Anthony Vidler** is a professor of architecture and the dean of the Irwin S. Chain School of Architecture at the Cooper Union for the Advancement of the Arts and Sciences. His most recent book is *Histories of the Immediate Present: Inventing Architectural Modernism* (2008).

**Johannes von Moltke** is an associate professor of German studies and screen arts and cultures at the University of Michigan. He is the author of *No Place Like Home: Locations of Heimat in German Cinema* (2005) and has published broadly on German film, theory, and cultural history. He is an executive editor of *The Germanic Review* and coeditor, with Gerd Gmuenden, of the book series Screen Cultures: German Film and the Visual, published by Camden House. He is currently at work on a book-length manuscript about film, history, and the politics of empathy.

# INDEX

**JULIA HELL** is an associate professor of German studies at the University of Michigan.

**ANDREAS SCHÖNLE** is a professor of Russian studies at Queen Mary, University of London.

Library of Congress Cataloging-in-Publication Data
Ruins of modernity / edited by Julia Hell and Andreas Schönle.
p. cm. — (Politics, history, and culture : a series from the International Institute at the University of Michigan)
Includes bibliographical references and index.
ISBN 978-0-8223-4456-8 (cloth : alk. paper)
ISBN 978-0-8223-4474-2 (pbk. : alk. paper)
1. Ruins, Modern. 2. Civilization, Modern—20th century. 3. Civilization, Modern—21st century. 4. Ruins in literature. 5. Ruins in motion pictures.
I. Hell, Julia. II. Schönle, Andreas.
III. Series: Politics, history, and culture.
CB425.R85 2009
909.83—dc22 2009035117